THE

MAURITIUS ALMANAC

FOR

1896

TWENTY-EIGHTH PUBLICATION

COMPILED BY

D. P. GARRIOCH

SUPERINTENDENT, INLAND REVENUE

MAURITIUS

ENGELBRECHT & CO.'S PRINTING ESTABLISHMENT, CORDERIE STREET.

1896

PREFACE

The Editor trusts, that this issue of the Mauritius Almanac may be found not less useful than its predecessors. The assistance he has received from many contributors has done much to aid him in making the work more accurate and complete than former Editions. In the Civil List an improvement has been made by inserting the date of the first appointment of each Officer; the exact service of every Civil Servant can thus be at once found out.

He desires to thank the Public for the continued favour with which each edition meets and asks their indulgence for many shortcomings which are almost inseparable from a work of this sort.

D. P. GARRIOCH.

Port Louis,
20th. March 1896.

ALPHABETICAL INDEX.

D

INDEX TO ORDINANCES OF 1895.

---

* These Ordinances although passed at the last day of the Session 1895, have not been signed by His Excellency the Governor. They will be put in force by a Proclamation.

LIST OF NEWSPAPERS.

PRINTED IN THE COLONY.

DAILY.

Le Cernéen.

The Merchants and Planters Gazette.

Le Journal de Maurice.

The Commercial Gazette.

Le Bien Public.

Le Vrai Mauricien.

The Daily Publisher and Les Petites Affiches.

Le Vrai Progrès Colonial.

Le XXe Siècle.

L'Express.

WEEKLY.

Le Mouvement à l'Ile Maurice.
La Croix du Dimanche et Annales de l'Union Catholique.

MONTHLY.

Revue Agricole.

PRINTING ESTABLISHMENTS.

The Central Printing Establishment, Poudrière Street.

Le Journal de Maurice, Corderie Street.

Imprimerie Co-opérative, Des Créoles Street.

Le Cernéen, Old Council Street.

The Merchants and Planters Gazette, Pope Hennessy Street.

The Commercial Gazette, Post Office Square.

Le Bien Public, Touraine Street.

Le Vrai Progrès Colonial, Bourbon and Touraine Streets.

Le XXe Siècle, Bourbon Street.

COMMON NOTES FOR THE YEAR 1896.

Golden Number	16	Rogation Sunday	May 10
Epact	XV	Ascension Day	,, 14
Solar Cycle	1	Birth of Queen Victoria (1819) ...	,, 24
Dominical Letters	E D	Pentecost, Whit Sunday	,, 24
Roman Indiction	9	Trinity Sunday	,, 31
Julian Period	6609	Corpus Christi	June 4
Sundays after Trinity	25	Accession of Queen Victoria (1837)	,, 20
Septuagesima Sunday	Feb. 2	Queen's Coronation (1838) ...	,, 28
Ash Wednesday	,, 19	Birth of Prince of Wales	Nov. 9
Good Friday	April 3	1st. Sunday in Advent	,, 29
Easter Sunday	,, 5	Christmas Day (Friday)	Dec. 25

The year 1314 of the Mahomedan Era commences on the 12th. June 1896.

Ramadân (month of abstinence observed by the Mahomedans) commences on the 14th. of February 1896.

The latitude of the Royal Alfred Observatory, from which the Time Ball on the Signal Mountain is dropped at 1 p.m. mean solar time, is 20° 5′ 39″ S., and the Longitude 3h. 50m. 12.6s. East of Greenwich. When the Ball drops at 1 p.m. Mauritius mean time, the Greenwich mean time is 9h. 9m. 47.4 a.m.

ASTRONOMICAL PHENOMENA.

Kindly furnished by the Honorable Dr. C. Meldrum, C.M.G., L.L.D., F.R.S., Director of the Royal Alfred Observatory.

Eclipses during the year 1896.

In the year 1896 there will be two Eclipses of the Sun, and two of the Moon.

I.—An Annular Eclipse of the Sun, February 13, 1896, invisible at Mauritius.

Begins on the Earth generally, February 13, 5h. 43.9m. P.M., mean time at Mauritius, in Long. 137° 32′ W. of Greenwich and Lat. 58° 33′ S.

Ends on the Earth generally, February 13, 10h. 43.3m. P.M., in Long. 7° 8′ W. of Greenwich, and Lat. 10° 35′ S.

This Eclipse is visible in the South Atlantic and parts of South Africa, South America, and the Antarctic Ocean.

II.—A Partial Eclipse of the Moon, February 28—29, 1896, visible at Mauritius.

			M. M. T.
First contact with the Penumbra,	February	28,	9h. 05m. 7 P.M.
First contact with the Shadow,	,,	28,	10h. 06m. 5 ,,
Middle of the Eclipse,	,,	28,	11h. 35m. 9 ,,
Last contact with the Shadow,	,,	29,	1h. 05m. 3 A.M.
Last contact with the Penumbra,	,,	29,	2h. 06m. 1 ,,

Magnitude of the Eclipse (moon's diameter =1) 0.870.

The first contact with the Shadow occurs at 85° from the Northernmost point of the Moon's Limb towards the East.

The last contact at 30° towards the West.

III.—A Total Eclipse of the Sun, August 9, 1896, invisible at Mauritius.

Begins on the Earth generally, August 9, 6h. 33.6m. A.M., mean time at Mauritius, in Long. 32° 30′ E. of Greenwich, and Lat. 47° 49′ N.

Ends on the Earth generally, Aug. 9, 11h. 25.1m. A.M., in Long. 158° 3′6 E., and Lat. 3° 34′ N.

This Eclipse is visible over parts of the North Pacific, Arctic Ocean, Asia and Europe.

IV.—A Partial Eclipse of the Moon, August 23, invisible at Mauritius.

			M. M. T.
First contact with the Penumbra,	August	23,	7h. 58m. 3 A.M.
First contact with the Shadow,	,,	23,	9h. 14m. 6 ,,
Middle of the Eclipse,	,,	23,	10h. 47m. 7 ,,
Last contact with the Shadow	,,	23,	0h. 20m. 8 P.M.
Last contact with the Penumbra	,,	23,	1h. 37m. 1 ,,

Magnitude of the Eclipse (Moon's diameter =1) 0.734.

The first contact with the Shadow occurs at 100° from the Northernmost point of the Moon's Limb towards the East.

The last contact at 153° towards the West.

Equinoxes		Solstices	
March 20	at 6h. A.M.	June 21	at 2h. A.M.
September 22	at 5h. P.M.	December 21	at 11h. A.M.

Sun in Perigee, January 1, at 11h. P.M. Sun in Apogee, July 4, at 2h. A.M.

Perigee, December 31, at 2h. P.M.

THE ARTICLES OF THE CALENDAR.

Golden Number.—The Golden Number indicates the place of the Year in the Lunar Cycle. The Cycle is a course of 19 years, in which the phenomena of the moon occur within an hour and about 29 minutes of the time at which they occurred 19 years before.

Epact.—The Epact indicates the moon's age on 1st. of January. The common Solar year of 365 days contains 12 moons and 11 days.

Solar Cycle.—The Solar Cycle is a period of 28 years during which the week days occur on the same days of the month as they did during the previous Solar Cycle. The number of the Solar Cycle shows the place of the year in that place.

Dominical Letter.—The first seven letters of the Alphabet are used in the Calendar to show the days of the week and the Dominical Letter is always marked by the letter A. In leap year. there are two letters : one till the end of February and then the preceding letter.

Roman Indiction.—A period of 15 years inst tuted by Constantine the Great, and originally a period of taxation. It dates from 1st. of January 313.

Julian Period.—A period of 7980 years obtained by multiplying together the Lunar Cycle. Solar Cycle, and Roman Indiction : 19 × 28 × 15=7980. This period was invented in 1553, and is used in calculations of astronomy and chronology.

Bissextile or Leap Year.—To make up the difference between the astronomical and the computed year, every fourth year is Leap year or a year of 366 days. But it was arranged by Pope Gregory XIII that in every 400 years three Leap Years should be omitted: and thus 1700, 1800 and 1900 should not be Leap Years but that 2000 should be a Leap Year.

Gregorian Calendar.—Previous to 1582 the year had been reckoned as containing 365 days and 6 hours; which space of time exceeded by some minutes the actual length of the year. The error which had consequently arisen in the Calendar was removed by Gregory XIII who ordered the day following Oct. 4 of the 1582, to be called Oct. 15; and by this arrangement be prevented the recurrence of the error. The OLD STYLE of reckoning according to the *Julian Calendar* was observed by England till 1752, when the day after Sept. 2 was called Sept. 14. It is still observed by Russia.

Besides the *Julian* or *Old Calendar* and the *Gregorian* or *New Calendar*, there are the Jewish and Mahomedan Calendars, and a variety of Calendar in the East, of which the most important are the Chinese, the Japanese, the Hindoo and the Parsee.

The year 1896 is the 6609th. of the Julian Period and the 2649th. from the foundation of Rome. According to the Jews the year 1896 is the latter part of the 5656th. and the beginning of the 5657th. year since the creation of the world.

PUBLIC HOLIDAYS

Observed by the Government and the Banks,

New Year's Day	1st. & 2nd. Jan.	Assumption Day	15th. August
Good Friday	3rd. April	St. Louis	25th. ,,
Easter Monday	5th. ,,	All Saints Day	1st. November
Queen's Birthday	24th. May	All Souls	2nd. ,,
Corpus Christi (Fête Dieu) ...	4th. June	Prince of Wales' birthday ...	9th. ,,
Queen's Accession	20th. ,,	Christmas Day	25th. December

Sugar Estate Holidays.

*New Year's Day	1st. January	*Christmas Day	25th. December
*Queen's birthday	24th. May	*Last day of Mohurrum (Yamsé)	

* If any of these days fall on a Sunday the following day shall be substituted.

NOTE.—Under Ordinance 4 of 1881 the Governor is empowered to declare, in addition to the above holidays, any day as a Bank, Office or Estate Holiday.

JANVIER, 31 JOURS.	JANUARY, 31 DAYS.
SOLEIL	LUNE
Lever / Coucher.	P. L. le 1er .... à 0h. 29m. 9 du matin
	D. Q. le 7 .... à 7h. 15m. 1 du soir
	N. L. le 15 .... à 2h. 09m. 6 du matin
	P. Q. le 23 .... à 6h. 32m. 5 du matin
	P. L. le 30 .... à 0h. 45m. 5 du soir
1er à 5h. 26m ....à 6h. 42m.	Périgée, le 4 à 8 du matin
15 à 5h. 35m....................à 6h. 44m.	Apogée, le 20 à 9h. du matin

Canon de la Diane.

Du 1er au 14 à 4h. 15m. — Du 15 au 31 à 4h. 20m.

The month is so named from the Roman deity Janus, who was supposed to preside over doors. He was represented with two faces, one of which looked back over the old year ; the other forward to the new. The Roman year was originally commenced in March ; at first it had but ten months, till Numa Pompilius, who died 672 B.C., added January and February.

1 M	La Circoncision de N. S. J. C.	1 W	Circumcision—New Year's Day.
2 J	Octave de S Etienne, 1er martyr	2 T	Sudden death at Réduit of Sir Lionel Smith [1842.
3 V	Octave de S Jean	3 F	
4 S	Octave des SS Innocents	4 S	
5 D	Vig. de l'Epiphanie	5 S	General Chanzy died, 1883.
6 L	**Epiphanie de N. S. J. C.**	6 M	Epiphany, Death of Poivre, 1788.
7 M	De l'Octave, 2me jour	7 T	Royal College founded, 1791.
8 M	De l'Octave, 3me jour	8 W	Arrival of Governor Higginson, 1851.
9 J	De l'Octave, 4me jour	9 T	Ordinance to Encourage " Bois Noirs," 1782.
10 V	De l'Octave, 5me jour	10 F	Penny Post introduced into England, 1840.
11 S	De l'Octave, 6me jour	11 S	Earl of Iddlesleigh died, 1887.
12 D	**1er ap. l'Epiphanie**	12 S	1st. Sun. after Epiphanny.
13 L	Baptême de N. S. J. C.	13 M	
14 M	S Hilaire, évêque	14 T	
15 M	S Paul, ermite	15 W	Introduction of Indian Laborers, 1835.
16 J	S Marcel, p.m.	16 T	
17 V	S Antoine, abbé	17 F	
18 S	La chaire de S Pierre à Rôme	18 S	German Empire proclaimed, 1871.
19 D	S nom de Jésus	19 S	2nd. Sun. after Epiphany. Arr. of Major Gen.
20 L	SS Fabien et Sébastien	20 M	[C. M. Hay as Actg. Governor 1855.
21 M	Ste Agnès, vierge et mart.	21 T	
22 M	S Vincent et Anatase, mm.	22 W	Lemaire the navigator died at Mauritius, 1617.
23 J	Les fiançailles de la B. V. M.	23 T	
24 V	S Timothée, évêque et martyr	24 F	Foundation of the *Cernéen* Newspaper, 1832.
25 S	La Conversion de S Paul	25 S	Conversion of St. Paul.— General Gordon [killed at Kartoum, 1885.
26 D	**3e ap. l Epiphanie**	26 S	3rd. Sun. after Epiphany.
27 L	S Jean Chrystôme, e. c. d.	27 M	
28 M	S Cyrille, év.	28 T	Murder of Mme Trambouze by Indians, 1854.
29 M	S François de Sales	29 W	1st. Reform Parliament met in England, 1838.
30 J	Ste Martine	30 T	Arbitral Justice established, 1794.
31 V	S Pierre Nolasque	31 F	

Janvier.—Semez : Brèdes Malgache et Bringelles. Pantez : Concombre, Cornichon, Giraumon Melon, Melon-d'Eau, Riz, Manioc, Safran, Gingembre, Callebasse, Piment, Margauze, Patolle, Pipangaille, Brèdes Malabar et d'Angolle, Ambrevade, Lalo, Cambare, &c.

Janvier.—Mois favorable pour faire les plantations d'arbres avec des plants préparés à l'avance en paniers, mottes ou vases. Bonne époque pour faire des provins. Plantez : Dahlias, chrysanthèmes, phlox decussata. Floraison des gloxinias, tydéas, bégonias. Bouturez les dahlias, œillets, géraniums, les chrysanthèmes de l'Inde et de Chine.

FÉVRIER, 29 JOURS.

SOLEIL

Lever	Coucher
1er à 5h. 46m.................	à 6h. 42m.
15 à 5h. 53m.................	à 6h. 35m.

FEBRUARY, 29 DAYS.

D. Q. le 6 à.......... 4h. 28m. 3 du matin
N. L. le 13 à............ 8h. 02m. 8 du soir
P. Q. le 22 à............ 1h. 04m. 7 du matin
P. L. le 28 à............ 11h. 41m. 6 du soir

Périgée, le 1er à 6h. du matin
Apogée, le 16 à minuit
Périgée, le 29 à 3h. du soir

Canon de la Diane.

1er au 14 à 4h. 39m. | 15 au 29 à 4h. 40m.

February is so named from Februa, supposed to be the same as Juno; "and the evident relation between the Februata Juno and the Purificata Virg. Maria, is one of the most striking instances of the connection between Pagan and Christian rites and festivities as to the periods of their occurrence."

1 S	S Ignace, e. m.	1 S	Emancipation of the Slaves, 1835.
2 D	**Septuagésime**	2 S	Septuagesima.
3 L	Purification de la B. V. M.	3 M	Candlemass.
4 M	Oraison de N. S. J. C.	4 T	Telegraphs transferred to Government, 1870.
5 M	Ste Agathe, vierge et martyr	5 W	
6 J	S André Corsini	6 T	Birth of Parny in Bourbon, 1753.
7 V	S Romuald	7 F	
8 S	S Jean de Matha	8 S	Death of Lislet Geffroy, Port Louis, 1835. [burnt by 4 slaves, 1695.
9 D	**Sexagésime**	9 S	Sexagesima Sunday.— Fort at Grand Port
10 L	Ste Scholastique	10 M	Marriage of Queen Victoria, 1840.
11 M	Com. de la Passion	11 T	Mahé de Labourdonnais born, 1699.
12 M	S Tite, év. et conf.	12 W	
13 J	S Cyrille d'Alexandrie	13 T	
14 V	S Valentin	14 F	St. Valentine.
15 S	S Faustin, mart.	15 S	
16 D	**Quinquagésime**	16 S	Shrove Sunday. [1869.
17 L	S Donat	17 M	Wreck of the *Théo & Lulu* on Ile de la Passe,
18 M	S Siméon	18 T	Dissolution of Districts Councils, 1820.
19 M	**Les Cendres**	19 W	Ash Wednesday.
20 J	S Eucher	20 T	
21 V	Ste Couronne d'Epines	21 F	First Municipal Elections at Mauritius, 1850.
22 S	Chaire de St Pierre à Antioche	22 S	Revolt of Malagasy slaves under Ratsitatane, [1822
23 D	**1er du Carême**	23 S	1st. Sunday in Lent.
24 L	S Pierre Damien, e. c. d.	24 M	Gutemberg (printer) d 1468.
25 M	S Mathias, ap.	25 T	Loss of the *Eugénie* at Passe Danoise, 1857.
26 M	Q. T., S Nector, év.	26 W	
27 J	Q. T., S Léandre, év.	27 T	
28 V	Q. T., Ste Lance et Clous	28 F	Streets of Port Louis renamed, 1828.
29 S	Q. T., S Romain	29 S	

Février.—Plantez : Concombre, Melon, Cornichon, Patate, Giraumon, Maïs, Bringelle, (on transplante celle de Décembre) Patolle, Calebasse, Margauze, Melon-d'Eau, Safran, Brèdes d'Angolle, Malabar et Malgache, Lalo, Pipangaille.

Février.—Mêmes travaux. Semez reines-marguerites qui fleuriront en mai ; pour obtenir de belles marguerites on doit les arroser chaque semaine pendant leur végétation avec un peu d'eau de guano. En cas de mauvais temps ou de p'uie, couvrir les semis avec des vitres.

MARS, 31 Jours.

SOLEIL

Lever.	Coucher.
1er à 5h. 59m.	à 6 h. 26m.
15 à 6h. 04m.	à 6 h. 14m.

Canon de la Diane.

Du 1er au 14 à 4h. 50m. Du 15 au 31 à 5h. 00m.

MARCH, 31 DAYS.

LUNE

D. Q. le 6 à .... 3h. 19m. 2 du soir
N. L. le 14 à .... 2h. 37m. 9 du soir
P. Q. le 22 à .... 3h. 46m. 9 du soir
P. L. le 29 à .... 9h. 11m. 7 du matin

Apogée, le 15 à 5h. du matin
Périgée, le 29 à 4h. du matin

The first month of the year, according to the ancient reckoning, was named in honour of Mars the supposed father of the founder of Rome. Our Anglo-Saxon ancestors called it Lenct Monath, Lent or Spring month.

1 D	**2e du Carême**	1 S	2nd Sunday in Lent. — Severe Hurricane, [1850.
2 L	St Simplice, pape	2 M	Pope Leon XIII b. 1810.
3 M	St Titien, év.	3 T	
4 M	St Casimir, roi, c.	4 W	Louis Léchelle, named 1st. Mayor of Port [Louis, 1850.
5 J	St Théophile, e.	5 T	Thames Tunnel opened, 1843.
6 V	St Suaire de N. S. J. C.	6 F	
7 S	St Thomas d'Aquin, c. d.	7 S	Epizootie broke out, 1848.
8 D	**3e du Carême**	8 S	3rd Sunday in Lent.
9 L	Ste Françoise, v.	9 M	
10 M	Les Sts 40 martyrs	10 T	Loss of the Bg. *Guess* at Cannonier's Point, [1870.
11 M	St Eutime, c.	11 W	
12 J	St Grégoire, pape	12 T	Arrival of Mr. Dumas, 1729.—Departure of [Sir John Pope Hennessy, 1887.
13 V	Les 5 Plaies de N. S. J. C.	13 F	
14 S	Ste Ma hilde	14 S	London & Paris Telephone completed, 1891.
15 D	**4e du Carême**	15 S	4th. Sunday in Lent.
16 L	St Héribert, e.	16 M	Queen created Empress of India, 1876.
17 M	St Patrice, e.	17 T	
18 M	St Cyrille de Jérusalem, e. c. d.	18 W	Suez Canal opened, 1869.
19 J	St Joseph, époux de la B. V. M.	19 T	
20 V	Précieux Sang	20 F	
21 S	St Benoît, abbé	21 S	
22 D	**La Passion**	22 S	P ssion Sunday.—5th Sunday in Lent.
23 L	St Victorien	23 M	
24 M	St Gabriel, archange	24 T	The *Sultany* arrived from Calcutta with [cholera on board, 1854.
25 M	Annonciation de la B. V. M.	25 W	
26 J	St Emmanuel, m.	26 T	
27 V	Les 7 douleurs de Marie	27 F	
28 S	St Jean de Capistran	28 S	Duke of Albany, died 1884.
29 D	**Les Rameaux**	29 S	Palm Sunday.—E. Swedenborg, died 1772.
30 L	St Quirin, m.	30 M	
31 M	Ste Balbine, v.	31 T	Prœdial apprentices freed, 1839.

Mars.—Plantez : Maïs, Giraumon, Brède Malgache ; on transplante les Bringelles plantées en Janvier. Et on peut aussi vers le 15 commencer à semer : Brède Martin, Choux, Laitue, Pomme d'Amour, Gros Oignons, etc., mais les fortes pluies sont à craindre pour ces sortes de légumes.

Mars.—On transplante les rosiers, on les nettoie ainsi que les autres arbustes, semez pensées, reines-marguerites, œillets, paquerettes, pois-fleurs, etc. Taillez les raisins en ville et sur le bords de mer, mais pas à Moka ni à Curepipe et les climats analogues.

AVRIL, 30 JOURS.	APRIL 30 DAYS.
SOLEIL	LUNE
LEVER COUCHER	D. Q. le 5 à .... 4h. 14m. 4 du matin
	N. L. le 13 à .... 8h. 13m. 0 du matin.
1er à 6h. 08m.................. à 5h. 59m.	P. Q. le 21 à .... 2h. 37m. 0 du matin.
	P. L. le 27 à .... 5h. 37m. 4 du soir.
15 à 6h. 12m.................. à 5h. 47m. 5'	Apogée, le 11 à 7h. du matin.
	Périgée, le 26 à 1h. du soir.
Canon de	la Diane.
Du 1er au 14 à 5h. 10m.	Du 15 au 30 à 5h. 15m.

The name of this month is by some said to be derived from Aperio, to open, on account of its being the month of opening buds. By others it is derived from Aphrodite, the Greek name of Venus, to whom it was dedicated. By the Saxons it was called Ostre (or Easter) month. The Dutch and Germans call it grass month.

1 M	St Hugues, e.	1 W	
2 J	JEUDI SAINT	2 T	Prince Bismark b. 1815. [1798.
3 V	**Vendredi Saint**	3 F	GOOD FRIDAY.—Insurgent troops sent away,
4 S	SAMEDI SAINT	4 S	Ordinance restricting the liberty of the press [1836.
5 D	**Pâques**	5 S	EASTER SUNDAY [Réunion to France, 1815.
6 L	De l'octave	6 M	EASTER MONDAY—Holiday.— Retrocession of
7 M	De l'octave	7 T	Prince Léopold b. 1853.
8 M	De l'octave	8 W	
9 J	De l'octave	9 T	Hurricane which overthrew the Church at
10 V	De l'octave	10 F	1st. Criminal Assize 1832. [Port Louis, 1773
11 S	De l'octave	11 S	Papal Jubilee at Rome, 1869.
12 D	**Quasimodo**	12 S	LOW SUNDAY.— Vaccination introduced by [Mr Déclos, 1803.
13 L	Ste Herménégilde	13 M	
14 M	St Justin, m.	14 T	Departure of Governor Higginson, 1854.
15 M	Ste Anastasie, m.	15 W	
16 J	St Paterne, év.	16 T	Thiers b. 1797.
17 V	St Anicet, p. m.	17 F	
18 S	St Parfait, p. et m.	18 S	Abbé de la Caille arrived, 1753.
19 D	**2e ap. Pâques.**—Le Bon Pasteur	19 S	2ND SUNDAY AFTER EASTER
20 L	St Sulpice, m.	20 M	Napoleon III b. 1808.
21 M	St Anselme, e. c. d.	21 T	
22 M	St Soter et Cajus, pp. mm.	22 W	Colonel Draper died 1851 & buried at B. River.
23 J	St Georges, m.	23 T	Shakespeare died, 1616.
24 V	St Fidèle de Sigmaringen, m.	24 F	Murder of Madame Lehec, Flacq, 1774.
25 S	St Marc, évang.	25 S	Bourbon declared English Possession in 1811.
26 D	**3e ap. Pâques.**—Pat. de St Joseph	26 S	3RD SUNDAY AFTER EASTER.
27 L	St Anastase, p.	27 M	
28 M	St Paul de la Croix	28 T	Queen gazetted Empress of India, 1877.
29 M	St Pierre, m.	29 W	Hurricane without precedent, 1892.
30 J	Ste Catherine de Sienne, v.	30 T	

AVRIL.—Semez : Ail, Brède, Echalotte, Oignon, Poireau, Oseille, Epinard, Amarante, Thym, Menthe, Marjolaine, Piment, Tomate, Pomme d'amour, Chicorée de toute espèce, Laitue, Salsifis, Carotte, Céléri, Persil, Choux, Choux-Fleur, Choux-Navet, Cresson, Moutarde, Choux-de-Chine, Navet, Radis, Petsai, Rave, Capucine, Lentille, Petit-Pois, Pois, Anis, Tabac, Bohëme et Asperges.

AVRIL.—Transplantez les reines-marguerites, semées en février dans une terre bien préparée. Semez toutes sortes de fleurs. Plantez griffes de renoncules et d'anémones. Plantez quinquina, cacao géroflier, muscadier, préparés d'avance en vases et en paniers.

MAI, 31 JOURS.	MAY, 31 DAYS.
SOLEIL	LUNE
LEVER — COUCHER	D. Q. le 4.........à 7h. 15m. 5 du soir
	N. L. le 12.........à 11h. 36m. 7 du soir
	P. Q. le 20.........à 10h. 11m. 3 du matin
1er à 6h. 18m. ....à 5h. 36m.	P. L. le 27.........à 1h. 46m. 8 du matin
	Apogée, le 8 à 7h. du soir
15 à 6h. 23m. ....à 5h. 29m.	Périgée, le 24 à 3h. du soir
Canon de la Diane	
Du 1er au 14 à 5h. 20m.	Du 15 au 31 à 5h. 25.

This month is by some said to derive its name from Maia, the mother of Mercury. Others explain that among the Romans it was named mensis maioram, and dedicated to the elder portion of the community, the following month, mensis junirum of June, being appropriated to the younger folk. The Saxons named the month Trimilchi, because they then began to milk their cows three times a day.

1	V	SS. Jacques, et Philippe, ap.	1	F	Jacoté attacked by Willoughby, 1810.—Archives Office established, 1815.
2	S	St Anathase, év. et conf.	2	S	
3	D	**4e après Pâques** Inv. de la Ste Croix	3	S	4th. SUND. AFTER EASTER.
4	L	Ste Monique, veuve	4	M	Livingstone died, 1873.
5	M	St Pie V, pape et conf.	5	T	Gov. Sir W. Gomm left for India, 1849.
6	M	St Jean à la Porte Latine	6	W	
7	J	St Stanislas, év. m.	7	T	Lord Brougham died, 1849.
8	V	App. de St Michel, arch.	8	F	
9	S	St Grégoire de Nazianze, év.	9	S	
10	D	**5e après Pâques** St Antonin, év. c.	10	S	5th. SUNDAY AFTER EASTER. *Rogation Sunday.*
11	L	*Rogat.* St Gengoulphe, m.	11	M	Earl Granville b., 1815.
12	M	*Rogat.* SS. Nérée et ses comp.	12	T	Anti-Drainage Meeting, 1870.
13	M	*Rogat.* St Servais, év.	13	W	Pope Pius IX, b. 1792.
14	J	**Ascension de N.S.J.C.**	14	T	ASCENSION DAY.
15	V	Ste Sophie, vierge	15	F	Cholera in Port Louis Prison, 1854.
16	S	Ste Ubald, év. et conf.	16	S	Special Tribunal at Seychelles abolished, 1827.
17	D	**6e après Pâques** St Pascal Baylon	17	S	6th. SUNDAY AFTER EASTER.
18	L	Ste Venance mart	18	M	Closing of the Port to foreign vessels, 1816.
19	M	St Pierre Célestin, p. m.	19	T	
20	M	St Bernardin de Sienne	20	W	Departure of Gov. Sir T. R. Farquhar, 1823.
21	J	St Jean Népomucène, m.	21	T	
22	V	Ste Julie, v. et mar.	22	F	
23	S	Vig. de la Pentecôte	23	S	
24	D	**La Pentecôte, Nais. de Sa Majesté**	24	S	QUEEN VICTORIA, b. 1819. Holiday.
25	L	St Grégoire VII	25	M	Remains of Adrien d'Epinay arrived from [France, 1840.
26	M	St Philippe de Néri	26	T	
27	M	St Mad. de Pazzi, v.—*Q. T.*	27	W	
28	J	St Augustin, év.	28	T	Strike of the Post Office Clerks, 1858.
29	V	St Maximin—*Q. T.*	29	F	
30	S	St Félix, p.m.—*Q.T.*	30	S	Foundation stone of R.A. Observatory laid by [the Duke of Edinburgh, 1870.
31	D	LA TRINITÉ	31	S	TRINITY SUNDAY.

MAI.—Semez et plantez en abondance toutes sortes de légumes : on œilletone les plants d'artichants : dans la première quinzaine de ce mois, on doit faire la grande plantation de haricots pour recolter en sec, ce qui n'empêche pas d'en semer tous les 15 ou 20 jours pour en manger vert, ainsi que des fèvres et de pois.

MAI.—Faire boutures d'œillets, d'héliotrope, verveines, véroniques, rosiers, on fait encore des semis de fleurs ; récolter les graines de dhalias qu'on resème ensuite, ces semis donnent de nouvellas variétés, continuer les mêmes plantations du mois dernier.

JUIN, 30 JOURS.	JUNE, 30 DAYS.
SOLEIL	LUNE
Lever — Coucher	D.Q. le 3.........à 11h. 52m. 7 a.m.
	N.L. le 11.........à 0h. 33m. 1 p.m.
	P.Q. le 18.........à 3h. 30m. 9 p.m.
1er à 6h. 29m. ....à 5h. 26m.	P.Q. le 25.........à 10h. 45m. 1 a.m.
15 à 6h. 34m. ....à 5h. 26m.	Apogée, le 5 à midi Périgée, le 20 à 8h. p.m.

Canon de la Diane

Du 1er au 14 à 5h. 30m.	Du 15 au 30 à 5h. 35m.

The probable origin of the name of this month has been given together with that of May.

1	L	St Juvence, m.	1	M	Prince Imperial killed, 1879.
2	M	St Erasme, év.	2	T	Poste du Cap at Savanne attacked, 1810.
3	M	Ste Clothilde	3	W	[ted to sittings of Council, 1841.
4	J	**FETE DIEU**	4	T	CORPUS CHRISTI. Holiday.—Public first admit-
5	V	St Boniface, év.	5	F	Derby Day. Epson Races.
6	S	St Norbert, e.c.	6	S	
7	D	**2e ap. Pent.** Oct. de la Trinité	7	S	1st. SUNDAY AFTER TRINITY.
8	L	St Médard, év.	8	M	Governor Sir George Anderson arrived, 1849.
9	M	SS. Prime et Felicité	9	T	
10	M	Ste Marguerite, reine	10	W	Crystal palace opened, 1854.
11	J	St Barnabé, ap.	11	T	
12	V	St Cœur de Jésus	12	F	
13	S	St Antoine de Padoue	13	S	Slave Trade Act of 1824, promulgated. Holiday.
14	D	**3e ap. Pent.** St Basile, e.c.d.	14	S	2nd. SUNDAY AFTER TRINITY.
15	L	Ste Germaine, c.	15	M	Militia established, 1769.
16	M	St François R.	16	T	
17	M	St Rainier, conf.	17	W	Governor Malartic arrived, 1792.
18	J	SS. Marc et Marcelin	18	T	
19	V	Ste Julienne de Falconieri	19	F	
20	S	**Av. de Sa Maj.,** S. Silvère, p.	20	S	QUEEN'S ACCESSION, 1837. Holiday.
21	D	**4e ap. Pent.**	21	S	3rd. SUNDAY AFTER TRINITY.
22	L	St Paulin, év.	22	M	
23	M	Vig. de St Jean Baptiste	23	T	
24	M	NATIVITÉ DE S. JEAN-BAPTISTE	24	W	President Carnot assasinated, 1894.
25	J	St Guillaume, abbé	25	T	Wreck of the Immig. ship *Randolph* and loss
26	V	SS. Jean et Paul	26	F	[of 18 lives, 1851.
27	S	St Ladislas, roi	27	S	[founded by Poivre, 1759.
28	D	**5e ap. Pent.**	28	S	4th. SUN. AFTER TRINITY. Botanical Gardens
29	L	SS. Pierre et Paul, **C. de S. M.**	29	M	CORONATION DAY. [James H. Higginson, 1853.
30	M	Com. de St Paul	30	T	First stone of Scotch Church laid by H. E.

JUIN.—On sème et on récolte de tous les légumes. Plantez : Pomme de terre, Poireau, Oseille, Echalotte, Betterave, Epinard, Amaranthe, Thym, Piment, Tomate, Pomme-d'Amour, Chicorée, Laitue, Salsifis, Artichaut, Céléri, Persil, Choux, Chou-Fleur, Choux-Navet, Choux-de Chine, Radis, Rave, Petsai, Capucine, Lentille, Pois, Petits-Pois, Brèdes, Boéme, Blé, Avoine, Gram, Tabac, &c., liez la Chicorée, étêtez les premiers Pois et les premières Fèvres, pour avancer leurs fruits.

JUIN.—Retirer de terre pendant ce mois les tubercules de dhalias, gloxinias, bégonias tubéreux, les fuschias doivent être traités comme les marguerites. Floraison des reines-marguerites.

JUILLET, 31 JOURS.

SOLEIL

Lever	Coucher
1er à 6h. 37m.	à 5h. 30m.
15 à 6h. 37m.	à 5h. 35m.

JULY, 31 DAYS.

LUNE.

D.Q. le 3 .... à 5h. 13m. 5 du matin
N.L. le 10 .... à 11h. 25m. 1 du soir
P.Q. le 17 .... à 7h. 54m. 5 du soir
P.L. le 24 .... à 9h. 35m. 3 du soir
Apogée, le 3 à 7h. du matin
Périgée, le 15 à 10h. du soir
Apogée, le 31 à 2h. du matin

Canon de la Diane.

Du 1er au 14 à 5h. 35m. | Du 15 au 31 à 5h. 30m.

The fifth month of the Roman year was called Quintilis. It became the seventh after the reform of the Calendar by Julius Cæsar, in whose honor it received its present name.

1	M	Oct. de St Jean Baptiste	1	W	First Steamer on Thames, 1801.
2	J	VISITATION DE LA B.V.M.	2	T	
3	V	St Anatole, év.	3	F	Bureau de Bienfaisance Established, 1790.
4	S	Ste Berthe, abb.	4	S	
5	D	**6e ap. Pentecôte,** Précieux Sang	5	S	5TH. SUND. AFTER TRINITY. Barristers allowed [to plead with sword on 1787.
6	L	St Isaie, prophète	6	M	
7	M	St Guillebaud, év.	7	T	
8	M	Ste Elizabeth, reine	8	W	
9	J	Ste Véronique, v.	9	T	Capture of Bourbon, 1810.
10	V	Les 7 frères, mart.	10	F	
11	S	St Pie I, pape	11	S	Opening of the Theatre, 1790.
12	D	**7e ap. Pentecôte,** St Jean Gualbert	12	S	6TH. SUND. AFTER TRINITY. Crimea evacuated, [1856.
13	L	St Anaclet, p.m.	13	M	Opening of the Mauritius Dry Dock, 1857.
14	M	St Bonaventure	14	T	Bernardin de St Pierre arrived, 1769.
15	M	St Henri, empereur	15	W	Cardinal Manning b. 1808.
16	J	N. D. du Mont-Carmel	16	T	
17	V	St Alexis, c.	17	F	Reopening of the Port to Foreign Vessel, 1820.
18	S	St Camille de Lellis, c.	18	S	Declaration of Papal Infallibility, 1870.
19	D	**8e ap. Pentecôte,** St Vin. de Paul	19	S	7TH. SUNDAY AFTER TRINITY.
20	L	St Jérôme Emilien	20	M	
21	M	Ste Praxède, v.	21	T	
22	M	Ste Marie-Madeleine	22	W	
23	J	St Apollinaire, év. et m.	23	T	Great fire destroying the Chaussée, 1893.
24	V	Ste Christine, v.	24	F	Death of Governor Malartic, 1800.
25	S	St Jacques, ap.	25	S	First cattle cargo left Van Dieman's land for [Mauritius, 1818.
26	D	**9e ap. Pentecôte,** STE ANNE	26	S	8TH. SUNDAY AFTER TRINITY.
27	L	St Pantaléon, mar.	27	M	
28	M	St Victor, pr. et m.	28	T	Reorganization of the Chamber of Commerce, [1828.
29	M	Ste Marthe, vierge	29	W	
30	J	St Germain l'Auxerois	30	T	Island divided into 9 Districts, 1773.
31	V	St Ignace de Loyola, c.	31	F	Ignatus Loyola, Jesuit died, 1556.

JUILLET.—Plantez et semez, Brède, Ail, Echalotte, Oseille, Betterave, Epinard, Amarante, Thym, Piment, Pomme-de-Terre, Pomme d'Amour, Chicorée, Laitue, Salsifis, Artichaut, Carotte, Céléri, Persil, Choux, Choux-fleur, Choux-Navet, Cresson, Moutarde, Choux-de-Chine, Navet, Radis, Rave, Capucine, Lentille, Petit-Pois, Gram, Manioc, Tabac, &c.

JUILLET.—Taillez des rosiers pour la floraison de Septembre, c'est le moment de greffer les roses et bouturer les œillets.

AOUT, 31 JOURS.	AUGUST, 31 DAYS.
SOLEIL.	LUNE
LEVER. — COUCHER.	D.Q. le 1er .... à 10h. 24m. 6 du soir
1er à 6h. 31m................ à 5h. 41m.	N.L. le 9.................... à 8h. 52m. 1 du matin
15 à 6h. 23m................ à 5h. 45m.	P.Q. le 16............... à 0h. 52m. 7 du matin
	P.L. le 23................. à 10h. 54m. 6 du matin
	D.Q. le 31.................. à 2h. 45m. 4 du soir
	Périgée, le 11 à 10h. du soir
	Apogée, le 27 à 7h. du soir

Canon de la Diane.

Du 1er au 14 à 5h. 25m. | Du 15 au 31 à 5h. 20m.

This month in the early Roman times was called Sextilic, or the sixth ; but became the eight by the Julian arrangement; and received its present title from Augustus, the second of the Cæsars.

1	S	St Pierre-ès-Liens	1	S	Slavery abolished, 1838.
2	D	**10e ap. Pentecôte,** St Alph. de Liguori	2	S	9TH. SUNDAY AFTER TRINITY.
3	L	Invent. de St Etienne, 1er m.	3	M	
4	M	St Dominique, c.	4	T	
5	M	N. D. des Neiges	5	W	First Atlantic Cable laid, 1858.
6	J	TRANSFIGURATION de N. S. J. C.	6	T	Lord Tennyson, born 1809.
7	V	St Gaëtan, conf.	7	F	
8	S	St Cyriaque et ses comp. mm.	8	S	
9	D	**11e ap. Pentecôte**	9	S	10TH. SUNDAY AFTER TRINITY.
10	L	St Laurent, mart.	10	M	Lord Moira, arrived 1813.
11	M	Ste Suzanne, m.	11	T	
12	M	Ste Claire, vierge	12	W	Creation of the Govt. Council, 1825.
13	J	St Jean Berchmans, c.	13	T	
14	V	Ste Philomène	14	F	Printing invented 1457. [laid, 1893. Holiday.
15	S	**Assomption de la T.S.V.**	15	S	1st. stone of the N. Ch. of St François Xavier,
16	D	**12e ap. Pentecôte,** St Joachim	16	S	11TH. SUND. AFTER TRINITY. Gas first used in
17	L	Oct. de St Laurent	17	M	[the streets of London, 1807.
18	M	Ste Hélène, impératrice	18	T	Wreck of the *St. Géran*, 1744.
19	M	St Louis, év.	19	W	Title of Hon. given to Memb. of Council, 1836.
20	J	St Bernard, c.d.	20	T	
21	V	Ste Jeanne de Chantal	21	F	
22	S	Oct. de l'Assomption	22	S	
23	D	**13e ap. Pentecôte,** St Philippe Benizi	23	S	12TH. SUND. AFTER TRINITY. Engagement of
24	L	St Barthélemy, ap.	24	M	[" Ile de la Passe," 1810.
25	M	**St Louis,** roi de France	25	T	Saint Louis—Holiday.
26	M	St Zéphyrin, pape	26	W	
27	J	St Joseph Calasanz, c.	27	T	
28	V	St Augustin, év.	28	F	
29	S	Décol. de St Jean Baptiste	29	S	Jeremie recalled, 1834.
30	D	**14e ap. Pentecôte,** Ste Rose de Lima	30	S	13th. SUND. AFTER TRINITY.
31	L	St Raymond Nonat, c.	31	M	

AOUT.—Semez et plantez : Brède, Echalotte, Poireau, Oseille, Betterave, Epinard, Amarante, Tomate, Pomme d'Amour, Chicorée, Laitue, Salsifis, Carottes, Céléri, Persil, Choux, Choux-Navet, Radis, Navet, Petsai, Rave, etc., semez l'Oignon qu'on récolte sec pour replanter en Mars, (l'Oignon de Mars), Pomme-de-Terre, Boëme, Thym, etc.

AOUT.—Mois favorable aux boutures de roses, camélias, azaléas, fuschias, franciscoeas et autres plantes. Taillez le raisin du 15 au 30 à Moka, à Curepipe et dans un climat analogue, là où on a taillé en mars on taillera en septembre.

SEPTEMBRE, 30 JOURS.

SOLEIL

Lever	Coucher
1er à 6h. 09m	à 5h. 50m.
15 à 5h. 57m	à 5h. 53m.

SEPTEMBER, 30 DAYS.

LUNE

N. L. le 7 .... à 5h. 33m. 5 du soir
P. Q. le 14 .... à 7h. 59m. 8 du matin
P. L. le 22 .... à 2h. 39m. 7 du matin
D. Q. le 30 .... à 5h. 48m. 7 du matin

Périgée, le 8 à minuit
Apogée, le 24 à 7h. du matin

Canon de la Diane.

Du 1er au 14.........à 5h. 15m. | 15 au 30.........à 5h. 10m.

This and three months following still retain the numeral names—seventh, eighth, ninth and tenth given them in the original Roman calendar, notwithstanding that the titles have been incorrect ever since the change from a decimal to a duo-decimal reckoning, instituted before the days of the Cæsars.

1 M	S Gilles, ab.	1 T	
2 M	S Etienne, roi de Hongrie	2 W	
3 J	S Sérapie, v.	3 T	
4 V	Ste Rose de Viterbe, v.	4 F	Introduction of the silkworm by Mr de
5 S	S Laurent Justinien, e. c.	5 S	Malta taken, 1800 [Chazal, 1815. [Seychelles by French, 1756.
6 D	**15e ap. Pentecôte**	6 S	14th. SUNDAY AFTER TRINITY.—Poss. taken of
7 L	Ste Reine	7 M	Ascent of P. Bothe by Snr. Genl. Lloyd, 1832
8 M	**Nativité de la T. S. V.**	8 T	
9 M	S Pierre Claver, c.	9 W	Death of Revd. Father Laval, 1864.
10 J	S Nicolas de Tolentin	10 T	Foundation Fort Adelaide laid, 1833.
11 V	SS Protus et Hya	11 F	
12 S	S Aimé, év. et conf.	12 S	Chamber of Commerce established, 1827.
13 D	**16e ap. Pentecôte,** Saint nom de Marie	13 S	15th. SUNDAY AFTER TRINITY.
14 L	Exaltation de la Ste Croix	14 M	Duke of Wellington died, 1852.
15 M	S Nicomède, m.	15 T	
16 M	Q. T., SS Corn. et Cyprien	16 W	
17 J	Stig. de St François d'Assise	17 T	
18 V	Q. T., S Joseph de Cuperti	18 F	Conseil Provincial replaced by Conseil Supe-
19 S	Q.T., St Janvier et ses comp.	19 S	[rieur, 1724.
20 D	**17e ap. Pentecôte,** N.D. des 7 douleurs	20 S	16th. SUNDAY AFTER TRINITY.— Mauritius
21 L	S Mathieu, apôtre et évan.	21 M	[taken poss. of by the Dutch, 1598.
22 M	S Maurice, m.	22 T	
23 M	S Lin, pâpe et mart.	23 W	
24 J	N. D. de la Merci	24 T	
25 V	S Cléophas, m.	25 F	Conflagration of Port Louis, 1816.
26 S	N. D. des Grâces	26 S	Races at Mont Choisy, 1891.
27 D	**18e ap. Pentecôte**	27 S	17th. SUNDAY AFTER TRINITY.
28 L	S Wenceslas, martyr	28 M	Races at Mont Choisy, 1891.
29 M	S Michel, arch.	29 T	
30 M	S Jérôme	30 W	

SEPTEMBRE.—Les Brèdes seules se sement encore pendant ce mois; on transplante les semis des mois précédents. C'est ordinairement pendant ce mois qu'on ramasse les belles semences.

SEPTEMBRE.—Greffez les roses en fente ou par inoculation, les azaléas par approche. Du 5 au 10 on taille les rosiers pour avoir des fleurs le 2 Novembre.

OCTOBRE, 31 JOURS.

—

SOLEIL

	Lever	Coucher
1er	à 5h. 42m	à 5h. 57m.
15	à 5h. 31m	à 6h. 01m.

OCTOBER, 31 DAYS.

—

LUNE

N. L. le 7.............. à 2h. 08m. 5 du matin.
P. Q. le 13.... .... à 6h. 37m. 6 du soir
P. L. le 21.............. à 8h. 07m. 5 du soir
D. Q. le 29.............. à 7h. 10m. 9 du soir

Périgée, le 7 à 9h. du matin
Apogée, le 21 à 10h. du matin

Canon de la Diane

Du 1er au 14 à........... 5h. 00m. | Du 15 au 31........... à 4h. 50m.

This month was known by the Saxons as Wynat-monat, or wine-month, it being the time for the annual importation of wines from Germany.

1 J	St Rémy, c. c.	1 T	Foundation stone of St John's Moka laid, 1846.
2 V	SS. Anges Gardiens	2 F	[Instance dismissed from Office, 1834.
3 S	St Candide, m.	3 S	Mr John Reddie, President of Court of 1st.
4 D	**19e ap. Pentecôte.**—N. D. du Rosaire	4 S	18TH. SUNDAY AFTER TRINITY.
5 L	St François d'Assise	5 M	Great Reform Meeting at the Union Catho-
6 M	St Bruno, c.	6 T	[lique, 1882.
7 M	St Marc, p.	7 W	Sir J. P. Hennessy, died 1891
8 J	Ste Brigitte, v.	8 T	
9 V	St Denis, c.	9 F	Rome incorporated with Italy, 1870.
10 S	St François Borgia, c.	10 S	Opening of the Port of Mahebourg, 1836.
11 D	**20e ap. Pentecôte.**—Maternité B.V.M.	11 S	19TH. SUNDAY AFTER TRINITY.
12 L	St Maximilien, e.	12 M	America discovered, 1492.
13 M	St Edouard, roi	13 T	Arrival of the *Sultana & Blue Jacket* with
14 M	St Calixte, p. m.	14 W	[cholera, 1855.
15 J	Ste Thérèse, v.	15 T	
16 V	St Gall, ab.	16 F	General Census of Slaves, 1826.
17 S	Ste Edwige, v.	17 S	
18 D	**21e ap. Pentecôte.**—Pureté de B.V.M.	18 S	20TH. SUNDAY AFTER TRINITY.—Arrival of Go-
19 L	St Pierre d'Alcantara, c.	19 M	[vernor Magalon, 1803.
20 M	St Jean de Cant. c.	20 T	Lord Palmerston, b. 1784.
21 M	Ste Ursule	21 W	
22 J	Ste Marie Salomé	22 T	
23 V	St Séverin, év.	23 F	Promulgation of the Civil Code, 1805.
24 S	St Raphaël, arch.	24 S	
25 D	**22e ap. Pentecôte.**— Pat. de la B.V.M.	25 S	21ST. SUNDAY AFTER TRINITY.
26 L	St Evariste, p.	26 M	Count Von Moltke, born 1800.
27 M	St Florentin, m.	27 T	
28 M	SS. Jude et Simon, ap.	28 W	Abolition of Slave Trade by Colonial Assem-
29 J	St Narcisse, év.	29 T	[bly, 1794.
30 V	St Quentin, m.	30 F	Sir J. P. Hennessy proclaimed the New Cons-
31 S	St Sirice, p. c.	31 S	[titution, 1885.

OCTOBRE.— Il n'y a aucune plantation à faire : on transplante les Brèdes sémées le mois passé qui demandent de fréquents arrosements, 4 fois par jours dans les quartiers secs.

OCTOBRE.—Plantez les gloxinias, dahlias, tydéas, gasnérias, caladium, bégonias, tubéreux et autres plantes qui ont reposé pendant l'hiver.

NOVEMBRE, 30 JOURS.

SOLEIL

Lever	Coucher
1er à 5h. 20m.	à 6h. 08m.
15 à 5h. 14m.	à 6h. 15m. 5

NOVEMBER, 30 DAYS.

LUNE

N.L. le 5............... à 11h. 17m. 2 du matin
P.Q. le 12............... à 9h. 30m. 8 du matin
P.L. le 20............... à 2h. 14m. 8 du sori
D.Q. le 28............... à 6h. 33m. 9 du matin.

Périgée, le 4 à 9h. du soir
Apogée, le 17 à 1h. du soir

Canon de la Diane.

Du 1er au 14 à 4h. 40m. | Du 15 au 30 à 4h. 30m.

Known as Wint-mount (wind month) by our Saxon ancestors.

1	D	**LA TOUSSAINT**	1	S	**All Saint's Day.**—Holiday.
2	L	**Fête des Morts**	2	M	All Souls. Arrival of first Indian Laborers,
3	M	St Hubert, év.	3	T	[1834. Holiday.
4	M	St Charles Borromée, c.	4	W	
5	J	St Zacharie	5	T	Gunpowder Plot, 1605.
6	V	St Léonard, ermite	6	F	
7	S	St Ernest, abbé	7	S	[1674.
8	D	**24e ap. Pentecôte,** Stes Reliques	8	S	23rd. Sund. after Trinity. John Milton died,
9	L	**Nais. du P. de Galles,** Bas. S. Sauv.	9	M	Prince of Wales born, 1841. Holiday.
10	M	St André Avellin	10	T	Martinmas.
11	M	St Martin, év.	11	W	Zanzibar-Seychelles Cables laid, 1893.
12	J	St Martin, p. m.	12	T	
13	V	St Stanislas Kostka, c.	13	F	
14	S	St Josaphat, év.	14	S	John Abercrombie died, 1844. [*Smith* at Rodrigues, 1847.
15	D	**25e ap. Pentecôte,** Déd. des Eglises	15	S	24th. Sund. after Trinity. Wreck of *Samuel*
16	L	St Edmond, év.	16	M	Court of Assizes established, 1831.
17	M	St Grégoire, th.	17	T	
18	M	Déd. de St Paul	18	W	
19	J	Ste Elisabeth, veuve	19	T	Governor Farquhar left for England, 1817.
20	V	St Félix de Valois, c.	20	F	Suez Canal opened, 1869.
21	S	Présentation de la B.V.M.	21	S	Governor Sir W. Gomm arrived, 1842. [Day.- -Mauritius Cable completed, 1893.
22	D	**26 ap. Pentecôte,** Ste Cécile, v.	22	S	25th Sunday after Trinity.—St. Cecilia's
23	L	St Clément, p. m.	23	M	Arr. of the *Sarah Sands* with part of 54th Regt.
24	M	St Jean de la Croix	24	T	Indian Immigration susp.,1856. [on board 1857.
25	M	Ste Catherine vierge et m.	25	W	Opening of the Maur. Submarine Cable, 1893.
26	J	St Silvestre abbé	26	T	
27	V	St Léonard de Pt. Maurice	27	F	[first printed by steam, 1814.
28	S	St Sosthène, év.	28	S	English landed at Mapou, 1810. *The Times*
29	D	**1er de l'Avent**	29	S	1st. Sun. in Advent. First London School
30	L	St André, ap.	30	M	St Andrew's Day. [Board elected, 1870.

Novembre.—Plantez : Bringelles, Concombres, Cornichons, Giraumons, Citrouilles, Melons, Melons-d'Eau, Calebasses, Marganzes, Patolles, Pipengailles, Pistaches Créoles, Pistaches Malgaches, Ambrevades, Lalos, Cambarres.

Novembre.—Plantez les gloxinias, dhalias, tydéas, gasnérias, caladium, bégonias tubéreux et autres plantes qui ont reposé pendant l'hiver.

DÉCEMBRE, 31 JOURS.

SOLEIL

Lever	Coucher
1er à 5h. 13m.	à 6h. 26m.
15 à 5h. 17m.	à 6h. 34m.

DECEMBER, 31 DAYS

LUNE

N.L. le 4.........à 9h. 41m. 3 du soir
P.Q. le 12..........à 4h. 19m. 6 du matin
P.L. le 20.........à 7h. 55m. 6 du matin
D.Q. le 27.........à 3h. 58m. 9 du soir
Périgée, le 3 à 7h. du matin
Apogée, le 15 à 4h. du matin
Périgée, le 31 à 5h. du matin

Canon de la Diane

Du 1er au 14 à 4h. 20m. | Du 15 au 31 à 4h. 10m.

The Saxon name for this month was originally Winta-monat the signification of which is evident. After the introduction of Christianity, it was called Heligh-monat or " Holy-month," in referrence to the festival of the Nativity on the 25th.

1	M	St Eloi, év.	1	T	Princess of Wales b. 1844.
2	M	Ste Bibiane, vierge	2	W	Mauritius taken by the British, 1810.
3	J	St François Xavier, c.	3	T	Mauritius capitulated, 1810.
4	V	St Pierre Crysologue	4	F	
5	S	St Sabas, abbé	5	S	R. T. Farquhar assumed the Government of [Mauritius, 1810.
6	D	**2e de l'Avent**	6	S	2nd. SUNDAY IN ADVENT,
7	L	St Ambroise, év. d.	7	M	Foundation stone of the New Royal College, [laid 1892.
8	M	L'IM. CONCEPTION	8	T	
9	M	Ste Léocadie, vierge	9	W	
10	J	Trans. de la s.m. de Lorette	10	T	
11	V	St Damase, pape et conf.	11	F	
12	S	St Synèse, martyr	12	S	Govt. Savings Bank established, 1836.
13	D	**3e de l'Avent**	13	S	3rd. SUNDAY IN ADVENT.
14	L	St Nicaise, mart.	14	M	Susp. of Gov. Sir J. Pope Hennessy, 1886.
15	M	Oct. de l'Im. Conception	15	T	Sir H. Robinson sworn in as Governor, 1886.
16	M	St Eusèbe, év.—*Q.T.*	16	W	
17	J	St Lazare, év.	17	T	
18	V	Attente de l'Enfant.—*Q.T.*	18	F	Slavery officially abolished in U.S. 1862.
19	S	St Némèse, m.—*Q.T.*	19	S	
20	D	**4e de l'Avent**	20	S	4th. SUNDAY IN ADVENT.
21	L	St Thomas, ap.	21	M	St. Thomas's Day.
22	M	St Zénon, mar.	22	T	Return of Sir J. Pope Hennessy, 1888.
23	M	Ste Victoire, vierge	23	W	
24	J	Vigile et jeûne	24	T	Withdrawal of paper money, 1824.
25	V	**NOEL**	25	F	**Christmas Day.**
26	S	St Etienne, premier martyr	26	S	Removal of bodies of Mme Labourdonnais & [child disc. in the Col. Secy's yard.
27	D	ST JEAN, apôtre et évangéliste	27	S	
28	L	LES SAINTS INNOCENTS	28	M	Holy Innocents.
29	M	St Thomas de Cantorbéry, e.m.	29	T	
30	M	St Sabin, év.	30	W	
31	J	St Silvestre, p. c.	31	T	St. Sylvester.

DÉCEMBRE.—Plantez : Mais, Manioc, Bringelles, Concombres, Melons, Melons-d'Eau, Pipengailles, Calebasses, Patolles, Margauzes, Lalos, Giraumon, Patates, Safran, Gingembre.

DÉCEMBRE.—Soignez les dhalias, les bégonias, qui sont en ce moment en pousse ; les activer avec de l'engrais liquide composé de bouse de vache. Le bégonia est une belle plante que l'on cultive à l'ombre et à laquelle il faut peu de soins ; vous en êtes dédommagé par ses feuilles et ses fleurs qui sont très belles. Ce mois est aussi le mois de fougères elles sont en pleine végétation. Les adiantum, asplénium, dicksonia, aspidum, ptéris, etc. sont dans toute leur beauté.

TOPOGRAPHY OF MAURITIUS.

The Island of Mauritius lies between Lat. 19° 58' and 20° 32, South and between Long. 57° 18' and 57° 49' East of Greenwich. Its extreme length is 38 statute miles and its breath 28 miles. The interior of the Island is chiefly high land composed of plains sloping each way to the sea the general elevation being over 500 feet above sea level.

The first systematic triangulation of Mauritius was made by the celebrated Abbé de la Caille, in 1753. After finishing the measurement of an arc of the meridian at Cape of Good Hope, he was sent by the Government of France to determine the Latitude and Longitude of Mauritius and Bourbon. He triangulated about 80 of the chief points of the Island.

During the period that the present General Manager of Railways (Mr. Connal) was Surveyor General, he had signals placed on certain principal elevated points of the Island; from these stations, readings were made by Mr. Parsons and others with a 12 inch theodolite on the other signals and also on all marked objects such as sugar mills chimnies, church towers, &c. From these Mr. Connal himself deduced their rectangular co-ordinates in English feet, the *initial line* being the Meridian passing thro' a stone column on the top of the Pouce Mountain. The results were printed in a small volume. Mr. Descubes then a draughtsman in the Survey Office using the above co-ordinates as a foundation and the materials to be found in the Survey Office together with all the Estate plans, &c., he could borrow, with remarkable industry, compiled a map of the Island on a scale of 1/63,360 (inch to mile) this Map was engraved in England in 1880 and was published by subscription. It has proved of great public utility and is remarkably free from error considering the materials on which it is based; its defect, if any, is overcrowding with detail. The great difficulty Mr. Descubes had to encounter with the plans at his command was not so much *error of measurement* as *distortion*. Mr Descubes is now in the Forest Department of the Indian Government and his name has of late been mentioned in official reports with high praise.

In 1877 Lieutenant Coglan, R. N., made a Coast Survey of the island. He also used for a foundation the above named co-ordinates. This is published as an Admiralty Chart and is on a scale of one inch to the nautical mile; amongst other things of interest in it, is to be found the " hundred fathom line. "

Since Descubes' map of the Island appeared, others have been published but they contain nothing new.

Districts of Mauritius, their approximate area and the names of the Towns and Villages in them: that of the Court house being in italics and first.

15 Port Louis, 15 sq. miles.—*Port Louis*, Grand River, Roche Bois, Vallée des Prêtes.

68 Pamplemousses, 68 sq. miles.—*Pamplemousses*, Long Mountain, Peterboth, Callebasses River, Piton, Bois Rouge, Mapou, Tombeau, l'Arsenal, Pointe aux Piments, Trou aux Biches.

55 Rivière du Rempart, 55 sq. miles.—*Poudre d'Or*, Bois Rouge, Mapou, Grand Baie, Piton, Plaine St Cloud, Rivière du Rempart, Plaine des Roches.

112 Flacq, 112 sq. miles.—*Flacq*, Mare aux Lubines, Quatre Cocos, Trou d'Eau Douce, Rivière Sèche, Mare aux Fougères, Trois Ilots, Camp de Masque.

98 Grand Port, 98 sq. miles.—*Mahébourg*, Mare d'Albert, Plein Bois, Mare Tabac, Cent Gaulettes, Rivière Lachaux, Rivière des Créoles, Les Anses.

92 Savanne, 92 sq. miles.—*Souillac*, Grande Savanne, Petite Savanne.

77 Plaines Wilhems, 77 sq. miles.—*Rose Hill and Curepipe*, Bas du quartier, Terre Rouge, Beau Bassin, Quatre Bornes, Phœnix, le Bassin, Vacoas, Mesnil.

88 Moka, 88 sq. miles.—*Moka*, Les Pailles, Terre Rouge, Quartier Militaire, St Pierre.

100 Black River, 100 sq. miles.—*Bambous*, Petite Rivière, Plaine St. Pierre, Tamarin, Black River, Coteau Raffin, Gorges du Cap.

705 Total area 705 English square miles.

Heights above the level of the sea of the principal Mountains of Mauritius, as found by Abbé de la Caille in the year 1753.

Mountains.

	Toises	Eng. feet
Coin de Mire	81	518
Isle of Serpents, called Parasol or small Round Island	83	531
Long Mountain	89	569
Piton	134	856
Great Round Island	165	1054
Signal Mountain, Port Louis	166	1061
Montagne des Créoles	188	1202
Piton de la Fayence, Eastern end	164	1048
Piton du Canot	274	1752
Piton du Fouge	276	1764
Piton de la Fayence	223	1425
Morne de la Rivière Noire	283	1809
Morne Brabant	283	1809
Piton du Milieu	302	1931
Morne du Grand Port	249	1592
Montagne de la Porte	309	1976
Piton du Bambou	322	2059
Highest of Trois Mamelles	342	2187
Corps-de-Garde Mountain	369	2359
Savanne Mountain	355	2270
Montagne du Rempart	396	2532
Pouce	416	2650
Pieter-Both	420	2685
Piton de la Rivière Noire	424	2711

Dependencies of Mauritius.

Nos. 1 to 3 nearer Dependencies
4 to 11 Chagos Archipelago
12 to 14 Detached Islands
15 Seychelles Archipelago
16 to 23 Dependencies of Seychelles

with Latitudes and Longitudes or relative positions and remarks, compiled from the following Authorities :

1st. Islands in the Southern Indian Ocean by Capt. H.A. Moriarty, R.N., C.B. (Edition 1891.)

2nd. The following Admiralty Charts.

For Dependency, No.	1	Chart No. 715
,,	2 and 3	,, ,, 1881
,,	4	,, ,, 920
,,	6 to 9	,, ,, 3
,,	5, 10 and 11	dated 10th. July 1839
,,	12, 22	,, No. 748 B
,,	13, 16, 17, 18	,, ,, 721 and 722 and 724
,,	14, 21, 23, 24	,, ,, 718
,,	19, 23	,, ,, 724

3rd. Certain official papers, as Mr. Magistrate Ackroyd's reports of 1877 and 1880, &c.

In this list as far as the information would allow nearly all the names of Islands, Islets and Rocks have been inserted, but Shoals, Banks and Reefs except where Islands exist on them have not been mentioned.

General observations. All the dependencies are situated in the Indian Ocean and within the tropics South of the line, between the parallels 3°.42' and 19°.50' (that is to about the latitude of Round Island a few miles North of Mauritius and between the meridiens 46°.12 and 72°.50 East of Greenwich. With the exception of Rodrigues and most of the Seychelles Islands they are of coral formation, the highest points being from 10 or 15 to 50 or 80 feet where sand hills have been formed.

Number.	Names of Islands or Groups.	Latitude South.	Longitude East of Greenwich.	Distance from Port Louis in Marine Miles.	Remarks.
	NEARER DEPENDENCIES. 1—3.				
1	Rodrigues with surrounding Islands and reefs.	Between 19° 38′ and 19° 50′	Between 63° 18′ and 63° 31′		Main Island about 11½ miles long (Statute) and 4 to 5 broad, Area 42 square miles, Mountainous, the highest point Mont Limon, 1,300 feet. Principal Village: Port Mathurin.—Products: Salt fish, cattle, sheep, goats, &a., and now some Tobacco. There are remarkable caverns to S. W. of the Island. Is governed by a resident Magistrate subordinate to the Government of Mauritius.
	(The transit of Venus of Dec. 9th. 1874 Observatory Station about ½ mile Eastward of Port Mathurin Village at) Venus Point is at	19° 40′ 23″	63° 26′ 15″	355	ISLETS WITHIN THE REEF. *On the North.* Booby, Diamond } rocks. *On the West.* Sandy, Coco } low; Marianne, Catherine, Frégate, Destinée, Crab, the largest } high. *On the South.* some very small Paille en queue, Misel, Gombrani, Pierrot or Cat, Flat } low. Hermitage, in Port Sud Est, a rock.
2	Cargados Carayos or St. Brandon Group of Islets, reefs and shoals.	Between 16° 14′ and 16° 50′	Between 59° 29′ and 59° 44′	231 to 265	All the Islands are small and low, many are liable to be submerged in heavy weather. Ths Eastern or outer side of the reef is about 34 miles long in a curved line.
	Islets within or Protected by the Reef.				
	1st. Les Iles Boisées ... ... Several intervening Islets... Cocos ... ... Baleines	Between 16° 25′ and 16° 50′			The most Southerly—a row of 12 to 19 Islets;—According to the Admiralty Chart 1881, there only three, the one at S. W. extremity being represented as a speck, and eleven succeeding patches as of Sand are put in place of the others. The Iles Boisées are the most Southern, they are also called Ile Pointe Requins and Ile Pointe du Sud, which is marked Coco Island in Chart 1881 and the most Northern of this row are the Cocos and Baleines. Some of the intervening ones are Capitaine, Longue, Petit et Grand Dagorne. The Iles Courson are another row of Sandy Islets also on inner side of reef at 4 to 6 miles E. N. Eastward of Baleines Id.

Number.	Names of Islands or Groups.	Latitude South.	Longitude East of Greenwich.	Distance from Port Louis in Marine Miles.	Remarks.
	(St. Brandon—*Continued*).				
	2nd. I. Veronge				3 miles N. E. of Baleines } A fishing station.
	aux Bois				$1\frac{3}{4}$,, ,, of Véronge } A fishing station.
	3rd. Petits Fous				
	Lavocaire				
	aux Fous				Three to seven miles North of aux Bois. These form a fishing station of which Lavocaire and aux Fous are the only ones sufficiently large for camping.
	du Gouvernement	Between 16° 25′ and 16° 50′	Between 59° 29′ 59° 44′		
	Grand Mapou				
	Petit Mapou...				
	4th. Mapare or Paul				On East side of reef, 3 miles East of Lavocaire. (See Admiralty chart 1881.)
	5th. Raphael Islands comprising				
	Pointe du Nord				Fishing establishment.
	Poulailler or Establishment				
	Puits à Eau (most Northern)				Brackish water is collected in sunk barrels.
	3 Islets				
	Islets to West of Reef.				
	6th. Frégate	16° 36′	59° 32′		
	7th. Perle	16° 33′	59° 31′		
	8th. Cirène	16° 28′	59° 36′		
	to North of Reef.				
	9th. North Island	16° 23′ 30″	59° 39′ 40″		About 3 miles N.W. of end of reef.
	10th. St. Pierre or Albatross ...	16° 15′	59° 36′ 30″		Largest of the Group, about ⅓ mile either way, stands apart at North end of bank.
3	Tromelin or Sandy I. North end	15° 51′ 37″	54° 24′ 48″	318	About 1 mile long × ⅛ wide-low, uninhabited.
	CHAGOS ARCHIPELAGO 4—11.				
4	Diego Garcia	Between 7° 13′ and 7° 27′	Between 72° 20′ and 72° 30′		The most important of the Oil Islands, a strip of land in some places very narrow and in others nearly $1\frac{1}{4}$ miles broad, nearly enclosing a vast lagoon which is 12 miles long. The Island is low but covered with tall cocoanut and other trees.
	Observatory Point inner side N. E. limb	7° 14′ 09″7	72° 26′	1181	

	Islands at entrance of Lagoon.				
	East Island				900 × 200 yards.
	Middle				Small } The Main Pass is between these two.
	West Island				Very small }
5	Egmont or Six Iles with reef ...	Between 6° 37′ and 6° 41′	Between 71° 22′ and 71° 27′	1165	Forming an oval 5½ miles × 2 enclosing a lagoon. The Isles are on the South side.
	Names.				
	Isle South East				The Establishment is on this Island.
	Tattamacca				
	Carapatte				
	Lubine				
	Sipaille				
	Rat...				Very small.
	On the Great Chagos Bank. 6—9				
6	Danger Island	6° 23′	71° 17′	1167	On Wn. extremity of the banki 1½ × ¾ miles—low, uninhabited.
7	Eagle Islands. 2 in number.				
	Main or Eagle	6° 11′	71° 23′	1173	2½ × ¾ miles—Cocoanut and other trees.
	Vache Marine				Two miles South of the Main Island. Small ; low.
8	Three Brothers or Trois Frères				
	The North Brother	6° 7′	71° 42′	1197	And within four miles, the Middle brother or Moyenne, (then a rocky Islet) and the South brother which is the largest, ¾ miles long,-- are covered with cocoanut trees, people from Eagle I. sometimes go there, but landing is difficult.
9	Nelson or Legour Island ...	5° 41′	72° 22′	1243	On Northern edge of Great Chagos Bank, about 1¼ miles long, uninhabited.
10	Peros Banhos	Between 5° 13′ and 5° 28′	Between 71° 46′ and 72° 01′		Important. The 27 Islands and Reefs form a rough square, the interior is a large lagoon.
	Diamond Island. Establishment.	5° 15′	71° 48′ 07″	1238	
	Islands on West side.				*Islands on North Side.* — *Islands on East side.*
	du Coin, at S.W. corner 2 miles long. Establishment ...				Diamond, at N.W. ; Establihment — Petit Coquillage
	Anglaise				Petit Ile la Passe — Grand ,,
	Mompatre				La Passe
	Poule				Morseby — *On South Side.*
	Pte. Sœur...				Parasol
	Grande Sœur				Longue — Coin de Mire
	Verte				Grand Bois Mangue — Vache Marine
	Pierre				Petit ,, — Fouquet
	Diable				Manuel — Mapou
	Petit Mapou				Yayé
	Grand Mapou				

Number.	Names of Islands or Groups.	Latitude South.	Longitude East of Greenwich.	Distance from Port Louis in Marine Miles.	Remarks.
11	Salomon or Onze Iles	Between 5° 17′ and 5° 22′	Between 72° 14′ and 72° 19′		On the sides of a reef 5 × 3 miles, six of them are very small, are planted with cocoanut and contain tall timber trees.
	Boddam	5° 22′	72° 14′	1251	Boddam, S.W., the principal; Diable very small; Anglaise, on N.W. side; Passe, Northernmost; Mapous very small; Tattamacca E. side; Fouquet S.E. part; Sepulture or Cimetière, Jacobin, Sel, Poule } very small on Sn. Side
	DETACHED ISLANDS (12—15)				
12	Agaléga	10° 30′	56° 30′	582	Among the most important of the Oil Islands; contains a large Establishment. Consists of two Islands the Extreme points being 12 miles apart, separated near the middle by a sand bank which can be traversed at lowtide by wading.
13	Coetivy	7° 08′	56° 15′	785	$5\frac{3}{4} \times 1\frac{1}{2}$ miles, produces oil.
14	St. Jean de Nove or Farquhar Isles with reefs	Between 10° 05′ and 10° 15′	Between 51° 02′ and 51° 12′		The lagoon $11\frac{1}{2}$ miles × 6 is generally shallow
	Names.				
	North Island, (the Manager's house 1879)	10° 06′ 45″	51° 10 03″	713	4 miles long × ½ to 1/6, planted with cocoanuts.
	South Island				3 " " × ½ " "
	The Manahas (three in number)				Islets between North and South Islands.
	Goelette				do. 2 miles S.W. of South Island.
	Trois Iles				Three small spots having brushwood on N.W. reef, (there are also three others).

15	Seychelles Archipelago				Partial Dependencies.—The Seat of Local Government is at Mahé. There are a resident Civil Commissioner, Executive and Legislative Councils, Judge, &a.
	Names				
	1st Mahé	Between 4° 33′ and 4° 49′	Between 55° 22′ and 55° 33′		Length 16 marine miles, breath 5 to 2, Area 50 square miles, the Town of Mahé is in Port Victoria. The Island is Mountainous the highest Peak, the Morne is 2,993 feet high, and there are several other high peaks, principal produce cocoanut oil.
	The end of Hodoul jetty in Port Victoria Harbour is at ...	4° 37′ 15″	55° 27′ 23″	940	In harbour, Hodoul Islet, very small, off Hodoul jetty and on South side of Victoria Pier.
	Islands surrounding Port Victoria				
	St Anne				2¼ miles from Shore, 1¾ long × ¾ wide, 847 feet high.
	Cerf				1 ,, ,, 1 ,, × ½ ,, 375 ,,
	The Fawn or Faon				An Islet close to Cerf.
	Longue, Moyenne, Ronde				N. E. of Cerf and standing on the same reef, and within one mile, each high and wooded.
	Beacon Island or Sèche				9/10 miles S. E. off Ste. Anne, 89 feet high, white cliffs.
	Harrison Rock				A little further off.
	Islets on Eastern Coast				
	Hodoul Rock				About 2 miles N. of Port Victoria at Anse l'Etoile, white in colour.
	South East Island				Off Pointe La Rue, 6 miles S. E. of P. Victoria.
	Brulé or Rat Island				½ mile N. of S. E. Island.
	Anonyme				1 ,, N. W. of do. covered with cocoanuts, boulder at summit, 130 feet high.
	Souris Islet				3 miles S. of S. E. Island, off Pointe du Sel.
	West Coast Islets				
	Chauve Souris Isle				Off Anse La Mouche, 27 feet high.
	Vache Marine				⅓ mile off Northern Point of Boileau Bay, 177 feet high.
	Thérèse				Conical, 541 feet high, covered with trees, off Anse Jeb.
	L'Ilot de l'Islette				Islet 300 × 100 yards near the coast of Anse l'Islette.
	Conception				Nearly 1 mile long, narrow, 432 feet high, about 1 mile off Cape Ternay.

Number	Names of Islands or Groups	Latitude South.	Longitude East of Greenwich.	Distance from Port Louis in Marine Miles.	Remarks.
	Islands surrounding Mahé (*Continued.*)				
	On North Coast				
	North Islet				Off Western side of North Point, small, 51 feet high.
	2nd. Nearer Islands off Mahé.				
	Silhouette	4° 29′	55° 14′	950	Most Western of the Seychelles Archipelago, 12 miles from N. W. point of Mahé, extends about 3½ × 3 miles, is 2473 feet high, is next in importance to Mahé for oil produce — well wooded and striking appearance.
	North Island				3½ miles North of Silhouette 1½m. × 1 moderate height, straggling wood, " a marked contrast to Silhouette " Establishment.
	Les Mamelles				8 miles N. E. from N. W. point of Mahé, a rock 140 feet high, forming two peaks.
	3rd. Praslin Island	Between 4° 17 and 4° 22′	Between 55° 41′ and 55° 49′	954	Next in size and importance to Mahé, length 7 miles, breath 2, Area 13 square miles, about 1,260 feet high. The " coco de mer " or double cocoanut is indigenous to this Island and Curieuse and was not found elsewhere.
	4th. Larger Islands near Praslin.				
	Curieuse				2 miles long × 1 mile off North coast, Establishment for lepers.
	La Digue	4° 21′	55° 51′	953	Next in importance and about 3 miles to East of Praslin. 3 miles × 2,1175 feet high.
	Félicité				About 2 miles N. E. of La Digue, 2 miles × 1, Produces tattamacca timber.
	5th. Smaller Islands surrounding Praslin.				
	Aride				5 miles N. by W. a barren rock about 500 feet high.
	Booby or Ile aux Fous ...				Small, 2 miles N. by W. of Praslin—low.
	Le Cousin or North Cousin...				" 2 " from S.W. side do.
	La Cousine or South Cousin..				" 3 " from do. do.
	Ave Maria				" 1½ " " E. do. do.

6th. Islets off Félicité.				A rock off S. E. point of Félicité.
Ronde				1 mile long × $\frac{1}{4}$ m., 2 miles Eastward of Félicité.
Marie Anne				Largest 1 m × $\frac{1}{2}$ m., $1\frac{1}{4}$,, North of Félicité } Rocky Islets.
The Sisters. Eastern and Western				$\frac{3}{4}$ mile × $\frac{1}{4}$ } Rocky Islets.
7th. Islets standing further off Praslin and Mahé				
Frigate or aux Frégates ...	4° 35′	55° 58′	939	The Easternmost of the Seychelles group. 31 m. East of N. Pt. of Mahé and 18 m. S.E. of Praslin—$1\frac{1}{2}$ m. long × $\frac{1}{2}$ m. 550 ft. high.
Lelot				2 m. W. by S. of Frégates, a rock 50 feet high.
Recif Island	4° 35′	55° 47′	940	20 miles E. of N. pt. of Mahé and 14 m. S. of Praslin, $\frac{1}{2}$ m. long × $\frac{1}{4}$ 150 feet high, white rock on Summit, uninhabited, a resort of Sea birds.
8th. Outlying Islands of the Seychelles Archipelago.				
Plate or Flat Island	5° 52′	35° 24′	867	Most Southern of the Seychelles group, 64 m. S. b. W. of South extreme of Mahé 1 m. long × $\frac{1}{4}$ broad, low, sand and coral, uninhabited.
Bird Island or Sea cow (centre)	3° 42′ 50″	55° 12′ 19″	996	Most Northern of the Seychelles group, 1 m. × $\frac{1}{2}$, low uninhabited but visited by fishermen—seal and turtle abound and a great many birds.
Dennis or Orixa	3° 48′	55° 40′	987	$1\frac{1}{4}$ m. × $\frac{3}{4}$, there is a lighthouse on this Island, 60 feet high.
DEPENDENCIES OF SEYCHELLES.				Under Ordinance No. 23 of 1881.
16 Amiralty Archipelago — including Desroches Islands ...	Between 4° 50′ and 6° 17′	Between 52° 50′ and 53° 45′		On a bank, 89 miles long and 6 to 23 broad, the Ile Desroches is on a separate bank.
Names.				
1st. African Isles or African Banks				
North Islet, (North Extreme of)	4° 52′ 26″	53° 23′ 33″	949	At N.E. end of the great bank, both very small, are joined at low water spring tides by a ridge of Sand, so that they may be considered as one Island of $2\frac{1}{2}$ miles in length—frequented by fishermen from Seychelles.
South Islet, (the larger)... ...				
2nd. Eagle of Remire Island (N.E. point of)	5° 06′ 23″	53° 18′ 41″	938	1 mile long × $\frac{1}{2}$ wide, uninhabited.
3rd. Darros, (N.E. point at ... with	5° 24′ 23″	53° 18′ 13″	921	1 mile long × $\frac{1}{2}$, oil establishment.
St. Joseph and group ...				Eight Islets on a reef surrounding a lagoon the whole $3\frac{1}{4}$ × 2 miles separated from Darros by a channel $\frac{1}{3}$ mile wide — (*Darros* being to the N.W.) but form part of same Establishment.

Number.	Names of Islands or Groups.	Latitude South.	Longitude East of Greenwich.	Distance from Port Louis in Marine Miles.	Remarks.
	St. Joseph and Group—(*Contd.*)				
	Names.				
	St. Joseph...				1 mile × ¼, on Eastern Edge of the reef, distant 3 miles from Darros, planted.
	Ressource, Fouquets ...				Small Islets on N. E. part of reef, planted, low.
	Benjamin, Carcassaye, Pelican, Aux Chiens, Poule or Pol ...				On Southern part of reef, low and sandy, covered with bushes — all very small.
	4th. Poivre Islands				Most important of the Amirantes, are upon a coral reef 3 × 2 miles which dries all over at low tide.
	The North Island (N.E.extreme)	5° 45′ 14″	53° 19′ 12″	900	Establishment,—about 1 mile long and narrow.
	,, South Island or Sud ...				Produces maize, about 1 mile either way.
	,, Western				Very small.
	5th. l'Etoile	5° 53′	53° 02′	897	Small, about 400 yards either way sandy, uninhabited, scattered bushes.
	6th. Boudeuse	6° 05′	52° 51′	890	About 300 yards either way, sandy, uninhabited — coarse grass — on S. W. extremity of Amirantes Bank.
	7th. Marie Louise Island, (N.W. point)	6° 10′ 22″	53° 09′	879	On S.E. edge of Amirantes Bank, ¾ × ⅓ mile some cocoanuts and filaos, landing difficult, uninhabited.
	8th. Ile des Neuf...	6° 14′	53° 03′	860	¾ × ¼ mile, low, sandy, uninhabited — most Southerly of the Amirantes.
	9th. Ile Desroches (centre of N. beach)...	5° 40′ 56	53° 40′ 58″	899	3½ × ½ mile, on Southern side of nearly circular coral bank of 11 miles diameter, forming an interior lagoon, this bank is separated from the Great Amirantes Bank being about 11 miles to the East of it, the Island produces oil and maize.
	10th. Lampériaire or King Ross Island...				Not identified on Charts.

17	Alphonse	7° 01'	52° 45'	839	About 2 miles long, on a detached reef, oil establishment.
	Bijoutier				3 miles to S. of Alphonse, deep channel between, is small and circular. } on the same reef $8\frac{1}{2} \times 5$ miles shallow and drying in patches at low water.
	St. François				6 miles to S. of Bijoutier, a ridge of sand $\frac{3}{4}$ m. long, planted with cocoanuts. } on the same reef $8\frac{1}{2} \times 5$ miles shallow and drying in patches at low water.
18	Providence Reef & South Banks		09"		Extend 24 miles nearly N. & S. by 2×6 wide, besides the islands named there are many sandy Islets or cays distributed over it, also banks that dry at half tide.
	Names.				
	Providence Island (W. extreme of Village)	9° 14' 04"	51° 02' 09"	762	2 miles × $\frac{1}{3}$, on Northern part of reef, oil establishment.
	Cerf Island or South Bank ...				Near the S. end of the bank, one of a number of Sandy Islets, visited from Providence for turtle.
19	St. Pierre N.W. extreme ...	9° 19' 10"	50° 43' 20"	768	1 mile either way— uninhabited— no fringing reef. "The sea breaks on it and will in time reduce it to its level."
20	Cosmoledo Group	Between 9° 37' and 9° 46'	Between 47° 30' and 47° 40'		Several coral Islands and Islets on a reef surrounding a central lagoon, uninhabited, visited by fishermen—$9\frac{1}{2}$ miles × 7.
	Names.				
	Menai				The Westermost, over 2 miles long, a small hill at each end.
	Observation Islet...	9° 41' 20"	47° 32' 25"	864	The 3rd large rock Eastward of Menai and about $\frac{3}{4}$ miles from the N. E. point.
	Middle Islet				Very small.
	The Eastern North Island ...				$\frac{1}{2}$ mile long. } on North part of reef.
	The Western " ...				400 yards either way } on North part of reef.
	Goeltte Island				Very small
	Polite "				1 mile long, narrow, 35 feet high at South end.
	Wizard "				2 miles long, a small hill near each end, at S.E. corner of the group.
	Pagodo "				Small.
	South "				$1\frac{3}{4}$ m. long, narrow.
	And several other rocks & Islets.				
21	Astove. Centre	10° 06' 30"	47° 45' 42"	840	About 3 miles × 2, uninhabited, visited by a vessel from Seychelles for turtle.
22	Assumption Island Hillock near S.E. extreme ...	9° 46' 20"	46° 31' 07"	908	$3\frac{1}{2}$ miles × $\frac{1}{2}$ to 1 m. broad—uninhabited, visited by fishing parties for turtle.
23	Aldabra Islands	Between 9° 21' and 9° 29'	Between 46° 12' and 46° 32'		The most Western of the Dependencies, is about 19 miles long (marine) by 5 to $7\frac{1}{2}$ broad, the interior lagoon about 15×2 to 5 m. is very shallow and partly dry at low water— the land is from $\frac{1}{4}$ to 3 miles wide round the lagoon and is divided into three or four larger Islands by narrow channels. Total area of land may be about 37 square miles.

Number.	Names of Islands or Groups.	Latitude South.	Longitude East of Greenwich.	Distance from Port Louis in Marine Miles.	Remarks.
	Aldabra Islands—Continued.				
	Names.				
	West Island (observation spot). (Eastern side) ...	9 o 22′ 35″	46 o 14′ 41″	236	2½ × 1m. or 2½ square miles, has a sandy beach, extending 1½ miles on Wn. coast.
	Middle Island (West part) ...				2 × ¼ m. or ½ square mile } narrow channel between, considered as one Island.
	,, (East part) ...				9½ × 2/3 m. or 6 ,, ,, } narrow channel between, considered as one Island.
	South Island				25 × ½ to nearly 3 or 4 square miles extends along the whole Southern and curves to the Wn. and round the N. En. side— mostly rocky surface covered with jungle and mangrove swamps.
					(the above:) "Useless for habita- " tion, the surface is " generally sharp " jagged coral with " no soil except sand, " and a thick tangled " bush difficult to get " through.
	Islets				
	Cocoanut Island				Very small, in the lagoon near the East end, " the only suitable place for building a house."
	Euphrates Island				Very small, on the lagoon, about 2 miles to the S. of Obsn. spot.
					Also several Islets and rocks in the space between West and South Islands forming the Western channels—" is visited for fish and " turtle, and for the large land tortoise which in this Island " alone in all the Indian Ocean still survives, but in very " diminished numbers."

Estimated Population of Mauritius from 31st. December 1892 to 1895.

Districts.	1892									1893								
	General Population.			Indian Population.			Total Population.			General Population.			Indian Population.			Total Population.		
	Males.	Females.	Total.	Males.	Females.	Total.	Males.	Females.	Total.	Males.	Females.	Total.	Males.	Females.	Total.	Males.	Females.	Total.
Port Louis	18356	18308	36664	13810	10481	24291	32166	28789	60955	18017	17869	35886	12840	9943	22783	30857	27812	58669
Pamplemousses	4726	4126	8852	16998	12950	29948	21724	17076	38800	4724	4078	8802	16443	12818	29261	21167	16896	38063
R. du Rempart...	2583	2237	4820	11429	8776	20205	14012	11013	25025	2647	2289	4936	11410	8872	20282	14057	11161	25218
Flacq	5982	5437	11419	26916	20009	46925	32898	25446	58344	6063	5446	11509	26521	19982	46503	32584	25428	58012
Grand Port ...	6596	6057	12653	21327	15246	36573	27923	21303	49226	6763	6095	12858	21080	15246	36326	27843	21341	49184
Savanne ...	3934	3428	7362	16639	11687	28326	20573	15115	35688	3980	3436	7416	16061	11533	27594	20041	14969	35010
Pl. Wilhems ...	10997	11372	22369	20357	16209	36566	31354	27581	58935	11192	11475	22667	19980	16271	36251	31172	27746	58918
Moka	3360	3289	6649	15096	11641	26737	18456	14930	33386	3420	3310	6730	14922	11753	26675	18342	15063	33405
Black River ...	2719	2350	5069	5928	4559	10487	8647	6909	15556	2772	2356	5128	5722	4469	10191	8494	6825	15319
Total ...	59253	56604	115857	148500	111558	260058	207753	168162	375915	59578	56354	115932	144979	110887	255866	204557	167241	371798

Districts.	1894									1895								
	General Population.			Indian Population.			Total Population.			General Population.			Indian Population.			Total Population.		
	Males.	Females.	Total.	Males.	Females.	Total.	Males.	Females.	Total.	Males.	Females.	Total.	Males.	Females.	Total.	Males.	Females.	Total.
Port Louis ..	17926	17871	35797	12601	9846	22447	30527	27717	58244	17824	17663	35487	12232	9668	21900	30056	27331	57387
Pamplemousses	4728	4105	8833	16577	12970	29547	21305	17075	38380	4689	4038	8727	16410	13028	29438	21099	17066	38165
R. du Rempart..	2701	2325	5026	11730	9146	20876	14431	11471	25902	2738	2347	5085	11964	9360	21324	14702	11707	26409
Flacq ...	6147	5520	11667	26926	20403	47329	33073	25923	58996	6165	5504	11669	27182	20546	47728	33347	26050	59397
Grand Port ...	6876	6201	13077	21478	15539	37017	28354	21740	50094	6985	6198	13183	21686	15844	37530	28671	22042	50713
Savanne ...	4042	3515	7557	16119	11609	27728	20161	15124	35285	4086	3504	7590	16455	11857	28312	20541	15361	35902
Pl. Wilhems ..	11349	11664	23013	20261	16654	36915	31610	28318	59928	11516	11678	23194	20214	16897	37111	31730	28575	60305
Moka ...	3465	3368	6833	15160	11969	27129	18625	15337	33962	3505	3375	6880	15304	12192	27496	18809	15567	34376
Black River ..	2813	2379	5192	5729	4507	10236	8542	6886	15428	2842	2392	5234	5673	4480	10153	8515	6872	15387
Total ..	60047	56948	106995	146581	112643	259224	206628	169591	376219	60350	56699	117049	147120	113872	260992	207470	170571	378041

Population of Mauritius at each Census and on 31st. December 1895.

Date of Census.	General Population.			Indian Population.			Total.		
	Males.	Females.	Total.	Males.	Females.	Total.	Males.	Females.	Grand Total.
August 1846 ...	58290	46554	104844	48925	7310	56245	107225	53864	161089
20 November 1851 ...	55059	47768	102827	64282	13714	7996	119341	61482	180823
8 April 1861 ...	61346	56070	117416	141615	51019	192634	202961	107089	310050
11 April 1871 ...	51771	48013	99784	141804	74454	216258	193575	122467	316042
3 April 1881 ...	57303	53578	110881	151352	97641	248993	208655	151219	359874
5 April 1891 ...	58539	56129	114668	147499	108421	255920	206031	164550	370581
31 December 1882 ...	58218	54283	112501	148165	98656	246821	206383	152939	359222
31 December 1883 ...	59035	54459	113494	147117	99600	245717	206152	154069	360221
31 December 1884 ...	60097	54924	115021	151001	102791	253792	211098	157715	368813
31 December 1885 ...	60811	55161	115972	148345	102791	251316	209156	158132	367288
31 December 1886 ...	60789	55635	116424	147612	104109	251721	208401	159744	368145
31 December 1887 ...	60928	55888	116816	146553	104809	251362	207481	160697	368178
31 December 1888 ...	61405	56337	117742	145752	105808	251560	207157	162145	369302
31 December 1889 ...	61499	56700	118199	146865	107600	254465	208364	164300	372664
31 December 1890 ...	62101	56900	119001	149264	109721	258985	211365	166621	377986
31 December 1891 ...	59354	56548	115902	148112	109971	258083	207466	166519	373985
31 December 1892 ...	59253	56604	115857	148500	111558	260058	207753	168162	375915
31 December 1893 ...	59578	56354	115932	144979	110887	255866	204557	161241	371798
31 December 1894 ...	60047	56948	116995	146581	112643	259224	206628	169591	376219
31 December 1895 ...	60350	56699	117049	147120	113872	260992	207470	170571	378041

Marriages from 1886 to 1895.

Districts.	1886			1887			1888			1889			1890			1891			1892			1893			1894			1895		
	General Population.	Indian Population.	Total.	General Population.	Indian Population.	Total.	General Population.	Indian Population.	Total.	General Population.	Indian Population.	Total.	General Population.	Indian Population.	Total	General Population.	Indian Population.	Total.	General Population.	Indian Population.	Total.	General Population.	Indian Population.	Total.	General Population.	Indian Population.	Total.	General Population.	Indian Population.	Total.
Port Louis.	359	151	510	333	146	479	290	126	416	321	116	437	320	115	435	381	118	499	332	121	453	237	101	338	307	91	398	287	97	384
Pamplem...	40	66	106	46	70	116	57	73	130	40	58	98	39	67	106	58	71	129	52	37	89	26	44	70	37	65	102	23	50	73
R. du Rem.	20	44	64	14	33	47	46	37	83	19	29	48	18	32	50	27	26	53	22	15	37	20	32	52	23	32	55	21	22	43
Flacq	64	103	167	88	100	188	75	103	178	77	75	152	58	79	137	86	102	188	73	81	154	46	70	116	56	93	149	30	98	128
Grand Port	78	79	157	71	71	142	104	103	207	81	87	168	57	75	132	92	79	171	69	45	114	52	94	146	51	76	127	49	71	120
Savanne ...	66	33	99	47	51	98	46	39	85	65	54	119	58	65	123	80	50	130	56	32	88	27	39	66	62	40	102	24	54	78
P. Wilhems	107	127	234	115	121	236	119	82	201	124	110	234	119	108	227	151	115	266	120	72	192	105	84	189	114	96	210	107	94	201
Moka	40	60	100	35	68	103	56	59	115	39	62	101	35	56	91	35	41	76	25	39	64	19	49	68	16	53	69	29	57	86
B. River ...	20	33	53	20	34	54	29	40	69	47	27	74	25	34	59	29	24	53	38	16	54	24	14	38	18	16	34	22	17	39
Total...	794	696	1490	766	694	1463	822	662	1484	813	618	1431	729	631	1360	939	626	1565	787	458	1245	556	527	1083	684	562	1246	592	560	1152

Births from 1886 to 1895.

Districts.	1886									1887									1888								
	General Population.			Indian Population.			Total.			General Population.			Indian Population.			Total.			General Population.			Indian Population.			Total.		
	Males.	Females.	Total.	Males.	Females.	Total.	Males.	Females.	Grand Total.	Males.	Females.	Total.	Males.	Females.	Total.	Males.	Females.	Grand Total.	Males.	Females.	Total.	Males.	Females.	Total.	Males.	Females.	Grand Total.
Port Louis.	661	649	1310	469	475	944	1130	124	2254	652	668	1320	473	438	911	1125	1106	2231	647	634	1290	440	888	828	1087	1031	2118
Pamplem...	182	150	332	495	487	982	677	637	1314	133	141	274	500	459	959	633	600	1233	175	131	306	447	469	916	622	600	1222
R. du Rem.	91	95	186	323	309	632	414	404	818	90	87	177	322	306	628	412	373	805	93	89	182	325	327	652	418	416	834
Flacq	246	227	473	862	772	1634	1108	999	2107	276	246	522	750	871	1824	1229	1117	2346	244	249	493	828	810	1638	1072	1050	2131
Grand Port	289	289	578	698	631	1329	987	920	1907	282	296	578	707	666	1373	989	962	1951	275	243	518	598	569	1167	873	812	1685
Savanne ...	148	135	283	462	437	899	610	571	1182	170	141	314	520	485	1005	690	629	1319	159	135	294	491	475	966	650	610	1260
P. Wilhems	357	326	683	718	736	1454	1075	1062	2137	351	363	714	783	781	1564	1134	1144	2278	382	416	798	780	695	1475	1162	1111	2273
Moka	122	113	235	469	417	866	591	530	1121	126	122	248	471	477	948	597	599	1196	122	121	246	444	422	866	566	546	1112
Bk. River..	84	92	176	146	162	308	230	254	484	108	102	210	180	165	345	288	267	555	27	103	176	157	152	309	230	255	485
Total...	2180	2076	4256	4642	4426	9068	6822	6502	13324	2188	2169	1357	4909	4648	9557	7097	6817	13914	2170	2133	4303	4510	4307	8817	6680	6440	13120
	1889									1890									1891								
Port Louis.	674	601	1275	457	416	873	1131	1017	2148	638	616	1254	410	410	820	1048	1026	2074	625	629	1254	383	366	749	1008	995	2003
Pamplem...	147	154	301	491	501	992	638	655	1293	140	141	281	523	508	1031	663	649	1312	145	118	263	557	499	1056	702	617	1319
R. du Rem.	89	89	178	358	372	730	447	461	908	96	89	185	358	360	718	454	449	903	101	94	195	416	372	788	517	466	983
Flacq	243	270	513	946	873	1819	1189	1143	2332	257	223	480	865	819	1684	1122	1042	2164	256	233	488	964	937	1901	1219	1170	2289
Grand Port	264	243	507	668	617	1285	932	860	1792	266	256	522	542	485	1027	808	741	1549	340	244	584	683	602	1285	1023	846	1869
Savanne ...	146	129	275	458	466	924	604	595	1199	150	141	291	456	448	904	606	589	1195	139	137	276	484	504	988	623	641	1264
P. Wilhems	362	337	719	790	771	1561	1152	1128	2280	349	379	728	768	774	1542	1117	1153	2270	401	403	804	767	730	1497	1168	1133	2301
Moka	118	111	229	472	524	996	590	635	1225	115	133	248	547	480	1027	662	613	1275	128	119	247	503	492	995	631	611	1242
Bk. River..	96	91	187	162	175	337	258	266	524	103	98	201	186	174	360	289	272	561	91	83	174	168	166	334	259	249	508
Total...	2139	2045	4184	4802	4715	9517	6941	6760	13701	2114	2076	4190	4655	4458	9113	6769	6534	13303	2225	2060	4285	4925	4668	9593	7150	6728	13195

Births from 1886 to 1895.—*Continued.*

Districts.	1892									1893								
	General Population.			Indian Population.			Total.			General Population.			Indian Population.			Total.		
	Males.	Females.	Total.	Males.	Females.	Total.	Males.	Females.	Total.	Males.	Females.	Total.	Males.	Females.	Total.	Males.	Females.	Total.
Port Louis	590	607	1177	448	423	871	1038	1030	2068	518	494	1012	347	330	677	865	824	1689
Pamplemousses.	156	151	307	631	613	1244	792	759	1551	120	127	247	525	478	1003	645	605	1250
R. du Rempart..	94	87	181	406	494	900	500	581	1081	87	101	188	378	391	769	465	492	957
Flacq	244	263	507	1055	1047	2102	1299	1310	2609	227	215	442	814	775	1589	1041	990	2031
Grand Port	263	266	529	753	728	1481	1016	994	2010	274	242	516	713	640	1353	987	882	1869
Savanne	156	146	302	567	498	1065	723	644	1367	136	119	255	471	484	955	607	603	1210
Pl. Wilhems ...	451	451	902	862	783	1645	1323	1224	2547	449	423	872	768	779	1547	1217	1202	2419
Moka	129	128	257	539	480	1019	668	608	1276	96	112	208	571	563	1134	667	675	1342
Black River... ..	97	88	185	155	136	291	252	224	476	91	78	169	139	120	259	230	198	428
Total	2180	2187	4367	5416	5202	10618	7611	7374	14985	1998	1911	3999	4726	4560	9286	6724	6471	13195

Districts.	1894									1895								
Port Louis	598	626	1224	386	379	765	984	1005	1989	583	557	1140	395	351	746	978	908	1886
Pamplemousses.	150	137	287	599	548	1147	749	685	1434	127	119	246	553	580	1133	680	699	1379
R. du Rempart..	112	87	199	477	471	948	589	558	1147	96	106	202	430	433	863	526	539	1065
Flacq	260	237	497	904	935	1839	1164	1172	2336	223	232	455	909	794	1703	1132	1026	2158
Grand Port	283	253	536	735	631	1366	1018	884	1902	288	245	533	688	704	1392	976	949	1925
Savanne	145	145	290	407	414	821	552	559	1111	135	133	268	479	446	925	614	579	1193
Pl. Wilhems ...	419	448	867	850	785	1635	1269	1233	2502	433	456	889	778	800	1578	1211	1256	2467
Moka	109	111	220	542	525	1067	651	636	1287	115	108	223	618	611	1229	733	719	1452
Black River... ..	88	79	167	131	156	287	219	235	454	93	97	190	122	133	255	215	230	445
Total	2164	2123	4287	5031	4844	9875	7195	6967	14162	2093	2053	4146	4972	4852	9824	7065	6905	13970

Still-Births from 1886 to 1895.

Districts.	1886			1887			1888			1889			1890			1891			1892			1893			1894			1895		
	General Population.	Indian Population.	Total.	General Population.	Indian Population.	Total.	General Population.	Indian Population.	Total.	General Population.	Indian Population.	Total.	General Population.	Indian Population.	Total.	General Population.	Indian Population.	Total.	General Population.	Indian Population.	Total.	General Population.	Indian Population.	Total.	General Population.	Indian Population.	Total.	General Population.	Indian Population.	Total.
Port Louis	115	61	176	118	70	188	88	64	152	81	53	134	78	71	149	87	56	143	90	67	157	63	51	114	91	43	134	76	52	128
Pamplemousses.	25	75	100	27	83	110	25	82	107	26	94	120	20	89	109	24	85	109	30	116	146	20	88	108	16	116	132	21	121	142
R. du Rempart..	9	36	45	8	46	54	11	55	66	11	49	60	11	51	62	11	44	55	16	69	85	19	48	67	13	69	82	9	71	80
Flacq	24	111	135	20	117	237	23	83	106	22	98	120	27	94	121	29	131	160	24	161	185	23	136	159	22	105	127	26	121	147
Grand Port	28	77	105	27	92	129	27	68	95	40	101	141	34	84	118	25	73	98	36	109	145	28	128	156	20	84	104	28	109	137
Savanne	17	80	97	21	55	76	27	71	98	23	80	103	26	77	103	31	82	113	33	88	121	32	87	119	21	77	98	22	89	111
Pl. Wilhems ...	31	80	111	30	63	93	32	49	80	26	70	96	28	77	105	32	81	113	65	107	172	47	95	142	48	103	151	48	94	142
Moka	7	68	69	15	67	82	16	55	68	10	54	64	12	60	72	12	67	79	11	74	85	15	69	84	10	70	80	7	75	82
Black River......	11	20	31	9	25	34	6	14	20	8	20	28	4	20	24	9	20	29	10	34	44	17	25	42	6	30	36	14	12	26
Total......	269	600	769	285	619	903	252	541	793	247	619	866	240	623	863	260	639	899	315	825	1140	264	127	991	247	697	944	251	744	995

Deaths from 1886 to 1895

Districts.	1886									1887									1888								
	General Population.			Indian Population.			Total.			General Population.			Indian Population.			Total			General Population.			Indian Population.			Total.		
	M.	F.	Total.	M.	F.	Total.	M.	F.	Grand Total.	M.	F.	Total.	M.	F.	Total.	M.	F.	Grand Total	M.	F.	Total.	M.	F.	Total.	M.	F.	Grand Total
Port Louis	684	645	1329	794	512	1306	1478	1157	2635	809	755	1564	808	588	1396	1617	1343	2945	767	696	1463	760	459	1219	1527	1155	2682
Pamplem	172	129	301	602	381	983	774	510	1284	202	151	353	723	468	1191	925	619	1544	193	137	330	557	355	912	750	492	1242
R. du Rempart.	45	49	94	226	158	384	271	207	478	68	76	144	358	260	618	426	336	762	71	70	141	227	154	391	298	234	532
Flacq	172	140	312	606	408	1014	778	548	1326	175	207	382	746	538	1284	921	745	1666	191	171	362	569	449	1018	760	620	1380
Grand Port......	178	168	346	556	413	969	734	581	1315	303	284	587	750	575	1325	1053	859	1912	240	194	434	636	390	1026	876	584	1468
Savanne	86	99	185	412	282	694	498	381	879	103	82	185	387	303	690	490	385	875	104	88	192	437	322	759	541	410	951
Pl. Wilhems ...	293	248	538	599	350	949	892	595	1487	302	238	540	680	392	1072	982	630	1612	286	272	558	612	431	1043	898	703	1601
Moka	84	67	151	324	242	566	408	309	717	94	59	153	394	286	680	488	345	533	107	96	203	357	288	645	464	384	848
Black River ...	50	39	89	232	182	414	282	221	503	76	77	153	222	373	373	298	228	526	67	68	133	230	134	364	295	202	409
Total	1764	1581	3345	4351	2928	7279	6115	4509	10625	2132	1929	4061	5068	8629	8629	7200	5490	12675	2024	1792	3816	4385	2992	7377	6409	4784	11193
	1889									1890									1891								
Port Louis	757	679	1436	692	461	1153	1449	1140	2589	893	812	1705	365	591	1456	1758	1403	3161	637	545	1182	603	364	967	1240	909	2149
Pamplem	150	133	283	715	447	1162	865	580	1445	174	152	326	754	483	1237	928	635	1563	139	117	256	462	319	781	601	436	1037
R. du Rempart.	76	60	136	252	195	447	328	255	583	76	82	158	301	247	548	377	329	706	50	50	100	222	180	402	272	230	502
Flacq	170	153	323	720	530	1250	890	683	1573	220	211	431	803	543	1346	1023	754	1777	165	183	348	613	466	1079	778	649	1427
Grand Port......	302	270	572	1049	757	1806	1351	1027	2378	230	185	415	751	468	1219	981	653	1634	185	159	344	578	403	981	763	562	1325
Savanne	132	117	249	570	428	998	702	545	1247	100	94	194	499	342	841	599	436	1035	100	89	189	458	314	772	558	403	961
Pl. Wilhems ...	243	241	484	616	372	988	859	613	1472	275	285	560	652	439	1091	927	724	1651	251	244	495	533	362	895	784	606	1390
Moka	82	92	174	330	278	608	412	370	782	92	79	171	336	259	595	428	338	766	90	76	166	285	226	511	375	302	677
Black River ...	58	56	114	217	167	384	275	223	498	58	62	120	229	139	368	287	201	488	63	61	124	214	170	384	277	231	508
Total	1970	1801	3771	5161	3635	8796	7131	5436	12567	2118	1962	4080	5190	3511	8701	7308	5473	12781	1680	1524	3204	3968	2804	6772	5648	4328	9996

Deaths from 1886 to 1895.—*Continued.*

Districts.	1892 General Population. Males.	Females.	Total.	1892 Indian Population. Males.	Females.	Total.	1892 Total. Males.	Females.	Total.	1893 General Population. Males.	Females.	Total.	1893 Indian Population. Males.	Females.	Total.	1893 Total. Males.	Females.	Total.
Port Louis ..	898	885	1783	858	573	1431	1756	1458	3214	973	831	1804	980	607	1587	1953	1438	3391
Pamplemousses	215	153	368	657	450	1107	872	603	1475	202	182	384	858	513	1371	1060	695	1755
Riv. du Rempart	63	81	144	292	208	500	355	289	644	70	58	128	374	280	654	444	338	782
Flacq	204	181	385	894	724	1618	1098	905	2003	223	200	423	1024	698	1722	1247	898	2145
Grand Port ...	231	219	450	559	406	965	790	625	1415	191	211	402	768	536	1304	959	747	1706
Savanne ...	119	118	237	472	376	848	591	494	1085	157	117	274	866	570	1436	1023	687	1710
Pl. Wilhems ...	365	340	705	685	425	1110	1050	765	1815	369	330	699	838	542	1380	1207	872	2079
Moka	98	67	165	352	286	638	450	353	803	89	101	190	565	364	929	654	465	1119
Black River ...	88	87	175	259	167	426	347	254	601	84	80	164	281	175	456	365	255	620
Total ...	2281	2131	4412	5028	3615	8643	7309	5746	13055	2358	2110	4468	6554	4285	10839	8912	6395	15307

Districts.	1894 General Population. Males.	Females.	Total.	1894 Indian Population. Males.	Females.	Total.	1894 Total. Males.	Females.	Total.	1895 General Population. Males.	Females.	Total.	1895 Indian Population. Males.	Females.	Total.	1895 Total. Males.	Females.	Total.
Port Louis ...	745	664	1409	609	458	1067	1354	1122	2476	835	695	1530	734	514	1248	1569	1209	2778
Pamplemousses	161	125	286	498	402	900	659	527	1186	196	166	362	727	517	1244	923	683	1606
Riv. du Rempart	68	61	129	230	215	445	298	276	574	79	74	153	335	250	585	414	324	738
Flacq	196	183	379	654	548	1202	850	731	1581	245	228	473	1063	795	1858	1308	1023	2331
Grand Port ...	190	167	357	552	400	952	742	567	1309	229	223	452	696	490	1186	925	713	1638
Savanne ...	98	76	174	399	336	735	497	412	909	121	129	250	553	378	931	674	507	1181
Pl. Wilhems ..	302	289	591	559	378	937	861	667	1528	406	392	798	785	535	1320	1191	927	2118
Moka	74	63	137	341	306	647	415	369	784	105	86	191	473	382	855	578	468	1046
Black River ...	57	66	123	190	132	322	247	198	445	81	75	156	199	167	366	280	242	522
Total ...	1891	1694	3585	4032	3175	7207	5923	4869	10792	2297	2068	4365	5565	4028	9593	7862	6096	13958

Regulations relating to the issue of Army Allowances, 1894.

PROVISIONS.

Commuted Allowance in lieu of Rations to officers of all ranks ... ... Rs. 0.35 per diem.

FORAGE ALLOWANCE.

Commuted allowance in lieu of Forage ... ... Rs. 1.40 per horse.

FUEL AND LIGHT.

Colonel Commanding	Rs. 1.50 per diem.
Colonel, Lieutenant-Colonel and Major	0.75 ,,
Captain	0.65 ,,
Subaltern	0.50 ,,
Warrant Officer, single	0.12 ,,
Warrant Officer, married	0.18 ,,

SERVANTS' ALLOWANCE.

For each personal servant allowed under parags. 501 and 502 of Allow. Regulations 1894... Rs. 0.80
For each authorized groom 0.80

COLONIAL ALLOWANCE.

Colonel Commanding	Rs. 8.75 per diem.
Other Ranks	1.65 ,,
Warrant Officer or Schoolmistress unmarried	0.55 ,,

LODGING ALLOWANCE.

Staff and Departmental.		*Regimental.*	
Colonel on the staff ...	Rs. 5.70 per diem.	Lieutenant Colonel Commanding ...	Rs 5.20 p. d.
Lieutenant Colonel ...	5.20 ,,	Lieutenant Colonel	3.55 ,,
Major	4.35 ,,	Major	3.55 ,,
Captain	3.55 ,,	Captain	2.75 ,,
Lieutenant	2.75 ,,	Lieutenant	2.75 ,,

STAFF AND REGIMENTAL.

Warrant Officer				Rs. 1.60 per diem.
Non Commissioned Officers and men included in Class 16 ...				1.60 ,,
Do.	do.	do.	Classes 17 and 18 ...	1.00 ,,
Do.	do.	do.	Classes 19 and 20 ...	0.50 ,,

Amount of Bills drawn during 1894 by the Treasury Chest Officer on account of Army Services ... ... £ 32,293 2. 6.

ALFRED H. LINDOP,

Captain, A.P.D.

15th. February 1895.

District Paymaster.

Statement of total Military Expenditure for the year 1894.

No. of vote.	PARTICULARS.	Amount. £	s.	d.
1	Pay &c., of the Army	26,539	...	...
2	Medical Establishment..	1,713	...	...
6	Transport and Remounnts	1,730	...	...
7	Provisions, Forage &c....	11,615	...	...
8	Clothing Services	710	...	...
9	Warlike and other stores	790	...	...
10	Works, Buildings and Repairs	7,364	...	...
	Imperial Defence Loan { Barracks	651	...	...
	Imperial Defence Loan { Fortifications	...	...	...
11	Establishments for Military Education	124	...	...
12	Miscellaneous Effective Services	21	...	...
14 to 16	Army Non-Effective Services	610	...	...
	Total ... £	51,867	...	...

By the Colony :	£	s.	d.
Colonial Contribution for Regulsr Troops...	13,804	13	9

ALFRED H. LINDOP,

Captain, A. P. D.

District Paymaster.

15th. February 1895.

I.—Government Debenture-Debt Account on 31st. December 1894.

Debts.	To whom due.	Rate of Interest.	When incurred and for what cause.	Provisions for Payment of Interest or Sinking Fund and enactments by which it is made.	Amount of original Debt.	Amount repaid.	Remarks.
					£	£	
Mauritius Railways.	1. Debenture Bond Holders.	6 o/o p.a.	In 1865 and 1866—For the construction of the Mauritius Railways.	Paragraph 2 of Article XIV of Ord. 15 of 1864 enacts that an annuity at the rate of 7 per centum per annum on the whole of the sum which shall be borrowed, shall be paid into the Sinking Fund half-yearly	......	5000	Converted into Consolidated 4 o/o Debentures under the provisions of Ord. 10 of 1879.
					245900	*79900	Converted into 4 o/o Inscribed Stock under provisions of Ordinance 1 of 1887. *£ 72,400—4 o/o Ins. Stock. 7,500—6 o/o Reg. Stock.
	2. Do.	4½ " ...	In 1876. — For the construction of the Mauritius Railways, Savanne Line.	Ordinance No. 10 of 1876 enacts that 1 o/o Cumulative Sinking Fund shall be applied either to annual drawing or to the purchase of the Bonds in the market, payable half-yearly and chargeable against the Revenues of the Colony		13800	Drawn Bonds.
					100000	33300	Converted into 4 o/o Inscribed Stock under the provisions of Ord. 1 of 1887.
	3. Do.	4 " ...	In 1879.—For the redemption of 4 o/o Debentures issued under the provisions of Ord. No. 10 of 1879.	Ordinance No. 10 of 1879 enacts the same provisions as Ordinance No. 10 of 1876		27100	Drawn Bonds.
					314600	217900	Converted into 4 o/o Inscribed Stock as per Ord. 1 of 1887.

I.—Government Debenture-Debt Account on 31st. December 1894.—*Continued.*

Debts.	To whom due.	Rate of Interest.	When incurred and for what cause.	Provisions for Payment of Interest or Sinking Fund and Enactments by which it is made.	Amount of Original Debt.	Amount repaid.	Remarks.
					£	£	
Maur. Railways.	4. Debenture Bond Holders.	4 o/o p.a.	In 1887.—To pay to the General Revenues, the funds spent for the construction of the Moka Railway Line under provisions of Ord. 1 and 2 of 1887.	Article 24 of Ord. No. 2 of 1887 enacts that the Governor shall appropriate out of the General Revenues and Assets of the Colony in each half year a sum for the formation of a Sinking Fund equal to Ten shillings per £100 on the total nominal amount of Inscribed Stock	......	100	Drawn Bonds.
					102900	100200	Converted into 4 o/o Inscribed Stock as per Ord. 1 of 1887.
Do. and Mare-aux-Vacoas Water Supply.	5. Stock Holders.	,, ...	In 1888.— To declare the terms and conditions applicable to Loans authorized to be raised in England by the Government of Mauritius, and to provide for the creation of Mauritius Inscribed Stock under the provisions of Ord. No. 1 of 1887. ...	Do do.	480749.13.0	...	Ord. 1 of 1887 £341687. 0.0 Do. 2862.13.0 344549.13.0 Ord. 2 of 1887 100200. 0.0 Ord. 22 of 1887 36000. 0.0 £480749.13.0
Maur. Loan Ord. 1892.	6. Stock Holders.	3 ,, ...	In 1893.—To meet the wants and necessities created by the hurricane of the 29th. April 1892 and to provide funds for certain public works.	Do do.	600000. 0.0	...	
				Total	1844149.13.0	473000	

A. FITZ PATRICK,

Head Accountant.

I.—Public Debts of Mauritius on 31st. December 1894.

SINKING FUND.

	Stock.	Market Value.	£	s.	D.
Ordinance No. 15 of 1864.					
Invested in 4 o/o Mauritius Debt. Inscribed Stock	£ 45,849.12.11	£ 53,529.19. 2			
,, 3 o/o Guaranteed	13,580.16. 3	14,701. 4. 7			
,, 2¾ o/o Consols	79,750.16. 1	82,442. 7.10			
,, 2½ o/o Annuities...	25,826. 7. 5	26,246. 0.11	176,919	2	6
	£ 165,007.12 8				
Ordinance No. 1 of 1887.	Stock.	Cost Price.			
Invested in 2½ o/o Annuities...	£ 8,206.11. 0	£ 7,939.16. 9			
,, 3½ o/o Cape of Good Hope	3,851·19. 5	4,227.10. 9			
,, 3 o/o Ceylon	4,259.16. 0	4,291.14.11			
,, 3½ o/o South Australia	5,473. 1. 9	5,459. 8. 1			
,, 3½ o/o Victoria	6,386. 4. 6	6,019. 0. 4			
,, 3½ o/o New South Wales	5,224.15.11	5,211.14. 9			
,, 3½ o/o Hong-Kong	2,911.16. 9	3,021. 0. 7	36,170	6	2
	£ 36,314. 5. 4				
Ordinances 4 and 12 of 1892.					
Invested in 4 o/o British Guiana	£ 44. 0. 0	£ 46.19. 4			
,, 3½ o/o New South Wales	1,148. 2. 9	1,145. 5. 5			
,, 3½ o/o New Zealand	2,638.19. 7	2,632. 7. 8			
,, 3½ o/o Victoria	4,336. 4. 0	4,086.17. 5	7,911	9	10
	£ 8,167. 6. 4				
In the names of the Trustees (Ordinances 10 of 1876, 10 of 1879 and 2 of 1887.)			1.440	18	9
		Total £	222,441	17	3

A. FITZ PATRICK,
Head Accountant.

II.—Debenture Debt of the Poor Law Commission on 31st. December 1894.

Debts.	To whom due.	Rate of Interest.	When incurred and for what cause.	Provision for payment of Interest or Sinking Fund and Enactments by which it is made.	Amount of Original debt.	Amount repaid.	Remarks.
					£	£	Debentures.
Poor Law Commission.	Debenture Bond Holders.	5 o/o p.a.	In 1873 for the purpose of erecting a hospital at Savanne, and infirmaries at the Barkly Asylum; and for the purpose of erecting a hospital at Grand Port and one at Flacq.	Provision for payment of interest due on debentures is made in the Budget of the Colony under Item No. 21, Sub-Item 16. "Poor Law Commission." Same provision is made towards the withdrawal of Debentures in the Budget under same item. Sub-Item No. 17.	*10,000	7,500	* Issued in April 1873 £ 3,000 *a* Do. July 1873 3,000 *b* Do. Oct. 1873 4,000 £ 10,000

(*a*) These Debentures were issued by virtue of a resolution adopted by the then Poor Law Commission at their Meeting held on the 28th. of November 1872, and with the sanction of the Government (Government Order No. 4,984 of 16th. December 1872.)

(*b*) These Debentures were issued by virtue of a resolution adopted by the then Poor Law Commission, at their Meeting held on the 5th. September 1873, and with the sanction of the Government (Col. Sec. Letter, A/1625 of the 29th. August 1873.)

E. AUBERT,

Poor Law Commissioner.

III.—Debenture Debt of the Municipal Corporation on 31st. December 1894.

Debts.	To whom due.	Rate of Interest.	When incurred and for what cause.	Provision for payment of Interest or Sinking Fund and Enactments by which it is made.	Amount of Original debt.	Amount repaid.	Remarks.
Municipal Corporation.	Debentures Holders.	5 o/o ...	On 28th. July 1884—To repay the public Debts contracted on Debentures by the Mayor and Corporation of Port Louis.	Provision for the payment of Interest and Sinking Fund is made in Ord. 33 of 1881, amended by Ordinance No. 16 of 1884-85.	£ 140,000	£ 4,700.0.0	Conversion Loan payable within the term of 49 years and 6 months from the 31st. December 1889.
		,, ...	On 15th. January 1889—To adjust the Accounts of 1885 and 1886 for the balance of expenses incurred for the Rectification Canal for the supply of water to the Eastern Suburb. To complete the Conversion Loan.	Provision for the payment of Interest and of principal is made in Ordinance No. 42 of 1888.	Rs. 156,000	Rs. 39,000	Colonial Loan payable within the term of 20 years from the year 1890 by yearly drawings by lot 78 Debentures.
	Maurit. Government.	By Annuities.	On 22nd. October 1892.—To pay the interest and Sinking Fund of the Conversion Loan out of a Loan of Rs. 150,000 to be made by Mauritius Government to the Municipal Corporation, on account of the hurricane of the 29th. April 1892, only a sum of Rs. 66,000 was paid.	Provision for the payment of Annuities is made in Ordinance No. 20 of 1892.	15,000	78,348	Part of Hurricane Government Loan payable within the term of 25 year from 1st. November 1893 by Annuities of Rs.9601.80.
		5 o/o ...	On 28th. December 1894—To pay the interest and Sinking Fund of the Conversion Loan.	Provision for the payment of instalments is made in Ordinance No. 19 of 1894.	28,500	......	Government Special Loan payable by four instalments of Rs.7,125 each, the 1st. to become due on 31st. Dec. 1895.
				Total ... £	162,200	7280.2.10	

Recapitulation :—

On Loan contracted in Sterling money £ 140,000 out of which £ 4,700 repaid.
Three Loans in Rupee currency amounting to Rs. 334,500 out of which Rs. 46,348 repaid.

Doger SPÉVILLE,
Town Treasurer.

E. FRANÇOIS,
Mayor of Port Louis.

From 1st. January to 31st. December.	Revenue.	Expenditure.	Surplus in Revenue.	Excess in Expenditure.
	£	£	£	£
1812	191355	364498	....	173143
1813	204221	349836	....	190618
1814	161717	310647	....	148030
1815	177165	286337	....	109172
1816	133750	232434	....	98683
1817	214501	304580	....	90070
1818	149190	143240	5949	....
1819	134928	156406	....	21477
1820	102875	135433	....	32558
1821	107596	188628	....	81032
1822	131606	186631	....	55024
1823	148131	201399	....	53268
1824	167272	208614	....	41342
1825	141167	178003	....	36836
1826	138459	151134	....	12675
1827	156257	142997	13260	....
1828	164371	158827	5544	....
1829	174473	160458	13914	....
1830	164542	153382	11159	....
1831	155580	191310	....	35730
1832	131873	178330	....	46457
1833	133334	161406	....	28072
1834	196888	181991	14997	....
1835	166575	169320	....	2745
1836	188552	164725	23828	....
1837	185139	188164	....	3025
1838	233398	182088	51310	....
1839	198375	189637	8737	....
1840	230522	181058	49513	....
1841	265704	218187	47517	....
1842	255209	188848	66361	....
1843	245547	436454	....	190906
1844	268255	351486	....	83231
1845	296828	280014	16816	....
1846	328719	378112	....	49101
1847	264059	289372	74687	....
1848	286714	342092	....	55378
1849	245954	272838	....	26884
1850	308550	254747	53803	....
1851	231389	240728	80661	....
1852	311854	283053	23881	....
1853	318750	285204	33546	....
1854	366867	(a) 372370	....	5503
1855	348452	(b) 317839	30693	....
1856	335103	(c) 326580	68522	....
1857	451209	(d) 381780	68429	....
1858	553166	(e) 521514	31652	....

(a) Including £ 21,614 taken from Accumulated Balances.
(b) ,, 7,503 ,, ,, ,,
(c) ,, 8,192 ,, ,, ,,
(d) ,, 24,863 ,, ,, ,,
(e) ,, 11,875 ,, ,, ,,

From 1st. January to 31st. December.	Revenue.	Expenditure.	Surplus in Revenue.	Excess in Expenditure.
	£	£	£	£
1859	609516	(*j*) 572479	37037	......
1860	553419	(*g*) 500853	52565	......
1861	482788	(*h*) 468849	13939	.....
1862	492324	(*ik*) 609942	......	117617
1863	518278	(*l*) 482521	35757	......
1864	638067	(*m*) 602279	35788	......
1865	646730	(*n*) 667715	......	20985
1866	639576	(*o*) 700048	......	60475
1867	534992	(*p*) 642601	......	197609
1868	577686	(*q*) 641272	......	63585
1869	595024	(*r*) 575180	19844	......
1870	683166	(*s*) 591579	16587	......
1871	616953	(*t*) 600962	15991	.....
1872	703159	650328	52831	.....
1873	690081	657110	32971	......
1874	720130	727063	......	6933
1875	692894	(*u*) 775826	......	82942
1876	732106	719539	12567	......
1877	748059	703608	44451	......
1878	Rs. 7,895,536	Rs. 7,345,786	Rs. 549,750	......
1879	7,637,295	7,461,998	175,297	......
1880	7,821,085	7,573,960	247,127	......
1881	7,813,910	7,600,176	213,733	......
1882	9,551,635	8,280,107	1,271,528	......
1883	8,892,655	8,379,344	513,311	......
1884	8,609,628	9,162,442	....	552,814
1885	7,309,233	8,391,059	....	1,081,826
1886	7,229,973	8,390,054	....	1,160,081
1887	6,858,918	7,985,909	....	1,126,991
1888	8,574,058	7,771,578	802,480	......
1889	8,744,864	8,560,074	184,790	......
1890	7,774,773	7,705,311	69,462	......
1891	7,595,650	8,192,265	....	596,614
1892	7,473,029	8,024,484	....	551,454
1893	8,103,922	7,872,096	231,825	......
1894	8,534,427	8,587,039	....	52,612

(*j*) Including £ 7405 taken from Accumulated Balances.
(*g*) " 5411 " " "
(*h*) " 12541 " " "
(*i*) " 10066 " " "
(*k*) £ 300,000 were taken in 1862 from Accumulated Balances for Railway purposes and not included in the Total Expenditure of that year.
(*l*) Including £ 5486 taken from Accumulated Balances.
(*m*) " 1575 " " "
(*n*) " 3492 " " "
(*o*) " 3886 " " "
(*p*) " 1303 " " "
(*q*) " 643 " " "
(*r*) " 333 " " "
(*s*) " 2433 " " "
(*t*) " 952 " " "
(*u*) " 67496 " " "

Receipts of the Mauritius Government from 1885 to 1894.

Heads of Revenue.	1885	1886	1887	1888	1889	1890	1891	1892	1893	1894
	Rs.	Rs.	Rs.	Rs.	Rs.	Rs.	Rs.	Rs.	Rs.	Rs.
Customs	2276450	2325094	2088452	2558677	2412875	2670420	2424414	2620282	2808085	3006819
Harbour Dues	126059	132799	122330	118340	122557	138833	156963	198419	179108	180959
Land Sales	4265	1814	3090	4077	5936	2901	18883	931	5942	921
Rent of Government property ...	918	1098	3606	968	48	776	52268	54294	58007	56920
Transfer, Registration and Mortgage Dues	264772	178463	138385	163025	160014	178031	159306	118448	179902	171361
Licenses and Permits	1919567	1958288	1913465	1869415	2240176	2142917	2272120	2055130	2120930	2016146
Stamps	89279	84506	78589	82623	108426	96083	96415	89787	90506	93493
Taxes	112615	109421	103594	102402	109390	105477	128515	119119	117714	......
Post Office and Telegraphs ...	70516	69430	68616	71852	78961	81592	73909	66842	65996	84276
Fines, Forfeitures and Fees of Court	102279	86674	81661	91962	79628	97184	39306	89790	284359	264122
Fees of Office	34238	34957	31469	31768	33482	32630	240234	112396		
Forests	......	55141	66360	60794	62753	45720	41761	5976	11429	32031
Sale of Government Property ...	44726	45647	42249	43332	48526	34005	9151	1019	......	......
Reimbursements in aid of expenses incurred by Government ...	342483	312812	297832	826367	266889	237299	*......	*......	*......	*......
Miscellaneous Receipts	38730	69082	112254	406931	753234	71392	73544	144473	228751	290561
Interest	237659	234773	216715	558366	509797	219136	226533	240638	404731	536330
Special Receipts	......	9629	4394	......	2921	......	26692	51607	*......	......
Sanitary Receipts	31330	28353	32102	30274	32532	30892	*......	4226	*......	......
Rodrigues	6760	5998	11116	13848	11254	9186	*......	*......	8617	5680
Oil Islands	4010	4170	4050	4096	4030	4402	*......	*......	4116	4000
Diego Garcia	552	2366	3833	1166	120	......	*......	*......	*......	......
Total	5765161	5752515	5424069	7040281	6943651	6198885	5998329	5982387	6518193	6743619
Railway Traffic	1544063	1477448	1434848	1533769	1801213	1575888	1597321	1490642	1585729	1790808
Grand Total	7309224	7229963	6858918	8574058	8744864	7774773	7595650	7473029	8103922	8534427

* Owing to a different classification of accounts begun in 1891 these items are included under other heads.

Expenditure of the Mauritius Government from 1885 to 1894.

Heads of Services.	1885	1886	1887	1888	1889	1890	1891	1892	1893	1894
Civil Establishments.	Rs.	Rs.	Rs.	Rs.	Rs.	Rs.	Rs.	Rs.	Rs.	Rs.
Total Establishments, viz: Fixed Salaries, Provisional and Temporary Salaries, Allowances and Contingencies	2397542	2373452	2365428	2310367	2268589	2309010	1403996	1641431	911475	1007935
Services exclusive of Establishments.										
Pensions, Retired Allowances and Gratuities ...	295721	345171	286841	331149	359764	337365	356737	422822	413355	463201
Harbours, Coast Services, &c.	56180	67537	49090	78910	65471	71121	*......	......	*......	*......
Revenue Services &c.	13189	10793	19295	12841	16984	9147				
Administration of Justice	91581	86442	73733	81520	72803	87046	519712	530387	521885	519343
Ecclesiastical...	27350	25579	23379	28497	28583	29708	144811	143594	142482	142314
Charitable Allowances	3449	3470	2733	2030	2060	1275	10444	11505	11027	12157
Education	146156	162908	168030	167770	164026	167533	459588	457040	469858	505648
Hospitals	138302	124089	111088	105857	129314	121739	428063	402146	494313	415044
Police	62422	53429	66936	45819	79316	55522	475169	474825	468026	493195
Gaols	3670	1443	1734	1374	1425	1905	191992	188417	179118	181716
Rent	62982	62290	65410	61881	54755	55700	*......	......	*......	*......
Transport	93432	96630	93312	93961	109001	54501	9824	6373	7315	6697
Conveyance of Mails	164165	158958	111661	96607	97306	109352	*......	......	220059	182290
Works and Buildings	514044	460628	254939	142718	257544	186589	477773	......	318534	338521
Roads and Bridges	214658	166937	165573	174453	188102	176416				
Forests	143020	115417	122825	116879	114788	100758	108435	103700	96241	104588
Miscellaneous	306240	564625	824010	598180	483968	361762	524883	537397	338442	460521
Interest and Exchange	179964	217723	169570	247833	326853	217857	91590	157285	329541	376773
Civil Store Department	628077	554267	445299	420500	488686	478851	37337	8068	35582	34163
Contribution towards Military Expenditure ...	185208	211750	208896	246840	307791	301761	347451	150787	259699	252718
Immigration	104322	70964	73150	42334	72133	58724	130794	147164	159570	132598
Drawback and Refund of Duties	15267	10073	20783	13039	16714	12531	*......	......	......	*......
Quarantine	12433	9066	37740	13600	127092	56158	335050	308356	101008	80828
General Board of Health	201868	194684	188987	193092	212731	197506	195343	196391	189010	186214
Poor Law Department	392697	367780	370907	384372	371195	330677	238935	230837	220352	207660
Rodrigues	11342	18610	19008	17724	21227	13664	26559	37412	46627	32158
Oil Islands	......	......	......	......	......	......	8289	6456	7473	7194
Total... ...	6465281	6504709	6340362	6030193	7172144	5904189	6414340	6192493	5941002	6143476
Railway	1207613	1100344	1047003	999806	1306393	1106304	1043707	984025	960717	1153969
Debenture Debt paid in England	718153	784980	598544	741609	815437	694818	734217	847966	970377	1289594
Grand Total	8391047	8390054	7985909	7771578	8560074	7705311	8192264	8024484	7872096	8587039

* Owing to a different classification of accounts begun in 1891, these items are included under other heads.

Heads of Revenue.	1885	1886	1887	1888	1889	1890	1891	1892	1893	1894
	Rs.	Rs.	Rs.	Rs.	Rs.	Rs.	Rs.	Rs.	Rs.	Rs.
Government contribution in lieu of quay dues	90000	90000	90000	90000	90000	90000	90000	90000	90000	90000
Licenses and permits. .	8086	7596	8818	8917	8233	8206	7955	12146	9782	14007
Taxes	177669	174435	176763	173419	167881	166341	176228	158428	165281	184134
Rents	54818	50893	57306	58083	58353	55646	53691	48154	47242	49430
Sale of Municipal property	2175	2002	2118	1018	1642	18598	4284	3195	2695	2192
Reimbursements in aid of expenses incurred	2047	841	1020	159	111	412	65	20133	14	1351
Fees of Office	1888	1732	1877	946	1035	598	22	264	558	729
Canals	23020	26206	20828	19870	22252	24275	22413	15000	17649	21047
Special Receipts	7030	6917	6677	5935	6620	7766	7227	6265	6741	4628
Miscellaneous Receipts	9050	11326	14439	12344	10345	10029	7677	19612	12198	14710
Interest	3740	420	248	162	343	409	517	320	452	812
Provisional Contribution for Exchange ...	......	......	......	......	15181	53382	......	41911	46802	56379
Total Revenue...	379562	378368	380097	370853	381996	435662	370079	415434	399414	439419
Sundry Debtors	......	......	......	1969	2688	1663	517	11	13133	7384
Advances recovered ...	11381	72259	10844	7541	11200	10357	13327	8488	11038	13520
Deposits received	1227615	23118	7735	7783	9260	12127	23041	5375	4329	11365
Investment of unclaimed monies	......	......	......	......	......	......	......	......	......	
Sinking Fund, &c.	......	......	......	......	......	......	......	......	......	
Loan	* 1182018	* 492978	* 802493	1147542	582710	46467	62221	66000	84000	28500
Total Receipts...	2800576	966723	1201120	1535688	987854	506276	469185	495308	511914	500088

* Including Bills payable, Conversion loan, and amount received from Corporation Agent, Paris.

Heads of Services.	1885	1886	1887	1888	1889	1890	1891	1892	1893	1894
	Rs.	Rs.	Rs.	Rs.	Rs.	Rs.	Rs.	Rs.	Rs.	Rs.
Establishment and Allowances	43795	46425	45500	47477	46264	46894	47053	47185	47096	47722
Office Contingencies...	6816	4653	3417	3813	5838	5730	4984	4484	7882	7786
Pensions and Gratuities	5566	5305	5676	6846	5736	8884	8591	9105	11397	9118
Revenue Services	12945	12607	32394	12474	.12565	12315	12961	13843	12296	13391
Works and Buildings...	60119	11043	...	5318	3269	4494	9688	20245	57743	31593
Streets, Bridges, and Gardens.	157983	110798	129123	112545	120801	137316	147876	114404	119459	106978
Canals	·3289	5086	...	7437	5194	21964	5695	5258	9393	10140
Fire Engine Establishment.	28738	27479	...	31441	35899	25699	20000	22307	27486	27953
Cemeteries	4989	4802	...	4881	4783	4924	5075	5450	5603	6004
Municipal Agents	10169	10212	...	8262	8288	8660	8753	9612	8142	8622
Theatre	4067	4416	...	2807	2304	2461	3458	1038	2686	16044
Interest, Debenture debt, &c.	324414	97223	77713	79360	67952	130595	138923	141849	165528	178474
Miscellaneous Services	11960	8693	10789	9469	10264	7613	7776	22252	17284	16033
Public Works Department—materials.	...	...	...	...	...	...	...	...	21325	779
Drawbacks and Refund of duties.	362	440	34	229	69	1053	118	526	74	100
Public Library	2408	1440	...	1364	2203	1951	2038	2022	2173	3210
Sundry Creditors	75709	43443	55863	77797	55112	54036	855	774	1019	170
New Oriental Bank Corp	...	...	...	...	...	...	...	15049	...	...
Total Expenditure...	753329	394765	360509	411580	395511	474589	423844	445410	516584	484117
Advances repaid.........	12999	73001	10003	6906	13001	12265	12479	10246	9628	22403
Deposits do.	13614	23248	7644	7657	7201	13691	22363	6171	2811	8573
Loan do.	2036218*	479297*	827900	1124227	566176	14750	...	...	...	...
Investment of unclaimed Monies.	...	...	...	...	...	...	...	...	...	...
Sinking Fund, &c.	...	...	...	...	...	...	...	...	...	...
Grand Total Expenditure	2788558	969611	1206056	1550370	981919	515295	458686	461827	529023	515093

* Including Bills payable, loans repaid, temporary loan.

Computed real value of Total Imports of Merchandize, &c., in Mauritius from the United Kingdom, British Possessions, and Foreign Countries, from 1885 to 1894.

Countries.	*1885	*1886	*1887	*1888	*1889	*1890	*1891	*1892	*1893	*1894
	Rs.	Rs.	Rs.	Rs.	Rs.	Rs.	Rs.	Rs.	Rs.	Rs.
United Kingdom	4531409	4962017	6272943	3010409	3670880	4051595	3622436	5189701	3349075	3709564
British Possessions.										
Australasia	23331[illegible]	1588187	2004023	939595	884708	1010367	1045023	726919	919199	1124656
Cape Colonies	328658	519730	567105	364306	230977	188738	173072	185850	90547	134286
Ceylon	68081	43091	11029	11542	7268	19865	25235	11430	1635348	20535
Continental India	8448914	8169484	6769146	7413129	7698034	7081729	7974875	13351147	10939093	12930404
Seychelles	250741	265854	315468	272013	256621	223081	......	233346	247658	225903
Hong-Kong	172036	100120	180162	145126	100654	82774	76672	84381	123961	110161
Jamaica	......	......	......	......	......	......	......	......	36	......
Natal	......	......	......	......	......	......	......	16540	9951	2277
Singapore	358996	365239	268495	185200	232714	225329	94183	210387	279907	274221
St. Helena	1200	......	......	......	......	......	......	......	......	......
Foreign Countries.										
Europe.										
Belgium	......	......	......	......	457	80000	......	968	14031	......
Denmark	......	......	......	......	......	......	......	......	2400	729
France	3771250	4641359	4323495	2406386	2269814	2450789	2085504	1915363	1950683	1836793
Holland	......	......	......	......	......	......	......	654	745	71
Italy	......	......	......	......	101500	......	......	2080	11225	6394
Germany	14566	237756	78537	142295	54100	1816	27853	325580	208552	70206
Norway	......	......	......	......	......	......	......	......	......	......
Sweden	22873	22102	22861	21997	22015	45399	7700	18147	66225	39867
Spain	......	......	......	......	......	......	......	1600	......	......
Africa.										
Abyssinia	......	......	......	......	......	......	......	......	......	......
Egypt	......	......	......	......	......	......	......	450	......	2
Johanna	98953	11507	174035	121967	156003	74631	174610	175430	226934	214068
Madagascar	1226769	1226769	864052	663458	382269	433634	427153	519301	407262	218296

Mozambique	......	......	......	......	......	......	......	......	......	......
Réunion	321203	311261	241559	171136	159185	227064	127642	117223	145514	121967
Zanzibar	132984	23775	12962	3553	9647	9668	5793	18407	21091	4851
Asia.										
Arabia	......	......	......	......	......	......	......	......	9842	6690
Bussorah	......	......	......	......	......	......	......	......	......	......
China	......	......	20	2	......	......	......	1642	2472	168496
Cochin China	45459	......	......	1245	2977	......	......	3950	......	......
Java	30591	......	25713	......	......	......	......	......	1210	......
Lombock	......	......	......	......	......	......	......	......	......	......
Muscat	18403	8880	......	......	11297	22314	81941	......	......	......
Persia	......	......	......	......	......	......	......	......	......	......
Philippine Islands	......	26375	5242	1967	......	560	......	......	......	256
Pondicherry	441300	532755	444539	296628	289408	206957	138920	209980	334311	332325
Sandalwood	......	5029	8220	10324	14525	20018	8002	......	19366	4500
Siam	......	......	......	......	......	......	......	......	......	......
Sumbawa	......	......	......	......	......	......	8300	......	......	......
Timor	......	......	......	......	......	......	......	......	......	......
America.										
Brazils	......	48527	......	......	......	......	......	......	......	......
Peru	6667	......	979523	200060	986020	......	......	......	......	......
Uruguay	51507	18210	34377	58161	44838	53549	11195	24320	36349	18604
States of Argentine Confed.	18867	45886	5806	30809	37129	23533	45248	9774	18636	99235
United States	39936	1648	20178	67079	51230	163992	71084	46606	288356	33[illegible]8[illegible]7
New Caledonia	171	1785	1308	82	......	......	360	......	......	......
The Fisheries	......	......	......	......	......	......	......	......	......	......
Total	22788727	7696401	17243427	16538469‡	17676556‖	16702818§	16477341**	23401176††	21388[illegible]01‡‡	2193[illegible]259

* The value of the Imports includes freight and other charges; in previous years only the invoice value at port of shipment is given. † Inclusive of Rs 2,053,611 amount of Specie imported. ‡ Inclusive of Rs. 1,197,267 amount of Specie imported. § Inclusive of [illegible] amount of Specie imported. ‖ Inclusive of Rs. 327,441 amount of Specie imported. ** Inclusive of Rs. 44,208 amount of Specie imported. †† Inclusive of Rs. 7,655,060 amount of Specie imported. ‡‡ Inclusive of Rs. 2,488,252 amount of Specie imported.

ARTICLES.	1885		1886		1887		1888	
	Quantities.	Value.	Quantities.	Value.	Quantities.	Value.	Quantities.	Value.
		Rs.		Rs.		Rs.		Rs.
Acid : Carbolic......kilo.	2823	2432	1091	646	4844	3390	8304	4432
Muriatic .... ,,	......	......	25	51	177	25	......	...
Sulphuric .... ,,	22503	4188	28152	6047	21249	4904	14260	4008
Phosphoric ...... ,,	......	......	......	......	......	......	75000	20288
Ammoniacal:								
Liquor .... ,,	......	72	1093	251	7443	914	1328	375
Salt................. ,,	......	......	......	......	......	......	117	83
Ammonia:								
Carbonate......... ,,	390	220	403	302	156	109	......	...
Muriatic .... ,,	......	......	......	......	......	......	......	...
Salts .... ,,	287	287	12210	2107	551	190	......	...
Sulphate .... ,,	1567140	336568	3294627	674949	5523934	797240	3727038	621398
Superphosphate.. ,,	......	......	1	1	......	......	......	...
Animals: Antelopes No.	1	26	......	......	......	......	......	...
Asses .... ,,	94	5411	72	2612	2	113	116	7219
Birds (not specified) ,,	......	......	......	......	......	......	......	...
Cows and Oxen... ,,	7970	389733	9730	524103	6088	308168	10135	503547
Dogs .... ,,	26	1135	37	2624	28	1067	37	2548
Gazelles........... ,,	......	......	1	8	......	......	1	26
Geese............... ,,	......	......	......	......	......	......	......	...
Goats .... ,,	7	26	2	8	3	43	23	193
Horses .... ,,	175	20684	177	20562	214	13902	369	54441
Mules............... ,,	473	56039	363	51900	386	31372	1160	123218
Ostriches .... ,,	......	......	......	......	......	......	......	...
Peacocks .... ,,	......	......	......	......	......	......	......	...
Sheep............... ,,	73	894	81	708	62	969	281	3942
Swine............... ,,	74	950	114	1436	109	2230	163	1839
Turtle.............. ,,	60	39	6	8	104	123	166	299
Apothecary Wares	......	300729	......	242872	......	260720	......	287423
Apparel	......	158390	......	188769	......	232191	......	291133
Arms and Ammunition:								
Caps	......	546	......	692	......	112	......	1404
Cartridges	......	4826	......	11445	......	3962	......	8422
Dynamite ....kilo.	......	......	......	......	......	......	1250	3262
Fowling Pieces...No.	55	2257	183	6234	103	4756	159	6438
Gunpowder.........kilo.	5068	8601	2454	5583	2427	4984	7529	16089
Guns	......	......	......	......	......	......	18	9683
Muskets ....No.	416	3352	4	81	......	......	......	...
Ordnance of Iron	......	......	......	......	......	......	......	...
Pistols...............No.	243	1302	178	1009	556	4263	283	1193
Rifles .... ,,	16	1187	324	11009	8	470	267	20835
Shell .... ,,	......	......	......	......	......	......	......	...
Shot Lead.........kilo.	4623	1036	8926	2474	8563	2211	9852	3124
Swords & Cutlasses ...	......	......	11	130	......	......	2	118
Arrowroot...........kilo.	298	179	797	135	100	47	318	111
Asphaltum .... ,,	20000	561	57125	1531	171000	4630	19000	1437
Bacon and Hams ... ,,	34521	47536	27472	40442	44244	65874	22277	31386
Bags, Empty: Gunny.No.	1386286	124791	1297107	126819	828984	78523	1576573	156536
Linen .... ,,	21000	3296	62512	9901	4500	923	27380	5099
Rabannas .... ,,	......	......	......	......	......	......	......	..
Straw.............. ,,	2418148	163658	1204728	94506	242375	24090	13600046	145374
Vacoa......... ... ,,	27600	2791	3860	511	3100	295	15276	1916
Bark for Tanners...kilo.	31381	3054	18550	2639	35732	6067	19872	3220
Baskets & Basket Work..	......	240	......	157	......	20	......	66
Beads, Ornamental	......	1339	......	74	......	115	......	1404
Baggage (dutiable articles	......	......	......	14408	......	19853	......	20095

1889		1890		1891		1892		1893		1894	
Quantities.	Value.	Quantities.	Value.	Quantities.	Value.	Quantities.	Value.	Quantities.	Value.	Quantities.	Value.
	Rs.		Rs.		Rs.		Rs.		Rs.		Rs.
9116	5290	9653	5207	7016	3885	11849	7059	6704	4075	7394	3564
......	...	700	33	......	...	1500	104	......	...	......	...
8140	2380	32435	4645	16706	2648	12875	2589	26059	2789	21539	2721
300	158	60	11	......	...	......	...	35100	10893	25469	6131
129	116	1001	484	1095	532	1201	535	778	598	......	...
......	...	......	...	......	...	7	3	......	...	......	...
56	38	150	121	......	...	......	...	560	148	500	365
......	...	......	...	......	...	......	...	......	...	......	...
401	266	2257	1140	450	259	......	...	1210	655	......	...
2700401	443774	3622651	630651	1523114	254537	2843487	646221	2877375	...	3553374	812226
16650	1518	......	...	......	...	......	...	200000	610278	......	...
......	...	......	...	......	...	......	...	......	...	......	...
486	35448	413	19067	140	3908	93	3027	1	138	1	90
......	...	......	...	......	...	......	...	......	...	......	...
6073	281665	7996	310530	7085	369047	9717	469598	9355	460084	7320	278904
32	1577	23	1235	18	383	19	986	1	79	10	510
2	143	3	101	......	...	......	...	......	...	......	...
......	...	......	...	......	...	......	...	......	...	......	...
2	41	35	207	8	24	3	20	2	4	......	...
713	78276	958	109424	709	112527	335	51180	362	54215	439	157899
1232	121755	975	109625	1125	92672	537	50566	1070	101435	1567	277760
......	...	......	...	......	...	......	...	......	...	......	...
......	...	......	...	......	...	......	...	......	...	......	...
250	4647	94	1071	237	2185	375	4009	83	1302	173	3464
54	976	38	546	23	362	47	569	36	406	239	4222
203	121	48	9	80	173	......	...	8	4	......	...
......	299335	......	302197	......	240828	......	265411	......	299966	......	132395
......	211468	......	174315	......	182441	......	149323	......	183846	......	171202
......	1809	......	325	189800	368	359000	582	438500	751	461000	830
......	64385	......	3512	125020	2623	110470	2350	67405	1571	183950	4382
......	...	1250	3112	3405	11687	4086	4092	......	...	2542	1894
91	3891	151	3805	96	4190	77	4270	78	3272	128	9157
16848	39068	25602	21771	4667	7787	7900	11027	5567	6666	5930	8128
......	...	......	...	1	17	15	93	......	...	2	102
......	...	8	44	40	283	......	...	......	...	......	...
......	...	......	...	......	...	......	...	......	...	......	...
352	1286	348	1357	641	2269	320	1346	179	1350	266	1225
59	2240	4	999	328	3056	30	198	1	195	120	2460
......	...	......	...	......	...	......	...	......	...	......	...
54580	15562	9250	2348	10399	2716	6913	1853	6535	1741	6595	1541
......	...	4	63	......	...	......	...	......	...	......	...
880	156	......	...	230	86	7	2	14	7	1948	258
72158	3970	14000	927	100	13	3000	117	2975	118	1600	93
35859	50809	37177	49062	30973	39611	29360	42101	28438	47791	31980	47329
2294685	259037	1143469	127393	1613259	176837	643202	95020	678275	124433	2388916	423446
67032	10097	12663	2546	10	69	400	706	......	...	......	...
......	...	......	...	......	...	......	...	......	...	......	...
1649314	148331	1799270	177127	2027893	162355	464080	44340	276800	22965	247560	16957
18135	2667	4300	375	9619	897	2440	130	7700	622	10304	1347
55274	14904	25214	5648	87137	19740	59192	12674	67143	11919	67388	9824
......	10	......	238	......	231	......	68	......	62	......	98
......	408	......	2850	......	119	......	941	......	246	......	244
......	25312	......	26512	......	21570	......	23332	......	29953	......	29673

Articles.	1885		1886		1887		1888	
	Quantities.	Value.	Quantities.	Value.	Quantities.	Value.	Quantities.	Value.
		Rs.		Rs.		Rs.		Rs.
Beef, salted ....kilo.	378547	177185	300139	156340	266093	136773	285824	146588
Beer and Ale :								
Of all sorts... Hectol.	2374	170013	3658	159878	1741	131183	4568	235525
Of all sorts... Bottles.	231318		148834		159289		219939	
Bellows, Smith's ...... No.	......	94	......	272	......	106	78	1285
Betel nuts ....kilo.	70840	11636	107300	15406	66143	8902	85775	13067
Blacking	......	14851	......	5585	......	7600	......	14866
Blocks for ships' rigging .... No.	625	1177	687	984	1358	2537	.. ...	......
Boats .... ,,	10	1073	29	3527	14	1368	14	8759
Books, printed ....kilo.	11043	42662	22598	67230	12257	63337	19702	79560
Bran....................... ,,	1262203	137113	1851364	132091	1124172	83421	1708319	127378
Bread and Biscuits ... ,,	5187	2880	4614	1166	5890	1082	1586	1753
Bricks and Tiles ...... No.	52914	2873	141939	7728	147647	14440	220854	14226
Brimstone ....kilo.	150026	19592	252245	34129	185700	21583	237910	26973
Brushes and Brooms ... ,,	......	5459	......	6254	......	6006	......	5001
Bunting ....M.	647	653	816	758	462	560	105	1800
Butter ....kilo.	66423	98151	79067	121104	97859	153915	44695	80082
Cabinet and Upholstery Wares	......	73585	......	36270	......	38269	......	64460
Camphor.................kilo.	5987	6990	15284	19071	7680	10126	3455	4504
Candles :								
Composition .... ,,	96259	61346	99750	80191	101195	67672	82898	55324
Tallow .... ,,	6860	4273	2651	1974	582	406	2109	1288
Wax and Sperm...... ,,	1415	2205	10821	9658	21662	16436	559	1015
Canes and Sticks	......	103	......	50	......	244	......	131
Caoutchouc ....kilo.	58170	129744	29858	61699	60331	147591	......	......
Manufacture of...........	......	7869	......	16552	......	8763	......	166731
Cards, playing	......	2700	......	2091	.. .	898	4	3688
Carriages .... No.	6	7100	......	...	2	4090	2	174
Carts and Waggons ... ,,	4	1969	......	..	19	1022	......	3134
Casts of Statutes and Busts	......	2454	......	805	......	1590	......	5823
Cement ....kilo.	309360	14900	1208939	56315	1041690	42390	1838841	72860
Charcoal, Animal ...... ,,	100	28	......	...	1333	194	1991	591
Vegetable .... ,,	2	2	......	...	100	6	......	......
Cheese .... ,,	43738	46364	36964	42121	52320	58016	51166	43421
Chocolate and Cocoa... ,,	6737	10116	9094	14220	10683	17037	6957	10986
Choorah .... ,,	69409	5959	71599	7410	86813	6884	63023	5111
Cider .... lit.	......	...	24	25	100	137	116	27
Clay..........................kilo.	1068	52	16125	482	23060	835	24408	716
Clocks and Watches... No.	674	11805	705	13205	2267	27165	1487	23485
Coals ....kilo.	38528010	1209065	55971983	1188516	43850995	1123596	44384395	944643
Coffee .... ,,	348700	170998	517270	209425	187282	108423	457443	390060
Confectionery	......	45055	......	56292	......	55313	......	50283
Copper Sheets, &c. ...kilo.	95344	82825	37652	29623	35697	34383	21412	21809
Old .... ,,	54730	28735	16661	7765	19993	12127	20737	12707
Rods .... ,,	860	923	328	272	......	...	......	......
Copperah & Poonac.kilo.	......	...	300	16	250	13	722400	38265
Cordage :								
Coir ....kilo.	73788	22320	131469	37140	49644	17278	57997	14353
Hemp .... ,,	24690	16518	42237	17032	41280	22715	66865	34606
Cordials and Liqueurs.. lit.	21223	40245	27700	50093	21905	39861	16807	26292
Cork ....kilo.	......	...	......	...	......	...	......	......
Corks and Bungs ...Gross	58635	83386	44579	28592	31195	18884	66949	36203
Corn, Grain, Meal, &c. :								
Barley ....kilo.	1380	227	2716	234	306	75	1275	87

1889		1890		1891		1892		1893		1894	
Quantities.	Value.	Quantities.	Value.	Quantities.	Value.	Quantities.	Value.	Quantities.	Value.	Quantities.	Value.
	Rs.		Rs.		Rs.		Rs.		Rs.		Rs.
217173	113992	422093	202925	192425	98335	206065	113181	214864	122813	241973	133391
3266 230124	214238	2860 140650	187870	154484	165676	3681 119288	187629	4503 90746	214722	3879 148563	220931
58	728	111	1719	46	646	28	178	18	514	27	1336
137708	28732	21415	4910	370	51	......	...	......	...	......	...
......	10564	......	15573	......	7549	......	18843	......	11615	......	18018
......	...	......	...	75	90	......	...	......	...	......	...
14	6047	13	3929	12	2252	27	4155	13	2035	19	1212
13894	42141	11047	30637	16493	41296	12455	37320	19089	45361	8591	50536
3144944	185582	2289047	241424	1294530	105828	2635801	203705	3168133	268207	1882689	145175
4757	2342	7194	4517	7533	4299	6766	4139	4225	2068	7353	2806
761965	43142	1023954	46269	197850	13005	255742	22718	157672	11182	289998	18445
170755	20299	50368	2789	50500	6398	127600	17765	70000	9583	50500	7032
......	6245	......	4713	......	4361	......	3392	......	3591	......	5381
801	1079	499	796	307	316	1691	1011	6	23	1334	538
56082	107744	106095	199533	35952	103100	28406	61067	63427	143931	62598	140890
......	49644	......	29157	......	35263	......	42281	......	36836	......	49473
10110	13856	4191	5614	7376	10574	5182	7626	10554	16168	4540	5339
47063	32911	69750	43176	51849	35817	52294	36275	101312	49774	78070	61255
1242	853	2758	1977	2173	1478	1469	1071	2644	2320	1356	1029
6544	8177	4214	3508	9289	6508	2325	3968	1339	2226	556	1160
......	189	......	524	......	433	......	183	......	236	......	99
......	...	......	...	15190	25384	44086	131200	21297	39407	5150	12148
......	29186	......	33529	3036	12884	2804	14579	2089	9040	3676	14946
......	1815	......	2116	......	421	......	1142	......	1780	......	1426
1	1056	1	1162	15	3526	......	...	6	1076	1	55
......	...	1	522	......	...	3	234	230	117128	......	...
......	1437	......	788	......	499	......	1177	......	828	......	1170
2400623	82114	1156383	30036	1028760	49019	767990	22921	1107592	32444	2269006	81725
2980	469	......	...	562	63	......	...	......	...	......	...
3000	335	......	...	3780	73	......	...	......	...	......	...
46705	52919	41312	45032	36176	42119	36652	47689	38939	50001	33362	41486
6280	10741	9298	16987	9638	15659	11783	19640	9220	16466	10720	20675
81842	7932	71723	4758	100427	8268	27090	2100	71671	8286	46506	4566
328	117	240	62	48	37	72	26	108	28	120	40
17213	547	139550	2712	19901	311	200	14	11004	568	6160	663
1692	31260	1908	23745	1661	19834	2065	19467	1545	21141	2450	26546
55272400	2274448	41931237	1408150	35258050	1620140	44498370	1637284	42959200	1149686	29480137	510957
274882	207076	313376	217939	302358	205375	371029	272811	206274	224374	299078	301398
......	67585	......	43161	......	41065	......	54330	......	...	......	49374
69141	42810	57056	56030	75646	86415	18452	23458	48139	58775	43553	51813
27010	15573	26429	15021	10431	7883	30430	20310	5253	4448	21515	23006
......	...	......	...	......	...	......	...	535	690	4858	5884
727033	56125	892937	56343	693754	44047	60587	4395	79695	4838	109226	9214
88111	20408	128404	25530	140184	24881	238535	46687	77737	19514	112176	31940
77468	43089	68117	46542	75491	29248	58066	35585	67163	55233	42213	17968
14635	27843	14422	28064	11214	24773	10370	25729	10820	29839	12053	35290
.....	...	......	...	......	...	......	...	......	...	......	...
59856	34599	55038	21477	2721538	12868	4963068	20149	3726742	16561	7990185	27979
460634	31900	9765	1112	16240	1133	291610	22934	1076352	95757	240859	14228

Articles.	1885		1886		1887		1888	
	Quantities.	Value.	Quantities.	Value.	Quantities.	Value.	Quantities.	Value.
		Rs.		Rs.		Rs.		Rs.
Corn, &c.—*Continued.*								
Beans ....kilo.	166380	20099	361814	44719	233237	34797	14382	27321
Dholl .... ,,	56557	241993	67125	282626	6091050	328461	3596625	219602
Gram .... ,,	97574	448359	152409	579703	10274850	498548	9281250	545464
Lentils .... ,,	......	......	......	......	......	......	1207650	70418
Maize .... ,,	116102	12575	169305	12679	25449	1694	20474	920
Oats .... ,,	4817891	356836	4861925	42490	3183294	279948	2935561	234239
Oatmeal .... ,,	65	64	134	207	48	17	145	53
Peas .... ,,	92957	7505	98742	6107	108590	8512	49912	6866
Pollard .... ,,	4500	672	17780	2213	......	......	10500	553
Rice* .... ,,	853132	3834139	983391	4185975	846774	3541653	87926925	5020470
Wheat........ .... ,,	25060	126658	52789	221419	1868575	97990	457725	35121
Wheat Flour..... ,,	5017198	919685	5928343	938170	5534542	908156	6227976	1017509
Cotton Manufactures:								
Plain .... M.	2916202	517145	467223	753096	4264125	614623	4801749	686034
Colored .... ,,	4165307	757489	5682542	938170	3604529	641985	4595519	849251
Counterpanes ... No.	150	308	5	9	179	398	50	67
Hoisery	......	38449	......	38347	......	45080	......	46876
Cotton for sewing.kilo.	10043	63257	13136	57814	6863	38226	10410	64898
Wick and Waste.. ,,	6485	3716	2691	1145	7503	3585	4395	2253
Wool .... ,,	15650	1830	1200	129	15470	763	11123	2245
Diamonds	......	......	......	......	......	......	......	...
Drawings	......	16	......	......	......	......	......	...
Earthen and China ware ....Pieces.	258873	28580	255036	34226	707610	53197	677448	77785
Eggs salted .... No.	......	......	4510	147	12050	261	6950	213
Feathers, Ornamental...	......	5326	......	1576	......	1365	......	513
Fibre Aloe ....kilo.	......	......	......	......	......	......	2933	857
Coir................. ,,	29550	1819	42250	3142	6045	483	25415	1794
Raffia .... ,,	102002	19244	262175	93554	129264	16944	5500	1914
Fireworks † .... ,,	......	25783	......	9169	.....	10896	... ..	17422
Fish:								
Dried or salted ... ,,	2874308	822052	1925183	373518	1967170	395476	2334892	544123
Pickled .... ,,	74575	19947	266064	63767	26517	20411	95568	23435
Salmon .... ,,	......	......	......	......	......	......	.. ...	...
Not otherwise described ...... ,,	......	......	......	......	......	256	.....	...
Fishing tackle ...... ,,	......	1978	......	1549	......	......	......	67
Flowers, artificial.........	......	4603	......	4741	......	7526	......	4846
Fruits, dried, viz:								
Almonds...........kilo.	5972	2201	8182	2645	8891	2712	8573	3797
Apples .... ,,	......	......	......	......	......	......	......	...
Cocoanuts .... No.	1070430	27132	698302	13557	855633	19358	1234507	25216
Dates ....kilo.	31915	2061	222848	12453	12630	1112	174076	13210
Figs................ ,,	20	16	11	8	301	138	... ..	...
Pistachio nuts ... ,,	2401	226	230	14	315	90	225	29
Prunes .... ,,	895	948	......	......	......	......	12	19
Raisins .... ,,	9859	3396	17528	4902	56399	15082	4763	1925
Walnuts .... ,,	1475	361	622	188	365	37	761	198
Not enumerated... ,,	442	274	1496	1058	1093	596	3777	1633
Fruits, Fresh..............	......	6514	......	5719	8373	3303	12747	3571
Gandia ....kilo.	131	171	810	1456	1579	1652	1932	7438
Ghee .... ,,	137678	97805	141555	106575	114723	89296	116347	95119
Ginger .... ,,	17443	1842	10227	1267	9195	839	2015	186
Glass, Window......Panes	36576	4958	55121	8235	91343	6033	56711	6586
,, Bottles empty..Gr..	8	61	21	168	21	128	16	306
Glasses, Looking & Mirrors .... No.	13055	6697	13996	5704	14749	7317	14624	5991

* In bags of 75 kilos.

† The duty on Fireworks has been increased since 1st, October 1893 to 15 o/o Ord. 12 of 1893.

1889		1890		1891		1892		1893		1894	
Quantities.	Value.	Quantities.	Value.	Quantities.	Value.	Quantities.	Value.	Quantities.	Value.	Quantities.	Value.
	Rs.		Rs.		Rs.		Rs.		Rs.		Rs.
105337	15246	236374	33565	94737	13773	307056	60036	199713	37953	257772	41327
4512638	251386	6428948	342297	3536775	263113	4539041	325958	5051235	482903	4810958	458427
11437602	655207	12264763	667851	9734007	734015	10246220	694958	9777913	772903	10806712	999747
1410906	83524	1940738	105390	1339023	99536	1796520	136286	2351895	213986	1192675	118828
60336	3191	9828	645	18108	1084	18533	1343	31649	2252	29849	1764
5930804	427519	4420134	319249	4545754	379254	4446070	344069	4455710	449453	4136082	502480
156	89	281	109	3388	1472	2265	1091	4413	2210	3335	1751
87152	8410	144169	14260	152252	15703	151542	25253	247805	28514	239502	30886
3545	580	10780	825	890	120	26136	3717	21966	2314	34986	6027
52003551	2840058	77729173	4304296	74118396	5726937	61953920	4592407	65699763	6848212	71597775	7692797
1685776	104398	485090	44892	265825	27787	65370	7092	140100	14867	288245	23474
6545771	992517	7221972	1094236	8119687	1301830	6994708	1046306	10591501	1738780	9799895	1387618
4529526	643360	5502276	750978	4893085	652579	3934317	560589	4713400	647602	5813553	611246
4751010	837734	5694501	1054170	3257197	661986	5457380	1085181	4858213	981348	4888269	942688
30	228	140	373	660	312	......	...	......	...	......	...
......	45214	......	549121	......	53507	......	40181	......	51273	......	31079
5306	11424	12808	89465	6869	46597	5772	32942	13245	45027	3980	23744
9689	3139	5460	2443	13881	2981	9248	4235	10470	3848	10583	5378
10262	2602	21448	3297	13930	2419	9469	1992	14558	3838	6891	2523
......	...	......	...	......	...	......	...	......	...	......	...
......	...	......	...	......	..	......	...	......	...	......	...
663791	61839	547764	60957	402265	45821	609948	66939	489951	56208	532263	58598
31000	721	35950	1035	5050	93	16800	483	15053	437	32675	1017
252	732	......	1530	......	152	......	65	......	74	......	102
......	...	10850	6910	......	...	......	...	......	...	......	...
27332	2761	33008	2777	51128	4216	67025	7221	44579	5918	46070	5336
......	...	280	52	52	10	......	...	13545	2483	......	...
......	14475	......	10856	......	16496	......	17761	......	17481	......	13931
1843340	367152	1583137	353227	1495648	311279	2032616	448628	1182784	277153	1206610	289847
65843	19029	80856	23529	30945	15806	94802	33701	78121	24391	92302	35190
......	...	......	...	......	...	......	...	......	...	......	...
......	...	......	...	......	...	......	...	......	...	......	...
......	272	......	...	......	...	......	...	......	...	......	...
......	5840	......	8270	......	8164	......	4419	......	7365	......	4223
6832	3527	6720	2431	6007	2883	6519	2227	11999	4026	10995	3462
......	...	......	...	......	...	......	...	......	...	......	...
946459	20542	64236	17441	948168	31983	1531142	43561	1354513	41042	1495935	45049
153748	13843	36013	3071	123972	10721	21206	1768	134555	13846	62978	6537
......	...	247	49	......	...	......	...	......	...	......	...
5805	946	33405	5653	34280	5458	25012	2164	43158	6640	13989	2618
......	...	......	...	......	...	......	...	......	...	......	...
15629	6198	11130	3306	3135	1564	5092	1511	12479	3873	4588	1512
42	26	188	113	701	164	330	285	569	289	952	248
3445	1109	5174	1534	22811	4210	18801	7351	24274	5333	72393	9389
12400	3618	14078	2749	22430	7673	23604	8274	47280	13922	35278	9398
2416	8392	2933	16275	2780	15406	2781	16670	2524	14741	2499	13162
133925	129535	171949	161741	149834	141269	109307	96353	119768	110320	160131	130343
7533	946	2661	340	8994	1804	5250	1044	3225	915	9608	1719
92801	7424	52540	5823	30829	9988	36199	11035	57313	18313	59945	15954
18	416	49	667	44105	3107	1738	764	7026	365	27053	2536
8145	8538	13607	6035	6915	6728	7202	7066	10751	9150	12927	13170

Articles.	1885		1886		1887		1888	
	Quantities.	Value.	Quantities.	Value.	Quantities.	Value.	Quantities.	Value.
		Rs.		Rs.		Rs.		Rs.
Glassware	101946	27990	82526	20944	143823	24879	166288	27820
Glue ....kilo.	1622	1442	1218	1168	2260	1397	1864	1499
Grease .... ,,	41651	4663	177537	12369	53347	7153	94779	9686
Groceries	......	20778	......	28240	......	11739	......	33009
Gum, Arabic ....kilo.	989	1675	1532	2403	1750	2442	1276	1369
Copal .... ,,	17169	27888	9581	12128	5626	10338	869	460
Haberdashery, Mercery and Milinery	......	411197	......	494280	......	515688	......	607385
Hair, Horse ....kilo.	75	96	138	200	98	164	652	784
Ornamental ...... ,,	......	299	......	69	......	53	......	120
Hardware and Cutley ...	......	456512	......	860198	......	567638	......	779710
Hats, Beaver .... No.	......	......	......	......	......	...	......	......
Felt .... ,,	39501	60275	30588	47515	50744	72903	36202	59303
Silk .... ,,	981	3478	199	1411	604	3902	272	1590
Solah .... ,,	424	668	359	511	1654	1291	1422	1558
Straw .... ,,	28770	16720	18771	13911	33838	14531	45174	13069
Of all sorts .... ,,	330	674	4641	2839	8765	8355	162	683
Hay and Straw ......kilo.	835	3062	317	1985	26825	1506	76333	4929
Hemp, undress ...... ,,	416	403	104	119	1162	1774	9630	2648
Hides, raw and tanned ,,	12748	74372	9827	67178	2692	5846	4590	13662
Honey .... lit.	92	124	92	78	24	11	13	6
Hoofs ....kilo.	......	......	......	......	15	6	......	......
Hops .... ,,	361	736	......	57	......	...	......	259
Horn, Cow or Bull... No.	3754	115	8051	270	4340	494	851	62
Hulls of vessels aban. ,,	2	3200	6	27880	5	20213	3	15416
Indigo ....kilo.	3147	3018	7569	5290	16636	8771	19481	13539
Iron Wrought: Anchors and Grapnels ...kilo.	4520	557	8832	1369	3950	485	6993	169
Bar .... ,,	248416	23177	484435	46120	569720	140640	304784	30155
Cast .... ,,	15812	19290	261967	19303	2471853	258607	553385	53230
Sheet .... ,,	241940	48602	358718	98870	463124	82017	395691	77545
Nails .... ,,	102709	27769	335100	54506	183674	49261	188058	56741
Of all sorts .... ,,	......	.....	15071	1755	3028	731	94408	18795
Old .... ,,	40	44	5700	153	920	59	1000	46
Iron, Sulphate of ... ,,	2889	206	......	114	307	54	6863	373
Ivory ware .... ,,	......	......	......	......	......	...	......	......
Jewellery .... ,,	......	39451	......	53620	......	73012	......	84689
Juice of Lemons...... lit.	899	501	1234	810	977	635	693	511
Jute .... kilo.	......	......	80550	4333	......	...	......	......
Lard .... ,,	520033	371034	368144	262216	539141	371039	656865	462469
Lead, old .... ,,	......	......	......	......	......	...	......	......
Sheets and pipes... ,,	44223	8691	214416	18808	50698	11696	132703	36019
Leather, Unwrought. ,,	28466	54460	19892	49296	35511	72768	31484	59496
Leather, Wrought:								
Boots and shoes ... prs.	112940	315597	116383	341769	115552	272441	126680	256771
Gloves .... doz.	697	11334	621	10230	529	9502	301	6086
Of all sorts ....kilo.	......	27739	......	43010	......	41618	......	48675
Leeches .... No.	4500	217	2000	95	1000	47	1100	97
Lentils ....kilo.	10955	42625	20322	86276	515025	28617	1207650	70418
Lime....................bags.	......	......	70	13	20010	1387	......	......
Carbonate ....kilo.	50	70	......	......	......	...	......	......
	1050	8	50	13	......	...	......	......
Chloride .... ,,	......	......	......	......	91	29	50	13
Nitrate .... ,,	......	......	......	......	......	...	......	......
Phosphate .... ,,	......	......	132263	17909	10185	926	......	......
Superphosphate ... ,,	451198	75971	271461	45109	905240	92319	1278198	177873
Sulphate .... ,,	......	......	......	......	......	...	78257	5764

1889		1890		1891		1892		1893		1894	
Quantities.	Value.	Quantities.	Value.	Quantities.	Value.	Quantities.	Value.	Quantities.	Value.	Quantities.	Value.
	Rs.		Rs.		Rs.		Rs.		Rs.		Rs.
137579	26589	161811	31923	191565	35856	150897	44519	247880	41985	192445	52341
2841	2424	1723	1024	2087	1230	1582	1117	2716	2078	1746	1319
96726	12074	61406	8891	80744	9278	102032	13444	70462	10804	112000	17543
......	30169	......	28297	......	7834	......	11978	...	14399	......	17657
3108	2175	167	386	803	705	722	368	2178	1441	1109	593
......	...	930	646	3058	5202	182	133	558	310	1245	524
......	575652	......	667080	......	610862	......	640473	...	744425	......	910894
3227	3203	7521	6362	547	691	804	1058	399	817	427	670
......	24	......	39	......	22	......	7	...	...	......	...
......	986724	......	1724692	......	688064	......	828199	...	129253	......	710484
......	...	......	...	......	...	......	...	...	...	......	...
23564	42644	45539	42532	41216	48561	30227	47042	36839	62616	34080	62602
816	3267	736	3104	195	1429	292	1973	406	2870	332	2160
753	873	348	451	893	1467	1246	1344	2315	2500	402	611
30795	11734	24339	11595	40255	16815	46082	17391	57582	15398	34652	19917
38	77	436	531	193	304	84	187	142	241	2302	2938
75362	1425	119046	6247	74955	2508	44576	2009	44944	1768	161308	21584
2192	2432	1797	1768	1730	1749	3505	3565	6319	...	7084	7608
655	3266	6215	9883	3	6	3300	2790	4850	5253	3717	6205
94	73	33	24	107	54	19	36	156	87	627	461
......	...	......	...	......	...	......	...	...	...	......	...
......	21	......	...	......	...	175	145	81	89	177	435
318	...	......	...	2314	255	86	18	100	39	......	...
2	6830	3	12482	2	10150	5	12592	2	6474	1	1000
5598	3329	12407	7991	10104	6554	18587	11115	11106	6573	2266	3178
1225	212	1140	145	874	197	12888	946	4750	1290	2641	632
587598	65392	681076	80397	401580	47044	513230	85740	697168	78339	688662	88646
579346	48611	329470	36930	232076	24367	118363	16500	52194	7183	......	...
427556	100515	425921	99794	386696	81942	1007925	224249	531222	117407	590748	110888
167044	44567	175234	56170	188686	43622	417198	108841	387901	105635	168590	72094
174932	18823	144797	22345	470464	81299	306146	55309	522583	76359	1228063	150693
1382	49	......	...	......	...	375	35	1000	37	......	...
9694	364	10383	597	29844	1459	22321	1262	5108	234	......	...
......	...	......	...	......	...	......	...	...	...	......	22
......	79447	......	55230	......	58936	......	59506	...	79560	......	69117
1249	674	2970	1642	636	535	9	489	615	590	3489	3276
18000	246	198650	5755	......	...	......	...	...	...	......	...
730233	513219	707703	479657	607103	432772	336503	250105	569489	471396	753712	393389
......	...	......	...	......	...	25	9	...	...	......	...
62225	16166	55288	14790	58687	13683	89348	19602	110677	24516	85043	16682
47144	86332	38528	76502	891	2262	2942	8059	...	...	9744	14236
128966	289370	138962	273162	101930	195263	127808	206901	133915	240117	97752	203573
252	5175	378	4172	492	9506	199	3425	184	3478	286	3888
......	67557	......	45408	10498	46958	......	55538	8512	73783	......	62188
......	49	2000	92	2000	71	1000	52	1000	54	1000	92
1410906	83524	......	...	1339923	99536	......	...	2351895	213986	1192675	118828
......	...	......	...	......	...	......	...	...	...	......	...
19000	3934	......	...	56	20	......	...	...	...	10000	146
......	...	160	20	......	...	......	...	...	...	......	...
525	96	......	...	31000	4896	......	...	...	...	2000	485
......	...	......	...	......	...	......	...	...	...	......	...
......	...	19650	3486	185037	36796	207753	43049	238026	51080	236439	63366
1447262	239518	1230432	148677	1285281	166951	1909465	271387	1725758	234908	922278	136929
23000	5214	23000	1920	65592	10013	11112	442	70067	6899	240700	44601

Articles.	1885		1886		1887		1888	
	Quantities.	Value.	Quantities.	Value.	Quantities.	Value.	Quantities.	Value.
		Rs.		Rs.		Rs.		Rs.
Linen Manufactures :								
Plain .... M.	37527	12982	49901	11897	50341	15547	10070	5624
Colored .... ,,	5696	1520	1401	431	3332	750	600	212
Sails .... No.	91	1904	306	6056	177	3737	112	2222
Sail Cloth .... M.	32926	23410	95347	59209	50709	38917	77583	56020
Tents .... No.	......	......	......	......	......	......	3	234
Thread for sewing kilo.	2357	7960	3490	11138	4052	10528	1419	4055
Matches .... gross	......	22443	......	88570	......	102788	89645	90443
Machinery & Mill Work..	......	60337	......	122337	125227	49955	359538	139224
Manure, viz :								
Guano ....kilo.	4121804	484052	6417239	912120	12697775	1602396	5084465	778724
Of all other sorts. ,,	3547114	465925	6474634	1017780	7977052	886243	3712679	507587
Maps and Charts	......	365	...	625	......	418	......	84
Mathem. & Opt. Insts. ...	......	4834	......	5872	......	3381	......	4334
Mats and Matting.........	......	3110	... ..	9920	......	8683	......	1702
Molasses..............kilo.	1286	51	100	3	......	......	......	...
Moss .... ,,	1037	1086	1546	1558	996	1080	177	254
Musical Instruments ...	......	8198	......	15165	......	12250	......	13557
Music Printed	......	3570	......	2230	......	2053	......	1311
Oakum ....kilo.	7520	368	3241	1355	1775	102	195	187
Oil, Cloth .... M.	2519	3383	2061	2805	1960	2116	2975	4464
Castor..............kilo.	431340	106072	381498	94498	448620	107080	371661	90290
Cocoanut .... lit.	1038206	181416	1073825	187239	1323745	234440	1302689	233434
Gingely ....kilo.	22647	5579	14510	5193	13490	4270	5498	1916
Mustard .... ,,	216052	67206	139285	43394	160613	48217	124505	37957
Neatsfoot .... lit.	5335	1653	8622	4852	4702	2472	5793	3490
Olive .... ,,	71738	62263	92645	94663	52857	51378	61616	59579
Petroleum .... ,,	730215	29641	33925	1674	1545423	111075	578498	41188
Pistachio ....kilo.	905805	253851	806808	247799	1070678	312078	1040400	307377
Sperm or Fish ... lit.	1433	252	517	224	111	28	195	60
Of all other sorts. ,,	25062	9991	15761	9711	19250	12418	77616	16399
Onions and Garlic...kilo.	117275	10358	154576	18497	61412	5116	110728	15612
Opium................ ,,	4866	157243	2445	99864	5736	111834	2275	80730
Printers' Colors, &c.......	......	.....	......	......	......	......	......	...
Painters and Dyers								
Colors and materials...	......	102026	......	187181	......	131510	......	172032
Papers, Manufactures of	......	11497	......	20303	......	22771	......	27916
Packing	......	......	......	......	......	......	......	19607
Printing	......	......	......	......	......	......	......	21923
Stained for hang..rolls	17487	4117	29442	9805	27514	7708	31213	8986
Pearl&Scotch Barley.kilo	3272	923	1461	436	2234	612	5458	1461
Perfumery	......	77238	......	73979	......	58843	......	65442
Pickles and Sauces	......	44183	......	23280	......	19995	......	12834
Pictures, Oil Paintings...	......	5100	......	700	......	3020	......	348
Pitch and Tar......kilos.	2722	5621	697	6933	30501	7495	5721	7617
Plants and Roots	......	1397	......	816	......	791	......	1604
Plaster of Paris ...kilo.	924	168	... 682	90	155	18	10500	809
Plate, Wrght. of Silver.k.	12	139	1	442	1	51	......	104
Plated & Gilt Wares......	......	14494	......	8200	......	10746	......	10490
Pork salted ....kilo.	151381	76668	51848	33965	57376	59408	58862	42823
Potash, Carbonate of ,,	175	57	1463	398	202	83	......	...
Nitrate of .... ,,	110756	23311	132365	27819	40975	1537	318711	48176
Sulphate of ...... ,,	......	......	......	......	190	42	3384	6552
Potatoes.............. ,,	894212	70583	473227	39729	647331	55245	573022	45472
Prints and Engravings...	......	6163	......	8596	......	10179	......	9630
Printing Types, &c.	......	6098	......	17761	......	10387	......	5875
Provisions preserved ...	......	76566	......	91473	......	93805	.. ...	91106

1889		1890		1891		1892		1893		1894	
Quantities.	Value.	Quantities.	Value.	Quantities.	Value.	Quantities.	Value.	Quantities.	Value.	Quantities.	Value.
	Rs.		Rs.		Rs.		Rs.		Rs.		Rs.
25565	12450	29563	8972	68675	17055	1451	794	25	8	4689	1966
157	28	2219	964	1600	332	215	72	......	...	...	...
77	11983	32	1996	10	207	174	11874	9	241	...	...
76337	45931	78939	42816	30463	52722	45837	89499	8256	10354	38300	59066
8	440	...	...	6	142	......	...	......	...	...	...
4095	6332	5463	11607	753	2269	1295	2693	43	177	...	...
55015	59351	17486	19407	11637	17506	58663	77764	93421	127694	72473	109537
498599	238097	592395	347947	286771	155084	606194	381696	289610	193633	725986	356202
10026489	2028220	1487500	125894	3590045	184762	2215051	166946	3333530	233849	1841510	201917
6982055	774863	5153455	559932	6164287	616930	6563940	741409	6918034	997524	9793724	1297359
......	271	...	86	...	40	......	...	......	175	...	999
......	3030	...	5206	...	2296	......	4216	......	5940	...	4609
......	8552	...	1913	8687	3052	30916	11965	24902	7174	8260	2347
......	...	10	4	...	...	300	18	2956	323	190	51
387	369	511	518	780	651	1894	2162	2019	983	955	705
......	19384	...	16208	...	17462	......	6450	......	10950	...	14113
......	2085	...	743	...	864	......	680	......	441	77	690
864	533	1807	1414	4163	963	969	280	642	298	1975	1234
2321	2502	3543	3140	1859	1440	3495	3011	5256	2215	2791	2229
407346	149870	496645	162379	462826	178953	359780	116010	352070	119206	542215	156483
995203	180186	990324	187334	139209	237578	11173	223161	10135	272080	929021	189211
8734	4526	17645	6732	10881	3305	8447	4671	13736	7029	108687	22545
199033	83469	246468	106158	347305	156411	192740	76893	322910	131453	331523	118991
3035	2032	8629	3258	2353	1669	69	3245	370	2870	5935	4018
42045	43979	78255	74232	48082	42781	3301	38185	5055	58305	56091	53510
1217749	104819	3306391	224930	824832	76398	13229	84262	967736	69079	1523205	180230
883135	341033	876106	346144	809925	264752	708125	262454	970349	463919	862562	223230
......	...	...	...	...	...	......	...	......	...	...	...
16663	11935	26812	10473	9996	5664	679	27354	68756	38033	147113	30284
317002	38703	304853	37619	103358	11230	135845	12333	213779	16780	135954	7750
1725	59872	3591	123811	2331	78975	2805	97834	2628	89707	1933	2[illegible]280
......	...	... ..	...	...	...	......	...	......	...	...	...
......	151168	...	130586	...	81106	......	126828	......	170717	...	130809
......	31110	...	33871	...	38684	......	14581	......	27926	...	36677
......	12588	...	23391	...	26599	......	14213	......	17090	...	10651
......	20562	...	16504	...	18951	.. ...	22535	......	22306	...	19428
44958	9162	28278	5800	53427	11889	62598	15294	39341	18618	34335	10255
4261	1133	2347	614	3779	1377	5920	2185	6657	2031	3605	1270
......	72148	...	83175	...	79447	......	73747	......	86125	...	78458
......	40955	...	38804	...	14490	......	3870	......	3122	...	1959
......	227	...	614	...	527	.....	2379	......	...	1	115
922	5497	2576	8130	62590	6094	54916	6286	116961	9258	99822	9887
......	784	...	1388	...	2408	......	1322	......	1083	...	1363
4276	160	92	34	300	66	841	126	2942	191	1514	151
10	1069	15	1801	...	792	......	557	.....	317	...	...
......	14793	...	11512	...	10629	.....	13933	......	9081	...	6273
56876	43408	78765	58419	26674	17111	35667	25224	19505	19148	26030	23982
200	99	162	69	400	136	......	...	1565	323	192	83
1628306	184176	1243245	236902	1989890	385735	2502948	423073	2363958	595567	2592395	645689
72200	13691	161980	26751	121937	20522	215912	34746	222954	41451	105925	29427
714926	77230	736654	60556	600885	37321	459085	36424	437696	82876	529013	87645
......	9418	...	9678	...	9770	......	10852	......	13819	...	11902
......	2578	...	4042	...	3304	......	6868	......	3783	...	3192
......	124172	...	133265	...	83000	.. ...	73652	......	102456	...	102315

Articles.	1885		1886		1887		1888	
	Quantities.	Value.	Quantities.	Value.	Quantities.	Value.	Quantities.	Value.
		Rs.		Rs.		Rs.		Rs.
Rabannes ....Pieces.	81035	19572	57545	21146	5545	1528	15101	4574
Rattans ....kilo.	51270	4569	119050	8449	145544	12327	157180	11793
Rosin : Red .... ,,	5320	630	100	68	345	104	3850	440
Rough .. .. ,,	18252	2462	50120	8131	51953	4126	46089	4012
Saddlery and Harness ,,	......	9875	......	11755	......	14397	......	12855
Sago .... ,,	19998	2571	29591	4038	31167	3819	25248	3461
Salt-Ammoniac ...... ,,	......	......	......	...	......	...	......	......
Salt .... ,,	1974326	24277	5574151	86309	4296108	42445	1892447	29746
Salpetre .... ,,	83734	11432	111305	16089	28157	7354	738539	167514
Sand .... ,,	42846	941	57536	970	67619	769	118021	2691
Sausages .... ,,	4562	5734	4281	5549	4952	8715	4770	6717
Seeds : Garden	......	3875	......	3349	......	2564	......	3110
Unenumerated	......	28340	......	24919	......	22001	......	25766
Sheating paper or felt Rolls	......	5708	......	5455	......	1451	......	6359
Silk Manufactures :								
Silk, Satin, &c. ......M.	37941	31317	42722	36360	74806	49153	57139	41109
Sewing Silks ....kilo.	11	112	11	141	6	287	4	93
Soap .... ,,	935960	210956	1785953	406471	795756	183603	837525	164727
Soda, Carbonate of ... ,,	2366	539	949	175	8116	524	638	51
Caustic	.....	......	......	...	......	...	......	......
Silicate	......	......	......	...	23850	2700	16067	1502
Nitrate	......	......	......	...	......	...	......	......
Phosphate ....kilo.	56	5	1140	78	......	...	......	......
Sulphate	12892	1307	16807	1700	......	...	......	......
Soda water, doz. bottles ...	......	......	......	...	......	...	......	.....
Solder ....kilo.	287	284	729	534	987	514	616	722
Specie, viz :								
Copper and Bronze	......	......	......	1	......	...	......	15300
Gold	......	16560	......	22361	......	1830	......	89401
Paper Currency............	......	......	......	15565	......	14697	......	714
Silver	......	2563903	......	724232	......	199168	......	1212168
Specimens Illust. of Nat. History	......	540	......	345	......	179	......	220
Spelter of Zinc ....kilo.	1443	438	1090	464	55	30	......	... ..
Spices, viz :								
Cinnamon ....kilo.	2865	663	825	449	7239	1343	3575	391
Cloves .... ,,	903	379	514	409	2401	1922	1070	667
Nutmegs .... ,,	......	......	......	...	......	...	......	.. ...
Pepper .... ,,	30493	9645	46745	15017	316119	11043	33906	14567
Of all other sorts ... ,,	154285	17183	127585	15185	118858	13998	131360	16709
Spirits, viz :								
Brandy .... lit.	69507	127694	62104	117986	66084	126780	54371	113318
Geneva .... ,,	4457	3727	8173	7658	7582	8529	4387	10052
Rum .... ,,	22046	4578	8393	2919	44104	22686	65486	27039
Whisky .... ,,	16389	27377	19730	35154	26507	50852	20236	39758
Of Wine .... ,,	3573	2534	2608	1652	1092	983	1874	1623
Of other sorts ...... ,,	......	......	......	...	......	...	688	734
Sponge ....kilo.	95	2168	109	1559	141	2013	215	3006
Stamps .... ,,	......	......	......	...	......	...	......	2296
Starch..................... ,,	......	......	80	23	17950	34	19050	2489
Stationery .... ,,	......	221109	......	155753	......	181523	......	196602
Steel, Unwrought...... ,,	4156	1625	3829	2387	256106	261724	30360	12220
Stones, viz :								
Filtering..............No.	57	508	119	1078	70	807	424	1210

1889		1890		1891		1892		1893		1894	
Quantities.	Value.	Quantities.	Value.	Quantities.	Value.	Quantities.	Value.	Quantities.	Value.	Quantities.	Value.
	Rs.		Rs.		Rs.		Rs.		Rs.		Rs.
20200	12749	58045	13717	6978	1489	9792	2750	16643	5805	112	73
130305	15120	117775	9105	52937	3717	79569	10162	182088	33526	116809	14010
1340	178	41199	3365	4910	570	20685	2376	31035	2957	19877	1870
6593	1601	...	...	...	...	...	...	......	...	......	...
...	13837	...	22129	...	16758	...	18012	......	7789	......	12853
54200	9432	68426	10206	1320	246	33801	4799	37876	4812	13390	1841
...	...	...	...	...	...	...	...	......	...	......	...
1572325	30853	3885754	42722	4566001	110178	4457622	159654	1037994	35059	1302488	78254
...	...	...	...	575	67	...	...	......	...	......	...
131633	1652	76291	978	30	1	31968	933	90017	1739	134973	4927
1536	3903	1670	2783	2486	3573	3037	4321	2247	3296	884	2293
...	3694	...	3116	...	3563	...	7399	......	8272	......	12515
...	58287	...	35912	504722	31584	1860	532	212051	42587	71431	6489
...	6036	...	4417	24150	4336	11650	2486	24080	6602	15394	3901
85394	49605	54615	35459	61694	38778	72768	39266	35992	27402	48028	25458
10	133	21	383	9	44	...	...	......	...	......	...
676744	138276	1158675	223112	1103442	244331	366739	78513	740620	194316	611182	129648
3532	332	7595	345	3100	340	15250	1194	4099	575	44062	4688
...	...	...	...	106189	25522	26945	5478	130932	29725	88899	19008
23875	2537	22313	3154	41840	5532	12789	1977	8758	1240	11528	1130
10000	1619	25500	3627	5100	807	60547	10948	2242389	390920	1273000	181418
...	...	250	21	..	...	7	10	......	...	......	...
...	...	...	...	...	...	...	...	......	...	......	...
...	...	...	...	...	...	...	...	......	...	......	...
2317	2291	26241	2710	1445	1575	1030	1080	1392	1677	2961	1986
...	...	...	15300	...	...	...	...	......	2140	......	...
...	43948	...	15596	...	19120	...	60972	......	20432	......	...
...	6351	...	9095	...	...	...	...	......	2989	......	...
...	2098528	...	326630	...	39715	...	9009710	......	2715930	......	902492
...	271	...	91	...	164	...	508	......	181	......	405
1544	663	5124	1364	50	52	2517	2230	5159	4026	7806	5916
4926	1172	2445	699	1164	262	3082	953	4402	1917	4055	1413
2835	1937	9677	7635	1017	485	2627	1162	16703	8060	2047	1106
...	...	...	...	...	...	...	...	......	...	......	...
64849	51581	73429	55568	32378	22232	20206	14690	36586	47889	67854	37681
189191	27800	148025	21275	5	270	202243	23683	82566	20071	......	...
71340	149444	57912	113683	70111	140781	58287	126093	76144	167822	7264394	159309
7670	16589	1217	23286	863	1805	7224	10429	4281	5990	976058	20877
6900	2619	1508	1917	1707	1729	1365	2525	......	17714	3225	4669
33990	67991	25680	48903	26102	51753	29642	65337	35833	81680	54970	128909
3348	3155	2958	994	3089	1746	3827	1566	3868	2381	3217	2288
9	14	351	96	14	17	440	1024	73	79	19	69
320	1577	127	1912	130	1302	137	1683	181	1979	73	1170
...	3854	...	507	...	255	...	2436	......	8999	......	1690
51026	6139	101398	12748	467	141	5232	916	98626	19168	68112	8529
...	152537	...	135957	...	157644	...	122361	......	138681	......	198747
260097	66792	81547	24485	7495	4450	12727	4380	9045	5253	8517	4817
102	1128	45	692	182	2424	1100	1530	137	2178	44	706

ARTICLES.	1885		1886		1887		1888	
	Quantities.	Value.	Quantities.	Value.	Quantities.	Value.	Quantities.	Value.
		Rs.		Rs.		Rs.		Rs.
Stones (*Continued*) viz:								
Grindstones ...... No.	317	386	700	1698	8058	2267	1435	2301
Marble .... ,,	199	1604	126	955	147	1134	1875	2917
Paving .... ,,	38652	2152	......	......	11200	507	6	20
Slates .... ,,	......	......	......	......	......	......	......	...
Tombstones ...... ,,	6	1764	4	1258	3	820	......	....
Straw-ware	......	1300	......	477	......	470	......	541
Sugar, viz: Candy... kilo.	281	129	1632	576	3514	1258	2612	765
Refined .... ,,	258	124	250	158	209	80	50	19
Raw .... ,,	759290	132172	1410766	314692	1121789	261828	853901	212306
Sulphur .... ,,	46159	7085	49629	5943	179888	19820	287848	28179
Tallow .... ,,	88501	48174	71027	33229	19964	11077	37678	15012
Tamarinds........... ,,	262936	15437	239924	13436	182365	9805	149022	9303
Tarpaulins........... No.	8	208	94	324	4	32	62	95
Tea ... . kilo.	31009	46324	39186	49422	31466	67646	53881	74661
Tin Unwrought...... ,,	5635	7440	5484	5683	8873	11551	12781	19806
Plates............... ,,	......	36490	......	38147	......	35498	......	31451
Tobacco, viz:								
Unmanufactured.. kilo.	267768	116475	177619	88499	199041	98993	277661	158561
Manufactured ... ,,	53345	85977	56005	99604	62083	102588	74823	127027
Segars............... ,,	1406	5393	1273	3648	879	4388	2241	6884
Snuff .... ,,	......	......	1	4	1	......	......	...
Tobacco, Pipes...... gross	166	1967	703	4600	1009	3608	665	4877
Tongues.............. kilo.	50	59	1533	1759	775	360	280	264
Tortoise shell ...... ,,	15	16	1	......	......	......	......	...
Toys	......	27535	......	33731	......	59296	......	58076
Turmeric .... kilo.	210406	24157	112981	14258	175637	20982	126775	50778
Twines of all sorts.. ,,	115640	28393	50377	19618	35815	21029	77183	17575
Umbrellas, viz: Cotton No.	4840	5718	5303	8692	13424	20702	27003	30475
Silk .... ,,	9848	28980	9730	28534	17254	45848	9581	28391
Of all other sorts.. ,,	168	545	1406	2891	1660	4441	241	757
Vanilla .... ,,	247	3495	54	434	1301	19411	1694	21829
Vegetables, fresh... kilo.	......	369	......	105	3730	748	130	43
Vermicelli & Maca.. ,,	18414	8175	13356	6452	14431	6135	18206	7856
Vinegar .... lit.	31183	7310	64019	14242	87677	19172	61819	11941
Wax, Bees'........... kilo.	47349	49739	109859	145805	46923	20804	25556	28192
Whalebone........... ,,	......	......	......	......	......	......	......	...
Wine of all sorts.. { lit. / bot.	H. 26502 / B. 48093	1061770	H. 22170 / B. 85824	932919	H. 25107 / B. 65168	1113028	H. 22695 / B. 93439	1050812
Wood, viz:								
Boards & Planks.. C.M.	4391	199616	6036	229327	4851	160124	14489	181500
Casks, empty...... No.	6081	20700	28989	65632	32033	60663	25892	47175
Firewood .... M 2	2	19	7	136	12	251	113	726
Masts & Spars ... No.	130	7264	123	12929	148	9402	67	3078
Oars .... ,,	289	1253	649	3695	64	379	641	24[illegible]5
Shingles............ ,,	4259150	61684	5119525	73184	383750	4569	2876875	45899
Timber .... C.M.	539	50523	25543	47493	8944	194816	1237	24047
Woodware .... ,,	......	16205	......	17882	......	18322	......	4916[illegible]
Woollen Manufact., viz:								
Cloth .... M.	10048	42643	22883	44416	2294	10007	12795	26903
Blankets .... No.	8367	8334	7888	9333	19829	26659	17252	20617
Carpets, &c. ...... ,,	681	3442	946	1330	1373	1687	404	1530
Mixed with Cotton or Silk .... M.	191680	149825	203512	162761	425676	256724	226104	191720
Shawls .... No.	5193	8967	6776	9752	14473	14486	7516	10051
Zinc, Sulfate of............	......	......	......	......	......	......	......	...

* The quantity of Pontac entered for the Colonial Government was 140 hect. 7 litres.

1889		1890		1891		1892		1893		1894	
Quantities.	Value.	Quantities.	Value.	Quantities.	Value.	Quantities.	Value.	Quantities.	Value.	Quantities.	Value.
	Rs.		Rs.		Rs.		Rs.		Rs.		Rs.
1579	2525	1926	2022	1031	11844	1220	2942	1305	3543	...	...
290	2782	162	1266	480	2225	128	941	2193	4221	1206	3362
127	21	1000	131	799	136	150	9	170	45	222	2277
280	18	...	...	...	...	...	...	...	...	...	...
...	...	...	...	2	397	...	..	...	...	...	...
...	1323	...	1335	...	664	...	1198	...	530	...	...
1456	700	1661	721	2147	708	1996	863	3611	2349	..	2387
400	144	151	58	344	170	405	214	302	140	2677	1526
1269082	308353	534722	124781	1010435	296812	1084586	366230	1114917	493109	236	100
151620	16142	275479	26877	155469	19105	224952	30194	282413	33984	1087206	444050
49989	22882	72732	30507	41580	20083	28137	12165	46369	22269	590820	74184
265973	16624	163717	10628	204692	15293	222041	3167	201734	5138	84576	57595
...	...	21	3838	2	32	21	375	6	107	156085	15579
33924	45625	30213	47010	27924	37469	45514	61483	51217	74827	...	...
13232	22361	23025	20117	125	200	20743	23466	13864	14487	55536	49315
...	78242	...	18660	126500	32371	978390	209622	238457	58359	106545	40721
172068	76554	217993	105353	168056	98199	222986	102836	127058	69640	136109	59125
76295	135063	106374	181528	56526	106123	99946	178972	122251	244777	75743	147006
4143	11878	3915	11901	2783	8128	11915	30082	7240	24705	6288	20406
...	...	...	...	...	...	1	5	...	...	...	...
1014	2354	1175	3386	589	1686	309	2242	214	1905	209	1125
84	133	25	8	34	49	2325	3024	1775	1136	2017	2112
160	140	10	16	205	985	...	...	...	...	...	...
...	57708	...	51679	...	65479	...	49047	...	60060	...	69290
62663	8848	120036	15875	157331	25441	128542	17988	157138	33412	198677	29158
92296	31814	47595	15031	38324	18920	39072	17706	58117	15085	41053	13640
27312	31547	14533	23134	20425	28909	21508	31996	22373	50381	27856	44253
16178	41077	17111	43761	10398	29672	4549	13444	7670	21656	5852	16163
871	2325	721	1591	198	613	502	1567	204	349	12	42
2296	43671	350	4725	...	...	414	5960	...	...	331	10380
2300	459	1120	217	1915	268	21875	5459	1400	177	...	...
20410	10536	16154	6403	13802	6955	24314	11561	13632	7050	15150	7969
78528	16338	71577	12547	429	5582	284	6077	100444	27382	37338	7163
10878	14620	11728	12409	2924	4109	5130	8081	4269	6915	871	1111
...	...	...	...	...	...	...	...	...	...	...	...
H.23816 B.56627	1052496	25071 73494	990482	*23191 101056	1007264	26933 47481	1131952	24587 63792	1134557	60651 25792	1142050
7918	190712	40538	220273	3209	95569	5201	222432	6403	244698	9688	251176
26691	46780	26119	47275	4263	15546	3228	14615	6661	21081	6139	19804
24	162	17	139	49	227	41	214	92	458	102	489
6	4079	87	4920	26	3358	52	2941	105	10683	99	7029
12	79	173	1286	130	642	51	256	92	569	80	526
2025100	26843	2797800	37637	253025	34428	4566375	109958	4023250	104524	4467500	113241
3551	134003	11657	161136	16070	241982	3225	177929	7136	355820	3684	275261
...	31662	...	30244	...	16603	...	44553	...	18973	...	32637
20640	43826	11284	21283	2210	7799	12076	24913	16235	14040	10830	7977
19647	21531	15393	21451	13345	17862	15441	19097	8971	5776	41053	38386
2835	4690	1557	1942	227	2530	1056	1413	582	1843	497	1300
329597	284060	339524	288138	288082	242323	282776	246526	290952	270879	349862	262094
5833	10255	10916	25477	16569	22461	12941	15420	5242	9940	5524	13313
...	...	...	...	91	425	...	...	64	15	140	51

Computed real value of Total Exports from Mauritius of Foreign and Colonial Produce and Manufactures, &c., to the United Kingdom, British Possessions and Foreign Countries, from 1885 to 1894.

Countries.	1885	1886	1887	1888	1889	1890	1891	1892	1893	1894
	Rs.	Rs.	Rs.	Rs.	Rs.	Rs.	Rs.	Rs.	Rs.	Rs.
United Kingdom	4894753	4808213	1761476	2901712	4237861	3155119	2774150	3212428	2304925	2870478
British Possessions.										
Australasia	8174405	5948215	6453725	7182826	10178486	7329528	4205172	1791942	1661452	3539414
Barbadoes	....	....	....	310800	37240	....	....	....	....	....
Canada	287520	726435	243941	....	72230	58490	....	....	....	....
Cape Colonies	1067905	1231504	984963	2212986	2489891	2593493	2742429	1428308	2375723	2587874
Ceylon	....	....	515705	675168	214041	150880	274516	874156	4930639	3005403
Continental India	14820235	17402479	13988469	15567854	11213389	11292967	11545399	8393967	12609864	15678606
Depend. of Mauritius (a)	6944*	4897*	355851	231451	(a) 3322	(a) 3772	*2824	4403	5928	8824
Gibraltar	....	....	....	....	....	....	....	....	....	....
Singapore	8896	8691	21566	8496	6705	4032	21108	49532	54307	74840
St. Helena	12738	17582	13042	22482	10826	25358	15723	358503	32381	29118
Hong-Kong	63039	137399	75875	374524	31190	122572	61346	115863	351354	429215
Natal	....	....	....	....	181118	121695	239868	81879	117113	78112
Seychelles	....	....	....	....	242500	211555	191082	153155	200701	202356
Foreign Countries.										
Europe.										
Denmark	....	....	....	....	....	....	....	....	....	....
France	548534	433343	525084	717146	790012	706648	517021	459917	756290	125968
Italy	....	....	....	....	....	....	....	....	....	....
Germany	....	....	....	200	100	....	....	....	....	....
Portugal	....	....	30697	....	152267	....	....	....	699418	....
Spain	....	....	....	....	....	....	....	....	....	....

Africa.										
Delagoa Bay	......	......	......	......	......	32533	......	1250	3278	2123
Bay of Benin	......	......	38765	4935	......	......	......	......	......	......
Johanna	55917	77382	39248	17354	127232	20929	69567	89467	82807	70228
Madagascar	855498	1047264	784665	715994	582559	440563	380816	528428	911852	736847
Mozambique	16035	73695	43175	......	......	......	......	......	......	......
Réunion	379362	606223	730823	1000035	710570	825647	539569	732236	706294	790093
Zanzibar	2928	26739	55986	39430	73436	37850	90292	50867	35751	129557
Madeira	121	......	......	......	......	......	......	......	......	......
Canary Island	......	......	......	......	1165	......	1218	......	......	......
Egypt	......	......	......	......	120	......	......	3020	......	500
Asia.										
China	......	353	......	......	......	......	......	......	......	......
Cochin China	......	......	......	......	......	......	......	......	......	......
Java	......	......	......	......	......	125	......	......	......	......
Muscat	......	......	3095	......	26925	19576	15362	3000	9083	......
Persia	......	......	......	......	......	......	......	......	......	......
Pondicherry	65740	88251	48869	35498	58453	35214	10311	15012	59701	30424
Samoa	......	......	......	......	......	......	......	......	......	......
Sandalwood	......	......	2414	......	......	760	909	......	4113	......
Sumbawa	......	......	......	......	......	......	1180	2266	......	......
Philippine Islands	......	......	......	......	......	20	80	......	......	......
America.										
States of Argentine Conf.	......	......	......	......	......	......	......	......	......	......
United States	3094366	441000	1160363	1088790	1755781	421726	608470	......	......	806095
Uruguay	68082	......	......	......	......	......	......	......	......	......
Oceania.										
New Caledonia	6378	18485	13624	12753	1290	7340	......	548	......	......
Total	34695469†	33348341	26263943	32840436‡	33198679§	27620824‖	2234786	18350147¶	27914463**	33390672

* Sugar only. † Inclusive of Rs. 579,753 amount of Specie and Bullion exported. ‡ Inclusive of Rs 548,458 amount of Specie and Bullion exported. § Inclusive of Rs. 391,864 amount of Specie exported. (a) Other than Seychelles. ‖ Inclusive Rs. 657,894 amount of Specie exported. ¶ Inclusive of Rs. 256,966 amount of Bullion exported. ** Inclusive of Rs. 5,737,377 amount of Specie and Bullion exported.

Articles.	1885		1886		1887		1888	
	Quantities.	Value.	Quantities.	Value.	Quantities.	Value.	Quantities.	Value.
		Rs.		Rs.		Rs.		Rs.
Acid : Muriatic.........kilo.	......	...	25	30	......	...	......	......
Carbolic.............. lit.	......	...	10	5	110	107	85	97
Sulphuric ....kilo.	3125	1820	3022	1314	1725	636	1566	597
Ammonia :								
Sulphate of ....kilo.	......	...	......	...	......	...	......	......
Liquor .... ,,	......	...	......	...	......	...	......	......
Animals :								
Asses................. No.	1	35	......	...	......	...	......	......
Cows .... ,,	8	455	4	290	5	200	2	200
Deer .... ,,	......	...	......	...	......	...	2	40
Dogs .... ,,	......	...	......	...	2	100	......	......
Goats................. ,,	......	...	......	...	36	190	45	246
Horses .... ,,	24	5030	11	1640	5	750	9	5050
Mules .... ,,	19	2900	6	1200	4	600	......	......
Sheep .... ,,	8	40	......	...	......	...	9	96
Swine .... ,,	2	100	24	480	......	...	......	......
Turtle .... ,,	......	...	......	...	......	...	......	......
Apothecary Wares	......	13041	......	13074	......	9229	......	6249
Apparel	......	7205	......	15440	......	4073	......	10746
Arms and Ammunition :								
Caps	......	...	......	172	......	...	......	30
Cartridges	......	...	......	214	......	...	......	3785
Fowling Pieces ... No.	......	...	32	1500	3	1200	15	750
Guns .... ,,	......	...	......	360	......	...	1	10
Gunpowder ....kilo.	8	15	324	239	350	571	175	217
Revolvers........... ,,	......	...	36	360	......	...	......	......
Rifles................. ,,	418	2136	......	...	234	6354	......	......
Ammunition	.. ...	...	......	...	......	...	......	4133
Shot Lead...........kilo.	875	219	2530	532	113	43	15262	6220
Swords .... No.	......	...	......	...	......	...	......	......
Dynamite ....kilo.	......	...	......	...	......	...	125	600
Arrowroot .... ,,	150	16	3579	372	750	250	2150	539
Artificial Flowers ... ,,	......	...	......	...	......	...	......	......
Bacon and Hams..... ,,	1052	995	1291	1577	697	685	1961	2000
Bags, Empty, viz :								
Gunny .... No.	41791	2957	103690	6106	158500	11561	190900	17422
Rabannas .... ,,	......	...	......	...	......	...	......	......
Straw .... ,,	1669348	149072	869100	59327	223290	19779	31050	2664
Vacoa .... ,,	19050	2522	34600	3008	21000	2200	29000	1988
Bark for Tanners...... ,,	4200	456	......	...	......	...	......	......
Basket & Basket work......	......	73	......	262	......	69	......	101
Beads, ornamental	......	186	......	200	......	...	......	......
Beef, salted ....kilo.	3500	1150	41764	13279	17169	7067	32860	9309
Beer and Ale { hectol....	Hec.2250	6954	19	...	13	7679	25	8383
Beer and Ale { litres ...	B, 22750		50665	15445	27005		27273	
Bellows, Smith's...... No.	2	76	6	320	4	116	1	50
Betelnuts ....kilo.	4433	1975	10460	2164	......	...	5420	2596
Blacking	......	715	......	354	......	263	......	217
Blocks for Rigging... No.	46	43	20	85	......	...	......	......
Boats.................... ,,	5	1350	12	8515	2	340	4	2050
Books, Printed........kilo.	487	1128	2520	3076	540	1970	4317	8126
Bran .... ,,	6180	639	6142	546	10792	664	3590	257
Bread and Biscuits ... ,,	12307	3204	6517	2035	3382	769	305	75
Bricks and Tiles ...... No.	14100	1706	42800	2034	6000	405	35600	2780
Brimstone ....kilo.	688	135	......	141	1350	196	98	27
Brushes and Brooms	......	36	......	175	......	84	......	32
Bullion, Silver ....kilo.	154	4760	......	3700	......	7790	......	600

1889		1890		1891		1892		1893		1894	
Quantities.	Value.	Quantities.	Value.	Quantities.	Value.	Quantities.	Value.	Quantities.	Value.	Quantities.	Value.
	Rs.		Rs.		Rs.		Rs.		Rs.		Rs.
......	...	......	...	......	...	103	66	......	...	......	...
5	17	100	80	105	24	163	70	100	90	28	23
325	190	446	368	865	614	1396	418	932	352	420	180
40000	9500	13760	1426	......	...	......	...	......	...	......	...
......	...	......	...	......	...	300	150	......	...	......	...
5	250	......	...	......	...	2	100	1	150	......	...
2	110	4	150	5	345	......	...	2	170	11	690
......	...	2	100	2	60	......	...	......	...	4	40
......	...	......	...	......	...	1	5	......	...	......	...
4	74	......	...	8	36	17	104	......	...	15	78
4	2550	17	5800	35	6850	35	6800	26	13650	22	8600
1	300	6	1200	537	6600	12	1750	2	400	7	1100
14	210	2	36	......	...	2	14	......	...	7	152
......	...	......	...	......	...	......	...	......	...	......	...
......	...	......	...	......	...	......	...	......	...	......	...
......	5594	......	5059	......	6692	......	4246	......	5971	......	7239
......	8874	......	9645	......	7828	......	8059	......	7497	......	8331
......	60	......	...	20000	50	......	...	......	...	3600	80
......	5591	......	...	......	...	......	...	156	20	500	5
2	200	3	200	......	...	......	...	......	...	5	600
25	14538	......	...	......	...	......	...	......	...	......	...
2100	2185	......	...	187	370	123	150	34	78	70	84
......	...	......	...	......	......	......	...	......	...	......	...
2	43	9	950	......	...	......	...	......	...	......	...
......	1279	......	5	......	...	......	...	......	...	......	...
50	36	2100	575	32	16	......	...	......	...	200	36
......	110	5	95	......	...	......	...	......	...	......	...
......	...	50	100	......	...	......	...	23	25	......	...
427	220	50	15	......	...	......	...	25	17	400	129
......	..	......	...	......	...	......	...	......	...	......	...
302	437	794	903	415	484	75	62	265	392	387	414
194600	14391	307425	23842	226330	17035	196275	16501	265930	13664	188200	18760
......	...	......	...	......	...	......	...	......	...	......	...
45737	2302	557850	37582	350000	27205	6300	533	7000	350	1000	105
112925	5470	9975	1495	87100	5290	30600	3970	33800	3173	26000	3017
5	2	......	...	200	20	......	...	......	...	......	...
......	454	......	484	......	170	......	389	......	304	......	183
......	40	......	265	......	...	......	250	......	...	.. ...	...
8885	3167	53417	25478	36697	10779	5422	2380	22063	7952	2255	980
22 16984	5459	83 20403	7568	56 17467	6222	136 13004	4095	14 12426	3729	5145 12060	4249
7	182	4	220	......	...	1	50	......	...	......	...
40864	6105	25831	5603	......	...	270	39	......	697	......	...
......	128	......	187	......	60	......	115	......	123	......	75
......	...	94	1118	......	...	......	...	......	...	......	...
......	...	4	1600	1	150	2	56	1	200	2	1110
1809	1700	715	830	1282	1799	1299	384	240	400	2370	1925
6219	558	9900	733	12790	1073	26688	1838	105030	8016	46199	3356
1105	322	1636	557	532	268	1210	372	1065	197	1220	325
69729	4266	13950	1230	6300	2125	7725	1283	4700	313	4270	527
560	80	1000	80	1420	190	......	...	......	...	......	...
......	59	......	...	......	83	......	34	......	145	......	185
......	...	......	880	......	200	......	6283	......	10326	......	4320

Articles.	1885		1886		1887		1888	
	Quantities.	Value.	Quantities.	Value.	Quantities.	Value.	Quantities.	Value.
		Rs.		Rs.		Rs.		Rs.
Bullion, Gold ......kilo.	......	......	......	3700	......	.....	.....	600
Butter .... ,,	7696	4356	1639	1787	887	575	3159	2211
Bunting.............. M.	......	......	......	5	......	......	3	17
Cab. & Upholst Wares...	......	8151	......	14406	......	13691	......	9753
Camphor ....kilo.	185	230	458	748	715	620	183	133
Candles :								
Composition...... ,,	1474	823	8817	5128	6283	3064	8644	3566
Wax & Sperm ... ,,	71	97	96	72	490	500	.. ...	...
Canes and Sticks	......	6	......	......	......	......	......	...
Caoutchouc ....kilo.	57814	80793	26362	36513	53685	106085	......	...
Manufacture of.........	......	......	......	200	17460	36344	38718	78389
Carriages .... No.	7	2900	2	50	2	700	3	800
Carts and Waggons ,,	2	120	4	200	4	415	1	50
Casts of Statutes & Busts	......	......	......	......	......	......	......	...
Cement ....kilo.	12617	731	14220	954	45715	2123	15600	1210
Cheese .... ,,	1442	1702	1918	2179	2558	1563	1239	1404
Chocolate & Cocoa. ,,	1175	1330	105	168	9	12	338	299
Choorah .... ,,	165	21	124	16	346	39	503	59
Clay ....kilo.	......	......	......	......	150	18	......	...
Clocks and Watches No.	4	527	9	1574	90	977	16	425
Coals ....kilo.	45250	1319	60960	1794	13300	350	12910	558
Coffee .... ,,	27116	12744	23445	14582	26376	18064	32962	22537
Confectionery	......	1085	......	4943	......	3013	......	3870
Copperah or Poonac.kilo.	30579	768	5630	443	3250	240	12450	490
Copper Old........... ,,	131033	41535	142697	53414	27736	22804	33042	16318
Rods .... No.	......	......	......	......	......	......	......	...
Sheets and Nails..kilo.	1898	1463	11618	4396	170	148	......	...
Cordage, Aloe ...... ,,	350	90	......	......	......	......	......	...
Coir .... ,,	22674	9868	2639	297	3933	520	639	228
Hemp.............. ,,	13414	9283	1633	600	9160	2411	2100	1202
Cordials & Liquour. lit.	4057	3878	7996	7860	7442	6893	8324	6919
Corks & Bungs...... No.	2288	1044	6008	1975	23301	1202	2831	937
Corn, Grain, Meal, &c. :								
Barley ....kilo.	......	......	......	......	......	... ..	375	40
Beans .... ,,	6870	510	22800	2205	6806	771	7405	715
Dholl .... ,,	543	3708	548	2683	81600	4822	86925	4932
Gram.............. ,,	9244	44713	10251	43767	988950	46361	1401600	64014
Lentils .... ,,	1095	7003	8286	36148	312375	16659	482400	23362
Maize.............. ,,	101125	6853	1715	114	10270	345	8873	268
Oats .... ,,	15180	2078	6254	675	15026	1297	8910	726
Peas .... ,,	10030	394	5495	449	274	32	7925	1053
Pollard .... ,,	......	......	......	......	150	48	......	...
Rice .... ,,	23296	141458	41647	203998	5689425	290945	9970060	430113
Wheat .... ,,	375	2743	730	2290	43425	1987	31500	4200
Wheat Flour...... ,,	186164	23772	602890	68636	540873	62936	793965	81415
Cotton Manufactures :								
Colored .... ,,	670413	71998	619032	84386	660440	33092	462776	67217
Counterpanes ... No.	......	.. ...	......	......	75	92	50	50
Hoisery	......	933	......	100	......	2	......	100
Plain .... M.	325036	39390	240912	59829	221374	21748	228604	27365
Stitched or sewing.kilo	140	202	250	1340	.....	......	......	...
Wick .... ,,	70	48	45	67	5	5	50	19
Wool .... ,,	400	92	600	110	......	......	......	...
Cutch .... ,,	......	......	......	......	......	......	......	...
Earthen & Chinaware P.	73799	8903	95252	14201	56255	8865	54556	4633
Earth, red	......	......	......	......	......	......	100	5

1889		1890		1891		1892		1893		1894	
Quantities.	Value.	Quantities.	Value.	Quantities.	Value.	Quantities.	Value.	Quantities.	Value.	Quantities.	Value.
	Rs.		Rs.		Rs.		Rs.		Rs.		Rs.
......	...	......	880	......	200	......	6283	......	...	......	...
148	299	2911	3652	600	765	775	915	1343	1554	1914	4944
......	...	......	18	......	...	......	...	......	...	......	...
......	5823	......	15688	......	5443	......	7526	......	5650	......	6413
555	605	168	308	480	685	315	409	185	235	652	872
367	245	1730	1298	1685	935	3709	1628	944	557	242	166
10	10	12	10	50	10	63	50	12	20	12	8
......	...	......	200	......	30	......	13	......	...	......	...
50	70	3918	4968	7650	8900	......	...	19228	19065	5317	6669
10297	13490	6195	6826	333	467	7935	705	3215	1910	1096	1150
6	2075	8	2330	7	740	6	1775	11	1710	8	1750
1	70	1	50	2	65	......	...	14	1060	......	...
......	...	......	...	......	...	......	...	......	...	......	...
61400	3782	88815	12000	11990	316	5775	713	21000	908	9385	1421
318	391	427	524	223	243	48	70	385	552	690	1415
......	...	......	...	50	60	32	68	......	...	825	1320
1400	156	825	68	55	12	200	30	780	126	300	125
......	...	......	...	......	...	75	23	......	...	......	...
10	757	205	2210	16	1080	15	2110	2	25	325	956
63250	2407	71880	2258	15080	595	44000	1469	21600	522	45500	1510
14383	11280	32694	25543	10323	11452	21656	16988	14054	7840	14495	16331
......	2589	......	2862	......	1385	......	2651	......	2737	......	4893
9310	482	1700	80	3300	118	3150	126	5000	200	4550	420
144543	53347	215894	54888	78414	20221	102013	40182	82126	33403	84875	36417
......	...	......	...	20	16	......	...	......	...	4950	2670
1220	1670	4330	1552	1176	1779	3506	2011	211	146	3688	3765
......	...	......	...	......	...	......	...	......	...	......	...
768	240	1310	1095	1397	864	775	220	1020	520	1465	555
3414	1450	539	340	3410	1391	2217	1500	1507	898	395	97
3188	3722	3137	2653	840	634	437	759	603	889	137	355
2137	616	1274	561	276172	488	293518	550	184710	543	185720	809
......	...	......	...	......	...	......	...	6020	799	......	...
2993	475	2790	554	3495	499	21820	2191	42451	4150	9895	1287
108192	7067	47250	4798	33635	2895	41830	2045	26742	2661	21560	2116
1379137	60597	1095950	44493	1191375	53186	1169595	76291	782400	51543	1406450	101408
581635	31304	888077	44735	788467	38243	935420	53327	738431	50819	710700	55162
765	58	540	38	5015	287	1350	110	345	31	140	14
9534	862	1957	206	7557	884	12404	1004	11477	1780	9228	953
7305	834	1125	153	940	128	603	81	4515	546	710	109
200	40	......	...	......	...	......	...	......	...	4628	520
3909927	229579	7118308	349989	3996400	256040	3872004	252831	4354188	458614	3049013	274103
......	...	87240	8165	43575	4067	90	24	......	...	525	70
696622	91413	670485	66097	598283	64237	1314209	148921	2290904	152499	1474575	168647
314168	41784	148592	16939	77371	9489	254079	28080	144810	22167	143029	24174
......	5	144	144	......	...	......	...	......	...	......	...
......	638	......	1717	......	601	......	281	......	1116	......	169
271127	31724	72148	8154	76760	4236	51275	6026	36633	4645	6280	652
10	...	......	...	......	...	......	...	......	...	......	...
500	60	50	10	5	4	25	20	880	176	......	...
757	185	92	384	30	9	......	...	340	74	......	...
......	...	......	...	......	...	......	...	......	...	......	...
30623	2823	10206	1358	4520	463	7055	2070	36018	2806	24159	3118
......	...	......	...	......	...	......	...	......	...	......	...

ARTICLES.	1885		1886		1887		1888	
	Quantities.	Value.	Quantities.	Value.	Quantities.	Value.	Quantities.	Value.
		Rs.		Rs.		Rs.		Rs,
Eggs salted............ No.	......	......	500	10	......	...	750	15
Feathers, Ornamental ...	......	......	......	......	......	...	......	...
,, Ostrich	......	4800	......	2000	......	...	......	...
Fibre Aloe ....kilo.	657540	165633	996792	217613	1959281	446176	2532115	690858
Raffia .... ,,	104195	13191	186528	42142	129750	10004	5500	1100
Cocoanuts .... ,,	2375	300	8550	348	......	...	......	...
Fireworks .... ,,	......	619	......	578	......	832	......	4897
Fish, dried or salted. ,,	309203	40302	481772	64364	442636	60755	669060	100469
dried herrings.. ,,	......	......	......	......	......	...	......	...
Fish, pickled not otherwise described...kilo.	1935	245	17930	1964	355	107	60	21
Fishing tackle ...... ,,	......	......	......	35	......	...	......	...
Fruits, dried, viz.								
Almonds ....kilo.	......	......	102	81	280	74	580	235
Cocoanuts .... No.	39108	2433	62228	3242	38094	2664	50430	3860
Dates..................kilo.	7377	735	21082	2125	14480	1261	33300	3335
Pistachio nuts...... ,,	3729	246	130	9	930	79	1689	184
Raisins .... ,,	......	......	55	62	......	......	......	...
Of all other sorts.. ,,	225	48	234	50	......	......	35	8
Fresh .... ,,	......	253	......	21	100	15	......	...
Ghee .... ,,	4598	3474	4955	4786	7821	6240	7608	5576
Ginger .... ,,	1318	138	1387	178	2902	261	1930	183
Glass, viz : broken... ,,	......	......	......	......	45	25	......	...
Bottles empty...Gross	12672	1836	127	1575	63	1282	182	2111
Window glass ...Panes	1660	430	300	52	280	70	460	364
Glassware ....Pieces	22465	2828	17202	7582	14863	4205	5383	1262
Glasses, Looking, &c. No.	19966	952	300	52	......	......	81	255
Glue ....kilo.	......	......	75	100	70	50	50	40
Grease .... ,,	......	......	75	170	......	......	......	......
Groceries .... ,,	......	9655	......	22960	......	10502	......	19346
Gum, Arabic .... ,,	......	......	5	3	......	......	5	8
,, Copal .... ,,	17429	17432	9591	7034	5588	6010	1000	600
Haberdashery .... ,,	......	79927	......	112248	......	71116	......	47910
Hair, Horse............ ,,	490	50	......	......	......	......	......	...
,, Ornamental ... ,,	......	......	......	......	......	......	......	...
Hardware and Cutlery ...	......	38972	......	48060	......	33360	......	118955
Hats, Felt .... No.	255	318	801	1698	21	120	678	901
Silk .... ,,	......	......	......	......	......	......	......	...
Solah .... ,,	......	......	......	......	......	......	154	179
Straw .... ,,	209	548	15	125	30	30	250	150
Of all other sorts... ,,	24	36	50	130	326	253	......	...
Hay and Straw ......kilo.	913	1174	70	159	245	851	162	27
Hemp, undressed ... ,,	25	5	133529	30245	7735	1710	13425	4500
Hides, raw .... ,,	24441	105841	23626	90770	14601	47481	8767	35071
Hoofs of Cattle ...... ,,	11741	226	162300	2288	31076	800	1600	520
Hops and Malt ...... ,,	......	......	......	......	40	40	......	...
Horn, Cow or Bull... No.	17204	955	28680	746	10968	910	29473	1498
Indigo ....kilo.	25	11	417	302	20	5	382	131
Iron, viz : Bar......... ,,	13949	1963	19838	2776	14282	1171	8782	1247
Cast .... ,,	780	274	1538	942	2948	511	1225	731
Sheet .... ,,	26534	8871	49803	10624	61598	14764	45717	7887
Wrought, Anchors and Grapnels ... ,,	......	......	205	40	570	106	1422	462
Nails .... ,,	6008	2161	6620	2828	5448	1664	5878	1837
Old .... ,,	427737	9517	336475	11020	246000	4880	69800	10280
Of all other sorts... ,,	......	......	......	......	34000	600	......	...

* Including Shipping Charges.

1889		1890		1891		1892		1893		1894	
Quantities.	Value.	Quantities.	Value.	Quantities.	Value.	Quantities.	Value.	Quantities.	Value.	Quantities.	Value.
	Rs.		Rs.		Rs.		Rs.		Rs.		Rs.
1000	40	1000	40	......	...	......	...	...	...	250	15
..	...	......	...	......	...	......	...	...	...	......	...
...	...	......	...	......	...	......	...	...	... *	......	...
2746799	1023351	1899126	623725	1485510	453530	1017236	309653	1324201	275433	857633	178387
...	...	1250	150	......	...	......	...	13710	2354	......	...
4350	435	......	...	166	35	......	...	14305	1653	46850	5746
...	3735	......	685	......	624	......	1489	...	1507	......	1701
440893	59736	359135	58866	410080	52557	823640	127329	415457	70955	286655	60273
...	...	......	...	......	..	......	...	...	...	......	...
7135	1274	3888	539	325	138	3130	1595	770	250	25	15
...	...	......	400	......	...	......	...	...	...	......	...
207	60	50	16	145	34	......	...	75	25	......	...
84804	4713	32750	2074	65106	5660	60632	4626	91837	4044	74075	3914
35475	3101	14406	1748	31507	1424	50	4	33496	2776	15990	1308
1262	195	3550	452	11892	1425	13030	1430	16305	1827	4007	522
5	5	......	...	75	20	......	...	...	...	......	...
12	10	1352	2380	110	62	200	10	50	20	3220	377
25	5	400	16	3150	60	50	15	235	27	60	20
14671	11849	12245	9620	23564	19167	5268	4518	5245	4669	1125	10030
2550	264	3840	452	5367	1240	4971	936	7947	1103	3723	628
...	..	... ..	...	......	...	......	...	...	...	......	...
326	1688	117	955	31274	1977	26981	909	38593	1957	27212	1860
627	145	1160	217	33	12	... ..	...	. .	...	153	145
6832	305	12590	802	8142	915	3161	993	35949	6580	20578	1423
2	40	2425	180	......	...	119	120	296	304	3955	751
1500	3000	......	...	.....	...	5	5	70	49	540	265
...	...	......	...	......	...	475	98	248	126	425	190
...	13218	......	10576	......	5580	......	5166	...	7613	......	9478
...	...	......	...	......	...	50	35	..	...	......	...
737	64	......	...	3565	3485	145	147	554	190	1008	160
...	30916	......	34676	......	17021	......	33670	...	55967	...	55157
...	...	......	...	......	...	......	...	...	...	......	...
...	...	......	...	......	...	......	...	...	...	......	...
...	38696	......	46394	......	22685	......	17112	...	25280	......	25320
114	113	136	170	36	72	......	...	334	335	492	833
...	...	......	...	......	...	......	...	...	...	......	...
...	...	129	129	122	81	382	345	473	452	......	...
...	...	252	92	1	5	......	...	570	190	512	34
...	...	......	...	......	...	......	...	. .	...	......	...
2170	315	22250	320	71156	2666	43000	835	2150	50	33100	653
175	40	......	...	......	..	30	18	...	...	......	...
23140	29896	75488	29179	90192	23594	126955	37837	97296	33539	150164	34317
8000	250	6000	180	6238	262	3865	293	...	...	......	...
...	. .	......	...	......	...	......	...	...	...	... ..	...
19708	1565	136606	1640	16911	1845	16285	1108	17260	1634	9876	1540
120	115	......	...	650	384	......	...	160	88	50	50
9022	1098	1769	396	2982	548	4119	742	5156	1170	4814	695
3930	1342	8338	1331	1055	659	5790	732	...	...	......	...
16798	4580	20498	5043	19873	5842	10878	2420	29655	7076	3510	896
5000	100	400	314	808	493	920	135	15	8	3640	1039
2615	566	6119	1560	6638	1381	2009	568	5468	1775	2210	843
45000	1040	519550	4413	314050	2742	112650	7583	375000	16280	193000	2005
1000	150	9489	632	13053	828	202523	20784	2907	586	5298	1449

Articles.	1885 Quantities.	1885 Value.	1886 Quantities.	1886 Value.	1887 Quantities.	1887 Value.	1888 Quantities.	1888 Value.
		Rs.		Rs.		Rs.		Rs.
Jewellery	......	1753	......	5195	......	1759	......	1150
Juice of Lemons ...... lit.	......	......	......	......	......	...	......	......
Jute .... kilo.	......	......	160700	16070	6075	192	......	......
Lard .... ,,	58694	26151	94023	37787	270477	85810	320674	33639
Lead, viz:								
Sheets & pipes ... ,,	1341	364	1411	547	2228	910	3450	989
Old .... ,,	300	80	9100	908	......	...	3921	440
Leather, Unwrought ,,	8760	6148	3335	991	14535	7587	7209	2550
Leather, Wrought:								
Boots and shoes...prs.	2952	6424	1878	6770	3283	5357	1569	3500
Of all sorts .... ,,	2	38	......	......	......	...	......	......
Gloves .... doz.	......	926	......	503	.....	1220	......	990
Lime .... kilo.	79432	1220	65350	1458	22440	603	96900	1422
Carbonate .... ,,	......	... ..	......	......	......	...	......	......
Superphosphate ... ,,	500000	5000	......	......	......	...	......	......
Linen Manufactures:								
Plain .... M.	......	......	5737	1495	36	22	......	......
Sail Cloth .... M.	3211	786	796	527	130	124	1375	550
Sails .... No.	......	......	10	60	1	20	......	......
Thread for sewing.kilo.	10	40	......	......	......	...	50	410
Tents .... No.	......	......	......	8668	......	...	1	100
Matches .... gross.	......	3100	......	7749	......	14145	8511	9343
Machinery & Mill Work...	......	9975	......	10325	......	4400	74910	34410
Manure, viz:								
Guano .... kilo.	15000	1500	10000	500	2000	180	310000	310000
Of all other sorts.. ,,	34256	945	5900	530	5435	119	30	10
Mathem. & Opt. Insts	......	102	......	192	......	160	......	......
Mats and Matting	......	181	......	402	......	174	......	64
Molasses .... kilo.	210365	11696	2670050	76479	3469830	84198	6060033	143644
Moss .... ,,	247	297	257	376	130	125	108	150
Musical Instruments ..	......	2178	......	2623	......	1660	......	3960
Music Printed	... ..	......	50	300	......	...	......	500
Oakum .... kilo.	845	196	700	117	720	216	312	46
Oil, Cloth .... M.	......	......	90	10	......	...	......	......
Castor .... kilo.	10785	3841	19459	6339	34419	10966	15309	4331
Cocoanut .... lit.	1005710	209644	953827	209701	1743842	218550	909913	179457
Gingely .... kilo.	2746	930	2957	1605	1952	760	2577	788
Mustard .... ,,	38	8	1357	559	2910	1069	1275	424
Olive .... lit.	3167	2290	5425	4005	3809	2483	1025	1156
Pistachio .... kilo.	35700	10390	31357	7857	25437	7857	31310	9595
Petroleum .... lit.	43787	4456	168563	16058	15271	2246	311500	34767
Of all other sorts. ,,	8076	2719	850	287	427	248	397	102
Onions and Garlic...kilo.	12258	1724	35433	4427	10052	1204	31990	2680
Opium .... ,,	455	12903	437	13222	493	13000	296	7800
Printers' Colors, &c.	......	5879	......	6461	......	8696	......	6041
Paper, Manufacture of ...	......	221	......	1896	......	1053	......	1863
,, for hang...rolls	1843	240	2179	931	150	25	......	......
Pearl & Scotch Barley.kilo	......	......	......	......	100	16	......	......
Perfumery	......	1565	......	1706	......	1097	......	426
Pickles and Sauces	......	4439	......	3975	......	1707	......	679
Pictures, Oil Paintings ...	......	15	......	......	......	50	......	......
Pitch and Tar .... kilo.	74	1049	50	967	232	547	475	869
Plants and Roots	......	1285	......	1297	......	427	......	3120
Plated & Gilt Wares	......	350	......	......	......	1550	......	638
Plate, Wrght. of silver..k.	7	400	......	1364	......	...	......	......

1889		1890		1891		1892		1893		1894	
Quanti-ties.	Value.	Quanti-ties.	Value.	Quanti-ties.	Value.	Quanti-ties.	Value.	Quanti-ties.	Value	Quanti-ties.	Value.
	Rs.		Rs.		Rs.		Rs.		Rs.		Rs.
...	6921	...	4025	...	3707	...	8501	...	3935	...	3990
...	...	...	...	...	...	...	...	...	...	...	...
13560	182	221500	19330	...	...	...	...	...	...	...	...
356838	153473	289235	126416	50744	28047	158571	109752	172686	77905	256346	133748
1800	647	295	116	272	675	1465	465	955	356	385	124
425	38	423	434	...	...	10668	1587	16408	2471	42520	6187
9021	5754	14996	5777	2111	661	32	30	500	230	...	...
2002	1950	1199	1069	804	1373	3681	1857	1170	1307	2342	3298
...	...	...	1120	10	893	...	1957	...	379	...	314
...	387	...	...	...	...	...	...	...	...	...	...
63880	1338	98560	631	43570	1220	28150	724	39800	696	96500	1670
...	...	...	...	...	...	...	...	...	...	...	...
...	...	...	...	1400	90	...	...	...	...	1800	356
...	...	...	...	...	...	...	...	...	...	...	...
952	304	438	438	855	500	209	120	310	376	500	1233
...	...	...	...	...	...	...	...	...	...	...	...
...	...	...	...	...	...	20	15	...	...	...	...
...	...	...	...	...	...	...	...	...	...	...	...
10254	7827	6472	5290	9373	7436	32649	8459	9488	5891	7777	6334
86567	140088	107817	44470	117276	38125	388213	172603	66342	59600	8744	9150
534000	37400	...	200	...	...	...	...	...	...	250	10
202567	44295	2000	100	52450	5335	50000	3000	1200	120	46000	5265
...	566	...	290	...	10	...	...	...	180	...	...
...	70	...	160693	1175	355	10540	1000	1900	1475	1390	408
3905250	130461	5893575	259	4689570	94313	5622100	104633	3356500	104625	7415350	217859
15	24	212	2750	250	225	10420	1755	90	155	107	165
...	360	...	...	...	2410	...	1630	...	2100	...	2124
...	50	...	203	...	20	...	...	...	...	...	...
3125	410	750	...	239	162	325	108	385	137	5	2
...	...	...	5568	...	...	...	...	...	...	...	...
45145	9111	16042	314850	17057	5281	12871	4143	21710	67[illegible]8	9403	3904
698819	138173	1134936	314850	714686	180587	1159280	215900	113980	257198	1039134	187116
2912	1290	3088	1175	1483	590	1901	788	3161	1398	2011	1066
970	373	970	472	5250	1363	420	180	420	192	4240	973
482	775	415	422	2348	1627	1049	795	715	576	7878	3576
24741	7585	27623	10909	39417	12442	18933	7555	20147	5706	20511	5282
350282	43951	433451	40065	94463	9287	751247	28197	2740	2171	305172	22047
240	65	425	191	4058	1333	650	307	255	89	561	404
43276	3515	58649	7515	19088	1922	19853	2254	50593	5688	66119	10897
246	6500	364	8044	412	10400	529	13010	363	9400	266	6550
...	7769	...	6072	...	9343	...	590	...	1931	...	781
...	2698	...	894	..	5213	...	877	...	1123	...	454
257	315	...	...	...	...	...	...	...	..	...	...
...	254	...	...	...	...	...	...	...	...	300	20
...	1998	...	320	...	320	...	1052	...	649	...	638
...	50	...	514	...	294	...	231	...	272	...	639
...	762	...	200	...	...	...	4	...	...	...	...
191	2478	63	947	5178	680	2365	423	4320	829	1575	412
...	525	...	2375	...	4244	...	1070	...	418	...	1216
...	...	...	1900	...	1364	...	427	...	...	...	300
...	...	14	230	...	...	...	...	...	...	...	...

Articles.	1885		1886		1887		1888	
	Quantities.	Value.	Quantities.	Value.	Quantities.	Value.	Quantities.	Value.
		Rs.		Rs.		Rs.		Rs.
Pork salted............kilo.	1375	626	2111	832	390	296	2335	1095
Potatoes................ ,,	9750	492	13275	1179	12308	890	12630	839
Prints and Engravings...	......	190	......	210	......	......	......	170
Potash Azote of.....kilo.	......	......	231	30	6	9	......	...
Printing Types, &c.......	......	......	......	......	......	1300	......	125
Provisions preserved.....	*......	19946	......	19583	......	14598	......	7117
Rabannas.... ......Pieces.	34300	6265	59775	14164	2200	913	48	222
Rags & Paper Stuff..kilo.	2240	428	......	......	1000	50	......	...
Rattans................ ,,	2075	335	22441	1307	34152	5016	16375	2793
Rosin . Red........... ,,	50	15	......	......	......	......	......	...
Rough................ ,,	2697	435	3860	731	4745	693	2062	353
Saddlery & Harness......	......	615	......	474	......	635	......	1079
Sago.....................kilo.	3765	982	6162	1145	1492	487	3280	679
Sand .... ,,	150	34	2725	115	......	......	......	...
Salt...................... ,,	615297	17998	1419179	40348	1050933	27460	697022	20244
Salpetre .... ,,	25	6	878	180	30378	6216	92379	15167
Sausages............... ,,	130	192	125	335	29	38	......	...
Seeds : Garden............	......	25	......	343	......	396	......	556
Unenumerated	......	3380	......	9602	......	4210	......	5034
Sheating paper or felt.ki	312	83	......	283	......	290	......	...
Silk anufactures :								
Satins & Ribbons... M.	3319	2465	4907	4444	2276	2019	463	452
Coooons ....kilo.	......	......	......	......	......	......	......	...
Soap .... ,,	57411	12127	77500	14613	37159	8986	49790	10389
Soda, Carbonate of ,,	1160	75	60	50	......	......	......	...
Soda Water, doz. bottles.	......	......	......	......	......	......	......	.
Solder..................kilo.	......	......	25	50	......	......	......	...
Specie, viz : Gold.........	......	16000	......	41100	......	343335	......	210000
Silver	......	443353	......	629445	......	1785290	......	480970
Copper & Bronze.......	......	......	......	2170	......	......	......	...
Paper Currency.........	......	115640	......	88547	......	63950	......	45888
Spec. Illn. of Nat. History	......	1237	......	1685	......	1610	......	2191
Spelter of Zinc ......kilo.	......	......	12200	1280	25023	3018	5000	200
Spices, viz :								
Cinnamon...........kilo.	85	45	70	16	50	8	......	...
Cloves.............. ,,	......	......	2505	1600	165	55	1050	524
Pepper .... ,,	6212	4660	7022	3779	5297	2570	7285	5835
Of all other sorts ,,	21570	2110	4064	770	13381	1763	10447	1947
Spirits, viz :								
Brandy............. lit.	5357	6467	7702	9106	4673	4189	2671	3047
Geneva .... ,,	.....	......	490	396	1404	833	74	72
Rum .... ,,	3733140	3749522	3444259	415827	3200454	366920	297881	297881
Whisky .... ,,	1343	904	2743	2381	1218	1362	1848	2037
Of Wine .... ,,	25	25	32	33	......	......	......	...
Sponge ....kilo.	......	......	......	......	......	......	40	699
Starch.................. ,,	131	46	7267	801	75	24	295	66
Stationery .... ,,	......	4176	......	3304	......	2496	......	1162
Steel, Unwrought ... ,,	100	50	29	24	150	92	694	291
Stones, viz :								
Building........... No.	6	18	16	40	69	140	6	20
Diamonds	......	......	......	......	......	......	......	...
Filtering .... No.	......	......	3	75	26	23	3	75
Gravestones ...... ,,	......	......	......	......	......	......	......	...
Grindstones ...... ,,	37	117	27	160	22	178	19	128
Marble .... ,,	1	25	8	192	2	30	......	...

* Including Shipping Charges.

1889		1890		1891		1892		1893		1894	
Quantities.	Value.	Quantities.	Value.	Quantities.	Value.	Quantities.	Value.	Quantities.	Value.	Quantities.	Value.
	Rs.		Rs.		Rs.		Rs.		Rs.		Rs.
455	325	4899	2065	1718	583	547	295	630	365	11460	2909
4365	509	9815	838	4117	461	7945	757	3275	367	12128	1168
......	28	...	25	...	7450	......	895	......	650	...	72
......	...	...	...	525	461	182	40	53950	14176	..	..
......	...	...	...	...	...	......	200	......	50	...	100
......	6766	...	9095	...	7450	......	6291	......	6340	...	9207
20200	2915	42125	5956	12452	1856	2829	548	3497	852	200	176
......	...	...	...	...	...	......	...	......	......	...	...
44560	3791	22085	2270	34560	3872	36835	2897	9500	2052	45291	7090
80	13	1090	234	1630	328	212	43	345	110	275	65
615	150	440	54	...	...	......	...	......	...	...	...
......	506	...	1104	...	398	......	648	......	1218	...	590
3768	1254	19552	3060	7042	801	3569	827	2720	603	3826	657
300	25	300	28	350	25	800	144	...	...	200	55
1234515	28303	780303	24909	421729	10912	974012	15108	502018	11656	162263	4887
40112	12800	815	296	82690	18560	......	...	......	...	...	...
75	80	412	100	...	...	......	...	......	...	...	...
......	635	...	682	...	143	......	245	......	357	...	225
......	22155	...	6213	37664	3709	......	...	43727	5261	2912	210
......	100	...	310	585	105	60	50	165	142	...	...
15253	4150	911	890	455	22[illegible]	4884	955	594	310	400	244
......	...	...	...	...	...	......	...	......	...	...	...
55482	12738	23095	5865	28284	5780	111882	20255	150506	38599	208665	81204
......	...	...	...	100	48	......	...	.. ..	...	...	...
......	...	...	...	...	...	......	...	......	...	...	...
......	...	...	...	...	...	......	...	......	...	...	...
......	...	...	510	...	6000	......	1756	......	...	...	17100
......	394864	...	657384	...	594115	......	246381	......	5727151	...	409562
......	..	..	...	...	...	......	...	......	500	...	...
......	...	...	...	...	3000	......	2545	......	...	...	...
......	840	...	2305	...	1255	......	1025	......	151	...	232
7000	560	5500	1050	3302	404	7403	1879	12382	3067	8669	2510
......	...	...	...	100	45	3	1	......	...	...	...
50	12	6250	3263	1425	559	......	...	1653	446	10341	4666
9792	6250	5179	3672	9821	5696	9703	4493	1060	591	6574	4309
11674	1871	10835	2084	55	55	......	...	100	200	3811	1099
1150	1523	760	1389	1408	1777	1372	2315	1348	1747	1496	1946
79	100	4460	3045	291	286	63	158	48	74	12	24
3345152	365112	3454019	313509	3812206	389926	2691751	303642	2557850	*344685	3054001	439559
372	688	678	517	569	774	568	760	562	730	546	874
45	45	...	...	167	417	......	...	......	...	...	...
......	...	...	...	..	...	......	...	......	...	...	...
480	115	95	21	26310	2521	117	34	595	76	...	...
......	387	...	1528	...	930	......	814	......	666	...	1644
238	38	299	262	44	17	......	...	......	...	169	276
6	12	7000	125	...	...	......	...	......	...	...	...
......	...	...	...	...	...	......	400	......	50	...	...
4	100	7	30	4	70	3	50	3	45	10	25
......	...	...	...	...	...	......	...	......	...	...	...
9	117	152	50	12	136	54	134	8	124	1007	164
1	6	...	...	...	...	4	329	16	193	...	...

Articles.	1885		1886		1887		1888	
	Quantities.	Value.	Quantities.	Value.	Quantities.	Value.	Quantities.	Value.
		Rs.		Rs.		Rs.		Rs.
Stones (*Continued*) viz:								
Paving .... No.	......	......	......	......	......	......	...	......
Rock Crystal ...... ,,	295	61	20	5	......	......	...	......
Slates .... ,,	......	......	240	10	......	......	...	......
Sugar, *..............kilo.	......	31301179	......	29290185	......	23129949	..	28872022
Candy .... ,,	58	16	10	4	75	25	60	30
Straw-ware	......	1	......	242	......	56	...	24
Tallow .... ,,	7047	1135	1838	192	1450	340	662	138
Tamarinds........... ,,	38424	2441	26222	1849	12405	1192	20278	2336
Tarpaulins........... No.	......	......	4	240	......	......	30	31
Tea ... .kilo.	2818	4244	5195	5871	8342	9162	5495	5210
Tin Unwrought...... ,,	808	530	866	337	1746	1945	1854	1984
Plates............... ,,	......	11343	......	7077	......	4972	...	2118
Tobacco, viz:								
Unmanufactured..kilo.	10929	3718	7328	2372	44111	12822	15352	6638
Manufactured ... ,,	531	983	1783	1373	784	708	959	1020
Segars............... ,,	1129	3399	1307	3351	1686	3512	110	387
Snuff .... ,,	20	36	......	......	......	......	...	......
Tobacco, Pipes......gross	......	......	......	......	......	......	...	......
Tongues..............kilo.	......	......	......	......	......	......	...	......
Tortoise shell ...... ,,	289	2832	459	6450	553	5299	464	7454
Toys	......	1148	......	3377	......	3959	...	2370
Turmeric ....kilo.	4045	593	6419	1125	5887	783	4043	515
Twines of all sorts.. ,,	4516	769	3769	1972	786	458	135	85
Umbrellas,viz:Cotton No.	685	893	2062	2523	936	671	3990	2000
Silk .... ,,	647	579	18	36	10	36	...	......
Of all other sorts.. ,,	......	......	......	......	......	......	...	......
Vanilla .... ,,	26524	309381	22792	312049	18501	236583	25948	326817
Vacoa Leaves ...... ,,	......	......	......	......	......	......	...	......
Vegetables, fresh...kilo.	......	140	......	69	......	10	1270	164
Vermicelli & Maca.. ,,	2657	1448	1585	1085	1043	354	1455	499
Vinegar .... lit.	7296	1198	5676	1513	3691	996	9525	1870
Wax, Bees'...........kilo.	52122	35807	102575	69808	42316	20100	11163	11714
Whalebone........... ,,	......	......	......	......	......	......	...	......
Wine of all sorts.. lit.	214262	53131	1970	43303	1329	33174	1547	39881
Wine of all sorts.. bot.	8784		7136		4708	12419	3939	
Wood, viz:	C.M. D.M.							
Boards & Planks..C.M.	632 550	17858	371	12526	395	30245	1009	18433
Casks, empty...... No.	6012	24243	6581	26883	6730	......	6749	30341
Deals .... M 3	......	......	......	......	......	......	...	......
Ebony...............C.M.	84500	3898	328	15470	43	1000	78	4300
Firewood .... M 2	......	......	......	1	5	500	...	......
Masts & Spars ... No.	......	......	......	......	......	......	...	......
Shingles............ ,,	64000	1245	163500	3778	200550	5282	220000	6446
Timber ............C.M.	107–025	5106	73	4865	17	879	808	6024
Oars .... ,,	8	44	27	140	16	115	4	40
Woodenware .... ,,	......	1109	......	933	......	616	...	6382
Woollen Manufact.,viz:								
Cloth .... M.	304	851	360	1160	......	......	...	......
Carpets, &c. ...... ,,	210	500	......	......	......	......	64	640
Shawls .... No.	193	770	140	337	......	......	...	......
Blankets .... No.	261	271	232	692	563	584	327	260
Cloth mixed with Cotton .... M.	2824	2502	2642	2488	2721	1658	83	93

* Vide page 68, 69, 70 & 71.
† Including Shipping Charges.

1889		1890		1891		1892		1893		1894	
Quantities.	Value.	Quantities.	Value.	Quantities.	Value.	Quantities.	Value.	Quantities.	Value.	Quantities.	Value.
	Rs.		Rs.		Rs.		Rs.		Rs.		Rs.
62	160	......	......	......	......	......	......	......	......	...	...
......	......	......	......	......	......	......	......	......	......	...	...
...... *	......	... ..	......	......	......	......	......	......	......	...	...
142794220	29123381	129443098	24041707	124759108	21216308	94097446	15346233	87408861	19655528	13944	9413
30	15	......	......	60	10	85	35	78	49	...	...
......	......	......	61	......	34	......	769	......	82	...	31
353	100	60	37	172	90	315	200	3577	1720	250	50
32693	2408	39112	2979	12258	1048	21688	2167	11725	1298	11601	1978
......	......	3	62	......	......	5	100	......	......	...	...
6517	5581	2468	2756	3174	3383	4386	4745	4602	5646	9729	8623
......	......	6340	1826	100	120	......	......	......	......	...	...
......	3043	60	1005	14564	4258	35250	5067	18680	2808	14075	2599
10381	3713	7029	9907	7140	2458	8713	3611	6660	1861	8692	3085
358	346	1480	1658	644	676	9325	3970	411	277	506	350
412	1053	110	415	1425	2372	780	1182	442	1025	382	557
......	......	......	......	......	......	......	......	......	......	...	...
......	......	......	......	12	21	2	15	1	25	...	...
......	......	......	......	......	......	......	......	......	......	...	...
3667	2110	709	11490	264	1885	80	355	485	7830	119	1899
......	2086	......	1109	......	2093	......	969	......	3825	...	739
10255	1330	1545	345	5580	1007	5010	788	3337	574	3161	643
7712	1565	1225	661	4669	708	4789	1388	1145	638	880	475
1260	701	2298	1160	72	42	120	50	760	1115	536	617
251	323	4	32	......	......	4	12	9	36	54	75
......	......	......	......	......	......	......	......	......	......	...	...
23126	860455	12874	235536	14873	221313	17100	174074	7041	*86472	4136	84374
......	......	......	......	......	......	......	......	......	......	...	...
95	35	881	93	400	160	1253	174	753	119	1296	292
227	99	409	320	275	146	701	284	780	387	188	133
1811	530	887	177	3653	88[illegible]	5	94	134	580	1418	359
27671	19340	8784	7035	3950	2732	17	1462	2185	1805	...	...
......	......	......	......	......	......	......	......	......	......	...	...
586 1836	15621	457 3031	13975	2667 5634	13814	1455 3280	10477	2200 559	5615	25363 1599	6404
6489	16101	220	9306	159	4779	56	3836	15	1771	101	4021
5098	22126	5089	24248	4064	20001	4306	21468	2754	15285	2334	10512
......	......	122	......	......	......	......	......	......	......	...	...
61	5090	......	8780	115	2551	15	900	18	2500	48	2334
......	......	......	......	......	......	......	......	......	......	...	...
......	......	6	40	......	......	......	......	......	......	...	...
184000	4963	2200	38	29600	982	73400	1692	......	......	2400	240
785	23921	234	11670	404	14980	189	7945	69	3760	236	11098
12	96	6	30	6	30	16	80	18	114	...	...
......	2487	......	3576	......	494	......	9885	......	1341	...	4664
125	. 393	640	700	6	14	......	......	......	......	...	...
......	......	2	15	......	......	6	55	138	589	...	...
......	......	24	30	......	......	54	105	66	25	...	...
56	57	100	163	......	......	84	124	93	148	1320	1320
1918	504	1436	1950	300	130	......	......	......	......	4194	1602

* Out of the above quantity 170,966 kilos were exported free of duty, owing to the same having been already legally exported in 1888, and afterwards returned—the vessel having put back in distress.

ARTICLES.	1885		1886		1887		1888	
	Quantities.	Value.	Quantities.	Value.	Quantities.	Value.	Quantities.	Value.
		Rs.		Rs.		Rs.		Rs.
Animals :								
Deer ....No.	...	......	......	......	......	......	2	40
Arrowroot ....kilo.	150	16	30	15	......	......	2100	525
Bags, Vacoa ....No.	19050	2522	......	......	......	......	......	......
Basket work .... ,,	...	73	......	......	......	......	......	......
Boats .... ,,	5	1330	......	......	......	......	......	......
Bricks and Tiles	...	......	......	......	......	......	......	......
Coffee ....kilo.	638	328	42	17	132	264	25	80
Confectionery	...	......	......	95	......	......	......	......
Cordage, Hemp..........kilo.	...	......	......	......	......	......	......	......
Cordials and Liqueurs. lit.	...	......	......	......	......	......	......	......
Feathers, Ostrich............	...	......	......	2000	......	......	......	......
Fibre, Aloe...............kilo.	648150	165633	877332	189503	1959281	446176	2532115	690858
,, Ramie .... ,,	...	......	......	......	......	......	......	......
Fish, dried or salted. ,,	...	......	......	......	259	122	8655	1790
Fruits, fresh .... ,,	...	......	......	......	100	15	......	......
,, dried .... ,,	...	......	......	......	......	......	......	......
Cocoanuts ....No.	5000	260	3253	1272	692	692	......	......
Groceries	...	......	......	......	......	......	......	......
Glue	...	......	......	......	......	......	......	......
Hardware	...	......	......	......	......	......	......	......
Hemp, undressed ......kilo.	...	.....	77779	20495	4500	1200	125	100
Hides, Raw ....No.	1355	11270	2646	10499	2572	20598	3255	13510
Honey.....................kilo.	...	......	......	......	......	......	......	......
Hoofs	...	......	......	......	......	......	......	......
Horns......................No.	...	......	......	......	......	......	......	......
Jewellery	...	......	......	......	......	......	......	......
Lime ....kilo.	32500	400	20500	228	610	130	1500	25
Leather	...	......	......	......	......	......	......	......
Machinery & Mill work ,,	...	......	......	......	......	......	......	......
Manure ....kilo.	...	......	......	.....	......	......	30	10
Molasses .... ,,	210365	11696	1195050	45497	3449830	83398	5060033	143644
Oil, Cocoanut............lit.	991715	209641	764795	174120	1042948	59346	517865	107274
Onions and Garlic......kilo.	1200	260	......	......	......	......	1550	132
Pickles and Sauces	...	20	......	20	......	......	......	......
Plants and Roots	...	135	......	167	......	......	......	......
Potatoes ....kilo.	...	......	......	......	......	......	800	53
Provisions, preserved	...	250	......	950	......	......	......	......
Seeds, Gardens...............	...	......	......	700	......	......	......	......
Skins (tanned)	...	......	......	......	......	......	......	......
Soap	...	......	......	......	......	......	......	......
Spices, Cinnamon, &c. kilo	...	......	......	......	......	......	......	......
Specim. of Nat. History ...	...	1237	......	745	......	......	......	......
Spirits, Rum ....lit.	3733140	483507	3445259	415827	3200454	366920	2515985	297881
Starch.....................kilo.	...	......	......	......	......	......	......	......
Stones, Paving ....No.	...	......	......	......	......	......	......	......
Sugar (a) ....kilo.	...	......	118007754	29126169	96938159	22969997	130066518	28754798
Tobacco, Segars ...... ,,	...	31207255	......	......	1505	4817	14	190
Tortoise Shell .... ,,	...	......	......	......	553	5299	105	1304
Vanilla .... ,,	26504	309301	22792	312049	17562	236583	24876	311639
Vegetables, fresh............	...	......	......	......	......	......	625	101
Wax, Bees ....kilo.	...	......	......	......	23062	16928	......	......
Wood :								
Boards and Planks	...	......	......	......	60	4260	......	......
Ebony.................C.M.	26500	1448	328	15470	3	100	36	1800
Woodenware	...	......	......	......	......	10	......	......

(a) For quantities vide page 71. (b) Including shipping charges.

1889		1890		1891		1892		1893		1894	
Quantities.	Value.	Quantities.	Value.	Quantities.	Value.	Quantities.	Value.	Quantities.	Value.	Quantities.	Value.
	Rs.		Rs.		Rs.		Rs.		Rs.		Rs.
......	......	......	......	2	60	......	......	......	......	......	......
302	200	......	......	......	......	......	......	5	2	400	79
25	4	......	......	87100	5290	......	......	......	......	26000	2897
......	151	......	...	......	170	......	......	......	......	......	......
......	......	2	800	1	150	......	......	......	......	2	1110
6254	438	4000	400	6300	2125	......	......	......	......	......	......
......	......	119	151	10323	11236	......	......	......	......	......	......
......	385	......	......	......	1385	......	......	......	......	......	......
......	......	......	......	3410	1391	......	......	......	......	......	......
......	......	......	......	840	634	......	......	......	......	......	......
......	......	......	......	......	......	......	......	......	......	......	......
2728991	967077	1895249	622252	1485510	453530	1017236	309653	1324201	*2655433	857633	171526
......	......	......	......	......	......	......	......	......	......	......	......
15775	1000	29145	4672	410080	51557	53720	14900	40080	11200	69226	14333
25	5	400	16	3150	60	5	15	235	27	60	20
										......	.....
......	......	......	......	65106	4805	......	......	2235	438	......	......
......	358	......	......	......	5580	......	......	......	......	......	......
1500	3000	......	......	......	......	......	......	......	......	......	......
......	50	......	......	......	22685	......	......	......	......	......	......
75	20	......	......	......	......	......	......	......	......	......	......
15230	10136	6365	2285	......	23594	13939	4500	74249	21776	148497	33499
10	10	......	......	......	......	......	......	......	......	......	......
8000	250	......	......	6238	262	3115	278	......	......	......	......
5750	440	636	636	16911	1845	540	39	1650	250	9864	1520
......	......	......	......	......	3707	......	......	......	......	......	......
4560	152	22850	480	43570	1220	28050	714	39800	696	96500	1670
8451	5250	13300	4981	2111	661	......	......	......	......	......	......
7650	4288	......	......	117276	38425	......	......	41942	43000	8744	2785
189	40	......	......	......	......	......	......	......	......	......	......
3905250	130461	5893575	160693	4689570	94313	5621350	104583	3356500	104625	7415350	217859
236395	57673	46256	16957	714686	180587	55665	13092	......	......	4207	59565
......	......	3200	450	4195	1922	4240	978	14381	1767	58177	9911
......	112	......	......	......	294	......	......	......	......	......	......
......	920	......	......	......	4244	......	......	......	......	......	......
100	12	2470	247	467	461	750	45	230	30	5293	512
......	......	......	......	......	7450	......	185	......	......	......	......
......	50	......	......	......	143	......	......	......	......	......	......
......	......	......	......	......	......	17030	6010	35727	10150	16194	6061
......	......	......	......	......	......	73991	13732	23809	7257	83186	18591
......	......	260	400	11401	1355	......	......	......	......	......	......
......	840	......	......	......	1255	......	30	......	......	......	......
3345134	363094	8453469	313314	3812206	389926	2691730	303618	2557241	344076	3053783	424642
......	......	......	......	26310	2521	......	......	......	......	......	......
......	......	2000	50	......	......	......	......	......	......	......	......
141783434	28994791	128405938	23483868	124759108	21216308	93091256	15154894	86067841	19409218	138431733	28461564
......	......	20	40	1425	2372	......	......	5	6	......	......
......	......	262	2900	264	1885	......	......	90	2500	119	1554
21523	337271	12574	232536	14873	211313	15154	169985	6991	*85572	4136	82720
95	35	250	31	400	160	225	15	753	119	1296	292
......	......	......	......	3950	2732	......	......	......	......	......	......
......	......	......	......	159	4779	......	......	......	......	......	......
61	5090	67	6740	115	2551	......	......	......	......	......	......
......	5	......	......	......	494	......	......	......	......	......	......

Exportation of Sugar from Mauritius from 1821* to 1894.

Years.	lbs. French.	English Weight.				Years.	lbs. French.	English Weight.			
		Tons.	cwt.	qrs.	lbs.			Tons.	cwt.	qrs.	lbs.
1821...	20,410,053	9,810	11	0	25	1858	246,229,138	118,717	12	1	17
1822...	23,403,644	11,283	17	3	27	1859	256,980,607	123,901	16	3	19
1823...	27,400,887	13,211	2	3	9	1860	271,807,107	134,049	17	0	11
1824...	24,334,553	11,732	14	2	13	1861	220,631,916	106,376	2	0	5
1825...	21,739,766	10,481	13	1	23	1862	268,162,551	129,292	13	0	19
1826...	42,489,416	20,485	19	1	13	1863	274,548,961	132,371	16	1	17
1827...	40,619,254	19,584	5	2	18	1864	233,440,106	112,551	9	2	10
1828...	48,350,101	23,311	13	0	13	1865	270,066,937	130,191	11	0	19
1829...	58,413,538	28,472	6	3	25	1866	247,383,011	118,273	19	0	3
1830...	67,926,692	32,750	7	1	15	1867	200,895,816	96,860	9	2	17
1831...	70,203,676	33,848	4	0	2	1868	198,601,676	95,754	7	2	10
1832...	73,594,778	35,483	3	3	20	1869	213,766,517	102,065	19	3	26
1833...	67,482,800	32,536	7	...	...	1870	204,761,631	98,724	8	0	16
1834...	71,143,851	34,301	9	3	27	1871	246,489,734	118,843	5	1	1
1835...	64,876,825	31,279	17	3	23	1872	253,634,822	122,288	5	1	...
1836...	63,333,513	30,535	16	0	2	1873	231,711,979	111,718	5	2	1
1837...	68,275,965	32,918	6	2	22	1874	193,693,291	93,387	16	2	26
1838...	72,002,226	34,715	7	0	20	1875	181,375,433	87,448	17	1	15
1839...	68 572,979	33,061	19	1	21	1876	240,188,439	115,801	5	2	8
1840...	82,048,509	36,559	2	0	5	1877	282,680,532	136,292	7	3	26
1841...	78,969,678	38,074	13	1	8	1878	kil. 132,824,609	130,732	17	3	5
1842...	71,225,151	34,340	13	3	23	1879	,, 105,233,273	103,576	0	2	1
1843...	55,026,564	26,530	13	1	5	1880	,, 110,210,678	108,475	1	2	3
1844...	72,656,720	35,030	18	1	13	1881	,, 110,538,894	108,798	2	1	25
1845...	87,561,994	42,217	7	3	5	1882	,, 117,124,065	115,279	11	3	9
1846...	127,531,510	64,488	8	0	14	1883	,, 115,800,056	113,976	8	2	18
1847...	118,291,246	57,033	5	2	9	1884	,, 125,655,946	123,677	2	0	27
1848...	114,653,469	55,279	7	0	2	1885	,, 115,656,096	113,834	14	3	5
1849...	133,418,250	64,326	13	0	14	1886	,, 118,007,754	116,148	7	2	11
1850...	114,393,293	55,163	17	2	...	1887	,, 96,928,159	95,401	14	2	14
1851...	138,123,365	66,595	3	3	14	1888	,, 130,066,518	128,018	4	1	3
1852...	148,550,169	71,622	8	0	6	1889	,, 141,783,434	139,550	12	1	25
1853...	190,242,546	91,722	5	3	25	1890	,, 129,443,098	127,384	7	0	11
1854...	176,116,461	84,913	5	3	13	1891	,, 124,759,108	122,678	9	2	..
1855...	264,081,115	127,324	16	1	24	1892	,, 94,097,446	92,528	3	1	12
1856...	244,667,523	117,964	13	3	24	1893	,, 87,408,861	85,951	2	2	10
1857...	240 910,000	116,153	0	2	24	1894	,, 139,449,413	137,123	15	3	13

This Return represents the annual exportation of Sugar from 1st. January to 31st. December of each year; the value of the same for the last 10 years will be found on pages 66—67. In the statement on page 71, the exportation of Sugar during each annual Crop is given.

* Previous years *Vide Almanac of* 1889.

Exportation of Sugar from Mauritius to different places from the Crop 1858—59 * to the Crop 1894—95.

Crops.	United Kingdom.	France.	Australian Colonies.	Cape of Good Hope.	India.	America.	Other Places.	Total.
1858—59 ...	lbs 133,213,960	lbs 41,944,694	lb 47,581,513	10,622,440	....	....	4,536,312	237,898,919
1859—60 ...	108,238,079	59,905,435	43,751,932	10,100,726	....	....	4,950,140	226,946,312
1860—61 ...	135,572,459	27,399,837	43,053,751	9,258,895	....	....	6,714,209	271,999,151
1861—62 ...	82,714,588	50,047,715	67,207,552	12,835,521	....	....	7,607,891	220,417,237
1862—63 ...	170,709,069	42,199,734	69,916,628	13,817,304	17,551,200	....	2,128,445	316,322,276
1863—64 ...	118,255,066	36,702,080	59,397,235	9,351,230	10,199,598	....	524,513	243,432,525
1864—65 ...	116,825,825	48,837,456	61,408,876	9,326,314	22,853,945	....	1,079,974	260,333,051
1865—66 ...	131,463,429	3,620,722	69,623,783	4,486,299	30,708,980	....	1,513,057	241,416,170
1866—67 ...	51,463,733	11,223,163	100,360,454	6,469,493	44,938,742	....	2,059,976	216,475,162
1867—68 ...	102,550,997	3,309,362	70,617,653	3,655,303	51,760,761	....	1,087,583	232,981,686
1868—69 ...	43,608,898	9,957,359	73,429,247	1,507,740	26,658,466	....	1,219,574	156,563,284
1869—70 ...	76,212,475	22,310,088	99,748,587	4,751,588	59,209,368	....	1,273,429	264,505,545
1870—71 ...	45,413,427	12,760,454	83,507,646	3,829,731	33,454,920	....	1,782,227	180,748,405
1871—72 ...	95,564,126	26,585,755	64,823,002	2,358,341	48,136,115	....	12,183,952	294,466,122
1872—73 ...	84,247,930	21,265,196	94,456,677	3,396,970	27,142,674	....	22,983,179	253,492,623
1873—74 ...	74,893,365	2,312,740	98,441,577	7,257,997	33,540,306	....	12,508,791	233,576,689
1874—75 ...	61,596,790	2,105	54,490,698	5,725,722	40,435,380	....	4,125,496	166,385,166
1875—76 ...	67,902,627	3,050,077	74,042,002	8,095,694	49,772,555	....	5,376,753	209,049,708
1876—77 ...	125,631,595	7,150,408	70,297,434	4,248,081	19,580,231	....	22,535,859	247,922,175
1877—78 ...	88,215,813	3,079,906	110.792,752	11,624,544	51,112,936	....	20,502,034	285,327,975
1878—79 ...	kil. 24,738,988	kil. 1,320,546	kil. 57,206,478	kil. 7,977,647	kil. 38,495,490	kil.	kil. 5,496,630	kil. 134,962,897
1879—80 ...	5,284,200	501,680	38,461,741	7,049,872	28,622,493	....	8,015,449	86,356,433
1880—81 ...	15,395,260	2,775,947	46,382,457	6,399,300	39,083,682	....	9,694,847	119,731,492
1881—82 ...	13,288,028	1,070,672	56,865,508	11,262,321	29,097,489	....	6,225,600	117,809,610
1882—83 ...	14,857,636	49,946	52,941,255	10,957,309	30,376,475	....	7,543,376	116,719,997
1883—84 ...	11,328,554	757,698	53,100,089	7,402,688	37,069,212	....	10,737,897	120,396,858
1884—85 ...	14,609,261	42,864	39,986,786	4,546,783	55,627,057	10,343,458	2,628,130	127,784,339
1885—86 ...	17,145,073	10,202	26,101,058	4,175,164	60,448,802	5,779,729	3,694,579	115.299.039
1886—87 ...	5,863,505	25,200	22,360,026	3,050,016	60,117,844	8,542,353	2,417,327	102,376,271
1887—88 ...	12,486,030	4,179	29,406,593	5,701,168	67,119,748	4,467,292	4,888,130	124,073,140
1888—89 ..	16,135,571	105,999	34,572,565	8,863,158	58,332,985	10,165,147	4,007,563	132,172,988
1889—90 ...	10,598,438	20,332	36,906,544.	11,196,137	62,759,666	1,792,440	1,291,394	124,564,951
1890—91 ...	14,995,667	17,745	30,185,866	11,741,487	68,260,803	1,505,126	2,736,404	129,443,098
1891—92 ...	11,858,823	1,160	19,217,225	13,711,113	72,870,213	4,148,689	2,891,885	124,759,108
1892—93 ...	14,238,769	,977	8,533,167	7,765,458	55,081,582	....	8,477,493	94,097,446
1893—94 ...	10,710,998	2,084,926	7,114,642	11,626,114	40,532,991	....	15,339,190	87,408,861
1894—95 ...	12,249,231	112,491	19,248,329	12,369,395	73,932,673	3,898,806	17,638,488	139,449,413

This Return represents the Exportation of Sugar of each annual Crop i. e. from 1st. August to 31st. July. In the Statement on Page 70 the Exportation of Sugar from 1st. January to 31st. December in each year is given.

* For previous years *Vide Almanac of* 1889.

Number and Tonnage of British and Foreign Vessels ENTERED with Cargoes and in Ballast from various countries at Port Louis,* Mauritius, from 1885 to 1894.

Years.	British.				Foreign.				Total.				Total.	
	With Cargoes.		In Ballast.		With Cargoes.		In Ballast.		With Cargoes.		In Ballast.			
	Vessels.	Tons.	Vessels.	Tons.	Vessels.	Tons.	Vessels.	Tons.	Vessels.	Tons.	Vessels.	Tons.	Vessels.	Tons.
1885	251	137464	31	17474	170	139191	18	6141	421	276655	49	23616	470	300271
1886	283	181093	12	8803	188	152923	14	5097	471	334016	26	13900	497	347916
1887	250	156499	12	5566	162	142585	4	1570	412	299084	16	1736	428	306220
1888	264	162509	19	9954	171	138896	11	3073	435	301405	30	13027	465	314432
1889	280	200844	22	10734	124	118447	10	6769	404	319291	32	17503	436	336794
1890	294	221440	27	12882	124	104267	11	4712	418	325707	38	17594	456	343302
1891	274	195239	12	5762	112	95081	9	4248	386	290320	46	34465	407	300330
1892	264	225302	16	10030	110	87989	9	4207	374	313291	25	14237	399	327528
1893	234	213662	4	1159	100	78633	2	536	334	292295	6	1695	340	293990
1894	210	219201	7	3765	110	90917	8	2467	320	310118	15	6232	335	316350

Number and tonnage of British and Foreign Vessels CLEARED with Cargoes and in Ballast from various countries at Port Louis,* Mauritius, from 1885 to 1894.

Years.	British.				Foreign.				Total.				Total.	
	With Cargoes.		In Ballast.		With Cargoes.		In Ballast.		With Cargoes.		In Ballast.			
	Vessels.	Tons.	Vessels.	Tons.	Vessels.	Tons.	Vessels.	Tons.	Vessels.	Tons.	Vessels.	Tons.	Vessels.	Tons.
1885	241	115654	58	45199	163	132806	26	15182	404	248460	84	60351	488	308841
1886	236	125666	59	61462	180	149362	17	7864	416	275028	76	69326	492	344354
1887	207	101147	54	61145	144	131755	25	15572	351	232902	79	76717	430	309619
1888	243	124225	36	47866	155	126541	15	9280	398	250766	51	57146	449	307912
1889	268	164715	35	38983	119	94544	19	30963	387	259299	54	69946	441	329245
1890	279	169944	49	66680	125	102072	10	8624	404	272010	59	74304	463	346320
1891	242	160798	40	39291	89	72504	25	22718	331	233302	65	62009	396	293311
1892	226	176200	54	55903	85	59870	33	35769	311	236070	87	91672	398	327742
1893	181	152497	59	59763	99	75294	8	5488	153	60539	67	65251	347	293042
1894	183	172728	48	62317	98	81869	11	7834	281	254607	41	41453	340	324748

* Port Louis is the only port in the Colony at which an import trade is carried on.

Working of the Distillery Branch of the Receiver General's Department, and Imports of Foreign Spirits, Duty received thereon, &c., from 1862* to 1894.

Year.	Number of Stills in operation.	Number of Gallons of Rum.			Amount of Duty received on quantity issued for Consumption	Value of Rum exported.	Foreign Spirits of all sorts.			
		Distilled.	Issued for Consumption	Exported.			Total number of Gallons or Litres imported.	Total number of Gallons entered for Home Consumption.	Total value of quantities imported.	Total duty received on quantity entered for Consumption
1862 ..	18	811539	334772	1207900	£ 86306	£ 25854	73175	73391	£ 24166	£ 22270
1863 ...	14	724620	310026	358399	89930	22487	135758	96707	46818	31430
1864 ...	15	721513	444523	325338	126180	21073	65865	59079	22438	19196
1865 ...	12	869182	395034	436303	109697	29449	48466	54174	16947	17521
1866 ...	11	779037	354964	474999	97808	28887	38634	38743	12754	12584
1867 ...	12	583991	230970	323824	63643	16470	28342	37080	10182	11984
1868 ...	15	690557	259986	423548	78066	22788	21678	32904	12571	11271
1869 ...	11	779479	253021	489298	82478	25891	28533	31916	11116	11934
1870 ...	14	963978	241150	769365	78396	46183	40765	38482	16157	15256
1871 ...	14	973565	284824	649514	92400	32445	82654	35858	12876	13443
1872 ...	15	968745	320084	656612	104126	39664	43823	37132	19489	13757
1873 ...	[illegible]	1167500	319195	918778	103628	47082	99464	38998	22423	14381
1874 ...	20	1253128	351004	869020	136355	49268	40959	35234	16069	13041
1875 ...	18	1072076	290421	835115	112043	40292	34308	34767	17242	14786
1876 ...	15	1234063	313081	1010410	120838	51099	[illegible] 28529	29872	14099	12785 [illegible]
1877 ...	18	1159050	279835	988831	107964	50090	50526	29674	18116	12489
1878 ...	15	Lit. 4991464	Lit. 1277885	Lit. 4329698	Rs. 1230676	Rs. 442409	Lit. 272823	Lit. 140324	Rs. 197838	Rs. 128015
1879 ...	27	4181251	1272794	3848628	1222810	384453	218848	172276	157815	170691
1880 ...	21	3982182	1334803	3099275	1282449	310459	180044	144987	187909	140977
1881 ...	23	4841989	1419508	3795909	1364505	422134	252152	164830	224877	154281
1882 ...	19	4804077	1661871	4119622	1616625	806329	180044	250915	‡ 257240	141060
1883 ...	19	4130102	1842690	2363938	1772355	†512985	243151	157202	‡ 263083	146273
1884 ...	13	4223391	1784546	3193085	1715981	448670	232370	159348	241887	147775
1885 ...	15	4326430	1324583	3693399	1273614	485501	115974	114575	165910	107899
1886 ...	11	4240135	1390387	3350355	1336940	415827	98400	98966	163717	92692
1887 ...	13	3571212	1300199	3234836	1302402	366920	144277	103081	208844	100039
1888 ...	11	3113118	1273235	2371543	1275179	297881	144475	148722	190169	148533
1889 ...	14	4155062	1450613	3293103	1532505	365112	123249	116121	136286	122610
1890 ...	12	4084012	1379466	3412501	1533018	313509	100526	109913	188869	120951
1891 ...	10	4705036	1289370	3815516	1566998	496017	101887	99622	222634	120532
1892 ...	14	3409737	1147604	2738505	1394528	303642	115366	110378	‡232701	133301
1893 ...	13	3459830	1083053	2606980	1321750	333050	161418	157366	‡275672	190279
1894 ...	7	3135605	1026839	3078159	1358634	439494	155887	128323	361462	169042

* For previous years *Vide Almanac* of 1889. † Value on board ship. ‡ Inc[illegible]ding charges and exchange.

ARRI

YEAR.	Calcutta.								Madras.							
	Males.	Females.	Boys.	Girls.	Infants.		Total.		Males.	Females.	Boys.	Girls.	Infants.		Total.	
					M.	F.	M.	F.					M.	F.	M.	F.
1842...	54	4	2	1	...	...	56	5	15	4	2	1	...	...	17	5
1843...	12446	1692	346	211	128	128	12920	2922	12723	1405	254	156	49	47	13026	1608
1844...	6152	980	402	166	223	123	6677	1260	1986	391	75	51	19	19	2080	461
1845...	7677	1462	885	261	356	360	8918	2053	...	...	...	...	...	...	...	...
1846...	4847	1150	588	207	286	264	5718	1621	...	...	...	...	...	...	...	...
1847...	4845	562	277	45	52	40	5184	656	...	...	...	...	...	...	...	...
1848...	4335	564	251	43	53	49	4739	650	...	...	...	...	...	...	...	...
1849...	5936	887	368	91	74	69	6378	1047	...	...	...	...	...	..	...	...
1850...	4909	704	483	82	106	99	5418	885	2902	621	113	58	3	3	3018	709
1851...	4986	773	281	83	95	88	5362	904	2712	687	126	78	57	57	2895	819
1852...	6050	1634	350	336	235	215	6845	2185	4115	894	340	177	101	84	4557	1155
1853...	5269	815	247	112	138	136	5654	1063	3134	796	236	178	87	84	3457	1053
1854...	8518	1201	379	177	139	143	9036	1421	4570	1359	559	411	162	190	5291	1948
1855...	4482	1043	298	160	118	133	4898	1336	4047	1417	545	354	155	163	4774	1934
1856...	4148	1438	410	211	160	132	4688	1780	2990	1035	412	224	107	126	3509	1385
1857...	3796	1851	558	378	162	180	4516	2409	2854	976	396	272	104	83	3254	1331
1858...	9702	3580	1021	686	345	672	11068	4638	6535	2463	895	664	174	209	7608	1330
1859...	15443	4606	1316	920	464	431	17223	5957	8896	3753	1442	1134	385	365	10723	5262
1860...	4167	1772	513	366	95	117	4775	2255	2540	1125	277	242	59	60	2876	1427
1861...	4953	1386	364	291	101	89	5418	1766	3129	1176	282	257	62	50	3477	1579
1862...	2921	597	133	87	49	44	3103	728	2983	1059	336	288	55	45	3374	1392
1863...	647	179	46	29	17	13	710	221	1882	756	304	262	33	49	2219	1076
1864...	3188	811	308	129	57	66	3453	1009	1091	456	140	136	20	20	1251	612
1865...	10773	3021	1025	791	138	142	11936	3954	1853	835	344	298	28	30	2225	1513
1866...	1434	479	116	120	27	31	1622	630	1619	835	431	396	30	34	2080	1264
1867...	...	...	...	...	...	...	...	...	...	...	...	...	...	...	...	...
1868...	992	377	73	58	22	6	1087	441	215	84	32	20	4	3	251	107
1869...	232	87	40	32	7	11	279	121	813	309	82	61	8	9	904	379
1870...	1905	770	163	107	41	32	2109	909	636	258	77	69	9	9	722	336
1871 a.	...	...	...	...	...	...	64169	23422	...	...	...	...	...	...	33198	15638
1871...	1471	567	9	41	26	38	1593	646	656	292	64	57	5	9	725	326
1872...	2676	1023	203	138	73	74	2952	1235	884	377	153	128	26	19	1063	524
1873...	3495	1454	259	140	151	124	3905	1718	1138	487	171	171	12	12	1321	670
1874...	3102	1287	314	280	190	158	3606	1645	1054	431	142	141	16	17	1212	589
1875...	1175	452	96	59	66	62	1339	573	556	248	89	87	12	10	657	350
1876...	801	141	16	16	13	15	330	172	...	...	...	..	...	...	...	...
1877...	939	340	72	55	28	49	1030	444	424	170	58	40	7	5	489	215
1878...	1153	581	171	111	128	128	1442	820	1067	657	145	134	9	13	1761	803
1879...	449	224	75	50	18	14	542	288	1309	628	140	136	17	19	1471	778
1880 ..	125	66	18	17	6	4	149	87	188	93	23	30	7	3	222	123
1881 b.	...	...	...	...	...	...	55653	24844	...	...	...	...	...	...	26186	12855
*1882...	388	176	42	31	10	15	440	222	302	155	61	50	2	9	365	214
1883...	771	325	74	43	21	26	866	394	362	176	44	58	10	4	417	238
1884...	2214	886	194	138	46	64	...	...	1825	663	168	161	28	27	...	...
1885...	...	...	...	...	...	...	...	...	212	83	31	21	3	5	246	112
1886...	...	...	...	...	...	...	...	...	466	174	41	51	4	10	511	235
1887...	...	...	...	...	...	...	...	...	189	58	10	14	2	1	191	75
1888...	...	..	...	...	...	...	...	...	433	178	41	41	2	12	482	231
1889...	1301	434	109	84	36	39	1446	557	1532	522	240	180	28	42	1800	744
1890...	775	250	33	15	13	8	821	273	1129	430	179	154	23	16	1331	600
1891...	422	143	35	31	6	9	473	183	208	69	21	21	7	5	240	95
1892...	...	...	...	...	...	...	...	...	...	...	...	...	...	...	...	...
*1893...	247	83	11	11	9	9	267	103	85	28	...	...	1	1	86	29
1894...	337	110	13	11	5	7	355	128	381	124	13	14	9	2	403	140
1895...	672	226	41	26	19	20	732	272	481	159	26	32	23	9	530	200

(a) In the Colony on the 19th. April, date of taking the Census.
(b) ,, 4th. ,, ,,
* No Indian Immigrants were introduced into the Colony in 1881 and 1892.

VALS.

Bombay								Reunion Island								Total Arrivals		Births	
Males.	Females.	Boys.	Girls.	Infants.		Total.		Males.	Females.	Boys.	Girls.	Infants.		Total.					
				M.	F.	M.	F.					M.	F.	M.	F.	M.	F.	M.	F.
...	...	...	...	...	...	...	...	...	...	...	...	...	...	...	...	73	10	94	86
4143	599	112	61	17	17	4272	677	...	...	...	...	...	...	...	...	30218	4307	109	91
935	109	11	5	6	5	952	119	...	...	...	...	...	...	...	...	9709	1840	235	213
...	...	...	...	...	...	...	...	...	...	...	...	...	...	...	...	8918	2053	346	359
...	...	...	...	...	...	...	...	...	...	...	...	...	...	...	...	5718	1621	529	477
...	...	...	...	...	...	...	...	...	...	...	...	...	...	...	...	5174	656	664	625
...	...	...	...	...	...	...	...	...	...	...	...	...	...	...	...	4739	656	652	643
...	...	...	...	...	...	...	...	...	...	...	...	...	...	...	...	6378	1047	687	727
...	...	...	...	...	...	...	...	...	...	...	...	...	...	...	...	8436	1594	675	650
...	...	...	...	...	...	...	...	...	...	...	...	...	...	...	...	8257	1763	737	670
2145	398	97	51	29	25	2271	474	...	...	...	...	...	...	...	...	13671	3814	925	744
728	118	28	14	10	14	766	146	...	...	...	...	...	...	...	...	9877	2267	974	960
640	102	24	11	5	7	668	126	...	...	...	...	...	...	...	...	14995	3489	1095	972
...	...	...	...	...	...	...	...	...	...	...	...	...	...	...	...	9645	3270	1183	1096
845	301	73	38	15	19	933	358	...	...	...	...	...	...	...	...	9130	3523	1326	1278
764	282	77	54	29	9	870	345	...	...	...	...	...	...	...	...	8640	4085	1475	1483
1983	858	188	117	85	68	2256	1010	...	...	...	...	...	...	...	...	20930	9014	1619	1644
3221	1214	375	228	101	103	3697	1545	...	...	...	...	...	...	...	...	31643	12754	2089	2018
1397	439	100	75	14	18	1421	532	...	...	...	...	...	...	...	...	9070	4216	2978	2787
1229	398	90	58	18	12	1337	468	...	...	...	...	...	...	...	...	10232	3753	2967	2949
900	277	58	38	5	18	963	333	...	...	...	...	...	...	...	...	7440	2453	3283	3262
693	244	38	41	7	14	738	299	...	...	...	...	...	...	...	...	3667	1537	3436	3359
866	261	58	40	11	7	945	308	...	...	...	...	...	...	...	...	5626	1936	3579	3502
706	179	41	25	2	2	749	206	...	...	...	...	...	...	...	...	14910	5373	3834	3688
...	...	...	...	...	...	...	...	...	...	...	...	...	...	...	...	3702	1894	3929	3703
...	...	...	...	...	...	...	...	310	22	6	9	1	2	317	93	317	33	3528	3545
...	...	...	...	...	...	...	...	594	62	32	62	4	...	639	92	1968	640	3076	3341
...	...	...	...	...	...	...	...	...	...	...	...	...	...	...	...	1182	590	3214	3014
...	...	...	...	...	...	...	...	...	...	...	...	...	...	...	...	2831	1245	3464	3503
...	...	...	...	...	...	7939	3348	...	...	...	...	...	...	...	...	...	...	...	...
...	...	...	...	...	...	...	...	...	...	...	...	...	...	...	...	2318	974	3752	3579
...	...	...	...	...	...	...	...	...	...	...	...	...	...	...	...	4015	1759	3644	3467
...	...	...	...	...	...	...	...	...	...	...	...	...	...	...	...	5226	2388	3839	3650
...	...	...	...	...	...	...	...	...	...	...	...	...	...	...	...	4818	2234	3528	3438
...	...	...	...	...	...	...	...	...	...	...	...	...	...	...	...	1996	923	4364	4232
...	...	...	...	...	...	...	...	...	...	...	...	...	...	...	...	330	172	3654	3638
...	...	...	...	...	...	...	...	...	...	...	...	...	...	...	...	1528	659	3509	3476
...	...	...	...	...	...	...	...	...	...	...	...	...	...	...	...	3203	1623	4222	4014
...	...	...	...	...	...	...	...	...	...	...	...	...	...	...	...	2013	1066	4419	4323
...	...	...	...	...	...	...	...	...	...	...	...	...	...	...	...	371	213	4572	4486
...	...	...	...	...	...	5137	2303	...	...	...	...	...	...	...	...	...	...	3473	3400
...	...	...	...	...	...	...	...	...	...	...	...	...	...	...	...	805	436	3270	3205
...	...	...	...	...	...	...	...	...	...	...	...	...	...	...	...	1283	632	3058	2989
...	...	...	...	...	...	...	...	...	...	...	...	...	...	...	...	4450	1939	3092	3086
...	...	...	...	...	...	...	...	...	...	...	...	...	...	...	...	246	115	2887	2821
...	...	...	...	...	...	...	...	...	...	...	...	...	...	...	...	511	233	2714	2605
...	...	...	...	...	...	...	...	...	...	...	...	...	...	...	...	191	71	2745	2512
...	...	...	...	...	...	...	...	...	...	...	...	...	...	...	...	482	231	2406	2283
...	...	...	...	...	...	...	...	...	...	...	...	...	...	...	...	3246	1301	2461	2382
...	...	...	...	...	...	...	...	...	...	...	...	...	...	...	...	2152	873	2094	2025
...	...	...	...	...	...	...	...	...	...	...	...	...	...	...	...	713	278	2065	2042
...	...	...	...	...	...	...	...	...	...	...	...	...	...	...	...	...	...	2328	2269
...	...	...	...	...	...	...	...	...	...	...	...	...	...	...	...	353	132	1810	1778
...	...	...	...	...	...	...	...	...	...	...	...	...	...	...	...	758	268	1852	1796
...	...	...	...	...	...	...	...	...	...	...	...	...	...	...	...	1262	472	1735	2110

* For previous years *Vide Almanac* of 1889.

DEPAR

Year.	Calcutta.								Madras								Bombay							
	Males.	Females.	Boys.	Girls.	Inf.		Total.		Males.	Females.	Boys.	Girls.	Inf.		Total.		Males.	Females.	Boys.	Girls.	Inf.		Total.	
					M	F.	M.	F.					M.	F.	M.	F.					M.	F.	M.	F.
1842	...	...	...	...	...	...	...	...	...	...	...	...	...	...	...	...	...	...	...	...	...	...	...	...
1843	...	...	...	...	...	...	...	...	...	...	...	...	...	...	...	...	...	...	...	...	...	...	...	...
1844	...	...	...	...	...	...	...	...	...	...	...	...	...	...	...	...	...	...	...	...	...	...	...	...
1845	...	...	...	...	...	...	...	...	...	...	...	...	...	...	...	...	...	...	...	...	...	...	...	...
1846	1792	125	44	20	...	...	1836	45	628	38	18	14	...	...	646	52	74	7	...	...	...	...	74	7
1847	1035	83	2	4	...	...	1037	87	549	21	5	...	...	...	554	41	68	5	...	...	...	...	60	5
1848	1854	278	37	23	...	...	1891	301	620	57	7	1	...	..	627	58	118	16	3	1	...	...	121	17
1849	2570	347	26	20	...	...	2596	367	1169	120	18	5	...	...	1187	125	510	100	5	2	...	...	515	102
1850	2069	357	38	8	...	...	2647	365	515	58	3	1	...	...	518	59	118	18	...	...	...	..	118	18
1851	2475	327	23	13	...	...	2498	340	264	27	3	2	...	...	266	29	41	5	...	...	...	...	41	5
1852	2445	318	38	26	...	...	2483	344	320	31	2	3	...	..	323	36	128	12	...	...	...	...	128	12
1853	...	...	...	...	...	...	...	...	...	...	...	...	...	...	...	...	...	..	...	...	...	...	...	...
1854	...	...	...	...	...	...	...	...	...	...	...	...	...	...	...	...	...	...	...	...	...	...	...	...
1855	...	...	...	...	...	...	...	...	...	...	...	...	...	...	...	...	...	...	...	...	...	...	...	...
1856	2602	357	124	94	62	45	2989	496	1084	124	38	33	18	13	1140	170	85	11	1	...	...	...	86	11
1857	2325	379	126	109	68	57	2519	545	1048	179	39	20	21	26	1008	225	139	20	6	9	7	1	252	30
1858	3935	631	236	209	72	65	4243	905	1703	303	70	98	26	21	1799	422	618	100	37	21	10	10	665	131
1859	2543	399	148	148	51	41	2741	588	1099	246	70	71	22	25	1191	342	210	36	3	2	1	3	214	41
1860	1380	197	104	87	18	13	1501	297	579	139	44	44	13	7	636	190	126	41	12	10	1	4	139	55
1861	1083	199	93	84	12	11	1188	294	424	96	29	30	5	4	458	138	84	27	6	9	1	2	91	38
1862	1098	191	78	88	13	8	1189	282	361	90	28	31	7	8	396	128	145	34	8	10	1	5	154	49
1863	1601	295	126	104	13	14	1740	413	461	98	41	41	6	1	508	140	230	71	6	12	3	5	239	88
1864	1816	327	165	123	25	19	2006	469	203	50	13	11	2	...	218	61	321	108	30	36	7	6	358	159
1865	1846	337	125	129	18	21	1989	487	428	110	36	40	2	5	466	155	326	85	23	19	6	3	355	107
1866	1558	302	148	142	16	21	1722	465	252	46	22	22	6	2	280	73	523	170	51	44	11	6	585	220
1867	1563	339	139	161	17	19	1719	519	310	81	30	27	5	...	345	108	418	136	46	50	6	3	470	189
1868	915	194	114	69	12	6	1031	269	136	30	6	8	...	1	145	39	257	116	52	48	2	4	315	168
1869	659	143	51	49	3	5	713	197	110	33	6	9	...	3	116	45	434	157	38	60	...	2	473	219
1870	1233	209	120	44	6	8	1359	301	238	69	29	32	1	1	268	102	266	121	47	44	8	1	321	166
1871	...	..	...	...	...	...	...	...	...	...	...	...	...	...	...	...	...	...	...	...	...	...	...	...
1871	1521	275	131	130	8	10	1660	415	351	100	32	31	4	3	387	134	165	63	26	37	8	1	194	101
1872	1355	301	114	133	12	11	1481	445	774	280	105	88	8	10	887	378	282	119	82	58	6	2	370	179
1873	1048	335	81	99	12	8	1141	342	713	301	70	109	8	5	797	415	146	74	16	21	1	1	163	96
1874	1437	357	180	130	15	14	1632	501	882	387	121	141	16	27	1019	555	170	86	28	40	3	5	201	131
1875	1078	278	136	182	16	21	1230	431	642	301	121	118	24	19	787	438	225	111	43	40	5	13	273	164
1876	1030	280	111	91	15	13	1156	384	528	228	89	97	15	10	632	335	221	112	28	35	2	...	251	147
1877	903	208	93	91	10	10	1006	309	368	168	62	63	11	4	441	235	41	23	7	14	...	2	48	39
1878	1024	220	85	85	11	10	1120	315	274	92	39	24	2	4	315	120	81	34	12	8	1	2	94	41
1879	1182	255	106	106	16	12	1304	345	426	169	57	61	12	4	495	234	96	30	19	15	...	1	115	46
1880	1058	214	96	91	17	7	1171	342	375	157	51	55	4	4	430	216	83	24	11	18	4	...	98	42
1881	645	128	41	50	4	3	690	181	311	95	20	27	3	3	343	125	107	37	20	19	2	3	129	59
1882	915	204	6	9	...	...	921	213	382	119	5	5	...	...	387	124	132	56	...	...	...	...	132	56
1883	878	231	95	77	7	9	980	317	352	148	38	43	4	4	394	195	318	74	20	27	3	4	341	105
1884	666	188	65	67	1	9	732	264	252	111	33	30	2	2	287	143	274	56	6	1	1	1	284	58
1885	955	266	114	123	13	19	1082	408	991	374	168	131	16	11	1175	516	587	162	14	6	...	1	601	169
1886	787	266	105	109	5	5	897	380	326	114	37	29	2	4	365	147	376	139	5	2	...	...	381	141
1887	736	220	90	83	6	7	832	310	643	205	71	62	3	5	71[illegible]	272	145	51	5	4	...	...	147	55
1888	526	146	45	23	2	1	573	170	380	147	45	31	2	7	427	185	237	63	...	2	...	...	237	65
1889	307	81	28	23	3	2	338	106	292	93	31	31	2	4	325	128	278	65	1	...	...	...	279	65
1890	297	63	9	8	...	...	306	71	225	58	16	20	3	...	243	78	251	69	...	1	...	...	251	70
1891	192	24	6	8	1	1	199	33	259	85	32	17	1	2	292	104	195	39	2	1	...	...	197	40
1892	495	95	23	19	2	3	520	117	429	150	47	50	4	1	480	201	114	26	...	...	1	...	115	26
1893	457	138	57	34	...	6	514	178	517	182	60	59	4	8	581	249	73	18	...	2	...	...	73	19
1894	175	46	18	13	5	1	198	60	214	65	33	15	2	...	248	80	298	67	1	3	...	...	299	70
1895	282	67	31	22	3	2	316	91	297	103	38	30	1	2	336	135	202	47	3	...	...	...	205	47

No record of Departures for several Presidencies from 1834 to 1845, and from 1853 to 1855.

* The Census of 1881 gives the Indian population of the Colony on the 4th. April of that year as 249,064 of whom 151,423 were males and 97,541 females.

|| For previous years *Vide Almanac* of 1889.

TURES.													
OTHER PLACES.								Total Departures.		Total Deaths.		Estimated Indian Population on 31st. Dec. in each year.	
Males.	Females.	Boys.	Girls.	Infants.		Tatal.							
				M.	F.	M.	F.	M.	F.	M.	F.	M.	F.
...	...	...	...	...	...	...	...	2021	94	373	45	18105	888
...	...	...	...	...	...	...	...	2884	108	1094	129	44454	5049
...	...	..	...	...	...	...	...	2312	149	3862	238	48224	6715
...	...	...	...	...	...	...	...	2492	170	2100	252	52896	8705
...	...	...	...	...	...	...	...	2556	204	1447	298	55140	10301
...	...	...	...	...	...	...	...	1651	133	1171	295	48156	11154
...	...	...	...	...	...	...	...	2639	376	1215	289	59673	11788
...	...	...	...	...	...	...	...	4298	594	1220	296	61240	12572
...	...	...	...	...	...	...	...	3283	442	1359	356	65718	14018
...	...	...	...	...	...	...	...	2895	374	1259	331	70658	15746
...	...	...	...	...	...	...	...	2034	392	1594	664	80727	19478
...	...	...	...	...	...	...	...	1767	291	2076	484	87725	21960
...	...	...	...	...	...	...	...	3166	509	4517	781	96142	25134
...	...	...	...	...	...	...	...	3702	565	2727	687	100541	28245
6	...	...	...	...	...	6	...	4220	677	3955	923	102826	31446
11	8	4	1	...	...	15	9	3794	809	2074	742	107072	35462
...	...	...	...	...	...	...	...	6707	1458	2582	992	120334	43970
...	...	...	...	...	...	...	...	4146	971	4075	1336	145844	56135
13	1	...	...	...	...	13	1	2290	543	3842	1442	151760	61153
48	1	1	...	...	...	49	1	1786	471	4181	1456	*141615	*51019
13	1	...	...	...	...	13	1	1752	460	6818	2009	151462	58250
62	21	4	5	...	...	66	26	2553	667	6505	1888	150220	60766
87	22	19	18	4	1	110	41	2692	721	6311	2166	150649	62424
41	18	2	...	1	...	44	48	2854	67	5938	2286	161307	69575
298	78	35	48	5	6	338	132	2925	890	5899	1787	161362	72348
34	7	3	4	...	1	37	11	2571	827	16973	6769	146391	68416
332	143	58	41	3	4	393	188	1880	694	8119	4967	141391	67508
336	139	47	32	6	4	383	175	1684	636	5356	5570	133853	67888
192	79	29	20	3	2	224	101	2172	670	3079	1687	140283	70353
...	...	...	...	...	...	...	...	......	......	......	......	†141804	‡74454
120	47	8	6	...	2	128	55	2369	705	3425	2026	‡109470	‡45617
43	24	6	5	1	...	50	29	2788	1031	3423	2174	‡107149	‡44105
58	21	1	1	...	...	59	22	2160	875	4264	2677	†107771	‡44771
20	10	2	4	...	...	22	14	2874	1201	2420	1073	‡107758	‡45103
64	16	11	5	3	1	78	22	2368	1055	3469	2143	‡105738	‡44491
303	40	11	10	1	1	315	51	2354	917	2428	1002	‡101650	‡43096
284	28	13	9	2	3	299	40	1794	623	2937	1098	‡ 69028	‡42281
284	35	11	11	1	2	296	48	1835	527	4083	2432	‡ 98110	‡42588
11	3	1	1	...	...	12	4	1926	629	5014	3106	‡ 95241	‡41854
27	11	4	3	1	...	32	14	1731	614	4085	2715	‡ 91793	‡40654
18	6	...	...	...	...	18	6	1180	371	2126	814	‡ 88239	‡39393
26	4	...	...	...	...	26	4	1704	624	2947	1052	‡ 84638	‡38282
44	16	7	7	...	...	51	23	1766	640	2754	1105	‡ 81650	‡37399
62	32	0	4	...	...	62	36	1362	491	2988	1284	‡ 82298	‡37943
33	17	...	...	...	...	32	17	2891	1110	2417	1084	‡ 74610	‡34515
6	2	0	1	...	...	6	3	1649	671	2443	1058	‡ 73729	‡24674
11	6	...	...	...	...	11	6	1707	643	2699	1215	‡ 69722	‡32077
45	28	1	...	...	...	46	28	1283	448	2201	915	‡ 66822	‡32001
59	27	1	1	...	...	60	28	1002	327	2666	1159	‡ 65646	‡31505
26	9	...	...	...	...	26	9	826	228	2795	1237	‡ 65423	‡31408
28	7	...	...	...	...	28	7	716	184	2036	899	§ 63473	§29899
14	5	...	...	...	...	14	5	1129	349	2332	1132	58583	27873
11	8	...	...	...	...	11	8	1179	454	3589	1508	54462	26231
9	4	...	...	...	...	9	4	754	214	1854	876	52664	25450
3	2	...	...	...	...	3	2	857	275	2454	1087	51153	24757

* According to Census taken on 8th. April 1861.

† ,, ,, ,, on 10th. April 1871.

‡ These figures give the estimated number of *Indian Immigrants* in the Colony at the end of the year, whereas those of the previous years comprise the *Indian Population* generally.

§ According to the Census of 1891,

Summary of the Mauritius Blue Book and Administration Reports for 1894.

I.—TAXATION.

Ordinance No. 1 of 1894 provided for the payment of fees for the measurement of Tonnage of British Merchant ships.

By Ordinance No. 8 of 1894, the License duties hitherto payable to Government by persons carrying on their trade in Markets, Cemeteries, Slaughterhouses or other Municipal Establishments within the limits of the Municipality of Port Louis, were made henceforth payable to the Municipal Corporation of Port Louis.

By that same Ordinance, the Municipality was authorized to levy a tax of 2 o/o and 4 o/o on tenants paying rents at the rate of Rs. 20 and Rs. 30 and upwards, respectively.

By Ordinance No. 17 of 1894:

1. Ordinance No. 20 of 1890 entitled: "An Ordinance to provide additional Ways and Means "for meeting the Public Expenditure of this Colony up to the end of the year 1891" was to continue and remain in force for one year from the 1st. January 1895;—with the proviso that instead of the surcharge of 10 per cent imposed upon Rum issued for Home Consumption and upon Spirits imported into this Colony, a surcharge of 20 per cent shall be levied.

2. An import duty of 8½ o/o was to continue to be levied on goods liable to *ad valorem* duty.

3. Ordinance No. 20 of 1893, entitled: "An Ordinance to provide additional ways and means "for meeting the public expenditure of this Colony up to the end of the year 1894" was to continue and remain in force for one year from the 1st. January 1895,—"Prussian Blue" being added to Item (*c*) of Article 1 of the said Ordinance.

Ordinance No. 20 of 1894 established the rates for supplies of water from the Mare-aux-Vacoas water supply.

By Ordinance No. 26 of 1894, the following were added to the Schedule of Custom duties leviable on goods imported into the Colony:—

After the word "Butter": Margarine or any other substances sold or used as Butter.

To Item 46 were added:

23. Solid Phosphoric Acid.

24. Carbonate of Baryte.

25. Substances imported to be used in the destruction of insects or other parasites prejudicial to agriculture.

Ordinance No. 27 of 1894 amended Ordinance No. 18 of 1856, chapter VII, with respect to travelling allowances payable to Ushers in Civil and Criminal cases before the Sûpreme Court of Mauritius.

By Ordinance No. 29 of 1894, a tax of five per cent was to be levied on premiums payable on Fire Insurance Policies,—the proceeds of the tax to be paid half-yearly to the Municipality in aid of their Fire Engine Establishment.

II.—Revenue and Expenditure.

The Revenue of 1894 was ... ... — ...	Rs.	8,534,427.49
Shewing an increase of		430,505.47
as compared with the Revenue of 1893 which was	Rs.	8,103,922.02
The Expenditure of 1894 was	Rs.	8,587,039.27
Showing an increase of		714,942.44
on the expenditure of 1893 which amounted to	Rs.	7,872,096.83

The ratio of the Revenue to the Population was Rs. 22.68 per head and that of the Expenditure Rs. 22.82 per head.

III.—Assets and Liabilities.

1o. Commissioners of Currency :—

Assets	Bs.	4,611,299.69
Liabilities		4,025,11500
Surplus... ...	Rs.	586,184.69

2o. Government Savings Bank :—

Assets	Rs.	4,307,871.78
Liabilities		3,341,066.45
Surplus... ...	Rs.	966,805.33

3o. Curatelle :—

Assets	Rs.	451,786.48
Liabilities		451,786.48

4o. Treasury Proper :—

Assets	Rs.	3,049,026.40
Liabilities		1,497,979.50
Surplus on 31st. December 1894	Rs.	1,551,046.90

IV.—Pubic Debts.

The Public Debts stood as follows on 31st. December 1894 :

Mauritius Railways debentures payable 15th. February 1895 and 15th. January 1896, and bearing interest at 6 o/o	£	161,000
Savane Railway 4½ o/o debentures payable by annual drawings ...		52,900
Moka Railway 4 o/o debentures payable by annual drawings in and from 1884		2,600
Consolidated 4 o/o debentures payable by annual drawings from 1882 ...		69,600
Mauritius Inscribed Stock under Ord. 1 of 1887 (including the loan made for the Mare-aux-Vacoas £ 36,000)		480,749.13.0
Poor Law Commission 5 o/o Debentures issued in 1873		3,000
Hurricane Loan 1892		600,000
Public Debts	£	1,369,849.13.0

Carried over ...		...£	1,369,849.13.0
For the redemption of the debentures and inscribed stock, the sinking fund accumulated up to 31st. December 1893 amounted to	£ 224,404.19.8		

SURPLUS BALANCES:

Treasury proper	Rs 1,551,046.90		
Savings Bank	966,805.33		
Commissioners of Currency	586,184.69		
	Rs. 3,104,036.92		
Converted into £ at 1/0 20/32 per Rupee		163,370.7.6	
Loan Commission Balance due		393,684.6.0	
			781,459.13. 2
Balance representing the debt. of the Colony		£	588,390.19.10

V.—CURRENCY.

Amount of Currency Notes in circulation on 31st. December 1893:

Issue of 1848 and 1849	£	483.16 5
Issue of 1860		3,640. 0. 0
Total...	...£	4,123.16. 5

Issue of 1870:

1. In the Financial Officers Vault	Rs.	1,008,865
2. In the hands of the Public including the Bank		3,016,250
	Rs.	4,025,115

VI.—SAVINGS BANK.

The amount deposited in 1894 was	Rs.	1,149,816
This amount compared with the deposits of 1893 shows a decrease of ...		15,014
The amount deposited in 1893 being	Rs.	1,164,830
The total sum standing to the credit of depositors at the end of 1894, including the interest due to them, was		3,253,538

Of this sum Rs. 1,510,308 belonged to the Indian Population.

The number of depositors increased from 22,365 in 1893 to 22,816 in 1894; of these 10,151 belonged to the Indian Population.

VII.—CURATELLE (*Admistration of Vacant Estates.*)

The deposits amounted to ... ... Rs. 451,786.48

The assets consisted of the following sums:

(a) Cash-balances in Mauritius Commercial Bank	Rs.	107,925.53
(b) Invested in England £ 18,097.18.11		180,979.44
(c) Exchange on above		162,881.51
	Rs.	451,786.48

VIII.—Financial Condition of the Municipal Corporation of Port Louis.

Balance on hand on 1st. January 1894	Rs.	37,734.27
Revenue and Receipts on account during 1894		500,087.76
	Rs.	537,822.03
Expenditure and Payments on account during 1894		515,093.11
Balance on hand on 31st. December 1894	Rs.	22,728.92

Debenture—debt of the Municipal Corporation on 31st. December 1894 :

		Principal.
Conversion Loan	£	135,300
Colonial Loan, 1889	Rs.	117,000
Hurricane Government Loan		142,652
Colonial Loan, 1894		28,500
Total...	Rs.	288,152

IX.—Military Expenditure.

The Military Contribution paid by the Colony in 1894 amounted to £13,804.13s.9d.

The Troops in the Colony at the end of the year, were as follows :

Staff	9
Royal Artillery	138
Mauritius Companies Royal Artillery	195
Royal Engineers	72
1st. Bn. " The Black Watch "	480
Army Service Corps...	3
Ordnance Store Corps	4
Medical Staff Corps...	13
Corps of Armourers...	1
	915

The total Military Expenditure amounted to £ 51,867.

X.—Imports and Exports.*

Exclusive of especie and bullion, the value of Imports in 1894 amounted to Rs. 21,096,011 and that of the Exports to Rs. 31,228,619.

In 1893 the Imports were valued at Rs. 18,899,939 and the Exports at Rs. 22,176,486, exclusive of specie and bullion.

The rate of Imports per head of population was as follows during 1893 and 1894 :

1893	Rs. 50.83
1894	56.07

* The value of Imports and Exports is given in Rupees at the rate of 2.s. per R., exclusive of exchange and of any other charges.

The rate of Exports per head of population was as follows ;

1893	Rs. 59.67
1894	83.00

The exports of Sugar manufactured in the Colony in 1893 and 1894 were as follows :

1893 ...	86,007,841 kilos	Rs. 19,409,218
1894 ...	138,431,793 ,,	28,461,564

The value of other local products exported in 1894 was as follows :

Rum	Rs. 424,632
Vanilla	82,720
Aloe-Fibre	171,526
Molasses	217,859
Cocoanut-oil	59,565
Raw hides	33,499

XI—SHIPPING.

Under this head, the year 1894, compared with 1893, shows the following differences :—

		1893	1894	Increases.
Inwards	Tons :	293,990	316,350	22,360
Outwards	,,	293,033	324,748	31.715

		1893	1894	Decrease.
Inwards	Ships :	340	335	5
Outwards	,,	347	340	7

XII.—POPULATION AND VITAL STATISTICS.

The Estimated Population at the end of 1894 was as follows :

	Males.	Females.	Total.
General Population...	60,047	56,948	116,995
Indian do.	146,581	112,643	259,224
Total ...	206,628	169,591	376,219

The Births registered in 1894 stand thus ;

	Males.	Females.	Total.
General Population	2,164	2,123	4,287
Indian do.	5,031	4,844	9,875
Total...	7,195	6,967	14,162

The Deaths registered at the Civil Status Office in 1894 were as follows :

	Males.	Females.	Total.
General Population	1,891	1,694	3,585
Indian do.	4,032	3,175	7,207
Total...	5,923	4,869	10,792

The number of registered deaths in 1894 shews a decrease of 4,515 compared with 1893.

The birth-rate in the total population was 38.1 and the death-rate 29.0 per thousand. The registered births throughout the Colony in 1894 exceeded the deaths by 3370.

The number of still-births in 1894 was 944, shewing a decrease of 47 compared with 1893 and of 1896 compared with 1892.

The number of suicides in 1894 was 30, or 6 more than in 1893—23 were males and 7 females —28 indians and 2 of the other classes.

XIII.—Immigration and Labor.

In 1894, 338 men were received from Calcutta and 381 men from Madras.

The number of coolies who left the Colony last year and during the four previous years are shown by the following figures :—

	Males.	Females.	Total.
1890...	826	228	1,054
1891...	716	184	900
1892...	1,129	349	1,478
1893...	1,197	457	1,654
1894...	754	214	968

Of the Coolies who left the Colony in 1894 :—

258	went to Calcutta.
328	,, Madras.
369	,, Bombay.
11	,, Nagapatam
2	,, Colombo.

The proportion of females to males in the departures of 1894 was 28.1 against 38.1 in 1893.

XIV.—Paupers.

Recipients of Indoor Relief.

Civil Hospital, Port Louis.

	Males.	Females.	Total.
Remaining on 31st. December 1893	66	26	92
Admitted in 1894	1724	721	2445
Discharged ,, ...	1500	661	2161
Died ,, ...	215	55	270
Remaining on 31st. December 1894	75	31	106

District Hospitals. (1)

	Males.	Females.	Total.
Remaining on 31st. December 1893	257	77	334
Admitted in 1894	5534	2021	7555
Discharged ,, ...	5050	1907	6957
Died ,, ...	448	128	576
Remaining on 31st. December 1894	293	77	334

(1) Barkly Asylum, Powder Mills, Poudre d'Or, Centre de Flacq, Mahebourg, Souillac and Moka.

Sister Barthélemy's Convent Hospital.

	Males.	Females	Total.
Remaining on 31st. December 1893	16	...	16
Admitted in 1894	229	13	242
Discharged "	195	11	206
Died "	34	2	36
Remaining on 31st. December 1894	16	...	16

Barkly Asylum (1).

	Males.	Females	Total.
Remaining on 31st. December 1893	174	108	282
Admitted in 1894	216	138	354
Discharged "	213	140	353
Died "	15	18	33
Remaining on 31st. December 1894	162	88	250

Lunatic Asylum.

	Males.	Females	Total.
Remaining on 31st. December 1893	226	145	371
Admitted in 1894	77	39	116
Discharged "	46	34	80
Died "	8	9	17
Remaining on 31st. December 1894	249	141	390

Leper Asylum.

	Males.	Females	Total.
Remaining on 31st. December 1893	132	36	168
Admitted in 1894	53	5	58
Discharged "	35	4	39
Died "	29	10	39
Remaining on 31st. December 1894	121	27	148

Convent Branch Infirmaries. (2)

	Males.	Females	Total.
Remaining on 31st. December 1893	195	48	243
Admitted in 1894...	113	40	153
Discharged in 1893	64	17	81
Died	52	20	72
Remaining on 31st. December 1894	192	51	243

Convent Orphanages. (3)

	Males.	Females	Total.
Remaining on 31st. December 1893	41	74	115
Admitted in 1894...	7	13	20
Discharged	16	15	31
Died	2	4	6
Remaining on 31st. December 1894	30	68	98

Recipients of Out-Door Relief.

Alimentary and pecuniary.

	Males.	Females	Total.
Remaining on 31st. December 1893	279	958	1237
Admitted in 1894...	104	276	380
Discharged	89	418	507
Died	22	79	101
Remaining on 31st. December 1894	272	737	1009

(1) Indian Orphans, and harmless Lunatics.

(2) Pamplemousses Convent, Old Reformatory Calebasses, Belle Rose Convent, Rose Hill, and Convent Rempart street, Port Louis.

(3) Convent Rempart street; Do. La Paix street; Do. Cotton street; Do. Canal street; Do. Grand Port; Do. Moka, and the Protestant Benevolent Institution, Wellington street.

Medical Dispensaries.

Attendances of paupers in 1894	35,734	36,518	72,252

Expenditure of 1893 *and* 1894.

1893	Rs. 223,820.83
1894	218,640.00

XV.—Education.

During the year 1894, there were 174 schools in operation—which are thus classified:

Government Schools.	1st. grade—1st. division	17	82
	,, ,, —2nd. ,, ...	31	
	2nd. ,, —(Full time	24	
	,, ,, —half time Schools	8	
	Reformatory Schools	2	
Aided Schools.	Roman Catholic	59	92
	Church of England	30	
	Presbyterian	2	
	Mahomedan	1	

In the Government Schools, 254 teachers and monitors were employed at the end of the year 1894. In the Aided Schools 88 head-teachers and 84 assistants were employed.

The average number of scholars on roll in 1894 was ;—

In Government Schools	9191
In Aided Schools	8510
Total	17701
Average number in 1893	16659
Increase	1042

Of the total number of pupils at the end of 1894, 71.76 o/o were creoles of either European, African, or Chinese descent, and 28.24 o/o were Indians or of Indian origin.

Divided according to their religious persuasion, they stood as follows :—

	Govt. Schools.	Aided Schools.	Total
Members of Church of England	266	298	564
Roman Catholics	6503	6423	12926
Belonging to other Christian creeds...	144	135	279
Mahomedans...	720	508	1228
Hindoos and others	1602	1321	2923

The relative numbers are shewn by the following percentages :—

Members of Church of England	3·15 o/o
Roman Catholics...	72.13 ,,
Members of other Christian creeds	1.56 ,,
Mahomedans	6.85 ,,
Hindoos and others	16.31 ,,

The average attendance of scholars was :

In Government Schools	5,734
In Aided Schools	5,602
Total	11,336

showing an increase of 1,159 as compared with 1893.

The cost to Government of each pupil on the roll was as follows : —

In Government Schools	Rs. 15.86	R. 0.80 less than in 1893
In Aided Schools	10.93	,, 0.66 less than in 1893

The average number of pupils in the Royal College and Royal College School in 1893 and 1894 were as follows :—

	1893	1894
Royal College proper	201	203
,, School, Port Louis	117	100
,, ,, Curepipe	179	195
Total	497	498

The sums disbursed for educational purposes in 1894 were as follows :

Royal College	Rs. 197,643.14
Expenditure on Government Schools exclusively	157,225.12
Expenditure on Aided Schools exclusively	92,992.72
Expenditure common to Government and Aided Schools	21,397.33
Industrial Education	3,446.16
Administration...	24,300.97
Total	Rs. 496,005.44
The total expenditure in 1893 was	476,089.24
Increase of expenditure in 1894	Rs. 19,916.20

XVI.—Judicial Statistics.

The total number of offences reported to the Police or to the Magistrates in 1894 was 51,103 —i.e. 11,756 more than in 1893.

The total number of convictions in the inferior Courts was 19,995—i.e. 2,105 more than in 1893.

The convictions in the Supreme Court were as follows :—

	1893	1894
For offences against the person	23	7
For offences against property	40	27
For other offences	4	11
	67	45

The acquittals were as follows :—

	1893	1894
In the Inferior Courts...	5,208	5,012
In the Supreme Court...	21	20
Total ...	5,229	5,032

XVII.—Gaols.

The total number of persons committed in 1894 was 8,765 against 9,057 in 1893.

5	were imprisoned for	debt.
2,471	,,	non-payment of fines and costs.
1,595	,,	safe custody till trial, or for not furnishing security.
4,694	,,	purposes of penal imprisonment.

The above-mentioned Committals include 365 removals to the Juvenile Reformatory, against 395 in 1893.

The imprisonment in 1894 from Criminal Offences stands as follows :—

For five years or more	9
,, one year or more and less than five years	109
,, more than three months and less than one year	778
,, three months or less	3798
Total...	4694

or 317 less than 1893.

XVIII.—Ecclesiastical Establishment.

In Mauritius (exclusive of the Dependencies) the adherents of the Churches supported by the Government were, according to the Censes of 1891, as follows :—

Roman Catholics	115,438
Protestants	7,307

The number of ministers at the end of 1894 were as follows :—

Roman Catholic Church	43
Church of England	10
Presbyterian Church	1

The expenses incurred in 1894 for the Ecclesiastical Establishments were as follows :—

	Personal Emoluments and travelling allowances.	Priests at Rs. 1500 and payment of ministers and Catechists.	Building grants.	Education, recruiting and passage of Priests whom not paid by Goverment &c., &c.	Total.	Rate per member of each church.
	Rs. c.	Rs. c.	Rs. c.	Rs. c.	Rs. c.	
Roman Catholic Church......	64.416.25	15,000.00	12,000.00	9,820.00	101,236.25	0.88
Church of England	31,162.09	3,333.00	......	......	34,495.09	} 5.62
Presbyterian Church	3,999.96	2,583.00	......	......	6,582.96	
	99,578.30	20,916.50	12,000.00	9,820.00	142,314.30	...

XIX.—Forests and Crown Lands.

Under this head, the total revenue derived from leases amounted in 1894 to Rs. 32,031.16 and from sale of dead trees to Rs. 12,795.56, and the total expenditure amounted to Rs. 102,247.57.

The sums disbursed from 1881 for the acquisition of lands for afforestation purposes, were as follows :—

1881	... ...	Rs. 72,301
1882	... ...	590,433
1883	... ...	688,363
1884	... ...	912,816
1885	... ...	20,203
1886	... ...	210,636
1887	... ...	33.189
1888	... ...	Nil.
1889	... ...	Nil.
1890	... ...	Nil.
1891	... ...	Nil.
1892	... ...	Nil.
1893	... ...	Nil.
1894	... ...	Nil.
		Rs. 2,527,941

In addition to the above the following sums have been paid as indemnity for lands included in the Mountain Reserves :

1881...	... ...	Rs. 2,344.42
1882...	... ...	1,185.00
1883...	... ...	4,504.02
1884 ..	... ...	4,301.97
1885...	... ...	5.970.74
1886...	... ...	26.00
1887...	... ...	768.24
1888...	... ...	3.00
1889...	... ...	1,419.19
1890...	... ...	1,619.75
1891...	... ...	327.07
1892...	... ...	426.59
1893...	... ...	359.07
1894...	... ...	353.00
		Rs. 23,608.06

XX.—Railways.

The Railway Revenue and Expenditure stood as follows :

	1893	1894	Increase
Revenue .. .. Rs.	1.585.720	1,790,808	205,088
Expenditure	1,010,565	1,085,429	74,864

XXI.—Post Office and Telegraphs.

The Revenue collected in 1894, was 65,614,29 against Rs. 66,367.86 in 1893.

The letters, post-cards and newspapers, which passed through the Office were as follows :—

	Letters.	Post-cards.	Newspapers.
1893...	1,115.853	20,520	1,176.296
1894...	1,188.295	22,630	1,195.634
Increase	72,442	2,110	19.338

The postal money-orders business, foreign and inland, showed a decrease of Rs. 22,833.85 as follows :—

1893	Rs. 408,753.15
1894	385,919.30

Subsidy paid for Mail service to Messageries Maritimes Company Rs. 60,000.

Telegraph Cable.

From Mauritius to Seychelles and Seychelles to Zanzibar.
Owned and managed by the Eastern and South African Telegraph Company Limited.
Subsidy paid by the Colony annually £7,000.

XXII.—OBSERVATORY.

Summary of Observations taken in 1894.

Mean temperature in shade between two open windows in a lofty room 73°.2, against an average of 73°.5 for the last 20 years; absolute maximum 86°.4 on January 6; absolute minimum 56°.8 on June 11.

Mean temperature in a screen on lawn 74°.3, against an average of 74°.5 for the last 10 years; absolute maximum 93°.5 on January 3; absolute minimum 50°.6 on June 10.

Highest temperature in the sun's rays 159°.4 on February 9; mean for year 141°.3.

Highest temperature of the soil, at a depth of 5 feet, 80°.0 on January 14 and April 6; lowest 74°.4 from August 26 to September 2. Highest at a depth of 10 feet, 77°.55 on May 28; lowest 75°.5 on January 1 and 2.

Actinometric observations were made when the weather permitted. The greatest mean effect for an exposure of 2 minutes was 10°.27 on December 23, the sun's mean altitude being 89°.00; and the least 8°.39 on June 29, the sun's mean altitude being 46°.35.

Total duration of bright sunshine 2783.3 hours, and mean proportion for years (constant sunshine being 1) 0.634.

Mean atmospheric pressure at sea-level 30.048 inches, against an average of 30.079 for last 20 years; greatest pressure 30.342 on August 13; least pressure 29.276 on February 22.

Mean dew-point 64°.7, against an average of 64°.6; highest 76°.2 on March 13; lowest 50°.6 on June 16.

Mean vapour tension .621, against an average of ·619; highest ·905 on March 13; lowest .369 on June 16.

Mean relative humidity 75.8 per cent., against an average of 74.6; highest 94.8 on July 10; lowest 44.4 on October 30.

Rainfall 48.91 inches on 196 days against an average of 48.43 inches on 205 days. Greatest fall in 24 hours 3.70 inches on January 11.

Wettest months January and April, and driest June. The fall in March was only one half of the average.

Thunder and lightning, or both, occurred on 27 days, against an average of 33.

Mean hourly velocity of wind 11·2 miles, against an average of 11·1. Greatest velocity for an hour 62·2 on February 22. Mean direction S.71° 07' E; against an average of S.74° 13' E.

So far as is yet known, there were nine tropical Cyclones in the South Indian Ocean in the course of the year, and their tracks have been determined as far as possible.

Storm warnings were issued daily from the 9th. to the 14th. January ; on the 21st., 22nd and 23rd. February ; and on the 8th., 9th. and 18th. December.

As usual, observations made on board vessels in the Indian Ocean were tabulated, and detailed accounts of gales and hurricanes at sea recorded ; 45 daily weather charts of the South Indian Ocean have been prepared.

The Magnetographs were at work throughout the year, and the absolute values of the magnetic elements determined weekly. Mean Declination 9° -59'.21"-0 West mean Dip. 54° -41.'63 South. Mean Horizontal Force 5.1960, mean Vertical Force 7.3370, and mean Total Force 8.9907 (foot-grain-second units.)

The number and intensity of magnetic disturbances increased during the year. The dates of the greatest were February 25 and 26, July 20 and 21, and August 20 and 21.

568 photographs of the sun were taken. The sun was observed on 344 days, and on each of these days spots were seen.

The Solar Eclipse of the 29th. September was observed and 18 photographs of it were taken.

Observations for Time were taken daily when the weather permitted, and the Time Ball on the Signal Mountain was dropped three times a week.

XXIII.—CONSTITUTION.

The Government is vested in a Governor and Commander-in-Chief aided by an Executive Council, of which the Senior Military Officer in command of Her Majesty's Troops, the Colonial Secretary, the Procureur General, the Receiver General, and the Auditor General are *ex-officio* members, with the addition of such persons as may be designated by the Queen, by any Instruction or Warrant under Her Majesty's Sign Manual and Signet, or as may be provisionally appointed by the Governor. There is also a Council of Government constituted by Letters-Patent, dated 16th. of September 1885 ;—it consists of the Governor, Eight *ex-officio* members, Nine nominated members, and Ten elected members. Of these members, one represents each of the eight rural district, and two are elected for Port Louis.

The number of Registered Electors in 1894 was 5,159.

XXIV.--LEGISLATION.

The following Ordinances were passed in 1894 :

1. To provide for the payment of fees for the measurement of Tonnage of British vessels.

2. To empower the Governor in Executive Council to make Regulations for securing order and the preservation of property in the Botanical Gardens of Pamplemousses and Curepipe.

3. To authorize the Inspectors of the Woods and Forests to prosecute offences against the Forests Laws.

4. To amend Ordinance 8 of 1893 entitled "An Ordinance to amend the Widows and Orphans' Funds Ordinance, 1886."

5. To prevent unauthorized persons from tresspassing on, taking drawings of, or disclosing information relating to, the National Defences of Mauritius, and to repeal Ordinance 6 of 1891.

6. * To define the expression of £ 1,000 used in the Section of the Order in Council of the

* Disallowed by Order in Council dated 12.12.94.

13th. April 1831 which regulates the conditions under which appeals may be made to Her Majesty in Council from judgments, decrees, orders or sentences given or pronounced by Her Majesty's Supreme Court of Mauritius.

7. To relieve the Treasury from further contributions to the Sinking Fund created under Ordinance No. 15 of 1864.

8. To make provision for increasing the Revenue of the Municipality of Port Louis.

9. To amend Ordinance 15 of 1893.

10. For applying a further sum not exceeding Rs. 297,353.33 to the service of the year 1893.

11. To authorize the incorporation of the Mauritius Cricket Club.

12. To remove doubts as to the validity of certain acts done by the Honourable C. A. King-Harman, C.M.G., as Officer Administering the Government of Mauritius and its dependencies.

13. To make further provision for the administration of the Funds set apart under Ordinances 12 of 1892 and 17 of 1893, for assisting Planters and Owners of houses damaged or destroyed by the Hurricane of 29th. April 1892.

14. To validate the proceedings of the Council of Government and to legalize the votes of the Honorable George Robinson in the said Council during the period in which he sat in the said Council as a Nominated Member under a provisional appointment.

15. To amend the Law on Civil Pledges (Gage).

16. To amend Ordinance 38 of 1881 and to authorize the refund to the Ushers of the Supreme Court of four fifths of the amount that has accrued to the Public Treasury under Article 9 of that Ordinance.

17. To provide additional ways and means for meeting the Public Expenditure of the Colony up to the end of the year 1895.

18. For making provision for the Public Service for the year 1895.

19. To empower the Governor to lend to the Municipality of Port Louis the sum of Rs. 28,500

20. To amend the law relating to the Mare-aux-Vacoas Water Supply.

21. To amend Ordinances Nos. 28 of 1866, 1 of 1877 and 6 of 1878, relative to the distillation and sale of Colonial spirits.

22. To constitute the Association called the Mauritius Civil Service Mutual Aid Association into an Anonymous Society with limited liability, and to authorize the Receiver General to deduct monthly abatements from the salary or pension of its Associates.

23. To continue in force for six months Ordinance No. 14 of 1893 entitled " An Ordinance to prohibit the pollution of the Rivers of Curepipe."

24. To amend Article 42 of Ordinance 13 of 1875.

25. To extend Ordinances 19 of 1892 and 3 of 1894 to Mountain and River Reserves.

26. To amend Schedule A of Ordinance No. 16 of 1886.

27. To amend Ordinance No. 18 of 1856, entitled: " An Ordinance for establishing a General Table of costs for proceedings before the Supreme Court of Mauritius and in matters connected with the same."

28. To amend Ordinance No. 30 of 1881, entitled: "An Ordinance for regulating Pensions, Compensations and Allowances to be granted in respect of Offices held in Her Majesty's Civil Service in this Colony."

29. To impose a tax on premiums of policies of Fire Insurance.

30. To provide for the carrying out of Drainage Works referred to in Ordinance No. 15 of 1893."

31. To amend Ordinance No. 21 of 1894, entitled "An Ordinance to amend Ordinances 28 of 1866, 1 of 1877 and 6 of 1878 relative to the distillation and sale of Colonial Spirits."

XXV.—Dependencies.

(a) Rodrigues.

Population on 31st. December 1894... 2,522

		1893	1894
Revenue	... Rs.	5,131.16	8,880.23
Expenditure	...	22,600.74	29,637.58

(b) Minor Dependencies.

The production of these Islands consists wholly of Cocoanut-oil, and Salt fish. The quantities thence imported into Mauritius in 1893 and 1894 were as follows:—

	1893		1894	
	Litres.	Value.	Litres.	Value.
Cocoanut Oil...	... 1,406,259	Rs. 238,957.08	1,587,144	Rs. 303,253.43
	Kilos.	Value.	Kilos.	Value.
Salt Fish ...	... 463,479	Rs. 50,602	363,814	Rs. 38,182.20

The Magistrate for the Lesser Dependencies visited the following Islands during 1894.

(1) Peros Banhos.

(2) Diego Garcia.

(3) Agalega.

C. A. KING-HARMAN,

Colonial Secretary.

12th. August 1894.

Report on the Rodrigues Blue Book for the year 1894.

I.- TAXATION.

In 1894 the taxation on cattle was reduced to R. 1 per head of cattle.

REVENUE AND EXPENDITURE.

The revenue of the year amounted to Rs. 8.880.23 against Rs. 5,131.06 in 1893.

The payments amounted to Rs. 29,637.58 against Rs. 22,600.74 in 1893.

Forest revenue. Land rent, Dog tax. Pasturage fees and Licenses are the principal heads of Revenue (Custom duties are collected in Mauritius).

The excess of payments is to be attributed to the New Buildings, Roads, Jetty, Water Reservoir, and to extra salaries.

ESTABLISHMENTS.

The cost of Establishments in 1893 and 1894 shows the following differences.

Salaries	... Rs. 14,409.84	Rs. 16,530.20
Allowances	... 1,170.80	1,415.57
Total ...	... Rs. 15,580.64	Rs. 17,945.77

PENSIONS.

The sum paid for pensions amounted to Rs. 1,336.32 in 1893, and to Rs. 1,577.55 in 1894.

Rs. 100 were paid as alimentary allowance to Mr. Julien pending the settlement of his pension.

EXPORTS AND IMPORTS.

The Exports exclusive of specie amounted to Rs. 105,729.46 against Rs. 94,972.20 in 1893.

The ratio of Export per head was Rs. 40.90 in 1893 and Rs. 41.92 in 1894.

The Imports show a total of Rs. 137,133.55 against Rs. 107,002.25 in the preceding year.

The ratio of Imports per head was Rs. 54.51 against Rs. 45.88 in 1893.

SHIPPING.

Under this head the year 1894 compared with 1893 shows the following differences :

1893...	10 ships inwards	11 outwards
1894...	10 do.	9 do.

The subventioned ship (S. S. Touareg) was wrecked in Port Mathurin creek on the 18th. December 1894.

The subsidy for postal service is always paid in Mauritius.

Population and Vital Statitics.

The population on the 31st. December 1893 was composed of 2,322 souls—i.e. 1,268 males and 1,054 females.

	Males.	Females.
Number of births in 1894	75	65
" arrivals "	197	39
	272	104=376

	Males.	Females.
Number of deaths in 1894	26	15
" departures in 1894	113	22
	139	37=176
Increase in 1894	133	67=200

Population on the 31st. December 1894, 2,522 souls i.e.—1,401 males and 1,121 females.

The birth-rate shows an increase of 12 births if compared with the previous years.

The death-rate an increase of 11 deaths.

There was 1 still-birth in 1893 and none in 1894.

Fifteen marriages were celebrated in 1894 against 20 in 1893.

There was 1 marriage in *articulo mortis* in 1893 and none in 1894.

Registration.

Fifty two documents were registered in 1893 and 17 in 1894.

The Revenue derived thereby amounted to Rs. 26.00 in 1893 and to Rs. 8.50 in 1894.

Education.

There are two Government Schools at Rodrigues, one at Port Mathurin, the other at St. Gabriel.

	Boys.	Girls.
Port Mathurin Schools, 1893—Average No. on roll	51	32
do. Average attendance	38	23
do. 1894—Average No. on roll	61	41
do. Average attendance	34	21
St. Gabriel School, 1893—Average No. on roll	47	42
do. Average attendance	26	24
do. 1894—Average No. on roll	44	48
do. Average attendance	26	36

The cost of both schools was Rs. 2,751.00 against Rs. 2,996.81 * in 1893.

Stationery and School books (sent from Mauritius) were sold to the pupils of both schools to the value of Rs. 90.46 in 1893 and of Rs. 86.32 in 1894.

* Without including Rs. 497.50 spent for the enlargement of St. Gabriel school.

School fees were abolished in 1892.

The annual cost to Government of each pupil inscribed on the roll at both schools amounted to Rs. 17.44 and a fraction in 1893 and to Rs. 13.88 and a fraction in 1894.

The creed of the pupils of both schools was as follows:—187 Roman Catholics and 11 Protestants.

JUDICIAL.

Criminal Side.

The total number of Criminal informations filed in 1894 was 53 and 68 in 1893 (applications for search warrants included).

	1893	1894
No. of adjudications	61	41
No. of cases abandoned	7	12
No. of persons convicted	50	43
No. of persons acquitted	25	9
No. of cases pending	...	1

The most numerous offences were—Breach of forest laws, Assault, Larceny, Blows, Abusive language, Drunkenness, Stray animals and possession of stolen property.

Civil Side.

The number of Civil causes was 71 in 1893 and 46 in 1894.

Most of the plaints entered were for damages and claims for amounts due on goods sold.

Stipendiary Side.

The number of Stipendiary cases amounted to 12 in 1893 and to 8 in 1894.

Most of the Stipendiary cases were for Breach of Contract.

Three engagements were passed in 1893 and 25 in 1894.

Discharges, none in 1893 and 3 in 1894.

Summing up.

The total number of Criminal Civil and Stipendiary cases amounted to 151 in 1893 and to 107 in 1894.

GAOL.

26 persons were committed to gaol in 1893 and 25 in 1894.

The prisoners extra rations cost Rs. 22.07 in 1893 and Rs. 24.88 in 1894.

Rice and salt for prisoners were sent from Mauritius.

The Chief Officer of Police is the keeper of the gaol and constables act as prison guards.

POLICE FORCE AND RANGERS.

The expenses for these branches amounted to Rs. 5,162.01 in 1894 against Rs. 4,598.13 in 1893. (Salaries allowances, and extra salaries included).

A sum of Rs. 50.00 was paid to Sub-Inspector Bettand for his silver medal. (Police Reward Fund).

The Police uniforms, clothing and boots were sent from Mauritius.

MEDICAL BRANCH.

The number of patients treated in the public hospital in 1893 was 47 and 117 in 1894.

2,318 persons received medical care at the Dispensaries in 1893 and 2,092 in 1894.

Three deaths occurred in the hospital in 1893 and 11 in 1894.

83 children were vaccinated in 1893 and 224 in 1894.

The receipts on account of in-patients amounted to Rs. 10.13 in 1893 and to Rs. 3 in 1894.

The total expenditure for the Medical Branch was Rs. 3,235.66 against Rs. 2,838.64 in the preceding year.

The rice given to the hospital servant to complete his rations (i.e. 547½ lbs) is sent from Mauritius.

POST OFFICE.

The revenue collected in 1894 for Postage and Commission on Money Orders was Rs. 195.16 against Rs. 219.12 in 1893.

There were 1 190 letters received from Mauritius and 76 foreign letters, 785 newspapers.

In 1893 there were 851 letters received from Mauritius, 54 foreign letters, 521 newspapers.

The letters despatched for Mauritius amounted to 1,385 in 1894 against 1,388 in 1893—for foreign places to 39 in 1894 and to 63 in 1893.

The Money Orders drawn on Mauritius amounted to Rs. 19,102.79 in 1893 and to Rs. 17,205.95 in 1894.

Orders drawn on Rodrigues were paid to the value of Rs. 4,350.62 against Rs. 1,795.27 in the preceding year.

STAMP PAPERS, LICENSES AND INTERNAL REVENUE STAMPS.

The sale of stamped papers and Receipt stamps produced Rs. 233.96 in 1893 and Rs. 177.22 in 1894.

The sale of Stamps for bills of lading, Trade licenses and Game licenses obtained Rs. 1,550.00 in 1893 and Rs. 1,615.00 in 1894.

ECCLESIASTICAL.

There are two Roman Catholic Churches at Rodrigues. The expenditure for the Roman Catholic Church was Rs. 1,999.92 against Rs. 1,999.92 in 1893.

The Catechist of the Church of England officiates at the Government School of Port Mathurin—he is paid by the London Missionary Society.

POOR LAW.

15 males and 4 females were provided for in 1893 and 15 males and 7 females in 1894.

Each pauper received 500 grams of rice per diem.

The suit of drill usually given to them at the end of the year will be delivered to them in 1895.

The rice and clothing are always sent from Mauritius.

Out of the relief rice sent to Rodrigues—two bags of rice were distributed to paupers in 1893 and 1 in 1894.

LEGISLATION.

Reg. No. 1 of 1893—Fixing a uniform scale of Pasturage fees at Rodrigues (to come in force on the 1st. May 1894).

Reg. No. 1 of 1894—Stamp duty on receipts.

Reg. No. 2 of 1894—Fishing regulations.

And lastly—Money Orders (Regulation relative to).

METEOROLOGICAL.

The Chief Officer of Police took daily observations which have been transmitted to the Director of the Royal Alfred Observatory, Mauritius.

			New Ther:	New Bar:
1o. Highest temperature (indoors)	6.5.94 -3 p.m.	...	87.00	30.168
2o. Lowest temperature (do.)	27.7.94 8.30 a.m.	...	70.00	30.270

3o. Heaviest rainfall in 24 hours from 9 a.m. 13th. to 9 a.m. 14th. January 1894.

4o. The month of January was the month in which there were the heaviest rainfalls, the raingauge marked 897 lines which is equivalent to a little short of 8 $\frac{87}{100}$ inches.

5o. A strong gale visited the Island on the 23rd. April 1894, lowest fall of the New Barometer 29.638 at 7.15 a.m. Old Barometer 29.680.

The Chief Officer of Police received, Rs. 182.50 in 1893 and a similar sum in 1894, for taking these observations.

FOREST AND CROWN LANDS.

617 (*a*) acres were leased in 1894 (In that number are included 1 acre paid in advance in 1893—4 acres leased at R. 1 per acre, and 2 acres leased at R. 0.25 for a saline.)

Revenue obtained Rs. 186.25 (*b*) for arrears of 1893 and Rs. 1,042.25 for 1894. Total Rs. 1,228.50

Nothing was paid for arrears of 1890 and 1891.

Outstanding on the 31st. December 1894, Rs. 35 for 1890 and 1891, Rs. 51 for 1893 and Rs. 182 for 1894.

(*a*) 1 acre was declared over and above the number of acres leased. Refunded Rs. 2. Voucher No. 51 of 18.5.94.
(*b*) Rs. 2 paid by error and refunded voucher No. 61 of 3.12.94.

Forty two fishing posts were leased in 1894 and 28 in 1893. They fetched Rs. 190 out of which Rs. 25 are for arrears of 1893.

Outstanding Rs. 5 for 1891, Rs. 5 for 1892 and Rs. 45 for 1894.

The Islands were leased for Rs. 51.62 in 1894 against Rs. 30.99 in 1893.

Nine town lots were leased at Rs. 5 in 1894 against 5 in 1893, and two at Rs. 10 each in 1893 and 1894.

Rs. 45 were paid for 1894 and Rs. 10 for arrears of 1893 leaving outstanding Rs. 20 for 1894.

Nothing has been paid on the arrears of 1891 and 1892.

Outstanding Rs. 5 for 1891 and Rs. 5 for 1892.

The number of Government lessees in 1894 was 316 against 345 in 1893.

The Revenue actually received under the heading of Land Rent amounted to Rs. 1,525.12 in 1894 against Rs. 1,078.99 in 1893. (Fishing posts, town lots, islands and other land leases are included therein.)

Pasturage—

The pasturage dues for 1894 brought a total sum of Rs. 662.26 against Rs. 458.15 in 1893.

In the above sum of Rs. 662.26 there are Rs. 148.45 for arrears of 1893, and a further sum of Rs. 214.01 paid by Mr. Martin at Rodrigues on a total sum of Rs. 1,090 due by him for pasturage fees of 1893.

(The difference has been paid by him in Mauritius).

Outstanding on the 31st. December 1894—Rs.1.80 for 1892, Rs. 111.10 for 1893 and Rs. 93 for 1894 (without including the sums due by Mr. Martin who has declared 2,000 bullocks and 100 goats. Nothing has been paid for his pasturage dues of 1894).

Forest Produce—

The amount derived from forest produce amounted to Rs. 377.26 in 1894 against Rs. 180.63 in 1893.

Land Sales—

In 1893 five acres of Crown Land were sold for Rs, 58.75—costs Rs. 13.87.

In 1894 town lot No. 31 was sold for Rs. 245 a fourth of which i.e. Rs. 61.25 has been paid cash and the costs to the amount of Rs. 13.87.

The costs paid in 1893 and 1894 have been forwarded to the Hon. Surveyor General.

BUILDINGS AND BOATS.

A sum of Rs. 584.31 was expended in 1894 for maintenance of buildings against Rs. 624.50 in 1893 (boards paint, glass, bolts, &c. were sent from Mauritius.)

A sum of Rs. 1,088.33 was spent in 1894 for New Buildings. (This item under a special vote) *Boats*, Rs. 50.45 were spent for repairs to boats against Rs. 162.50 in 1893.

RICE ACCOUNT.

In 1889 six hundred bags of rice were sent to Rodrigues and the price fixed for the sale thereof, was Rs. 6,073.10 (charges included).

Amount paid up to the 31.12.93	Rs. 4,656.64
Amount paid in the year 1894	265.85
Probably unrecoverable	498.93
Carried to paupers account	5.59
	Rs. 5,427.01
Sum recoverable and outstanding	646.09
Total	Rs. 6,073.10

In 1891 six hundred bags of rice were offered for sale for Rs. 5,958.92.

Amount paid up to the 31.12.93	Rs. 3,599.63
Amount paid in the year 1894	513.08
26 bags and 78 lbs. damaged...	239.72
Carried to paupers' account	135.00
9 lbs. missing	0.90
Probably unrecoverable	167.00
	Rs. 4,655.33
Sum outstanding and recoverable	1,303.59
Total	Rs. 5,958.92

Nothing is due on the rice sent to Rodrigues in December 1891 and December 1892.

Six hundred bags of rice were sent here in December 1893 and sold in 1894 for Rs. 7,350 (charges included).

Amount paid up to the 31.12.94	Rs. 2,972.68
2 bags rotten and thrown away	24.50
1 bag distributed to paupers	12.25
Probably unrecoverable	43.00
	Rs. 3,052.43
Outstanding and likely to be recovered	4,297.57
Total	Rs. 7,350.00

SUMMING UP OF THE RICE DEBT.

The amount still due for Rice amounts to Rs. 6,956.18.

Rs. 708.93 probably unrecoverable.

6,247.25 likely to be recovered.

Total ... Rs. 6,956.18

GENERAL REMARKS.

The crop of 1894 has been very poor, owing to the gale of the 23rd. April last.

Tobacco plantations are increasing considerably. If the "*Touareg*" had not been wrecked, the exportation of tobacco would have amounted to about 20,331½ kilos.

By the wreck of the subventioned ship a loss of about Rs. 35,000 is incurred by the population.

A water Reservoir has been constructed and if pipes are sent in time, the population of Port Mathurin will have pure water by the end of 1895.

A road leading to St. Gabriel has been begun, as well as a jetty to facilitate the discharging of cargo.

The Government Surveyor has surveyed numerous lots of Crown Lands, many of which will be sold in the course of the year 1895.

Several buildings have been repaired.

B. H. COLIN,

Magistrate of Rodrigues.

15th. January 1895.

Scientific and local names.	Remarks.
Semeacarpus Anacardium—" Noix à marquer."	Small tree. Wood used as fuel.
Calophylum Inophyllum—"Tatamaka blanc" (Mauritius.)	A large tree. Wood tough curly grained, used in ship and house building, shafts or carts and in all things where strength and toughness are required, seeds yield a valuable oil, and the gum resine that issues from the trunk is the *tacamhaca* resine of commerce.
Bursera obtusifolia — " Colophane bâtard" (Mauritius.)	The wood of this small tree which is about 20 feet in height is mostly used for palissades and rafters in hut building, &c.
Eugenia mespiloides--"Bois de Néfle", (Mauritius.)	Middle sized tree, timber used for boards, planks, and flooring and boarding inside of houses, will not bear moisture.
Eugenia continifolia— " Bois clou ' (Mauritius.)	A tree which frequently attains large dimensions, timber used for boards, planks and flooring, and boarding inside of houses; will not bear moisture.
Eugenia jambosa—" Jamrosa" (Mauritius.)	Wood strong, elastic, tough, much resembles that of the Ash in color and grain, used for handles of tools, &c., and is reputed for the excellent charcoal which it makes. Tree small or large bush.
Mimusops Erythroxyen--" Makak" (Mauritius.)	A large growing tree. The wood excellent, hard, durable, which is smooth, dark in colour and takes an excellent polish. and is much used in shingles, frames of houses, boards for flooring, ship building, cabinet works, &c.
Antirrhœa verticillata--" Bois Lousteau" (Mauritius.)	Small sized tree. Wood used as palissades, and small timber in house and hut building.
Canarium colophania—" Bois Colaphane (Mauritius.)	Large growing tree, often attaining a diameter of 6 feet. Pirogues, canoes are frequently hollowed out of its trunk.
Cinnamomum zeylanicum — " Cinnamon" (Ceylon, India, and the East; grown in Mauritius.)	Small tree. Timber not much used, yellow and close grained. The roots yield an excellent yellow dye.
Lagerstrœmia Reginæ — " Goyavier fleur marbre (Ceylon, Burmah and grown in Mauritius.)	This tree is very ornamental. The timber is tough and very durable under water, it is much used by the natives for building purposes and in boat making, and in the manufacture of gun carriages, in felloes and cart naves, framing of boards and of waggon binders, and platform carts and ammunition box boards. It is prized for the fitting of boats, hull of canoes, house posts, planking, beams, carts and various other purposes.
Mespilodaphe Neissi D. C.—" Bois Canelle" (Mauritius.)	This is a middling sized tree. Wood excellent, smooth and even-grained, dark coloured, finely veined, polishes well, and much prized by cabinet makers.
Noronbia Broomeana—"Bois sandal" (Mauritius.)	A large tree. Timber excellent and highly prized by turners, house carpenters and wheelwrights: takes a fine polish, odoriferous, resembling sandalwood.
Weinmannia tinctoria—"Bois lalloo" (Mauritius.)	Small tree or large bush. Timber only used as firewood and sometimes as palissades.
Pterocarpus indicus—"Sang dragon" India, &c., grown in Mauritius.)	Large tree, very handsome. It yields a valuable red coloured beautiful timber used for gun carriages; cart wheels, furniture and musical instruments.
Inga dulcis— " Cassis de Manille" (Java, Singapore, &c., grown in Mauritius.)	Hardly middle sized timber. Timber hard, knotty and coarse grained brown, good but not much used.
Tetranthera laurifolia — " Bois d'oiseau" (India, grown in Mauritius.)	Tree middle size, naturalized in Mauritius. Wood soft and not durable.
Tecoma pentaphylla — " Tecoma" (West Indies, grown in Mauritius.)	Rapid growing middle size shade tree. Wood soft white and not much used.

Scientific and local names.	Remarks.
Ficus mauritiana—"Figuier" (Mauritius).	The wood of this fig tree is only used as firewood in the colony, sometimes its trunk is hollowed out for canoes in Seychelles Islands.
Diospyros ebenum—"Bois d'ébène" (Mauritius).	This tree yields the best kind of ebony. Generally gets black but sometimes streaked with yellow or brown, it is very heavy, close and even grained, stands a high polish; it is used for inlaying and ornamental turnery and sometimes for furniture.
Foetida mauritiana—"Bois Puant" (Mauritius).	A large size but slow growing tree. Timber excellent, very durable and used for all purposes in house and ship building, &c., now very scarce.
Labourdonnaisia calophylloides.—"Bois de nattes petites feuilles" (Mauritius).	In Mauritius, "Bois de Natte" is a common generic name for four varieties of Labourdonnaisia and three species of Mimusops. They all yield excellent, hard, durable timber which is smooth, dark in colour and takes an excellent polish, and is much used for shingles, frames of houses, board for flooring, ship building, cabinet works, &c. Bark used in tanning and dying, and seeds make excellent bird lime.
Erythrospermum verticillatum.—"Bois gros coco" (Mauritius).	Big bush or small tree. Wood good, useful for palissades for huts, &c.
Tabernaemontana Mauritiana.—"Bois de lait à fleurs jaunâtres" (Mauritius).	Small tree. Timber used as rafters and palissades in common house and hut building.
Polyscias repanda—"Bois papaye" (Mauritius).	Small tree. Wood soft, not durable, used as palissades in constructing huts, &c.
Labourdonnaisia glauca.—"Bois de natte à grendes feuilles" (Mauritius).	(Vide Labourdonnaisia calophylloides.
Doratoxylon mauritianum—"Bois de sagaya" (Mauritius).	Small middle sized tree. Wood good and used in a great variety of purposes.
Mangifera indica—"Manguier" (India).	This is the well known Mangoo tree. The wood is coarse and often grained, not durable, and is soon attacked by insects. It is much in use for coffee case planks, &c. The natives use it for building purposes.
Nuxia verticillata—"Bois maigre" (Mauritius).	Middle sized tree. Timber occasionally used for palissades short grained, and decomposes readily; when young it makes excellent walking sticks which are much sought after.
Psiloxylon mauritianum—"Bois Bigaignon" (Mauritius).	Wood very hard and durable, and used for a great variety of domestic purposes. Tree small and middle sized.
Pongamia glabra — (Polynesian Islands).	Middle sized tree. Wood light and fibrous, coarse and even grained, light yellowish, brown colour not easily worked, nor giving a smooth surface, and is used for a variety of purposes. Solid wheels of the wooden carts are often made of it. An oil is extracted from the seeds, which is used by the natives for the lamp purposes.
Elacodendron orientale—"Bois d'olive" (Mauritius).	Large sized tree. Wood soft, used as flooring boards and planking inside houses, and as skirting under shingles, &c.
Artocarpus integrifolia—"Jacquier" (India).	Large growing tree. Quatity of timber excellent, yellow when newly cut, changing to brown with age. Highly prized for furniture, durable and resisting extremes of moisture and dryness well.
Heritiera littoralis—"Bois de table" Seychelles and India &c.)	Large tree, yields good timber which is much used in Seychelles and in house building.
Harounga madagascariensis—"Bois Haroungue" (Mauritius).	Small tree. Wood soft, only fit for firewood.
Terminalia Benzoin — "Benzoin" (Mauritius).	Large tree, now scarce in Mauritius. Wood good, used for a variety of purposes. Some parts of this tree were once much burnt in Mauritius as an incense.

Scientific and local names.	Remarks.
Geniostomo borbonicum—" Bois Piment " (Mauritius).	This wood of this big bush or small tree is used for palissades or rafters for huts and inferior kinds of houses. When grown in dense forests it is drawn up by surrounding trees, and has a trunk like a small tree; when grown on open ground, the branches spread out and form a bush.
Adenanthera pavonina—" Bois noir à graine rouge " (India)	Large tree. Timber when fresh cut much ressembles the red sanders and has a pleasant smell, is strong but not stiff, hard, durable, tolerably coarse and even grained; takes a good polish, is of beautiful red colour, streaks of darker shade but turns purple and ressembles rose wood.
Leea sambucina— " Bois de sureau " (Mauritius).	Small tree or big bush. Wood soft, not durable, used occasionally for want of better in inferior kinds of hut building and for firewood, charcoal, &c.
Dalbergia Sissoo—" Sissoo " (India).	Handsome tree of considerable size. Wood tolerably light and remarkably strong, and greyish brown colour with darker colored veins, and is used in ship building, gun carriages and mail carts and furniture. White ants seldom if ever attack it.
Erythroxylon laurifolium—" Bois de ronde " (Mauritius).	Small tree. Timber hard and durable, used for palissades, posts, and for making hurdles or trelisses to grow vanilla upon.
Imbricaria coriacea—"Pomme Jacot" (Madagascar).	Small tree. Timber strong, durable, planted generally in Mauritius as a forest tree.
Stadtmania sideroxylon — " Bois de fer " (Mauritius).	Middle sized growing tree. Timber hard and durable, used for square pieces in building, &c.
Erythroxylon hypericifolum—" Bois à balais " (Mauritius).	Small tree or large bush. Wood used generally as fuel.
Sideroxylon boutonianum — " Tambalacoque " (Mauritius).	Tree common, grows to a large size. Timber hard and strong, durable when felled during cold season; cross and curled grain, used generally for large beams and poles but occasionally for shingles and boards, verandah posts and frames of houses, &c.
Quivisia oppositifolia — " Bois café marron " (Mauritius).	Small tree or large bush. Timber generally small, elactic, durable, used for tool handles, &c.
Sideroxylon Bojerianum—"Manglier"	Sometimes attains large dimensions, but generally a small tree. Wood good and hard, and used for planks, boards and in house building.
Swietenia mahogany—" Bois d'acajou " (Mahogany — West Indies and Central America).	The Mahogany tree has been introduced into Mauritius where it thrives well and now bears seeds. It is being extensively planted. Timber is so well known as not to need description.
Psidium pomiferum — " Goyavier " (Tropical America).	Small tree or big bush. Wood hard generally used as fuel.
Ochrosia borbonica — " Bois jaune " (Mauritius and Seychelles).	Large bush or small tree. Common wood, soft, not much used, chiefly for palissades, rafters, &c., in hut and house building and for fuel.
Eugenia jambolana—" Jamlongue " (Asia).	Middle sized tree. Timber white, close grained, soft, good turning wood, used for boards inside of houses. Said to resist moisture well and used in India largely for well curbs, &c. Introduced into Mauritius but now growing spontaneously in many places of the colony.
Melia azaderach—" Lilas de l'Inde " (India, &c.)	This is a very ornamental tree. The wood of older trees is handsomely marked, rather durable and in use for furniture but is apt to warp and split. Planted largely and grows spontaneously.
Frenelia buxifolia—"Bois de Chauvesouris " (Mauritius).	Small tree, very variable in size and character of leaves and slow of growth, and wood of some of the varieties hard and durable that of others, from its smallness, worthless for constructing purposes.

Scientific and local names.	Remarks.
Schmidelia racemosa — "Bois Merle" (Mauritius).	Tree small, or slow growth. Wood good, hard and durable used for a variety of purposes.
Tetranthera monopetala—"Telfairia" —Yatti—(India).	Small tree. Wood when old used in a great variety of domestic purposes.
Erythrospermum mauritianum—'Bois manioc' (Mauritius).	Small tree when grown in dense forest. Large bush when growing in open ground. Wood generally used as fuel, Rafters in house and hut building, palissades, &c.
Terminalia catappa — "Badamier" (India).	A large ornamental tree. Wood light but tolerably durable and is used for various purposes, and the levers of Pakottahs are often made of it. The kernels of the nuts are eaten and are very palatable. The oil of the seeds is like almond oil, and the cake is used to feed pigs.
Imbricaria sps.	Middle sized tree planted. Timber good, used as that of all the Imbricarias is for a variety of purposes.
Pithecolobium saman—" Rain Tree" or Guanga — (Central America, West Indies, &c.)	Introduced and planted for shade, wood soft, and useless for construction, &c. Pod is an excellent fodder for cattle horses, &c.
Nephelum Longan — " Longanier " (India).	Large tree, naturalised in Mauritius, planted generally as a fruit tree. Timber not durable, little used.
Spondeas sps.	Large growing tree. Wood only used for charcoal and firewood.
Albizzia Lebbeck — " Bois noir " (Western India to Arabia).	An introduced but now naturalised tree, common in all the low and dry parts of Mauritius. Timber (heart wood) durable and hard, in great repute for making naves of wheels and charcoal.
Flacourtia ramontchi—" Prunier " ...	Large bush or small tree, planted as fences, &c., for its fruit. Wood used as fuel.
Diospyros melanda — " Bois d'ébène marbré ".	Tree middle sized. Timber generally used in square pieces for frames of houses. It will not bear exposure and is useless for boards as it invariably splits.
Casuarina equisitifolia — " Filao " (Madagascar, Polynesia, &c.)	Middle sized tree, generally planted throughout the colony; grows fast, wood tough, durable when well seasoned, used for a variety of purposes such as rafters, boarding.
Camphora officinarum—"Camphrier" (Eastern Asia, &c.)	Large tree, planted extensively in Mauritius. Timber used for planks, beams, poles, construction purposes.
Morinda citrifolia — " Bois jaune " (Asia, Polynesia, &c.)	Small tree. Timber not much used, yellow and close grained. The roots yield an excellent yellow dye.
Terminalia tomentosa—India ...	This is a most useful timber tree. Wood very hard, heavy and strong, much used in house building and for boats, canoes, solid wheels of carts, furniture, &c.
Averrohoa carambola—" Carambole" (India).	Small tree introduced. Planted generally for its fruit which is eaten raw and made into tarts, &c.
Hornea mauritiana—" Bois l'huile " (Mauritius).	......
Swietenia Senegalensis	......
Acacia algaroba—" Algarob " ...	......
Santalum album—" Sandalwood " ...	Quick growing tree. Heart wood used for carving, incense and perfume. It has been found to be well suited for engraving.
Bassis latifolia—" Illipe "	Large tree. Wood used for naves of wheels, for furniture, &c. The flowers are an important article of food. They are also distilled into a coarse spirit. From the kernel a greenish-yellow oil is obtained, used to adulterate ghee and soap making.
Michelia champaca—" Champee " ...	Middle sized tree. Wood very durable and used for furniture, house building, carriage work and native drums.
Sterculia balanghas—" Cavalum " ...	Wood very soft and light.
Guazima tomentosa—" Thainpuche "	Large tree. Light brown wood used in Southern India, for furniture and packing cases.

Scientific and local names.	Remarks.
Berrya Hammonilla	A large tree. Wood very durablo, used for carts, agricultural implements, spear handles, and in Madras for Massilia boats.
Chikrassia tabularis—"Chrikassi" ..	A large tree. The wood is used in furniture and for carving. The bark is a powerful astringent and the flowers give red or yellow dye.
Cedrela toona—"Toona"	A large tree. Growth rapid. The wood is very durable and is used for furniture of all kinds, also for door panels and carving. The flowers yield a red or yellow dye.
Cedrela odorata "Trinidad Cedar" ...	....
Dalbergia latifolia "Rosewood" ...	A large deciduous tree. It is a valuable furniture wood and exported in large quantities to Europe. It is also used for cart wheels, &c., and for furniture.
Prosopsis spiecgera	A moderate sized strong tree. Wood used for carts, agricultural implements, &c., is very valuable for fuel. The pods are used as fodder for cattle, goats, &c.
Afzolia bijuja—"Faux Gayac" ...	A moderate sized tree. Wood used for bridge and house building.
Brexia madagascariensis	....
Macadamia ternifolia	....
Grevillea robusta—"Cape oak" ..	A moderate sized tree. Wood used for cask staves.
Aleurites triloba—"Candle-nut tree"	....
Oldfieldia africana	....
Cryptomeria japonica—"Japan Cedar".	....
Pterocarpus marsipium "Gum kin"	A large deciduous tree. The wood is durable. It is much used for doors and window frames, furniture, &c., and also for sleepers. It yields from wounds in the bark a red gum resin called "kin" a valuable astringent much used in medecine
Pinus Sinensis	....
Pinus longifolia	A large tree, yields large quantities of resin and tar. The bark is used for tanning and as fuel for iron smelting. The wood is made into charcoal.
Pinus merkusii	....
Lagerstroemia parviflora	Large tree. Wood tough, elastic and fairly durable; used as sleepers, ploughs and other agricultural implements. The bark is used for tanning. Leaves used to feed tassar silkworms.
Cassia Flonda	A moderate sized tree. Wood used for mallets, walking sticks, &c,
Eucalyptus globulus—"Blue gum" ..	....

Fibre Yielding Plants growing in the Colony.

Botanical Names.	Common Names.
Areca sps.	Cabbage palm.
,, lutescens	
,, sapida	
,, catechu	Betel nut.
,, sps.	
Agave Augustifolia	Aloes à petites feuilles.
,, mexicana	
,, variegata	
Alpinia calcarata	
,, magnifica	
Artocarpus intergrifolia	Jack fruit.
,, incisa	Bread fruit.
Aloë sps.	Aloes.
,, macra	
,, sps.	
Aralia papyrifera	Rice paper plant.
,, pentaphylla	
Ananassa sativa	Pine apple.
,, species creole	
,, bracteata	
Acrocomia sps.	
,, sclerocarpa	
Argyrea nervosa	
,, sps.	Liane d'argent.
Amomum nemorosum	Zédoaire du pays.
,, cardamomum	Cardomome.
Arum macrorizhum	
,, violreeum	
Astrapea wallichii	
Arenga sps.	
,, sps.	
Aleurites triloba	Candle-nut tree.
Attalia macrocarpa	
Averrhoa carambola	
Andansonia digitata	Sour Gourd, Baobad.
Acanthophœnix crinita	
Alacis guinensis	Oil palm.
Azerderachta indica	Niem.
Bracteolaria racemosa	
Barringtonia asiatica	
Boehmeria nivea	China grass.
Butea superda	
,, frondesa	
Bixa orellana	Roucou
Bauhinia acuminata	
Bromelia sceptrum	
Bignonia unguis	
Bombax edulis	
,, species	
Cajanus sps.	Abrevade.
Cocos nucifera	Cocoa-nut.
,, flexuosa	
Caryota rumphiana	

Botanical Names.	Common Names.
Caryota urens	Caryota.
,, rumphiana	
Corypha elata	
Carludovica palmetto	
Curculigo seychellensis	
Chrysophyllum cainito	Star apple.
Cocculus palmetta	Colombo root-Colombo.
Clusir species	
Canna indica	Indian shot.
Costo elegans	
Calamus Roxbourgii	Rotin.
Dracaena refiera	Bois Chandelle.
,, concinna	
,, ferrea	
,, Brazilliensis	
Dombeya acutangula	Dombeya.
,, Natalensis	
,, ferruginea	
,, umbellata	
Dictyosperma aurea	
rubra	
Duriozebith inos	
Doryanthes palmerii	
Desmoncus elegans	
,, horridus	
Deckenia nobilis	
Demonorops melanochcites	
Entada foetida	
,, gigantea	La liane de la Baie du Cap Laocoon.
Euterpe oleracea	
Ficus mauritiana	
,, nymphiafolia	
,, lucida	
,, nitidus	
,, sps.	
,, dealbata	
,, sps.	
,, sps.	
,, sapotoides	
,, elastica	
,, sps.	
,, mangifolia	
,, rubra	
,, macrophylla	
,, stipulata	
,, carica	
,, religiosa	
,, lucida	
Flimingia strobilifera	
Fourcroya gigantea	Aloes vert.
,, cubensis	
Gossypium Babadense	
,, herbaceum	
Hibiscus sps.	Foulsapate-Hibiscus.

Botanical Names.	Common Names.
Hibiscus mutabilis	
,, esculentus	
,, sps. C. Africa	
,, sinensus	
,, species	
Hernandia ovigera	
Hyophorbe verschaffeltii	
,, amaricaulis	
Hyphaene schatan	Doom palm.
Heritiera littoralis	Bois de Table.
Heliconia sanguinea	
Hydrophyllum Lindlejii	
Ipomea sps	Ipomea.
,, tuberosa	Liane de Gondelour.
Inga haematoxlyon	
Kigelia piunata	
Latania Commersonii	Latanier.
,, Mauritiana	,,
,, Loddigesii	,,
Lodoicea Seychellarum	Coco de mer Seychelles.
Lagerstroemia indica	Goyavier fleur.
Licuala horrida	
Musa coccinea	Bananier fleurs.
,, chinensis	Bananier nain.
,, otahite	Tahiti.
,, vert	Verte.
,, matala	Banane Matelot.
,, nain	Nain.
,, textelis	Graines.
Maranta zebrina	Maranta.
,, sanguinea	
Malvaviscus arboreus	Gde. Mauve.
Macrozamia spiralis	
Morus alba	
Mucuna sps.	
Monocera lanceolata	
Murraya exotica	
Nerium Oleander	
Nephrospernia Van Haulteau	
Oreodoxa regia	Palmiste de Cayenne.
,, oleracea	
Pandanus microcarpus	Vacoa.
,, Seychellarum	
,, Maritimus	
,, palustris	
,, variegata	
,, utilis	
,, pyramidalis	
,, odoratissimas	
Phœnix dactylifera	Date palm.
,, rupicola	
,, sylvestris	Wild date.
Pongamia glabra	Pongam.

Botanical Names.	Common Names.
Pteraspermum accrifolium	
Phormium tenax	New Zealand Flax.
Phyllarthron Bojerianum	
Pancratium giganteum	
Plantago major	
Philodendron lacerum	
Pitcairnia Olfersii	
Rapolocarpus lucidus	
Rubus moluccanus	
Ravenola madagascariensis ...	Arbre du Voyageur.
Sterculia Balangas	
Strelitzia augusta	
,, regina	
Sagus ruffia from leaves... ...	Ruffia.
,, lœvis	
,, raffia from leafstalk ...	Ruffia.
Arenga saccharifera	Sugar palm.
Swietenia mahogany	Mahogany.
Sida glutinosa	
,, carpinifolia	
Sanserviera zeylanica	Bow string Hemp.
,, pungens	
,, cylindrica	
Sapindus longifolius	
Sabal Adansonii	
,, sps.	
,, umbraculifera	
Theobroma cacao	Chocolate nut tree.
Thunbergia grandiflora	
Thespesia populnea	Bois Marie.
Triumfeltia glandulosa	
Typha augustifolia	
Wrightia tomentosa	
Wikstromia virideflora	
Yucca variegata	
,, filamentosa	
,, gloriosa	
,, sps.	
Zinziber species	Ginger.

Tables of distances for the various districts of Mauritius.

District of Port Louis.

Table giving the distance by the road, to half a kilometer from the Supreme Court, Port Louis, to the Chief points in the Port Louis District.

No.	Description of Chief points.	Distance from Court House.		Remarks.
		Kilometers.	Miles.	
1	Western Cemetery—Gate	3	1¾	
2	Salines—Mr. Lemière's house	3	2	
3	Cassis Church—" St. Sacrement "	3	1¾	
4	Plaine Lauzun Railway workshop	3	1¾	
5	Grand River Suspension Bridge	4	2½	
6	Pointe au Sable—Martello Tower	5	3¼	
7	Brabant Street—Middle	2	1¼	
8	Pailles road Bridge	4½	2¾	
9	Tranquebar, Vallée du Ponce—Gausseran's property	2	1¼	
10	Chateau d'Eau—House	3	1¾	
11	Boulevard Victoria, Vallée Pitot where Magon Street joins	2	1¼	
12	Jardin Despeaux—Centre	2	1¼	
13	Lataniers Bridge, Pamplemousses Road ...	2½	1½	
14	Briqueterie, Abercrombie Police Station ...	3½	2¼	
15	Ste. Croix Church	3½	2¼	
16	Le Hochet property	4	2½	
17	Petit Bois	6½	4	
18	Namdarkhan's property...	6½	4	
19	Village Estate	6	3¾	
20	Caroline Estate—the old sugar house ...	7	4¼	
21	Montagne Jacot	7	4½	
22	Cocoterie Road Distillery	5½	3½	
23	Rochebois Railway Station	4	2½	
24	Fort George...	3½	2¼	
25	Mer Rouge—Bruniquel's property	3	2	
26	Bell Buoy	3½	2¼	

Distrist of Pamplemousses.

Table giving the distance by the road, to nearest half kilometer from the Pamplemousses Court House, to the Chief points in the Pamplemousses District.

No.	Description of Chief points.	Distance from Court House.		Remarks.
		Kilometers.	Miles.	
	Pamplemousses Court House from Port Louis...	11	7	
1	Alma Distillery	8	5	
2	Auchandrayen Sugar house	8	5	
3	Arsenal Police Station	9½	6	
4	Do. Sea shore Batterie Mortiers ...	10	6¼	
5	**Balaclava Distillery**	9½	6	

District of Pamplemousses.

No.	Description of Chief points.	Distance from Court House. kilo-meters.	Distance from Court House. Miles.	Remarks.
6	Belle Vue Harel Sugar house	6	3¾	
7	Belle Vue Sugar house	8	5	
8	Bon Air Sugar house	6½	4	
9	Bon Air (Arsenal)	6	3¾	
10	Beau Plan Sugar house	2	1¼	
11	Boulingrin part of L'Industrie	9½	6	
12	Bois Mangue Estate Centre	7	4¼	
13	Bois Rouge Estate limit of District	13	8	
14	Briqueterie Police Station	8	5	
15	California Sugar house	9½	6	
15 a	Canoniers Point	15	9¼	
16	Constance Sugar house	12	7½	
17	Calebasses Railway Station	2½	1½	
18	Crêve-Cœur	14½	9	
19	Fond du Sac Sugar house	9½	6	
20	Fair Fund Sugar house	5	3	
21	Grand'Garde L'Amitié Sugar house	5	3¼	
22	Hermitage Sugar house	12½	7¾	
23	Ilot (extreme limit)	6½	4	
24	Jouvance (Ville Bague)	6½	4	
25	La Louise (Mauricia) Sugar house	3	2	
26	La Paix at Piton Police Station	7	4½	
27	La Rosalie Sugar house	6½	4	
28	L'Espérance Sugar house	1½	1	
29	L'Espoir Sugar house	3	2	
30	Les Mariannes	14½	9	
31	Les Roches (St. André) Sugar house	5	3	
32	L'Etoile (Ruisseau des Citrons)	5	3	
33	L'Industrie Sugar house	12	7½	
34	L'Unité	6½	4	
35	Long Mountain Police Station	9½	6	
36	Do. (at Chapel)	6½	4	
37	Maison Blanche (Clémentine Sugar house)	2	1½	
38	Mont Choisy Sugar house	15	9¼	
39	Mont Piton Sugar house	5½	3⅛	
40	Mon Désir	3	2	
41	Mon Choix Sugar house	7	4½	
42	Mount Sugar house	3	1¾	
43	Mon Goût	2½	1½	
44	Mon Rocher Sugar house	1½	1	
45	Mapou Station	5½	3½	
46	Montagne Bonamour	8	5	
47	Nicolière Sugar house	13	18	
48	Nouvelle Découverte (la Coupée)	16	10	
49	Piton Police Station	7	4½	
50	Piton (Hanning's property)	9	5½	
51	Pic de la Vierge	13	8	
52	Pieter Both	13	8	
53	Plessis Sugar House	3	2	
54	Petite Rosalie Sugar house	5	3	
55	Petit Triolet	9½	6	
56	Powder Mills	3	2	
57	Plaine Papayes (extreme limit)	8	5	
58	Pointe aux Piments Grenadier's Battery	10½	6½	

District of Pamplemousses.—*Continued*

No.	Description of Chief points.	Distance from Court House.		Remarks.
		Kilometers.	Miles.	
59	Plaine St. Cloud	13	8	
60	Pont Praslin	13	8	
61	Rouge Terre (near Fond du Sac)	9½	6	
62	River Citrons	6½	4	
63	Riche Terre Railway Station	14	9	
64	Roche Bois (Sea Shore)	11	7	
65	Ruisseau Rose (Baillache's property	13	8	
66	Solitude Sugar House	7½	4¾	
67	Sottise	13½	8½	
68	Salazie	16	10	
69	Triolet Sugar house	11½	7¼	
70	Tombeau Police Station at Rochebois ...	11	7	
71	Tombeau Bay	8	5	
72	Tombeau Bridge	5½	3½	
73	Trou aux Biches Village Centre	14½	9	
74	Terre Rouge Police Station	5½	3½	
75	Villevalio	9½	6	
76	Walton	9½	6	
77	Villebague, Police Station & Chapel	9¼	6	
78	Windsor (Long Mountain)	7	4½	

District of Rivière du Rempart.

Table giving the distance by road, to nearest half kilometer from the Rivière du Rempart Court House, to the Chief points in the Rivière du Rempart District.

No.	Description of Chief points.	Distance from Court House.		Remarks.
		Kilometers.	Miles.	
	Poudre d'Or Court House from Port Louis ...	27	17	
1	L'Amitié Estate Sugar house	9	5¾	
2	Antoinette „ Sugar house	14½	9	
3	Belmont „	3	2	
4	Beau Séjour „ Sugar house	6½	4	
5	Bon Espoir „ „	8	5	
6	Belle Vue „ Maurel Sugar house... ...	11	7	
7	Do. „ Cugnet „	9½	6	
8	Belle Rive „	11	7	
9	Beau Manguier Estate	14½	9	
10	Cottage Estate	6½	4	
11	Cap Malheureux Village	16	10	
12	Camp Maçons do.	13	8	
13	Espérance Estate Sugar house	5	3	

DISTRICT OF RIVIÈRE DU REMPART.—*Continued.*

No.	Description of Chief points.	Distance from Court House. Kilometers.	Miles.	Remarks.
14	Eau Blanche Estate	3	2	
15	Forbach ,, ...	6½	4	
16	Figette ,, ...	5	3	
17	Goodlands ,, ...	6½	4	
18	Grand Gaube Village	9½	6	
19	Grand Baie Estate Sugar house	14½	9	
20	Grand Baie Village (extreme limit) ...	16	10	
21	Haute Rive Estate Sugar house	5	3	
22	Hermitage (Hamlet)	3	2	
23	Ile d'Ambre Estate Sugar house	2	1¼	
24	Labourdonnais Estate Sugar house... ...	8	5	
25	Mon Triomphe Estate	3	2	
26	Moulins Estate	6½	4	
27	Mapou ,, ...	6½	4	
28	Melville Estate Sugar house	5½	3½	
29	Mon Loisir Estate Rouillard and Harel ...	9½	6	
30	Do. Fadhuile, D. de Riquebourg & Co. Sugar house	9	5½	
31	Mont Mascal Estate	13	8	
32	Mare Sèche ,, ...	14½	9	
33	Mon Songe ,, Sugar house	14½	9	
34	Piton Police Station	6½	4	
35	Pointe Bourrique (Hamlet)	3	2	
36	Poudre d'Or Estate	2	1¼	
37	Pointe Lascars Village	5	3	
38	Plaine des Roches	8	5	
39	Railway Station Rivière du Rempart ...	7	4¼	
40	Ravin Estate	7	4¼	
41	Railway Station Mapou...	7	4¼	
42	Do. Poudre d'Or	3	2	
43	Réunion Estate	8	5	
44	Roche Noire Estate Sugar house	7	4½	
45	Ravensworth ,, ...	13	8	
46	St. Antoine Sugar house	5	3	
47	St. François Estate	9½	6	
48	Shœnfeld Estate Sugar house	5	3	
49	Union Estate	11	7	
50	L'Union Estate	13	8	
51	The Vale Estate Sugar house	13	8	
52	Von Moltke Distillery	6½	4	
53	Woodford Estate	13	8	

District of Flacq.

Table giving the distance by the road, to nearest half kilometer from Flacq Court House to the Chief points in the Flacq District.

No.	Description of Chief points.	Distance from Court House.		Remarks.
		Kilometers.	Miles.	
	Flacq District Court House from Port Louis ...	34	21	
1	Argy Sugar house	2	1¼	
2	Australia Sugar house	14½	9	
3	Beau Bois Sugar house	5½	3½	
4	Beau Rivage Sugar house	12	7½	
5	Beau Champ Sugar house	13	8	
6	Beau Vallon (Fabre) Sugar house	14	8¾	
7	Beau Vallon (Dubois) Sugar house... ...	21	13	
8	Bel Etang Sugar house	9½	6	
9	Belle Etoile Sugar house	7½	4¾	
10	Belle Mare Sugar house...	7	4½	
11	Belle Roche Sugar house	6	3¾	
12	Belle Rose Sugar house...	9	5¾	
13	Belle Vue (D'Arifat) Sugar house	1½	1	
14	Belle Vue (Allendy) Sugar house	4½	2¾	
15	Belle Rive Sugar house...	17	10½	
16	Bonne Mère Sugar house	3	2	
17	Bras d'Eau Sugar house...	7	4½	
18	Belle Source...	9½	6	
19	Bon Accueil Sugar house	9½	6	
20	Brisée Verdière	9½	6	
21	Bassin Bleu	6	3¾	
22	Bon Espoir Sugar house...	6	3¾	
23	Bois d'Oiseau (Petite Retraite)	6½	4	
24	Caroline Sugar house	9	5½	
25	Choisy Sugar house	5	3	
26	Clémencia Sugar house	10	6½	
27	Constance (d'Arifat) Sugar house	2	1¼	
28	Constance (Manès) Sugar house	2½	1½	
29	Camp de Masque Police Station	8½	5¼	
30	Do. (Mare Triton)	9½	6	
31	Deep River Sugar house	13	8¼	
32	Grand River South East Police Station ...	13½	8½	
33	Haut de Flacq Police Station	8	5	
34	L'Etoile Sugar house	21	13	
35	La Louise Sugar house	17	10½	
36	La Gaiété Sugar house	3	2	
37	La Mare	15	9½	
38	La Grande Retraite Sugar house	7½	4¾	
39	La Lucie Sugar house	10	6¼	
40	L'Unité Sugar house	7	4½	
41	L'Union Sugar house	5½	3½	
42	Mare Triton Sugar house	9½	6	
43	Mon Rêve Sugar house	6½	4	
44	Montagne Blanche	14	8¾	
45	Magenta	13	8¼	
46	Mon Ida	12	7½	
47	Montagne Rava	17	10½	
48	Mare aux Lubines	5	3	
49	Olivia Sugar house	17½	11	
50	Palma Sugar house	8	5	
51	Petite Retraite Sugar house	5½	3½	

DISTRICT OF FLACQ.—*Continued*

No.	Description of Chief points.	Distance from Court House.		Remarks.
		Kilometers.	Miles.	
52	Petit Victoria Sugar house	10½	6½	
53	Providence Sugar house	4	2½	
54	Pont Blanc	4	2½	
55	Pont Angibont	6½	4	
56	Pont Bon Dieu	10½	6½	
57	Post de Flacq Military Post	4½	2¾	
58	Pont Praslin...	13½	8½	
59	Quatre Sœurs Sugar house	15	9½	
60	Queen Victoria Sugar house	4½	2¾	
61	Riche Mare Sugar house	3	1¾	
62	Riche Fund Sugar house	7	4½	
63	Rivière Profonde	12	7½	
64	Rivière Sèche Police Station	8½	5¼	
65	Sébastopol Sugar house...	17½	11	
66	St. Julien Sugar house	12	7½	
67	Sans-Souci Sugar house...	17	10¾	
68	Trou d'Eau Douce Distillery	9½	6	
69	Trois Ilots Bois d'Oiseau	20	12½	
70	,, La Nourrice...	21	13	
71	,, Baie Manioc	20	12½	
72	,, Montagne Jacot	21½	13½	
73	,, Le Bouean	19	12	
74	Woodlands	12½	7¾	

DISTRICT OF GRAND PORT.

Table giving the distance by the road, to nearest half kilometer from the Grand Port Court House, to the chief points in the Grand Port District.

No.	Description of Chief points.	Distance from Court House.		Remarks.
		Kilometers.	Miles.	
	Mahebourg Court House from Port Louis ...	49½	31	
1	Astræa Estate Sugar house	9½	6	
2	Anse Jonchée Sugar house	13	8	
3	Beau Vallon (Rocheconste) Sugar house ...	2	1¼	
4	Bel Air Village Centre	3½	2¼	
5	Bon Espoir Estate	4	2½	
6	Beau Vallon Estate (Dauban)Sugar house ...	7	4¼	
7	Belle Vue ,, Sugar house	10½	6½	
8	Beau Fond ,, Sugar house	9	5½	
9	Bouchon Village (Centre)	12	7½	
10	Bonne Source Estate Sugar house	13	8	
11	Choisy, Bissy	4	2½	
12	Cluny Sugar house	14½	9	
13	Camp Lassime	20	12½	

DISTRICT OF GRAND PORT.—*Continued.*

No.	Description of Chief points.	Distance from Court House. Kilo-meters.	Miles.	Remarks.
14	Cent Gaulettes (Sénèque)	8	5	
15	,, Ste. Philomène Chapel ...	9	5½	
16	,, P. Magnien	10	6¼	
17	,, Estate (Montocchio & Co.) ...	11	7	
18	,, Buttié	11	7	
19	Deux Bras Estate Sugar house	12½	7¾	
20	Eau Bleue ,, Sugar house	12	7½	
21	Ferney Estate Sugar house	7	4¼	
22	Gros Bois Estate Sugar house	12	7½	
23	Grand Sable...	22½	14	
24	Joli Bois Village Centre...	14	8¾	
25	,, Estate Sugar house	15	9¼	
26	La Barraque Estate Sugar house	11½	7¼	
27	Le Chaland (Cloupet)	5½	3¼	
28	Les Bambous Sugar house	17	10½	
29	Les Mares Sugar house	8	5	
30	La Rosa Sugar house	11	7	
31	La Providence (Portal)	12	7½	
32	L'Escalier Village Centre	15	9¼	
33	La Forêt (Rouillard)	14	8¾	
34	Le Val Sugar house	11½	7¼	
35	Mon Repos (Cantin)	4	3¾	
36	Mon Désert Sugar house	8	5	
37	Mon Trésor	8	5	
38	Mare d'Albert (Molliere)	9½	6	
39	,, (Constantin)	11	7	
40	Mont Fertille (Sauzier)...	12½	7¾	
41	Mont Fernand (Paul Rochecouste)... ...	11	7	
42	Mare Chicose Village Centre	11½	7¼	
43	Mare d'Albert (Pelte)	14	8¾	
44	Mare d'Albert (Baramia)	13½	8¼	
45	Mare Tabac Village Centre	15	9¼	
46	New Grove Estate Sugar house	13½	8¼	
47	New Grove Road Village Centre	13½	8¼	
48	Nouvelle France (Pellegrin)	22½	14	
49	Oriole Village Centre	11½	7¼	
50	Old Grand Port Village Chapel	9½	6	
51	Plaisance Estate Sugar house	5	3	
52	Pointe Brocus (Coureau)	4	2½	
53	Plaine Magnien	6½	4	
54	Plein Bois (Robillard)	12	7½	
55	Petit Sable Sugar house	21	13	
56	Pont Colville	18½	11½	
57	Rivière Créole Estate Sugar house	3	1¾	
58	Riche-en-Eau Estate Sugar house	7	4¼	
59	Ruisseau Copeaux (Morel & Bardet) ...	5½	3½	
60	,, ,, (Amadis Thérèse) ..	6	3¾	
61	Rose Belle Estate Sugar house	14½	9	
62	Rivière Citrons (Barbeau)	22½	14	
63	Rivière La Chaux Estate Sugar house ...	3	1¾	
64	,, ,, Village Centre	5	3	
65	St. Antoine Village Centre	5	3	
66	St. Hélène Estate (Lalouette)	5	3	
67	Solitude Estate Sugar house	6	3¾	

DISTRICT OF GRAND PORT—*Continued.*

No.	Description of Chief points.	Distance from Court House.		Remarks.
		Kilometers.	Miles.	
68	St. Roch Estate Monneron	7½	4¾	
69	Sauve Terre Estate Sugar house	10	6¼	
70	Savinia Estate Sugar house...	12½	7¾	
71	Souffleur ,, Sugar house	13	8	
72	St. Hubert Estate Sugar house	10	6¼	
73	St. Flour Macquet	20	12½	
74	Trois Boutiques Village Centre	11	7	
75	Union Vale Estate Sugar house	9	5½	
76	Union Park ,, Sugar house	15½	9½	
77	Ville Neuve ,, (Casteries)	9	5½	
78	Virginia ,, Sugar house	11	7	

DISTRICT OF SAVANNE.

Table giving the distance by road, to nearest half kilometer from the Savanne Court House, to the Chief points in the Savanne District.

No.	Description of Chief points.	Distance from Court House.		Remarks.
		Kilometers.	Miles.	
	Souillac Court House from Port Louis ...	50	31½	
1	Baie du Cap (le grand Cap)...	20	12½	
2	Bain des Négresses	2	1¼	
3	Beau Bois Sugar house	11	7	
4	Beau Champ Sugar house	10½	6½	
5	Bel Air (Rouillard) Sugar house	5	3	
6	Bel Air (Hardouin) Sugar house	9½	6	
7	Bel Ombre Sugar house	14½	9	
8	Bel Vue (Micouin)...	6½	4	
9	Bénarès Sugar house	10½	6½	
10	Bois Chéri Sugar house	14½	9	
11	Bois Sec Shooting box	12½	8½	
12	Bon Accueil Estate	9	5½	
13	Bon Courage	20	12½	
14	Bassin Blanc	10	6¼	
15	Camp Diable Village Centre	11	7	
16	Camp Berthaud	13	8	
17	Chamouny Sugar house	8½	6¼	
18	Chemin Grenier Police Station	9½	6	
19	Choisy Sugar house	19	11¾	
20	Colmar Sugar house	12	7½	
21	Combo Sugar house	5	3	
22	Constance ,, ...	9½	6	
23	Fontenelle Sugar house	3	1¾	
24	Grand Bassin	15	9¼	

District of Savanne—*Continued*

No.	Description of Chief points.	Distance from Court House.		Remarks.
		Kilometers	Miles.	
25	Gros Bois (Chardonillet)	14½	9	
26	Gros Ruisseau	6½	4	
27	Jacotet	10	6½	
28	La Chaumière	6¼	4	
29	La Flora Sugar house	15½	9½	
30	La Prairie (Black River District)	24	15	
31	L'Abondance	22	13¾	
32	L'Hermitage	24	15	
33	Les Rouleaux	25	15½	
34	L'Union (Rouillard) Sugar house	8	5	
35	L'Union (Constantin do.	3	1¾	
36	Luchon (ex La Forêt) do.	12	7½	
37	Maisonnette	5½	3½	
38	Mexico	19	11¾	
39	Mont Blanc	11	7	
40	Petit Bien (Chamonny	9	5½	
41	Pont Colville	26	16	
42	Petit Cap	18½	11½	
43	Riche Bois	12	7½	
44	Rivière des Anguilles (Village Centre ...	6½	4	
45	Rivière des Galets do.	8½	5¼	
46	Rivière Dragon	10½	6½	
47	Rivière du Poste Railway Station	14½	9	
48	Riambel	3½	2¼	
49	Rochester	3	1¾	
50	Ruisseau Créole	15½	9½	
51	Ruisseau Michel	1½	1	
52	Savannah Sugar house	14	8¾	
53	Surinam	1½	1	
54	St. Amand Bridge	11½	7¼	
55	St. Aubin Sugar house	4½	2¾	
56	St. Avold do.	12½	7¾	
57	St. Félix do.	7½	4¾	
58	St. Joseph (ex-Frederica) Sugar house ...	13	8	
59	St. Martin...	16	10	
60	Ste. Marie Sugar house	10	6¼	
61	Terracine...	1½	1	
62	Terrain Dada	3	1¾	
63	Trois Cascades	11	7	

DISTRICT OF BLACK RIVER.

Table giving the distance by the road, to nearest half kilometer from the Black River Court House, to the Chief points in the Black River District.

No.	Description of Chief points.	Distance from Court House.		Remarks.
		Kilo-meters.	Miles.	
	Bambous District Court from Port Louis ...	16	10	
1	Albion Sugar house (by road near Petite Rivière Police Station)	13	8	
2	Barachois (Gautier's)	9½	6	
3	Bon Asile	11	7	
4	Belle Vue (Keisler)	25½	15¾	
5	Belle Vue (Albion)	11	7	
6	Belle Vue (Bellogaet) Sugar house... ...	4½	2¾	
7	Belle Vue (Nayl)	8½	5¼	
8	Beaux Songes Sugar house	5½	3½	
9	Baie du Cap...	36	22½	
10	Brigault (near Beaux Songes)	7	4¼	
11	Chamarel Sugar house	28½	17½	
12	Case Noyal Police Station	23	14¼	
13	Camp Benoit (Grand River)	11	7	
14	Camp des Embrevades do.	10	6¼	
15	Casse Cavelle Village Centre	6½	4	
16	Chaumière (La) do.	5	3	
17	Clarens (on Main Road) Village	5½	3½	
18	Cantine (La) Aloes fibre manufactory ...	5	3	
19	Cressonville	7½	4¾	
20	Gros Cailloux Sugar house	6½	4	
21	Flic-en-Flacq Village Centre	11½	7½	
22	Les Gorges (shooting box)	21	13	
23	Les Salines	19	11¾	
24	Le Bosquet Sugar house	8	5	
25	Medine Sugar house	3	1¾	
26	Morne Village Centre	32	20	
27	Mon Désir	6½	4	
28	Moka (Chamarel)	35	21¾	
29	Mon Vallon	6½	4	
30	Nermont (Ferme Expérimentale)	9½	6	
31	Pierrefond Sugar house...	8	5	
32	Palmyre Aloes fibre manufactory	5	3	
33	Petit Verger...	10	6¼	
34	Petite Rivière	9½	6	
35	,, Railway Station	8½	5¼	
36	,, Police Station	8½	5¼	
37	,, Church	9½	6	
38	Pointe au Sable	15	9¼	
39	Petite Rivière Noire Sugar house	21	13	
40	Rivière Noire Sugar house	18	11¼	
41	Raffin	27	16¾	
42	Richelieu Sugar house	10	6¼	
43	St. Patrice (at stream)	32½	20¼	
44	St. George Est. (by Pce. Sn. & Albion Sug. house)	9½	6	
45	Tamarin Sugar house	8	5	
46	,, Bay Village Centre	11	7	
47	Wolmar Sugar house	8½	5¼	
48	Walhalla Sugar house	11½	7¼	
49	Yemen Sugar house	11½	7¼	

District of Plaines Wilhems.

Table giving the distance by the road, to nearest half kilometer from the Plaines Wilhems Court House, to the Chief points in the Plaines Wilhems District.

No.	Description of Chief points.	Distance from Court House. Kilometers.	Distance from Court House. Miles.	Remarks.
	Rose Hill Court House from Port Louis ...	12	7½	
1	Allée Brillant Centre	8½	5¼	
2	Bagatelle Estate Sugar house	6	3¾	
3	Bananes	23	14¼	
4	Bassin Estate Sugar house	8	5	
5	Beau Bassin Village Centre	3	1¾	
6	Camp Créole Centre	4½	2¾	
7	„ Fouquereau	10	6¼	
8	„ Franky „	12	7½	
9	„ Malgache „	12	7½	
10	„ Mapou „	11½	7¼	
11	„ Margoze „	11	7	
12	„ Roche „	11	7	
13	Cancaval	13½	8¼	
14	Chébel Estate Main dwelling house	7	4¼	
15	Clairfond Estate Sugar house	5½	3½	
16	Eau Coulée	9	5½	
17	Ebène Estate	2½	1½	
18	Eighteenth Mile Mark	17	10½	
19	Henrietta Estate Sugar house	12	7½	
20	Highlands „ „	6	3¾	
21	La Caverne Village Centre	8	5	
22	La Caférie—Gillibert	14½	9	
23	La Louise Estate Sugar house	4	2½	
24	La Marie	12½	7¾	
25	Mesnil Centre	8	5	
26	Midlands Estate Sugar house	23	14¼	
27	Military Camp Curepipe	15	9¼	
28	Mill Vale Estate Sugar house	14	8¼	
29	Palma „ „	8	5	
30	Phœnix „ „	4	2½	
31	Plaisance (D'Unionville)	3	1¾	
32	Plaine Sophie	18½	11½	
33	Railway Station Coromandel	7	4¼	
34	„ Beau Bassin	2½	1½	
35	„ Quatre Bornes	3	1¾	
36	„ Phœnix	5	3	
37	„ Vacoa	8	5	
38	„ Curepipe Road	10	6¼	
39	„ Curepipe	11	7	
40	„ Forest Side	13	8	
41	Rivière Sèche	12	7½	
42	Réunion Estate Sugar house...	10	6¼	
43	Stanley „ „	2	1¼	
44	Solférino „ „	7	4½	
45	Tamarin Falls Estate Sugar house	14½	9	
46	Trianon „ „	2½	1½	
47	Terrain Perier	20½	12¾	
48	„ Laing & Wilson	22	13¾	
49	Vacoa Village Centre	10	6¼	
50	Curepipe Court House from Port Louis ...	21½	13½	

District of Moka.

Table giving the distance by the road, to half a kilometer from the Moka Court House to the Chief points in the Moka District.

No.	Description of Chief points.	Distance from Court House.		Remarks.
		Kilo-meters.	Miles.	
	Moka District Court from Port Louis... ...	10½	6½	
1	Pailles extreme limit of District on main road...	7	4½	
2	Guibi (Anse Courtois)	10	6¼	
3	Hermitage Sugar house	10	6¼	
4	Quartier Militaire Village Police Station ...	11	6¾	
5	Union Estate Sugar house	17½	11	
6	Nouvelle Découverte Pont Bondieu	18	11¼	
7	Rivière Dubois Mr. Fenouillot's house ...	23	14½	
8	Petit Verger Village Centre...	4½	2¾	
9	Mon Désert Sugar house	3½	2¼	

The Royal Alfred Observatory.

The Observatory is about 3 miles from the west coast and stands on a plain which is 179 feet above the sea-level. From W.S.W., through West to North, there is an interrupted view of the sea; and from North through East, to S. E., the ground generally slopes from the Piton, the summit of which bears about four miles E. b. S. and is 917 feet above the sea-level. Between S.E. and S.W., there is a chain of mountains, the highest peak of which, the Pieterboth, bears nearly six miles due South, and has an altitude of 2874 feet above the sea. The nearest extremities of two spurs, which run N. and N.W. from the Pieterboth, are at distances of three to four miles, and have an elevation of about 560 feet.

The island is of volcanic origin, and the rocks are more or less magnetic. Around the Observatory the soil has a dept of 3 to 14 feet, below which is solid basalt.

The standard barometer (Newman, No. 128) has no error, and the cistern is 180.86 feet above the sea-level.

All the thermometers have been verified at the Kew Observatory. They have been frequently compared with the Observatory Standards and, when necessary, corrections have been applied for their respective errors.

Continuous records of the temperature and pressure of the air and of the temperature of Evaporation (wet bulb thermometer) are obtained by photography.

The amount of bright sunshine is recorded by an improved "Campbell Sunshine Recorder" placed on the roof of the Observatory 42½ feet above the ground.

The direction and velocity of the wind are recorded by self-registering Kew anemometer by Casella, the caps of which are 51.2 feet above the surface of the ground.

The rim of Beckley's self recording rain gauge is 11.283 inches in diameter and 23 inches above the surface of the ground.

The rim of Glaisher's raingauge is 8 in. in diameter and 10 in. above the surface of the ground. The rainfall is measured at 9 h., and the amount is set down to the day on which it is measured.

During the year four eye-observations of the principal elements have been taken daily, viz :—at 6, 9, 13, 15 hours, the day commencing at midnight and the hours being counted from 0 to 23.

Daily readings have been taken of Solar and Terrestrial radiation thermometers and of thermometers the bulbs of which are 5 feet 2 inches and 10 feet below the surface of the ground.

The minimum thermometers have been read daily at 9 and the maximum at 15 hours.

Self registering thermometers by Negretti and Zambra are exposed in a Stevenson screen on the lawn, the thermometers being four feet from the ground. Readings have also been taken of dry and wet bulb thermometers by Negretti and Zambra exposed in ordinary hygrometric screens on the lawn, the thermometers being 4½ feet from the ground.

Care of Boilers.

Compiled from Rules issued by various Boiler Companies.

1.—Safety Valves.

See these are ample in size, and in working order. *Overloading or neglect* may lead to disastrous results. Examine every day to see that they act freely.

2.—Pressure Gauge.

Should be at zero when pressure is off, and should shew same pressure as the safety valve when that is blowing off. If not, then gauge should be tested by one known to be correct.

3.—Water Level.

See that water is at proper height. Do not rely on gauge glasses, flots or water alarms, but try the cocks. If they do not agree with water gauge, learn cause, and correct it.

4.—Gauge Cocks and Water Gauges.

Keep clean. Blow off water gauge frequently ; glasses and passages to gauge should be kept clean. There are more accidents attributable to inattention to water gauges than all other causes, put together.

5.—Feed Pump or Injector.

Keep in perfect order ; no pump is continuously reliable without regular and careful attention, Safe to have two means of feeding boiler. Check valves, self acting feed valves examine and clean frequently. See frequently that the valve is acting when feed pump is at work.

6.—Low Water.

Immediately cover fire with ashes (wet if possible) or earth. Draw fires as soon as can be done without increasing heat. Neither turn on the feed, start, or stop the engine, or lift safety valve *until* fires are out, and the boiler cooled down.

7.—Blisters and Cracks.

When first indication appears, there must be no delay in having boiler examined.

8.—Fusible Plugs.

Must be examined when boiler is cleaned, carefully scraped clean on both water and fire sides or they are liable not to act.

9.—Firing.

Fire evenly and regularly, little at a time. Moderately thick fires are most economical ; this firing must be used when draught is poor. Do not " clean " fires oftener than necessary.

10.—Cleaning.

All heating surfaces must be kept clean outside and in or there will be waste of fuel. Hand holes should be frequently removed and surfaces examined.

11.—Hot feed water.

Cold water should never he fed into any boiler if it can be avoided. When necessary mix it with the heated water before coming in contact with any portion of boiler.

12.--Foaming.

Check outflow of stream. If cause by dirty water blowing down and pumping up will generally cure it. In cases of violent foaming, check draught and cover the fire.

13.—Air Leaks.

All these to boilers or flues, except through the fire, should be carefully stopped.

14.—Blowing off.

If water be muddy or salt, blow off a portion frequently ; empty boiler every week or two and refill. When surface blow cocks are used, often open for a few minutes. Make sure no water is escaping from blow off cocks where it is supposed to be closed. Examine cocks whenever the boiler is cleaned. Never empty the boiler when brickwork is not.

15—Leaks.

When discovered repair at once.

16.—Rapid Firing.

In boilers with thick plates or seams exposed to the fire, steam should be raised slowly, rapid and intense firing avoided.

17.—Standing unused.

Empty and dry thoroughly, or fill quite full of water and put in quantity of common washing soda.

18.—General Cleanliness.

Everything about boiler should be kept thoroughly clean and in good order.

A Table to find the number of Days, from any Day of any one month to the same Day of any other month.

From	Jan.	Feb.	March	April	May	June	July	Aug.	Sept.	Oct.	Nov.	Dec.
To January	**365**	334	306	275	245	214	184	153	122	92	61	31
February	31	**365**	337	306	276	245	215	184	153	123	92	62
March	59	28	**365**	334	304	273	243	212	181	151	120	90
April	90	59	31	**365**	335	304	274	243	212	182	151	121
May	120	89	61	30	**365**	334	304	273	242	212	181	151
June	151	120	92	61	31	**365**	335	304	273	243	212	182
July	181	150	122	91	61	30	**365**	334	308	273	242	212
August	212	181	153	122	92	61	31	**365**	334	304	273	243
September	243	212	184	153	123	92	62	31	**365**	335	304	274
October	273	242	214	181	153	122	92	61	30	**365**	334	304
November	304	273	245	214	184	153	123	92	61	31	**365**	335
December	334	308	275	244	214	183	153	122	91	61	30	**365**

EXAMPLE.—What is the number of days from 10th. October to 10th. July ?

Look in the upper line for October, let your eye descend down that column till you come opposite to July, and you will find 273 days, the exact number of days required.

Again, required the number of days from 16th. February to 14th. August ?
Under February and opposite to August is ... ... 181 days
From which subtract the difference between 14 and 16 ... 2 days

The exact number of days required is ... ... 179 days

N.B.—In Leap Year, if the last day of February comes between, add one day to the number in the Table.

Commercial Commission as revised by the Chamber of Commerce of Mauritius, September 1868.

Art. 1.—On sales of Goods imported of all descriptions, on the net amount, if sold by auction, and on the gross amount of all other sales	... ...	5 per cent.
Art. 2.—On sales on Colonial Sugar and other Colonial Produce	...	2½ ,,
Art. 3.—Purchase of Goods :		
On purchase effected when the Agent is in funds	...	2½ ,,
On purchase of do. when funds are provided by the Agent		5 ,,
Art. 4.—On the sale of Specie of Encashment of Bills of Exchange		1 ,,
Art. 5.—On remittances of proceeds of the sale of Goods, Specie, Bills of Exchange, &c.	... ...	1 ,,
Art. 6.—On Goods consigned and afterwards withdrawn, on Invoice value	... ...	2½ ,,
Art. 7.—On Goods landed on account of damage incurred by the vessel and reshipment of the same :—		
When the value does not exceed Rs. 20,000...	...	2½
Exceeding Rs. 20,000 and not exceeding Rs. 50,000	...	Not less than Rs. 500 or 2 per cent. (At the option of the Consignee.)
,, 50,000 ,, ,, 100,000	...	Not less than Rs. 1,000 or 1½ per cent. (At the option of the Consignee.)
,, 100,000 ,, ,, 200,000	...	Not less than Rs. 1,500 or 1 per cent. (At the option of the Consignee.)
,, 200,000...	... ...	Not less than Rs. 2,000 or ¾ per cent. (At the option of the Consignee.)

(The Chamber of Commerce consider this sliding scale not as a commission, but as a means of fixing a fair remuneration for the risk and trouble incurred).

Art. 8.—On Freight of Passage Money	... ...	5 per cent.
Art. 9.—For collecting Freight or Passage Money	... ...	2½ ,,
Art. 10.—On Ships disbursements, when the Agent is in funds	...	2½ ,,
Art. 11.—On Ships disbursements, when the Consignee furnishes the funds...	... ...	5 ,,
Art. 12.—On disbursements for vessels under repairs...	...	5 ,,
Art. 13.—On letters of credit and advances of funds from which no other Commission is derived	... ...	2½ ,,
Art. 14.—On affecting Marine Insurances, on the amount insured.		½ ,,
Art. 15.—On sales or purchase of houses, or other immoveable property under Power of Attorney	... ...	5 ,,
Art. 16.—On sales or purchase of vessels, whether abandoned or whether purchased or sold under power of Attorney	...	5 ,,
Art. 17.—For recovery of rent...	... ...	5 ,,
Art. 18.—On affairs in dispute...	... ...	5 ,,
Art. 19.—On affairs before the Courts and attended with legal proceedings, according to the delay and trouble, but not less than 5 per cent, on the amount received.		
Art. 20.—On affairs in dispute and withdrawn before being brought to a settlement, upon the actual value of the claim	...	2½ ,,
Art. 21.—On protested Bills returned for recovery on the amount recovered...	... ...	2½ ,,
Art. 22.—On funds employed at interest for parties absent, on the amount of interest received	... ...	10 ,,
Art. 23.—On guarantee of sales (del credere) where the term does not exceed six months.	... ...	2½ ,,
and half per cent additional on each month beyond 6 months.		
Art. 24.—Indorsement of Bills of Exchange or Local Bills	...	2½ ,,
Art. 25.—For the delivery of Goods from a cargo when the freight has been paid before-hand	... ...	2s. per ton.

N.B.—Brokerage and Action dues are a reparate charge.

Value of the rupee.

Indian Quotation.	Equivalent Mauritius Quotation.		Indian Quotation.	Equivalent Mauritius Quotation.		Indian Quotation.	Equivalent Mauritius Quotation.	
s.d.	Rs.		s.d.	Rs.		s.d.	Rs.	
1.0	20	...	1.1$\frac{3}{8}$	17	94	1.2$\frac{3}{4}$	16	27
1.0$\frac{1}{32}$	19	94	1.1$\frac{13}{32}$	17	90	1.2$\frac{25}{32}$	16	24
1.0$\frac{1}{16}$	19	89	1.1$\frac{7}{16}$	17	86	1,2$\frac{13}{16}$	16	20
1.0$\frac{3}{32}$	19	84	1.1$\frac{15}{32}$	17	81	1.2$\frac{27}{32}$	16	17
1.0$\frac{1}{8}$	19	79	1.1$\frac{1}{2}$	17	77	1.2$\frac{7}{8}$	16	13
1.0$\frac{5}{32}$	19	74	1.1$\frac{17}{32}$	17	73	1.2$\frac{29}{32}$	16	10
1.0$\frac{3}{16}$	19	69	1.1$\frac{9}{16}$	17	69	1.2$\frac{15}{16}$	16	07
1.0$\frac{7}{32}$	19	64	1.1$\frac{19}{32}$	17	65	1.2$\frac{31}{32}$	16	03
1.0$\frac{1}{4}$	19	59	1.1$\frac{5}{8}$	17	60	1.3	16	...
1.0$\frac{9}{32}$	19	54	1.1$\frac{21}{32}$	17	57	1.3$\frac{1}{32}$	15	97
1.0$\frac{5}{16}$	19	49	1.1$\frac{11}{16}$	17	53	1.3$\frac{1}{16}$	15	93
1.0$\frac{11}{32}$	19	44	1.1$\frac{23}{32}$	17	49	1.3$\frac{3}{32}$	15	90
1.0$\frac{3}{8}$	19	39	1.1$\frac{3}{4}$	17	45	1.3$\frac{1}{8}$	15	87
1.0$\frac{13}{32}$	19	34	1.1$\frac{25}{32}$	17	40	1.3$\frac{5}{32}$	15	84
1.0$\frac{7}{16}$	19	29	1.1$\frac{13}{16}$	17	37	1.3$\frac{3}{16}$	15	80
1.0$\frac{15}{32}$	19	24	1.1$\frac{27}{32}$	17	33	1.3$\frac{7}{32}$	15	77
1.0$\frac{1}{2}$	19	20	1.1$\frac{7}{8}$	17	29	1.3$\frac{1}{4}$	15	74
1.0$\frac{17}{32}$	19	15	1.1$\frac{29}{32}$	17	25	1.3$\frac{9}{32}$	15	71
1.0$\frac{9}{16}$	19	10	1.1$\frac{15}{16}$	17	22	1.3$\frac{5}{16}$	15	67
1.0$\frac{19}{32}$	19	05	1.1$\frac{31}{32}$	17	18	1.3$\frac{11}{32}$	15	64
1.0$\frac{5}{8}$	19	01	1.2	17	14	1.3$\frac{3}{8}$	15	61
1.0$\frac{21}{32}$	18	96	1.2$\frac{1}{32}$	17	10	1.3$\frac{13}{32}$	15	58
1.0$\frac{11}{16}$	18	91	1.2$\frac{1}{16}$	17	07	1.3$\frac{7}{16}$	15	55
1.0$\frac{23}{32}$	18	86	1.2$\frac{3}{32}$	17	03	1.3$\frac{15}{32}$	15	52
1 0$\frac{3}{4}$	18	82	1.2$\frac{1}{8}$	16	99	1.3$\frac{1}{2}$	15	48
1.0$\frac{25}{32}$	18	77	1.2$\frac{5}{32}$	16	95	1.3$\frac{17}{32}$	15	45
1.0$\frac{13}{16}$	18	73	1.2$\frac{3}{16}$	16	92	1.3$\frac{9}{16}$	15	42
1.0$\frac{27}{32}$	18	68	1.2$\frac{7}{32}$	16	88	1.3$\frac{19}{32}$	15	39
1.0$\frac{7}{8}$	18	64	1.2$\frac{1}{4}$	16	84	1.3$\frac{5}{8}$	15	36
1.0$\frac{29}{32}$	18	59	1.2$\frac{9}{32}$	16	81	1.3$\frac{21}{32}$	15	33
1.0$\frac{15}{16}$	18	55	1.2$\frac{5}{16}$	16	77	1.3$\frac{11}{16}$	15	30
1.0$\frac{31}{32}$	18	50	1.2$\frac{11}{32}$	16	73	1.3$\frac{23}{32}$	15	27
1.1	18	46	1.2$\frac{3}{8}$	16	70	1.3$\frac{3}{4}$	15	24
1.1$\frac{1}{32}$	18	41	1.2$\frac{13}{32}$	16	66	1.3$\frac{25}{32}$	15	21
1.1$\frac{1}{16}$	18	37	1.2$\frac{7}{16}$	16	62	1.3$\frac{13}{16}$	15	18
1.1$\frac{3}{32}$	18	32	1.2$\frac{15}{32}$	16	59	1.3$\frac{27}{32}$	15	15
1.1$\frac{1}{8}$	18	28	1.2$\frac{1}{2}$	16	55	1.3$\frac{7}{8}$	15	12
1.1$\frac{5}{32}$	18	24	1.2$\frac{17}{32}$	16	52	1.3$\frac{29}{32}$	15	09
1.1$\frac{3}{16}$	18	19	1.2$\frac{9}{16}$	16	48	1.3$\frac{15}{16}$	15	06
1.1$\frac{7}{32}$	18	15	1.2$\frac{19}{32}$	16	45	1.3$\frac{31}{32}$	15	03
1.1$\frac{1}{4}$	18	11	1.2$\frac{5}{8}$	16	41			
1.1$\frac{9}{32}$	18	07	1.2$\frac{21}{32}$	16	38			
1.1$\frac{5}{16}$	18	02	1.2$\frac{11}{16}$	16	34			
1.1$\frac{11}{32}$	17	98	1.2$\frac{23}{32}$	16	31			

Foreign Money and their English Equivalents.

Country.	Chief Coin.	English Value. £	s.	d.
Argentine, Chili and Uruguay	Dollar	0	4	2
Austria and Hungary	Florin, silver	0	1	11
Belgium	Franc	0	0	9½
Brazil	Milrei	0	2	1½
Canada and United States	Dollar	0	4	2
China	1 Tael of Silver	0	6	8
Do.	Dollar, varies	0	4	6
Cuba	Dollar	0	4	2
Denmark and Sweden	Kronor	0	1	1¼
Egypt	Piastre	0	0	2½
Do.	50 Piastres piece, gold ...	0	10	2½
Do.	98 Piastres	1	0	0
France	Franc	0	0	9½
Germany	1 Mark	0	1	0
Do.	20 Marks, gold	0	19	7
Greece	Drachma, 100 lepta ...	0	0	9½
Holland and Java	Florin	0	1	8
Do.	10 Florins, gold	0	16	8
India	Rupee, about	0	1	4
Do.	Mohur, 15 do. gold... ...	1	9	2
Italy	Lira	0	0	9½
Japan	1 Yen	0	4	1¼
Do.	10 Yens piece	2	1	0
Mexico, Chili and Peru	Dollar, about	0	4	2
Persia	Toman	0	10	6
Portugal	Milrei, about	0	4	10
Russia	Silver Rouble pr. 2/6 ...	0	3	0
Spain	1 Peseta	0	0	9½
Sweden and Norway	18 Kronor...	1	0	0
Switzerland	Franc	0	0	9½
Turkey	1 Piastre, nearly	0	0	2¼
Do.	£—Turkish	0	18	0
West Indies	Dollar	0	4	2

Table for the Conversion of Metric Weights and Measures into English.

Mètres into Yards.		Kilomètres to miles and yards.			Litres into gallons and quarts.			Hectolitres into quarters and bushels			Kilogrammes into cwt. qrs. lbs. ozs.					Hectares into acres. r. p.			
1	1.094	1	0	1094	1	0	0.880	1	0	2.751	1	0	0	2	3¼	1	2	1	35
2	1.187	2	1	427	2	0	1.761	2	0	5.502	2	0	0	4	6½	2	4	3	31
3	3.281	3	1	1521	3	0	2.641	3	1	0.254	3	0	0	6	9¾	3	7	1	26
4	4.374	4	2	855	4	0	3.521	4	1	3.005	4	0	0	8	13	4	9	3	22
5	5.468	5	3	188	5	1	0.402	5	1	5.756	5	0	0	11	0¼	5	12	1	17
6	6.562	6	5	1282	6	1	1.282	6	2	0.507	6	0	0	13	3½	6	14	3	12
7	7.655	7	4	615	7	1	2.163	7	2	3.258	7	0	0	15	7	7	17	1	8
8	8.749	8	4	1709	8	1	3.043	8	2	6.010	8	0	0	17	10¼	8	19	3	·3
9	9.843	9	5	1043	9	1	3.923	9	3	0.761	9	0	0	19	13½	9	22	0	28
10	10.936	10	6	376	10	2	0.804	10	3	5.512	10	0	0	22	0¾	10	24	2	34
20	21.873	20	12	753	20	4	1.608	20	6	7.024	20	0	1	16	1½	20	49	1	28
30	32.809	30	18	1129	30	6	2.412	30	10	2.536	30	0	2	10	2½	30	74	0	21
40	43.745	40	24	1505	40	8	3.215	40	13	6·048	40	0	3	4	3	40	98	3	15
50	54.682	50	31	122	50	11	0.019	50	17	1.560	50	0	3	26	3¾	50	123	2	9
60	65.618	60	37	498	60	13	0.823	60	20	5.072	60	1	0	20	4½	60	148	1	3
70	76.554	70	43	874	70	15	1.627	70	24	0.585	70	1	1	14	5¼	70	172	3	37
80	87.491	80	49	1251	80	17	2.431	80	27	4.097	80	1	2	8	6	80	197	2	38
90	98.427	90	55	1627	90	19	3.325	90	30	7.609	90	1	3	2	6½	90	222	1	24
100	109.363	100	62	243	100	22	0.039	100	34	3.121	100	1	3	24	7	100	247	0	18
200	218.727	200	124	487	200	44	0.077	200	68	6.242	200	3	3	20	15	200	494	0	37
300	328.090	300	186	730	300	66	0.116	300	103	1.362	300	5	3	17	6	300	741	1	15
400	437.453	400	248	973	400	88	0.155	400	137	4.483	400	7	3	13	14	400	988	1	33
500	546.816	500	310	1217	500	110	0.193	500	171	7.604	500	9	3	10	5	500	1235	2	11

Rules for converting Metric to English Measures and Weights.

To convert kilogrammes to pounds multiply by 1,000 and divide by 454.
To convert litres to gallons multiply by 22 and divide by 100.
To convert litres to pints multiply by 88 and divide by 50.
To convert millimetres to inches multiply by 10 and divide by 254.
To convert metres to yards multiply by 70 and divide by 64.

French Metrical System of Weights and Measures.

The Metric System is based upon the length of the fourth part of a terrestrial meridian. The ten-millionth part of this arc was chosen as the unit of measures of length, and called a *Mètre*. The cube of the tenth part of the mètre was adopted as the unit of capacity, and denominated a *Litre*. The weight of a litre of distilled water at its greatest density was called a *Kilogramme*, of which the thousandth part, or *Gramme* was adopted as the unit of weight. The multiples of these, proceeding in decimal progression, are distinguished by the employment of the prefixes *deca*, *hecto*, *kilo*, and *myria*, from the Greek, and the subdivisions by *deci*, *centi*, and *milli* from the Latin :

MEASURES OF LENGTH (UNIT MÈTRE.)

EQUAL TO	Inches.	Feet.	Yards.	Fathoms.	Miles.
Millimètre	0.03937	0.003281	0.0010936	0.0005468	0.0000006
Centimètre	0.39371	0.032809	0.0109363	0.0054682	0.0000062
Décimètre	3.93708	0.328090	0.1093633	0.0546816	0.0000621
MÈTRE	39.37079	3.280899	1.0936331	0.5468165	0.0006214
Décamètre	393.70790	32.808992	10.9363306	5.4681653	0.0062138
Hectomètre	3937.07900	328.089917	109.3633056	54.6816528	0.0621382
Kilomètre	39370.79000	3280.899167	1093.6330556	546.8165278	0.6213824
Myriamètre..................	393707.90000	32808.991667	10936.3305556	5468.1652778	6.2138242

CUBIC, OR MEASURES OF CAPACITY (UNIT LITRE.)

EQUAL TO	Cubic Inches.	Cubic Feet.	Pints.	Gallons.	Bushels.
Millilitre, or cubic centimètre	0.06103	0.000035	0.00176	0.0002201	0.0000275
Centilitre, 10 cubic do...	0.61027	0.000353	0.01761	0.0022010	0.0002751
Décilitre, 100 do. do...	6.10271	0.003532	0.17608	0.0220097	0.0027512
LITRE, or cubic Décimètre.	61.02705	0.035317	1.76077	0.2200967	0.0275121
Décalitre, or Centistère ...	610.27052	0.353166	17.60773	2.2009668	0.2751208
Hectolitre, or Décistère ...	6102.70515	3.531658	176.07734	22.0096677	2.7512085
Kilolitre, or Stère, or cubic mètre	61027.05152	35.316581	1760.77341	220.0966767	27.5120846
Myrialitre, or Décastère...	610270.51519	353.165807	17607.73414	2200.9667675	275.1208459

MEASURES OF WEIGHT (UNIT GRAMME.)

EQUAL TO	Grains.	Troy oz.	Avoir du poids lb.	cwt=112 lbs.	Tons=10 cwt
Miligramme..................	0.01543	0.000032	0.0000022	0.0000000	0.0000000
Centigramme	0.15432	0.000322	0.0000220	0.0000002	0.0000000
Décigramme	1.54323	0.003215	0.0002205	0.0000020	0.0000001
GRAMME	15.43235	0.032151	0.0022046	0.0000197	0.0000010
Décagramme	154.32349	0.321507	0.0220462	0.0001968	0.0000098
Hectogramme...............	1543.23488	3.215073	0.2204621	0.0019684	0.0000984
Kilogramme	15432.34880	32.150727	2.2046213	0.0196841	0.0009842
Myriagramme...............	154323.48800	321.507267	22.0462126	0.1968412	0.0098421

SQUARE OR MEASURES OF SURFACE (UNIT ARE.)

EQUAL TO	Sq. Feet.	Sq. Yards.	Sq. Perches.	Sq. Roods.	Sq. Acres.
Centiare, or square mètre	10.764299	1.196033	0.0395383	0.0009885	0.0002471
ARE, or 100 square mètres......	1076.429934	119.603326	3.9538290	0.0988457	0.0247114
Hectare, or 10,000 sq. mètres...	107642.993419	11960.332602	395.3828959	9,8845724	2,4711431

NOTE :—The Colonial (Mauritius) Arpent contains... 45,433⅓ English feet.
The English Acre .... 43,560 ,,

Difference...... 1,873⅓

Rates per word to be charged at Seychelles and Mauritius.

To	Seychelles.				Mauritius.			
	Direct.		*Viâ* Capetown.		Direct.		*Viâ* Capetown.	
EUROPE.	RS.	C.	RS.	C.	RS.	C.	RS.	C.
Austria-Hungary	5	75	13	12	7	...	14	37
Azores	6	25	12	87	7	37	14	12
Belgium	5	75	12	87	7	...	14	12
Bosnia-Herzegovina	5	62	13	...	6	87	14	25
Bulgaria	5	62	13	...	6	87	14	25
Denmark	5	75	13	...	7	...	14	25
France	5	75	13	...	7	...	14	25
Germany	5	75	13	12	7	...	14	25
Gibraltar	5	62	12	37	6	87	13	62
Great Britain	5	87	12	75	7	12	14	...
Greece	5	37	13	...	6	62	14	25
Holland	5	75	13	...	7	...	14	25
Italy	5	50	13	...	6	75	14	25
Luxembourg	5	75	13	12	7	...	14	25
Malta	5	50	12	87	6	75	14	...
Montenegro	5	62	13	...	6	87	14	25
Norway	6	...	13	...	7	12	14	25
Portugal	5	75	12	37	7	...	13	62
Roumania	5	75	13	12	7	...	14	37
Russia in Europe	6	...	13	50	7	12	14	75
,, Caucasus	6	12	13	75	7	37	15	...
Servia	5	62	13	...	6	87	14	25
Spain	5	75	12	37	7	...	13	62
Sweden	5	87	13	12	7	12	14	37
Switzerland	5	62	13	12	6	87	14	25
Turkey in Europe	5	50	13	...	6	75	14	25
,, Asia	5	87	13	25	7	12	14	50
Crete	5	25	12	87	6	50	14	12
Rhodes	5	50	13	...	6	75	14	25
Chios, Lemnos and Tenedos	5	37	12	75	6	62	14	...
Cyprus	5	...	13	37	6	25	14	62
Other Turkish Islands	5	87	13	25	7	12	14	50
AFRICA.			*Viâ* Aden & Malta.				*Viâ* Aden & Malta.	
East Coast—								
German East Africa	1	75	—		3	37	—	
Imperial British East Africa Co's Stations ...	2	...	—		3	62	—	
Laurenço Marques	5	...	13	50	6	62	14	75
Mombassa	1	62	—		3	25	—	
Mozambique	3	37	14	37	5	...	14	62
Zanzibar	1	62	—		3	25	—	
Seychelles	—		—		1	62	—	
Mauritius	1	62	—		—		—	
			Viâ Capetown.				*Viâ* Capetown.	
North—								
Algeria	5	50	13	12	6	75	14	37
Egypt, Alexandria	5	...	13	37	6	25	14	62
,, Other places	5	...	13	62	6	25	14	87
Tangier	5	75	12	50	7	...	13	75
Tripoli, Tripoli	5	75	13	37	7	...	14	50
,, Other places	5	87	13	37	7	12	14	62
Tunis	5	50	13	12	6	75	14	37

To	Seychelles.				Mauritius.			
	Direct.		*Viâ* Capetown.		Direct.		*Viâ* Capetown.	
AFRICA—*Continued.*	Rs.	c.	Rs.	c.	Rs.	c.	Rs.	c.
Red Sea Ports—								
Aden	2	87	15	12	4	12	16	37
Assab	3	37	15	25	4	62	16	50
Hedjaz, viâ Jeddah	5	12	15	12	6	37	16	37
Massowah	3	37	15	25	4	62	16	50
Obock	3	37	15	25	4	62	16	50
Perim	3	25	15	12	4	50	16	37
Suakim	4	12	14	12	5	37	15	37
Yemen, via Sheik Seyd	3	75	15	62	5	...	16	87
			Viâ Aden and Malta.				*Viâ* Aden and Malta.	
South—								
British South Africa Coy's Stations ...	6	12	13	...	7	75	14	25
Cape Colony	5	87	12	87	7	50	14	...
Natal, Durban	5	75	12	75	7	37	14	...
,, Other places	5	87	12	87	7	50	14	...
Orange Free State	5	87	12	87	7	50	14	...
Transvaal	5	87	12	87	7	50	14	...
	Viâ Capetown.				*Viâ* Capetown.			
West Coast and adjacent Islands—								
Accra	10	75	11	62	12	37	12	87
,, Government Stations	10	87	11	75	12	50	13	...
Bathurst	13	...	10	...	14	62	11	25
Benguella	8	37	13	75	10	...	15	...
Bissao	13	37	9	25	15	...	10	50
Bolama	13	37	9	25	15	...	10	50
Bonny	10	67	12	87	12	37	14	12
Braqs	11	62	12	87	13	37	14	12
Cameroons	10	87	13	12	12	50	14	25
Canaries	12	...	6	25	13	25	7	50
Conakry	12	...	9	37	13	62	10	62
Gaboon	10	50	11	12	12	12	12	37
Grand Bassam	11	50	9	75	13	12	11	...
Kotonou	10	50	10	75	12	12	12	...
Lagos	11	62	12	25	13	37	13	50
Loanda	8	37	12	62	10	...	13	87
Madeira	12	25	6	25	13	50	7	50
Mossamedes	8	37	14	37	10	...	15	62
Principe	10	50	11	37	12	12	12	62
St. Jago	14	25	8	12	16	12	9	25
St. Thomé	10	...	11	...	11	62	12	25
St. Vincent...	15	62	7	37	16	87	8	62
Senegal	11	37	6	87	12	62	8	12
Sierra Leone	11	62	10	62	13	37	11	87
ASIA.	Direct.		*Viâ* Capetown.		Direct.		*Viâ* Capetown.	
Annam	7	25	17	...	8	50	18	25
China—								
Hong-Kong...	8	62	17	87	9	87	19	12
Shanghai, Amoy and Foochow	9	87	17	87	11	12	19	12
Canton and Macao	8	87	18	12	10	12	19	37
Other places	11	25	19	12	12	50	20	37

To	Seychelles.				Mauritius.			
	Direct.		*Viâ* Capetown.		Direct.		*Viâ* Capetown.	
	Rs.	c.	Rs.	c.	Rs.	c.	Rs.	c.
Cochin China	6	62	16	37	7	87	17	62
Corea, via Shanghai	11	50	19	37	17	75	20	62
Dutch Indies—								
Java	7	37	17	12	8	62	18	37
Other Islands	7	75	17	62	9	...	18	87
Japan	11	87	21	12	13	12	22	37
India—								
India	5	12	15	50	6	37	16	75
Burmah	5	37	15	75	6	50	16	87
Ceylon	5	25	15	62	6	50	16	87
Persia	6	50	14	...	7	75	15	25
Persian Gulf—								
Bushire	6	...	13	62	7	25	14	87
Other Places	6	...	14	50	7	25	15	75
Philippine Islands	10	12	19	25	11	25	20	50
Russia—								
I. Region	6	62	14	25	7	87	15	50
II. ,, ...	7	37	15	...	8	62	16	25
Siam, via Singapore	7	...	16	87	8	25	18	...
,, Moulmein	6	12	15	87	7	37	17	12
Straits Settlements—								
Jelebu	7	12	16	87	8	37	18	12
Malacca	7	...	16	87	8	25	18	...
Penang	6	50	16	37	7	75	17	50
Perak	6	62	16	50	7	87	17	75
Selangor	7	12	16	87	8	37	18	12
Singapore	7	25	17	...	8	50	18	25
Sunjie-Ujong	7	12	16	87	8	37	18	12
Tonquin	7	62	17	37	8	75	18	62
AUSTRALASIA.								
New South Wales	7	...	16	25	8	12	17	50
New Zealand	7	12	16	50	8	37	17	75
Queensland	11	...	19	87	12	25	21	...
South Australia...	6	87	16	12	8	...	17	37
Tasmania	7	37	16	62	8	62	17	87
Victoria	6	87	16	25	8	12	17	50
West Australia	6	87	16	12	8	...	17	37
SOUTH AMERICA.					11	25		
Argentine Republic, via St. Vincent	10	...	15	25	12	...	16	50
Bolivia, via Galveston	10	75	17	50			18	75
Brazil—					11	...		
Pernambuco, via St. Vincent	9	75	13	87	11	25	15	12
Other places	10	...	14	62	12	...	15	75
Chili, via Galveston	10	75	17	50			18	75
Colombia via Galveston—								
Isthmus of Panama	9	75	16	62	11	...	17	87
Buenaventura	10	25	17	...	11	50	18	25
Other Places	10	37	17	25	11	62	18	50
Ecuador, via Galveston	10	75	17	50	12	...	18	75
Guiana British, via Galveston	15	75	22	50	16	87	23	75
,, Dutch, via Galveston	13	75	20	62	15	...	21	87
,, French, via St. Vincent	13	12	18	25	14	25	19	50
Paraguay, via St. Vincent	10	...	15	25	11	25	16	50
Peru, via Galveston	10	75	17	50	12	...	18	75
Uruguay, via St. Vincent	10	...	15	25	11	25	16	50
Venezuela, via Galveston	14	62	21	50	15	87	22	75

Regulations.

The following Regulations are used by the Eastern and South African Telegraph Company Limited :—

Telegrams are classed in three categories :

1o. Government Telegrams— those which emanate from the Chief of the State, Ministers, Commanders-in-Chief of Land and Sea forces and diplomatic or Consular Agents of the Contracting Governments ; also the replies to such telegrams.

2o. Service telegrams— those which emanate from the Telegraph Administrations of the Contracting States, and which relate either to telegraphy, or to objects of public interest agreed upon between the said Administrations.

3o. Private telegrams.

In transmission, Government telegrams take precedence of other telegrams.

Messages can be forwarded in the following languages :—

English, French, German, Italian, Spanish, Dutch, Portuguese, and Latin.

All that the sender writes in his telegram to be transmitted is included in resolving the cost, except the indication of route, signs or punctuation, apostrophes, fresh paragraphs, and hyphens.

Words, numbers, or signs forming the preamble, and inserted in the copy by the office in the interest of the service, are not charged for.

In plain language, the maximum length of a word is fixed at fifteen characters, according to the " Morse Alphabet," any excess, up to fifteen additional characters, is counted as a word. For traffic under the Extra-European system, the maximum is fixed at ten characters ; any excess, up to ten additional characters, is counted as a word.

In preconcerted language under both systems the maximum length of a word is fixed at ten characters.

Words in plain language inserted in the body of a mixed telegram composed of words in plain language and words in preconcerted language, are counted as a word up to ten characters, any excess being counted as a word by indivisible series of ten characters. If the mixed telegram contains in addition a part in cipher, the parts in cipher are counted according to the stipulations of paragraph 7 hereafter.

If the mixed telegram is composed partly of plain language and partly of cipher language, the parts in plain language are counted according to the stipulations of paragraph 1 of the Regulation, under the convention, and the parts in cipher language according to the stipulations of paragraph 7.

In all languages and under both systems, must be counted respectively as one single word :

a. The name of the Telegraph Office of delivery, the name of the country and the name of the territorial sub-division of destination, but in the address only, whatever number of words or characters be employed to express them, provided always that these names be written as they appear in the official nomenclature of the International office of the telegraph Administrations ;

b. Each separate character, each separate letter, each separate figure.

c. An underline.

d. Parenthesis (the two signs which serve to form it.)

e. Inverted commas (distinctive signs placed at the commencement and end of a single word or phrase.)

Expressions joined by a hyphen are counted for the number of words employed in their formation. Words separated by an apostrophe are counted as so many separate words.

Decimal points and commas, used in the formation of numbers, and bars of division, are each counted as a figure.

Letters added to figures to form ordinal numbers are each counted as a figure.

Charges for messages are prepaid, except as provided for in the following cases, *i. e.*, the supplementary charge for messages to follow the charge for express, and the charge for semaphoric telegrams which are collected by the delivery office.

In every case where charges have to be collected on arrival, the telegram is only given over to the addressee upon payment of the amount due.

Any sender can, by proving his indentity, stop, if in time, the transmission of a telegram deposited by him.

When a sender withdraws or stops his telegram before transmission has been commenced, the charges are returned to him, less a fixed sum of 5d., the fee of the sending office.

Any sender can prepay the reply which he requests his correspondent to return ; but the prepayment cannot exceed the tariff of a telegram, of whatever kind it may be, of 30 words for the same journey, unless it be to obtain the repetition of a telegram previously transmitted.

The sender of any telegram may request that a notice of the date and time at which his telegram is handed to the receiver be transmitted to him by telegraph immediately after its delivery. He inserts before the address the notice acknowledgment of receipt or (C.R.)

The charge for an acknowledgment of receipt is equal to that of an ordinary telegram of ten words by the same route.

The originals of telegrams and documents relating to them, retained by the Administrations, are preserved during at least six months, counting from their date, with all necessary precautions to secure their secrecy.

This period is extended to twelve months in the case of telegrams under the extra-European system.

Refunds will be made in the following cases :—

The full cost of every telegram which has experienced serious delay, or failed to reach its destination, through the fault of the telegraph service ;

The full cost of every collated telegram which has manifestly been unable to fulfil its object, in consequence of errors made in its transmission ;

In traffic under extra-European system, the cost of every word omitted in the transmission of an ordinary telegram, through the fault of the telegraph service.

This rule, however, is not applicable when the receiver has discovered the omission and had it rectified.

Every claim for refund should be made, under penalty of rejection, within two months of the date of the telegram. This period is extended to six months for telegrams under the extra-European system.

Greatest Velocity of the Wind for one hour in each month of the year for the period 1876—1894.

Months.	1876-94 Greatest velocity for 1 hour.	Days of Months.	Years.	Months.	1876-94 Greatest velocity for 1 hour.	Days of Months.	Years.
	Miles.				Miles.		
January	49.8	21	1881	July	34.3	12	1877
February ...	77.5	19	1876	August	34.4	11	1879
March	80.3	21	1879	September ...	35.4	6	1878
April	103.3	29	1892	October... ...	33.2	13	1880
May...	32.4	17	1878	November ...	34.0	12	1891
June	41.5	30	1881	December ...	44.9	7	1883

INTERNAL REVENUE.

Authority under which levied.	Description of Tax.	Rates. Rs.	c.
	RECEIVER GENERAL'S DEPARTMENT.		
Ord. No. 6 of 1878.	DIRECT TAXES.	Rs.	c.
Ord. 24 of 1895.	*Carts, Carriages, Horses, &c. possessed in 1st. Quarter of the Year.*		
Ord. No. 28 of 1883.	1. Every Carriage on 4 wheels	22	
Received by the Municipality of Port Louis in cases where the proprietor resides in Port Louis.	2. ,, ,, on 3 ,, ...	16	50
	3. ,, ,, on 2 ,, ...	13	50
	4. ,, Break on 4 ,, ...	22	...
	5. ,, ,, on 2 ,, ...	13	50
	6. ,, Traction-engine	600	...
	7. ,, Truck attached thereto	132	...
	8. ,, Triqueballe	44	...
	9. ,, Cart or Waggon on 4 wheels.	26	50
	10. ,, ,, Dray, Tumbrel, or large Cart on 2 wheels drawn by more than one animal ...	13	50
	11. ,, ,, on Springs on 2 wheels	13	50
	12. ,, ,, ,, on 4 ,, ...	16	50
	13. ,, Other dray or cart drawn by one animal ...	11	...
	14. ,, Horse or Mule used wholly or occasionally for the saddle or in carriage	6	75
	15. ,, ,, used only in a Cart, Dray, Drumbrel or Waggon	4	50
Ord. 6 of 1892.	16. ,, Donkey	3	50
Regulation No. 31 of 1879 under Ordinance 18 of 1879.	An additional tax of 10 o/o is payable on the Direct Tax on every Traction-Engine or Truck attached thereto, when such Traction-Engine or Truck is declared in Port Louis. The proceeds thereof to be paid over by the Receiver General to the Mayor of Port Louis on the 30th. June, and the 28th. of December of every year.		
	Dog Tax.		
	Every Dog of the age of 4 months and upwards or attaining the age of 4 months at any time during the year not being kept within the Municipal boundaries of Port Louis.	2	75

On animals and vehicles kept within the boundaries of the Municipality of Port Louis, such tax shall be paid as shall be imposed by the Municipal Law in force for the time being.

Proportion of Taxes payable on Vehicles and Animals bought or otherwise obtained and taken possession of after the 1st. April.

Period within which the Vehicle or Animal has been bought or otherwise obtained by its possessor.	Proportion of Tax payable by possessor.
1—From 1st. April to 15th. May inclusive	Six-Eighths.
2— „ 16th. May to 30th. June „	Five „
3— „ 1st. July to 15th. August „	Four „
4— „ 16th. August to 30th. Sept. „	Three „
5— „ 1st. October to 15th. Nov. „	Two „
6— „ 16th. Nov. to 31st. Dec. „	One „

List of licenses in force in 1896.

No.	Business, Profession, or Trade.	Duty for 6 calendar months. Port Louis and Curepipe.		Country Districts.		Remarks.
		Rs.	c.	Rs.	c.	
1	Agent (House Land and Cattle) ...	27	50	27	50	
2	Assurance or Insurance Company ...	137	50	137	50	
3	Assurance or Insurance Agency ...	137	50	137	50	For each Agency.
4	Attorney-at-Law	33	...	33	...	
5	Auctioneer (keeping no Auction Room)	82	50	38	50	
6	do. (keeping an Auction Room)	125	...	125	...	With right to sell by retail, but only goods received from residents or local importers and not goods imported by himself or received direct from manufacturers outside the Colony.
7	Baker (with more than two workmen or assistants.	11	...	11	...	
8	Banker	550	...	...	...	
9	Banker's Agent	250	...	...	...	For each Agency.
10	Basket-seller	4	...	3	...	Selling baskets purchased for his trade.
11	Billiard Room (not public) ...	165	...	130	...	Kept by a Club or Society.
12	Billiard Room (public)	330	...	220	...	
13	Billiard Table in an Hotel (each Table)	100	...	65	...	
14	Blacksmiths and Farriers.					
	a. With not more than 2 assistants...	5	...	4	...	
	b. With more than 2 assistants ...	10	...	8	...	
15	Book-binder	8	25	8	25	
16	Brick and Tile maker	22	...	22	...	
17	Broker-Sworn (1st. class)... ...	110	...	110	...	
18	do. (2nd. class) ...	27	50	27	50	
19	do. (Custom House) ...	27	50	...	...	
20	Builder of Houses	...	...	...	...	See Job Contractor.
21	Builder of Funeral Monuments (employing more than one workman.)	22	...	22	...	
22	Butcher (in a market)	8	...	8	...	Exclusive of a separate duty of Rs. 2.75 every 6 months for each stall exceeding one.

NOTE.—License duties payable to Government by persons who carry on their trade, profession or calling in Markets, Cemeteries, Slaughter-Houses or other Municipal Establishments within the limits of Port Louis in virtue of Ord. 6 of 1878 or of any other law now in force are now paid over to the Municipal Corporation of Port Louis in virtue of Ord. 8 of 1894.

No.	Business, Profession, or Trade.	Duty for 6 calendar months. Port Louis and Curepipe.		Country Districts.		Remarks.
		Rs.	c.	Rs.	c.	
23	Butcher (elsewhere than in a market)...	8*	...	8	...	* Curepipe only.
24	Cabinet-maker	9	...	7	...	
25	Cake seller (in a market)... ...	3	50	3	50	Exclusive of a separate duty of Rs. 2.20 every 6 months for each stall exceeding one.
26	do. (elsewhere than in amarket)	3	50	3	50	
27	Carrier by Land	5	...	5	...	For each cart.
28	Cartwright	11	...	11	...	
29	Chocolate maker	6	...	6	...	
30	Manufactures of Cigars, Cigarettes, Snuff & Plug (employing no assistant)	20	...	20	...	License to be issued only to Licensed Retailers of Tobacco.
31	Manufacturers of Cigars, Cigarettes, Snuff & Plug (employing not more than 5 assistants).	30	...	30	...	
32	do. (employing more than 5 assistants.)	50	...	50	...	
33	Coach builder...	12	...	9	...	
34	Coffee house keeper	...	...	...	...	See Refreshment Room Keeper.
35	Comb maker	5	...	5	...	
36	Commission Merchant — Agent who buys, or sells, or orders from abroad Goods on accounts of others—whether the Goods are imported in his own name or not.	100	...	100	...	
37	Company Public (under Ord. 31 of 1865.)	220	...	220	...	
38	Company, Joint Stock or other not provided for in Ord. 31 of 1865.)	66	...	66	...	
39	Compounder (not furnishing any bond, and not using any still or distilling apparatus.)	80	...	...	...	
40	do. (using still or distilling apparatus and furnishing bond.)	170	...	...	...	
41	Confectioner	27	50	22	...	
42	Cooper	10	...	10	...	
43	Co-operative Societies	...	...	...	...	According to nature of Business and selling to its own members only.
44	Coppersmith	27	50	27	50	
45	Cutler	7	...	7	...	
46	do. (itinerant)	8	...	8	...	
47	Distiller	550	...	550	...	
48	Engineer (Civil and Mechanical) ...	33	...	33	..	
49	Fishing for shrimps, sprats and other small fish of sizes authorised by Ord. No. 42 of 1881 and with nets of the dimensions authorized by Ord. 11 of 1883.	2	25	2	25	With or without boats and whatever the number of fishermen employed in fishing with nets.
50	Fishing with large nets (*Grandes Seines*) and three boats or less.	14	...	14	...	An additional duty of Rs. 2 per half year, for every extra boat.
51	Fishing with one large net (*Grande Seine*) without boat.	6	...	6	...	Whatever the number of Fishermen.
52	Seller of fish from private Barachois (sold at the Barachois or elsewhere.)	27	...	27	...	

No.	Business, Profession, or Trade.	Duty for 6 calendar months.				Remarks.
		Port Louis and Curepipe.		Country Districts.		
		Rs.	c.	Rs.	c.	
53	Fishmonger (in a market) ...	7	...	4	...	Exclusive of a separate Licence duty of Rs. 2, every 6 months for each stall exceeding one.
54	do. (elsewhere than in a market) ...	...	...	4*	...	* And Curepipe.
55	Founder or Proprietor of Engineering shop	55	...	44	...	
56	Do. not having an Engineering shop	12	...	7	...	Having the right of preparing or manufacturing only small pieces of iron and copper not usually prepared by Engineers.
57	Manufacturer of Gold and Silverware.	40	...	40	...	With right to sell on Licensed premises only.
58	Gilder or Plator	9	...	8	...	
59	Gunsmith	11	...	11	...	
60	Hawkers of :*					
	a. Brass and Copper jewels	6	...	4	...	
	b. Earthenware and Crockery	3	50	3	50	
	c. Firewood and Charcoal	5	50	5	50	
	d. Fish, Shrimps and Shell fish. ...	...	...	*3	50	*And Curepipe.
	e. Haberdashery...	4	50	4	50	
	f. Ice-creams	3	...	3	...	
	g. Imported Jewellery	27	50	27	50	Issued only when Receiver General is satisfied that holder is *bonâ fide* importer of jewellery.
	h. Jewellery	16	50	16	50	Only issued to manufacturers of gold and silverware made in the Colony.
	i. Lemonade and Soda water	3	30	3	30	
	j. Dairy produce (or seller)	1	25	1	25	
	k. Toddy (*Calou*) (or seller)	2	50	2	50	
	l. Cakes	3	50	3	50	
	m. Poultry	3	50	3	50	
	n. Timber	10	...	10	...	
	o. Tinware	3	50	3	50	
	p. Tobacco (manufactured or not) ...	30	...	30	...	
	q. All other goods, wares and merchandize—except Opium, Jewellery, Tobacco, Spirits, Wine, Beer and Gandia.	8	25	8	25	
61	Hair dresser	8	50	5	...	
62	Harness maker	11	...	7	...	
63	Hatter and Glover.	7	...	6	...	
64	Hotel-keeper (or Inn-keeper)	200	...	140	...	

* An additional duty of Rs. 2 shall be charged for every porter; Rs. 2 for every beast of burden; and Rs. 5 for every vehicle employed by any hawker under Article 80 of Ordinance No. 6 of 1868.

No.	Business, Profession, or Trade.	Duty for 6 calendar months. Port Louis and Curepipe. Rs.	c.	Country Districts. Rs.	c.	Remarks.
65	Ironmonger	55	...	33	...	With right to sell hardware either by wholesale or retail.
66	Do. Selling by retail only small ironware such as Jeweller's and Watchmaker's tools.	20	...	15	...	
67	Job Contractor ;	...	...	...	...	Notwithstanding the provisions of Article 32 of Ordinance 6 of 1878 licenses to Job-Contractors may at any time be issued for several consecutive periods of six months but so that the last of such consecutive licenses shall in no case extend two years beyond the date of the first issue.
	a. Employing more than 50 laborers or artisans.	82	50	82	50	
	b. Employing more than 25 but not more than 50.	50	...	50	...	
	c. Employing more than 10 but not more than 25.	25	...	25	...	
	d. Employing more than 5 but not more than 10.	15	...	15	...	
	e. Employing not more than 5 ...	6	...	6	...	
68	Land Surveyor	16	50	16	50	
69	Lemonade, Soda water and Ginger-beer maker.	15	...	15	...	With right to sell on Licensed premises only.
70	Do. seller	5	...	5	...	
71	Lime burner	16	50	16	50	With right to sell lime in any quantity at his kiln or elsewhere.
72	Lime seller	8	...	8	...	An additional duty of Rs. 4 per half-year for each depot in excess of the one for which the license is granted.
73	Livery stable keeper.—					
	For each carriage	7	...	7	...	
	For each carriole	5	...	5	...	
74	Lodging-house keeper	13	50	13	50	When the number of lodgers is in excess of 6 ; and for every lodger in excess of 6, R. 1.
75	Manufacturer of Copper and Brass Jewels.	8	25	8	25	
76	Manufacturer of Fireworks ...	13	75	13	75	With right to sell on the licensed premises only.
77	Manure manufacture	27	50	27	50	
78	Market Auctioneer	33	...	26	50	With right to sell fish, fruits and vegetables only at public markets.

No.	Business, Profession, or Trade.	Duty for 6 calendar months. Port Louis and Curepipe. Rs.	c.	Country Districts. Rs.	c.	Remarks.
79	Marine Surveyor	16	50	...	...	
80	Merchant	...	...	...	...	See Wholesale dealer.
81	Miller (corn)	22	...	22	...	
82	Milliner (or Dress maker)					
	(a) Employing 5 but not more than 8 assistants.	16	50	8	25	
	(b) Employing more than 8 assistants.	33	...	13	...	
83	Money changer	10	...	10	...	
84	Musical Instrument maker and mender.	11	...	7	50	
85	Mussel-bed keeper	5	50	5	50	
86	Notary Public	165	...	55	...	
87	Notary (English)	55	...	...	...	
88	Oil vendor	25	...	25	...	Selling Oil only.
89	Opium Seller	...	...	...	...	See Retailer of Opium
90	Optician	8	25	8	25	
91	Oyster-bed keeper	5	50	5	50	
92	Painter and Glazier	8	25	8	25	
93	Painter of badges and sign-boards ...	5	...	5	...	
94	Partner in any Commercial Firm or Company whether such partner be dormant or not.	5	50	5	50	Joint Stock Companies excepted.
95	Pawnbroker	165	...	165	...	
96	Pharmacist	110	...	88	...	
97	Printer	22	...	22	...	
98	Proctor in Admiralty not practising as an Avoué.	38	50	...	...	
99	Refreshment Room keeper ...	120	...	120	...	
100	Retailer of :					
	a. Spirits, Wine and Beer ...	165	...	132	...	
	b. Groceries	22	...	16	50	
	c. Drapery & haberdashery ...	27	50	16	50	
	d. Gold & Silver wares	33	...	33	...	
	e. Tobacco (manufactured or not) ...	27	50	27	50	
	f. Opium	110	...	110	...	
	g. Earthenware, China and Glassware.	27	50	22	...	This license not to be issued to importers of Gandia.
	h. Gandia	110	...	110	...	The sale of any quantity not exceeding 20 grammes to be considered a sale by retail.
101	Retailer (General)	75	...	50	...	Authorising the retail of all Goods, Wares and Merchandize (except Spirits, Wines, Beer, Tobacco, Gold & Silver wares, Opium and Gandia.
102	Retailer (Consolidated License) ...	220	...	200	...	Not authorised to retail Gold and Silver wares, Opium and Gandia.
103	Sail maker	11	...	11	...	
104	Seller of :					
	Cattle (in a market or elsewhere) ...	4	50	4	50	
	Poultry (in a market, shop, or public place.	5	50	5	50	

No.	Business, Profession, or Trade.	Duty for 6 calendar months.				Remarks.
		Port Louis and Curepipe.		Country Districts.		
		Rs.	c.	Rs.	c.	
105	Seller of Dunnage wood	8	25	8	25	
	,, Firewood and charcoal ...	5	...	5	...	
106	Scavenger	11	...	5	50	
107	Shipchandler	55	...	55	...	
108	Shipwright	33	...	33	...	
109	Shoemaker employing not more than 2 assistants.	5	...	5	...	
110	do. with more than 2 assistants ...	10	...	10	...	
111	Soap-maker	10	...	10	...	
112	Stationer	11	...	8	25	
113	Stevedore	10	...	10	...	
114	Supplier of fresh water to ships ...	1	10	...	...	Per ton of Tank boat.
115	Tailor :					
	a. Employing not more than 2 assistants.	7	50	5	...	
	b. Employing more than 2 assistants	15	...	10	...	
116	Tanner	11	...	11	...	
117	Tavern keeper or keeper of a Restaurant	132	...	132	...	
118	Timber Merchant	50	...	25	...	
119	Tinsmith					
	With not more than 2 assistants ...	5	...	4	...	
	With more than 2 assistants ...	10	...	8	...	
120	Undertaker	30	...	30	...	
121	Upholsterer	8	25	7	...	
122	Usher :					
	a. Supreme Court	22	...	...	...	
	b. District Court	16	50	16	50	
123	Vegetable and Fruit seller :					
	a. In a market or shop	3	25	3	25	*a.* Exclusive of a separate license of Rs. 2 every six months for every extra stall.
	b. Elsewhere than in a market or shop	3	30	3	30	
124	Victualler selling cooked food to be consumed :					
	a. Off the premises	10	...	7	50	
	b. On the premises	12	...	12	...	
	c. On or off the premises ...	20	...	15	...	
125	Warehouseman (not issuing Dock-warrants.)	27	50	27	50	
126	Watchmaker	11	...	5	50	With right to sell watches and watch cases.
127	Sworn-Weigher	11	...	11	...	
128	Wharfinger	25	...	25	...	
129	Wholesale Dealer or Merchant ...	165	..	165	...	Has the right to sell all goods, wares and merchandize—except Gandia.
130	Wholesale Retailer, Consolidated License.	360	...	360	...	Authorising the sale of all goods, wares and merchandize by wholesale, except Gandia, and of all goods, wares and merchandize, except Gold and Silver wares, Opium & Gandia by Retail.
131	Wholesale Seller of Gandia ...	500	...	500	...	This License to be issued only to importers of Gandia. A sale of more than 20 grammes to be considered wholesale.

TARIFF OF FEES.

		Rs.	c.
Schedule K of Ordinance 6 of 1878. Art. 88.	For every duplicate License	2	00
	For every endorsement of transfer on License	1	00
	For every Certificate under Article 106	2	00
	Yearly Licenses.		
Ordinance No. 24 of 1895.	License to shoot Game	11	00
Ordinances 6 of 1878 and 24 of 1895.	License to deal in Game	5	50
	Warehouseman issuing Dock Warrants	66	00

EXEMPTIONS.

1. Hawkers or sellers of any produce of the soil of the Colony grown or manufactured by himself except Spirits, Timber and Tobacco.
2. Hawkers or sellers of any Animal reared by himself, or eggs of poultry reared by himself.
3. Hawkers of Bread only.
4. Baker employing only one assistant or none.
5. Brush makers.
6. Washermen and Laundresses.
7. Shoemakers employing one assistant.
8. Milliners employing fewer than five assistants.
9. Tailors employing one assistant only.
10. Mattress makers.
11. Umbrella menders.
12. Blacksmiths and Farriers employing one assistant.
13. Tinsmiths employing one assistant.
14. Barbers.
15. Holders of Tea and Coffee stalls.

TABLE OF FEES TO BE LEVIED IN THE IMMIGRATION OFFICE.

	Rs.	c.
1. For every duplicate of a ticket, cost of Photograph included (Art. 15.)	5	00
2. For every Photograph of an Immigrant	0	25
3. For every passport (Art. 16)	1	00
4. For every release from Industrial Residence	1	00
5. For every Certicate of engagement Photograph included (Art. 27)	0	75
6. For every transfer of a Contract (Art. 62)	1	00
7. For every Certificate under Arts. 104 and 106 of Schedule 22	0	50

TARIFF PAID FOR THE STORAGE OF GUN POWDER AT THE MARTELLO TOWER.

Per hundred kilos ... ... Rs. 4.00

Authority under which levied.	Description of Tax.	Rates. Rs.	c.
	COLONIAL SPIRITS.		
	Excise duty on Rum sold for Home Consumption.		
Ordinances No. 21 of 1895.	Colonial Spirits, on delivery for Home Consumption, shall be liable to an excise duty of One Rupee and twenty cents per litre of 23 degrees of strength according to Cartier's Areometer; and to an additional duty of 4 cents per litre for every degree in excess of the said strength.		
	Storage of Rum in Central Warehouse.		
Ordinance No. 19 of 1877. Sch. D. Section (B) III.	On the storage of Rum in the Central Rum Warehouse, Rent shall be charged at the following rates :		
	(1) On every 4 Gallons or Lit. 18.17 issued for Home Consumption.	0	25
	(2) Do. 24 Gallons or Lit 109.04 deposited in the Central Rum Warehouse per month	0	25
	PATENTS.		
Ordinance No. 6 of 1875.	Every Certificate under Article 10	100	
	Every Patent under Article 11	20	
	ROAD TAX.		
	Pamplemousses.		
Ord. No. 33 of 1858.	6 per cent Direct Tax levied on the inhabitants for repairs to road from Villebague to L'Ilot.		
	STAMP DUTIES.		
	Schedule A.		
	Stamp duty in proportion to the size of the paper used.		
	Large Register paper (Royal)	...	75
	,, paper (demi-Royal	...	50
Ord. No. 2 of 1869.	Middle size paper (Foolscap	...	38
	Small size paper (Letter)	...	24
	Half sheet	...	12
	Schedule B.		
Ord. No. 2 of 1869.	Instruments and writings subject to a Fixed Stamp duty :		
	Charter-parties or any agrement or Contract for the Charter of any sea-going ship or vessel, or any Memorandum, Letter or other Writing being equivalent to a charter-party, for each copy....	1	...
	Bills of lading of or for any goods, &c., for each part of every set....	...	25
	Survey Reports on ships, each copy	...	50
	Do. do. on Goods, do.	...	50
	Each Marine Protest	...	50
	Each extension of Protest	2	...
	Transfer or Registration or transfer in the books of any Company of each Share of any Financial, Commercial, Industrial or Civil Society, Partnership or Association whatsoever	...	50
	Every Dock Warrant	2	...
	Each legalisation of Signature	5	...

Authority under which levied.	Description of Tax.	Rates. Rs.	c.
	Each Passport when required	2	...
	Security Bonds for Public Officers when salary does not exceed 2,000 Rupees	5	...
	In all other cases	10	...
	Security Bonds for the performance of any Public Contract &c ...	10	...
	Do. against any Breach of the Law	2	50
	Do. taken in any Court of Law for any purpose whatsoever	2	50
	Custom-House Bonds	..	50
	All other Bonds and Obligations taken as securities and not hereinbefore specified	...	50
	Any foreign Bill of Exchange drawn in and payable out of the colony on demand	...	50
	Each Debenture, Title (Titre) or Certificate of Share (Action) in any Financial, Commercial, Industrial or Civil Society, Company, Partnership or Association whatever	...	90
	Schedule C.		
	Instruments and Writings subject to an *ad valorem* Stamp Duty :		
	Inland Bills of Exchange and Promissory notes payable to Order or to Bearer, each Account or Obligation accepted and payable to Order or Bearer, except Cheques or Money Orders, payable on demand :		
	First scale.		
	Not exceeding Rs. 500	...	25
	Exceeding 500 but not exceeding Rs. 1000	...	50
	1000 ,, 2000	1	...
	2000 ,, 3000	1	50
	3000 ,, 4000	2	...
	4000 ,, 5000	2	50
	5000 ,, 7500	3	75
	7500 ,, 10000	5	...
	10000 ,, 15000	7	50
	15000 ,, 20000	10	...
	20000 ,, 30000	15	...
	30000 ,, 40000	20	...
	And for every additional Rs. 10,000 or part of Rs. 10,000 the duty shall increase by Rs. 5.		
Ord. No. 2 of 1869	Foreign Bills of Exchange drawn in, but payable out of this Colony not being payable on demand, if drawn singly, or otherwise than in a set of three, shall be subject to a stamp duty according to the following scale :		

Authority under which levied	Description of Tax.	Rates. Rs.	c.
	STAMPS—(*Continued*).		
	Second Scale.		
	Not exceeding Rs. 500	...	15
	500 and not exceeding Rs. 1000... ...	...	25
	1000 ,, 2000... ...	...	50
	2000 ,, 3000... ...	...	75
	3000 ,, 4000... ...	1	...
	4000 ,, 5000... ...	1	25
	5000 ,, 7500... ...	1	85
	7500 ,, 10000... ...	2	50
	10000 ,, 15000... ...	3	75
	15000 ,, 20000... ...	5	...
	20000 ,, 30000... ...	7	50
	30000 ,, 40000... ...	10	...
	For each additional Rs. 10,000 or part of Rs. 10,000 an additional duty of 2 Rupees and 50 cents.		
	The said Foreign Bills of Exchange drawn in sets of three, shall for every bill of each set, pay a duty according to the following scale:		
	Third Scale.		
	When not exceeding Rs. 500	...	05
	Exceeding 500 and not exceeding Rs. 1000 ...	...	10
	1000 ,, 2000 ...	...	15
	2000 ,, 3000 ...	...	25
	3000 ,, 4000 ...	...	35
	4000 ,, 5000 ...	...	40
	5000 ,, 7500 ...	...	65
	7500 ,, 10000 ...	...	85
	10000 ,, 15000 ...	1	25
	15000 ,, 20000 ...	1	65
	20000 ,, 30000 ...	2	50
	30000 ,, 40000 ...	3	35
	For each additional Rs. 10,000 or part of Rs. 10,000 an additional duty of Eighty-five cents shall be paid.		
	Foreign Bills of Exchange drawn out of, and payable in this Colony, shall pay a Stamp-Duty according to the second scale.		
	Each account or Obligation accepted and payable to Order or Bearer, except Cheques or Money Order payable on demand shall pay duty according to the first hereinbefore mentioned scale.		
	Policies of Insurance or Assurance upon any life or lives shall pay a Stamp-Duty at the rate of Fifty cents per Rs. 1,000, or part of Rs. 1,000.		
	Instruments and Writings, subject to an *ad valorem* Stamp-Duty of Thirteen cents for every Rs. 1,000 or part of Rs. 1,000.		
	Policies of Insurance of any Ship, Vessel, Coaster, Sloop, Lighter Boat or the like or of any Goods, or property on board, or upon freight of any Ship, Vessel, Coaster, Sloop, Lighter, Boat or the like upon any interest relating thereto or upon any voyage.		
	Policies of Insurance for loss or damage by fire. The duty being payable on each policy if the Insurance be for one year or less and yearly if the Insurance extends beyond one year.		
	All policies of Insurance or Assurance not above specified.		

Authority under which levied.	Description of Tax.	Rates.	
	STAMPS—*Continued*	Rs.	c.
	Every Convention subsequent to a policy of Insurance of any kind whatsoever, and containing either the prolongation of the Insurance or an augmentation in the premium in the Capital insured.		
	Instruments and Writings subject to an *ad valorem* duty of Fifty cents per Rs. 1,000 or part of Rs 1,000.		
	Bonds and other Obligations concerning Respondentia or Bottomry.		
Ord. 29 of 1894.	On every Fire Insurance Company, whether entirely established or having merely an Agency in this Colony, a tax of five per cent is levied on the premiums on all Fire Insurance policies entered into, issued or renewed by such Company or Agency after the coming into force of this Ordinance relating to property situate within the District of Port Louis.		
	Proceeds of this tax are to be paid over to the Mayor of Port Louis on the 1st. March and 1st. September of every year in aid of the Fire Engine Establishment of the Municipality.		
	NATURALIZATION OF ALIENS.		
Ordinance 26 of 1871 & Ordinance 17 of 1877.	Levied through Stamps. 1. Certificate of Naturalization	60	...
	2. Declaration of Alienage of British Nationality ...	1	...
	3. Certificate of re-admission to British Nationality ...	10	...
	4. Transmitting a declaration without Oath of Allegiance...	...	25

TUITION FEES.

ROYAL COLLEGE.

Govt. Notice No. 32 of 1879.—Each pupil per mensem ... ... Rs. 12

ROYAL COLLEGE SCHOOL.

Each pupil over 10 years per mensem ... ... Rs. 10

In case of brothers or half-brothers attending the Royal College and Royal College School, a reduction of Two Rupees is made.

CUREPIPE COLLEGE SCHOOL.

Each pupil over 10 years per mensem ... ... Rs. 10

Each pupil under 10 years per mensem ... ... Rs. 10

In case of brothers, the fee for each brother is Rs. 10 a month.

FEES FOR MARKING WEIGHTS AND MEASURES.

GOVERNMENT NOTICE No. 47 OF 1878.

Fees for stamps and marks affixed by the Inspector of Weights and Measures on all Measures of Length.

1. For every Stamp or Mark on wood ... ... 10 c.
2. For every Stamp or Mark on metal ... ... 20 c.

Fees for stamps and marks affixed on all Weights and Measures.

1. For every Stamp or Mark on wood on a single Weight or Measure of Capacity ... 10 c.
2. For every Stamp or Mark on metal on a single Weight or Measure of Capacity... 20 c.

For Stamps or Marks on a series of Weights or Measures of Capacity, the above rates shall be reduced by 20 per cent.

FEES CHARGEABLE FOR PASSENGERS IN QUARANTINE.

1st. Class passengers	Rs. 4.00	per diem
2nd. „	1.50	„
3rd. „	0.75	„

TARIFF FOR LARGE HACKNEY COACHES IN PORT LOUIS.

§ IV—Limits.

Art. 33.—The town shall be divided into large and small limits.

The large limits shall include the space existing between the "Place d'Armes" and the Church Square, or other Stationing places, which may be appointed hereafter and :

On the North.—The Terre Rouge River from its mouth up to the Briqueterie Bridge.

On the East.—The Vallée des Prêtres Road, as far as the Police Station at the foot of the mountain.

On the West.—The Pailles Road up to the Municipal Post, the Grand River Road as far as the Boundaries of the Municipality.

The Small limits shall include the space existing between the Stationing Places above designated and ;

On the North.—The Sea Shore at the Trou Fanfaron and the old Slaughter House ;

On the East.—The Lataniers River and the Municipal Post on the Vallée des Prêtres Road, near Mr. Duffau's seat.

On the South.—The Upper part of the Champ de Mars and Champ de Lort ;

On the West.—The end of Brabant street, at the point of junction of the Pailles and Grand River Roads, the Cemetery, the Cassis, the Bathing places of the Sea Shore;

§ V—Tariff.—Fares by the Job.

LARGE LIMITS		SMALL LIMITS	
For 1 or 2 persons....................	R. 1.00	For 1 or 2 persons....................	R. 0.50
For every additional person	0.25	For every additional person	0.25

FARES BY THE HOUR.

Within the large as well as the small limits, and whatever may be the number of persons provided it shall not exceed the number of seats in the Carriage.

For every hour... ... ... R. 1.50

The first hour shall not be fractioned, every subsequent hour may be fractioned by quarter.

Art. 36.—It shall be lawful for any person having hired a Carriage for a job, either in the small or large limits, to avail himself of the Carriape going back to its Station, on his paying half the fare, provided he shall not cause the same to wait more than a quarter of an hour.

Art. 37.—Any person who shall send for a Carriage for the purpose of employing it, and who shall decline to do so, shall be bound to pay the Coachman half the price of the job according to the Tariff.

SMALL HACKNEY COACHES.

§ VI—Limits.

Art. 33.—The Town shall be divided into large and small limits.—(*Same as* Large Hackney Coaches which see.)

TARIFF.—FARES BY THE JOB.

Large Limits.		*Small Limits.*	
For 1 or 2 persons...	R. 0.50	For 1 or 2 persons...	R. 0.25
For every additional person...	0.25	For every additional person...	0.12

FARES BY THE HOUR.

Within the large as well as the small limits, and whatever may be the number of persons provided it shall not exceed the number of seats in the Carriage.

For every hour ... R. 1.00

The first hour shall not be fractioned, every subsequent hour may be fractioned by quarter.

ART. 36.—It shall be lawful for any person having hired a Carriage for a job, either in the small or large limits, to avail himself of the Carriage going back to the Station; on his paying half the fare, provided he shall not cause the same to wait more than a quarter of an hour.

ART. 37.—Any person who shall send for a carriage for the purpose of employing it, and who shall decline to do so, shall be bound to pay to the Coachman half the price of the job according to the tariff.

HACKNEY CARRIOLES.

§ VI—LIMITS.

ART. 33.—The town shall be divided into large and small limits. -(*Same as for* LARGE HACKNEY COACHES with see).

TARIFF.—FARES BY THE JOB.

Large Limits.		*Small Limits.*	
For 1 or 2 persons...	R. 0.50	For 1 or 2 persons...	R. 0.25
For every additional person...	0·25	For every additional person...	0.12

FARES BY THE HOUR.

Within the large as well as the small limits, and whatever may be the number of persons provided it shall not exceed the number of seats in the Carriole.

For every hour ... ... R. 0.75

The first hour shall not be fractioned, every subsequent hour may be fractioned by quarter.

ART. 36.—It shall be lawful for any person having hired a Carriole for a job, either in the small or large limits, to avail himself of the Carriole going back to the Station; on his paying half the fare, provided he shall not cause the same to wait more than a quarter of an hour.

ART. 37.—Any person who shall send for a Carriole for the purpose of employing it, and who shall decline to do so, shall be bound to pay to the Coachman half the price of the job, according to the Tariff.

TARIFF FOR PLYING BOATS IN THE HARBOUR OF PORT LOUIS.

Fares for the hire of Plying boats shall be chargeable at the following rates.

For a boat with a pair of oars; to the inner harbour (that is: within a line supposed to be drawn from the extremity of " Reserves " street near the Chinese Mosque, to the Canal passing through the Chaussée of Tonneliers Island ") and returning.

For one person	R. 0.50
,, each additional person	0.12
,, luggage weighing 25 lbs and under 100 lbs ...	0.12
,, every additional 100 lbs	0.08

For the outer harbour (that is: between the line abovementioned, and a line supposed to be drawn from the flag staff at Fort George to that at Fort William) and returning:

For one person	R. 1.00
,, each additional person	0.25
,, luggage weighing 25 lbs and under 100 lbs ...	0.25
,, each additional 100 lbs	0.17

To the outer anchorage and returning:

For one person	R. 2.00
,, each additional person	1.00
,, luggage weighing 25 lbs and under 100 lbs ...	0.33

For a boat with four oars, double the amount allowed above.

The above rates are applicable for Boats employed from gun fire in the morning till the firing of the evening gun; after which time and until gun fire in the morning, double the above rates are allowed to be charged.

CUSTOMS DUES.

No. of Law.	Title.	Extent of repeal.
Ord. No. 17 of 1881 ...	To increase the import and license duties on Opium.	Article 1 modified by substituting a duty of twenty-two rupees and forty four rupees per kilogram respectively, in lieu of a duty of twenty rupees and forty rupees as therein mentioned.
Ord. No. 5 of 1886 ...	To abolish Quay Dues and to substitute Customs Duties in lieu thereof.	The whole Ordinance.
Ord. No. 16 of 1886 ...	To substitute amended Schedules for the Schedules annexed to Ord. No. 5 of 1886, entitled "An Ordinance to abolish Quay Dues, and to substitute Customs Duties in lieu thereof.	The whole Ordinance.
Ord. No. 7 of 1887 ...	To amend the law permitting and regulating the importation and sale of Gandia.	Article 7 modified by substituting a duty of twenty two rupees per kilogram in lieu of the duty of twenty rupees as therein provided.
Ord. No. 34 of 1888 ...	To exempt from Customs Dues Tobacco grown in Rodrigues.	Article 2 only.
Ord. No. 20 of 1890 ...	To provide additional ways and means for meeting the public expenditure of this Colony up to the end of the year 1891.	Item 1 of Article 1 only.
Ord. No. 29 of 1890 ...	To provide for the levying of Customs Duty according to weight, measurement or number, on certain articles now liable to duty according to value.	The whole Ordinance.
Ord. No. 12 of 1893 ...	To increase the Import duty on Fireworks and to impose a license duty on Manufacturers of Fireworks.	Article I only.
Ord. No. 20 of 1893 ...	To provide additional ways and means for meeting the Public Expenditure of the Colony up to the end of the year 1894.	The whole Ordinance.
Ord. No. 17 of 1894 ...	To provide additional ways and means for meeting the Public Expenditure of the Colony up to the end of the year 1895.	The whole of the unrepealed part of the Ordinance.
Ord. No. 26 of 1894 ...	To amend Schedule A of Ordinance No. 16 of 1886.	The whole Ordinance.

IMPORTS

Description of Goods.	Duty how chargeable.	Rate of Duty Rs.	c.
1.—Ale, Beer, Porter, Cider and Perry... In casks ...	per hectolitre ...	7	85
In bottles...	per dozen bottles, each bottle not to exceed one litre.	1	20
	per dozen bottles, each bottle not to exceed five decilitres.	...	60
2.—Almonds	per 100 kilos ...	3	85
3.—Anchors and Grapnels	do. ...	1	65
4.—Animals: Dogs	per head ...	6	05
Asses, horses, mules	do. ...	...	60
Cattle and Oxen	do. ...	...	25
Other live stock	do. ...	...	10
5.—Animal charcoal	per 1,000 kilos ...	...	30
6.—Arrowroot	per 100 kilos ...	2	75
7.—Asphaltum	per 1,000 kilos ...	1	40
8.—Assafœtida	per 100 kilos ...	7	...
9.—Bacon, Hams, Sausages and Tongues	do. ...	5	...
10.—Bags, Pockets linen (empty)	per 100 pockets ...	...	80
,, Vacoa and Madagascar Straw (empty) ...	per 100 bags ...	...	10
,, Of all other descriptions (empty)	do. ...	1	20
11.—Bark	per 1,000 kilos ...	11	...
12.—Barley	per 100 kilos ...	1	...
Do. Pearl	do. ...	2	85
13.—Beans	do. ...	1	...
14.—Beef and Pork salted	do. ...	2	...
Beer (see Ale)			
15.—Biscuits (not sweetened)	do. ...	1	10
16.—Bitumen	per 1,000 kilos ...	1	40
Blue Prussian (see Indigo)			
17.—Bran	per 100 kilos ...	...	80
18.—Brassware	do. ...	12	10
19.—Bread	do. ...	1	...
20.—Bricks and Tiles	per 100 bricks or tiles ...	...	10
21.—Brimstone or Sulphur: common	per 100 kilos ...	...	70
refined	do. ...	1	30
Bungs (see Cork)			
22.—Bunting	per metre ...	...	15
23.—Butter, Margarine, or any other substance sold or used as butter...	per 100 kilos ...	4	50
24.—Camphor: crude...	do. ...	9	...
refined and in powder	do. ...	12	50
25.—Candles ...: parafine	do. ...	3	...
Sperm	do. ...	3	...
Wax	do. ...	10	...
composition and all other sorts ...	do. ...	3	...
26.—Canvas...	do. ...	3	...
27.—Caoutchouc (manufactured)	do. ...	18	...
28.—Caps (percussion)...	per 1,000 caps ...	...	20
29.—Capsules (bottling)	per 100 capsules ...	1	10
30.—Cardamonds: common	per 100 kilos ...	2	30
small	do. ...	33	...
31.—Cards, playing	ad valorem ...	25 o/o	...
32.—Cartridges...: empty	per 100 cartridges ...	...	20
loaded	do. ...	...	25

Description of Goods.	Duty how chargeable.	Rate of Duty. Rs.	c.
33.—Casks, empty, old or new	per cask		55
34.—Cement	per 100 kilos... ...		30
Cider (see Ale)			
35.—Cinnamon	per 100 kilos... ...	3	...
36.—Charcoal	do.		10
37.—Cheese	do.	5	...
38.—Chillies	do.	2	...
Chocolate (see Cocoa)			
39.—Choorah	per 100 kilos... ..		70
40.—Cloves	do.	5	...
41.—Clay, pipe and fire...	per 1000 kilos ...	5	...
42.—Coals, Coke & Patent Fuel	per 1000 kilos ...		55
43.—Cocoa & Chocolate...	per 100 kilos... ...	13	20
44.—Cocoanuts	per 100 cocoanuts ...		05
45.—Coffee	per 100 kilos... ...	5	...
46.—Coir fibre	per 100 kilos... ...		85
Coke (see Coals)			
47.—Copper old	per 100 kilos... ...	3	...
sheets, bars, bolts, nails &c., (red) ...	do.	8	80
Do. (yellow metal	do.	4	40
48.—Copperah or Poonac	per 100 kilos... ...		10
49.—Cordage { Coir	do.	2	...
do. oiled	do.	4	10
Hemp	do.	2	20
do. oiled	do.	5	...
50.—Corks and bungs	per 1000		55
51.—Corn flour	per 100 kilos... ...	5	...
52.—Cotton { Wool	do.	1	90
Wick	do.	2	75
Waste	do.	1	95
Cutch (see Gambier)			
53.—Detonators	per 1000	5	...
54.—Dholl	per 100 kilos... ...	1	10
55.—Dye wood	per 1000 kilos ...	11	...
56.—Dynamite	per 100 kilos... ...	14	...
57.—Eggs (fresh or preserved)	per 1000	2	20
58.—Felt sheathing	per 100 sheets ...		60
59.—Fibre, jute, rafia and all other sorts	per 100 kilos ...	3	30
60.—Firewood	per 2 cubic metres ...		15
61.—Fireworks	ad valorem	16.50 per o/o	
62.—Fish { dried or salted	per 100 kilos... ...	1	00
pickled	do.	1	35
63.—Fruits { dried (except cocoanuts)	do.	2	50
and vegetables (fresh	per pkge of 50 kilos ...		25
64.—Gambier or Cutch...	per 100 kilos ...	2	20
65.—Gandia	per kilo	22	...
66.—Ghee	per 100 kilos... ...	12	...
67.—Ginger, dry	do.	1	65
68.—Glass { window	per 100 metres ...	2	20
bottles, empty	per 100 bottles ...		10
69.—Glue	per 100 kilos... ...	3	30
70.—Gram	do.	1	10
Grapnels (see Anchors)			
71.—Grease, Cart	do.	1	10
72.—Gum { arabic	do.	2	20
copal	do.	8	80
73.—Gunpowder { sporting	do.	6	...
blasting	do.	1	10
Hams (see Bacon)...			
74.—Hay and Straw	do.		15
75.—Hemp, undressed	do.	2	75
76.—Hides { raw and salted	do.	3	30
tanned	do.	4	95

Description of Goods.	Duty how chargeable.	Rate of duty. Rs.	c.
77.—Hogslard	per 100 kilos ...	4	15
78.—Honey	per hectolitre ...	3	...
79.—Hops	per 100 kilos ...	1	65
80.—Horns	per 1,000 horns ...	...	85
81.—Horse hair	per 100 kilos ...	5	50
82.—India rubber (manufactured)...	do. ...	17	60
83.—Indigo, Prussian Blue, Ultramarine Blue and any like preparation sold or used for laundry purposes ...	per kilo ...	1	10
84.—Iron { wire netting and galvanized	per 100 kilos ...	3	...
84.—Iron { pig	per 1,000 kilos ...	2	20
84.—Iron { bars, hoops, pipes, wire, nails, galvanized sheets, ridging, chains, &c.	do. ...	8	...
85.—Jams	per 100 kilos ...	3	50
86.—Jellies	do. ...	3	50
87.—Lead, sheet and pipes	do. ...	1	40
88.—Lead, shot	do. ...	3	...
89.—Leather, sole	do. ...	8	...
90.—Lemon juice	per hectolitre ...	3	30
91.—Lentils	per 100 kilos ...	...	65
92.—Lime	do. ...	...	20
93.—Lime juice	per hectolitre ...	3	30
94.—Macaroni	per 100 kilos ...	3	30
95.—Mace	per kilo ...	...	60
96.—Machinery & Apparatus for the manufacture & improvement of Sugar, Rum or other produce of the Colony...	per 1,000 kilos ...	1	10
Do. when using the Crane	do. ...	2	10
97.—Maize	per 100 kilos ...	...	80
98.—Malt	do. ...	1	65
99.—Manure of all sorts: and the following substances when imported for the purpose of being used in the preparation of Manures, or of other Colonial Produce or as Disinfectants :			
1.—Ammoniacal Liquor			
2.—Bones, Bonedust, Bone oil and Dissolved bones ...			
3.—Carbolic Acid			
4.—Carbonate of Baryte			
5.—Chloride of Lime and of Potassium			
6.—Chloride of Manganese			
7.—Chloride of Soda, Solution of Soda			
8.—Chloride of Zinc			
9.—Coal and Wood Soot			
10.—Dried Muscular Flesh and Dried Blood			
11.—Ether			
12.—Fish and other substances damaged and condemned by the Customs San. Offic. as fit for Manure only ...			
13.—Lime, Carbonate of Lime, Sulphate of Lime or Gypsum, Phosphate and Superphosphate of Lime ...	per 1,000 kilos ...	...	30
14.—Nitrates, Silicates and Carbonate of Potash and Soda.			
15.—Perchloride of Iron			
16.—Permanganate of Potash			
17.—Phosphate of Soda			
18.—Phosphoric Acid (Solid)			
19.—Substances imported by Agriculturists and to be issued in the destruction of insects or other parasies prejudicial to agriculture			
20.—Sulphate of Iron			
21.—Sulphate and Muriate of Ammonia and other Ammoniacal Salts			
22.—Sulphate of Potash and Sulphate of Potassium ...			
23.—Sulphate of Zinc...			
24.—Sulphuric Acid			
25.—Urate and Sulphurated Urine			
Margarine (see Butter)			
100.—Marmalade	per 100 kilos ...	3	50

Description of Goods.	Duty how chargeable.	Rate of duty.	
		Rs.	c.
101.—Matches	per gross, on boxes containing each not more than 100 matches and a proportional duty on boxes containing more than 100 matches.	1	10
102.—Mats and Matting	per 100 kilos	2	75
103.—Molasses	do.	1	10
104.—Moss	do.	10	...
105.—Mustard (prepared)	do.	3	30
106.—Nuts { Areca	do.	2	...
do. boiled	do.	5	...
Gall	do.	2	50
107.—Nuts { Pistachio	do.	1	10
Walnuts	do.	3	60
All other sorts	do.	2	50
108.—Nutmegs	do.	4	50
109.—Oakum	do.	3	30
110.—Oatmeal	do.	1	65
111.—Oats	do.	1	10
112.—Oils { Castor	do.	3	30
Gingely, Mustard and Pistachio	do.	2	75
Cocoanut (when not imported from the Oil Is.*)	per hectolitre	1	65
Do. (when imported from the Oil Islands)	do.	...	06
Olive in cases	per case not exceeding 12 litres	...	55
Neatsfoot	per hectolitre	4	...
Petroleum	do.	3	30
Colza	do.	2	75
Linseed	do.	1	95
All other sorts (except perfumed)	do.	2	75
113.—Opium { Crude	per kilogram	25	...
Refined	do.	50	...
114.—Paper Cigarette	per kilog: (gross weight)	4	40
Patent Fuel (see Coals)			
115.—Peas	per 100 kilos	1	...
116.—Pepper { White	do.	16	50
Black	do.	11	...
Perry (see Ale)			
117.—Pitch	do.	...	55
118.—Plaster of Paris	do.	4	10
Pockets (empty see Bags)			
119.—Pollard	do.	1	...
Poonac (see Copperah)			
Pork salted (see Beef)			
Porter (see Ale)			
Prussian Blue (see Indigo)			
120.—Rabannahs, not exceeding 2 metres each	per 100 pieces	1	65
121.—Rattans	per 100 kilos	...	55
122.—Rice	do.	...	60
123.—Rope { coir	do.	2	...
do. oiled	do.	4	10
hemp	do.	2	20
do. oiled	do.	5	...
124.—Rosin	do.	...	75
125.—Sago	do.	1	...
126.—Salt	per 100 kilos	1	...
127.—Sand, moulding	per 1,000 kilos	...	85
Sausages (see Bacon)			
128.—Seeds { Aniseed	do.	3	...
Coriander	do.	3	...
Gingely, Linseed, Mustard, Metty, Millet, Poppy and all others.	do.	1	...

* In addition to a sum of Rs. 4,000 paid under Ordinance No. 41 of 1875.

Description of Goods.	Duty how chargeable.	Rate of duty. Rs.	c.
129.—Shooks, per bundle containing not more than sufficient to make one barrel, cask or tierce (tierçon) and a proportional duty on bundles containing more than the above quantity	per bundle	...	55
130.—Skins, sheep and goat (tanned)	per 100 kilos... ...	6	60
131.—Slates and Stones for building and paving ...	per 100	...	15
132.—Soap (ordinary not including scented)	per 100 kilos... ...	1	40
133.—Soda, caustic	do.	...	80
134.—Solder...	do.	3	85
135.—Spirits, plain or compounded, of any strength not exceeding proof according to Syke's Hydrometer, and a further proportional duty for any greater strength...	per litre	1	20
136.—Starch	per 100 kilos... ...	...	85
137.—Steel, unwrought...	do.	2	20
Stones, for building and paving (see Slates			
Straw (see Hay)			
138.—Sugar ... { raw	do.	1	65
refined and sugar candy	do.	5	25
139.—Sulphate { iron	do.	...	55
copper	do.	1	65
Sulphur (see Brimstone)			
140.—Tallow	do.	2	20
141.—Tamarinds	do.	...	75
142.—Tapioca	do.	1	65
143.—Tar	do.	...	55
144.—Tea	per kilo	...	10
Tiles (see Bricks)			
145.—Tin plates	per 100 kilos... ...	1	40
146.—Tin-slabs	do.	8	80
147.—Tobacco { Manufactured	per kilo	2	45
Unmanufactured	do.	1	85
Unmanufactured, grown and produced in any of the Dependencies of Mauritius except Seychelles	do.	...	35
Cigars and Snuff	do.	3	30
Tongues (see Bacon)			
148.—Treacle	per 100 kilos... ...	1	10
149.—Turmeric	do.	2	...
150.—Turpentine	per hectolitre ...	2	20
151.—Twines { hemp	per 100 kilos... ...	2	45
of all other sorts	do.	1	65
152.—Vanilla	per kilog.	1	65
153.—Varnish (all kinds)	per hectolitre ...	5	50
Vegetables fresh (see fruits)			
154.—Vermicelli	per 100 kilos... ...	3	30
155.—Vinegar	per hectolitre ...	1	40
156.—Wax { bees	per 100 kilos... ...	6	60
sealing and bottling	do.	2	20
157.—Wheat	do.	...	60
158.—Wheat flour	do.	...	90
159.—Wines { In casks	per hectolitre* ...	7	65
In bottles	per dozen bottles, each bottle not to exceed 1 litre	1	20
	per half doz, bottles, each half bottle not to exceed 5 decilitres.	...	60
Do. Sparkling Champagne and others ...	Per bottle not exceeding 1 litre	...	10
	Per half bottle not exceeding 5 decilitres ...	...	05

* When not exceeding 18° of Gay Lusac's Areometer and each degree above to pay the duty upon spirits per litre as per hectolitre of wine.

Description of Goods.	Duty how chargeable.	Rate of duty. Rs.	c.
160.—All goods, wares and merchandize not otherwise charged with Duty, or not mentioned above, or not specially exempted, shall be liable to an *ad valorem* duty of per centum	....	10o/o	

EXPORTS.

Description of Goods.	Duty how chargeable.	Rate of duty. Rs.	c.
1.—Sugar, the produce of Mauritius	per 100 kilos ...	...	30
2.—Goods exported from Bond	per 1,000 kilos or per ton metric measure.	1	...
3.—Goods landed at this Port in transit for other ports ...			
4.—Goods landed from Vessels in distress, and reshipped...			

SCHEDULE C.

Exemptions.

No.	Description of Goods.
1	Ballast, when the same consists of Sand or Stone.
2	Glass bottles, imported full, (except fancy bottles or decanters).
3	Instruments for Regimental Bands.
4	Ice.
5	School Materials for the use of Free Schools.
6	Articles imported for the use of His Excellency the Governor.
7	Articles of Civil, Naval, and Military Uniform, intended for the personal use of the Importer.
8	Provisions and Stores of every description imported or supplied from Bond for the Colonial Government, or, under special authority from the Governor, for the use of Ships of war of Foreign nations.
9	Wearing Apparel, Luggage, or any instrument intended for Professional use, if it be the property of a person coming to the Colony, and if it arrives within *three months* before or after the arrival of such person.
10	All goods upon which the full amount of Duty shall have been paid on their first importation into Mauritius, legally exported hence and afterwards returned: provided such goods shall be returned within *three years* from the date of their exportation, and it be proved, to the satisfaction of the Collector of Customs that they are the identical goods exported from Mauritius; and provided the property of such goods continue in the person by whom or on whose account the same were exported.
11	Objects and Specimens (Animal, Mineral and Vegetable) illustrative of Natural History, including live plants and vegetable productions connected with the study of Botany.
12	Animals and Goods (except Oil, Spirits and Tobacco) the produce of any of the Dependencies of Mauritius other than Seychelles.
13	Books and Music.
14	Coin and Bullion.
15	Leeches.
16	Seeds intended for Agricultural and horticultural purposes.
17	Poultry.
18	Goods imported into Mauritius by the proper Military authorities for the public use of Her Majesty's land Forces (Ord. 9 of 1887).
19	Goods in Transit transhipped direct from vessel to vessel.

Prohibitions.

Vine-Plants.—Affected with any disease or brought from a place, beyond the limits of this Island, where any disease of Vine-plants is existing or is supposed to exist or may hereafter exist. Ord. 14 of 1882 and Proclamation No. 9 of 1888.

Base or Counterfeit Coin.

Articles of Foreign Manufactures, and any Packages of such Articles bearing any Names, Brands or Marks, being or purporting to be the Names, Brands or Marks of Manufacturers resident in the United Kingdom.

Indecent or Obscene prints, Paintings, Books, Cards, Lithographic or other Engravings, or any other indecent or obscene Articles.

Infected Cattle, Sheep or other Animals.

Cast-off clothes.—Ordinance No. 22 of 1883.

Goods referred to in Article 14 of merchandize marks—Ordinance 1888.

Restrictions.

Foreign Reprints of Copyright works are admitted under Her Majesty's Order in Council dated 1st. April 1853; but they are liable to a poundage of 20 per cent upon their estimated value. —Ordinance No. 24 of 1851.

The shell of the "Tortue de mer" or "green Turtle" known as "Kakonane," and Turtle Oil, cannot be landed, removed, or imported into Mauritius from any of its Dependencies, except in virtue of a special permit issued by the Collector of Customs in Mauritius.—Ordinance No. 21 of 1871.

☞ *If any goods are imported or brought into Mauritius contrary to any of the Prohibitions or Restrictions mentioned in the above Tables, the same will be forfeited.*

Sworn Weighers.

Sworn Weighers are appointed under and subject to the provisions of Proclamation dated 29th April 1846.

Crane Dues.

Government Order A/951 of June 1869. For the use of the Crane for lifting heavy goods per 1000 kilos Rs. 2.00 (except in the case of machinery imported and paying duty when the charge is R. 1.00 per 1000 kilos.)

Queen's Warehouse.

(*Government Notice of 8th. May 1827 and Ordinance No. 19 of 1877 Section IV, Schedule B.*)

All articles introduced for sale, private use, or amongst Passenger's Luggage, when secured in the Queen's Warehouse for Examination or for the Duties, if not removed within Three days after the authorisation of their delivery, are charged as follows:

	Not exceeding 15 days.		Above 15 days and not exceeding a month.		Exceeding a month, for every 30 days.	
	Rs.	c.	Rs.	c.	Rs.	c.
If not exceeding 250 kilograms	...	25	...	50	...	50
If above 250 and not exceeding 500 kilograms	...	50	1	...	1	...
If above 500 and not exceeding 750 kilograms	...	75	1	50	1	50
If above 750 and not exceeding 1,000 kilograms.. ...	1	...	2	...	2	...
If above 1,000 kilograms, at the rate, per 1,000 kilos of	1	...	2	...	2	...

All goods landed by Sufferance and by Bills of Sight are liable to the above charges for Ren from the date of their being lodged in the Queen's Warehouse.

Boat Licenses.

Proclamation of 16th. December 1823 and Ordinances Nos. 12 of 1848 and 19 of 1877 Section V.	Rs.	c.
Boats, Barges, Lighters, or other Craft employed in loading or unloading vessels, or in supplying or discharging ballast. } per ton, per annum ...	2	...

Careening Hulks.

Ordinances Nos. 24 of 1875 and 19 of 1877.— Section VI.	Rs.	c.
For every hulk moored in any spot in the Trou Fanfaron, there shall be paid a License duty of, per annum	1000	...
For every hulk moored outside the limits of the Harbour of Port Louis, and moored in the shallow parts of the Harbour of Port Louis, there shall be paid a license duty of, per annum	600	...

Examination of Animals.

Fees chargeable by Veterinary Health Officer attached to the Custom-House.	Rate of duty.	
Ordinance No. 11 of 1879.	Rs.	c.
1.—*Examination within the Harbour.*		
For examination of and Report on the following animals :—		
Dogs, not exceeding five	3	...
Do. exceeding 5 and not exceeding 10	4	...
Do. do. 10	5	...
Asses, Mules, Horses (including Ponies) not collectively exceeding 10 head ...	4	...
Do. exceeding 10 and not exceding 20 head	6	...
Do. do. 20 50 ,, ...	10	...
Do. do. 50 100 ,, ...	15	...
For every additional 50 or less	7	50
Horned Cattle, and all Animals other than those above enumerated :—		
Not collectively exceeding 10 head	2	...
Exceeding 10 and not exceeding 20 head	4	...
Do. 20 do. 50 ,, ...	5	...
Do. 50 do. 100 ,, ...	8	...
For every additional 50 or less	3	...
2.—*Examination outside of the Harbour.*		
The above charges to be increased by 25 o|o.		
☞ In all cases a boat for the Veterinary Health Officer must be supplied by Importers.		

Harbour Dues.

Ordinance No. 3 of 1890.

Particulars.	Charges.	
	Rs.	c.
(1) PILOTAGE.		
a. For pilotage inwards, and mooring: per ton of register	...	12
b. For unmooring, and pilotage outwards: per ton of register...	...	12
c. For the pilotage inwards and mooring, of any steamer entering the harbour merely for the purpose of taking coals, provisions, or water: per ton of register ...	...	06
d. For the mooring and pilotage outwards of any such steamer: per ton of register...	...	06
e. For taking a pilot to the Bell Buoy and not entering the harbour:		
For vessels under 500 tons	15	...
For vessels above 500 tons and under 1,500 tons	20	...
For vessels above 1,500 tons	25	...
(2) TOWAGE.		
a. For every vessel not above 100 tons...	20	...
b. For every vessel above 100 and not exceeding 200 tons	25	...
c. For every vessel above 200 and not exceeding 400 tons: per ton of register ...	...	15
d. For every vessel above 400 tons: Sixty Rupees (Rs. 60) for the first 400 tons, and for every ton in excess of 400 tons	...	10
(3) ANCHORAGE.		
a. For every vessel breaking bulk or receiving cargo: per ton of register ...	...	20
b. For every colonial registered vessel trading with Madagascar, Reunion, or the Dependencies of Mauritius; per ton of register	...	07
Provided the last charge of R. 0.07 per ton on any such vessel shall not be levied on any vessel more than twice in one year.		
c. For every vessel not breaking bulk nor receiving cargo: per ton of register ...	...	05
d. For moving any vessel from one berth to another in the harbour: per ton of register	...	05
e. For swinging any vessel alongside of a hulk	20	...
f. For remooring any vessel	20	...
g. For any vessel remaining swung on warps above 24 hours, or above 48 hours when the Harbour Master has certified in writing that the vessel was prevented by unfavorable winds from leaving the harbour at the end of 24 hours after having been swung:—		
If under 100 tons	10	...
If above 100 tons but under 1,000	30	...
If above 1,000 tons but under 1,500 tons	60	...
Above 1,500 tons	70	...
(4) HIRE OF CHAINS, ANCHORAGE AND BOATS.		
a. For every vessel not above 150 tons—		
One Anchor, per diem	...	50
One Chain, per diem	...	50
b. For vessels above 150 tons:—		
One Anchor, per diem	1	25
One Chain, per diem	1	25

Harbour Dues.—*Continued.*

Particulars.	Charges.	
(4) Hire of chains, anchors, and boats.—*Continued.*	Rs.	c.
c. For the use of mooring-chains or anchors placed around Trou Fanfaron :—		
For each vessel not above 100 tons ;—per diem	...	50
For each vessel above 100 tons and not above 400 tons :—per diem ...	1	...
For each vessel above 400 tons :—per diem	2	...
d. For the use of a Launch (manned) :—per diem...	15	...
e. For the use of Mud boats not to be detained over 4 hours alongside the vessel ...	50	...
If kept longer than 4 hours :—per hour	10	...

Vessels in Distress.

Vessels in distress shall henceforth be charged pilotage and other Harbour Dues.

Exemptions.

No pilotage or anchorage dues shall be charged on the following vessels :—

a. British or Foreign Men-of-War or Transports, and vessels belonging to the Government of Mauritius.

b. Vessels breaking bulk at the Bell-Buoy, and discharging cargo to the extent of not more than 25 tons, or landing not more than 5 horses, mules, donkeys, or horned cattle; or 20 sheep, pigs or goats.

c. Vessels touching at Port Louis without entering the Harbour, on their way to some other port, unless the master of any vessel referred to in the preceding section (b) and section (e) of article 1 headed " Pilotage " has requested to be supplied with a pilot.

Abolition.

The charges hitherto levied on port clearances are hereby abolished.

Vessels abandoned.

All vessels abandoned in the Harbour, and sold, shall either be broken up or fitted for sea within six months from the date of sale, subject to a charge of Rs. 10 per diem for every day that every such vessel shall remain not broken up or not fitted for sea after the lapse of six months.

Light Dues.

	Rs.	c.
Local Light-Dues. *Ordinance No. 3 of 1890.*		
There shall be levied on all vessels (excepting Coasters employed on the Coast of Mauritius(entering the Harbour, or discharging or shipping cargo or Immigrants in the Roadstead of Port Louis, per ton	...	09
The above dues shall not be levied more than twice within Twelve Calendar months, on any one vessel.		
Light-Dues for the Great Basses Light House and the Light Basses Light House. *Ordinance No. 23 of 1883—Section II.*		
For every ton of Register of the vessel liable to the Dues	...	07½
Light Dues for the Minicoy Light House. *Ordinance No. 23 of 1883—Section III.*		
For every ton of Register of the vessel liable to the Dues	...	02½

Note: From and after the 1st. July 1892, an abatement or discount of 50 o/o is made on the duties heretofore levied in respect of The Great Basses, The Little Basses and the Minicoy Light Houses. (Her Majesty's Order in Council dated 9th day of May 1892.)

Rates of Postage levied in Mauritius and its Dependencies upon Correspondence addressed to Countries and Colonies, forming part of the Postal Union.

Union Countries.	Letters.				Registration Fee.	Post Cards.	Reply Post Cards.	News-papers.		Commercial Documents.			Printed papers Samples or Patterns of Merchandize.		
	Not exceeding 15 grammes.	Exceeding 15 grammes and not exceeding 30 grammes.	Exceeding 30 grammes and not exceeding 45 grammes.	Every additional 15 grammes.				Not exceeding 50 grammes.	Every additional 50 grammes.	Not exceeding 50 grammes.	Exceeding 50 grammes and not exceeding 100 grammes.	Every additional 50 grammes.	Not exceeding 50 grammes.	Exceeding 50 grammes and not exceeding 100 grammes.	Every additional 50 grammes.
	R. C.	R. C.	R. C.	R. C.	R. C.	R. C.	R. C.	R. C.	R. C.	R. C.	R. C.	R. C.	R. C.	R. C.	R. C.
Africa, West Coast (*A*) ...															
Do. East Africa (*B*) ...															
Argentine Republic ...															
Australian Colonies (*C*) ...															
Australia, Western ...															
Austro-Hungary															
Barbadoes															
Belgium															
Bermuda															
Bolivia															
Brazil															
British Borneo															
British Guiana															
British Honduras... ...															
British India (*D*)															
Bulgaria, Principality of...															
Cameroons...															
Canada, Dominion of (*E*)...															
Canary Islands															
Cape of Good Hope ...															
Cape Verde Islands ...	0.15	0.30	0.45	0.15	0.12	0.06	0.12	0.03	0.03	0.15	0.18	0.03	0.06	0.09	0.03
Ceylon															
Chili															
Columbia, Republic of ...															
Congo															
Costa Rica															
Cyprus															
Denmark															
Danish Colonies (*F*) ...															
Dominica, Republic of ...															
Ecuador, Republic of ...															
Egypt															
France and Algeria ...															
French Colonies (*G*) ...															
Falkland Islands															
Germany															
German Colonies (*H*) ...															
Gibraltar (*I*)															
Grenada															
Grenadine															
Greece															
Guatemala, Republic of ...															

Union Countries.	Letters.							News-papers.		Commercial Documents.			Printed papers Samples or Patterns of Merchandize.		
	Not exceeding 15 grammes.	Exceeding 15 grammes and not exceeding 30 grammes.	Exceeding 30 grammes and not exceeding 45 grammes.	Every additional 15 grammes.	Registration fee.	Post Cards.	Reply Post Cards.	Not exceeding 50 grammes.	Every additional 50 grammes.	Not exceeding 50 grammes.	Exceeding 50 grammes and not exceeding 100 grammes.	Every additional 50 grammes.	Not exceeding 50 grammes.	Exceeding 50 grammes and not exceeding 100 grammes.	Every additional 50 grammes.
	R. C.	R. C.	R. C.	R. C.	R. C.	R. C.	R. C.	R. C.	R. C.	R. C.	R. C.	R. C.	R. C.	R. C.	R. C.
Hawaii ... ... Hayti ... ... Heligoland... ... ... Hong-Kong (*J*) ... ... Honduras, Republic of ... Italy ... ... Jamaica ... ... Japan ... ... Labuan ... ... Leeward Islands (*K*) ... Liberia, Republic of ... Luxembourg ... ... Madeira ... ... Malta ... ... Mexico ... ... Montenegro ... ... Natal ... ... Newfoundland ... ... Netherlands and Netherlands Colonies (*L*) ... Nicaraguay ... ... Norway ... ... Paraguay, Republic of ... Persia ... ... Peru ... ... Portugal ... ... Portuguese Colonies (*M*)... Roumania ... ... Russia ... ... St. Vincent... ... ... Salvador ... ... San Domingo, Republic of Servia ... ... Seychelles ... ... Siam ... ... Spain ... ... Spanish Colonies (*N*) ... Shanghai ... ... Sweden ... ... Switzerland ... ... Straits Settlements ... Tamatave ... ... Trinidad ... ... Turkey	0.15	0.30	0.45	0.15	0.12	0.06	0.12	0.03	0.03	0.15	0.18	0.03	0.06	0.09	0.03

Union Countries.	Letters. Not exceeding 15 grammes.	Letters. Exceeding 15 grammes and not exceeding 30 grammes.	Letters. Exceeding 30 grammes and not exceeding 45 grammes.	Letters. Every additional 15 grammes.	Registration Fee.	Post Cards.	Reply Post Cards.	News-papers. Not exceeding 50 grammes.	News-papers. Every additional 50 grammes.	Commercial Documents. Not exceeding 50 grammes.	Commercial Documents. Exceeding 50 grammes and not exceeding 100 grammes.	Commercial Documents. Every additional 50 grammes.	Printed Papers Samples or patterns of Merchandize. Not exceeding 50 grammes.	Printed Papers Samples or patterns of Merchandize. Exceeding 50 grammes and not exceeding 100 grammes.	Printed Papers Samples or patterns of Merchandize. Every additional 50 grammes.
	R. C.	R. C.	R. C.	R. C.	R. C.	R. C.	R. C.	R. C.	R. C.	R. C.	R. C.	R. C.	R. C.	R. C.	R. C.
State of North Borneo ...															
United Kingdom															
United States of America...															
Uruguay, Republic of ...	0 15	0 30	0 45	0 15	0 12	0 06	0 12	0 03	0 03	0 15	0 18	0 03	0 06	0 09	0 03
Venezuela															
West Indies (O)															
Zanzibar viâ Aden (P) ...															
Réunion															
Soldiers' Letters	0 08	...	...	...	...	...	...	...	...	...	...	...	...	...	...
Unpaid Lettert from Union Countries	0 26	0 52	0 78	0 26	...	...	...	...	...	...	..	...	...	...	...
Do. from Réunion ...	0 20	0 40	0 60	0 20	...	...	...	...	...	..	...	...	...	...	...

REMARKS.

A Acra, Gold Coast, Gambia, Lagos, Sierra Leone — Sette, Cama, Nyanza, Majumba, Grand Bassam Assinie and Black Point (places under French protection).

B Bagamoyo, Dar es Salaam, Tanga and Lindi (German Agencies).

C New South Wales, Victoria, South Australia, Western Australia, Queensland, British New Guinea, Tasmania, New Zealand and Fiji.

D Bagdad, Bundor Abbas, Bushire, Bussora, Gaudhur, Lingo, Muscat, Mandalay, the correspondence for these places is assimilated to that of British India.

D Cashmere, Cabul, Djulja, Ladakh, Teheran, the correspondence for these places is assimilated to that of British India, but on condition of compulsory prepayment.

E New Brunswick, Nova Scotia, Prince Edward Island, Vancouver's Island and British Colombia.

F St. Thomas, St. Croix, St. John, Greenland, Faroe Island and Iceland.

G Chandernagor, Cochin China, French Guiana, Gabon, Guadeloupe, Cayenne, Karikal, Martinique, Mayotte, Mahé, Marquisers Island, New Caledonia, Pondicherry, Senegal, Tamatave, Ste. Marie de Madagascar, St. Pierre and Miquelon, Tahiti, correspondence for Camboge and Tonkin is assimilated to that of Cochin China.

H Viz—Marshall Islands, Shanghai (German Agencies) at New Guinea (portion of) Samoa (Apia) Tongo Territory, including Bageida, Little Popo, Lome and Porto Seguro, and territory in South West Africa. Viz—Grand Namaqua, the Damaras Country and Southern portion of Ovambo.

I Including the British Port Office at Tangier, Laraiche, Labat, Casablanca, Staffi, Muzagan and Modagor.

J Kiung Chow, Canton, Swatow, Amoy, Too Chow, Hanknow and Nengpo viâ Hong-Kong.

K Antigua, Dominica, Montserrat, St. Christopher, (St. Kitts), Nevis and Virgin Islands.

L 1st *Group* : East Indies, Archipelago and Banco, Archipelago of Riouw, Billiton, Borneo, (except N.W. part) Celebes, Java, Madura, Sumatra, Sunda Islands, Bali, Lombock, Sambawa, Floris and the S.W. part of Timor, the Archipelago of the Moluccas, and the N. W. part of New Guinea, (Papua). *2nd. Group* : Dutch Guiana (Surinam). *3rd. Group* : Curaçao, Bonaire, Aruba, the Netherland portion of St. Eustatius and Saba.

M Azores (Madeira, Goa, Damao and Diu) Macao, Timor, Cap de Verd, Bissau and Caclea), Island of St. Thomas and Prince (in Africa), with the Establishment of Rjuda, Mozambique and Agola.

N Balearic Islands, Cuba, Fernando Po, Marian Islands, Phillippine Islands, Porto Rico, Marqueza Islands, and Annobon and Dependencies.

O Bahamas, Cariacon, Grenada, St. Lucia, Tobago, Tortola and Turks Islands.

P The correspondence is assimilated to that of British India.

Regulations.

Prepayment of Letters. I.— Prepayment of Postage on every description of Articles shall be effected only by means of Postage Stamps.

Official correspondence on Postal matters alone exempt from Postage. II.— Official Correspondence relative to the Postal Service is alone exempt from all liability of charge.

Prohibition of Letters containing Gold, &c. III.—It is forbidden to the Public to send by Post :

1o. Letters or Packets containing Gold or Silver Bullion, Pieces of Money, Jewellery or precious Articles.

2o. Any Packets whatever containing Articles liable to Customs duty.

Post Cards. IV.—Post Cards must be forwarded openly :

1o. Post Cards for circulation within the Union must have an impressed stamp, and the superscription *Union Postale Universelle.*

2o. Rely Post Cards will consist of a double card folded in the centre, one portion to be used by the original sender and the other to be torn off and used for reply.

The reply Post Cards will be impressed with Six cents stamp on each portion.

3o. The front is reserved for the address only.

4o. The communicction is written on the back.

5o. It is forbidden to join or attach to Post Cards, any articles whatsoever.

6o. No Post Cards other than those issued by the Post Office, can be allowed to pass.

Commercial papers. V.—The following are considered as Commercial Papers and admitted as such :

All papers and documents written or drawn wholly or partly by hand will have not the character of an *actual* and *personal correspondence*, such as papers of legal procedures, Deeds of all kinds drawn up by public functionaries, Way Bills, or Bills of lading, Invoices, the various documents of Insurance Companies, Copies of Extract of Deeds under Private Seal written on Stamped or Unstamped Paper, Scores or Sheets of Manuscript Music, Manuscript of Works forwarded separately. Commercial papers must be forwarded under band or in an open envelope.

No Commercial papers under 50 grammes can leave the Colony without having paid the initial rate of 15c. and an additional rate of 03c. for every 50 grammes.

Printed papers of every kind. VI.—The following are considered as printed papers and admitted as such :

1o. Periodical works, Books stitched or bound Pamphlets, Sheets of Music, visiting Cards Address Cards, proofs or printing, with or without the Manuscripts relating thereto' engravings, photographs, drawings, plans, maps, catalogues, prospectuses, announcements and notices of various kinds, whether printed, engraved and lithographed and in general all impressions or copies obtained upon paper, parchment or card board, by means of printing, lithographing or any other mechanical process easy to recognize, except the copying press.

2o. The following are excluded, viz : Stamps for prepayment, whether obliterated or not, as well as all printed articles constituting the representative sign of the monetary value.

VII.—The character of *actual* and *personal correspondence* cannot be ascribed to the following, viz :

1o. To the signature of the Sender or to the designation of his name or of his social standing, or his rank, of the place of origin, and of the day of despatch.

2o. To the figures or signs by the aid of which the passages of a text are marked in order to draw attention to them.

3o. To a declaration or mark of respect offered by the author.

4o. To the prices added, whether to stock and share lists, or price-current and market reports.

5o. Lastly to anotations or corrections made upon proofs or printing or Musical composition, and relating to the text or to the completion of a work.

Patterns of Merchandize. VIII.—Patterns of Merchandize are admitted under the following conditions.

1o. They must be placed in Bags, Boxes or open Envelopes, in such a manner as to admit of easy inspection.

2o. They must possess no saleable value, nor bear any manuscript beyond the name or the social position of the senders, the address of the addressee, a manufacturer's trade mark, number and price, or words such as may be necessary to indicate the place of origin or the nature of the merchandize.

No Patterns of Merchandize under 50 grammes can leave the Colony without having paid the initial rate of 0.06c. and an additional rate of 0.03c. for every 50 grammes.

Printed Papers. IX.—Printed Papers must be either placed under band upon a roller between boards, in a cover open at one side at both extremities, or in an enclosed envelope, or simply folded in such a manner as not to conceal the nature of the packet, or lastly, tied by a string easy to unfasten.

Address Cards. X.—Address Cards and all printed papers presenting the form and consistency of an unfolded Card, may be forwarded without band, envelope, fastening or fold.

Registered. XI.—The articles specified in the foregoing paragraphs may be registered.

Every registered article is liable at the charge of the sender :—

1o. To the ordinary prepaid rate of postage on the article, according to its nature.

2o. To a fixed registration fee of 12 cents, including the issue of an acknowledgment of posting to the sender.

3o. The sender of the registered article may obtain an acknowledgment of the delivery of such article, by paying in advance 15 cents, in addition to the ordinary registration fee and postage mentioned above.

In case of the loss of a registered article addressed to Countries and Colonies forming the Postal Union except in the case "*force majeure*" there is to be paid an indemnity of 50 francs to the sender, or, at his request, to the addressee, by the administration of the Country in the territory or in the Maritime Service of which the loss has occurred, that is to say, where the trace of the article has ceased.

If it is impossible to discover the service in which the loss has occurred, the indemnity is borne in equal proportions between the two corresponding offices.

Payment of this indemnity is made with the least possible delay, and, at the least, within a year dating from the date of application.

Every claim for an indemnity is excluded if it be not made within one year, counting from the date on which the registered article was posted.

XII.—There shall not be forwarded :

Partial prepayment of Letters. 1o. Articles other than letters which are not prepaid at least partly, or which do not fulfill the condition required above.

Injury to correspondence. 2o. Articles of such a nature likely to stain or injury to correspondence.

Limits of weight for Patterns. 3o. Patterns exceeding 250 grammes in weight, or measuring more than 20 centimetres in length, ten in breadth, and five in depth.

Weight of printed papers. Lastly, packets of Commercial papers, and printed papers of every kind the weight of which exceeds 2 kilogrammes, or the length of which exceeds 31 inches (79 centimetres).

Insufficient prepayment. XIII.—In case of insufficient prepayment, correspondence of every kind whether from Union or Non-Union Countries, is liable to a charge equal to double the amount of the deficiency, to be paid by the addressees.

INLAND LETTERS.

Not exceeding 15 grammes	4 cents.
Above 15, and not exceeding 30 grammes	8 ,,
,, 30, ,, 45 ,, ...	12 ,,

and so on, four cents being charged for every additional 15 grammes, or fractional part thereof.

Unpaid letters are charged with double the above rates, and insufficiently prepaid letters with double the deficiency.

INLAND POST-CARDS.

Post-Cards, impressed upon two cents, may be transmitted from any place to any other place in the Colony.

INLAND NEWSPAPERS.

Newspapers are transmitted free from Post Office to Post Office, if not exceeding 100 grammes in weight; if above 100 grammes they are charged book-rate of postage.

Newspapers sent out for delivery at the domicile of the addressee are charged two cents each.

INLAND BOOK-POST.

Not exceeding 50 grammes	2 cents.
Above 50 and not exceeding 100 grammes	4 ,,
,, 100 ,, 150 ,, ...	6 ,,

and so on, two cents being charged for every additional 50 grammes or fractional part thereof.

Unpaid books are charged double the above rates, and insufficiencyly paid books double the deficiency.

INLAND REGISTRATION.

By payment of eight cents in addition to the ordinary postage, any letter or other postal packet may be registered.

Postal Parcels for United Kingdom, viâ Marseilles.

Limit of weight. 1.—The weight of a parcel must not exceed 3 kilos 175 grammes.

Rates of postage. 2.—The rates of postage chargeable on parcels addressed to the United Kingdom shall be as follows:

For a parcel not exceeding 1 kilo 361 grammes in weight	Rs. 1.58
Exceeding 1 kilo 361 grammes and not 3 kilos 175 grammes	1.88

A parcel must not exceed 3 feet 6 inches in length or 6 feet in girth and length combined.

In addition to the exceeding rates, the parcels will bear an extra charge, computed according to the rate of exchange, ruling on the day such parcels are posted.

No parcels will be received on the days fixed for the departure or arrival of the Mails.

Rates of postage on transit parcels through United Kingdom. 3.—Rate of postage chargeable on parcels addressed to the British Possessions or Colonies or Foreign Countries in transit through the United Kingdom:—

For a parcel not exceeding 3 kilos 175 grammes in weight, R. 1.38 in addition to the postage for the time being payable on a parcel of like weight transmitted from the United Kingdom to such British Possession, Colony or Foreign Country.

In addition to the existing rates, the parcels will bear an extra charge, computed according to the rate of exchange, rulling on the day such parcels are posted.

List of Postage Stamps now in use in Mauritius

Stamps on Sale.---1c., 2c., 3c., 4c., 8c., 15c., 16c., 25c., 50c., and Rs. 2.50

Envelopes.—8c., 25c., 50c. *Reg. Envelopes.*—F. Size 08., G. Size 12c.

Post Cards. –2c., 6c. Reply 12c.

Postal Parcels for France, (M. M. Steamers.)

Limit of Weight. 1.—The weight of a parcel must not exceed 5 kilos.

Rates of postage to France. 2.--For each parcel addressed to France if not exceeding 5 kilos in weight R. 1.25.

Rates of postage to Réunion 3.--For each parcel addressed to Réunion not exceeding 5 kilos in weight R. 0.50.

Rates of postage to places via France. 4.—For each parcel addressed to French Colonies and Foreign Countries in transit through France, if not exceeding 5 kilos in weight, R. 1.25 in addition to the postage for the time being payable on a parcel of like weight transmitted from France to such French Colony or Foreign Country.

In addition to the existing rates, the parcels will bear an extra charge, computed according to the rate of exchange, ruling on the day such parcels are posted.

Postal Parcels for Seychelles.

Not exceeding 11 pounds ... ... R. 0.80

Parcel Post between Mauritius and The United Kingdom and other Countries, viâ Colombo.

Limit of Weight :--The weight of a parcel must not exceed eleven pounds.

Dimensions :--No parcel may exceed three feet six inches in length or six feet in girth and length combined, such girth being measured round the thickest part of the parcel,

Rates of Postage :—The Rates of Postages chargeable on Parcels addressed to the United Kingdom are as follows :

For a parcel not exceeding three pounds in weight ... ... R. 1.00c.
Exceeding three pounds but not exceeding seven pounds ... ... ,, 1.50
,, seven pounds but not exceeding eleven pounds ... ... ,, 2.00
plus exchange at the ruling rate

To Colombo.

Not exceeding three pounds... ... ... R. 1.00c.
Exceeding three pounds but not exceeding seven pounds ... ... ,, 1.50
,, seven ,, ,, eleven ,, ... ,, 2.00

The Rates of Postage chargeable on Parcels addressed to any other British Colony or Possession or any Foreign Country with which a Parcel Post is established (viâ the United Kingdom) are as above, in addition to the Postage from the United Kingdom to the place of destination, for which see the Tariff annexed to Government Notice No. 292 of the 22nd. September 1891, pages 7, 8, 9 and 10.

No parcels will be received or delivered on the days fixed for the departure or arrival of any of the subsidized Mail Steamers and after four o'clock p.m. on any day.

Under reservation of the above rules, all provisions contained in Government Notice No. 185 of 1889, apply to this Parcel Post.

Foreign Money Orders are issued on the United Kingdom, France, the Continent of Europe America, English Colonies and India at the current rate of Exchange, plus 1 o/o commission.

Rates of Commission to be charged on Money Orders issued and payable in this Colony, as well as those issued on Rodrigues and Seychelles.

Inland Money Orders.

				Rate of Commission.
For a Money Order not exceeding Rs. 5...			.. ...	R. 0.05
Exceeding Rs. 5 and not exceeding Rs. 10			... ...	0.10
,,	10	,, 15	... ...	0.15
,,	15	,, 20	... ...	0.20
,,	20	,, 25	... ...	0.25
,,	25	,, 30	... ...	0.30
,,	30	,, 35	... ...	0.35
,,	35	,, 40	... ...	0.40
,,	40	,, 45	... ...	0.45
,,	45	,, 50	... ...	0.50

No single Money Order payable in this Colony can be issued for more than Rs. 50; but as many Money Orders of Rs. 50, may be given as the Remitter many require.

Money Orders drawn in Seychelles and Rodrigues

				Rate of Commission.
For a Money Order not exceeding Rs. 10			... ...	Rs 0.20
Exceeding Rs. 10 and not Rs. 20			... ...	0.40
,,	20	,, 30	... ...	0.60
,,	30	,, 40	... ...	0.80
,,	40	,, 50	... ...	1.00

No single Money Order payable in Seychelles and Rodrigues, can be issued for more than Rs. 50, but as many Money Orders of Rs. 50 may be given as the remitter requires.

Persons authorized to send and receive telegrams or correspondence free

His Excellency the Governor.
Private Secretary
Aide de Camp.
Bishop of Mauritius.
,, of Port Louis.
Judges Supreme Court.
Colonial Secretary.
Assistant Colonial Secretary.
Chief Clerk Colonial Secretary's Office.
Procureur and Advocate General.
Substitute Procureur General.
Crown Solicitor.
Chief Clerk Procureur General's Office.
Receiver General.
Assistant Receiver General.
Superintendent Inland Revenue.
Inland Revenue Inspectors.
Secretary Royal College.
Superintendent Distilleries and Inspectors.
Auditor General.
Collector of Customs.
Deputy Collector of Customs.
Tide Surveyors.
Protector of Immigrants.
Inspectors of Immigrants.
Immigration Medical Officer.
Mayor of Port Louis.
Surveyor General and Superintendent Public Works.
Assist. Engineer, Mare aux Vacoas Water Works,
Storekeeper, Mare aux Vacoas Water Works.
Government Engineer and Architect.
Government Surveyor.
Chief and other Inspectors of Roads.
Master Supreme Court.
Receiver Registration Dues.
Inspector General of Police.
Superintendent and Inspectors of Police.
Other Members of Police Force.
Storekeeper and Assistant Storekeeper General.
Superintendent and Chief Warders of Prisons.
Sanitary Guards.
Registrar Supreme Court.
Rector Royal College.
Headmaster Royal College Curepipe.
Harbour Master and Chief Pilot.
Secretary to Council.
Colonial Postmaster.
Chief Medical Officer.
Chief Clerk, Medical Department.
Government Medical Officers.
Superintendent Lunatic Asylum.
Civil Service Commissioners.
Manager of Railways.
Director Royal Observatory.
Registrar General.
Officers Civil Status.
District Magistrates.
Stipendiary Magistrates.
Curator Vacant Estates.

District Cashiers.
Director and Assistant Director Forests and Gardens.
Forests Inspectors and Rangers.
President General Board of Health.
Sanitary Warden.
Sanitary Guardians.
Sanitary Inspectors and Guards.
Poor Law Commissioner.
Poor Law Guardians.
Superintendent of Schools.
Inspectors of Schools.
Secretary General Board of Health.
Members Legislative Council.
Chief Clerk Public Works Department.
Inspector of Works.
Overseer Parc-à-Boulets.

Military.

His Honor Officer Commanding Troops.
Commanding Officers of Regiments.
Deputy Commissary General.
Deputy Assistant Adjudant and Q. M. Gl.
Principal Medical Officer.
Paymasters of Regiments.
Officers in command of Posts.

Telegraph Tariff.

	R. c.
Message not exceeding 20 words	0 25
Over 20 but not over 30 ,, ...	0 38
,, 30 ,, 40 ,, ...	0 50
,, 40 ,, 50 ,, ...	0 63

and so on, increasing by 13 and 12 cents alternately, for every additional 10 words or fraction of 10 words.

PORTERAGE.

25 cents per mile by foot messenger. But no foot messenger will be employed to convey a message beyond 2 miles. 38 cents per mile by carriole.

A fraction of a mile is counted as a whole mile.

No porterage is payable for a message addressed to a Telegraph Office for delivery there.

Delivery of Carriers, Port Louis.

1st. delivery	8.00 A.M.
2nd. ,, ...	11.00 ,,
3rd. ,, ...	2.00 P.M.
4th. ,, ...	4.00 ,,

Pillar letter Boxes cleared at Royal, Pope Hennessy, St. George, Desforges and Nabob streets, Champ de Mars and Railway Terminus and Moka Street—Port Louis.

1st. clearing	8.00 A.M.
2nd. ,, ...	11.30 ,,
3rd. ,, ...	2.30 P.M.
4th. ,, ...	6.00 ,,

LIST OF POST OFFICES IN EACH DISTRICT.

TO WHICH CORRESPONDENCE ADDRESSED TO ESTATES SHOULD BE DIRECTED.

Pamplemousses.

	Estate.	*Nearest Station.*
1	Beau Plan	Pamplemousses.
2	Belle Vue (Pilot)	Do.
3	Belle Vue (Mauricia) ...	Do.
4	Constance	Do.
5	Industrie	Terre Rouge.
6	L'Amitié	Pamplemousses.
7	La Rosalie	Do.
8	L'Espérance	Do.
9	Le Plessis	Do.
10	Maison Blanche	Do.
11	Mon Repos...	Do.
12	Mon Rocher	Do.
13	Mon Piton	Mapou.
14	Petite Rosalie	Pamplemousses.
15	St. André (*a*)	Do.
16	St. André (*b*) alias Solitude.	Terre Rouge.
17	The Mount	Pamplemousses.

Rivière du Rempart.

	Estate.	*Nearest Station*
1	Antoinette	Riv. du Rempart
2	Beau Séjour ...	Mapou.
3	Belle Vue (Maurel)	Riv. du Rempart.
4	Bon Espoir... ...	Mapou.
5	Espérance	Poudre d'Or.
6	Forbach	Mapou.
7	Haute Rive, Ile d'Ambre S. E. Cy. ...	Riv. du Rempart.
8	Ile d'Ambre Sugar Estate Company ...	Poudre d'Or.
9	L'Amitié	Riv. du Rempart.
10	La Bourdonnais ...	Mapou.
11	Mon Loisir Sugar Estate Company Limited	Riv. du Rempart.
12	Mon Songe... ...	Ville Bague.
13	St. Antoine ...	Mapou.
14	Schœnfeld	Poudre d'Or.

Flacq.

Estate.	Nearest Station.
1 Argy	... Argy.
2 Beau Bois ...	... Flacq.
3 Beau Champ S. E. Cy.	... Grand River S. E.
4 Beau Vallon (Fabre)	... Camp de Masque.
5 Bel Etang... ..	... Camp de Masque.
6 Belle Rive ...	... Olivia.
7 Belle Rose ...	... Bel Air.
8 Belle Vue... ..	... Flacq.
9 Bon Accueil ...	... Do.
10 Bon Espoir ...	... Do.
11 Bonne Mère, Companie Sucrière de Queen Victoria et Bonne Mère.	Argy.
12 Caroline	... Rivière Sèche.
13 Clémencia ...	... Bel Air.
14 Constance (Manès)	... Flacq.
15 Constance & La Gaieté S. E. Cy.	Do.
16 Deep River ...	... Olivia.
17 Grande Retraite...	... Flacq.
18 La Gaieté S. E. Cy.	... Argy.
19 La Lucie	... Olivia.
20 L'Etoile M. S. E. Cy.	... Do.
21 Olivia, Beau Champ S. E. Cy.	Do.
22 Petite Retraite ...	... Flacq.
23 Queen Victoria, Compagnie Sucrière de Queen Victoria et Bonne Mère.	Argy.
24 Rich Fund ...	... Flacq.
25 St. Julien... ...	... Quartier Militaire.
26 Sans Souci ...	... Montagne Blanche.
27 Sébastopol ...	... Do.
28 Union	... Flacq.
29 Unité & Mon Rêve	... Do.

Plaines Wilhems.

Estate.	Nearest Station.
1 Bassin	... Quatre Bornes.
2 Bagatelle ...	... Rose Hill.
3 Fressanges ...	... Fressanges.
4 Fressanges S. E. Cy. (Midlands).	Do.
5 Henrietta ...	... Vacoa.
6 Highlands ...	... Phœnix.
7 La Louise ...	... Quatre Bornes.
8 Mare-aux-Vacoas	... Vacoa.
9 Rénnion ...	... Do.
10 Solferino ...	... Quatre Bornes.
11 Stanley...	... Rose Hill.
12 Tamarind Falls.	... Vacoa.
13 Trianon ...	... Rose Hill.

Grand Port.

Estate.	Nearest Station.
1 Anse Jonché ...	... Mahebourg.
2 Astrœa M. S. E. Cy.	... Rose Belle
3 Belle Vue... ...	... Mahebourg.
4 Beau Fond ...	... Union Vale.
5 Beau Vallon (D)...	... Mahebourg.
6 Beau Vallon (R)...	... Do.
7 Cluny	... Cluny.
8 Cent Gaulettes (E.R.)	... Do.
9 Cent Gaulettes (L.R.)	... Do.
10 Cent Gaulettes S. E. Cy..	Do.
11 Deux Bras ...	... Rose Belle.
12 Eau Bleue ...	... Cluny.
13 Ferney	... Mahebourg.
14 Gros Bois ...	... Mare d'Albert.
15 Joli Bois... ...	... Rose Belle.
16 La Baraque ...	... Union Vale.
17 La Rosa	... Mare d'Albert.
18 Les Bambous ...	... Mahebourg.
19 Mon Désert ...	... Union Vale.
20 Mare d'Albert ...	... Mare d'Albert.
21 Mon Trésor (closed)	... Do.
22 New Grove ...	... Do.
23 Plaisance ...	... Union Vale.
24 Rose Belle ...	... Rose Belle.
25 Rivière Créole ...	... Mahebourg.
26 Riche en Eau ...	... Do.
27 Savinia	... Union Vale.
28 St. Hubert ...	... Cluny.
29 Union Park ...	... Rose Belle.
30 Union Vale ...	... Union Vale,
31 Virginia	... Do.

Moka.

Estate.	Nearest Station.
1 Alma	... Verdun.
2 Bar-le-Duc ...	... Do.
3 Bon Air	... Moka
4 Bonne Veine ...	... Quartier Militaire
5 Côte d'Or ...	... Moka.
6 Helvetia ...	... St. Pierre
7 Hermitage ...	... Moka.
8 La Laura ...	... St. Pierre.
9 L'Agrément ...	... Do.
10 Melrose	... Camp de Masque.
11 Minissy	... Moka.
12 Mon Désert ...	... St. Pierre.
13 Valetta	... Verdun.

Savanne.

Estate	Nearest Station.
1 Beau Bois	Riv. des Anguilles.
2 Beau Champ	Chemin Grenier.
3 Bel Air	Riv. des Anguilles.
4 Bel Ombre	Chemin Grenier.
5 Bénarès...	Riv. des Anguilles.
6 Britannia	Rivière Dragon.
7 Caledonia	Rose Belle.
8 Chamouny	Chemin Grenier.
9 Colmar	Rivière Dragon.
10 Combo, Highlands S.E.C.	Riv. des Anguilles.
11 Frederica	Chemin Grenier.
12 Fontenelle	Riv. des Anguilles.
13 La Flora	Rose Belle.
14 La Forêt	Chemin Grenier.
15 Riche Bois, M.S.E. Cy.	Rivière Dragon.
16 Rivière des Anguilles...	Riv. des Anguilles.
17 St. Aubin, Société de St. Aubin	Do.
18 St. Avold	Rivière Dragon.
19 St. Félix	Riv. des Anguilles.
20 Savannah S.E. Cy. Ld.	Union Vale.
21 Surinam	Souillac.
22 Terracine	Do.
23 Union & Bel Air ...	Chemin Grenier.
24 Union	Riv. des Anguilles.
25 Sainte Marie	Chemin Grenier.

Black River.

Estate.	Nearest Station.
1 Albion...	Petite Rivière.
2 Belle Isle	Bambous.
3 Belle Vue & Rivière Dragon	Do.
4 Chamarel	Chamarel.
5 Clarens S. E. Cy. ...	Bambous.
6 Médine	Do.
7 Rivière Noire M.P. Cy.	Black River.
8 Tamarin, Clarence S.E.	Bambous.

RAILWAYS.

Kindly supplied by the late A. H. Vandermeersch, C. E. Government Engineer and Architect.

The Mauritius Railways consist of two main lines, the NORTH and the MIDLAND having a common terminus in Port Louis, and of two branch lines, the MOKA-FLACQ and the SAVANNE.

The *North Line*, 31 miles in length runs through the Districts of Port Louis, Pamplemousses, Rivière du Rempart and Flacq, to Grand River South East ; it was the first one open to traffic (May, 1864) ; the principal bridge on this line is an iron viaduct over the "Trou Fanfaron," composed of 16 spans of 36 feet each, supported on cast iron screw piles filled with concrete, and built on a curve of 2,000 feet radius. The maximum gradient on this line is 1 in 80, and the highest level attained is 329 feet above the sea.

The *Middland Line*, 35½ miles in length, traverses the centre of the island, it runs through the Districts of Port Louis, Plaines Wilhems and Grand Port to Mahebourg. The highest level above the sea is attained between the stations of Curepipe and Forest Side, viz : 1828 feet. The gradients on this line are of peculiar steepness, one in 27 occurring repeatedly. The principal bridges (wrought iron girders) are the bridge over River St. Louis with one span of 90 feet and a height of 25 feet ; the viaduct over Grand River N. W. in five spans of 126 feet each, supported on cast iron columns filled with concrete and having a height of 140 feet above the bed of the River. (This viaduct was partially blown down in the great hurricane of 1868, and the trafic for two years was carried over a wooden bridge ; it is now completely restored). There is also the viaduct over River La Chaux of three spans, viz : two of 75 feet and one of 50 feet.

The *Moka-Flacq-Branch*, 26¼ miles in length, begins at Rose Hill Station on the Midland Line and runs through the districts of Plaines Wilhems, Moka and Flacq, to Rivière Sèche on the North Line. The ruling gradient is one in 40. The two principal bridges on this branch are built in masonry, viz ; the bridge over River Plaines Wilhems, with two circular arches of 50 feet span and a height of 30 feet above the river bed, and the Reduit viaduct over River Cascade, with three arches, the central one of 70 feet span with a rise of 27 feet, and the two sides one, semi-circular, of 50 feet span. The rail level on this viaduct is 80 feet above the bed of the river. It was opened to traffic as far as Quartier Militaire on 2nd. October 1880. To Montagne Blanche on 6th. June 1882 and throughout on the 15th. April 1893.

The *Savanne Branch*, 11 miles long, begins also on the Midland Line at Rose Belle Station, and runs through the Districts of Grand Port and Savanne to Souillac. The ruling gardients is one in 40. The principal bridge is the viaduct over River des Anguilles, of three spans, two of seventy feet, and a central one of 85 feet, with iron girders supported on masonry piers. The rail level on this viaduct is 105 feet above the bed of the river. It was opened for traffic throughout, on 1st. January 1878.

Ledger Accounts.

Accounts are rendered within 15 days after the close of the month and 3 months thereafter if credit is allowed.

Parcel Rates.

From any Station to any Station irrespective of distance :

		Rs. c.
Not exceeding	15 kilograms	0 25
Do.	50 ,, ...	0 50
Do.	75 ,, ...	0 75
Do.	100 ,, ...	1 00
Note :	A bag of oats, bran, gram, sugar or rice	0 50

Parcels of fresh meat, fish, oysters, crabs, fowls, eggs, fruits and vegetables other than 'private bazars will be charged as follows :

From any Station to any Station irrespective of distance :

		Rs. c.
Not exceeding	25 kilograms	0 50
Do.	50 ,, ...	1 00
Do.	75 ,, ...	1 25
Do.	100 ,, ...	1 50

Parcels are forwarded to the address of persons who reside within the short limits of Port Louis.

Each parcel as forwarded must not weight more than 20 lbs., be legibly addressed and the cost of transport, plus a charge of 6d. for porterage, be prepaid by the sender.

Parcels for delivery are sent out from the Central Station at

9.00 A.M. 10.45 A.M. 1.40 P.M. 3.00 P.M.

Passenger Fares from Port Louis.

To	Single.			Return.	
	1st.	2nd.	3rd.	1st.	2nd.
North Line.	Rs. c.	Rs. c.	Rs. c.	Rs. c.	Rs. c.
Roche Bois	0 24	0 16	0 08	0 36	0 24
Riche Terre	0 36	0 24	0 12	0 54	0 36
Terre Rouge	0 48	0 32	0 16	0 72	0 48
Calebasses	0 72	0 48	0 24	1 08	0 72
Pamplemousses	0 84	0 56	0 28	1 26	0 84
Mapou	1 20	0 80	0 40	1 80	1 20
Poudre d'Or	1 56	1 04	0 52	2 34	1 56
Riv. du Rempart	2 04	1 36	0 68	3 06	2 04
Flacq	2 64	1 76	0 88	3 96	2 64
Argy	2 88	1 92	0 96	4 32	2 88
Rivière Sèche	3 48	2 32	1 16	5 22	3 48
Grand River S. E.	3 72	2 48	1 24	5 58	3 72

Passenger Fares from Port Louis.

To	Single. 1st.	Single. 2nd.	Single. 3rd.	Return. 1st.	Return. 2nd.
Midland Line.	Rs.	Rs.	Rs.	Rs.	Rs.
Cassis Road	0 12	0 08	0 04	0 18	0 12
Pailles	0 24	0 16	0 08	0 36	0 24
Coromandel	0 36	0 24	0 12	0 54	0 36
Petite Rivière	0 60	0 40	0 20	0 90	0 60
Beau Bassin	0 84	0 56	0 28	1 26	0 84
Rose Hill	1 08	0 72	0 36	1 62	1 08
Quatre Bornes	1 20	0 80	0 40	1 80	1 20
Phœnix	1 44	0 96	0 48	2 16	1 44
Vacoas	1 56	1 04	0 52	2 34	1 56
Curepipe Road	1 80	1 20	0 60	2 70	1 80
Curepipe	1 92	1 28	0 64	2 88	1 92
Forest Side	2 04	1 36	0 68	3 06	2 04
Midlands	2 28	1 52	0 76	3 42	2 28
Fressanges	2 40	1 60	0 80	3 60	2 40
Cluny	2 76	1 84	0 92	4 14	2 76
Rose Belle	3 00	2 00	1 00	4 50	3 00
Mare d'Albert	3 24	2 16	1 08	4 86	3 24
Union Vale	3 60	2 40	1 20	5 40	3 60
Mahebourg	4 32	2 88	1 44	6 48	4 32
Moka-Flacq Line.					
Réduit	1 32	0 88	0 44	1 98	1 32
Moka	1 44	0 96	0 48	2 16	1 44
St. Pierre	1 68	1 12	0 56	2 52	1 68
Verdun	1 80	1 20	0 60	2 70	1 80
Quartier Militaire	2 28	1 52	0 76	3 42	2 28
Camp de Masque	2 76	1 84	0 92	4 14	2 76
Montagne Blanche	3 00	2 00	1 00	4 50	3 00
Olivia viâ Rose Hill	3 84	2 56	1 28	5 76	3 84
Bel Air viâ North Line	3 84	2 56	1 28	5 76	3 84
Savanne Line.					
Rivière du Poste	3 36	2 24	1 12	5 04	3 36
Rivière Dragon...	3 60	2 40	1 20	5 40	3 60
Rivière des Anguilles	3 84	2 56	1 28	5 76	3 84
Souillac	4 32	2 88	1 44	6 48	4 32

1st. Class Contract Tickets.

Port Louis to	One Month.		Three Months.		Six Months.		One Year.		Miles.
	Rs.	c.	Rs.	c.	Rs.	c.	Rs.	c.	
North Line.									
Roche Bois	8	...	23	...	45	...	80	...	2
Riche Terre	13	...	35	...	70	...	125	...	3
Terre Rouge	17	50	50	...	95	...	170	...	4
Calebasses	22	50	65	...	120	...	215	...	6
Pamplemousses	25	...	70	...	130	...	250	...	7
Mapou	31	50	90	...	170	...	320	...	10
Poudre d'Or	37	50	105	...	195	...	370	...	13
Rivière du Rempart...	43	...	122	...	225	...	415	..	17
Flacq	44	50	125	...	240	...	425	...	22
Argy	47	50	135	...	260	...	460	...	24
Rivière Sèche	55	...	155	...	295	...	525	...	29
Grand River S. E.	57	...	165	...	305	...	550	...	31
Midland Line.									
Cassis	4	...	11	75	20	...	40	...	1
Pailles	8	...	23	...	45	...	80	...	2
Coromandel	13	...	35	...	70	...	125	...	3
Petite Rivière	20	...	55	...	105	...	195	...	5
Beau Bassin	25	...	70	...	130	...	250	...	7
Rose Hill	29	50	85	...	160	...	285	...	9
Quatre Bornes	31	50	90	...	170	...	320	...	10
Phœnix	35	...	100	...	185	...	350	...	12
Vacoa	37	50	105	...	195	...	370	...	13
Curepipe Road	42	50	120	...	220	...	400	...	15
Curepipe...	42	50	120	...	220	...	400	...	16
Forest Side	42	50	120	...	220	...	400	...	17
Midlands	43	50	125	...	235	...	420	...	19
Fressanges	43	75	126	...	240	...	425	...	20
Cluny	45	...	130	...	245	...	435	...	23
Rose Belle	48	50	137	...	265	...	465	...	25
Mare d'Albert	50	...	145	...	280	...	480	...	27
Union Vale	56	25	160	...	305	...	540	...	30
Mahebourg	60	...	170	...	320	...	580	...	36
Moka-Flacq Branch.									
Réduit	33	50	95	...	180	...	340	...	11
Moka	35	...	100	...	185	...	350	...	12
St. Pierre	39	...	110	...	210	...	375	...	14
Verdun	40	50	115	...	215	...	390	...	15
Quartier Militaire	43	50	125	...	235	...	420	...	19
Camp de Masque	45	...	130	...	245	...	435	...	23
Montagne Blanche	48	50	137	...	265	...	465	...	25
Olivia / Bel Air }	57	75	165	...	310	...	555	...	32
All Stations	60	...	170	...	320	...	580	...	

Contract Tickets are issued at the Central, Beau Bassin, Rose Hill, Quatre Bornes, Phœnix, Vacoas, Curepipe Road, Curepipe, Forest Side, Moka, St. Pierre, Verdun, Terre Rouge and Pamplemousses Stations.

Yearly, Half-yearly and Quarterly Contract Tickets are issued at any month in the year.

A fine of Rs. 2.50 is levied on any person losing his contract ticket and wishing to renew the same, irrespective of the class of ticket lost.

All Contract tickets are issued subject to the condition that the Government are able to provide Carriages for the conveyance of the Contract Ticket holders. Every exertion will be made to provide suitable accommodation, but Government cannot guarantee that room will always be available.

2nd. and 3rd. Class Contract Tickets available by Industrial Trains only.

Port Louis To	Monthly. 2nd. Class.		3rd. Class.		*Port Louis* To	Monthly. 2nd. Class.		3rd. Class.	
	Rs.	c.	Rs.	c.		Rs.	c.	Rs.	c.
Rochebois	4	50	3	...	Cassis	2	...	1	50
Riche Terre	7	...	5	..	Pailles	4	50	3	...
Terre Rouge	8	75	6	50	Coromandel	7	...	5	...
Calebasses	14	...	8	...	Petite Rivière	12	25	7	...
Pamplemousses	17	50	9	50	Beau Bassin	17	50	9	50
					Rose Hill	21	25	11	...
					Quatre Bornes	22	50	12	...
					Phœnix	24	50	12	50
					Vacoa	26	25	13	50
					Curepipe Road... ...	29	75	15	...
					Curepipe	29	75	15	...
					Forest Side	29	75	15	...
					Reduit	23	50	12	...
					Moka	24	50	12	50
					St. Pierre	28	...	14	...
					Verdun	28	75	14	50
					Quartier Militaire ...	32	50	16	50
					Camp de Masque ...	33	50	18	...
					Montagne Blanche ...	34	...	19	...

Industrial Contract Tickets confer a right to travel solely by the Industrial Train and by no higher class than that for which issued. If a holder chooses to travel by another train he has to pay one third of regular fare.

The term " Industrial train " is confined strictly to that ordinary Passenger Train which is due first to arrive from the country each week day morning at Port Louis to that ordinary Passenger Train which is notified to leave Port Louis at night. It follows that on each line there are only two Industrial trains per diem, on each way.

Second and Third Class Monthly Contract Ticket available for travelling by Ordinary or Industrial Trains between Port Louis and the following Stations are issued, viz :

MIDLAND LINE

SECOND CLASS.

Stations.	Monthly.		Quarterly.		Half-yearly.		Yearly.	
Midland Line.	Rs.	c.	Rs.	c.	Rs.	c.	Rs,	c.
Cassis Road	2	85	8	20	15	50	27	55
Pailles	5	75	16	35	31	...	55	10
Coromandel	8	60	24	55	46	50	82	65
Petite Rivière	15	10	43	...	81	50	144	85
Beau Bassin	18	30	52	15	98	75	175	60
Rose Hill	22	40	63	85	120	95	215	05
Quatre Bornes	24	25	69	05	130	85	232	60
Phœnix	27	45	78	20	148	10	263	35
Vacoas	28	35	80	75	153	05	272	05
Curepipe Road	32	...	91	20	172	80	307	20
Curepipe	32	...	91	20	172	80	307	20
Forest Side	32	...	91	20	172	80	307	20

MIDLINE LINE.

SECOND CLASS.—*Continued.*

Stations.	Monthly.		Quarterly.		Half-yearly.		Yearly.	
Midland Line.	Rs.	c.	Rs.	c.	Rs.	c.	Rs.	c.
Midlands	33	30	94	90	179	80	319	70
Fressanges	33	50	95	50	180	95	321	70
Cluny	34	15	97	30	184	35	327	75
Rose Belle	35	25	100	45	190	35	338	40
Mare d'Albert	36	...	102	55	194	30	345	40
Union Vale	37	70	107	50	203	70	362	10
Mahebourg	40	70	115	95	219	75	390	60
Savanne Branch.								
Rivière Dragon	37	70	107	50	203	70	362	10
Rivière des Anguilles	39	...	111	15	210	60	374	40
Souillac	40	70	115	95	219	75	390	60

THIRD CLASS.

Stations.	Monthly.		Quarterly.		Half-yearly.		Yearly.	
Midland Line.								
Cassis Road	2	...	5	70	10	80	19	20
Pailles...	4	...	11	40	21	60	38	40
Coromandel	6	...	17	10	32	40	57	60
Petite Rivière	9	70	27	60	52	30	92	95
Beau Bassin	11	45	32	60	61	80	109	80
Rose Hill	14	50	41	40	78	40	139	40
Quatre Fornes	15	85	45	15	85	55	152	05
Phœnix	18	90	53	90	102	15	181	65
Vacoas	19	80	56	45	106	90	190	10
Curepipe Road	22	...	62	70	118	80	211	20
Curepipe	22	...	62	70	118	80	211	20
Forest Side	22	...	62	70	118	80	211	20
Midlands	23	70	67	50	127	95	227	45
Fressanges	24	20	68	95	130	70	232	30
Cluny	25	30	72	10	136	60	242	90
Rose Belle	25	65	73	10	138	50	246	25
Mare d'Albert	25	75	73	35	139	...	247	10
Union Vale	26	40	75	25	142	55	253	45
Mahebourg	27	60	78	65	149	...	264	85
Savanne Branch.								
Rivière Dragon	26	40	75	25	142	55	253	45
Rivière des Anguilles	26	95	76	85	145	65	258	90
Souillac	27	60	78	65	149	...	264	85

The Industrial, and 2nd. and 3rd. class Contract Tickets extend from the 5th. of one month to the 4th. of the next both days inclusive, and will be examined on the 5th. of each month, but 1st. class Contract Tickets and School Tickets will run from the first to the last day of the month and be examined on the 2nd.

Second and Third Class Contract Tickets.

NORTH LINE.

SECOND CLASS.

Stations.	Monthly.		Quarterly.		Half-yearly.		Yearly.	
North Line.	Rs.	c.	Rs.	c.	Rs.	c.	Rs.	c.
Roche Bois	5	75	16	35	31	00	55	10
Riche Terre	8	60	24	55	46	50	82	65
Terre Rouge	12	35	35	20	66	70	118	55
Calebasses	16	00	45	60	86	40	153	60
Pamplemousses	18	30	52	15	98	75	175	60
Mapou	24	25	69	05	130	85	232	60
Poudre d'Or	28	35	80	75	153	05	272	05
Rivière du Rempart	32	40	92	35	174	95	311	05
Flacq	33	95	96	75	183	30	325	85
Argy	34	75	99	...	187	60	333	50
Rivière Sèche...	37	05	105	55	199	95	355	50
Grand Rivière S. E.	38	40	109	45	207	35	368	65
Moka-Flacq Line.								
Réduit	25	85	73	60	139	50	247	95
Moka	27	45	78	20	148	10	263	35
St. Pierre	29	70	84	70	160	45	285	20
Verdun	31	10	88	65	167	95	298	55
Quartier Militaire	33	30	94	90	179	80	319	70
Camp de Masque	34	15	97	30	184	35	327	75
Montagne Blanche	35	25	100	45	190	35	338	40
Bel Air, Olivia... }	39	...	111	15	210	60	374	40

THIRD CLASS.

Stations.	Monthly.		Quarterly.		Half-yearly.		Yearly.	
North Line.								
Roche Bois	4	...	11	40	21	60	38	40
Riche Terre	6	...	17	10	32	40	57	60
Terre Rouge	7	90	22	60	42	75	76	05
Calebasses	10	10	28	85	54	65	97	15
Pamplemousses	11	45	32	60	61	80	109	80
Mapou	15	85	45	15	85	55	152	05
Poudre d'Or	19	80	56	45	106	90	190	10
Rivière du Rempart	22	45	63	95	121	20	215	45
Flacq	25	...	71	30	135	05	240	10
Argy	25	50	72	75	137	80	245	...
Rivière Sèche	26	05	74	30	140	80	250	25
Grand River S. E.	26	70	76	15	144	25	256	45
Moka-Flacq Line.								
Reduit	17	15	48	90	92	65	164	75
Moka	18	90	53	90	102	15	181	65
St. Pierre	20	55	58	55	110	95	197	30
Verdun	21	35	60	80	115	25	204	90
Quartier Militaire	23	70	67	50	127	95	227	45
Camp de Masque	25	30	72	10	136	60	242	90
Montagne Blanche	25	65	73	10	138	50	246	25
Olivia..., Bel Air }	26	95	76	85	145	65	258	90

The Industrial and 1st., 2nd. and 3rd class Contract Tickets extend from the 5th. of one month to the 4th. of the next, both days inclusive and will be examined on the 5th. of each month, but School Tickets will run from the first to the last day of the month and be examined on the 2nd.

Second Class Contract Tickets for persons under 18 years not School Children.

Second Class Contract Tickets are issued monthly, at the following reduced rates, for children and for young persons under 18 years of age, being members of the same families and residing with their parents or guardians :

Stations.	Miles.	Number of Children of the same family.					
		1	2	3	4	5	6
Port Louis to :		Rs. c.	Rs. c.	Rs. c.	Rs. c.	Rs. c.	Rs. c.
Roche Bois	2	4 ...	6 50	9	11 50	14 ...	16 ...
Terre Rouge	4	6 ...	10 ...	13 75	17 50	21 25	25 ...
Calebasses	6	7 50	12 ...	16 50	21 ...	25 50	30 ...
Pamplemousses	7	10 ...	15 50	21 ...	26 50	31 ...	37 50
Mapou	10	15 ...	20 50	26 ...	31 50	37 ...	42 50
Poudre d'Or	13	18 50	24 50	30 50	36 50	42 ...	47 50
Pailles	2	4 ...	6 50	9 ...	11 50	14 ...	16 ...
Coromandel	3	5 ...	8 ...	11 ...	14 ...	17 ...	20 ...
Petite Rivière	5	7 50	12 ...	16 50	21 ...	25 50	30 ...
Beau Bassin	7	10 ...	15 50	21 ...	26 50	31 ...	37 50
Rose Hill	9	13 75	19 25	24 75	30 25	35 75	41 25
Quatre Bornes	10	15 ...	20 50	26 ...	31 50	37 ...	42 50
Phœnix	12	17 50	23 ...	28 50	34 ...	39 50	45 ...
Vacoa	13	18 50	24 50	30 50	36 50	42 ...	47 50
Curepipe Road	15	20 ...	26 ...	32 ...	38 ...	44 ...	50 ...
Curepipe	16	20 ...	26 ...	32 ...	38 ...	44 ...	50 ...
Forest Side	16	20 ...	26 ...	32 ...	38 ...	44 ...	50 ...

The same scale of charges will apply for equal mileage between Intermediate Stations.

Second Class Contract Tickets for School Children.

North Line.			MIDLAND LINE.		
	Miles.	Per Ticket.		Miles.	Per Ticket.
		Rs. c.			Rs. c.
Port Louis to Roche Bois ...	2	2 50	Port Louis to Pailles ...	2	2 50
,, Terre Rouge ...	4	3 65	,, Coromandel ...	3	3 ...
,, Calebasses ...	6	5 25	,, Petite Rivière..	5	4 25
,, Pamplemousses .	7	6 25	,, Beau Bassin ...	7	6 25
,, Mapou	10	7 75	,, Rose Hill ...	9	7 25
,, Poudre d'Or ...	13	9 25	,, Quatre Bornes.	10	7 75
,, Riv. du Rempart	16	10 50	,, Phœnix ...	12	8 75
			,, Vacoa ...	13	9 25
			,, Curepipe ...	16	10 50
			For	1	1 25
			,, ...	4	3 65
			,, ...	6	5 25
			,, ...	11	8 25

These reduced rates apply *solely to school children* and those Tickets will only be issued on the production of a certificate of a Schoolmaster vouching that the applicant is his scholar.

The charges for Tickets between intermediate Stations will be in proportion to the above reduction.

First Class contract tickets for school children are also issued at one half of the rate detailed on page 172.

Fares for Contract Tickets for Intermediate Stations.

Number of Miles.	1st. Class.		2nd. Class.		3rd. Class.	
	Rs.	c.	Rs.	c.	Rs.	c.
1	4	...	2	85	2	...
2	8	...	5	75	4	...
3	13	...	8	60	6	...
4	17	50	12	35	7	90
5	20	...	15	10	9	70
6	22	50	16	...	10	10
7	25	...	18	30	11	45
8	27	50	20	55	13	20
9	29	50	22	40	14	50
10	31	50	24	25	15	85
11	33	50	25	85	17	15
12	35	...	27	45	18	90
13	37	50	28	35	19	80
14	39	...	29	70	20	55
15	40	50	31	10	21	35
16	42	50	32	...	22	...
17	43	...	32	40	22	45
18	43	25	32	90	23	10
19	43	50	33	30	23	70
20	43	75	33	50	24	20
21	44	...	33	60	24	65
22	44	50	33	95	25	...
23	45	...	34	15	25	30
24	47	50	34	75	25	50
25	48	50	35	25	25	65
26	49	25	35	65	25	75
27	50	...	36	...	25	75
28	52	...	36	25	25	75
29	55	...	37	05	26	05
30	56	25	37	70	26	40
31	57	...	38	40	26	70
32	57	75	39	...	26	95
33	58	25	39	60	27	25
34	59	...	40	15	27	40
35	60	...	40	70	27	60

Height of Stations on the North, Midland, Savanne and Moka Lines.

North Line. Stations.	Miles from Central Station, Port Louis.	Height of rails above Mean Sea Level.
	Miles.	Eng. feet.
1 Roche Bois ...	2	44
2 Richeterre ...	3	106
3 Terre Rouge...	4	137
4 Calebasses ...	6	192
5 Pamplemouss.	7	208
6 Mapou...	10	296*
7 Poudre d'Or ...	13	172
8 R. du Rempart	17	134
9 Flacq	22	78†
10 Argy	24	146
11 Riv. Sèche......	29	100
12 Gd. River S. E.	31	38

Midland Line. Stations.	Miles from Central Station, Port Louis.	Height of rails above Mean Sea Level.
	Miles.	Eng. feet.
Port Louis ...	...	8
1 Cassis	1	19
2 Pailles	2	165
3 Coromandel...	3	175
4 Petite Rivière	5	392
5 Beau Bassin...	7	737
6 Rose Hill	9	923
7 Quatre Bornes	10	1083
8 Phœnix	12	1311
9 Vacoa	13	1371
10 Curepipe Road	15	1784
11 Curepipe	16	1806
12 Forest Side ...	17	1812‡
13 Midlands	19	1467
14 Fressanges ...	20	1313
15 Cluny	23	1000
16 Rose Belle ...	25	874
17 Mare d'Albert	27	559
18 Union Vale ...	30	253
19 Mahebourg ...	36	4

Savanne Branch. Stations.	Distance from Rose Belle Station.	Height of rails above Mean Sea Level.
	Miles.	Eng. feet.
Rose Belle ...	...	874
1 Riv. du Poste...	3	920
2 ,, Dragon ...	5	753
3 ,, des Anguil.	7	426
4 Souillac	11	42

Moka Branch. Stations.	Distance from Rose Hill.	Height of rails above Mean Sea Level.	*Moka Branch* Stations.	Distance from Rose Hill.	Height of rails above Mean Sea Level.
	Miles.	Eng. feet.		Miles.	Eng. feet.
1 Rose Hill	...	923	6 Quartier Militaire.	10	1337
2 Réduit (Pass: platform).	2	1031	7 Camp de Masque..	14	995
3 Moka	3	1130	8 Montagne Blanche	19	906
4 St. Pierre	5	1320	9 Olivia	22	376
5 Verdun	9	1420§	10 Bel Air	24	242

The height above the sea of any residence can easily be determined approximately from the above tables, by means of an aneriod Barometer, it is only necessary to observe the *fall* of the *Barometer* when removed from the nearest station and allow a *rise* at the rate of 1,000 feet to the inch or *vice versâ*.||

Example : The Barometer at Phœnix Station reads.................. 28,710 inches.
At A's house .... 28,620 ,,

Fall......... 0,090 ,,

Height of Phœnix Station .... 1,311 feet.
Add for fall of barometer 0,090............................. 90

Height of House above mean level .... 1,401 English feet.

* Summit 327 feet. † Second summit 146 feet. ‡ Summit 1,822 feet. § Summit 1,515 feet

|| If the aneriod be graduated metrically allow 40 feet to the mm.

ORDINANCES OF 1895.

Ordinance No. 32 of 1894-95.

To amend the constitution and functions of the General Board of Health, to create a Medical and Health Department, and to amend and consolidate the Laws relating to the Public Health.

(28*th. June* 1895.)

Be it enacted by His Excellency the Governor, with the advice and consent of the Council of Government, as follows ;—

I.

PRELIMINARY.

Short title. 1.—This Ordinance may be cited as the "Public Health Ordinance, 1894-95."

Repeal of existing laws. 2.—The several Ordinances and parts of Ordinances mentioned in Schedule A of this Ordinance are hereby repealed.

Provided always that all Regulations and Bye-Laws made in virtue of any of the said Ordinances or parts of Ordinances and in force at the date of the passing of this Ordinance shall remain in operation, so far as they are not inconsistent with the provisions of this Ordinance, until they shall have been repealed or replaced by Regulations framed in accordance with the provisions of this Ordinance.

Provided further that all powers, authority and duties vested in or imposed upon the General Board of Health as heretofore constituted, under any of the said Regulations or Bye-Laws, shall vest in and be exercised by the Sanitary Authority as constituted under this Ordinance: and all powers, authority and duties vested in or imposed by the said Regulations or Bye-Laws, upon the Sanitary Warden, or any Sanitary Guardian, Inspector, or other officer or servant of the General Board of Health as heretofore constituted, shall vest in and be exercised by such officer of the Medical and Health Department created by this Ordinance, as may be designated by the Director of the said Department.

(2) Such repeal shall not affect :

(a) Anything duly done or suffered under any enactment hereby repealed.

(b) Any right or liability acquired, accrued or incurred under any enactment hereby repealed.

(c) Any judgment, conviction, sentence or order pronounced, any enquiry, prosecution or other legal proceeding commenced ; but any such judgment, conviction, sentence or order shall remain valid, and every such proceeding may be continued and completed, as if this Ordinance had not been passed.

(3) Any unrepealed enactment referring to any enactment hereby repealed shall be construed to apply to the corresponding provision of this Ordinance.

Interpretation Clause. 3.—In this Ordinance, and in any Regulation or Order made thereunder, the following words and expressions shall have the meanings hereinafter assigned to them, unless the context otherwise requires :—

1o.—"The Sanitary Authority" means the Sanitary Warden or the Assistant Sanitary Warden ;

2o.—"Owner" means the person for the time being receiving or who would be entitled to receive the rent of any premises, if such premises were let whether for his own behoof or that of any other person : and shall, in the case of property belonging to the Crown, mean the Surveyor General; and in all other cases of public property, the person to whom the management thereof is entrusted; and in case of property in the possession or under the management of the Municipal Corporation, the Mayor and Municipal Council of Port Louis;

3o.—"Occupier" means every person in actual occupation of the premises; and shall include the Owner of such premises when such Owner is in actual occupation of the same;

4o.—"Person" and words applied in this Ordinance to any person or individual shall apply to and include Corporations, Companies, Joint Tenants and Tenants in common, Communities, lay or religious, and Females as well as Males;

5o.—"City of Port Louis" means the District of Port Louis and every part thereof as defined in Schedule A of Ordinance No. 27 of 1875;

6o.—"Premises" shall include Lands, Houses, Buildings, Structures of any kind, Rivers, Streams, Beds of Rivers or Streams, Ponds, Pools, Marshes, Drains, Ditches, Wells, Reservoirs, Canals, Conduits, Streets or Roads, or Places open, covered or enclosed;

7o.—"Ship" means any sailing or steam Ship, Vessel, Lighter, Hulk or Boat;

8o.—"Food" means any Carcase, Meat, Poultry, Game, Flesh, Fish, Fruit, Vegetables, Bread, Grain whole or ground, and every other alimentary substance whether solid or liquid;

9o.—"Structural Work" means any Building, Erection or Construction, or any repairs thereto the cost of which shall, as estimated by the Sanitary Authority, be fifty Rupees (Rs. 50) or upwards;

10o.—"Village" means any Area or Locality in the rural districts of the Island proclaimed by the Governor to be a Village under the Building Acts.

Duties of Municipal Council.

4.—The Municipal Council shall, for the purposes of this Ordinance, and subject to the provisions thereof, continue to be charged with the construction, maintenance and management of roads, bridges, streets, footpaths and squares, and with the maintenance and management of areas or spaces of land devoted to the public use, and not required by Government or for Military purposes, within the area of Port Louis.

Provided that it shall not be lawful for the Municipal Council to object to or oppose any digging, or other works, consequent on or incidental to the construction, repairing, maintenance and general management of drains, sewers, and gutters, within the said area, the construction, repairing, maintenance and general management of which are hereby vested in the Sanitary Branch of the Medical and Health Department.

II.

Constitution and Duties of the General Board of Health.

Constitution of General Board of Health.

5.—The General Board of Health shall henceforth cease to be an administrative, executive, and quasi-judicial body, and shall be a purely consultative and deliberative body as provided by the present Ordinance.

All powers, authority and duties vested in and imposed upon the General Board of Health as heretofore constituted by any Ordinance or Regulation, shall cease and determine.

Composition of the Board.

6.—The General Board of Health as established by this Ordinance, shall consist of the Director of the Medical and Health Department, the Protector of Immigrants, the Mayor of Port Louis, the Surveyor General, and the Poor Law Commissioner for the time being, and six other persons to be annually appointed, as follows:—

One, not being an official, by the Governor.

One by the Municipal Council of Port Louis.

One by the Chamber of Agriculture.

One by the Chamber of Commerce.

Two by the duly qualified Medical practitioners, as defined by Ordinance No. 22 of 1869, resident in the Island.

President of the Board.

7.—The Director of the Medical and Health Department shall be the President of the General Board of Health.

Delay for intimating appointment to the Governor.

8.—On the day before the coming into force of this Ordinance, and within the first fifteen days of January in each subsequent year the Mayor of Port Louis, the President of the Chamber of Agriculture, the President of the Chamber of Commerce and the Director of the Medical and Health Department respectively, shall transmit to the Governor the names of the persons respectively appointed as aforesaid. In the event of such names or any of them not being transmitted as aforesaid, on or before the twentieth of January in any future year, it shall be lawful for the Governor to appoint such number of persons as shall be rendered necessary by such failure.

Names of members of the Board to be notified in Government Gazette.

9.—The names of the persons appointed members of the Board as aforesaid for the current year shall be forthwith notified in the Government Gazette, and the notification in the Gazette shall be sufficient evidence thereof.

Temporary vacancies to be filled up by Governor or elective Bodies.

10.—If any member of the Board be at any time temporarily prevented from acting, the Governor or the Body which shall have appointed such member, as the case may be, may appoint some person to replace such member until he shall be able to resume his functions.

Provided that if the Mayor of Port Louis is temporarily prevented from acting, he shall be replaced by the Deputy Mayor.

Vacancy not to affect constitution of Board. Vacancy how to be filled up.

11.—The Board shall be held to be legally constituted notwithstanding any vacancies occurring therein by the death, resignation or incapacity of any member, if the number of members be not reduced at any time by such vacancies below five. Provided always that every such vacancy may be filled up by a person appointed by the Governor, or, as the case may be, by the Body who shall have appointed the member whose death, resignation or incapacity shall have caused such vacancy. The appointment of persons to fill up such vacancies shall be made and shall be notified as nearly as may be in the manner hereinbefore provided.

(2) In case of failure by the said Body to fill up the vacancy as aforesaid within fifteen days, it shall be lawful for the Governor to do so in lieu of the said Body.

Board to continue in Office until the appointment of new Board.

12.—The persons forming the General Board of Health at the expiry of any year shall continue in office until the notification in the Government Gazette of the names of the persons who shall have been appointed members of the General Board of Health for the current year.

Quorum. Casting vote.

13.—Five members of the Board shall be a quorum for the despatch of business. At every meeting the President, or in his absence such member of the Board as the members present may appoint as Chairman, shall preside. The Chairman at every meeting shall have a deliberative and a casting vote.

Board may make Rules to regulate its proceedings.

14.—The Board shall meet once every month, and oftener if need be, and may adjourn from time to time. The Board may from time to time make rules for regulating the mode and order of proceeding at its meetings, and may, from time to time, alter such rules.

Property of existing Board of Health to vest in Government.

15.—All property whether moveable or immoveable, and all rights, claims or liabilities which at the time when this Ordinance comes into operation are vested in the General Board of Health as heretofore constituted, shall be transferred to, and shall vest in the Government.

Duties of the Board. 16.—It shall be the duty of the General Board of Health to advise upon all questions connected with the sanitary law, or with the sanitary administration of the Colony, or with Regulations made or to be made or amended under Article 24, which are referred to it by the Governor; and further it shall be competent for the Board to make suggestions to the Governor on similar questions without previous reference from the Governor.

(2) The General Board of Health shall further appoint annually a Quarantine Committee as defined in Part VII of this Ordinance.

III.

CONSTITUTION AND DUTIES OF THE MEDICAL AND HEALTH DEPARTMENT.

Abolition of existing Departments and offices; and creation of new Department. 17.—The Medical Department and the Department of the General Board of Health as now existing shall be abolished, and in lieu thereof there shall be created a Government Department called the Medical and Health Department.

The following posts shall be abolished, provided that the holders thereof shall not be entitled to any compensation by reason of such abolition, if they are appointed to any other office in the colonial service to which at least an equivalent salary is attached:

a. *In the Medical Department*: the Chief Medical Officer, the Chief Clerk, the Clerk Poor Law Branch, the Visiting and Superintending Surgeon of the Civil Hospital.

b. *In the Department of the General Board of Health*; Secretary, Financial Clerk, Assistant Financial Clerk, Copyist, Clerk to Sanitary Warden, the three Sanitary Guardians, the Harbour Sanitary Inspector.

c. The Engineer of the "Building Acts" section of the General Board of Health, and the Medical Officer of the Immigration Department.

Until the appointment of officers to fill the new posts created in the Medical and Health Department, the officers whose posts are to be abolished shall perform, under this Ordinance, the duties assigned to them by the Governor.

Composition of the Medical and Health Department. 18.—The head of the Medical and Health Department shall be styled the Director of the Medical and Health Department; he shall have the general control of the Department and of all public hospitals, including the hospital of the Barkly Asylum, and shall be directly responsible to Government; he shall also be vested with and exercise the same powers as the Sanitary Authority.

The Medical and Health Department shall consist of two Branches: the Medical Branch and the Sanitary Branch.

The Sanitary Branch shall be sub-divided into two sections:

a. the Sanitary Police section; and

b. the Sanitary Works and Building Acts section.

Officers of the Medical and Health Department. 19.—The Officers of the Medical and Health Department, shall be as follows, and shall be appointed by the Governor

Director,

Medical Inspector,

Sanitary Warden,

Assistant Sanitary Warden,

Health Officer,

Dispensary Medical Officer,

Police and Prison Surgeon,

Medical Superintendent of the Civil Hospital,

Assistant Superintendent of the Civil Hospital,

Medical Superintendent of the Barkly Asylum,

Assistant Superintendent of the Barkly Asylum,

Medical Superintendent of the Lunatic Asylum,

all of whom shall be medical men as defined by Ordinance No. 22 of 1869; and a Sanitary Engineer, at a salary to be determined by the Governor, with the advice and consent of the Council of Government.

Provided, however, that after the 1st. January 1900, no person shall be appointed to the office of Sanitary Warden or Assistant Sanitary Warden unless he be legally qualified for the practice of medicine and shall in addition hold a diploma in Sanitary Science, Public Health, State Medicine or Hygiene; and meanwhile for the selection of such officers, preference shall be given whenever practicable and saving superior claims, to candidates holding both the qualifications aforesaid.

There shall be also attached to the Medical and Health Department, officers, clerks and servants to be appointed by the Governor at salaries to be determined by the Governor, with the advice and consent of the Council of Government.

Except as provided in Article 27, any officer, clerk or servant of the Medical and Health Department who has to travel in the discharge of his duties shall be entitled to the refund of the actual amount of his travelling expenses.

Transfer of existing powers.

20.—The powers, authority and duties vested in the General Board of Health as heretofore constituted, in the President or Vice-President of the said Board, or in the Chief Medical Officer, under the following Ordinances or Regulations made thereunder, viz:—

Nos. 20 of 1868 and 34 of 1881, relating to Public Hospitals and Dispensaries,

No. 39 of 1881—"The Cattle Plague Ordinance, 1881,"

No. 28 of 1887—"The Cremation Ordinance, 1887,"

No. 9 of 1889—"The Water Pollution Ordinance, 1889,"

the laws relating to Quarantine, or under any other existing Ordinance or Regulation, are, unless otherwise provided in this Ordinance, hereby transferred to and shall vest in and be exercised by the Director of the Medical and Health Department.

(2) The powers, authorities and duties vested in the General Board of Health, as heretofore constituted, under Ordinance No. 39 of 1881—"The Cattle Plague Ordinance, 1881"— and under Ordinance No. 22 of 1883 entitled "And Ordinance to prohibit the introduction of cast off clothes into the Colony," are hereby transferred to, and shall vest in the Director of the Medical and Health Department, and shall be exercised by him after consulting the Quarantine Committee, appointed under Part VII of this Ordinance.

(3) Article 29 of Ordinance No. 39 of 1881—"The Cattle Plague Ordinance, 1881"—is hereby repealed and replaced by the following provision :—

The Director of the Medical and Health Department, the Sanitary Warden, the Assistant Sanitary Warden or any Sanitary or Police Officer shall have the right to enter any land or premises in order to carry out the provisions of this Ordinance or of any Regulations made, or Order given thereunder.

Provided that it shall not be lawful to enter any dwelling house between sunset and sunrise without a warrant from the District Magistrate.

(4) Article 2 of Ordinance No. 27 of 1883, entitled "An Ordinance to amend the laws on "Rivers and Forests," is hereby repealed and replaced by the following provision :—

The powers and duties of the Surveyor General under Articles 24, 25 and 68 of Ordinance No. 35 of 1863 are hereby transferred to the Director of the Medical and Health Department; and the Articles aforesaid shall henceforth be read and construed as if the words "Director of the Medical and Health Department" were substituted therein for the words "General Board of Health."

Any certificate required by any of the Articles aforesaid may be signed by the Director of the Medical and Health Department, or the Sanitary Authority.

(5) Article 4 of Ordinance No. 28 of 1887,—"The Cremation Ordinance, 1887,"— is hereby repealed and replaced by the following provision :—

It shall be lawful for the Government, with the advice of the General Board of Health, to build crematories in connection with public cemeteries or elsewhere, provided that such crematory be not situated within one and a half kilometres from any town or proclaimed village.

(6) Article 8 of Ordinance No. 9 of 1889 entitled "An Ordinance to make further provision "for preventing the pollution of Rivers and Streams," is hereby repealed and replaced by the following provision :—

Offences against this Ordinance may be prosecuted by the Sanitary Warden, the Assistan Sanitary Warden or other officer of the Medical and Health Department, any of whom may enter and inspect lands and premises not being private dwelling-houses.

(7) The right vested in any member of the General Board of Health as heretofore constituted, by Article 6 of Ordinance No. 20 of 1868, relating to Public Hospitals and Dispensaries, is hereby vested in any member of the General Board of Health as constituted by this Ordinance.

Pensions.

21.—The provisions of Ordinance No. 30 of 1881, as amended by Ordinance No. 5 of 1891, and of Ordinance No. 32 of 1891, as amended by Ordinance No. 30 of 1892, shall continue to apply to those officers of the General Board of Health, and of the Medical Department respectively, as constituted at the time of the passing of those Ordinances, who shall continue in the service of the Government under this Ordinance.

The expressions "General Board of Health" and "Medical Department" in those Ordinances respectively, shall, after the coming into force of this Ordinance, be construed to mean the Medical and Health Department, as constituted by this Ordinance.

Widows and Orphans' Pensions.

22.—The provisions of Ordinance No. 2 of 1886 and of Ordinance No. 8 of 1893, shall continue to apply to those officers of the General Board of Health, and of the Medical Department respectively, as constituted at the time of the passing of those Ordinances, who shall continue in the service of the Government under this Ordinance. The expressions "Board of Health" and "Public Hospitals" in Ordinance No. 8 of 1893 shall, after the coming into force of this Ordinance, be construed to mean the Medical and Health Department, as constituted by this Ordinance.

Persons to act for and during absence of Director.

23.—During the absence of the Director of the Medical and Health Department from the office of the said Department, the Medical Inspector, or in his absence the Sanitary Warden, shall have power to perform all duties, and to do all acts and things and to execute all deeds and writings, which by any law or practice in the Colony are required to be performed, done or executed by the said Medical Inspector, or the said Sanitary Warden, shall be as valid and binding as if they had been done, signed, and executed by the said Director himself.

Provided that, in the absence of the Director of the Medical and Health Department, the Medical Inspector, and the Sanitary Warden, the Chief Clerk shall have power to perform such duties as shall be defined by Regulations to be made in the form and manner provided for by Articles 24 and 25.

Director to make Regulations on certain matters.

24.— It shall be the duty of the Director of the Medical and Health Department from time to time to make Regulations either on his own initiative or when directed by the Governor, in respect of the following matters, and from time to time, to amend or repeal the same : and further to determine the localities to and within which such Regulations are to be applied.

a. The execution of the Laws relating to Quarantine ; and of all matters mentioned in Articles 3, 32, 33 and 38 of Ordinance No. 6 of 1887.

b. The drainage and cleansing of Towns, Villages and Districts.

c. The cleansing, ventilation or drainage of Premises, of Water-closets, Privies and Cesspools, and generally the night soil service of Towns, Villages and Premises : the closing of buildings or structures unfit for human habitation : and the prohibition of their use as such.

d. The erection of Public Fountains, Lavatories, Wash-houses and Bathing Places.

e. The erection of Water-closets, Privies and Urinals for Public use.

f. The supply of water for Public use in any District.

g. The prevention of the exposure for sale or of the hawking of of unwholesome food.

h. The prohibition of the establishment within certain limits, and the control of any Trade, Business or Process calculated to be injurious to Public Health.

j. The management and control of slaughter houses in the rural districts, and the sanitary control of slaughter-houses in Port Louis.

k. The prevention of overcrowding in premises intended or employed for the accommodation of men or animals.

l. Burials, Dead-houses and Cemeteries in the rural districts, and sanitary control of the same in Port Louis.

m. The management, interior administration, discipline and general control of Public Markets, except those within the jurisdiction of the Municipality of Port Louis, and the imposition of rates and duties for the hire of stalls or for permission to sell in such markets, and in respect of all other matters in connection therewith, or in respect of the sale of articles of food (to be specified in the Regulations) and similar to those sold in such market within a distance of one kilometre therefrom.

Provided that such Regulations shall not be applicable to licensed Shopkeepers, or to hawkers, except hawkers of meat, poultry or fish.

n. The carrying out of the provisions of Ordinance No. 39 of 1881, and the providing for the seizure and destruction of goods and chattels, the destruction of infected huts, pens and stables, the shares of penalties recovered under the said Ordinance to be given to informers, and for all other measures necessary to ensure the object of the said Ordinance.

o. The application of all or any of the provisions of Ordinance No. 39 of 1881 to horses, asses and mules, and glanders and farcy, and other diseases thereof.

p. The prevention of the pollution of the sea within the waters of Mauritius by any trade, business or process calculated or likely to be injurious to fish.

q. The matters referred to in Ordinance No. 28 of 1887 relating to Crematories, cremation and the burning of the dead.

r. The prohibition for certain fixed periods of bathing and washing clothes and animals in specified parts of any river, the water of which is used for domestic purposes.

s. And generally with respect to all matters relating to public health and sanitation.

Such Regulations may further provide the penalties following for any breach or contravention thereof, that is to say :—

In respect of paragraph (*a*) of this Article a fine not exceeding five hundred Rupees (Rs. 500), and imprisonment not exceeding three months, as provided by Article 3 (2) of Ordinance No. 6 of 1887.

In respect of paragraphs (*b*) to (*l*) inclusive, a fine not exceeding one hundred Rupees (Rs. 100).

In respect of paragraph (*m*) a fine not exceeding one hundred Rupees (Rs. 100).

In respect of paragraphs (*n*) and (*o*) a fine not exceeding one thousand Rupees (Rs. 1000), and to imprisonment not exceeding three months.

In respect of paragraphs (*p*), (*q*) and (*r*) a fine not exceeding one hundred Rupees (Rs. 100).

In respect of paragraph (*s*) a fine not exceeding five hundred Rupees (Rs. 500) and imprisonment not exceeding three months.

The Director shall prepare and sanction Forms of the various orders, notices and other papers, which may be required for the carrying out of this Ordinance and the Regulations made thereunder and may from time to time alter such Forms.

Regulations to be laid before Council.

25.—All Regulations in respect of any of the above matters not being inconsistent with the provisions of this Ordinance, or with any other law in force in the Colony, and all orders amending or repealing the said Regulations, shall, as approved by the Governor in Executive Council, be laid before the Council of Government at its next meeting, and may be disallowed or amended by resolution of the said Council at any time within one month thereafter, and if not so disallowed within such period shall be published in the Government Gazette and have the same force of law and be equally binding and valid as if they had been contained in this Ordinance.

Provided that whenever the Governor in Executive Council shall consider it necessary that any such Regulations be put in force immediately, he may order such Regulations to be published in the Government Gazette, and, on such publication, such Regulations shall be and remain in force so long as they are not disallowed by the Council of Government.

Duties of Officers of the Medical and Health Department.

26.—The Medical Inspector shall rank immediately after of Director of the Medical and Health Department and shall assist the Director generally in matters connected with the Department. It shall be his special duty to visit all Public Hospitals and Dispensaries, and perform the duties now performed by the Medical Officer to the Immigration Department under Article 26 of Ordinance No. 12 of 1878; provided that the reports directed to be made to the Protector of Immigrants, and the requisitions for visits to sugar estates which may be made by the Protector under the said Article, shall be made through the Director of the Medical and Health Department.

The Sanitary Warden shall be the head of the Sanitary Police Section of the Medical and Health Department.

The Sanitary Engineer shall be the head of the Sanitary Works and Buildings Acts Section of the Medical and Health Department, and shall be entrusted with the contruction, maintenance and management of drainage and water works, and of all works and structures connected with sanitation and shall also direct the application of technical clauses of the Building Acts.

The Police and Prison Surgeon shall also be the Vaccinator for the Police, Prison and other Government Departments in Port Louis. He shall also be the Commissioner of Lunacy for the town of Port Louis and shall be debarred from private practice.

The Health Officer shall be the Superintendent of Vaccination and shall also be a Relieving and Assistant Medical Officer for Port Louis and shall be debarred from private practice. He shall also exercise and perform all the powers and duties vested in the Health Officer referred to in the Ordinances and Regulations relating to Quarantine: and the words "Health Officer" therein used shall be construed to mean the Health Officer as created by this Ordinance.

The Public Vaccinator shall perform the duties laid down by Ordinance No. 12 of 1875 in Port Louis and continue to be paid as provided by the said Ordinance, and shall not be debarred from private practice.

The Medical Superintendent and Assistant Superintendent of the Barkly Asylum, in addition to their duties connected with the Asylum, shall continuq to perform as heretofore the duties under the Poor Law Commission.

The Assistant Superintendent of the Civil Hospital, the Medical Superintendent and the Assistant Superintendent of the Barkly Asylum, and the Medical Superintendent of the Lunatic Asylum shall have quarters at the Civil Hospital, the Barkly Asylum and the Lunatic Asylum respectively, and shall reside there.

Any of the members of the clerical staff of the Medical and Health Department may be called upon to perform the duties of Secretary and Assistant Secretary to the General Board of Health and Quarantine Committee.

Appointment of two Government Medical Officers in each district.

27.—In each District there shall be two Medical Officers, one to be called the Government Medical Officer, and the other Assistant Government Medical Officer.

The Government Medical Officer shall perform the following duties:

(*a*) He shall be in charge of the Public Hospital and Hospital Dispensary, and of the Prison Hospital;

(*b*) He shall act as one of the Commissioners in Lunacy;

(*c*) He shall medically examine the members of the Police Force, and afford medical aid to them and to their families;

(*d*) He shall report on all criminal cases referred to him;

(*e*) He shall make post mortem examinations and autopsies;

(*f*) He shall attend Court as witness in criminal casses;

(*g*) He shall be a member of the Medical Board for medical examination of public servants; and shall afford medical aid to the Forest Rangers and their families;

(*h*) He shall visit the paupers in his district and perform all other Government Medical work in his district except vaccination and attendance at Dispensaries.

He shall be debarred from private practice, and shall not be entitled to any travelling allowance.

(2) The Assistant Government Medical Officer shall be Public Vaccinator for his district. He shall perform the duties laid down by Ordinance No. 12 of 1875, and shall be paid as provided by the said Ordinance and by Ordinance No. 19 of 1877.

He shall also, saving vested rights, have charge of Dispensaries in his district (except the Hospital Dispensary) and shall replace and assist the Government Medical Officer in case of need.

He shall receive in respect of his Dispensary duties such sum as the Governor shall determine. He shall also receive the usual fee for assisting the Government Medical Officer in the performance of operations, but he shall receive no fee for replacing that officer in case of unavoidable or temporary absence from duty. He shall be entitled to private practice.

Employment of Chemical Analysts.

28.—There shall be employed from time to time by the Government in criminal cases Chemical Analysts to be paid by fees, provided that any analyses may be made by the officers employed at the Station Agronomique.

Provided also that none of the Government Medical Officers who owe the whole of their time to Government shall be employed in making these analyses.

IV.

REMOVAL OF NUISANCES.

Definition of Nuisance.

29.—The word "Nuisance" as used in this Ordinance shall include:

(*a*) Any failure to supply or any inadequate or defective provision or employment of drain, water-closet, privy or cess-pool accommodation, and any other matter or circumstance whereby any premises, or any part thereof is rendered injurious to health;

(*b*) Any street or road or any part thereof, or any water course, ditch, gutter, drain, ashpit, sewer, privy, urinal, or cess-pool, so foul as to be injurious to health;

(*c*) Any well, tank, pond, reservoir, canal, or conduit, the water of which is so tainted with impurities, or which is otherwise so unwholesome as to be injurious to the health of persons living near or using such water, or which is calculated to promote or aggravate epidemic disease:

(*d*) Any stream, canal, pond or water in which animals or clothes shall have been washed, or into which water used in the washing of clothes shall have escaped, or shall have been discharged, and which from these or any other causes is in such a state as to be injurious to health;

(*e*) Any stable, cow-house, pigstye, or other premises for the use of animals which is in such a condition as to be injurious to health; or any animal so kept as to be injurious to health;

(*f*) Any accumulation or deposit of water, manure, dirt, or other matter wherever situated injurious to health;

(*g*) Any manufactory, trade or business, so conducted as to be injurious to health;

(*h*) Any premises or part of premises so overcrowded as to be injurious to health;

(*j*) Any churchyard, cemetery or place of burial, so situated or so overcrowded with bodies, or otherwise so conducted as to be injurious to health.

Power to enter and inspect premises.

30.—It shall be lawful for the Sanitary Authority or any Sanitary Inspector, within his jurisdiction, or any person authorized in writing by the Sanitary Inspector, together with any assistant or assistants, to enter and inspect any premises other than private dwelling houses at any time between six in the morning and six in the evening.

Order for entry and inspection of dwelling-house.

31.—Whenever any person mentioned in the foregoing Article shall have reasonable ground for believing that there exists a nuisance in any private dwelling house, he may apply to the District Magistrate of the locality for an order to enter and inspect the said dwelling house. On any such application being made to the said District Magistrate by any person aforesaid, and on oath being made by the applicant that he has reasonable grounds for believing that a nuisance exists in such dwelling house, the Magistrate shall grant an order under his hand empowering such person to enter and inspect such dwelling house during the hours specified in the said order.

If nuisance exists Order to continue in force until it be removed.

32.—If, on any inspection made under such order, it be ascertained that a nuisance exists in such dwelling house, such order shall be a sufficient warrant for entry by the person named therein and by such other persons as shall be necessary, so long as the said nuisance shall not have been abated, remedied or removed, or until steps shall have been taken to prevent its recurrence; or to verify that the said nuisance has been abated, remedied or removed, or that steps have been taken to prevent its recurrence.

Sanitary Authority may issue notice for removal of nuisance.

33.—It shall be lawful for the Sanitary Authority in any case where the existence of a nuisance is ascertained to his satisfaction, to issue a notice in writing calling on the person by whose act, default, or sufferance the nuisance arises or continues, or if such person cannot be found, on the owner or occupier of the premises on which the nuisance arises, requiring him to abate, remedy or remove such nuisance within a reasonable time to be named in such notice, not being less than twenty-four hours or more than one month from the time of service of such notice, unless cause be shown to the Director of the Medical and Health Department for prolonging such time: Provided—

1o. That when the nuisance arises from the want or defective construction of any structural convenience or where there is no occupier of the premises, notice under this Article shall be served on the owner.

2o. That where the person causing the nuisance cannot be found, and the Sanitary Authority is satisfied that the nuisance does not arise or continue by the act, default, or sufferance of the owner or occupier of the premises, such Authority may himself abate the same without further order.

Nature of notice.

34.—Such notice may require the person on whom it is served to provide water-closet or privy accommodation, or to employ sufficient means of cleansing, draining, or ventilating the same: or to pave, cleanse, disinfect or purify any premises, or to drain, empty, cleanse, fill up, cover repair, alter or remove, any ditch, gutter, drain, ashpit, sewer, privy, urinal or cesspool, or to provide a sufficient substitute therefor; or to fill up, cleanse or cover any well; or to abstain from any operation which may pollute any stream, canal, pond or water; or to remove or provide for the wholesome keeping of any animal; or to carry away any accumulation or deposit of matter injurious to health; or to discontinue any work, manufactory, trade, or business; or to limit the number of persons who may be accommodated in any premises, or the number of separate dwellings or apartments into which any premises may be divided, or let to, or used by different persons or families; or to prevent the use of any churchyard, cemetery or place of burial; or to do such other works or acts as are necessary to abate, remedy or remove any nuisance ascertained to exist as aforesaid in such manner and within such time as shall be specified in the notice; and if the Sanitary Authority is of opinion that such or the like nuisance is likely to recur, he may further prohibit the recurrence thereof and issue a notice as aforesaid for the execution of such works as may be necessary in his opinion to prevent such recurrence.

If notice be not complied with, Sanitary Authority may execute necessary works.

35.—In cases of non-compliance with any such notice, and if no appeal has been made to the Magistrate within the delay specified [in Article 39, it shall be lawful for the Sanitary Authority, or any person authorized by him in writing with all proper assistants, workmen and servants, from time to time, and forcibly if need be, to enter the premises in respect of which such notice shall have been issued, and to do whatever may be necessary in execution of such notice for the abatement, remedy or removal, or for the prevention of the recurrence of such nuisance.

Sanitary Authority may certify to Director of the Medical and Health Department necessary works in Port Louis.

36.—If the Sanitary Authority shall ascertain that any nuisance exists upon or in respect of any premises, roads, bridges, streets, footpaths, squares, areas or spaces of land in the city of Port Louis belonging to, or in the possession of or under the management of the Municipal Council thereof; or if he shall be of opinion that it is expedient for the public health that any premises, road, bridge, street, footpath, square, area or space of land, should be altered or repaired, he shall certify in writing to the Director of the Medical and Health Department the existence of such nuisance, or the works necessary as aforesaid; and such certificate shall forthwith be transmitted by the Director to the Mayor of Port Louis, and shall have the same effect as a notice by such Sanitary Authority to abate, remedy, or remove such nuisance, or to prevent the recurrence thereof, or to execute such work as may be mentioned in such certificate, within the space of one month from the day of the delivery of such certificate to the Secretary of the Municipal Council.

If the certificate be not complied with, the Director of the Medical and Health Department may abate nuisance at the expense of the Municipal Council.

37.—If the Municipal Council of Port Louis shall fail to abate, remedy, remove or prevent the recurrence of any nuisance, or to execute any work mentioned in any certificate of the Sanitary Authority within the time specified therein, or within such extended time as the Director of the Medical and Health Department may allow on any application for the revision as hereinafter mentioned of any such certificate, the Sanitary Authority shall certify such failure to the said Director who shall thereupon do whatever may be necessary to abate, remedy, remove or prevent the recurrence of such nuisance, or for the execution of such work; and the expenses incurred in abating, remedying, removing or preventing the recurrence of such nuisance, or in executing such work shall, after being certified by the Director of the Medical and Health Department, be paid from the Colonial Treasury, and shall be a debt due to Her Majesty by the Municipal Council of Port Louis, recoverable by the Receiver General.

When notice is not complied with and costly works are necessary, Sanitary Authority may certify to the Director of the Medical and Health Department.

38.— Whenever any notice in respect of any nuisance within the city of Port Louis shall not be complied with within the time specified in such notice, and it shall appear to the Sanitary Authority that the total expenses attending the execution of such notice would exceed one year's rent of the premises, or that the execution of structural works is required for the abatement, remedy or removal, or for preventing the recurrence of the nuisance, such Sanitary Authority shall certify in writing to the Director of the Medical and Health Department that such notice has been made and has not been complied with; and the Director may thereupon take such steps as he shall deem fit to ensure compliance with such notice; and to this end may, by a warrant in writing, authorize any person to abate, remedy, remove or prevent the recurrence of the nuisance, and to do whatever may be necessary for the execution of such notice, and the completion of such structural works.

Power to appeal against notice or certificate to the Magistrate.

39.—If the person on whom a notice under Articles 33 and 34 has been served, is dissatisfied with any of the requisitions thereof, or if the Municipal Council shall be dissatisfied with the certificate given under Article 36 by the Director of the Medical and Health Department, it shall be lawful for such person within the time specified in such notice for complying therewith, or for the Municipal Council within seven days after the service of such certificate on the Secretary thereof, to cause a summons to be served upon the said Director calling upon him to show cause before the Magistrate of the District in which the said nuisance is alleged to exist, why such notice or certificate should not be discharged, modified or suspended as the case may be. Thereupon it shall be lawful for the said Magistrate to hear and determine the case whatever may be the amount involved, and, after having heard the evidence produced on both sides in the form and manner provided for by Ordinance No. 22 of 1888, to confirm, modify, suspend or discharge the said notice or certificate, or enlarge the time allowed for compliance therewith.

Provided that in any such action a party to the suit may appeal to the Supreme Court from the judgment of the said Magistrate, whatever may be the amount involved. Provided further that such appeal shall be proceeded with in the form and manner enacted by Ordinance No. 22 of 1888.

Articles removed from premises to be sold or destroyed.

40.—Any article removed from premises in consequence of a notice issued under this Ordinance may be sold by public competition by the Usher of the District Court of the locality under a warrant granted by the Sanitary Authority, provided that not less than five days' public notice of any such sale be given by such Authority. Provided that in the case of perishable articles, or articles the value of which does not exceed twenty Rupees (Rs 20), the Sanitary Authority may order the immediate sale thereof: or where such delay would be prejudicial to health, he may, with the consent of the Director of the Medical and Health Department, order the immediate destruction thereof. The proceeds of every such sale shall be retained by the Sanitary Authority and employed to defray the expenses of the removal and sale, and the surplus, if any, shall on demand, within one month from the date of sale, be delivered by the Sanitary Authority to the owner of the articles aforesaid.

Local Authority may enter shops, &c., to inspect food.

41.—The Sanitary Authority or any person authorized by him in writing may, at any time between the hours of six in the morning and six in the evening, enter any shop or premises used for the sale or preparation for sale, or for the storage of food, to inspect and examine any food found therein, which he shall have reason to believe is intended to be used as human food; and, in case any such food appear to the Authority or to such person so authorized by him to be unfit for such use, he may seize the same, and such Sanitary Authority may order it to be destroyed or to be so disposed of as to prevent the same from being exposed for sale or used as human food.

Provisions as to ships.

42.—For the purpose of the provisions of this part of the Ordinance relating to nuisances, any ship or vessel lying in any river, harbour, creek, or other inland waters of the Colony, shall be subject to the jurisdiction of the Sanitary Authority in the same manner as if it were a house.

The master or other officer in charge of any such ship shall be deemed for the purpose of the said provisions to be the occupier of such ship or vessel.

This Article shall not apply to any ship or vessel under the command or charge of any officer bearing Her Majesty's commission, or to any ship or vessel belonging to any foreign Government.

Jurisdiction of the Medical and Health Department Officers with respect to the town of Curepipe.

43.—The powers given to the Board of Curepipe under paragraph e of Article 7 of Ordinance No. 12 of 1889 to take measures for the cleansing and draining of the Town of Curepipe, for the cleansing, ventilation and drainage of premises, water-closets and privies, and generally the night soil service of the Town, shall be subject to the Rules and Regulations, now in force, of the General Board of Health as heretofore constituted, or hereafter to be made by the Director of the Medical and Health Department under Articles 21 and 25 of this Ordinance.

(2) The powers given to the Sanitary Authority or to any officer of the Medical and Health Department under this Ordinance, with regard to the Municipality of Port Louis, shall extend to the Town of Curepipe, and nothing in Ordinance No. 12 of 1889 contained shall be deemed to affect such powers.

(3) Any officer of the Board of Commissioners shall have power to prosecute for any breach of the Building Acts, or of any Bye-Laws made by the said Board, and shall further have power, concurrently with officers of the Medical and Health Department, to prosecute for any breach of any Regulations now in force made by the General Board of Health as heretofore constituted, or hereafter to be made by the Director of the Medical and Health Department.

V.

Prevention and Mitigation of Diseases under Proclamation of the Governor in Executive Council.

In case of formidable disease Part V. may be put in force.

44.—Whenever any part of the Colony appear to be threatened with, or is affected by any formidable epidemic, endemic, or contagious disease, the Governor, with the advice of the Executive Council may, by Proclamation from time to time, direct that the provisions contained in this Part of this Ordinance be put in force in the Colony or such part thereof as by such Proclamation may be specified, and may from time to time revoke or renew any such Proclamation; and, subject to such revocation or renewal, every such Proclamation shall be in force for such period as in such Proclamation shall be expressed, and every such Proclamation shall be published in the Government Gazette, and such publication shall be conclusive evidence thereof.

After Proclamation Director may issue Orders or Regulations.

45.—From time to time after the issuing of such Proclamation as aforesaid, and while the same continues in force, the Director of the Medical and Health Department may, with the advice of the Quarantine Committee, issue such Orders and Regulations as he shall think fit, for the prevention or mitigation of such epidemic, endemic or contagious disease, and from time to time may revoke, renew, and alter any such Orders and Regulations; and may impose for any infraction thereof a penalty not exceeding five hundred Rupees (Rs. 500) and imprisonment not exceeding six months. The said Orders and Regulations shall extend to all parts or places in which Part V of this Ordinance shall for the time being be in force, as aforesaid; and shall continue in force so long as the said Part V shall, under such Proclamation, be applicable to the said parts or places. All such Orders and Regulations as approved by the Governor in Executive Council shall be published in the Government Gazette, and such publication shall be conclusive evidence thereof:

Provided that whenever the Director of the Medical and Health Department considers that a case of Cholera, Yellow Fever, Plague, Typhus or Small-Pox, or of a disease which is suspected to be Cholera or any of the diseases above mentioned, has occurred in any part of the Colony, it shall be lawful for him, with or without the previous advice of the Quarantine Committee, to take or to order for the purpose of preventing the spread of the disease, any measures which he might take or order with the advice of the Quarantine Committee if such Proclamation had been published:

Provided further that the said Director, when he has in such cases deemed it expedient to act without the advice of the Quarantine Committee, shall forthwith report to the Governor any measure ordered or taken by him, and the Governor in Executive Council may, at any time, cancel, disallow, or amend any such measure. Such cancellation, disallowance or amendment shall not affect the validity of anything done, or of any measure ordered or taken by the said Director prior to such decision as may have been taken by the Governor in Executive Council.

Nature of Orders and Regulations.

46.—The Director of the Medical and Health Department by the Orders and Regulations referred to in the preceding Article, may provide

a. For the speedy and safe interment of the dead;

b. For house to house visitation;

c. For the dispensing and distribution of medicines and for affording to persons affected by or threatened with such epidemic, endemic, or contagious disease such medical aid and such accommodation as may be required;

d. For any such matters or things as may to him appear advisable for preventing or mitigating such disease.

Sanitary Authority to carry out directions of the Director.

47.—The Sanitary Authority shall superintend the execution of such Orders and Regulations and shall do and provide all such acts, matters and things as may be advisable for mitigating such disease or for superintending or aiding in the execution of such Orders and Regulations, or for executing the same as the case may require.

Sanitary Authority may enter and inspect any premises.

48.—The Sanitary Authority, acting in the execution of such Orders or Regulations, or the officers or persons by such Authority in this behalf authorized, may enter at any reasonable time during the day or night, and inspect any premises where they have ground for believing that any person has recently died of any such disease, or that necessity may otherwise exist for executing in relation to the premises, any of such Orders or Regulations.

Order to abate overcrowding.

49.—When any such Proclamation is in force in any place, on the certificate of the Authority, Sanitary Inspector or of any duly qualified Medical Practitioner, or on other sufficient evidence that any premises or part of premises are so overcrowded as to be dangerous to health, the Director of the Medical and Health Department shall have power to make such Order as he may see fit to abate such overcrowding; and the owner or occupier of such premises who shall permit such overcrowding after such Order or a copy thereof shall have been served on him shall be liable on conviction to a fine not exceeding twenty Rupees (Rs. 20) for each day during which such overcrowding shall continue.

Proclamation to extend to Harbours.

50.—All Proclamations of the Governor in Executive Council for executing the provisions of Part V of this Ordinance shall extend to all ports and harbours of the Island: and the Director of the Medical and Health Department may issue under the said Proclamation Orders and Regulations for cleansing, purifying, ventilating and preventing disease in ships within the ports and harbours of the island.

All such Orders and Regulations as approved by the Governor in Executive Council shall be published in the Government Gazette, and such published in the Government Gazette, and such publication shall be conclusive evidence thereof.

Proclamations, Orders and Regulations to be laid before Council of Government.

51.—Every Proclamation of the Governor in Executive Council and every Order and Regulation of the Director of the Medical and Health Department under Part V of this Ordinance as approved by the Governor in Executive Council, shall be laid before the Council of Government at its next meeting, and every such Regulation may be amended or disallowed by the said Council of Government.

VI.

LEGAL PROCEEDINGS.

Expenses arising from non-compliance with Certificate or Notice to be recovered from person in default.

52.—All expenses incurred by the Director of the Medical and Health Department or by the Sanitary Authority in consequence of any default in complying with any Notice, Certificate or Order issued under the provisions of this Ordinance, shall be deemed to be money paid for the use and at the requirement of the person on whom the said certificate or order was made, and shall be recoverable from the said person at the suit of the Director of the Medical and Health Department or the Sanitary Authority in the ordinary course of law.

Expense of Rs. 50 or under may be recovered by warrant of the Director of the Medical and Health Department.

53.—When the expenses incurred as aforesaid shall not exceed fifty Rupees (Rs. 50) the sum shall, without further formality, be recoverable from the said person by warrant under the hand of the Director of the Medical and Health Department, specifying the amount of such expense and the purpose for which it was incurred. Every such warrant may be executed by seizure and sale of the property real or personal belonging to the said person, or by opposition in the hands of his debtors.

Obstructing Officers of the Medical and Health Department.

54.—Whoever assaults, obstructs molests or hinders the Sanitary Authority, or any Inspector, Officer or Servant of the Medical and Health Department in the execution of the duties or exercise of the powers imposed or conferred upon him by this Ordinance or any other Ordinance, shall be guilty of an offence, and, on conviction thereof, shall be liable to a penalty not exceeding five hundred Rupees (Rs. 500) or to imprisonment not exceeding three months, without prejudice to the right of the Procureur General to institute any criminal proceedings against such offender under any law in force in this Colony.

Penalty for damage to property.

55.—Any person wilfully damaging any property or works under the charge of any officer of the Medical and Health Department, shall be guilty of any offence and shall ye liable on conviction to a fine not exceeding one hundred Rupees (Rs. 100), in addition to the cost of repairing or making good such property or works.

Limitation of actions and prosecutions.

56.—Every civil or criminal action, suit or proceeding, against any person for anything done or omitted to be done in pursuance of this Ordinance or in the execution of the powers or authority under this Ordinance, shall, under pain of nullity, be instituted within three calendar months from the date of the fact, act or omission, which shall have given rise to such action, suit or other proceeding.

Judge may certify probable cause of action.

57.—In any such action if the Judge or Court before whom such action shall be tried shall certify upon the record that the defendant or defendants in such action acted upon reasonable and probable cause, then the plaintiff in such action shall not be entitled to more than a cent of a Rupee damages nor to any costs of suit.

Notice of such action.

58.—No such civil action, suit, or proceeding shall be competent unless one calendar month before its institution written notice thereof and of the subject of complaint shall have been given to defendant.

If sufficient indemnity be offered, action to be dismissed.

59.—If, previous to the institution of any such civil action, suit or proceeding, the defendant shall have offered to the complainant any indemnity which shall be determined to be sufficient by the Court or Magistrate before whom the case shall be brought; or if, after any such action or other aforesaid shall have been commenced, the defendant therein shall have deposited with the Registrar or Clerk of the Court or Magistrate aforesaid a sum of money which such Court or Magistrate shall determine to be sufficient as damage or indemnity to the complainant, such action, suit or proceeding respectively shall be dismissed, subject to the award of such Court or Magistrate in respect of costs.

Notice, Certificate, or Order to be signed by the Director of the Medical and Health Department or Sanitary Authority.

60.—Whenever, under this Ordinance any Notice, Certificate of Order is issued to the owner or occupier of any premises or to the author of any nuisance, such Notice, Certificate or Order shall be signed by the Director of the Medical and Health Department or by the Sanitary Authority as the case may be.

Form of Notice, Certificate or Order.

61.—Every Notice, or Certificate shall be in the form contained in Schedule B annexed to this Ordinance or to the like effect.

Service of Notice, Certificate or Order.

62.—Every such Notice, Certificate and Order may be served by any officer of the Medical and Health Department by delivering the same or a true copy thereof to or at the residence of the person to whom it is addressed: and when addressed to the owner of any premises, it may also, if such owner cannot be found, be served by delivering the same or a true copy thereof to some person upon the premises, or, if there be no person upon the premises who can be so served, by affixing the same to some conspicuous part of the said premises.

Notice or other proceeding may be partly printed and partly written.

63.—Any Notice, Certificate, Order, or other proceeding under this Ordinance, may be partly written and partly printed.

Penalty for failure to comply with Notice, Certificate or Order of the Director of the Medical and Health Department.

64.—Any person on whom there shall be served any Notice or Certificate or Order issued by the Sanitary Authority under the provisions of this Ordinance, and who shall fail within the time specified to bring the matter before the District Magistrate as provided by Article 39, or who, after final judgment in such matter, shall fail to comply with such Notice, Certificate, or judgment, as the case may be, shall be deemed to be guilty of an offence, and shall, on conviction thereof, be liable to a penalty not exceeding ten Rupees (Rs. 10) for every day during which such non-compliance shall continue, unless the Director of the Medical and Health Department certifies that due diligence has been used to comply with the Notice, Certificate or Order.

Penalty for possession of food unfit for human food.

65.—Any person in whose possession there shall be found any food liable to seizure under Article 41 hereof, shall be deemed to be guilty of an offence, and shall, on conviction thereof, be liable to a penalty not exceeding two hundred Rupees (Rs. 200) or to imprisonment not exceeding three months.

General penal clause.

66.—Any person who shall contravene any provision of this Ordinance for which no special penalty is hereinbefore provided shall be guilty of an offence, and shall be liable, on conviction thereof, to a penalty not exceeding one hundred Rupees (Rs. 100).

Ordinance not to interfere with other Penal Laws.

67.—Nothing in this Ordinance contained and no prosecution entered thereunder shall be construed as in any way affecting any liability arising in respect of any crime or misdemeanor (*délit*) committed against the provisions of Ordinance No. 6 of 1838, commonly called "The Penal Code of the Colony" or under any other Ordinance in force in the Colony.

Title to sue.

68.—All penalties imposed by this Ordinance or by any sanitary enactment may be recovered on complaint at the instance of the Director of the Medical and Health Department, the Sanitary Authority or any Inspector of the said Department made to the District Magistrate of the District wherein the offender shall reside.

Provided always that any complaint in respect of the existence of any nuisance may be instituted by the owner or occupier, not being himself the author of the nuisance, of the premises in respect of which the offence is committed.

Transfer of existing powers of prosecution.

69.—All other powers of prosecution vested in the Sanitary Authority, Sanitary Inspector, Guardian, Warden or officer or servant of the General Board of Health as heretofore constituted, by any existing Ordinance or Regulation, are hereby transferred to and shall vest in the Sanitary Authority, and shall be exercised by him or by such officers of the Medical and Health Department as may be designated by the Director in Regulations to be made in the form and manner provided for by Articles 24 and 25.

Proceedings in certain cases against nuisances

70.—Where any nuisance under this Ordinance appears to be wholly or partially caused by the acts or defaults of two or more persons, it shall be lawful for the Sanitary Authority or other complainant to institute proceedings against any one of such persons, or to include all or any two or more of such persons in one proceeding; and any one or more of such persons may be ordered to abate such nuisance, so far as the same appears to the Court having cognizance of the case to be caused by his or their acts or defaults, or may be prohibited from continuing any act or defaults which, in the opinion of such Court, contribute to such nuisance or may be fined or otherwise punished notwithstanding that the acts or defaults of any one of such persons would not separately have caused a nuisance; and the costs may be distributed as to such Court may appear fair and reasonable.

Proceedings against several persons included in one complaint shall not abate by reason of the death of any among the persons so included, but all such proceedings may be carried on as if the deceased person had not been originally so included.

Whenever in any proceeding under the provisions of this Ordinance relating to nuisances, whether written or otherwise, it becomes necessary to mention or refer to the owner or occupier of any premises, it shall be sufficient to designate him as the "owner" or "occupier" of such premises, without name or further description.

Nothing in this Article shall prevent persons proceeded against from recovering contribution in any case in which they would now be entitled to contribution by law.

No proceeding to be removed by certiorari or quashed for want of form.

71.—No complaint, conviction, notice, certificate order or other proceeding, matter or thing, made or done in the execution of this Ordinance, shall be removed by certiorari, or by any other writ or process whatsoever, into any Court, or be vacated, quashed, or set aside for want of form.

Provided that when under this Ordinance any person or persons shall have been condemned to imprisonment an appeal shall in every case lie to the Supreme Court against such conviction; and the formalities to enter and prosecute, hear and determine the said appeal shall be the same as are provided for by Ordinance No. 23 of 1888 intituled "An Ordinance to consolidate and amend the law relating to the jurisdiction of District Courts in Criminal matters."

Amount of taxation of officers not entitled to fees to accrue to Treasury.

72.—Whenever any officer is summoned under this Ordinance to give evidence before a Court of Justice and is not entitled to fees for his attendance before such Court, his attendance shall be taxed by the proper officer of the Court, and the amount of such taxation shall accrue to the Treasury.

VII.

QUARANTINE.

Constitution of the Quarantine Committee.

73.—The Quarantine Committee of the General Board of Health, as constituted by Article 4 of Ordinance No. 6 of 1887, shall cease to exist, and shall be replaced by a Quarantine Committee to be appointed by the General Board of Health under Article 16, sub-section 2 of this Ordinance, which shall be a consultative and deliberative body for the purpose of advising the Government on all Quarantine matters.

Until such Committee is appointed by the Board, the Quarantaine Committee appointed under Ordinance No. 6 of 1887 shall be deemed the Quarantine Committee under this Ordinance.

Composition of the Quarantine Committee.

74.—The Quarantine Committee shall be composed of the President, three or more members of the Board, and the Mayor of Port Louis.

The President of the Board shall be the President of the Quarantine Committee.

Three members shall form a quorum.

Duties of the Quarantine Committee.

79.—The Quarantine Committee shall be consulted by the Government or by the Director of the Medical and Health Department on all matters relating to Quarantine, and the recommendations of the Committee shall be acted upon unless set aside or amended by the Governor in Executive Council.

Duties of Director of the Medical and Health Department with respect to Quarantine matters.

76.—The Director of the Medical and Health Department shall also be bound, in all cases, (save in the case of making Regulations) to consult the Quarantine Committee in the exercise and discharge of all powers and duties which were exercised and discharged by the General Board of Health in Quarantine matters as heretofore constituted, and which are hereby transferred to and vested in him.

Amendment of article 62 of Ordinance 6 of 1887.

77.—In Article 62 of Ordinance No. 6 of 1887 instead of the words "Board", there shall be read the words "Medical and Health Department."

Application of Part VI.

78.—The provisions of Part VI of this Ordinance shall apply in case any person is obstructed in the execution of any of the Quarantine Ordinances or Regulations, or in case such person is sued for or on account of anything done by him in execution of the aforesaid Ordinances or Regulations.

Commencement of Ordinance.

79.—This Ordinance shall come into force on a day to be fixed by Proclamation. *

---

* This Ordinance was brought into force by Proclamation No. 36 of 8th. November 1895.

SCHEDULE A.

Repeal.

The following enactments :—

(a.)	Ordinance	No.	8 of 1874.
(b.)	,,	,,	6 of 1875.
(c.)	,,	,,	6 of 1876.
(d.)	,,	,,	17 of 1883.
(e.)	,,	,,	2 of 1888.
(f.)	,,	,,	19 of 1888.
(g.)	,,	,,	23 of 1892.
(h.)	,,	,,	5 of 1893.

The following Articles in the following enactments :—

(j.)	Ordinance	No.	39 of 1881,	Articles	23, 32 and 39.
(k.)	,,	,,	27 of 1883	,,	2
(l.)	,,	,,	6 of 1887	,,	4, 5 and 56.
(m.)	,,	,,	28 of 1887	,,	4 and 7.
(n.)	,,	,,	9 of 1889	,,	8 and 9.
(o.)	,,	,,	12 of 1889	,,	9 and 10.

SCHEDULE B.

Form of Notice requiring abatement of Nuisance.

To [*person causing the nuisance, or owner or occupier of the Premises whereon the nuisance exists, as the case may be.*]

Notice is hereby given to you that I have ascertained that the following nuisance exists in the premises situate [*describe premises or place where the nuisance exists*] namely [*here describe the nuisance.*]

Now, you are hereby required within a delay of from the time of service upon you of the present Notice to [*here describe what is required to be done*] ; and if you fail to comply with this Notice, you will be liable to a fine not exceeding ten Rupees (Rs. 10) for every day during which such non-compliance shall continue.

Date

A. B.

[*Title of party signing.*]

SCHEDULE C.

Form of certificate to be used by the Sanitary Authority under Article 36.

To the Director of the Medical and Health Department.

I, the undersigned *Sanitary Authority* hereby certify that the following nuisance exists in [*here describe the place*], namely [*here describe the nuisance*] or, [*as the case may be*] that I am of opinion that it is expedient for the public health that [*here describe what should be done and the locality.*]

A. B.,

Sanitary Authority.

Ordinance No. 1 of 1895.

To provide for the engagements of persons wishing to join the Municipal Fire Engine Establishment of Port Louis.

(21*st. June* 1895.)

Whereas it is expedient that persons wishing to join the Municipal Fire Engine Establishment of Port Louis should enter into engagements with the Municipal Corporation of Port Louis for a certain number of years; the said engagements not being subjected to the provisions of Ordinance No. 12 of 1878;

Be it enacted by the Governor, with the advice and consent of the Council of Government, as follows:—

Short title.

1.—This Ordinance may be cited as "The Municipal Fire Brigade Ordinance, 1895."

Engagements not subjected to Ordinance 12 of 1878.

2.—The engagements made between the Municipal Corporation of Port Louis, and persons who wish to join the Municipal Fire Engine Establishment, shall not be subjected to the Provisions of Ordinance No. 12 of 1878.

Duration of engagements.

3.—Any one wishing to join the Fire Engine Establishment shall be bound to enter into an engagement with the Municipal Corporation of Port Louis for any period not exceeding five years.

Regulations applicable to engagements.

4.— The Regulations respecting the Fire Engine Establishment published on 19th. February 1884 as well as any other Regulations for the management of the Fire Engine Establishment which have been made and passed by the Municipal Corporation and approved by the Governor shall apply to every person who shall have entered into an engagement as aforesaid with the Municipal Corporation of Port Louis; provided that in the said engagement a special reference be made to such Regulations.

Amendment and repeal of Regulations.

5.—In Article 1 of Chapter I of the Regulations respecting the Fire Engine Establishment published on 19th. February 1884 for and instead of the words *for a period of three years*, the following words shall be read *for any period not exceeding five years.*

Chapter V of the aforesaid Regulations is hereby repealed.

Commencement of Ordinance.

6.—This Ordinance shall come into force on the day of its publication in the Government Gazette.

Ordinance No. 2 of 1895.

To amend the third Schedule of Ordinance No. 26 of 1890 entitled: "An Ordinance to consolidate "and amend the Law relating to the Civil Status."

(21*st. June* 1895.)

Whereas it is expedient to amend the third Schedule of Ordinance No. 26 of of 1890;

Be it enacted by the Governor, with the advice and consent of the Council of Government, as follows:—

Short title.

1.—This Ordinance may be cited as "The Civil Status Amendment Ordinance, 1895."

Fee to be paid for change of name.

2.—The following section is hereby added to the third Schedule of Ordinance No. 26 of 1890:

8.—For any change in, or addition to name, surname, or family name... ... ... Rs. 25

Provided that such fee may be remitted by the Governor whenever it shall be shewn to his satisfaction that the person applying for change of name is unable to pay the fee and that he would suffer any prejudice or hardship by being compelled to continue the use of his name without such change or addition as applied for.

Prepayment of fee. 3.—The Colonial Secretary shall, after prepayment of the said fee, cause to be gazetted any decision of the Governor in Executive Council authorizing any such change and addition.

Thereupon the name authorized to be borne by the applicant shall thenceforth be deemed his name, and the surname or family name as altered or added to, in conformity with such decision, shall thenceforth be the surname or family name of the applicant and that of his wife and children and of any other person by law entitled to bear the surname or family name of such applicant.

Article 110 of Ordinance No. 26 of 1890 is hereby repealed.

Ordinance to be read and construed with previous Ordinance. 4.—This Ordinance shall be read and construed with Ordinance No. 26 of 1890.

Commencement of Ordinance. 5.—This Ordinance shall come into force on the day of its publication in the Government Gazette.

Ordinance No. 3 of 1895.

To amend sub-section No. 9 of Article 1 of Ordinance No. 26 of 1852 and Ordinance No. 19 of 1877.

(21*st. June* 1895.)

Whereas it is expedient to amend sub-section No. 9 of Article 1 of Ordinance No. 26 of 1852 and Ordinance No. 19 of 1877.

Be it enacted by the Governor, with the advice and consent of the Council of Government, as follows :

Short title. 1.—This Ordinance may be cited as "The Succession Duties Amending Ordinance, 1895."

Amendment of sub-section 9 of Article 1 of Ordinance No. 26 of 1852. 2.—From the date this Ordinance shall come into force, the expression " Rs. 1,5000 " shall be read in lieu and stead of the expression " £1,000 " wherever it occurs in sub-section No. 9 of Article 1 of Ordinance No. 26 of 1852.

Amendment of Ordinance 19 of 1877. 3.—Ordinance No. 19 of 1877 is amended accordingly.

Ordinance to be read with previous Ordinance. 4.—This Ordinance shall be read and construed with Ordinance No. 26 of 1852.

Commencement of Ordinance 5.—This Ordinance shall come into force on the day of its publication in the Government Gazette.

Ordinance No. 4 of 1895.

To provide for the granting of pensions, compensations and allowances to the Officers of the Loan Office.

(21*st. June* 1895.)

Whereas it is expedient to give to the persons appointed to offices in the Loan Office, under Ordinance No. 13 of 1894, the same rights as to pensions, compensations and allowances as if those offices had been permanent and included in Schedule A annexed to the Pensions Ordinance No. 30 of 1881;

Be it enacted by the Governor, with the advice and consent of the Council of Government, as follows:—

Short title.

1.—This Ordinance may be cited as "The Pension to Officers of Loan Office Ordinance, 1895."

Ordinance 30 of 1881 applicable to Loan Officers under certain exceptions.

2.—From the commencement of this Ordinance, the provisions of Ordinance No. 30 of 1881, entitled: "An Ordinance for regulating pensions, "compensations and allowances to be granted in respect of offices held in "Her Majesty's Civil Service in this Colony" shall extend and apply to the Officers forming part of the Loan Office, referred to in article 7 of Ordinance No. 13 of 1894, and who draw salaries of Rs. 250 per annum or more, and pensions, compensations and allowances authorized by Ordinance No. 30 of 1881 may be granted to all such Officers in the same manner as if the offices held by them were permanent and had been included in Schedule A annexed to the said Ordinance.

Provided however that article 12 of Ordinance No. 30 of 1881 shall not apply to the aforesaid Officers and no addition of years shall be made to the service of the said Officers for the purpose of computing pension on the ground of abolition of office when the functions of the Loan Office shall come to an end.

Commencement of claim to pension, compensation or allowance.

3.—The claim of a person, who was not previously a member of the covenanted service of the Colony, to pension, compensation or allowance under this Ordinance shall be considered to have commenced from the date of his first appointment to one of the offices mentioned in article 7 of Ordinance No. 13 of 1894, whether such appointment has taken place before or after the commencement of this Ordinance.

Provided further that the Government shall in no case, except in the case of those Officers of the Loan Office who have joined the covenanted service of the Colony before the 1st January 1887, bear any loss for exchange in respect of the payment out of this Colony of any pension or other retiring allowance granted to any person under this Ordinance, but any such payment shall be made in Mauritius Currency.

Ordinance to be read and construed with previous Ordinances.

4.—This Ordinance shall be read and construed with Ordinances Nos. 30 of 1881 and 13 of 1894.

Commencement of Ordinance.

5.— This Ordinance shall come into force on a day to be fixed by Proclamation.

Ordinance No. 5 of 1895.

To authorize in certain cases judicial investigations into the causes of Fire.

(27*th. June* 1895.)

Whereas it is expedient to authorize in certain cases judicial investigations into the cause of Fire at the request of the Procureur General or on the application and at the expense of private parties;

Be it enacted by the Governor, with the advice and consent of the Council of Government, as follows :—

Short Title. 1.—This Ordinance may be cited as "The Fire Enquiry Ordinance, 1895."

Judicial investigation into causes of fire. 2.—(1) In any case of fire by which any house or building shall have been burnt down or damaged in the island of Mauritius, it shall be lawful for the Procureur General to require in the form of Schedule C the District Magistrate of the district within which the property burnt down or damaged is situated, to proceed to a judicial investigation into the cause of such fire, without charging any person with any offence against the law in connection with such fire.

(2) It shall also be lawful for any Company of Insurance, under-writers or persons suffering any prejudice from such fire to apply to the District Magistrate of the District within which the fire took place for a judicial investigation into the cause of such fire as mentioned above. Such application shall be made in the form of information in Schedule A, and the said information shall be sworn to by the person laying it.

Order of inspection. 3.—On receiving such requisition from the Procureur General or on the exhibition of the information mentioned in the preceding Article, the Magistrate shall issue an order in the form of Schedule B to the Chief Officer of Police in charge of the District, to cause an inspection of the locality where the fire took place and an enquiry into the causes of the fire, to be made as soon as possible. The order shall be complied with and report thereon made to the Magistrate.

Provided that, when the application for an investigation is made by any other person than the Procureur General, the Magistrate before issuing the aforesaid order shall require the deposit of a sufficient sum with the District Cashier to cover all the costs mentioned in Article 10.

Investigation to be made by the District Magistrate. 4.—The District Magistrate shall then proceed to make an investigation into the said case of fire, and shall within the shortest possible delay take the depositions upon oath of all persons likely to know the facts and circumstances of such case, and of all other persons who in his opinion may furnish information in respect thereof.

Examination of witnesses. 5.—It shall be lawful for any person deputed by the Procureur General, for any officer of Police, or, with the leave of the Magistrate, for any interested party present at such investigation, to examine the witnesses, and to cause such persons to be examined as may give due and proper information touching such case or fire.

Powers of the District Magistrate. 6.—The District Magistrate shall carry on such investigations with the same powers as are vested in him by Ordinance No. 23 of 1888 for investigating Criminal offences.

Any person making any false declaration before the Magistrate in any such investigation shall be liable to the penalties of articles 276, 279 and 282 of Ordinance No 6 of 1838, commonly called the Penal Code.

Appointment of Guardian. 7.—In every case of fire, it shall be lawful for the District Magistrate, at the request of any interested party, as aforesaid, to appoint a person duly sworn before him to take provisional charge of the premises where the fire has taken place or has been attempted, and of the property upon the said premises, during the time that the said Magistrate carries on his investigation ; the fees of such person shall be paid by the said interested party, and shall not exceed three rupees (Rs. 3) per diem.

Proceedings to be referred to Procureur General. 8.—At the close of the investigation, all proceedings under this Ordinance shall in all cases be referred to the Procureur General who may, in his discretion after examining the depositions, file an information before the Magistrate against any person or persons whom he shall suspect of being guilty of an offence against the law in connection with such fire, and order the Magistrate to proceed by way of preliminary enquiry under the District Court (Criminal Jurisdiction) Ordinance, 1888.

Previous enquiry not to be evidence. 9.—No previous enquiry taken by the Magistrate under the provisions of articles 3, 4, and following of this Ordinance shall, in any way, be evidence against the person or persons against whom any criminal information shall be filed, but the said Magistrate shall investigate the charge and carry on a new enquiry in the manner directed by Ordinance 23 of 1888.

Costs to be borne by applicants. 10.—(1) The costs of the information and order provided by articles 2 and 3 of this Ordinance, and of the judicial investigation provided by articles 4, 5 and 6 of this Ordinance shall be borne by the applicant out of the sums deposited by him, or if they be insufficient, in addition thereto, and such additional costs may be recovered as costs are by law recovered in a criminal case before the District Courts.

(2) If the judicial investigation is proceeded to at the request of the Procureur General the costs, if any, shall be borne by the Crown.

(3) Such costs shall be taxed according to the tariff of fees in force in the District Courts.

Judicial investigation shall not be a cause of challenge. 11.—No Magistrate shall be prohibited from making an enquiry under the District Court (Criminal Jurisdiction) Ordinance 1888, by the fact that he shall have made a judicial investigation under articles 3, 4 and following of this Ordinance.

Repeal. 12.—Ordinance No. 13 of 1882 entitled : " An Ordinance to authorize " in certain cases judicial investigations into the causes of fire, " is hereby repealed.

Commencement of Ordinance. 13.—This Ordinance shall come into force on the day of its publication in the Government Gazette.

SCHEDULE OF FORMS.

A.

Mauritius, in the District of

Be it remembered that of in the District of a maketh and saith as follows :

That on the day of in the year in the District of house (or as the case may be) situated in the locality of was by fire and that the he represents have thereby suffered prejudice; and that he hath reasonable cause to suspect and doth suspect that the said fire is the result of a crime; wherefore he prays that a judicial investigation be made into the cause of such fire, and is willing and ready to deposit the sum of to cover the expense of such investigation according Law.

Signed :

Exhibited and sworn on the day of in the year at in the District of

Before me

District Magistrate in and for
the District of

B.

Mauritius, In the District of
To of Police of the district.

Whereas information upon oath has this day been made before me Magistrate in and for the district of by of in the district of that a situated in the locality of in the district of has been by fire, and that there is reasonable cause to suspect that such fire is the result of a crime.

These are therefore in Her Majesty's name to require you to make or cause to be made an inspection of the premises where the fire has taken place, (or has been attempted,) and also an enquiry into the causes of such fire, and a search for the perpetrators if any of any crime which may have been the cause of such fire, and further to report to me on the matters aforesaid with as due diligence as possible.

Given under my hand at in the District of on the day of in the year

Magistrate in and for the
District of

C.

In the District of

In virtue of the powers conferred upon me by Ordinance No. of 189 , I hereby require the District Magistrate in and for the District of to proceed to a judicial investigation into the cause of the fire by which the house (or building as the case may be) situate in the locality of was , as there is reasonable cause to suspect that the said fire is the result of a crime.

Procureur and Advocate General.

Ordinance No. 6 1895.

To authorize the interment of the remains of Archbishop Léon Meurin, the late Roman Catholic Bishop of Port Louis in the Roman Catholic Cathedral of that city.

9th. July 1895.

Whereas the Church Wardens of the Roman Catholic Cathedral of Port Louis are desirous that the remains of Archbishop Léon Meurin, the late Roman Catholic Bishop of Port Louis, be interred within the walls of the Roman Catholic Cathedral of that city.

Be it enacted by the Governor, with the advice and consent of the Council of Government, as follows :

Short title.

1.—This Ordinance may be cited as "The Ordinance authorizing the interment of the late Roman Catholic Bishop of Port Louis in the Roman Catholic Cathedral of Port Louis."

Interment of the remains of the late Archbishop Meurin in the Roman Catholic Cathedral of Port Louis permitted.

2.—Permission is hereby given for the interment of the remains of the Archbishop Meurin, in his lifetime Roman Catholic Bishop of Port Louis, within the walls of the Roman Catholic Cathedral of Port Louis, notwithstanding any legal enactment to the contrary, and subject to such precautions as may be suggested by the General Board of Health.

Commencement of Ordinance. 3.—This Ordinance shall come into force on the day of its publication in the Government Gazette.

Ordinance No. 7 of 1895.

To make provision for the more efficient suppression of Common Gambling Houses.

(*15th. July* 1895.)

Be it enacted by the Governor, with the advice and consent of the Council of Government as follows:

Short title. 1.—This Ordinance may be cited as "The Common Gambling Houses Ordinance, 1895."

Definition of terms. 2.—In this Ordinance, unless the context otherwise requires, —

"Common Gambling House" means any place kept or used for gambling to which the public has or may have access whether freely, or upon the payment of an entrance fee, or upon the presentation of persons interested or associated therein, and includes any place kept or used for the purpose of a public lottery,

"Lottery" includes any game, method or device whereby money or money's worth is distributed or alloted in any manner depending upon or to be determined by chance or lot, whether the same be drawn, exercised, or managed within or whithout Mauritius.

"Public lottery" means a lottery to which the public or any class of the public has or may have access.

"Lottery ticket" includes any paper or figure or writing or symbol or other article whatsoever which either expressly or impliedly entitles or purports to entitle the holder or any other person to receive any money or money's worth on the happening of any event or contingency connected with any public lottery.

"Place" means any house, office, room or building, and any place or spot whether open or enclosed and includes a ship, boat, or other vessel, whether afloat or not, and any vehicle.

A place in which lottery tickets are sold or distributed shall be deemed to be "used for the purpose of a public lottery."

A place shall be deemed to be "used" for a purpose if it is used for that purpose, even on one occasion only.

When a place belongs to a minor, emancipated minor, or to an interdicted person or to a person absent from the Colony, the guardian or the curator of such interdicted person, or the agent of such absent person, shall be deemed the owner of the place.

The expression "Instruments or appliances for gaming" includes all articles which are used in or for the purpose of gaming or a lottery.

Offences. 3.—Whoever:

(*a*) Keeps or uses a place as a common gambling house; or

(*b*) permits a place of which he is occupier or of which he has the use temporarily or otherwise, to be kept or used by another person as a common gambling house; or

(*c*) has the care or management of, or in any manner assists in, the management of a place kept or used as a common gambling house or assists in carrying on a public lottery; or (*d*) receives directly or indirectly any money or money's worth for, or in respect of, any chance in or event or contingency connected with a public lottery or sells or offers for sale or gives or delivers any lottery ticket; or

(*e*) draws, throws, or exhibits the winning number ticket, lot, figure, design, symbol or other result of any public lottery, or declares the winner expressly or otherwise; or

(*f*) writes, prints, or publishes, or causes to be written, printed or published any lottery ticket or list of prizes or any announcement of the result of a public lottery or any announcement relating to a public lottery; or

(*g*) announces, or publishes, or causes to be announced or published either orally or by means of any print, writing, design, sign or otherwise that any place is opened kept or used as a common gambling house or in any other manner invites or solicits any person to commit a breach of or to infringe any of the provisions contained in any of the above paragraphs,

shall be punishable with a fine not exceeding one thousand rupees (Rs. 1,000) or with imprisonment with or without hard labour for a period not exceeding twelve months.

Playing in a gambling house punishable.

4.—(1) Whoever plays in a common gambling house shall be punishable with a fine not exceeding fifty rupees (Rs. 50).

(2) A person found in a common gambling house or found escaping therefrom on the occasion of its being entered under this Ordinance shall be presumed, until the contrary be proved, to be or to have been playing therein.

Search Warrants.

5.—A Magistrate on being satisfied upon written information on oath and after any further inquiry which he may think necessary, that any place is kept or used for gambling and that the public has access to it may, by warrant, authorize any person therein named or any Police officer with such assistance and by such force as may be necessary by night or by day to enter or go to such place and to search the same and to seize all instruments or appliances for gambling and all money securities for money and other articles reasonably supposed to have been used or intended to be used for any game or lottery which may be found in such place and also to detain all such persons until the said place shall have been searched. If any of the things or circumstances which are made by this Ordinance presumptive evidence of guilt are found in such place every person found therein shall be taken before a Magistrate to be dealt with according to law.

(2) All instruments or appliances for gambling, money, securities for money and other articles found in a common gambling house and which the Magistrate is of opinion were used or intended to be used for any game or lottery shall be declared by him to be forfeited to the Crown and shall be dealt with accordingly.

Presumptive proof against house and occupier.

6. If any instruments or appliances of gambling are found in any place under this Ordinance or if persons are seen or heard to escape therefrom on the approach or entry of a Police Officer, or if any person having authority under this Ordinance to enter or go to such place is unlawfully prevented from or obstructed or delayed in entering or approaching the same or any part thereof, it shall be presumed, until the contrary be proved, that the place is a common gambling house and that the same is so kept or used by the occupier thereof.

Presumptive proof against house occupier and owner.

7.—If in the case of a place entered under this Ordinance any passage, staircase, or means of access to any part thereof is unusually narrow or steep or otherwise difficult to pass or any part of the premises is provided with unusual or unusually numerous means for preventing or obstructing an entry or with unusual contrivances for enabling persons therein to see or ascertain the approach or entry of persons or for giving the alarm or for facilitating escape from the premises, it shall be presumed until the contrary be proved that the place is a common gambling house and that the same is so kept or used by the occupier thereof; and if notice as is next hereinafter provided shall have been served on the owner of the premises at least one month before such entry, it shall further be presumed till the contrary be proved that the place is so kept with the permission of the owner thereof.

Notice by Police officer.

8.— Whenever it comes to the knowledge of a Police officer that and place is fitted or provided with any of the means or contrivances mentioney in the preceding article in such a way as to lead to a presumption that the place is used or intended to be used for the purposes of a common gambling house, it shall be the duty of such Police officer to cause notice thereof to be served on the owner of such place as well as on the occupior thereof; and if the names of the owners and occupiers or owners or occupiers are not known, then the notice may be served by being affixed to the principal outer door or any outer door or window or any conspicuous part of the place.

(2) Every sub-tenant receiving a notice under this article shall forthwith inform in writing the owner or the person from whom he rents the premises of the receipt of such notice who shall in like manner inform the owner or the person from whom he rents the premisos and so on till the notice is brought to the knowledge of the owner, each tenant being responsible to bring the notice to the knowledge of his immediate lessor; and any sub-tenant refusing or omitting to make known to the owner or the person from whom he rents the premises the fact that such notice has been received, shall be liable to a fine not exceeding five hundred rupees (Rs. 500).

Order of destruction of means and contrivances.

9.—Whenever it appears to a Magistrate upon the trial of any offence under this Ordinance that the place in or in respect of which the offence is alleged to have been committed is a common gambling house and that the same is fitted or provided with any of the means or contrivances mentioned in the last preceding articles, he shall order the demolition and destruction of such of them as consist of staircases, doors and partitions, ladders, planks, platforms, posts, palings, bars, bolts and other things which appear to him to have been specially erected or constructed for the purpose of facilitating the carrying on of gambling on the premises.

Commencement of Ordinance.

10.—This Ordinance shall come into force on the day of its publication in the Government Gazette.

Ordinance No. 8 of 1895.

To amend Ordinance No. 7 of 1893.

(*15th. July* 1895.)

Be it enacted by the Governor, with the advice and consent of the Council of Government, as follows :—

1.—This Ordinance may be cited as "The Quarantine Ordinance, 1895."

Article 2 of Ordinance No. 7 of 1893 amended.

2.— Article 2 of Ordinance No. 7 of 1893 shall not apply to vessels caming direct from ports beyond the Cape of Good Hope or from any of the Australian ports, when such vessels shall have been twenty-one clear days at sea previous to their arrival at Mauritius.

Commencement of Ordinance.

3.—This Ordinance shall come into force on the day of its publication in the Government Gazette.

Ordinance No. 9 of 1895.

To amend Ordinance No. 28 of 1887.

(*19th. July* 1895.)

Be it enacted by the Governor, with the advice and consent of the Council of Government, as follows :

Short title.

1.— This Ordinance may be cited as "The Cremation Amendment Ordinance, 1895."

Conditions of Cremation. 2.—Except with the permission of the Director of the Medical and Health Department, no cremation or burning shall take place before twenty-four hours shall have elapsed since the death of the person to be cremated or burnt.

Penal Clause. 3.—Whoever shall cremate or burn or allow or cause to be cremated or burnt any corpse without having obtained the special permit required under Article 3 of Ordinance No. 28 of 1887, or before the required delay under Article 2 of this Ordinance shall be punished by a fine not exceeding five hundred rupees (Rs. 500) and by imprisonment not exceeding six months.

Further conditions required for issue of permit. 4.—(1) No permit for the cremation or burning of the body of a person who was not attended by a duly qualified Medical Practitioner shall be granted, until after an enquiry held by the Police with the assistance of a duly qualified Medical Practitioner appointed and paid by the person or persons applying for such permit.

(2) The application for the permit of cremation or burning shall set forth: The date and hour of the death. The name, sex and age of the deceased. The crematory at which the operation is to be carried out, and, in case no such establishment exists, the spot chosen for the burning and its distance from the nearest inhabited locality.

(3) With the application shall also be forwarded the certificate of the probable cause of death from the Medical Practitioner appointed as above, and also certificates from two persons who knew the deceased stating that, to the best of their knowledge and belief, the deceased died from natural causes.

(4) Provided that in cases when a judicial enquiry followed by an autopsy shall have been performed, a certificate from the Medical Practitioner who had charge of the operation shall be deemed proof of the nature of the cause of death, sufficient to dispense with the aforesaid certificates.

(5) The Police enquiry under paragraph 1 shall be forwarded to the Director of the Medical and Health Department who, before granting a permit, may further require such information as he may deem necessary, and may require that an autopsy be performed by a Medical Practitioner other than the Medical Practitioner appointed by the parties under paragraph 1 of this Article.

Commencement of Ordinance. 5.—This Ordinance shall come into force on the day of its publication in the Government Gazette.

Ordinance No. 10 of 1895.

To empower the Police to search more effectually for stolen property.

(19*th. July* 1895.)

Be it enacted by the Governor, with the advice and consent of the Council of Government, as follows:

Short title. 1.—This Ordinance may be cited as: "The search for stolen property amending Ordinance, 1895."

Issue of Warrants. 2.—Any Constable may, under the circumstances hereafter mentioned in article 4 of this Ordinance, be authorised in writing by a District Magistrate to enter, and if so authorised may enter, any house, shop, warehouse, yard, or other premises, in search of stolen property, and search for and seize and secure any property he may believe to have been stolen, in the same manner as he would be authorised to do if he had a search-warrant and the property seized, if any, corresponded to the property described in such search-warrant.

Summons before Magistrate.

3.—In every case in which any property is seized in pursuance of article 2 of this Ordinance, the person on whose premises it was at the time of the seizure, or the person from whom it was taken, if other than the person on whose premises it was, shall, unless previously charged with having been found in possession of the same without sufficient excuse or justification, or with receiving the same knowing it to have been stolen, be summoned before the Magistrate of the District in which such premises are situate, to account for his possession of such property, and such Magistrate shall make such order respecting the disposal of such property, and may award such costs, as the justice of the case may require.

Powers of the Magistrate.

4.—It shall be lawful for any Magistrate to give such authority as described in article 2 of this Ordinance, in the following cases, or either of them :

(1) When the premises to be searched are, or, within the preceding twelve months have been, in the occupation of any person who has been convicted of having been in possession of stolen property, or of receiving stolen property, or of harbouring thieves.

(2) When the premises to be searched are in the occupation of any person who has been convicted of any offence involving fraud or dishonesty, and punishable by penal servitude or imprisonment.

And it shall not be necessary for such Magistrate, on giving such authority, to specify any particular property, but he may give such authority if he has reason to believe generally that such premises are being made a receptacle for stolen goods.

Commencement of Ordinance.

5.—This Ordinance shall come into force on the day of its publication in the Government Gazette.

Ordinance No. 11 of 1895.

To make further provision in matters relating to Vaccination.

(*6th. August* 1895.)

Be it enacted by the Governor, with the advice and consent of the Council of Government, as follows :—

Short title.

1.—This Ordinance may be cited as "The Vaccination Ordinance, 1895."

Remuneration to Public Vaccinators.

2.—There shall be paid to each Public Vaccinator, from the Colonial Treasury, such fee as is provided for by article 4 of Ordinance No. 12 of 1875, for each unvaccinated child who shall have been under the age of ten months when first presented for vaccination, and whom he shall have successfully vaccinated or found insusceptible of successful vaccination, whether or not such child is at the time of each vaccination or at the date of the final certificate of insusceptibility of vaccination under ten months of age, or not.

Provided that no fee has already been charged by the Public Vaccinator in respect of such vaccination or attempt at vaccination.

Further remuneration to Public Vaccinator.

3.—There shall also be paid to each Public Vaccinator from the Colonial Treasury for each unvaccinated person older than ten months when presented for vaccination whom he shall have successfully vaccinated, or who shall be found insusceptible of successful vaccination, and for whom no fee shall have been charged by such Public Vaccinator, such fee as is provided for under article 4 of Ordinance No. 12 of 1875.

Duty of Public Vaccinator.

4.—Such Public Vaccinator shall be bound to take down the name and address of the person having the custody of the unvaccinated person, together with all particulars about the facts of the case, and no action under article 23 of Ordinance No. 12 of 1875 shall be begun against such person after the date when the child has been vaccinated or presented for vaccination.

Penalty for false declaration.

5.—The person having the custody of the unvaccinated child who shall wilfully make a false declaration to the Public Vaccinator with regard to his name and address, or to particulars which it is proper or necessary for such Public Vaccinator to know as such Vaccinator, or who shall refuse to give such information to the Public Vaccinator, shall be liable to a fine not exceeding fifty rupees (Rs. 50).

Penalty against Public Vaccinator.

6.—Every Public Vaccinator who shall fail to comply with any of the provisions of article 4 of this Ordinance, shall be liable to a fine not exceeding fifty rupees (Rs. 50).

Ordinance to be read as part of Ordinance No. 12 of 1875.

7.—This Ordinance shall be read as part of Ordinance No. 12 of 1875.

Commencement of Ordinance.

8.—This Ordinance shall come into force on the day of its publication in the Government Gazette.

Ordinance No. 12 of 1895.

To amend Ordinance No. 28 of 1892 entitled : "An Ordinance to provide for the management of the Customs of the Colony of Mauritius."

(*6th. August* 1895.)

Be it enacted by the Governor, with the advice and consent of the Council of Government, as follows :

Article 22 of Ordinance 28 of 1892 amended.

1.—In article 22 of Ordinance No. 28 of 1892, after the word " Provided " in the eleventh line thereof, there shall be read the words : " that if such goods be not duly warehoused within one month after the " date of the report of the Ship importing the same or " ; the word " that " in the twelfth line thereof shall be deleted, and the following words shall be added to the said article : " Provided " further that it shall be lawful for the Collector in special circumstances to extend the delay of " one month abovementioned for a period not exceeding three months."

Article 65 of Ordinance 28 fo 1892 amended.

2.—In Article 65 of Ordinance No. 28 of 1892, after the word "that" in the twenty-eighth line thereof, there shall be read the words : " if the said goods be entered for home consumption.

Ordinance to be part of Ordinance 28 of 1892.

3.—This Ordinance shall be read and construed as part of Ordinance No. 28 of 1892.

Commencement of Ordinance.

4.—This Ordinance shall come into force on the day of its publication in the Government Gazette.

Ordinance No. 13 of 1895.

To amend the Police Ordinance of 1893 with regard to the re-engagement of Policemen.

(*6th. August* 1895.)

Whereas it is necessary to amend the Police Ordinance, 1893 with regard to the re-engagement of Policemen ;

Be it therefore enacted by the Governor, with the advice and consent of the Council of Government, as follows :

Short title. 1.—This Ordinance may the cited as "The re-engagement of Policemen Ordinance, 1895."

2.—Article 9 of Ordinance No. 16 of 1893 is hereby repealed and replaced by the following provision :

Re-enlistment. 2.—Sergeants, Corporals and Constables of good character shall be eligible for re-engagement for a period of five years. Provided that if such re-engagement takes place within the three months next following the expiry of the previous term of enlistment, such previous term of enlistment shall count towards pension and discharge.

All re-engagements shall be dependent on the approval of the Inspector Genral, and on the candidates passing the usual medical examination.

Ordinance to be read with Ordinance 16 of 1893. 3.—This Ordinance shall be read as part of Ordinance No. 16 of 1893.

Commencement of Ordinance. 4.—This Ordinance shall come into force on the day of its publication in the Government Gazette.

Ordinance No. 14 of 1895.

To provide that Ordinances No. 8 of 1876 and No. 7 of 1895 do not extend to certain matters which may be regarded as coming within their purview.

(8*th. August* 1895.)

Whereas it is expedient to provide that Ordinances No. 8 of 1876 and No. 7 of 1895 should not extend to Sweepstakes organized, during the Race week and the week preceding the same, by, or under the control of the Mauritius Turf Club, whether under the name of *Pari Mutuel*, or otherwise, in view of or in connexion with the races held by the said Club ;

Be it therefore enacted by the Governor, with the advice and consent of the Council of Government, asfollows :—

Ordinances No. 8 *of* 1876, *and No.* 7 *of* 1895 *not to extend to Sweepstakes organized by the Mauritius Turf Club.* 1.—Ordinances No. 8 of 1876, and No. 7 of 1895 shall not extend to Sweepstakes organized, during the Race week and the week preceding the same, by, or under the control of, the Mauritius Turf Club, whether under the name of *Pari Mutuel* or otherwise, in view of or in connexion with the races held by the said Club.

Commencement of Ordinance. 2.—This Ordinance shall come into force on the day of its publication in the Government Gazette.

Ordinance No. 15 of 1895.

To authorize the levying of a stamp duty on certain Proclamations.

(8*th. August* 1895.)

Whereas it is expedient to levy a stamp duty on certain Proclamations ;

Be it enacted by the Governor, with the advice and consent of the Council of Government, as follows :

Short title. 1.—This Ordinance may be cited as "The Stamp Duty on Proclamations Ordinance, 1895".

Stamp duty. 2.—From the date this Ordinance shall come into force, a stamp duty of fifty Rupees (Rs. 50) shall be charged for the issuing of a Proclamation in the following cases:

Under articles 37 and 46 of the Code de Commerce, for:

(*a*) Authorizing the formation of Anonymous Societies.

(*b*) Authorizing the continuation of Anonymous Societies.

(*c*) Authorizing modifications in the articles of agreement of Anonymous Societies.

Commencement of Ordinance. 3.—This Ordinance shall come into force on the day of its publication in the Government Gazette.

Ordinance No. 16 of 1895.

To provide for the levying of a surcharge of 10 o/o on Transcription, Inscription and Registration dues and fees.

(23*rd August*, 1895.)

Be it enacted by the Governor, with the advice and consent of the Council of Government, as follows:

Short title. 1.—This Ordinance may be cited as "The Transcription, Inscription "and Registration Dues Ordinance, 1895."

Surcharge 2.—On and from the date on which this Ordinance shall come into force, a surcharge of 10 o/o shall be levied upon all sums payable to the Government in virtue of any laws now in force or to be put in force hereafter with respect to the following dues and fees:

(1) Dues and fees on Transcriptions and Inscriptions.

(2) Registration dues, except fixed dues.

Repeal clause. 3.-Sub-section 5 of article 1 of Ordinance No. 20 of 1890 is hereby repealed.

Commencement of Ordinance. 4.—This Ordinance shall come into force on the day of its publication in the Government Gazette.

Ordinance No. 17 of 1895

To render permanent the posts of Crown Prosecutors created in virtue of a Report of the Finance Committee of the Council of Government as amended and adopted by the said Council on the 18th. December 1891,—and to define more clearly the powers and duties of those Officers.

(5*th. September* 1895.)

Be it enacted by the Governor, with the advice and consent of the Council of Government, as follows:—

Short title. 1.—This Ordinance may be cited as "The Crown Prosecutors' Ordinance, 1895."

Appointment of two Crown Prosecutors.

2.—(*a*) It shall be lawful for the Governor (subject to the approval of Her Majesty, Her Heirs or Successors) to appoint two Crown Prosecutors who shall be officers of the Procureur General's Department.

(*b*) They shall be chosen amongst practising Barristers or Advocates of not less than three years' standing and shall be debarred from the right of private practice.

(*c*) They shall each receive such salary as may be determined by the Governor with the advice and consent of the Council of Government, and shall be entitled to the refund of their travelling expenses.

Duties of Crown Prosecutors.

3.—(*a*) The primary duty of the Crown Prosecutors shall be to control Criminal prosecutions on behalf of the Crown before the inferior Courts and to conduct such criminal prosecutions whenever they shall be directed to do so by the Procureur General, or whenever they shall consider it necessary to do so, provided that whenever they shall conduct prosecutions on their own initiative they shall report to the Procureur General the action taken by them.

(*b*) The Crown Prosecutors shall also be liable to be employed without any extra remuneration in any matter in which the Crown is concerned provided this additional work does not interfere with their primary duty.

Powers of Crown Prosecutors.

4.—The Crown Prosecutors shall continue to exercise all the powers conferred upon them by Ordinance No. 16 of 1893.

Oaths to be taken by Crown Prosecutors.

5.—The Crown Prosecutors shall, as soon as possible, after their acceptance of office, take the oath of allegiance and the official oath in the form prescribed by the "Promissory Oaths Ordinance, 1869"; and such oaths shall be tendered to them by the Registrar of the Supreme Court at a sitting of the Court, in term time, or before a Judge in Chambers, during vacation.

Ordinance No. 30 of 1881 shall apply to Crown Prosecutors.

6.—The provisions of Ordinance No. 30 of 1881 entitled: "An Ordinance for regulating pensions, compensations and allowances to be granted in respect of offices held in Her Majesty's Civil Service in this Colony" shall extend and apply to the Crown Prosecutors, and the number of years to be added to their period of service under article 13 of the said Ordinance for the purpose of computing their retiring allowance, shall be seven years.

Commencement of Ordinance.

7.—This Ordinance shall come into force on a day to be fixed by Proclamation.

Ordinance No. 18 of 1895.

To prohibit the pollution of the Rivers of Curepipe.

(*12th. September* 1895.)

Be it enacted by the Governor, with the advice and consent of the Council of Government, as follows:

Short Title.

1.—This Ordinance may be cited as "The Curepipe Rivers Ordinance, 1895".

Washing &c., prohibited.

2.—The washing of clothes is hereby prohibited in all the streams and rivers of Curepipe, with the exception of the following specified places:

(*a*) Rivière du Mesnil, from Manès Bridge, downwards;

(*b*) Rivière Sèche, from the bridge in Cox street, downwards;

(c) Rivière Eau Bleue, after the property Bradshaw, downwards.

Provided that the washing of clothes may take place in the places specified under (a) (b) and (c) only between the hours of 9 a.m. and 4 p.m.

The bathing and washing of animals in any part of the streams and rivers of Curepipe are absolutely prohibited.

Penalty. 3.—Any person acting in breach of this Ordinance shall be liable to a fine not exceeding one hundred Rupees (Rs. 100).

Commencement of Ordinance. 4.—This Ordinance shall come into force on the day of its publication in the Government Gazette and shall remain in force for six months.

Ordinance No. 19 of 1895.

To amend the law relating to the "Pas Géométriques."

(*27th. September* 1895).

Be it enacted by the Governor, with the advice and consent of the Council of Government, as follows :—

Short title. 1.—This Ordinance may be cited as "The Pas Géométriques Ordinance, 1895."

Pas Géométriques part of "Domaine Public." 2.—The reserved lands along the sea coast commonly called the "Pas Géométriques" and referred to in the Arrêté of General Decaen of 5th. May 1807 shall, as heretofore, form part of the "Domaine Public" and be inalienable and imprescriptible.

This provision shall apply to such "Pas Géométriques" as have reverted or may revert to the Crown by cession, surrender or otherwise.

But this provision shall not apply to such "Pas Géométriques" as may have become private property by prescription before the Arrêté of 5th. May 1807, or by grant or conveyance from the Crown made heretofore.

Breadth of Pas Géométriques. 3.—(1) The breadth of the "Pas Géométriques" is reckoned from the line of the sea-shore which is reached by high water at spring tide, and shall never be less than 81 metres and 21 centimetres.

(2) The boundary line of the "Pas Géométriques" shall, as far as the locality shall admit, be paralled to the lines of the coast considered as a whole and without regard to the small irregularities of the same.

Annexes of Pas Géométriques. 4.—The ponds of sea water, salt water marshes, lakes, bogs and basins situate wholly or partly upon the "Pas Géométriques", the islets adjacent to the shore and which can be reached on foot at low tides, the creeks at the mouths of rivers, and the mouths of rivers, shall be deemed "Annexes" of the "Pas Géométriques" and as such shall form part of the "Domaine Public" and shall be inalienable and imprescriptible.

This provision shall apply to such "Annexes" as have reverted or may revert to the Crown by cession, surrender or otherwise.

But this provision shall not apply to such "Annexes" as may have become private property by prescription before the Arrêté of 5th. May 1807 or by grant or conveyance from the Crown made heretofore.

Survey of Pas Géométriques.

5.—It shall be lawful for the Surveyor General to make, or cause to be made by any Government or other Sworn Land Surveyor delegated by him, the survey and plan of any "Pas Géométriques", and for this purpose he or any such Surveyor shall have power to enter any adjoining private land.

Notice of Survey to Occupier.

6.—(1) Whenever the Surveyor General will deem it expedient to survey or cause to be surveyed any portion of the "Pas Géométriques", it shall be lawful for the Procureur General, on the application of the Surveyor General, to cause a notice to be served upon any Occupier of the portion of the "Pas Géométriques" intended to be surveyed, in order that such Occupier should produce his permission of settlement or title deed within a reasonable delay. Such notice shall be served one month at least before the survey actually takes place.

(2) If the person so called upon to produce his permission of settlement or title deed refuses or neglects or is unable to do so within the specified time, the Surveyor General or his delegate under Article 4 of this Ordinance shall, after four days' notice given to the parties interested of the day of survey, proceed to survey the said portion of the "Pas Géométriques" *ex parte*, and the memorandum of survey signed by the Surveyor General or his delegate shall, upon production of the notice duly served and an affidavit that the party summoned to produce his permission of settlement or title deed has not produced the same within the specified delay, be evidence before all the Courts of this Colony, of the boundaries and extent of such portion of the "Pas Géométriques."

Provided that within a delay of six months a party who may have been prevented from producing his titles, shall be entitled to claim a new survey, at his own expense.

Governor may grant leases.

7.—(1) Subject to the provisions of this Ordinance, it shall be lawful for the Governor to grant leases of any portion of the "Pas Géométriques" or "Annexes" for any period not exceeding twenty years and upon such terms as to the payment ot rent and other conditions as shall be approved by the Governor.

(2) Such rents shall in all cases be payable in advance and in default of payment of any instalment by lessee within one month after service of a notice claiming payment, the Governor may, by an order in writing, cancel the lease, and thereupon the Government shall be entitled without any further formality to resume possession of the land.

Lessee to plant trees.

8.— In every lease of "Pas Géométriques" which are not already planted with trees, a clause shall be inserted, unless the Governor otherwise orders after consulting the Woods and Forests Board, imposing on the lessee the obligation of planting every year one-fifth of the land not planted until the whole has been planted, and of maintaining the trees so planted in a proper state of cultivation.

Transfer of lease.

9.—In all leases of portions of the "Pas Géométriques" to be made by the Governor, after the passing of this Ordinance, there shall be inserted a condition that if any transfer of any such lease is made without the express consent in writing of the Governor, the said lease shall be held to be forfeited along with the buildings and the plantations existing upon the land leased.

Leases of small portions of "Pas Géométriques.

10.—(1) It shall be lawful for the Governor from time to time to grant by private contract leases of certain limited portions of the "Pas Géométriques" not exceeding two hectares in any case to any person without imposing on the lessee the condition of planting trees on such "Pas Géométriques."

Provided that no such lease shall be granted except after notice published in two daily newspapers two weeks at least before any decision in the matter.

(2) Any such lessee may, with the permission of the Woods and Forests Board, and subject to such conditions as shall be approved by the Governor, cut and remove any trees growing on such "Pas Géométriques" which, for the purpose of erecting any building, it is necessary to cut or remove.

(3) When any person to whom any such lease as is referred to in this Article has been or shall be granted before or after the commencement of this Ordinance shall have erected any building thereon, the Governor may if he deems fit, grant to such person (or to any other person holding his rights) a renewal of such lease for any period not exceeding 20 years from the commencement of this Ordinance without complying with the provision of Article 11.

Notices in Gazette before granting lease.

11.—No lease of any portion of the "Pas Géométriques" shall be granted except after a public auction, notice of which shall be given in the Government Gazette and two daily Newspapers two weeks at least before the day of the sale; and the owner of the adjoining land shall have the preference over any other person, if be be willing to offer the same terms as the applicant for the said lease.

This provision shall not apply to leases granted under the preceding article.

Lease may be granted to tenants at will.

12.—It shall be lawful for the Governor without complying with the provisions of the preceding Article to grant to tenants at will or temporary grantees, who being fishermen or villagers near a fishing station or in a village are in possession of "Pas Géométriques,', leases of the portion of the "Pas Géométriques" by them actually held and possessed free from the obligation of planting trees.

When lessee entitled to cut trees.

13.—(1) The lessee of any portion of "Pas Géométriques" shall not be entitled to cut any trees on such "Pas Géométriques" unless he is expressly authorized so to do by the lease.

(2) The right to cut trees will not be granted in any lease unless the Governor, after consulting the Woods and Forests Board, has approved of its being granted.

(3) The right when granted shall be subject to such restrictions and conditions as may be recommended by the Woods and Forests Board and approved by the Governor.

Lessee bound to watch over the property.

14.—(1) The lessee of any "Pas Géométriques" shall be bound to watch over the property leased to him and to prevent and cutting or removal of any trees thereon growing not authorized by his lease, or by the Governor, or in breach of any condition subject to which the right of cutting trees may have been granted in the lease.

(2) If any trees growing on such "Pas Géométriques" be cut or removed when such cutting is not authorized, or is in breach of any condition of the lease, the Government, on proof of the fact and without being bound to prove that such cutting or removal took place with the knowledge or sanction of the lessee, shall be entitled to obtain judgment condemning the lessee to pay to the Public Treasury the value of the trees cut, or cancelling the lease with damages.

Such judgment, however, will not be given if the lessee proves that such trees were cut or stolen without any neglect on his part or in spite of proper supervision by him.

Provided that, in the case referred to at the end of the above clause, the lessee shall be bound to inform the Government within a delay of seven days of any such destruction or removal of trees.

When permission to occupy "Pas Geométriques" may be granted.

15.—Whenever buildings have been erected on any portion of the "Pas Géométriques" more than twenty years before the commencement of Ordinance No. 18 of 1874, the Governor in Executive Council may grant to any person by whom such buildings have been erected, or being in the right of any person by whom such buildings have been erected, permission to occupy such portion of the "Pas Géométriques" with or without payment of rent for such time and under such conditions as may seem just.

Disposal of dead and broken trees

16.—(1) The Government is entitled to remove and dispose of any dead, broken or fallen trees on any "Pas Géométriques," although such "Pas Géométriques" are leased, unless it is otherwise provided in the lease.

In case the Government decide to sell such trees, the sale shall be by public auction unless the Woods and Forests Board shall otherwise advise.

(2) It shall be lawful for any officer of the Government or any person authorized by the Surveyor General or, for any person, other than the lessee, who has purchased at a public auction or otherwise from Government the right of removing dead, fallen or broken trees or branches which the Government is entitled to remove or dispose of, or for the agents of such person, to enter any "Pas Géométriques" although such "Pas Géométriques" are leased, for the purpose of cutting and removing any such trees or branches.

The time necessary for cutting and removing such trees shall be fixed by the Woods and Forests Board.

Provided nothing herein contained will have the effect of conferring on the Government or any person aforesaid any right of way across private property.

Provided further that if such entry and the works necessary for the removal of trees aforesaid prevent the lessee from enjoying the said lease in conformity with his contract, the lessee shall be entitled to claim from the Government either a reduction of the rent payable for the current year or the cancellation of the lease.

Unauthorized cutting of trees an offence.

17.—(1) Any lessee of any portion of the "Pas Géométriques" who shall cut, destroy or remove or cause to be cut, destroyed or removed any tree on such "Pas Géométriques," unless he is expressly granted the right of cutting trees in his lease, shall be guilty of an offence.

(2) Any lessee authorized to cut trees who shall cut, destroy or remove or cause to be cut destroyed or removed any tree on any "Pas Géométriques" without having complied with the conditions of his lease, or in breach of any such condition shall be guilty of an offence.

(3) Any person who shall cut, destroy or remove or cause to be cut, destroyed or removed any tree on any portion of the "Pas Géométriques" which is either not let by the Government or which is let to another person by whom he is not authorized so to act, shall be guilty of an offence.

Penalty.

18.—Any person guilty of an offence under this Ordinance shall, on conviction, be liable to a fine not exceeding five hundred Rupees (Rs. 500) in addition to the value of any tree cut, destroyed or removed, with or without imprisonment not exceeding six months.

Lands in Villages excluded from operation of the Ordinance.

19.—(1) Lands situate within the limits of the District of Port Louis or in any Village mentioned in the Schedule annexed to this Ordinance and which would fall within the definition of "Pas Géométriques" given in article 2 are hereby excluded from the operation of this Ordinance, and shall be deemed and may be dealt with as Crown Lands which are not "Pas Géométriques."

(2) The boundaries of the Villages in the Schedule annexed to this Ordinance shall be fixed by the Governor, by Proclamation, after consulting the Council of Government.

Provided no new lease of "Pas Géométriques" shall be granted under this Ordinance of lands contiguous to any Village, before such Proclamation has been published.

(3) The Governor may, after consulting the Council of Government, order by Proclamation that any Village be added to the Schedule.

Meaning of the word "tree."

20.—The word "tree" in this Ordinance shall include live and dead timber, and the branches of trees but shall not include brushwood, shrubs, underwood, twigs and creepers.

Repeal.

21.—The following articles of Ordinance No. 18 of 1874 are hereby repealed; Articles 2, 3, 4, 5, 6, 7, 8, 9 and 10 only.

Ordinance No. 30 of 1876 entitled an Ordinance "To give to the Governor in Executive Council power to lease certain portions of the "Pas Géométriques" of this Colony under other conditions than those enacted by Ordinance No. 18 of 1874", is also repealed.

Provided that this repeal shall not affect

(*a*) Anything duly done or suffered under any enactment hereby repealed.

(*b*) Any right or liability acquired, accrued or incurred under any enactment hereby repealed.

(*c*) Any judgment, conviction, sentence or order pronounced, any enquiry, prosecution or other legal proceeding commenced, but any such judgment, conviction, sentence or order will remain valid, and every such proceeding may be continued and completed, as if this Ordinance had not been passed.

Commencement of Ordinance. 22.—This Ordinance shall come into force on the day of its publication in the Government Gazette.

SCHEDULE.

List of villages referred to in Article 19

District.	*Village.*
1. Pamplemousses	Trou-aux-Biches
2. Rivière du Rempart	Grand Bay.
3. ,, ...	Cap Malheureux.
4. ,, ...	Grand Gaube.
5. ,, ...	Poudre d'Or.
6. ,, ...	Pointe des Lascars.
7. ,, ...	Roche Noire.
8. Flacq	Post of Flacq.
9. ,, ...	Mare aux Lubines.
10. ,, ...	Trou Maho and Trou d'Eau Douce.
11. ,, ...	Grand River South East.
12. Grand Port	Grand Sable.
13. ,, ...	Bois des Amourettes.
14. ,, ...	Old Grand Port.
15. ,, ...	Mahebourg.
16. ,, ...	Pointe d'Esny.
17. Savanne	Souillac.
18. ,, ...	Riambel.
19. ,, ...	Ruisseau Créoles.
20. Black River	Morne Brabant.
21 ,, ...	Tamarind Bay.
22 ,, ...	Flic en Flac.

Ordinance No. 20 of 1895.

To reduce to 4 o/o the rate of Interest on all moneys belonging to the Widows and Orphans' Pension Fund and invested with the Government of this Colony.

(18*th. October* 1895.)

Be it enacted by the Governor, with the advice and consent of the Council of Government, as follows :—

Short Title. 1.—This Ordinance may be cited as "The Widows and Orphans' Pension Fund Amendment Ordinance, 1895."

Rate of Interest reduced to 4 *o/o.* 2.—The rate of Interest on all moneys belonging to the aforesaid Fund, whether arising from contributions, fines, interest or otherwise, and invested with the Government of this Colony under article 7 of Ordinance No. 2 of 1886 shall be four per centum per annum for ten years on and after the 25th. of September 1896.

Article 7 *of Ordinance* 2 *of* 1886 *amended.* 3.—Article 7 of Ordinance No. 2 of 1886 is amended accordingly.

Commencement of Ordinance. 4.—This Ordinance shall come into operation on the 25th. of September 1896.

Ordinance No. 21 of 1895.

To reduce the duty on Spirits and to amend the law relative to the sale of Spirits.

(22*nd. October* 1895.)

Be it enacted by the Governor, with the advice and consent of the Council of Government, as follows :—

Short Title. 1.—This Ordinance may be cited as : "The Duty on and Sale of Spirits Amendment Ordinance, 1895."

Excise-duty reduced. 2.—Instead of the excise-duty now levied on Colonial Spirits issued from the Central Rum Warehouse for home consumption, there shall henceforth be levied an excise-duty of one Rupee and twenty cents (R. 1.20) per litre of twenty three degrees strength according to Cartier's Areometer, and an additional duty of four cents per litre for every degree above the said strength.

Import duty reduced. 3.—Instead of the import duty now levied on Spirits, there shall henceforth be levied on Spirits plain or compounded of any strength not exceeding proof according to Sikes' Hydrometer, an import duty of one Rupee and twenty cents (R. 1.20) per litre and a proportional duty for any greater strength.

Article 12 *of Ordinance No.* 21 *of* 1894 *amended.* 4.—In lieu and stead of the words "any Distillery Officer" in the first and second lines of article 12 of Ordinance No. 21 of 1894, the following words shall be read : "The Superintendent or Chief Inspector of Distilleries."

Repealing clause. 5.—The following Ordinances or parts of Ordinances are hereby repealed :

(*a*) Ordinance No. 17 of 1889.

(*b*) Paragraph 3 of article 1 of Ordinance No. 20 of 1890.

(*c*) Paragraph 2 of article 1 of Ordinance No. 17 of 1894.

(*d*) Article 3 of Ordinance No. 21 of 1894.

(*e*) Ordinance No. 31 of 1894—95.

Commencement of Ordinance. 6.—This Ordinance shall come into force on the day of its publication in the Government Gazette.

Ordinance No. 22 of 1895.

To amend Ordinance No. 5 of 1887.

(29*th. October* 1895.)

Whereas it is expedient to amend Ordinance No. 5 of 1887 in certain respects;

Be it enacted by the Governor, with the advice and consent of the Council of Government, as follows:

Short title. 1.— This Ordinance may be cited as "The Registration of Voters Amendment Ordinance, 1895."

Article 12 of Ordinance No. 5 of 1887 repealed. 2.—Article 12 of Ordinance No. 5 of 1887 is hereby repealed, and the following article is substituted therefor:—

" On or before the 3rd. November in every year (either before or subsequently to the publication of the notice above referred to) every person duly qualified who is not already on the Register, or who being on the Register, shall not retain the same qualification as described in the Register may appear before any District Magistrate including in Port Louis the Junior District Magistrate and the Police and Additional District Magistrate and present his claim to be registered."

Provided that such person shall subscribe and fill in his claim as in Article 6 of Ordinance No. 5 of 1887 provided.

Provided also that when the third of November is an Office or an Estate holiday under Ordinance No. 4 of 1881, then the last day for the registration of Electors shall be the fourth of November.

Provided further that claims already made or hereafter to be made by persons desirous of being registered as Electors in any District, which claims may have been received or may hereafter be received by any District Magistrate, shall be considered as valid as if such claimant had appeared before the District Magistrate of the District in which he seeks to be registered and had presented his claim.

Costs how dealt with. 3.—It shall be lawful for the Magistrate, when acting under the provisions of article 13 of Ordinance No. 5 of 1887 to order any person who shall have presented a claim to be registered as an Elector, and who shall be found not to possess the required qualifications, to pay the costs which may have been incurred for ascertaining if such person is duly qualified.

Provided that in cases when the Magistrate shall be satisfied that such person had reasonable ground for making such application, the said Magistrate may order that the costs shall be borne by the Crown.

Article 14 of Ordinance 5 of 1887 repealed. 4.—Article 14 of Ordinance No. 5 of 1887 is hereby repealed, and the following article is substituted therefor:—

On or before the tenth of November the Magistrate shall publish a copy of the List of Claimants.

Within twenty-one days from the tenth of November any person on the Register or on the List then in force may object to any person whose name appears on the Register or on the List. The Magistrate shall also on or before the tenth of November publish a notice fixing a day for hearing any such objections.

Article 15 of Ordinance 5 of 1887 repealed. 5.—Article 15 of Ordinance No. 5 of 1887 is hereby repealed, and the following article is substituted therefor:

Any person on the Register then in force, wishing to object, as provided for in article 14 of Ordinance No. 5 of 1887, shall within twenty-one days after the publication of the notice, give notice in writing of his objection to the Magistrate, and the said Magistrate shall thereupon cause a copy of such notice to be served on the person objected to, and such objection shall be adjudicated upon by the Magistrate on the day fixed as above, or any subsequent day which he may fix for hearing such objection, and the Magistrate in trying any such objection, shall have all the powers mentioned in article 13 of Ordinance No. 5 of 1887.

If the Magistrate admits the objection he may order the person objected to, to pay the costs of service and of the witnesses, if any.

If the Magistrate rejects the objection he may order the person who has made the objection to pay the costs of service and of the witnesses.

Provided that, in any case, if the Magistrate is satisfied that the party making or resisting the objection was of good faith, he may order that the costs, if any, be borne by the Crown.

Provided also that if the person objected to, leaves default or admits the objection, the costs if any, shall be borne by the Crown.

All proceedings under this article shall be held publicly.

The Registrar General in Port Louis, and the Civil Status Officers in the rural Districts shall, within twenty-one days after the tenth of November, furnish to the District Magistrate a statement of the names of all persons deceased whose names appear on the List of Claimants or in the Register, and the Magistrate shall, thereupon, after enquiry, if necessary, expunge the name of such deceased person from the said List or Register.

Further duties and powers of Magistrate. 6.—It shall further be the duty of the Magistrate within twenty-one days from the tenth of November, to examine the Register and the List with a view to ascertain whether all the persons whose names appear on the said Register or on the said List are qualified as Electors; and in case he finds that there is reason to believe that any person whose name appears on the said Register or List is not qualified as an Elector, to cause a notice to be served on such person: the said notice calling upon such person to show cause why his name should not be expunged: and the Magistrate shall thereupon proceed as is provided for in the preceding article.

Service of Summons by Registered Letter. 7.—It shall be competent to the Magistrate in all cases when he shall require any person to appear before him for any of the purposes connected with this Ordinance to cite such person by means of a summons transmitted in a Registered Post Letter.

Any person, to whom such registered letter is addressed and tendered who shall neglect or refuse forthwith to sign a receipt therefor to be presented to him together with such letter, shall be liable to a fine not exceeding fifty Rupees (Rs. 50).

Upon production of such receipt for any such letter the person summoned shall be liable to the same penalties in case of non-appearance as if he had been personally served by an Usher.

Ordinance to be construed with Ordinance No. 5 of 1887. 8.—This Ordinance shall be read and construed with Ordinance No. 5 of 1887.

Commencement of Ordinance. 9.—This Ordinance shall come into force on the day of its publication in the Government Gazette.

Ordinance No. 23 of 1895.

To authorize the transfer and interment of the remains of the late Father S. Botta into the Parish of "Notre Dame de la Délivrande" at Long Mountain.

(21st. *November* 1895.)

Whereas the Church Wardens of the Parish of "Notre Dame de la Délivrande" are desirous that the remains of the late Reverend S. Botta, Curate of the said Parish, be buried and interred in the yard of the Church near the cross of "La Mission" or any other place in the yard of the said Parish to be designated by the Sanitary Warden;

Be it enacted by the Governor, with the advice and consent of the Council of Government, as follows:—

Short title. 1.—This Ordinance may be cited as "The Ordinance authorizing the interment of the late Reverend Father S. Botta, Curate of "Notre Dame de la Délivrande."

Interment of the remains of the late Father S. Botta in the Parish of "Notre Dame de la Délivrande" at Long Mountain permitted. 2.—Permission is hereby given for the burial and interment of the remains of the late Reverend Father S. Botta, in his life-time Curate of "Notre Dame de la Délivrande", Long Mountain, within the yard of the said Parish near the cross of "La Mission" or any other place in the said yard to be designated by the Sanitary Warden; notwithstanding any legal enactment to the contrary, and subject to such precautions as may be suggested by the Medical and Health Department.

Commencement of Ordinance. 3.—This Ordinance shall come into force on the day of its publication in the Government Gazette.

Ordinance No. 24 of 1895.

To amend and consolidate the Law relating to the amount of duty payable for Licenses.

(29th. *November* 1895.)

Whereas it is expedient to establish in one Ordinance the amounts to be paid in future for licenses at present computed and paid under various Ordinances and in other respects to amend the Law;

Be it enacted by the Governor, with the advice and consent of the Council of Government, as follows:

Short title. 1.—This Ordinance may be cited as "The License Law Amendment Ordinance, 1895."

Schedules repealed. 2.—Schedules A, B, E, F and G of Ordinance No. 6 of 1878 are hereby repealed.

Repealed Schedules replaced. 3.—The Schedules hereunto annexed and designated respectively A, B, E, F and G, shall be substituted for Schedules A, B, E, F and G of Ordinance No. 6 of 1878 respectively and shall have the same force and effect as if they had been annexed to and had formed part of the said Ordinance.

Ordinance repealed. 4.—Ordinance No. 25 of 1890 is hereby repealed, and Ordinance No. 20 of 1890 so far as it relates to Licenses and taxes on vehicles and animals.

Enactments modified. 5.—The following enactments are hereby repealed only so far as regards the amount of duty payable for licences issued thereunder or so far as they may otherwise be inconsistent with the present Ordinance :

Article 2 of Ordinance No. 17 of 1881.

Article 4 of Ordinance No. 7 of 1887.

Article 1 of Ordinance No. 6 of 1888.

Articles 1 and 2 of Ordinance No. 40 of 1888.

Article 1 of Ordinance No. 8 of 1890.

Article 1 of Ordinance No. 7 of 1891.

Article 1 of Ordinance No. 18 of 1891.

Article 1 of Ordinance No. 6 of 1892.

Article 2 (Section 1) of Ordinance No. 12 of 1893.

and any other laws and Ordinances whatsoever that may be repugnant to or inconsistent with the present Ordinance.

Provided always that the repeal or modification of all such laws as aforesaid shall in no way affect or prejudice any right of action or prosecution which before the promulgation of this Ordinance may have accrued under the said laws.

Provided also that all licenses issued under all such laws shall likewise remain in full force and effect until their expiry anything in this Ordinance to the contrary notwithstanding.

Provided further that nothing herein contained shall entitle any person having paid the the license fixed by any such laws aforesaid to claim the refund of any part of the amount so paid.

Commencement of Ordinance 6.—This Ordinance shall come into force on the day of its publication in the Government Gazette.

SCHEDULE A.

To replace Schedule A of Ordinance No. 6 of 1878.

HALF-YEARLY LICENSES.

No.	Business, Profession, or Trade.	Duty for 6 calendar months. Port Louis and Curepipe		Country Districts.		Remarks.
		Rs.	c.	Rs.	c.	
1	Agent (House Land, and Cattle) ...	27	50	27	50	
2	Assurance or Insurance Company ...	137	50	137	50	
3	Assurance or Insurance Agency ...	137	50	137	50	For each Agency.
4	Attorney-at-Law	33	...	33	...	
5	Auctioneer (keeping no Auction Room).	82	50	38	50	
6	Auctioneer, (keeping an Auction Room).	125	...	125	...	With right to sell by retail, but only goods received from residents or local importers and not goods imported by himself or received direct from manufacturers outside the Colony.
7	Baker (with more than two workmen or assistants).	11	...	11	...	
8	Banker	550	...	...	...	
9	Banker's Agent	250	...	...	...	For each Agency.
10	Basket-seller	4	...	3	...	Selling baskets purchased for his trade.
11	Billiard Room (not public... ...	165	...	130	...	Kept by a Club or Society.
12	Billiard Room (public)	330	...	220	...	
13	Billiard Table in an Hotel (each Table).	100	...	65	...	
14	Blacksmiths and Farriers.					
	a. With not more than 2 assistants ...	5	...	4	...	
	b. With more than 2 assistants ...	10	...	8	...	
15	Book-binder	8	25	8	25	
16	Brick and Tile maker	22	...	22	...	
17	Broker-Sworn (1st class)	110	...	110	...	
18	Do. (2nd class) ...	27	...	27	50	
19	Broker-Sworn (Custom House) ...	27	50	...	...	
20	Builder of Houses	...	...	...	...	See Job Contractor.
21	Builder of Funeral Monuments (employing more than one workman) ...	22	...	22	...	
22	Butcher (in a market)	8	...	8	...	Exclusive of a separate duty of Rs. 2.75 every 6 months for each stall exceeding one.
23	Butcher (elsewhere than in a market).	8*	...	8	...	* Curepipe only.
24	Cabinet maker...	9	...	7	...	
25	Cake seller (in a market)... ...	3	50	3	50	Exclusive of a separate duty of Rs. 2.20 every six months for each stall exceeding one.
26	Do. (elsewhere than in a market).	3	50	3	50	
27	Carrier by Land	5	...	5	...	For each cart.
28	Cartwright	11	...	11	...	
29	Chocolate maker	6	...	6	...	

SCHEDULE A.—Continued.

No.	Business, Profession, or Trade.	Duty for 6 calendar months. Port Louis and Curepipe. Rs.	c.	Country Districts. Rs.	c.	Remarks.
30	Manufacturers of Cigars, Cigarettes, Snuff & Plug (employing no assistant).	20	...	20	..	License to be issued only to Licensed Retailers of Tobacco.
31	Manufacturers of Cigars, Cigarettes, Snuff & Plug (employing not more than 5 assistants	30	...	30	...	
32	Do. (employing more than 5 assistants)	50	...	50	...	
33	Coach builder	12	...	9	...	
34	Coffee house keeper	...	...	...	...	See Refreshment Room Keeper.
35	Comb maker	5	...	5	...	
36	Commission Merchant — Agent who buys, or sells, or orders from abroad Goods on account of others—whether the Goods are imported in his own name or not.	100	...	100	...	
37	Company Public (under Ord. 31 of 1865).	220	...	220	...	
38	Company, Joint Stock or other not provided for in Ord. 31 of 1865.	66	...	66	...	
39	Compounder (not furnishing any bond, and not using any still or distilling apparatus).	80	...	...	...	
40	Do. (using still or distilling apparatus and furnishing bond).	170	...	...	...	
41	Confectioner	27	50	22	...	
42	Cooper	10	...	10	...	
43	Co-operative Societies	...	...	...	...	According to nature of Business and selling to its own members only.
44	Coppersmith	27	50	27	50	
45	Cutler	7	...	7	...	
46	Do. (itinerant)	8	...	8	...	
47	Distiller	550	...	550	...	
48	Engineer (Civil and Mechanical) ...	33	...	33	...	
49	Fishing for shrimps, sprats and other small fish of sizes authorised by Ordinance No. 42 of 1881 and with nets of the dimensions authorized by Ord. 11 of 1883.	2	25	2	25	With or without boats and whatever the number of fishermen employed in fishing with nets.
50	Fishing with large nets (*Grandes Seines*) and 3 boats or less.	14	...	14	...	An additional duty of Rs. 2 per half year, for every extra boat.
51	Fishing with one large net (*Grande Seine*) without boat.	6	...	6	...	Whatever the number of Fishermen.
52	Seller of fish from private Barachois (sold at the Barachois, or elsewhere.)	27	...	27	...	
53	Fishmonger (in a market)... ...	7	...	4	...	Exclusive of a separate License duty of Rs. 2, every 6 months for each stall exceeding one.
54	Do. (elsewhere than in a market) ...	...	...	4*	...	* And Curepipe.

SCHEDULE A.—Continued.

No.	Business, Profession, or Trade,	Duty for 6 calendar months.				Remarks.
		Port Louis and Curepipe.		Country Districts.		
		Rs.	c.	Rs.	c.	
55	Founder or Proprietor of Engineering shop.	55	...	44	...	
56	Do. not having an Engineering shop.	12	...	7	...	Having the right of preparing or manufacturing only small pieces of iron and copper not usually prepared by Engineers.
57	Manufacturer of Gold and Silver ware.	40	...	40	...	With right to sell on Licensed premises only.
58	Gilder or Plater	9	...	8	...	
59	Gunsmith	11	...	11	...	
60	Hawkers of :*					
	a. Brass and Copper jewels. ...	6	...	4	...	
	b. Earthenware and Crockery ...	3	50	3	50	
	c. Firewood and Charcoal... ...	5	50	5	50	
	d. Fish, Shrimps and Shell fish ..	...	...	*3	50	* And Curepipe.
	e. Haberdashery.	4	50	4	50	
	f. Ice-creams	3	...	3	...	
	g. Imported Jewellery	27	50	27	50	Issued only when Receiver General is satisfied that holder is *bonâ fide* importer of jewellery.
	h. Jewellery	16	50	16	50	Only issued to manufacturers of gold and silver ware made in the Colony
	i. Lemonade and Soda Water ..	3	30	3	30	
	j. Dairy produce (or seller) ...	1	25	1	25	
	k. Toddy (*Calou*) (or seller) ...	2	50	2	50	
	l. Cakes	3	50	3	50	
	m. Poultry	3	50	3	50	
	n. Timber	10	...	10	...	
	o. Tinware	3	50	3	50	
	p. Tobacco (manufactured or not) ...	30	...	30	...	
	q. All other goods, wares and merchandize— except Opium, Jewellery, Tobacco, Spirits, Wine, Beer and Gandia.	8	25	8	25	
61	Hair dresser	8	50	5	...	
62	Harness maker...	11	...	7	...	
63	Hatter and Glover	7	...	6	...	
64	Hotel-keeper (or Inn-keeper) ...	200	...	140	...	
65	Ironmonger	55	...	33	...	With right to sell hardware either by wholesale or retail.
66	Do. Selling by retail only small ironware such as Jewellers' and Watchmakers' tools.	20	...	15	...	

***** An additional duty of Rs. 2 shall be charged for every porter ; Rs. 2 for every beast of burden ; and Rs. 5 for every vehicle employed by any hawker under Article 80 of Ordinance No. 6 of 1878.

SCHEDULE A.—Continued.

No.	Business, Profession, or Trade.	Duty for 6 calender months. Port Louis and Curepipe. Rs.	c.	Country Districts. Rs.	c.	Remarks.
67	Job Contractor :					Notwithstanding the provisions of Article 32 of Ordinance 6 of 1878 licensed of Job-Contractors may at any time be issued for several consecutive periods of six months but so that the last of such consecutive licenses shall in no case extend two years beyond the date of the first issue.
	a. Employing more than 50 laborers or artisans.	82	50	82	50	
	b. Employing more than 25 but not more than 50.	50	...	50	...	
	c. Employing more than 10 but not more than 25.	25	...	25	...	
	d. Employing more than 5 but not more than 10.	15	...	15	...	
	e. Employing not more than 5 ...	6	...	6	...	
68	Land Surveyor...	16	50	16	50	
69	Lemonade, Soda waters and Gingerbeer maker.	15	...	15	...	With right to sell on Licensed premises only.
70	Do. seller ...	5	...	5	...	
71	Lime burner	16	50	16	50	With right to sell lime in any quantity at his kiln or elsewhere.
72	Lime seller	8	...	8	...	An additional duty of Rs. 4 per half-year for each depot in excess of the one for which the license is granted.
73	Livery stable keeper.—					
	For each carriage	7	...	7	...	
	For each carriole	5	...	5	...	
74	Lodging-house keeper	13	50	13	50	When the number of lodgers is in excess of 6; and for every lodger in excess of 6, R. 1.
75	Manufacturer of Copper and Brass Jewels.	8	25	8	25	
76	Manufacturer of Fireworks ...	13	75	13	75	With right to sell on the licensed premises only.
77	Manure manufacturer	27	50	27	50	
78	Market Auctioneer	33	...	26	50	With right to sell fish, fruits and vegetables only at public markets.
79	Marine Surveyor	16	50	...	...	
80	Merchant	...	...	...	...	See wholesale dealer.

SCHEDULE A.—Continued.

No.	Business, Profession, or Trade.	Duty for 6 calendar months. Port Louis and Curepipe.		Country Districts.		Remarks.
		Rs.	c.	Rs.	c.	
81	Miller (corn)	22	...	22	...	
82	Milliner (or Dress maker)					
	a. Employing 5 but not more than 8 assistants.	16	50	8	25	
	b. Employing more than 8 assistants...	33	...	13	...	
83	Money changer	10	...	10	...	
84	Musical Instrument maker and mender.	11	...	7	50	
85	Mussel-bed keeper	5	50	5	50	
86	Notary Public	165	...	55	...	
87	Notary (English)	55	...	...	...	
88	Oil vendor	25	...	25	...	Selling Oil only.
89	Opium seller	...	...	...	...	See Retailer of Opium.
90	Optician	8	25	8	25	
91	Oyster-bed keeper	5	50	5	50	
92	Painter and Glazier	8	25	8	25	
93	Painter of badges and sign-boards ...	5	...	5	...	
94	Partner in any Commercial Firm or Company whether such partner be dormant or not.	5	50	5	50	Joint Stock Companies excepted.
95	Pawnbroker	165	...	165	...	
96	Pharmacist	110	...	88	...	
97	Printer	22	...	22	...	
98	Proctor in Admiralty not practising as an Avoué.	38	50	...	...	
99	Refreshment Room keeper ...	120	...	120	...	
100	Retailer of :					
	a. Spirits, Wine and Beer... ...	165	...	132	...	
	b. Groceries	22	...	16	50	
	c. Drapery and haberdashery ..	27	50	16	50	
	d. Gold and Silver wares	33	...	33	...	
	e. Tobacco (manufactured or not) ...	27	50	27	50	
	f. Opium	110	...	110	...	
	g. Earthenware, China and Glassware..	27	50	22	...	
	h. Gandia	110	...	110	...	This license not to be issued to importers of Gandia. The sale of any quantity not exceeding 20 grammes to be considered a sale by retail.
101	Retailer (General	75	...	50	...	Authorising the retail of all Goods. Wares and Merchandize (except Spirits, Wines, Beer, Tobacco, Gold & Silver wares, Opium and Gandia.
102	Retailer (Consolidated License) ...	220	...	200	...	Not authorised to retail Gold and Silver wares, Opium and Gandia.
103	Sail Maker	11	...	11	...	
104	Seller of :					
	Cattle (in a market or elsewhere) ...	4	50	4	50	
	Poultry (in a market, shop, or public place).	5	50	5	50	
105	Seller of Dunnage wood	8	25	8	25	
	Do. Firewood and charcoal ...	5	...	5	...	
106	Scavenger	11	...	5	50	
107	Shipchandler	55	...	55	...	

SCHEDULE A.—Continued.

No.	Business, Profession, or Trade.	Duty for 6 calendar months. Port Louis and Curepipe. Rs.	c.	Country Districts. Rs.	c.	Remarks.
108	Shipwright	33	...	33	...	
109	Shoemaker employing not more than 2 assistants	5	...	5	...	
110	Do. with more than 2 assistants ...	10	...	10	...	
111	Soap-maker	10	...	10	...	
112	Stationer	11	...	8	25	
113	Stevedore	10	...	10	...	
114	Supplier of fresh water to ships ...	1	10	...	...	Per ton of Tank boat.
115	Tailor.					
	(a) Employing not more than 2 assistants.	7	50	5	...	
	(b) Employing more than 2 assistants.	15	...	10	...	
116	Tanner	11	...	11	...	
117	Tavern keeper or Keeper of a Restaurant.	132	...	132	...	
118	Timber Merchant	50	...	25	...	
119	Tinsmith.					
	With not more than 2 assistants ...	5	...	4	...	
	With more than 2 assistants ...	10	...	8	...	
120	Undertaker	30	...	30	...	
121	Upholsterer	8	25	7	...	
122	Usher :					
	a. Supreme Court	22	...	...	...	
	b. District Court	16	50	16	50	
123	Vegetable and Fruit seller .					
	a. In a market or shop	3	35	3	25	a. Exclusive of a separate license of Rs. 2 every six months for every extra stall.
	b. Elsewhere than in a market or shop	3	30	3	30	
124	Victualler selling cooked food to be consumed :					
	a. Off the premises	10	...	7	50	
	b. On the premises	12	...	12	...	
	c. On or on the premises ...	20	...	15	...	
125	Warehouseman (not issuing Dock-warrants)	27	50	27	50	
126	Watchmaker	11	...	5	50	With right to sell watches and watch cases.
127	Sworn-Weigher	11	...	11	...	
128	Wharfinger	25	...	25	...	
129	Wholesale Dealer or Merchant ...	165	...	165	...	Has the right to sell all goods, wares and merchandize—except Gandia.
130	Wholesale Retailer, Consolidated License	360	...	360	...	Authorising the sale of all goods, wares and merchandize by wholesale, except Gandia and of all goods, wares and merchandize except Gold and Silver wares, Opium and Gandia by Retail.
131	Wholesale Seller of Gandia ...	500	...	500	...	This License to be issued only to importers of Gandia. A sale of more than 20 grammes to be considered wholesale.

EXEMPTIONS.

1. Hawkers or sellers of any produce of the soil of the Colony grown or manufactured by himself except Spirits, Timber and Tobacco.
2. Hawkers or sellers of any Animal reared by himself, or eggs of poultry reared by himself.
3. Hawkers of Bread only.
4. Baker employing only one assistant or none.
5. Brush makers.
6. Washermen and Laundresses.
7. Shoemakers employing one assistant.
8. Milliners employing fewer than five assistants.
9. Tailors employing one assistant only.
10. Mattress makers.
11. Umbrella menders.
12. Blacksmiths and Farriers employing one assistant.
13. Tinsmiths employing one assistant.
14. Barbers.
15. Holders of Tea and Coffee stalls.

SCHEDULE B.

To replace Schedule B of Ordinance No. 6 of 1878.

Annual Licences.

		Duty for 12 calendar months.
License to shoot Game :		
(1) To Master	Rs.	11.00
(2) To Servant		11.00
License to deal in Game		5.50
Warehouseman issuing Dock-warrants		66.00

SCHEDULE E.

To replace Schedule E of Ordinance No. 6 of 1878.

Annual Taxes Due on Animals and Vehicles.

	Rs.	c.		Rs.	c.
1. For every Carriage on 4 wheels...	22	...	13. For every Dray or Cart drawn by one animal	11	...
2. For every Carriage on 3 ,, ...	16	50			
3. For every Carriage on 2 ,, ...	13	50	14. For every Horse or Mule used wholly or occasionally for the saddle or in carriage	6	75
4. For every Brake on 4 ,, ...	22	...			
5. For every Brake on 2 ,, ...	13	50			
6. For every Traction Engine ...	600	...	15. For every Horse or Mule used only in a Cart, Dray, Tumbrel or Waggon	4	50
7. For every Truck attached thereto	132	...			
8. For every Triqueballe	44	...			
9. For every Cart or Waggon on 4 wheels	26	50	16. For every Dog of the age of 4 months and upwards or attaining the age of 4 months at any time during the year not being kept within the Municipal boundaries of Port Louis	2	75
10. For every Dray, Tumbrel or large Cart on 2 wheels drawn by more than one animal ...	13	50			
11. For every Spring Cart on 2 wheels	13	50			
12. For every Spring Cart on 4 wheels	16	50	17. For every Donkey	3	50

On Animals and Vehicles kept within the boundaries of the Municipality of Port Louis such tax shall be paid as shall be imposed by the Municipal Law in force for the time being.

SCHEDULE F.

To replace Schedule F of Ordinance No. 6 of 1878.

(ARTICLE 48 OF ORDINANCE No. 6 OF 1878.)

Declaration of the Vehicles and Animals liable to Taxation possessed by (A)
(B) residing at (C)
in the District of between the 1st. day of January and the day
of and which he is bound to declare by Article 48 of Ordiance No. 6 of 1878.

	Rate of Tax.		Number in possession of or owned by Declarant. For use on the Public Road.	Number in possession of or owned by Declarant. Employed exclusively upon Proprietor's Estate or Estates possessed by him, and upon public or other Roads intersecting or bordering such Estates.	Amount of Assessment.	
	Rs.	c.			Rs.	c.
Carriages, Four Wheels...	22	...				
do. Three „	16	50				
do. Two „	13	50				
Brakes, Four „	22	...				
do. Two „	13	50				
Traction Engine	600	...				
Trucks attached thereto	132	...				
Triqueballes	44	...				
Carts or Waggons, Four wheels	26	50				
„ large Two „ and Drays or Tumbrels drawn by more than one animal,.	13	50				
Spring-Carts on Two wheels	13	50				
„ on Four „	16	50				
Carts, small, drawn by one animal	11	...				
Horses, used wholly or occasionally for the Saddle or in Carriage...	6	75				
Mules	6	75				
Horses, used only in Carts or Waggons ...	4	50				
Mules, „ „ ...	4	50				
Dogs	2	75				
Donkeys	3	50				
Road Tax						
Church Tax						
			TOTAL ... ... Rs.			

I do solemnly declare and affirm that the above is a true and correct return of the number of Vehicles and Animals liable to taxes possessed by me during the period above stated.

Mauritius, this day of 189 .

Signature of Declarant.

(A) All the names of the Declarant should be written at length.
(B) Here state the occupation or calling of the Declarant.
(C) Here state name of the Estate or the designation of the place where Declarant resides.

SCHEDULE G.

To replace Schedule G of Ordinance No. 6 *of* 1878 (*Article* 49 *of Ordinance No.* 6 *of* 1878.)

Declaration of the Vehicles and Animals liable to Taxation possessed by (A) (B) residing at (C) in the District of since the day of 189 and which he is bound to declare by Article 49 of Ordinance No. 6 of 1878.

PARTICULARS.	Rate of Tax. From 1st. April to 15th. May inclusive. Rs.	c.	From 16th. May to 30th. June inclusive. Rs.	c.	From 1st. July to 15th. August. inclusive. Rs.	c.	From 16th. August to 30th. September inclusive. Rs.	c.	From 1st. October to 15th. November inclusive. Rs.	c.	From 16th. November to 31st. December inclusive. Rs.	c.	Number in possession of or owned by Declarant. For use on the Public Roads.	Employed exclusively upon Proprietors' Estate or Estates possessed by them, and upon public or other Roads *intersecting or passing alongside* of such Estates, and so exempt.	Amount of Assessment.
Carriages, Four Wheels.	16	50	13	75	11	...	8	25	5	50	2	75			
do. Three „	12	50	10	50	8	25	6	25	4	25	2	25			
do. Two „	10	...	8	25	6	75	5	...	3	50	1	75			
Brakes, Four „	16	50	13	75	11	...	8	25	5	50	2	75			
do. Two „	10	...	8	25	6	75	5	...	3	50	1	75			
Traction Engines ...	450	...	370	...	300	...	230	...	140	...	80	...			
Trucks attached thereto.	100	...	80	...	70	...	50	...	35	...	17	...			
Triqueballes	35	...	28	...	22	...	17	...	11	...	6	...			
Carts or Waggons, Four Wheels	20	...	17	...	13	50	10	...	6	75	3	50			
Carts large, Two Wheels and Drays or Tumbrels	10	...	8	25	6	75	5	...	3	50	1	75			
Spring-Carts on Two Wheels	10	...	8	25	6	75	5	...	3	50	1	75			
Spring-Carts on Four Wheels	12	50	10	25	8	25	6	25	4	25	2	...			
Carts, small to be drawn by one animal ...	8	25	7	...	5	50	4	25	2	75	1	50			
Horses, used wholly or occasionally for the Saddle or in Carriage.	5	...	4	25	3	50	2	50	1	75	1	...			
Mules, do. do. ...	5	...	4	25	3	50	2	50	1	75	1	...			
Horses, used only in Carts or Waggons ...	3	50	2	75	2	25	1	75	1	25	...	50			
Mules, do. do. ...	3	50	2	75	2	25	1	75	1	25	...	50			
Donkeys...	2	50	2	...	1	75	1	25	...	75	...	50			
Dogs	2	10	1	75	1	25	1	...	...	75	...	50			
Surcharge for late declaration and payment...	...	...	...	...	...	...	...	...	...	...	...	...			
Church Tax	...	...	...	...	...	...	...	...	...	...	...	...			
Road Tax	...	...	...	...	...	...	...	...	...	...	...	...			
														Total ... ...Rs.	

I do solemnly declare and affirm that the above declaration is a true and correct return of the number of Vehicles and Animals liable to taxation possessed by me since

Mauritius, this day of 189 .

Signature of the Declarant.

(A) All the names of the Declarant should be written at length.
(B) Here state the occupation or calling of the Declarant.
(C) Here state the name of the Estate or the designation of the place where declarant resides.

Ordinance No. 25 of 1895.

For applying a further sum not exceeding Rs. 513,559.02 to the Service of the year 1894.

(*5th. December* 1895.)

Whereas certain sums, in addition to those by law provided, were required for the service of the Government of this Colony for the year 1894 and were paid and applied to the service of the said year, but without legislative authority having been obtained therefor;

And whereas it is proper that the said payments be now legalized;

Be it therefore enacted by the Governor, with the advice and consent of the Council of Government, as follows:

Legalization of excess expenditure for 1894.

1.—Five hundred and thirteen thousand five hundred and fifty nine Rupees and two cents, (Rs. 513,559.02) consisting of the sums specified in the Schedule to this Ordinance appended, which sum was duly paid and applied for the Public Service of the Island of Mauritius during the year 1894 and was paid out of the Revenue of the Colony, is hereby enacted and declared to be a valid and legal charge upon the said Revenue.

Commencement of Ordinance.

2.—This Ordinance shall come into force on the day of its publication in the Government Gazette.

SCHEDULE REFERRED TO

Item No.	Services.	Personal Emoluments.		Other Charges.		Total.	
		Rs.	c.	Rs.	c.	Rs.	c.
1	Charge on account of Public Debt ...	...	...	86,701	95	86,701	95
2	Pensions	...	...	37,908	13	37,908	13
3	Governor and Legislature	...	...	4	55	4	55
4	Colonial Secretary's Dept	...	...	3,913	63	3,913	63
13	Postal and Telegraph Dept	...	...	4,906	31	4,906	31
18	Royal College	...	...	15,415	07	15,415	07
30	Miscellaneous	...	...	135,360	44	135,360	44
31	Charitable allowances	...	...	862	87	862	87
32	Interest and Exchange	...	...	112,973	86	112,973	86
34	Railways	...	...	115,512	21	115,512	21
	Rs...	...	...	513,559	02	513,559	02

Ordinance No. 26 of 1895.

To appropriate five per cent of the Revenue of Mauritius to the use of the Imperial Government as a Military Contribution.

(*13th. December* 1895.)

Whereas it is expedient to appropriate a percentage out of the Revenues of the Colony as a Military Contribution;

Be it enacted by the Governor, with the advice and consent of the Council of Government, as follows:

Short title. 1.—This Ordinance may be cited as "The Military Contribution Ordinance, 1895."

Sum to be appropriated. 2.—There shall be appropriated every year, out of the Revenue of the Colony, a sum of money to the use of the Imperial Government as a Military Contribution, to be calculated at the rate of five per cent of such Revenue.

Percentage to be struck on Revenue. 3.—The Revenue on which such percentage shall be struck shall be brought to account in gross, and shall include all existing sources of income, except the proceeds of land sales, premia on leases and the sum entered in the annual accounts as exchange on Revenue collected by the Crown Agents.

Provided that sums equivalent to the amounts of the following items annually appearing in the Estimates shall be deducted from the Revenue for the purposes of this Ordinance and the percentage herein before referred to shall not be paid thereon:

a. For interest and sinking fund of the Savanne Line unconverted debentures, for the inscribed stock, for the Moka Line unconverted debentures and for the Moka extension;

b. For interest and sinking fund on the Hurricane Loan;

c. For interest on Treasury Bills issued to meet the cost of the work on the Chaussée;

d. For interest and sinking fund on the Mare-aux-Vacoas Loan;

Commencement of Ordinance. 4.—This Ordinance shall come into force on the 1st. January 1896.

Ordinance No. 27 of 1895.

For making provision for the Public Service for the year 1896.

(*12th. December* 1895).

Whereas further sums in addition to those already by Law provided and amounting to Six millions, two hundred and forty-five thousand, one hundred and sixty-five Rupees and eighty-seven cents, are required for the service of the Mauritius Government for the year 1896;

Be it therefore enacted by the Governor, with the advice and consent of the Council of Government, as follows:

Supply. 1.—A sum not exceeding Six millions, two hundred and forty-five thousand, one hundred and sixty-five Rupees and eighty-seven cents, shall be, and the same is hereby charged upon the revenue and other fund of this Colony for the service of the year 1896, and the said expenditure shall be in conformity with the Schedule of this Ordinance of which the following is an abstract:—

Item No.	Services.	Personal Emoluments.		Other Charges.		Total.	
		Rs.	c.	Rs.	c.	Rs.	c.
2	Pensions	...	...	343,745	61	343,745	61
3	The Governor and Legislature	588	...	18,830	...	19,418	...
4	Colonial Secretary's Department ...	14,320	...	8,350	...	22,670	...
5	Receiver General's Department... ...	53,052	...	25,600	...	78,652	...
6	Audit Department	29,512	...	2,220	...	31,732	...
7	Customs Department	66,370	...	20,986	...	87,356	...
8	Port & Marine Department	79,745	50	91,911	...	171,656	50
9	Meteorological Observatory	12,218	..	6,373	...	18,591	...
10	Museum	2,344	...	1,180	...	3,524	...
11	Registrar General...	10,364	...	3,062	...	13,426	...
12	Registration and Mortgage Department..	19,288	...	13,604	...	32,892	...
13	Post and Telegraph	79,030	...	105,052	...	184,082	...
14	Botanical Gardens	10,936	...	4,783	...	15,719	...
15	Woods and Forests Department... ...	76,270	...	31,710	...	107,980	...
16	Judicial Departments	201,106	11	107,020	...	308,126	11
18	Education	208,656	...	209,483	...	418,139	...
19	Medical and Health Department ...	248,106	...	411,384	...	659,490	...
20	Quarantine	10,782	...	45,400	...	56,182	...
21	Poor Law Department	26,980	...	206,496	...	233,476	...
22	Police	720	...	92,794	...	93,514	...
23	Gaols	63,340	...	94,500	...	157,840	...
24	Storekeeper General	21,386	25	5,815	...	27,201	25
25	Immigration Department	39,044	...	83,735	...	122,779	...
26	Dependencies	16,332	...	19,034	...	35,366	...
27	Crown Agents	1,100	...	2,350	...	3,450	...
28	Writers and Copyists	7,200	...	......	...	7,200	...
29	Transport	......	...	7,000	...	7,000	...
30	Miscellaneous	......	...	250,626	...	250,626	...
31	Charitable Allowances	......	...	12,640	...	12,640	...
32	Interest	......	...	124,900	...	124,900	...
33	Military Expenditure	......	...	380,500	...	380,500	...
34	Railway Department	539,737	...	562,960	...	1,102,697	...
35	Surveyor General's Department... ...	29,360	...	11,198	...	40,558	...
36	Public Works, Recurrent...	......	...	301,318	...	301,318	...
37	,, Extraordinary	......	...	75,406	...	75,406	...
39	Mar-aux-Vacoas, Water Works	15,692	...	16,007	...	31,699	...
40	Exchange	......	...	663,614	40	663,614	40
	Total	1,883,578	86	4,361,587	01	6,245,165	87

Short Title.

2.—This Ordinance may be cited as "The Supply Ordinance, 1896."

Commencement of Ordinance.

3.—This Ordinance shall come into force on the day of its publication in the Government Gazette.

Schedule.

ITEM 1.—PERSONAL EMOLUMENTS.

Services.	Salaries.		Personal allowance.		Total.	
	Rs.	c.	Rs.	c.	Rs.	c.
Governor and Legislature	588	...	......	...	588	...
Colonial Secretary	13,460	...	860	...	14,320	...
Receiver General	46,632	...	6,420	...	53,052	...
Audit	29,032	...	480	...	29,512	...
Customs	59,154	...	7,216	...	66,370	...
Port and Marine	70,646	...	9,099	50	79,745	50
Observatory	11,018	...	1,200	...	12,218	...
Museum	2,344	...	......	...	2,344	...
Registrar General	8,364	...	2,000	...	10,364	...
Registration	16,628	...	2,660	...	19,288	...
Post Office	77,910	...	1,120	...	79,030	...
Gardens	10,936	...	......	...	10,936	...
Forests	76,270	...	.....	...	76,270	..
Judicial	191,092	...	10,014	11	201,106	11
Education	207,906	...	750	...	208,656	...
Medical annd Health Department ...	246,366	...	1,740	...	248,106	...
Quarantine	10,782	...	......	...	10,782	...
Poor Law	26,980	...	......	...	26,980	...
Police...	......	...	720	...	720	...
Prisons	59,700	...	3,640	...	63,340	...
Storekeeper General	20,886	25	500	...	21,386	25
Immigration...	37,344	...	1,700	...	39,044	...
Dependencies	16,332	...	......	...	16,332	...
Crown Agents	1,100	...	......	...	1,100	...
Writers and Copyists.	7,200	...	......	...	7,200	...
Railway Department.	527,903	...	11,834	...	539,737	...
Surveyor General	26,300	...	3,060	...	29,360	...
Mare-aux-Vacoas Water Works	15,692	...	......	...	15,692	...
	1,818,565	25	65,013	61	1,883,578	86

Carried over... ... Rs. 1,883,578.86

Brought forward...... ...... Rs. 1,883,578.86

ITEM 2.—PENSIONS.

Pensions ... ... Rs.	343,745.61	343,745.61

ITEM 3.—THE GOVERNOR & LEGISLATURE.

Petty supplies, Flags, Implements and Stores ... ...Rs.	1,325.00	
Maintenance of "Le Reduit" Gardens	4,100.00	
Insurance	972.00	
House allowance to Guardian of stables and a courier ...	96.00	
Conveyance of Messengers	200.00	
Lunch to members of Council	1,200.00	
Books for Council Library	500.00	
Short-hand Writer's fees	4,000.00	
Furniture	5,700.00	
Uniforms for Messengers	160.00	
Fitting "Le Reduit" residence with Electric bells ...	25.00	
Laborers, Government House, Port Louis	552.00	
		18,830.00

ITEM 4.—COLONIAL SECRETARY.

Binding, Petty Supplies, Newspapers & Advertisements ...Rs.	2,850.00	
Books, Newspapers, &c., from United Kingdom and Colonies.	500.00	
Telegrams to and from Europe	5,000.00	
		8,350.00

ITEM 5.—RECEIVER GENERAL.

Extra Inspectors of Distilleries ... ...Rs.	4,800.00	
Transport	3,800.00	
Subsistence and Baggage Allowances	650.00	
Binding, Newspapers, Petty Supplies, Advertisements and Lighting	1,470.00	
Gallon measures, etc.	300.00	
Paper for Stamping purposes and printing I. R. Stamps ...	3,200.00	
Returns of Carriages, &c.—Fees for collecting	680.00	
Secret Service	3,000.00	
Uniforms	200.00	
Repairs to Pirogues	400.000	
Withdrawal of Old Currency Notes from circulation and surplus Balances from Bank	600.00	
New Currency Notes	4,000.00	
Computation of Interest (Savings Bank)	1,500.00	
Special Repayments and Refund of Taxes	500.00	
Extra Clerical Assistance (Savings Bank)	500.00	
		25,600.00

ITEM 6.—AUDIT.

Subsistence Allowances ... ...Rs.	1,500.00	
Binding, Petty Supplies and Newspapers	420.00	
Transport	300.00	
		2,220.00

ITEM 7.—CUSTOMS.

Subsistence Allowance ... ...Rs.	700.00	
Binding, Petty Supplies and Newspapers	746.00	
Repairs to Boats	1,200.00	
Secret Service	1,000.00	
Uniforms	1,140.00	
Carried over ... ...Rs.	4,786.00	Rs. 2,282,324.47

	Brought forward	...Rs. 4,786.00	Rs. 2,282,324.47
ITEM 7.—CUSTOMS (*Continued*).			
Hired Laborers...	...	50.00	
Lodging Allowance and Transport	...	630.00	
Rent of Telephone	...	420.00	
Provisions and Lightning ...	...	2,100.00	
Refund of Dues, Drawback and over entries	...	13,000.00	
			20,986.00
ITEM 8.—PORT AND MARINE.			
General Expenditure	...Rs.	56,210.00	
Steam Vessels and Dredgers	...	11,450.00	
Light Houses and Light Ship	...	24,251,00	
			91,911.00
ITEM 9.—OBSERVATORY.			
Books, Petty Supplies and Printing	...Rs.	700.00	
Extra Clerical Assistance ...	...	2,300.00	
Lodging allowance	...	1,450.00	
Chemicals, Stores and Instruments ...	...	1,500.00	
Meteorological Observations in the Dependencies...	...	423.00	
			6,373.00
ITEM 10.—MUSEUM.			
Petty supplies ...	...Rs.	500.00	
Keeping Museum clean	...	480.00	
Duty on Rum ...	...	200.00	
			1,180.00
ITEM 11.—REGISTRAR GENERAL.			
Petty supplies and Binding	...Rs.	1,200.00	
Subsistence allowance	...	92.00	
Rent of offices ...	...	1,260.00	
Transport	...	500.00	
Insurance	...	10.00	
			3,062.00
ITEM 12.—REGISTRATION.			
Binding, Newspapers an l Petty Supplies	...Rs.	374.00	
Law Books	...	150.00	
Extra Assistance	...	13,000.00	
Tin Boxes	...	80.00	
			13,604.00
ITEM 13.—POST OFFICE.			
Sea & Territorial transit of correspondence abroad	...Rs.	14,000.00	
Remuneration to Telegraph Operators for Night Work	...	450.00	
Extra Assistance	...	4,600.00	
Subsistence Money	...	1,050.00	
Clerk for regular night duty	...	470.00	
Binding, Petty supplies and printing of Postage Stamps	...	3,000.00	
Additional boats	...	50.00	
Poundage on sale of I. R. Stamps	...	700.00	
Uniforms	...	1,600.00	
Transport	...	450.00	
Rent	...	120.00	
Porterage of Telegraphic Messages	...	9,000.00	
Conveyance of Mails by sea	...	60,000.00	
Do. do. by road	...	1,830.00	
Gratuities to Masters of Vessels for taking care of Mails	...	1,200.00	
Telegraph instruments and Batteries and maintenance, &c.	...	4,300.00	
Provision, &c., and Lighting	...	450.00	
Special Stationery	...	800.00	
Scales	...	300.00	
Additional Post Offices	...	682.00	
			105,052.00
	Carried over...	... .	Rs. 2,524,492.47

Brought forward...		Rs. 2,524,492.47
ITEM 14.—GARDENS.		
Books	Rs. 200	
Petty Expenses	950	
Tools and Repairs	748	
Uniforms	75	
Maintenance of Curepipe Gardens	2,000	
Do. of Apprentices	810	
		4,783.00
ITEM 15.—FORESTS.		
Sanitary Plantations	Rs. 500	
Surveying and opening Lines	3,500	
Compensation for Land taken (Mountain Reserves) ...	500	
Transport and Subsistence Allowance, &c.	9,100	
Buildings and Tools	3,000	
Medical Treatment of Rangers and Keepers	50	
Uniforms	6,960	
Petty Supplies, Stationery, Printing, &c.	1,000	
Planting, &c.	5,100	
Rearing and Thinning Plants	2,000	
		31,710.00
ITEM 16.—JUDICIAL.		
Supreme Court...	Rs. 23,605	
Procureur General	2,930	
District Courts...	76,313	
Stipendiary Courts	4,172	
		107,020.00
ITEM 18.—EDUCATION.		
Royal College	Rs. 30,746	
Government and Grant-in-Aid Schools	178,737	
		209,483.00
ITEM 19.—MEDICAL & HEALTH DEPARTMENT.		
Medical Branch	Rs. 23,225	
Civil Hospital	56,240	
Lunatic Asylum	59,675	
Public Hospitals, &c.	165,980	
Sanitary Branch	106,264	
		411,384.00
ITEM 20.—QUARANTINE.		
Implements and Petty Stores	Rs. 1,000	
Clothing and Bedding	1,500	
Provisions, Fuel and Oil	12,000	
Stores, Boat and Petty Supplies, &c.	900	
Quarantine Services	30,000	
		45,400.00
Carried over		Rs. 3,334,272.47

Brought forward		Rs. 3,334,272.47
ITEM 21.—POOR LAW DEPARTMENT.		
Petty Supplies, Binding, Uniforms, &c. ... ...Rs.	1,275	
Rent and Insurance	1,287	
Transport	7,000	
Maintenance and care of Sick and Infirm Paupers, Orphans, Lepers and Return Passages	100,000	
Out-door Relief to Paupers and Relief in Cash	55,000	
Implements, Clothing, &c. (Barkly Asylum)	4,500	
Burial Expenses	2,000	
Sanitary Service and Fees Examination of Lunatics ...	3,280	
Interest on and withdrawal of Debentures	5,938	
Guardianship of Canals	216	
Provisions, Fuel and Oil, &c.	26,000	
		206,496.00
ITEM 22.—POLICE.		
Lodging Allowance and Rent ... ...Rs.	19,092	
Provisions, &c., and Lighting	7,000	
Uniforms for Constables	33,000	
Secret Service	2,000	
Transport	2,150	
Forage Allowance	11,520	
Canteen (Annual Grant)	4,000	
Miscellaneous petty expenses	13,532	
Fire Engine, Mahebourg	500	
		92,794.00
ITEM 23.—GAOLS.		
Provisions, Fuel, Oil and Lighting ... ...Rs.	64,500	
Clothing and bedding and uniforms	13,000	
Implements and materials for trades	11,000	
House Allowance	2,220	
Remuneration to prisoners on discharge	1,500	
Miscellaneous petty expenses	2,280	
		94,500.00
ITEM 24.—STOREKEEPER GENERAL.		
Binding, Freight, Advertisements, and Petty stores and Supplies ... ...Rs.	650	
Transport and House Allowance	2,520	
Dynamite and Gunpowder Magazine, and Subsistence Allowance to Inspecting Officers	985	
Lighterage and Boat hire	200	
Miscellaneous Services in Government yards	1,460	
		5,815.00
ITEM 25.—IMMIGRATION.		
Mauritius ... ...Rs.	35,530	
Calcutta	445	
Madras	1,200	
Other charges, India	46,560	
		83,735.00
ITEM 26.—DEPENDENCIES.		
Rodrigues —Miscellaneous Services ... ...Rs.	3,150	
Water Supply & Maintenance of Buildings ...	3,500	
Postal Communication	7,500	
Miscellaneous expenses	4,864	
Oil Islands —Petty supplies	20	
		19,034.00
Carried over		Rs. 3,836,646.47

	Brought forward...	...	...Rs. 3,836,646.47
ITEM 27.—CROWN AGENTS.			
General charges	...Rs.	2,350.00	
			2,350.00
ITEM 29.—TRANSPORT.			
Conveyance of Committees, etc.	...Rs.	2,000.00	
½ passage allowance	...	3,000.00	
Passage of Public officers to the Colony ...	...	2,000.00	
			7,000.00
ITEM 30.—MISCELLANEOUS.			
Annual grant to several Societies	...Rs.	8,605.00	
Experimental Farm	...	6,275.00	
Fees to Avoués, Notaries and Examiners in Pharmacy	...	3,400.00	
Curepipe Board of Commissioners	...	30,000.00	
Printing and Stationery	...	50,000.00	
Government Clocks	...	1,200.00	
Firing morning, evening and alarms guns ...	...	2,000.00	
Sub-Marine Cable	..	70,000.00	
Subsidy Beuter's Telegraphic Agency... ...	..	8,000.00	
Seamstresses' work rooms	...	1,954.00	
Uniforms	...	2,600.00	
Furniture	...	2,000.00	
Emancipated invalids	...	2,547.00	
Station Agronomique	...	25,500.00	
Special repayments	...	2,000.00	
Commission on sale of Government properties ...	...	1,000.00	
Special Committees : breakfasts and refreshments	...	1,500.00	
Register of Electors	...	45.00	
General Election expenses	...	6,000.00	
Contribution to Fire Engine Establishment ...	...	6,000.00	
New Edition of Colonial Laws	...	20,000.00	
			250,626.00
ITEM 31.—CHARITABLE ALLOWANCES.			
Governor's Fund	...Rs.	2,000.00	
Fixed allowances	...	8,640.00	
Allowances to maimed and disabled Artizans ...	...	2,000.00	
			12,640.00
ITEM 32.—INTEREST.			
Savings Bank	...Rs.	100,000.00	
Widows and Orphans' Fund	...	16,000.00	
Curatelle Deposits	...	8,900.00	
			124,900.00
ITEM 33.—MILITARY EXPENDITURE.			
Contribution	...Rs.	360,000.00	
Allowance in lieu of rebate on Customs duties ...	...	20,500.00	
			380,500.00
ITEM 34.—RAILWAYS.			
Maintenance of way	...Rs.	119,419.00	
Locomotive power	...	348,523.00	
Carriage and Waggon	...	46,074.00	
Traffic charges	...	39,973.00	
Police	...	550.00	
General Manager's Office	...	8,421.00	
			562,960.00
ITEM 35.—SURVEYOR GENERAL.			
Transport	...Rs	6,800.00	
Binding, Newspapers, Petty Supplies and Advertisements...		498.00	
Survey of Crown Lands	...	3,600.00	
Stationery	...	300.00	
			11,198.00
	Carried over	...	Rs. 5,188,820.47

		Brought forward	...			...Rs 5,188,820.47
ITEM 36.—PUBLIC WORKS RECURRENT.						
Maintenance and Repairs ...	...	...	...Rs	60,648.00		
Sanitary Works	...	...	...	46,500.00		
Miscellaneous ...	...	...	...	4,870.00		
Roads ...	...	...	...	144,200.00		
Bridges and Canals	...	...	...	45,100.00		
						301,318.00
ITEM 37.—PUBLIC WORKS, Extraordinary		...	...	75,406.00		
ITEM 39.—MARE-AUX-VACOAS, Water Works		...	...			16,007.00
ITEM 40.—EXCHANGE	...	...	...			663,614.40
		Total	...	...		Rs 6,245,165.87

Ordinance No. 28 of 1895.

To amend certain Ordinances relating to Municipal Elections.

(*13th. December 1895.*)

Be it enacted by the Governor, with the advice and consent of the Council of Government, as follows :

Short Title.

1.—This Ordinance may be cited as "The Municipal Elections Amendment Ordinance, 1895."

Article 17 of Ordinance No. 21 of 1851 repealed and replaced by another provision.

2.—Article 17 of Ordinance No. 21 of 1851 is hereby repealed and replaced by the following article :

The Mayor and Assessors shall on the next day following the day of the election, and if such day be a Sunday or a holiday, on the day next following not being a holiday or a Sunday, attend at the polling place, which polling place shall be open to the public, and shall examine and scrutinize the voting papers so delivered as aforesaid, for the purpose of ascertaining which of the several persons so voted for are elected : and so many of such persons, being equal to the number of persons then to be chosen, as shall have the greatest number of votes, shall be deemed to be elected : and, in case of an equality of votes for any two or more persons, the Mayor and Assessors shall cast lots and declare duly elected such persons, in whose favor the lot is determined, as may be necessary to complete the requisite number of persons to be chosen. The names of the persons elected shall be entered in a minute drawn up and signed by the Mayor and Assessors, who shall publish a list of them on the day next following the day of such election ; unless such day be a Sunday or a public holiday then on the day next following not being a Sunday or a public holiday.

Article 1 of Ordinance No. 15 of 1890 amended.

3.—Instead of the words " and two out of four Assessors " in the first line of article 1 of Ordinance No. 15 of 1890, the following words shall be read : the Duputy Mayor and four out of six Assessors ".

Article 3 of Ordinance No. 37 of 1853 amended.

4.—Instead of the words " and then on the Monday following ", in the second line of article 3 of Ordinance No. 37 of 1853, the following words shall be read : " or a public holiday and then on the day following."

Provision added to Article 3 of Ordinance No. 33 of 1875.

5.—The following provision is hereby added to article 3 of Ordinance No. 33 of 1875 :

The aforesaid names of candidates, as well as their abodes, professions or callings, shall be printed on the paper either in English or French ; provided that the said names shall also be printed in the Indian dialects most spoken in the Colony and in the Chinese language."

Article 4 of Ordinance No. 33 of 1875 amended.

6.—The second paragraph of Article 4 of Ordinance No. 33 of 1875 is hereby repealed and replaced by the following provision :

The polling place shall have two proper platforms and seats for the Mayor, the Deputy Mayor and the Assessoral Committee. There shall be two polling places presided by the Mayor, and Deputy-Mayor and in their absence by the senior Assessors.

There shall be suitable comhartments, at least six in number, each furnished with a table and seat and a pencil for the voters, and completely separated from each other, so as totally to prevent any communication whatever between the voters occupying the said compartments.

Commencement of Ordinance.

7.—This Ordinance shall come into force on the day of its publication in the Government Gazette.

Ordinance No. 29 1895.

To amend and consolidate the Customs Tariff.

(*19th. December* 1895.)

Whereas it is expedient to amend and consolidate the Tariff under which duties are now levied on goods imported into Mauritius ;

Be it therefore enacted by the Governor, with the advice and consent of the Council of Government, as follows :—

Short Title.

1.—This Ordinance may be cited as " The Customs Consolidate Tariff Ordinance, 1895."

Repeal of existing laws, Schedule of

2.—On and after the promulgation of the present Ordinance, the Ordinances mentioned in the Schedule A hereunto appended shall be repealed.

New Customs duties to be substituted for existing duties.

3.—Instead of the Customs duties payable under the laws mentioned in the preceding article, there shall, on and after the promulgation of this Ordinance, be levied the several Customs duties set forth in Schedule B hereunto annexed.

Goods exempted from duty.

4.—The goods enumerated in Schedule C of this Ordinance shall *de facto* be exempted from Customs Duties.

Duty on certain goods may be remitted or refunded by the Governor in Executive Council.

5.—It shall be lawful for the Governor in Executive Council, upon the report of the Collector of Customs, to remit or refund the whole or any portion of the duties set forth in Schedule B of this Ordinance, in the case of any goods imported under special circumstances, or for an object or enterprise beneficial to the Colony.

When goods exempted from duty are sold, duty to be brought to account.

6.—Whenever any goods have been exempted from duty or upon which the whole or any portion of the Customs duties have been remitted or refunded under the preceding articles 4 and 5 shall be sold, the person selling the same shall be bound to apprise the Collector of Customs of the quantity, weight, description, and value of such goods, and shall at the same time pay into the hands of the Collector the amount of Customs duties leviable on the same goods.

Duty on Wines according to strength to affect Wines shipped on or before the 15th. December.

7.—Provided that the item in the Schedule of Duties (B) hereunto annexed imposing an additional duty on certain Wines according to their strength shall not apply to Wines shipped on or before the 15th. December 1895.

Commencement of Ordinance.

8.—This Ordinance shall come into force on the day of its publication in the Government Gazette.

Schedule A to Ordinance No. 29 of 1895.

No. of Law.	Title.	Extent of repeal.
Ord. No. 17 of 1881 ...	To increase the import and license duties on Opium.	Article 1 modified by substituting a duty of twenty-two rupees and forty-four rupees per kilogram respectively, in lieu of a duty of twenty rupees and forty rupees as therein mentioned.
Ord. No. 5 of 1886 ...	To abolish Quay Dues and to substitute Customs Duties in lieu thereof.	The whole Ordinance.
Ord. No. 16 of 1886 ...	To substitute amended Schedules for the Schedules annexed to Ord. No. 5 of 1886, entitled "An Ordinance to abolish Quay Dues, and to substitute Customs Duties in lieu thereof.	The whole Ordinance.
Ord. No. 7 of 1887 ...	To amend the law permitting and regulating the importation and sale of Gandia.	Article 7 modified by substituting a duty of twenty two rupees per kilogram in lieu of the duty of twenty rupees as therein provided.
Ord. No. 34 of 1888 ...	To exempt from Customs Dues Tobacco grown in Rodrigues.	Article 2 only.
Ord. No. 20 of 1890 ...	To provide additional ways and means for meeting the public expenditure of this Colony up to the end of the year 1891.	Item 1 of Article 1 only.
Ord. No. 29 of 1890 ...	To provide for the levying of Customs Duty according to weight, measurement or number, on certain articles now liable to duty according to value.	The whole Ordinance.
Ord. No. 12 of 1893 ...	To increase the Import duty on Fireworks and to impose a licence duty on Manufacturers of Fireworks.	Article 1 only.
Ord. No. 20 of 1893 ...	To provide additional ways and means for meeting the Public Expenditure of the Colony up to the end of the year 1894.	The whole Ordinance.
Ord. No. 17 of 1894 ...	To provide additional ways and means for meeting the Public Expenditure of the Colony up to the end of the year 1895.	The whole of the unrepealed part of the Ordinance.
Ord. No. 26 of 1894 ...	To amend Schedule A of Ordinance No. 16 of 1886.	The whole Ordinance.

Schedule B. to Ordinance No. 29 *of* 1895.

(Consolidated Customs' Tariff).

IMPORTS.

No.	Description of Goods.	Duty how chargeable.	Rate of duty. Rs.	c.
1	Ale, Beer, Porter, Cider and Perry.—In Casks ...	per hectolitre ...	7	85
	In Bottles	per doz. bottles, each bottle not to exceed one lit.	1	20
		per doz. bottles, each bottle not to exceed 5 decilitres ...		60
2	Almonds	per 100 kilos ...	3	85
3	Anchors and Grapnels	do. ...	1	65
4	Animals ... Dogs	per head ...	6	05
	Asses, Horses, Mules	do. ...		60
	Cattle and Oxen	do. ...		25
	Other live stock	do. ...		10
5	Animal Charcoal	per 1,000 kilos ...		30
6	Arrowroot	per 100 kilos ...	2	75
7	Asphaltum	per 1,000 kilos ...	1	40
8	Assafœtida	per 100 kilos ...	7	...
9	Bacon, Hams, Sausages and Tongues ...	do. ...	5	...
10	Bags, Pockets linen (empty)	per 100 packets ...		80
	,, Vacoa & Madagascar Straw (empty) ...	per 100 bags ...		10
	,, of all other descriptions (empty)	do. ...	1	20
11	Bark	per 1,000 kilos ...	11	...
12	Barley	per 100 kilos ...	1	...
	do. pearl	do. ...	2	85
13	Beans	do. ...	1	...
14	Beef and Pork, salted	do. ...	2	...
	Beer see Ale.			
15	Biscuits (not sweetened)	per 100 kilos ...	1	10
16	Bitumen	per 1,000 kilos ...	1	40
	Blue Prussian (see Indigo).			
17	Bran	per 100 kilos ...	...	80
18	Brassware	do. ...	12	10
19	Bread	do. ...	1	...
20	Bricks and Tiles	per 100 bricks or titles ...	...	10
21	Brimstone or Sulphur common	per 100 kilos ...	...	70
	refined	do. ...	1	30
	Bungs, see Corks.			
22	Bunting	per metre ...	...	15
23	Butter, Margarine or any other substance sold or used as butter...	per 100 kilos ...	4	50
24	Camphor ... crude	do. ...	9	...
	refined & in powder	do. ...	12	50
25	Candles ... parafine	do. ...	3	...
	sperm	do. ...	3	...
	wax	do. ...	10	...
	composition and all other sorts ...	do. ...	3	...
26	Canvas...	do. ...	3	30
27	Caoutchou (manufactured)	do. ...	18	...
28	Caps (percussion)...	per 1000 caps ...	...	20
29	Capsules (bottling)	per 100 capsules ...	1	10
30	Cardamonds (common)	per 100 kilos ...	2	30
	do. (small)	do. ...	33	...
31	Cards, playing	ad valorem ...	25 o/o	
32	Cartridges... empty	per 100 cartridges ...	...	20
	loaded	do. ...	...	25
33	Casks, empty, old or new	per cask ...	...	55
34	Cement	per 100 kilos ...	...	30
	Cider (see Ale)			
35	Cinnamon	per 100 kilos ...	3	...

No.	Description of Goods.	Duty how chargeable.	Rate of duty. Rs.	c.
36	Charcoal	per 100 kilos ...	...	10
37	Cheese...	do. ...	5	...
38	Chillies	do. ...	2	...
	Chocolate (see Cocoa)			
39	Choorah	per 100 kilos ...	...	70
40	Cloves	do. ...	5	...
41	Clay, pipe and fire...	per 1,000 kilos ...	5	...
42	Coals, Coke and Patent Fuel	do. ...	...	55
43	Cocoa and Chocolate	per 100 kilos ...	13	20
44	Cocoanuts	per 100 cocoanuts ...	...	05
45	Coffee	per 100 kilos ...	5	...
46	Coir fibre	do. ...	...	85
	Coke (see Coals)			
47	Copper old	per 100 kilos ...	3	...
	sheets, bars, bolts, nails, &c., (red) ...	do. ...	8	80
	do. (yellow metal)	do. ...	4	40
48	Copperah or Poonac	per 100 kilos ...		10
49	Cordage ... Coir	do. ...	2	...
	do. oiled	do. ...	4	10
	Hemp	do. ...	2	20
	do. oiled	do. ...	5	...
50	Corks and bungs	per 1000 ...		55
51	Corn flour	per 100 kilos ...	5	...
52	Cotton ... Wool	do. ...	1	90
	Wick	do. ...	2	75
	Waste	do. ...	1	95
	Cutch (see Gambier)			
53	Detonators	per 1000 ...	5	...
54	Dholl	per 100 kilos ...	1	10
55	Dye wood	per 1000 kilos ...	11	...
56	Dynamite	per 100 kilos ...	14	...
57	Eggs (fresh or preserved)	per 100 ...	2	20
58	Felt sheathing	per 100 sheets ...		60
59	Fibre, jute, rafia and all other sorts	per 100 kilos ...	3	30
60	Firewood	per 2 cubic metres ...		15
61	Fireworks	ad valorem ...	16	50 o/o
62	Fish ... dried or salted	per 100 kilos ...	1	00
	pickled	do. ...	1	35
63	Fruits ... dried (except cocoanuts)	do. ...	2	50
	and vegetables (fresh)	per pkge of 50 kilos ...		25
64	Gambier or Cutch...	per 100 kilos ...	2	20
65	Gandia...	per kilogram ...	22	...
66	Ghee	per 100 kilos ...	12	...
67	Ginger, dry	do. ...	1	65
68	Glass ... window	per 100 metres ...	2	20
	bottles, empty	per 100 bottles ...		10
69	Glue	per 100 kilos ...	3	30
70	Gram	do. ...	1	10
	Grapnels (see Anchors)			
71	Grease, Cart	do. ...	1	10
72	Gum ... arabic	do. ...	2	20
	copal	do. ...	8	80
73	Gunpowder ... sporting	do. ...	6	...
	blasting	do. ...	1	10
	Hams (see Bacon)			
74	Hay and Straw	do. ...		15
75	Hemp, undressed	do. ...	2	75
76	Hides ... raw and salted	do. ...	3	30
	tanned	do. ...	4	95
77	Hogslard	do. ...	4	15
78	Honey	per hectolitre ...	3	00
79	Hops	per 100 kilos ...	1	65
80	Horns	per 1000 horns ...		85

No.	Description of Goods.	Duty how chargeable.	Rate of duty. Rs.	c.
81	Horse hair	per 100 kilos ...	5	50
82	India rubber (manufactured)...	per 100 kilos ...	17	60
83	Indigo, Prussian Blue, Ultramarine Blue and any like preparation sold or used for laundry purposes.	per kilo ...	1	10
84	Iron, wire netting and galvanized	per 100 kilos ...	3	...
	do. Pig	per 1000 kilos ...	2	20
	do. Bars, hoops, pipes, wire, nails, galvanized sheets ridging chains &c....	per 1000 kilos ...	8	...
85	Jams	per 100 kilos ...	3	50
86	Jellies	do. ...	3	50
87	Lead, sheet and pipes	do. ...	1	40
88	Lead, shot	do. ...	3	...
89	Leather, sole	do. ...	8	...
90	Lemon juice	per hectolitre ...	3	30
91	Lentils...	per 100 kilos ...	...	65
92	Lime	do. ...	...	20
93	Lime juice	per hectolitre ...	3	30
94	Macaroni	per 100 kilos ...	3	30
95	Mace	per kilo ...	...	60
96	Machinery and Apparatus for the manufacture and improvement of Sugar, Rum or other produce of the Colony	per 1000 kilos ...	1	10
	Do. when using the Crane	do. ...	2	10
97	Maize	per 100 kilos ...	...	80
98	Malt	do. ...	1	65
99	Manure of all sorts; and the following substances when imported for the purpose of being used in the preparation of Manures, or of other Colonial produce, or as Disinfectants ... ... 1. Ammoniacal Liquor ... ... 2. Bones, Bonedust, Bone oil and Dissolved bones... 3. Carbolic Acid... ... ... 4. Carbonate of Baryte ... ... 5. Chloride of Lime and of Potassium ... ... 6. Chloride of Manganese ... ... 7. Chloride of Soda, Solution of Soda ... ... 8. Chloride of Zinc ... ... 9. Coal and Wood Soot ... ... 10. Dried Muscular Flesh and Dried Blood ... 11. Ether ... ... 12. Fish and other substances damaged and condemned by the Customs Sanitary Officers as fit for Manure only ... ... 13. Lime, Carbonate of Lime, Sulphate of Lime or Gypsum, Phosphate and Superphosphate of Lime ... ... 14. Nitrates, Silicates and Carbonates of Potash and Soda ... ... 15. Perchloride of Iron ... ... 16. Permanganate of Potash... ... ... 17. Phosphate of Soda .. .. 18. Phosphoric Acid (Solid) ... ... 19. Substances imported by Agriculturists and to be used in the destruction of insects or other parasites prejudicial to agriculture. 20. Sulphate of Iron ... ... 21. Sulphate and Muriate of Ammonia and other Ammoniacal Salts ... ... 22. Sulphate of Potash, Sulphate of Potassium ... 23. Sulphate of Zinc ... ... 24. Sulphuric Acid ... ... 25. Urate and Sulphurated Urine	per 1000 kilos ...	...	30

No.	Description of Goods.	Duty how chargeable.	Rate of duty. Rs.	c.
	Margarine (see Butter)			
100	Marmalade	per 100 kilos ...	3	50
101	Matches	per gross, on boxes containing each not more than 100 matches and a proportional duty on boxes containing more than 100 matches. ...	1	10
102	Mats and Matting...	per 100 kilos ...	2	75
103	Molasses	do. ...	1	10
104	Moss	do. ...	10	...
105	Mustard (prepared)	do. ...	3	30
106	Nuts ... Areca	do. ...	2	...
	Nuts ... do. (boiled)	do. ...	5	...
	Nuts ... Gall	do. ...	2	50
107	Nuts ... Pistachio	do. ...	1	10
	Nuts ... Walnuts	do. ...	3	60
	Nuts ... All other sorts	do. ...	2	50
108	Nutmegs	do. ...	4	50
109	Oakum	do. ...	3	30
110	Oatmeal	do. ...	1	65
111	Oats	do. ...	1	10
112	Oils Castor	do. ...	3	30
	Oils Gingely, Mustard and Pistachio	do. ...	2	75
	Oils Cocoanut (when not imported from the Oil Islands.	per hectolitre ...	1	65
	Oils *Cocoanut (when imported from the Oil Islands)	do. ...	...	06
	Oils Olive in cases	per case not exceeding 12 litres ...	...	55
	Oils Neatsfoot	per hectolitre ...	4	...
	Oils Petroleum	do. ...	3	50
	Oils Colza	do. ...	2	75
	Oils Linseed	do. ...	1	95
	Oils All other sorts (except perfumed) ...	do. ...	2	75
113	Opium Crude	per kilogramme ...	22	...
	Opium Refined	do. ...	44	...
114	Paper Cigarette	per kilogram (gross weight)	4	40
	Patent Fuel (see Coals)	......		
115	Peas	per 100 kilos ...	1	...
116	Pepper White	do. ...	16	50
	Pepper Black	do. ...	11	...
	Perry (see Ale)	......		
117	Pitch	per 100 kilos ...	...	55
118	Plaster of Paris	do. ...	4	10
	Pockets (empty see Bags)	......		
119	Pollard	per 100 kilos ...	1	...
	Poonac (see Copperah)	......		
	Pork salted (see Beef)	......		
	Porter (see Ale)	......		
	Prussian Blue (see Indigo)	......		
120	Rabannahs (not exceeding 2 metres per 100 pieces each)	per 100 pieces ...	1	65
121	Rattans	per 100 kilos ...	...	55
122	Rice	do. ...	...	60
123	Rope coir	do. ...	2	...
	Rope do. oiled	do. ...	4	10
	Rope hemp	do. ...	2	20
	Rope do. oiled	do. ...	5	...
124	Rosin	do. ...	...	75
125	Sago	do. ...	1	...
126	Salt	do. ...	1	...

* In addition to a sum of Rs. 4,000 paid under Ordinance No. 41 of 1875 by the proprietors of the Oil Islands.

No.	Description of Goods.	Duty how chargeable.	Rate of duty. Rs.	c.
127	Sand, moulding	per 1000 kilos ...	...	85
	Sausages (see Bacon)			
128	Seeds { Aniseed	per 100 kilos ...	3	...
	Seeds { Coriander...	do. ...	3	...
	Seeds { Gingely, Linseed, Mustard, Metty, Millet, Poppy and all others... ...	do. ...	1	...
129	Shooks, per bundle containing not more than sufficient to make one barrel, cask or tierce (tierçon,) and a proportional duty on bundles containing more than the above quantity	per bundle ...	...	55
130	Skins, sheep and goat (tanned)	per 100 kilos ...	6	60
131	Slates and Stones for building and paving ...	per 100 ...	...	15
132	Soap (ordinary not including scented)	per 100 kilos ...	1	40
133	Soda, caustic	do. ...	...	80
134	Solder	do. ...	3	85
135	Spirits, plain or compounded, of any strength not exceeding proof according to Syke's Hydrometer, and a further proportional duty for any greater strength	per litre ...	1	20
136	Starch	per 100 kilos ...	...	85
137	Steel, unwrought	do. ...	2	20
	Stones, for building and paving (see Slates) ...			
	Straw (see Hay)			
138	Sugar ... { raw	do. ...	1	65
	Sugar ... { refined and Sugar candy	do. ...	5	25
139	Sulphate { of iron	do. ...	...	55
	Sulphate { of copper	do. ...	1	65
	Sulphur (see Brimstone)			
140	Tallow...	do. ...	2	20
141	Tamarinds	do. ...	...	75
142	Tapioca	do. ...	1	65
143	Tar	do. ...	...	55
144	Tea	per kilogram ...	...	10
	Tiles (see Bricks)...			
145	Tin Plates	per 100 kilos ...	1	40
146	Tin Slabs	per 100 kilos ...	8	80
147	Tobacco ... { Manufactured	per kilogram ...	2	45
	Tobacco ... { Unmanufactured	do. ...	1	85
	Tobacco ... { Unmanufactured, grown and produced in any of the Dependencies of Mauritius, except Seychelles ...	do. ...	...	35
	Tobacco ... { Cigars and Snuff	do. ...	3	30
	Tongues (see Bacon)			
148	Treacle	per 100 kilos ...	1	10
149	Turmeric	do. ...	2	...
150	Turpentine	per hectolitre ...	2	20
151	Twines ... { hemp	per 100 kilos ...	2	45
	Twines ... { all other sorts...	do. ...	1	65
152	Vanilla	per kilogram ...	1	65
153	Varnish (all kinds)	per hectolitre ...	5	50
	Vegetables fresh (see fruits)			
154	Vermicelli	per 100 kilos ...	3	30
155	Vinegar	per hectolitre ...	1	40
156	Wax ... { bees	per 100 kilos ...	6	60
	Wax ... { sealing and bottling	do. ...	2	20
157	Wheat	do. ...	...	60
158	Wheat Flour	do. ...	...	90

No.	Description of Goods.	Duty how chargeable.	Rate of duty.
			Rs. c.
159	Wines — In Casks	per hectolitre and a further duty of R. 1.20 per degree, or fraction of a degree, of Alcohol and per hectolitre above 18 degrees, according to Gay Lussac's alcohometer contained in *Bordeaux*, *Provence* and similar wines. Provided this duty do not affect Wines shipped on or before the 15th. of December 1895. (See Article 7 of the Ordinance.)	7 65
	In Bottles	per doz. bottles, each bottle, not to exceed 1 litre	1 50
		per doz. half bottles, each half bottle not to exceed 5 decilitres	... 75
	do. Sparkling — Champagne and others	Per bottle not exceeding 1 litre	... 10
		Per half bottle not exceeding 5 decilitres	... 05
160	All Goods, wares and merchandize not otherwise charged with duty, and not mentioned above, or not specially exempted, shall be liable to an *ad valorem* Duty of per centum	....	10 o/o

EXPORTS.

No.	Description of Goods.	Duty how chargeable.	Rate of duty.
			Rs. c.
1	Sugar, the produce of Mauritius	per 100 kilos	... 30
2	Goods exported from Bond	per 1,000 kilos or per ton metric measure.	1 ...
3	Goods landed at this Port in transit for other ports		
4	Goods landed from vessels in distress, and reshipped..		

CRANE DUES.

For the use of the Crane for lifting heavy goods (Except in the case of machinery imported and paying duty when the charge is R. 1.00 per 1,000 kilos).	per 1,000 kilos	2 ...

Schedule C.

EXEMPTIONS.

No.	Description of Goods.
1	Ballast, when the same consists of Sand or Stone.
2	Glass bottles, imported full, (except fancy bottles or decanters).
3	Instruments for Regimental Bands.
4	Ice.
5	School Materials for the use of Free Schools.
6	Articles imported for the use of His Excellency the Governor.
7	Articles of Civil, Naval and Military Uniform, intended for the personal use of the Importer.
8	Provisions and Stores of every description imported or supplied from Bond for the Colonial Government, or, under special authority from the Governor, for the use of Ships of war of Foreign nations.
9	Wearing Apparel, Luggage, or any instrument intended for Professional use, if it be the property of a person coming to the Colony, and if it arrives within *three months* before or after the arrival of such person.
10	All goods upon which the full amount of Duty shall have been paid on their first importation into Mauritius, legally exported hence and afterwards returned: provided such goods shall be returned within three years from the date of their exportation, and it be proved, to the satisfaction of the Collector of Customs that they are the idential goods exported from Mauritius; and provided the property of such goods continue in the person by whom or on whose account the same were exported.
11	Objects and Specimens (Animal, Mineral and Vegetable) illustrative of Natural History, including live plants and vegetable productions connected with the study of Botany.
12	Animals and Goods (except Oil, Spirits and Tobacco) the produce of any of the Dependencies of Mauritius other than Seychelles.
13	Books and Music.
14	Coin and Bullion.
15	Leeches.
16	Seeds intended for Agricultural and horticultural purposes.
17	Poultry.
18	Goods imported into Mauritius by the proper Military authorities for the public use of Her Majesty's land Forces (Ordinance 9 of 1887).
19	Goods in Transit transhipped direct from vessel to vessel.

Ordinance No. 30 of 1895.

To amend Ordinance No. 8 of 1869 and to repeal Ordinance No. 26 of 1884-85.

(*27th. December* 1895.)

Whereas it is expedient to amend Ordinance 8 of 1869 and to repeal Ordinance No. 26 of 1884-85;

Be it therefore enacted by the Governor, with the advice and consent of the Council of Government, as follows:

Short Title. 1.—This Ordinance may be cited as "The Game Law Amendment Ordinance, 1895."

Addition to Section 9 of Ordinance No. 8 of 1869. 2.—The following paragraph shall be added to and read with Section 9 of Ordinance No. 8 of 1869;

Every person offending against the provisions of this article and the preceding article shall, when the offence is committed between the hours of eight in the evening and four in the morning incur a penalty not less than one hundred Rupees (Rs. 100) and not more than five hundred Rupees (Rs. 500); such offender shall besides be liable to imprisonment for a term of not less than one month and not exceeding six months with labor.

Amendment of Section 11 of Ordinance No. 8 of 1869. 3.—Paragraph 1 of Article 11 of Ordinance No. 8 of 1869 is amended by substituting to the expression: "15th. of May following inclusive."

Forfeitures. 4.—Article 29 of Ordinance No. 8 of 1869 is hereby repealed and in lieu and stead thereof the following shall be read:

Besides the fines or penalties provided for by this Ordinance for the punishment of any offence against the provisions of articles 8, 9 11 and 12, the conviction of any offender shall carry with it the forfeiture and destruction of any gun, net, gin, snare, or other engine and of any game found in his possession at the time of the offence.

Such destruction shall take place in presence of the District Magistrate, and, in the case of a gun, shall mean the destruction of the stock, of the lock and of the barrel.

Repeal clause. 5.—Ordinance No. 26 of 1884-85, entitled "An Ordinance to give to Magistrates the power of awarding penalties less than the minimum penalties fixed by Ordinance No. 8 of 1869 "To amend and consolidate the laws on Game" is hereby repealed.

Commencement of Ordinance. 6.—This Ordinance shall comme into force on the day of its publication in the Government Gazette.

Ordinance No. 31 of 1895. *

To provide for the appointment of a Board of Commissioners for the Villages of Beau Bassin and Rose Hill.

Passed in Council on Friday 20.12.95.

Ordinance No. 32 of 1895. *

To provide for the appointment of a Board of Commissioners for the Town of Quatre Bornes.

Passed in Council on Friday 20.12.95.

* These Ordinances will come into force on a day to be fixed by Proclamation.

PROCLAMATIONS FOR 1895.

No. 1. To appoint Commissioners for the Town of Curepipe ... ... 4th. January 1895.

" 2. To appoint The Honorable A. P. Ambrose, The Honorable L. de Rochecouste, Edouard Montocchio, Esquire, and the Engineer and General Manager of Railways to be Members of the Railway Board for 1895 ... ... 4th. January 1895.

" 3. To put in force Ordinance No. 20 of 1894, entitled : An Ordinance "To amend the law relating to the Mare aux Vacoas Water "Work Supply." ... ... 11th. January 1895.

" 4. To authorize the renewal of the Limited Liability Company (Société Anonyme) known under the name of "The Mauritius Fire Insurance Company" and certain modifications in its Bye Laws. 25th. January 1895.

" 5. To put in force the Order in Council dated 12th. December 1894 ... 28th. January 1895.

" 6. To hold a District Court on the premises of the woman Sunkree in the village of Poudre d'Or ... ... 4th. February 1894.

" 7. To modify the boundaries of the village of Coromandel ... ... 5th. February 1895.

" 8. To put in force Ordinance No. 22 of 1894 entitled an "Ordinance "To constitute the Association called the Mauritius Civil Ser- "vice Mutual Aid Association into an Anonymous Society." ... 14th. February 1895.

" 9. To authorize Mamode Aly Tchian Miathiane to bear the name of David Nathaniel Martin ... ... 14th. February 1895.

" 10. Prorogation of the Council of Government until 9th. April 1895 ... 26th. February 1895.

" 11. To authorize Jean Baptiste Vyavoory to bear the name of Jean Baptiste Ramin... ... ... 27th. February 1895.

" 12. To put in force Ordinance No. 30 of 1894 entitled "An Ordinance "to provide for the carrying out of drainage works referred to "in Ordinance No. 15 of 1893." ... ... 8th. March 1895.

" 13. To authorize the formation and establishment as a Limited Liability Company (Société Anonyme), of the Hammond's Co-operative Stores." ... ... 21st. March 1895.

" 14. Prorogation of the Council of Government until 7th. May 1895 ... 6th, April 1895.

" 15. To authorize Vassoodeven Tirveedian to bear the name of Vassoodeven Pinagapany ... ... 3rd. April 1895.

" 16. To place the Estates "Réunion" and "Henrietta" within the limits of the Curepipe Division of the District Court of Plaines Wilhems... ... ... 17th. April 1895.

" 17. To place the Estates "Réunion" and "Henrietta" within the limits of the Curepipe Division of the Stipendiary Court of Plaines Wilhems ... ... 17th. April 1895.

No. 18. To fix the 1st. of May 1895 as the date when the Drainage Works are to begin ... ... 26th. April 1895.

„ 19. To authorize Ahmun to bear the name of Ahmun Chanpow ... 29th. April 1895.

„ 20. To declare the Estate " Bel Etang " to be within the District of Moka ... ... 3rd. May 1895.

„ 21. Amending the Letters Patent dated 22nd. March 1879 constituting the Office of Governor and Commander-in-Chief of the Colony of Mauritius and its Dependencies ... ... 14th. May 1895.

„ 22. To authorize Louis Elysée Roussety to bear the name of Louis Elysée ... ... 28th. May 1895.

„ 23. To authorize Giles Dominique Dorothée and Victor François Xavier Dorothée to bear the name of Jules Walter, and Victor François Xavier Walter respectively ... ... 28th. May 1895.

„ 24. To authorize certain modifications made to the Bye laws of the Limited Liability Company (Société Anonyme), named " The Ile d'Ambre Sugar Estates Company Limited ." ... ... 12th June 1895.

„ 25 To authorize Louis Henry Le Merle, and Daniel Edmond Le Merle to bear the name of Louis Henry de Chapuiset Le Merle and Daniel Edmond de Chapuiset Le Merle respectively ... ... 25th. June 1895.

„ 26 To grant a charter of Incorporation to the " Société des Hospitaliers Sauveteurs de Maurice " ... ... 5th. July 1895.

„ 27 To exempt Mr. Ernest Brine, Resident Engineer, Mare aux Vacoas Water Works from being inscribed on the Jury List, or called on to serve on any Jury ... ... 22nd. August 1895.

„ 28 To order that Monday the 26th. day of August 1895 be observed as a Bank and Office Holiday ... ... 23rd. August 1895.

„ 29 To exempt the Officials and Operators of the Eastern and South African Telegraph Company Limited from serving on the Jury. 6th September 1895.

„ 30 To put in force Ordinance No. 17 of 1895. Entitled an Ordinance to render permanent the Posts of Crown Prosecutors, and to define more clearly the powers and duties of those offices ... ... 10th. September 1895.

„ 31 To protect the shooting killing taking in any place and also the purchase, sale or exhibition for sale in any public place of certain birds during five years from 24th. October 1895 ... ... 17th. September 1895

„ 32 To put in force Ordinance No. 4 of 1895 entitled " An Ordinance to provide for the granting of pensions compensations and allowances to the officers of the Loan Office ... ... 1st October 1895.

„ 33. To authorize the renewal of the Limited Liability Company (Société Anonyme) known under the name of " The Albion Dock Company and certain modifications in the Bye laws ... ... 1st. October 1895.

„ 34. To authorize the formation and establishment as a Limited Liability Company (Société Anonyme) of the " Imprimerie Co-opérative " 16th. October 1895.

„ 35. To authorize the formation and establishment as a Limited Liability Company (Société Anonyme) of the " Librairie and Papeterie des Habitants." ... ... 29th. October 1895.

No. 36. To put in force Ordinance No. 32 of 1894—95 entitled "An Ordinance to amend the constitution and the function of the General Board of Health, to create a Medical and Health Department and to amend and consolidate the laws relating to the Public Health." ... ... 8th. November 1895.

,, 37. To authorize Mondésir Célina to bear the name of Mondésir Bagrin. 8th. November 1895.

,, 38. To authorize certain modifications in the bye laws of the Limited Liability Company (designated in the law of Mauritius "Société Anonyme") The Engrais Mauricien Company Limited ... ... 8th. November 1895.

,, 39. To authorize the Honorable Hamilton Stein, Consul for the German Empire to catch one dozen pairs of birds called "Martins" ... 12th. November 1895.

,, 40. To authorize the formation and establishment as a Limited Liability Company (designated in the law of Mauritius "Société Anonyme") of the Immoveable Co-operative Society ... ... 27th. November 1895.

,, 41. To exempt the Chief Fireman, the Officers, Sub-Officers and Enginemen of the Municipal Fire Brigade from serving on the Jury ... ... 28th. November 1895.

,, 42. To put in force Ordinance No. 24 of 1851 entitled "An Ordinance for securing in this Colony the rights on works entitled to copyright in the United Kingdom... ... ... 13th, December 1895.

,, 43. To authorize the formation and establishment as a Limited Liability Company (Société Anonyme) of the "Mon Rocher" Sugar Estate Company Limited ... ... 18th. December 1895.

,, 44. To authorize the formation and establishment as a Limited Liability Company (Société Anonyme) of "The Société de L'Express" ... 19th. December 1895.

" 45. Prorogation of the Council of Government until the 4th. January 1896 ... ... 20th. December 1895.

,, 46. To To fix the boundaries of the villages mentioned in the Schedule annexed to the Pas Géométriques Ordinance 1895 ... ... 20th. December 1895.

GOVERNMENT NOTICES FOR 1895.

No. 21 of 1895.

Amended Article 3 of the revised conditions and Syllabus of the Government and Aided Schools' Scholarship Examinations.

Amended Article 3 of the revised conditions and Syllabus of the Government and Aided Schools' Scholarship Examinations.

3. Candidates must have attended a Government or an Aided School for a period of not less than two years immediately preceding the thirty first of January of the year following that in which the examination is held. None will be eligible for the Senior Scholarship Examination who shall be more than 16 years of age and none for the Junior Scholarship Examination who shall be more than 12 years of age on the last day of the year in which the examination is held.

Passed in Executive Council at a meeting held on the 7th. day of December 1894.

WM. C. RAE,
Clerk of the Executive Council

Laid on the Table of the Council of Government at a meeting held on the 11th. December 1894 and not disallowed within one monther after.

WM. C. RAE,

Clerk of the Council of Government.

No. 22 of 1895.

Amended Article 73 of the Prison Regulations published under Government Notice No. 16 of 1891.

PRISON REGULATIONS.

Amended Article 73 of the Prison Regulations published under Government Notice No. 16 of 1891.

False accusations of Prisoners. 73.—Any prisoner who shall bring any false and malicious accusation against a prison officer or against the Medical Officer attached to a Prison shall be dealt with under Article 37 of the abovenamed Ordinance.

Passed in Executive Council at a meeting hold on the 7th. day of December 1894.

WM. C. RAE,

Clerk of the Executive Council.

Laid on the Table of the Council of Government at a meeting held on the 11th, December 1894 and neither annulled nor amended at any of the three meetings held thereafter.

WM. C. RAE,

Clerk to the Council of Government.

No. 32 of 1895.

Order in Council amending the Order in Council of 13th. April 1831, by fixing Rs. 10,000 instead of £1,000 as the amount or value of the property in respect of which an appeal may be made from the Supreme Court of Mauritius.

At the Court at Windsor.

The 12th. day of December 1894.

PRESENT :

The Queen's Most Excellent Majesty.
Lord Steward.
Marquess of Ripon.
Mr. Secretary Fowler.
Mr. Arnold Morley.
Sir John Thompson.

Whereas by an Order of His late Majesty King William the Fourth in Council, dated the 13th. day of April 1831, it was ordered, among other things, that appeals might be made to His Majesty in Council, His heirs and successors, against any final judgment, sentence, or decree of the Court of the Colony of Mauritius, then styled the Cour d'Appel, subject to the rules, regulations, and limitations obtained in the said Order :

And whereas by an Ordinance of the Legislature of Mauritius, No. 2 of 1850, which was ratified, confirmed, and finally enacted by an Order of Her Majesty in Council, dated the 23rd.

day of October 1851, it was enacted that the said Cour d'Appel should be called the Supreme Court of the Colony of Mauritius :

And whereas by the said Order in Council of the 23rd. day of October 1851, it was ordered that all appeals which should be made to Her Majesty in Council from any sentence, judgment, decree, rule, order, or other act of the said Supreme Court should, until otherwise ordered, remain and be made subject to such rules, and regulations, and limitations as were prescribed by the said Order of the 13th. day of April 1831 :

And whereas it is expedient to amend the said Order of the 13th. day of April 1831 :

Now therefore, Her Majesty, by and with the advice of Her Privy Council, doth order and declare, and it is hereby ordered and declared, as follows :—

1. The said Order in Council of the 13th. day of April 1831 shall be read and construed and have effect as if the words and figures "ten thousand rupees (Rs. 10,000)" had been inserted therein in substitution for the words and figures one thousand pounds (£1,000) sterling."

2. This Order shall apply to judgments, sentences, decrees, and orders given, pronounced or made before the day on which it comes into operation as to which the time for applying for leave to appeal limited by the said Order of the 13th. day of April 1831 has not then expired.

3. This Order shall come into operation from such day as shall be fixed by a Proclamation of the Governor of Mauritius.

And the Most Honourable the Marquess of Ripon, K. G., one of Her Majesty's Principal Secretaries of State, is to give the necessary directions herein accordingly.

C. L. PEEL.

No. 53 of 1895.

Levying of a rate of ½ o/o on the value of properties assessed in the town of Curepipe.. 19th. February 1895.

No. 72 of 1895.

Revised Regulations for the Examination of and grant of Certificates, to Masters and Mates of British Ships.. 18th. March 1895.

No. 82 of 1895.

Appointment of Mr. E. Brine, Resident Engineer of the Mare-aux-Vacoas Water Works to be the Drainage Authority.................................... 27th. March 1895.

No. 92 of 1895.

Special Rates for the conveyance of Goods by Railway .... 5th. April 1895.

No. 98 of 1895.

Parcels Post Convention between the Cape of Good Hope and Mauritius. 8th. April 1895.

No. 99 of 1895.

Transmission of Postal Parcels to British Bachuanaland, the South African Republic the Orange Free States and Mashonaland .... 8th. April 1895.

No. 109 of 1895.

Resignation of Mr. Maurice Maingard as a Notary Public for Port Louis. 24th. April 1895.

No. 110 of 1895.

Regulations for the Water-Supply and for the Distribution thereof ..... 25th. April 1895.

No. 111 of 1895.

Appointment of Mr. Edgar de Robillard to be a Notary Public for Port Louis .... 26th. April 1895.

No. 127 of 1895.

Letters Patent amending Letters Patent dated 22nd. March 1879, constituting the office of Governor and Commander-in-Chief of the Colony of Mauritius and its Dependencies.

Mauritius.

General.

Downing Street,

23rd. February 1895.

Sir,

With reference to the last paragraph of my despatch No. 168 of the 9th. July and to Mr. King Harman's despatch No. 227 of the 10th. of July 1894, I have the honour to transmit to you Letters Patent passed under the Great Seal of the United Kingdom amending the Letters Patent of the 22nd. of March 1879 constituting the Office of Governor and Commander-in-Chief of the Colony of Mauritius and its Dependencies.

These Letters Patent have been passed for the purpose of removing the difficulties which have arisen as to the administration of the Government of Mauritius after the Governor has arrived at Seychelles on his return from leave of absence and before his arrival in Mauritius.

I have, &c.,

RIPON.

Governor Sir H. E. H. Jerningham, K.C.M.G.,

&c., &c., &c.

MAURITIUS.

Letters Patent passed under the Great Seal of the United Kingdom, amending Letters Patent dated 22nd. March 1879, constituting the Office of Governor and Commander-in-Chief of the Colony of Mauritius and its Dependencies.

Letters Patent dated 21st. February 1895.

VICTORIA by the Grace of God of the United Kingdom of Great Britain and Ireland, Queen Defender of the Faith, Empress of India :

To all to whom these Presents shall come,

Greeting.

Preamble.

Recites Letters Patent of 22nd. March 1879.

Whereas We did, by certain Letters Patent under the Great Seal of Our United Kingdom of Great Britain and Ireland, bearing date at Westminster the Twenty-second day of March 1879, (hereinafter referred to as the Principal Letters Patent), constitute the office of Governor and Commander-in-Chief in and over Our Island of Mauritius and the Dependencies there of which said Island and its Dependencies are in the Principal Letters Patent and hereinafter referred to as the Colony :

And whereas We are minded to amend the Principal Letters Patent ;

Now know ye that We do hereby declare Our will and pleasure, and direct and ordain as follows :

Clauses XIII and XIV of Letters Patent of 22nd. March 1879, revoked.

I. Clauses XIII. and XIV. of the Principal Letters Patent are hereby revoked and rescinded.

Succession to the Government.

Lieutenant Governor, &c., to take oaths of office.

Power, &c., of Administrator.

II. Whenever the office of Governor of the Colony is vacant, and whenever the Governor becomes incapable or is absent from the Colony, Our Lieutenant Governor of the Colony, or, if there shall be no such officer in the Colony, then such person or persons as We may appoint under Our Sign Manual and Signet, and in default of any such appointment the Senior Civil Member of the Council of Government shall during Our pleasure administer the Government of the Colony, first taking the oaths by the Principal Letters Patent directed to to be taken by the Governor in the manner therein prescribed, which being done We do hereby authorize, empower, and command Our Lieutenant Governor, or any other such Administrator as aforesaid, to do and execute during Our pleasure all things that belong to the office of Governor and Commander-in-Chief according to the tenor of Our said Principal Letters Patent, and according to any other Our Letters Patent for the time being in force relating to Our said Colony.

Proviso.

Absence on voyages to and from Dependencies not to be deemed absent from the Colony.

Provided always that when the Governor is on a voyage between any of the Islands under his Government, or is in any place at which he has landed in the course of any such voyage, he shall be deemed not to be absent from the Colony.

Administration of Government in the Island of Mauritius when Governor absent from the Island but not from the Colony.

III. Whenever the Governor shall be absent from the Island of Mauritius, but shall by virtue of Clause II. of these Letters Patent be deemed not to be absent from the Colony, then such person as the Governor may by Commission under the Public Seal of the Colony appoint, shall, and is hereby empowered and required to, exercise in the said Island during such absence such of the powers and authorities granted to the Governor by the Principal Letters Patent (except the power of granting a pardon or remission of sentence) as the Governor shall think fit to assign to him by such Commission, and if there shall be no person in the Island so appointed, the Senior Civil Member of the Council of Government shall, and is hereby empowered and required to, exercise in the said Island during such absence all the said powers and authorities (except as aforesaid).

Letters Patent to be construed with Letters Patent of 22nd. March 1879.

IV. These Letters Patent shall be construed as one with the Principal Letters Patent.

Power reserved to revoke, alter, or amend Letters Patent.

V. We do hereby reserve to Ourselves, Our heirs and successors, full power and authority, from time to time, to revoke, alter, and amend these Our Letters Patent as to Us or them shall seem meet.

Publication of Letters Patent.

VI. And We do direct and enjoin that these Our Letters Patent shall be read and proclaimed at such place or places within the Colony as the Governor shall think fit.

In witness whereof We have caused these Our Letters to be made Patent, Witness Ourself at Westminster, the Twenty-first day of February, in the Fifty-eighth year of Our Reign.

By Warrant under the Queen's Sign Manual.

MUIR MACKENZIE.

Letters Patent amending the Letters Patent constituting the Office of Governor and Commander-in-Chief, Mauritius.

No. 135 of 1895.

Regulations for the town of Curepipe framed in conformity with Art. 8 of Ordce. No. 12 of 1889.

Regulations for the Town of Curepipe framed in conformity with Art. 8 of Ord. No. 12 of 1889.

CHAPTER I.

Cadastre.

I.—A Cadastre of the immoveable properties in the Town of Curepipe shall be made to serve for the collecting of the taxes on the immoveable property situate within the limits of the said Town.

II.—The valuer appointed by the Board to make the said Cadastre shall immediately proceed to the estimation of each immoveable property.

III.—On the notice which shall be published for that purpose in four newspapers, all proprietors in Curepipe shall be bound to give every facility to the valuer of the Board on his examination of their immoveable properties and to furnish their title deeds, plans or other necessary information to arrive at an accurate evaluation.

IV.—The valuer shall estimate every immoveable property at its full and fair value, taking in consideration its locative value. Such estimation shall serve as the basis for the perception of the tax which shall be collected from the date which shall be fixed by a resolution of the Board.

V.—The valuer shall proceed to such estimation of the immoveable properties in conformity with Article 13 of Ordinance No. 12 of 1889.

VI.—The estimation of the Cadastre may, at all times, be revised according to the increas in the value of the properties, arising for new buildings and constructions, and to the decrease in the value caused by fire or other serious circumstances.

But the new estimation shall begin to have its effects in the next ensuing year only.

VII.—A penalty not exceeding one hundred Rupees shall be awarded against any person refusing to produce to the valuer his title deeds, plans or other necessary information to arrive at an accurate valuation of his property; or who shall make a false declaration of ownership of the said property.

CHAPTER II.

Management and maintenance of Roads.

VIII,—A fine not exceeding One hundred Rupees shall be awarded against:

1st. Any person who shall obstruct a public thoroughfare by leaving thereon any materials or things whatsover which may hinder or obstruct the free and safe passing on the same;

2nd. Any person who shall encroach on any street, footway or public thoroughfare by means of trees or bushes planted upon his property or by erecting any building, fence enclosure or work of any description, or who shall injure, fill up or obstruct any ditch or drain along any such street or thoroughfare, or shall dig on any such street or thoroughfare any ditch, or commit any other act by which any such street or thoroughfare may be injured or the level thereof altered;

3rd. Any person who shall neglect to place a light upon or to enclose the materials which he may have heaped up, or the excavation which he may have made in any street, road or public place with the sanction of the Board of Commissioners; and also any person who, without such sanction, shall make any such heap or excavation:

4th. Any person who shall with the authority of the Board construct or establish enclosures or make excavations on a public thoroughfare and who, after completion of the works shall not fill in the said excavations in such a manner as to restore the said thoroughfare to its original condition and to the satisfaction of the Town Architect;

5th. Any person who shall neglect or refuse to comply with the laws and regulations concerning public roads or streets;

6th. Any person who shall erect a privy along a public thoroughfare or in view thereof. without prejudice to the right of the Board to remove the said privy at the expense of the offender:

7th. Any person who shall place upon a window, balcony, or elsewhere, any articles the fall of which may hurt persons passing by:

8th. The owner or occupier of any premises who shall neglect to destroy weeds on the footway along his premises, if there be no footway along the premises, the owner or occupier shall be bound to keep clean at all times the slope extending from his enclosure (wall or hedge) down to the gutter or ditch exclusively:

9th. Any person occupying any property within the limits of the Town, or the proprietor, if the property be not occupied, who shall neglect or refuse to trim the hedges of bambous or other similar plants bordering on a street or public thoroughfare, so as not to encroach either on the footway, street, gutter, ditch, or thoroughfare, or in a perpendicular line to the inward edge of the footway, and to leave the footway, street, gutter, ditch or thoroughfare entirely free at all times;

10th. Any person who shall allow Bambous hedges, at any time to grow at a height of more than three metres from the level of the road, and the hedges of the "bambou flora, or bambou balai" (melica latifolia) now existing, at a height of more than two metres from the level of the road;

The Board in order to secure the cleanliness of the streets, footways and public thoroughfares of the Town, has fixed the following periods for the cutting of the hedges of Bambous or other plants within the limits of the Town of Curepipe : 1o. from April 1st. up to May 31st. and 2o. from September 1st. up to October 31st. Before or after the above periods the occupier or proprietor of any property shall be bound to remove immediately at his own expense the cuttings of his hedges ;

11th. Any person who shall not cause the trees growing on his premises and projecting on a public street or thoroughfare to be lopped, so as to admit of a free passage perpendicular to the inward edge of the footway and to prevent them from being noxious to the preservation of the street ;

12th. Any person who, when trimming hedges, trees or shrubs shall place on the footway or public road within the same day or for more than three days in succession, more than one cartload of the cuttings of such hedges, shrubs or trees ;

13th. Any person who, without the permission of the Board of Commissioners, shall erect, fix, or set up, in public thoroughfares or places, any tent, rope, stake or post ;

14th. Any person who, without the said permission shall set up any prop or enclosure, encroaching on the public way, or any shed, table for exposing goods, trap-door, or other work, calculated to obstruct or impede the passage ;

15th. Any person who shall leave in any public thoroughfare or place, or in any field, or open yard, any crowbar, arms weapon or other instrument of which any improper use may be made by malefactors ;

16th. Any person who shall not fasten the shutters of his house or out-houses, or the gate of his enclosure, in such manner as persons passing by may not be obstructed or hurt by the same ;

17th. The owner or occupier of any premises who shall neglet to cause the footway along his premises to be swept, and to collect the sweepings together, in sufficient time for the removal thereof by the carts used for that purpose ;

All sweepings and house refuse must be placed before 11 A.M. near the public roadway adjoining every dwelling situate in the Town ; and no such sweepings or house refuse shall be so placed after 11 A.M. ; nor in places inaccessible to the scavengering carts, nor on Sundays. If such sweepings and house refuse are placed in any box, bag or other receptacle, the Contractor shall be bound to empty those receptacles into his carts and to leave them on the spot, and the proprietor or occupier shall be bound to remove them within an hour after the passing of the scavengering carts ;

18th. Any person who shall deposit in public thoroughfares or places any earth, rubbish or other thing which the Contractor for cleaning the streets is not bound to remove or of a nature to obstruct the free passage or to impair the salubrity of public thoroughfares ;

19th. Any person who through want of proper care, shall throw filth, water or any other thing whatsoever upon another person ;

20th. Any person who shall throw or deposit filth or any other noxious thing into or near any stream, canal, running-water, fountain or public reservoir ;

21st. Any person who shall wash or bathe himself or any animal in any canal, fountain, or public reservoir, or who shall wash or bathe any animal in any of the Town streams or sources except in the places specially specified ;

22nd. Any person who shall make, throw, or deposit in any road-way, public thoroughfare or place, or in any premises belonging to another person, any dung, filth, offal, or any other offensive matter whatsoever ;

23rd. Any person who shall throw in the street or footway any fruit rind, fruit stone, waste vegetable or such other refuse, without prejudice to the right of the sufferer, in case of accident caused by that offence to sue the offender before the competent Court ;

24th. Any person who shall allow any fetid or filthy water to run or flow on any footway, street or public thoroughfare, from his premises ;

25th. Any person who shall spring a mine though with the authority of the Board, but without having taken all requisite precautions to protect passers by or the neighbourhood, and three minutes previous notice being given of the firing, even though no harm or injury should ensue therefrom to persons or property ;

26th. Any person who shall fire off any fireworks or ignite any explosive substance upon a street or public thoroughfare or upon either side thereof ; as also whoever shall do either of the said acts within such proximity to a street or public thoroughfare as to cause injury to any person or property, to any carriage travelling along the street, or to startle or injure any animal upon the same ;

27th. Any person who shall destroy, break, injure or remove any lantern or lamp hung up by authority upon or near to any public street or thoroughfare, or who shall extinguish the light in such lantern or lamp without authority from the Board or the person in charge thereof ;

28th. Any person who shall, without due authority, break, cut, throw or pull down or injure any sign-post, stake, barrier, parapet, plate bearing the names of the streets or other works of any description placed or which shall be placed on above or near any street or public thoroughfare for the public convenience : or who shall efface, change, alter or destroy any of the letter or marks inscribed or painted on any of the aforesaid articles or works.

CHAPTER III.

Paving and cleaning of the Town.

IX.—The streets, roads, and places of the Town of Curepipe which are within the province of the Board, shall be maintained and repaired by the Board of Commissioners, according to their means and in conformity with the regulations which the said Board shall issue for that purpose.

X.—The Board of Commissioners shall determine the line of all footways according to the title deeds of the proprietors or to the lawful width of the street, and also the dimension and level of such footways in each street of the Town.

XI.—Any proprietor who shall be desirous to have a footway constructed at his own expense, must previously ask the Board to fix the line, dimension, and level thereof, and must have it made in accordance thereto and within the delay which shall be assigned to him by the Board.

XII.—If a proprietor does not follow the dimensions, line, or level given to him, or does not make his footway within the prescribed delay, the Board of Commissioners shall have the same reconstructed, or completed at the expense of the said proprietor.

XIII.—Any proprietor desirous to place before the entrance of his premises small bridges in stone or other materials must apply to the Board for an authority and shall pay to the Treasurer of the Board the rates specified in the Tariff published and deposited at the office of the Board.

XIV.—Any person having before his door small bridges in stone or other materials placed over the kennel, in the street, so as to obstruct the course of the water in the said kennel, shall be bound to have the same bridges removed, and shall be allowed to have them rebuilt, provided the drain be not obstructed in any manner, notice shall be given to house-holders to have such works removed as may be a nuisance or an obstruction in the streets. If any person shall not comply with the said notice, within the delay of ten days, the Board shall cause the said removal to be made at the expense of the offender, who shall morever, be liable to a fine not exceeding Ten Rupees.

XV.—Any person who shall fill up or obstruct the ditches or gutters placed along the roads, streets or places, or shall dig on the roads, streets, places or footways, any ditch or drain, or perform any other work calculated to destroy or injure the same shall be liable to a fine not exceeding one hundred rupees.

Chapter IV.

Protection of Canals.

XVI.—It is forbidden to cause any carriage or vehicle, cattle or heavy body to pass on the canals which provide or shall be made to provide the Town of Curepipe with water, in the places where they are out of the ground, to deteriorate the masonry to lift up the coverings, to deposit any filth, or to cause water to stagnate in the vicinity thereof, without any prejudice to the correctional punishments prescribed by the Penal Code against any person who shall deteriorate any work of public utility.

XVII.—It is also forbidden to introduce into the said canals any planking or other obstacles calculated to obstruct the course of the water, or to open the fire-plugs, or to turn the cocks existing therein, without permission of an officer of the Board or of a person authorized by the Board of Commissioners, except in case of absolute necessity.

XVIII.—All persons offending against the provisions set forth in the present chapter shall be liable to a fine not exceeding One hundred Rupees.

Chapter V.

Laying out of streets & public thoroughfares.

XIX.—Any proprietor desirous to erect any building whatsoever at the legal distance of the public road or to alter or make repairs to any buildings existing at such legal distance shall be bound previously to apply to the Board of Commissioners for a line to be laid out, and to pay to the Treasurer of the said Board the rates specified in the Tariff published and deposited at the office of the Board.

XX.—Any proprietor of any building which, before the creation of the Board, shall have been erected without lawful authority within the legal distance of the public road shall be bound before making any alteration or repairs to any such building to apply to the Board for authority to alter or make such repairs to any such building and the Board shall have power to refuse such authority, if such building constitutes an encroachment on the public road or on the footway thereof.

XXI.—Any person wishing to raise a balcony, shed, pentice or any construction projecting over the public road, shall be bound to obtain the permission of the Board of Commissioners, and to have his plan of construction approved by the said Board. He shall pay to the Treasurer of the Board the sum specified in the above-mentioned Tariff.

XXII.—Any person or co-partnership desirous to erect lamp-posts or props to support electric wires in or over any public thoroughfare shall be bound previously to ask for the authorization of the Board of Commissioners, which shall in case of approval point out the spots where such lamp-posts or props shall be erected. A fee of Fifty cents of a Rupee shall be paid for the permit to erect each such lamp-post or prop.

XXIII.—All lamp-posts and props now existing along the public roadways shall not be renewed or removed from one place to another without applying to the Board for authority to do so.

XXIV.—The removal of a lamp-post or prop, the erection of which shall have been lawfully authorized, shall be made by the Board, at the expense of the Board, when required for public utility.

XXV.—In case of non compliance with the present regulations the lamp-posts or props unlawfully erected or renewed may be removed by order of the Board, at the expense of the offender who shall moreover be liable to the fine undermentioned.

XXVI.—Any owner or occupier of premises within the Town of Curepipe desirous to enclose the frontage of his property bordering on a street or public thoroughfare, with hedges of bambous or other plants, shall be bound to apply to the Board for laying out the line of the street or thoroughfare, and for authority to plant such hedges and he shall be bound to plant such hedges one metre and thirty centimetres (4 feet) at least inside the boundary line of his property in order that such hedges, by their growth may not encroach on the width of the gutter, ditch, footway, road or thoroughfare.

XXVII.—It shall not be lawful to enclose the frontage of a property bordering on a street or public thoroughfare with hedges of *Melica latifolia* commonly called "bambou Flora" or "bambou balai".

XXVIII.— Any owner or occupier of a property situate within the Town of Curepipe desirous to enclose the frontage of his property bordering on a street or public thoroughfare, with any wall, fence, quickset hedge, palisade or enclosure of any description shall be bound previously to apply to the Board of Commissioners for the line to be laid out.

XXIX.—In case of non compliance with the above regulations the proprietor or occupier shall be liable to the fine hereafter set forth, and besides, in case of any encroachment on the street or thoroughfare, the Board shall have power to order the trimming or removing of such hedges or enclosures at the expense of the proprietor.

XXX.—All persons offending against the provisions contained in this present Chapter shall be liable to a fine not exceeding one hundred rupees. It shall moreover be lawful for the District Magistrate, as the case may be, to order the suppression of any construction made in contravention of the present chapter.

Chapter VI.

Thatched Buildings.

XXXI.—It shall not be lawful to erect any house or building covered or lined with straw, leaves or any thatch whatsoever or to cover or line with straw, leaves or thatch whatsoever any house or building already erected in the thickly inhabited parts of the Town of Curepipe, or in any other locality within the limits of the Town, without special leave of the Board; no such leave shall be given in places where the Board may consider a thatched building to become in the future dangerous or noxious.

XXXII.—Thatched buildings or coverings of buildings made with straw, now existing shall not be renewed without leave of the Board; any person who shall not comply with that provision shall be liable to the fine hereafter mentioned.

XXXIII.—No new thatched building duly authorized by the Board, shall be erected at less than one foot above the level of the ground, and the Board shall have in any case, a right to order such ground floor to be raised higher than one foot so as to allow the drainage of the surface or waste water or refuse of the premises.

XXXIV.—Every building that shall be enlarged or newly built and which shall be intended to be used as a human habitation shall, if erected in stone, bricks, rough-walling or metal, and if covered with straw, be at least seven feet in height from the floor to the top of the exterior wall.

XXXV.—Such height shall be nine feet if the building is of straw and covered with metal and shall be, at least, seven feet if the said building is of straw or wood and covered with straw.

XXXVI.—It shall not be lawful to erect any straw building intended to be used as a human habitation, the interior surface of which shall be less than thirteen cubic metres (one hundred and twenty square feet.)

XXXVII.—Three sides at least of the aforesaid building shall have doors, windows, or other openings for the free circulation of air equal to one-sixth of the surface of each side.

XXXVIII.—If any straw building to be enlarged, or newly built, is not intended for human habitation, such building shall have openings for the free circulation of air equal to one-eighth of the surface of each side.

XXXIX.—No straw building shall be newly built or enlarged unless a distance of thirty feet be left between such new construction or the building to be enlarged and any neighbouring building; and at least ten feet between the building newly erected or enlarged and the boundary line of the premises.

XL.—Any person not complying with the Regulations contained in the present chapter shall be liable to a fine not exceeding one hundred rupees and the Board may cause the building unlawfully constructed, enlarged or removed to be pulled down and the expense incurred by it in so doing shall be recoverable against the offender as provided for in article 99 of Ordinance No. 26 of 1875.

CHAPTER VII.

Opening of streets or thoroughfares.

XLI.—Any landowner in the Town of Curepipe intending to parcel out his property or a part of his property, or intending to open on his property a street or thoroughfare for the use of the public, must previously submit to the Board of Commissioners a plan of his intended parceling with a plan of any street or thoroughfare he may intend to open thereon, which plan must, in either case, be previously approved of by the Board of Commissioners.

XLII.—Any proprietor not complying with the foregoing regulation, shall be liable to a fine not exceeding one hundred Rupees, reserving the right of the Board of Commissioners to compel the offender to modify the plan of his road or roads in such manner as the Board may deem expedient in the public interest.

CHAPTER VIII.

XLIII.—It shall be lawful for any member or officer of the Board of Commissioners to require from any person causing a building to be constructed or augmented within the limits of the Town of Curepipe, to produce the authorization prescribed by law, and any person who shall not comply with the said request or who shall not be in possession of an authorization delivered by the Board, shall be liable to a fine not exceeding one hundred Rupees, without prejudice to the enforcements of the provisions of the Building Act; in case the building should not have been erected in conformity with such provisions or in conformity with the requirement of any sanitary law.

CHAPTER IX.

Erection of buildings along boundary lines.

XLIV.—Whereas the distance from a building to another building required by Article 8 of Ordinance 13 of 1877 is Twenty feet, subject to the 1st. proviso of the said Article 8, it shall not be lawful for any proprietor constructing, enlarging or adding to any building or removing any building from one place to another, under the provisions of Article 8 of the said Ordinance, to erect, enlarge or remove any such building or new building at a distance of less than ten feet from his own boundary line, except with the express and written consent of the adjacent proprietor. The main object of such prohibition is to empower such adjacent proprietor, if he wishes to erect or enlarge a building in the vicinity of his own boundary line, by doing so at Ten feet of his own boundary line to have the required distance of twenty feet between his own building and those of his neighbour.

XLV.—The Board, however, shall have power to reduce such distance in such manner as shall be deemed just and expedient in any particular case, in conformity with Article 16 of Ordinance No. 26 of 1875, and a fee of one Rupee shall be paid to the Treasurer of the Board for every such reduction.

XLVI.—Any person not complying with the Regulations contained in the present Chapter shall be liable to a fine not exceeding one hundred Rupees accruing to the Board of Commissioners and the Board in conformity with Article 21 of Ordinance No. 26 of 1875, may cause the building unlawfully constructed, enlarged or removed to be pulled down, and the expense incurred by it in so doing shall be recovenable against the offender as provided for in Article 99 of the same Ordinance.

CHAPTER X.

Forges, Ovens and Furnaces

XLVII—No forge, fire-place, oven furnace, bake-house or such other trade, business or process as described in Article 55 of Ordinance No. 26 of 1875 shall be built erected or established in the Town, except in pursuance of a written License delivered by the Board of Commissioners and under such conditions as the said Board may deem expedient to annex to such license for the prevention of Fire or for the protection of the Public Health. No such license as aforesaid shall be granted by the Board, except after a notice has been published in two daily newspapers in conformity with Article 58 of the said Ordinance and given by the Board at the expense of the petitioner, to each bordering proprietor or occupier of the premises on which the said forge, fire-place, oven, bake-house or such other Trade, business or process shall be established, erected or built. The notices in the newspapers shall be inserted by the Board, at the expense of the petitioner, who shall moreover pay a fee of one Rupee for the notice to be given to the bordering proprietors or occupiers.

XLVIII—A fine not exceeding one hundred Rupees shall be awarded against any person offending against the Regulations contained in the present chapter without prejudice to the enforcement of the provisions of the Building Act, in case any forge, fire-place, oven &c., should not have been erected in conformity with the requirement of the law.

Tariff of the duties to be paid to the Board of Commissioners for the laying out of buildings, and the performance of works in the line of any public street or place, or projecting over or encroaching on any public road, or for the planting of hedges :

Laying out (*alignement*) of any building in the Town of Curepipe, per metre in length ... Rs.	1.00
Laying out of an enclosure wall in masonry	1.50
Laying out of an enclosure wall made of boards	1.00
Laying out of an enclosure of hedges	1.00
Balcony, per metre in length	1.00
Enclosure around excavations, yards, constructions and repairs per diem (the breadth of the enclosure to be determined by the Town Architect)	1.00
Opening of doors, windows, on the ground floor within 2.50 metres from the outer edge of the street, for each	1.00
Pontice (*auvent*) for every metre in length the breadth to be determined by the Town Architect	0.25
Partial obstruction of a street for private works, per diem	1.00
Small bridges in front of houses	1.00

MISCELLANEOUS.

Permits for firing mines in the Town, per diem	0.50
Permits for erecting lamp-posts or wire-supports along public thoroughfares, each ...	0.50
Notice to bordering proprietors in case of erection of forge, oven &c., to be paid by the petitioner, Chapter X of the present Regulations	1.00

Scale of fees established in the Building Act (Schedule A) and to accrue to the Board of Curepipe.

Fee for surveying a dangerous structure	10.00
For drawing up Memorandum of Survey	5.00
For Service of Notice by Usher	0.50
For every permit issued under Ordinances 26 of 1875 and 13 of 1877	1.00
For every special permit in conformity with Chapter XV of the present Regulations ...	1.00
For registration of any lodging house	2.00

(Collectors and Bearers of Warrant to accrue to tho Board of Commissioners.)

Assessment	0.50
For serving a Warrant	2.00
For every execution of Judgment, order or warrant against goods and Memorandum of Seizure	2.00
Guardianship of seizure (not to exceed 10 days) unless the delay is caused by the debtor	0.50
For drawing up a memorandum of sale including attendance	1.50
Witnesses, each	1.00
Attachment	2.00
For each copy of attachment includingly the serving	1.00

Stamps, Registration, Crier, Trumpet and Notices in the Government Gazette to be at the charge of the debtor.

No. 162 of 1895.

General Orders in which the Army (Annual) Act, 1895 has been promulgated to the Troops serving in the Colony .... 11th. June 1895.

No. 167 of 1895.

The Merchant Shipping Act, 1894 .... 21st. June 1895.

No. 186 of 1895.

Regulations relative to the hours of working on the Quays............... ... 8th. July 1895.

No. 187 of 1895.

Regulations to provide means to put a stop to depredations in Tobacco Plantations at Rodrigues .... 8th. July 1895.

No. 188 of 1895.

Railway Bye-Law for the conveyance of Canes.................................. 12th. July 1895.

No. 189 of 1895.

Railway Bye-Law to regulate the conveyance of Molasses during the "Entre Coupe" .... 12th. July 1895.

No. 222 of 1895.

Additional Regulations of the Mauritius Government Savings Bank made under the provisions of Section 15 of Ordinance 10 of 1865........ 7th. August 1895.

No. 233 of 1895.

Amended charges for Meter Rent, Mare-aux-Vacoas Water Works ...... 28th. August 1895.

No. 237 of 1895.

Tables of rates for the conveyance of goods between certain stations on the Moka-Flacq Branch Railway .... 2nd. September 1895.

No. 247 of 1895.

Railway Bye-law to regulate the conveyance of Molasses for export ...... 9th. September 1895.

No. 282 of 1895.

Additional General Rules and Orders of the Supreme Court .... 15th. October 1895.

No. 313 of 1895.

Amended Municipal Regulations concerning Markets........ 15th. November 1895.

No. 320 of 1895.

Addition to the Mauritius Railways Bye-Law respecting monthly Contract Tickets........ 22nd. November 1895.

No. 322 of 1895.

Amended Rules for the application of the grant for the training of Teachers for Aided Schools .... 22nd. November 1895.

No. 337 of 1895.

Amended Rules and Regulations to be observed in future during Cyclone or Hurricane weather........ 12th. December 1895.

No. 348 of 1895.

Amended Articles 35, 42, 60, 61 and 62 of the Royal College Rules and Regulations .... 19th. December 1895.

List of Aliens naturalized under Ordinances No. 8 of 1868, 26 of 1871 and 20 of 1872 with the date of their taking the Oath of Allegiance.

Names.	Oath of Allegiance when taken.
Achack	20th. September 1895
Achard, Jules	22nd. May 1871
Achin	20th. September 1895
Acyokoo, Venpin	5th. May 1886
Adeline, The Reverend J. B.	17th. July 1889
Adolphe, Samuel	9th. June 1891
Affan-Tank-Wen	28th. November 1873
Affoy, Cham	20th. December 1886
Ah-Cheng	28th. December 1880
Ah-Chin	3rd. July 1889
Ah-Chong Cock Mineses	5th. May 1886
Ah-Foo	27th. January 1890
Ah-Fook, James	15th. March 1881
Ah-Hang	27th. October 1871
Ah-Hee-Koo-Lave	19th. December 1894
Ah-huon-Lai-Cheng	6th. December 1894
Ahime	18th. February 1879
Ah-Khon *alias* Chou-Ah-Kon	19th. September 1871
Ah-King	16th. November 1880
Ah-Loon	3rd. February 1874
Ah-Mun	29th. December 1874
Ah-Sing	13th. June 1873
Ahson	11th. May 1883
Ah-Tack	22nd. October 1878
Ahvan Lequetake	5th. May 1886
Attack, Cham Yoki	20th. December 1886
Ah-Thim	17th. October 1887
Ah-Tin	23rd. February 1887
Ah-Tin	27th. January 1890
Ah-Wan	16th. November 1880
Ah-Wan-Leung Sam	18th. January 1890
Ah-Weng	17th. December 1878
Akee, Semlum	10th. January 1895
Amelot, Auguste	1st. August 1871
Ameng	17th. March 1880
Anghow	30th. November 1869
Aug-Hoe-Po	7th. September 1894
Anglaw	22nd. December 1871
Angnoyee	13th. June 1873
Angtive	13th. June 1873
Ankave	2nd. February 1872
Ankresamy	9th. June 1891
Arnaud, Jean Alexandre	10th. June 1870
Ashingue *alias* Assène	17th. March 1874
Assouan	31st. October 1871
Atchan *alias* Atchaw	14th. May 1869
Athion	20th. July 1894
Atchiop *alias* Assop	27th. February 1877
Athonne	4th. June 1875
Atheeng	4th. January 1878
Athoy Chan Kaw	27th. December 1889
Attime Fockling	18th. January 1890
Aubergé, L. R.	5th. December 1885.
Audouin, Mrs. E. L. A. (widow of Félix Devinot) ...	3rd. July 1893
Awohoa	29th. December 1874
Aycho	21st. September 1887
Ayow	22nd. December 1873
Bailly, Laure Henriette	7th. August 1868

Names.	Oath of Allegiance when taken.
Baretty, Jean Georges Ferdinand	2nd. December 1873
Baud, Revd. Jean Marie	13th. April 1894
Baumgarten, Lazare Ephraim	25th. October 1870
Bazin, Ernest Victor	9th. June 1891
Beaugendre, Marie Josephine	30th September 1880
Berne, Revd. Regis Abel	6th September 1881
Binger, Revd. Aloysius	29th December 1894
Biberon, Jean Baptiste	6th March 1877
Boi, Justin	31st October 1876
Bolcovich, Antonio	9th June 1891
Bonnier, Edouard Marie Charles	10th May 1871
Bonnier, Marie Thérèse	10th May 1871
Boquillon, Jules Edmond	11th November 1870
Bordas, Jean Baptiste	13th December 1870
Bornard, George Ami Albert	27th August 1890
Bossy, Revd. Joseph François	Taken at Seychelles
Both	12th November 1879
Boot, Joseph	9th June 1891
Botta, Revd. Secondo	30th August 1871
Boucherit, Revd. F. A.	27th October 1882
Bouis, Léon	25th October 1870
Bouis, Marie Auguste	13th January 1874
Boujon, Revd. Alphonse	19th December 1892
Boulé, Revd. Félix Marie	17th April 1894
Bouquet, Charles Joseph Jules	24th March 1894
Boyer, Louis Aristide	24th February 1888
Bozelle, Louis Alfred	28th May 1872
Brabant, Léopold Marie Heuri	22nd December 1871
Brandi, Jean Baptiste	23rd December 1891
Brangeon, Jean Baptiste	30th September 1870
Bret, Mrs. Cécile Rose, wife of P. V. P. Pellorce	18th January 1873
Bretesché, Revd. Pierre Stanislas	13th December 1890
Brodard, G.	22nd February 1884
Bronner, Charles	19th July 1877
Bronner, Delia	19th July 1877
Bruel, Revd. Cyprien	18th April 1890
Bruneau, Jean Etienne	8th March 1881
Brunet, Charles	2nd June 1885
Buguel, Revd. Victor	17th August 1888
Buhler, John	9th June 1891
Bungchin	27th June 1871
Burg, Aloyse Edouard	9th April 1872
Cabannes, Antoine Isidore	10th October 1873
Canal, Jean Emile	30th June 1892
Caniel, André Prosper	9th April 1872
Carl, Sébastian Steinmetz	31st October 1895
Cassiau, Pierre Cassette	25th October 1870
Castelin, Louis Marie	25th April 1876
Chalvet, Revd. Guillaume Emile	13th March 1890
Chan Chi Lon	4th October 1889
Cham Ming	6th May 1891
Cham Cam	10th January 1895
Chan-Fun	11th January 1895
Chang-Ko	20th September 1895
Chanman	19th December 1895
Chantok	15th October 1895
Chang Wing	2nd September 1891
Chan Loh	7th May 1894
Chapelle, Revd. Jérémie Pierre Edouard de la	4th February 1895
Charrette, Jean Charles	9th August 1870
Chastellier, Dr. Evenor	4th December 1885
Chang Soone	28th July 1893

Names.	Oath of Allegiance when taken.
Chausiom	27th. June 1871
Chauvet, Pierre Hyacinthe	12th. June 1890
Chaw-Keem	20th. September 1895
Cheong Long Leong Pew	24th. September 1892
Chevalier, Isidore	28th. October 1870
Ching-Pow	19th. March 1872
Chion Kin	18th. December 1874
Chitchongthingee	1st. December 1894
Chong Mason	25th. October 1895
Choo-Tong	20th. September 1895
Choo Sek	8th. October 1889
Chouson, James	15th. March 1881
Chou-ah-Son	1st. June 1875
Chou-ah-Men	29th. December 1868
Chua-Appion	19th. September 1871
Chü-Ham	26th. September 1895
Church, George Franklyn	3rd. July 1893
Cimiotti, Joseph Karl	8th. December 1871
Clarenc, Louis Hector	16th. December 1870
Codabux, Corsetjee	17th. January 1871
Corbet, Revd. François Xavier	11th. February 1879
Cotonea, Revd. Jacques Henri	14th. January 1892
Courtaux, Mathias Frédéric	25th. October 1870
Crosnier, Réné	12th. March 1875
Cugnet, Charles Eugène	28th. October 1870
Daniel, Ah-King	21st. February 1889
Darribère, Revd. Auguste	6th. September 1881
Davidsen, Ole Severin	8th. June 1892
Dee-Thowlipgee	1st. December 1894
Deylere, Pierre Ernest	7th. August 1868
D'Abbadie de Barrau, Charles	3rd. March 1893
D'Abbadie de Barrau, Roger	3rd. March 1893
D'Emmerez, Joseph Julien *alias* Jules D'Emmerez	22nd. June 1880
Descours	27th. August 1868
Desprez, Georges Augustin Ludovic Aurel	13th. August 1872
Dioré de Perigny, Georges	14th. January 1890
Ditner, Revd. F. X.	4th. April 1882
Deymié, Pierre Auguste	16th. March 1869
Drouart, Charles	2nd. July 1872
Duboisée de Ricquebourg, Joseph Hyacinthe Henry	16th. May 1873
Duclerc des Rauches, M. A. A. C. F.	4th. December 1885
Dyrr, Frederick	19th. June 1868
Edmond, Revd. Joseph Alfred Dardanel	29th. March 1889
Elorza, Revd. Henry	23rd. September 1891
Eminet, Joseph	9th. August 1870
Engelbrecht, Paul Bernard Ulysse	22nd. December 1871
Erhart, Antoine	1st. November 1870
Erhmann, Michel Léon Bernard	11th. May 1880
Espallac, Revd. Joseph	15th. September 1871
Estingoy, Joseph Eugène	14th. July 1871
Etchevery, Revd. Jean Baptiste Marie Justin	6th. September 1881
Etienne, Paul	9th. June 1891
Eynaud, Paul Marie	23rd. June 1869
Fernal, Francis	23rd. April 1872
Ferran, Eugène	11th. August 1882
Fidelia, Alexandre Gaston Paul	19th. February 1873
Filippini, Revd. Jean Benoit	16th. March 1880
Fitch, Henry Newton	28th. May 1873
Fleury, Mrs. Benoite Marie	17th. March 1874
Florentin, Louis Alfred	8th. September 1886
Floret, Jules Simon	4th. November 1870
Florigny, Edouard Paul Eugène	12th. December 1890

Names.	Oath of Allegiance when taken.
Fock Sam...	5th. May 1886
Franchon, Mrs. Widow	20th. December 1886
Frank, Nicholas	9th. June 1891
Frélicot, Henry Désiré	22nd. November 1870
Galibardy, Thos. L.	4th. September 1885
Gardette, Cristophe	4th. April 1882
Garmy, Revd. A.	31st. October 1871
Gaspard, Joseph Anatole	2nd. March 1875
Gausserand, Revd. Auguste	1st. March 1893
Giroday, Elie Pierre Boyer de la...	18th. March 1879
Glen, Henry	9th. June 1891
Gonnet, Louis Michel Auguste	16th. June 1869
Gordon, Ulysse Mark	9th. June 1891
Goze, Félix	25th. October 1870
Grafelmann, Johann Hermann Otto	9th. June 1891
Grassett, Joseph Fortuné	29th. January 1878
Green, Carl	2nd. August 1892
Grimaud, Eugène	16th. October 1888
Grimaud, Revd. J. B....	28th. June 1893
Guilemin, O.	4th. December 1885
Guilhen, Revd. François	7th. February 1894
Guilloux, Revd. Victor Marie	23rd. August 1876
Gullifer, Walter Leo	9th. June 1891
Gun-Chit	19th. March 1872
Guyon, Revd. Pierre	13th. January 1880
Guyot, Revd. Joseph Marie	3rd. March 1891
Haaby, Revd. Marie Auguste	19th. April 1891
Hadjee	27th. October 1868
Halais, Edouard Félix Marie	29th. December 1868
Hakuy, Tidkoe	15th. August 1872
Hang-Tchen	19th. March 1871
Hatler, Revd. Louis	13th. July 1880
Hayotte, Louis Hippolyte	20th. October 1870
Henry, Joseph Etienne	23rd. June 1879
Henty, Henry	9th. June 1891
Hertogs, Gustave Charles César...	3rd. December 1868
Hilaire, Revd. Emile Adolphe	6th. October 1871
Hoefat, Acone	3rd. June 1879
Hong-Gee-Hing	19th. October 1894
Hook, Thomas	9th. June 1891
Hosing	4th. December 1895
Howe, Daniel John	25th. November 1890
Hudrisier, Right Revd. Mark Michel	28th. July 1893
Hung-Pete	19th. March 1872
Ipshaw	7th. May 1894
Isambert, *alias* Isambert Simon, Adolphe Amilcar	23rd. December 1873
Jaillet, Antoine	9th. June 1891
Jodun, Emile Eugène	17th. March 1892
Johnson, Auguste Nicolai Janus...	9th. June 1891
Johnson, Charles	9th. June 1891
Jonckeer, Léopold	9th. June 1891
Joseph, Revd. Jean Marie Sadoux	29th. March 1889
Jouane, Joson	9th. June 1891
Judais, Camille	20th. May 1881
Junghans, John Julius Christophe	28th. November 1891
Keemyang, Keekiane...	6th. April 1886
Koch, Albert	9th. June 1891
Laborde, L.	14th. July 1885
Lafitte, Jean Marie Théodore	17th. January 1873
Lagier, Revd. Adrien...	19th. October 1877
Lagreula, André	7th. November 1879
Lainé, Revd. Pierre Joseph	9th. March 1880

Names.	Oath of Allegiance when taken.
Laisné de la Couronne, Jean Louis Théodore ...	1st. May 1871
Lai-Yat	14th. January 1895
Lamanie, Louis	9th. June 1891
Lamothe, Marie Fanny	31st. August 1875
Langavant, Revd. A. C. de	8th. September 1893
Langlois, Henry Alcide Marie	5th. May 1871
Lanier, Edouard	10th. June 1879
Lanux, Joseph Crécy de	13th. July 1877
Larose, Louis Jean Baptiste	28th. January 1892
Laperrousaz, Revd. Joseph	12th. March 1891
Lapeyre, Louis	15th. January 1875
Laventure, Revd. Anthony	13th. April 1893
Lay Kamp Chee Kamp	8th. October 1889
Lay-hing	29th. June 1875
Lauratet, Victorin	29th. October 1888
Le Breton, Henry	9th. June 1891
Leconte, Paul	15th. July 1879
Lecoultre, Marie Hector	8th. November 1872
Lecoultre, Patrice Albert	8th. November 1872
Lee-Hanglin	20th. September 1895
Lee Payn	2nd. March 1887
Lee Hare Chonge	31st. May 1887
Lefeuvre, Revd. Jean Baptiste	9th. June 1890
Lejeune, Charles Henry Dr.	25th. February 1873
Lemarchand, Joseph Camille	11th. October 1871
Lemoine, Revd. Jean François	13th. January 1880
Lepervanche, Paul de	28th. February 1882
Lèques, Théodore	31st. October 1876
Lescure, Revd. J. L.	29th. December 1893
Lesport, Jean Baptiste François Appolydore ...	13th. May 1873
Levasseur, Auguste	27th. August 1868
Levinvillle, Ferdinand Oswald	16th. May 1873
Lian-Hok Cheng	23rd. February 1887
Lifocksam	25th. October 1895
Limteng	23rd. February 1887
Lim-Tin-Lap	27th. January 1890
Lim-Tock	23rd. February 1887
Lim-Bok	23rd. February 1887
Lincoln, Eugène Lionel	18th. May 1869
Lock Chew	2nd. October 1889
Loan Yean	2nd. October 1889
Losun	20th. September 1895
Lousier, Jacques Henry	6th. August 1875
Lowtny	3rd. February 1864
Lupo, César	9th. June 1891
Lutzemberger, Charles Hyacinth	25th. April 1871
Lye Foah	12th. October 1892
Lysoon	17th. October 1873
Malaizé, Jean Pierre	3rd September 1878
Malaval, Revd. Victor	23rd. January 1890
Malécage, Louis Gustave	16th. May 1870
Mallet, Jules Antoine	3rd. June 1869
Manach, Revd. Jean Louis	28th. January 1891
Manang	2nd. February 1894
Mancini, Alexandre Bastien	27th. January 1890
Manning, John Edward	9th. June 1891
Maroelli, Revd. Sebastino	2nd. August 1881
Marquez, Revd. Antoine	18th. January 1890
Marquet, Jean François Victor	2nd. May 1879
Martin, Andrew	9th. June 1891
Martin, Grégoire Marius Pierre	15th. March 1869
Martin, Revd. Marius	23rd. October 1890

Names.	Oath of Allegiance when taken.
Masméjean, Charles Emilien Paul Joseph	7th. November 1876
Mason, Robert Charles Nathaniel	19th. May 1892
Meyer, John Christian Adam	9th. June 1891
Maubert, Edmond	14th. July 1871
Maurel, Louis Dominigue Marie Joseph	3rd. September 1878
Mazars, Revd. Louis	27th. September 1880
Mazuy, Revd. Xavier...	11th. May 1869
Mérandon, Pierre	29th. October 1873
Mérandon, Emile Nicolas	19th. December 1873
Merian, Alfred	29th. November 1895
Merlet, Adolphe	25th. October 1870
Michel, Augustin Albert	13th. February 1872
Miller, Louis Carl August	9th. June 1891
Monferran, Revd. Léon	2nd. February 1894
Mourgue, Jules Louis...	28th. December 1875
Nallès, Nicolas Pierre Henry	16th. May 1873
Neyroles, Revd. Charles	4th. July 1895
Newpon, Chuck Ling Jib	2nd. October 1889
Nicault, Hippolyte Amédée	20th. July 1868
Nicolas, Jean Marie	10th. February 1892
Numa, Marie Uranie	3rd September 1880
Ormières, Louis Auguste	24th. February 1874
Orsatoni, Hyacinthe	9th. June 1891
Ousset, Jean Bertrand	11th. June 1869
Pangchuk...	20th. September 1895
Papon, Paul Gustave...	4th. January 1878
Payet, Arnold	30th. May 1876
Pellorce, Mrs. Pierre Vincent Paul	18th. January 1873
Pérard, Jules Joseph	30th. July 1873
Péguillan, Jean	29th. June 1875
Pellerin, Revd. Jean Marie Joseph	13th. December 1890
Perraud, Revd. Alphonse Clément	22nd. November 1881
Pezzani, Emile Anatole	5th. December 1879
Philippe, St. Cylia Marchand	9th. June 1891
Piffoux, Revd. Charles	29th. August 1888
Pochard, Ernest Erançois Marie...	21st. December 1869
Pol, Revd. Ambroise Eugène	29th. July 1881
Poculot, J.	31st. March 1885
Praud, Hilarion	4th. November 1870
Presbourg, Mrs. Marie Clothilde de Belland de ...	24th. February 1874
Pressigny, Eugène Prévost de	6th. August 1879
Queefond	27th. June 1871
Ramin, Vitelingom	9th. June 1891
Raoul, Joseph	9th. June 1891
Rasmussen, S. William	9th. June 1891
Raverat, Revd. Alexandre	30th. December 1880
Rebreyen, Revd. Eugène	13th. August 1873
Reibel, Revd. Emile	18th. July 1895
Rellier, Revd. François	17th. October 1892
Rhea, Robert Théodore Moskoff	9th. June 1891
Rial, Carl...	9th. June 1891
Richard, Auguste Jean	20th. October 1870
Rivière, François Emile	28th. September 1870
Rivière, Jean Auguste	10th. March 1871
Rochette de Lampdès, Revd. Jérôme	17th. August 1888
Roger, Joséphine Adam, Widow Louis Eugène ...	17th. August 1869
Roserot, Revd. Paul Joseph Louis	5th. December 1879
Rouhier, Jules Joseph	8th. February 1889
Rousselet, Paul George	25th. October 1870
Saint Félix, Joseph Gaston de	18th. October 1881
Salaffa, André Théobald	14th. October 1868
Samson	15th. March 1881

Names.	Oath of Allegiance when taken.
Schrooder, William Frederick Godfried	9th. June 1891
Schulthess, Emile	29th. November 1895
Seichan, Revd. Louis...	7th. November 1879
Seleff, Jean	9th. June 1891
Selleir, Etienne Auguste	30th. August 1870
Serres, Jean Baptiste Albert Poublon	14th. September 1869
Sew Waiking	25th. October 1895
Sham Tong	3rd. July 1889
Simian, Charles Joseph	9th. August 1870
Simonette, Mrs. Eugénie	7th. May 1895
Sinching, John	15th. November 1870
Skydeberg, William Christian Alexander	9th. June 1891
St. Aubin, Dehaulme...	28th. November 1873
Smith, Henry	9th. June 1891
Soit-Ah-Thian	11th. January 1895
Sorenso, Christian	9th. June 1891
Spangenberg, Adolphe Wilhem	3rd. October 1892
Spielman, Revd. J.	4th. December 1882
Talibard, Henry Armand	9th. June 1891
Tanaw, No. 4104	29th. August 1876
Tawchien	13th. September 1886
Tan-Foh	28th. January 1895
Tan-Yan	11th. January 1895
Teck-Young	20th. September 1895
Técheney, Pierre Raymond	15th. January 1875
Thomas, Alfred Louis Alexandre	28th. October 1870
Thies, John William Louis	15th. July 1873
Thienseng	30th. April 1872.
Thok-Long *alias* Tok-Long	6th. November 1874
Thinkoe Hakuy	29th. December 1868
Toulet, Bernard Gaston	19th. September 1871
Toulet, Paul	24th. October 1876
Toulet, Pierre Adrien	11th. April 1871
Tourneur, John	9th. June 1891
Touyé, Jean Marie	23rd. December 1873
Trillaut, *alias* A. S. Manoury	23rd. May 1872
Trumpy, Barthélemy...	8th. October 1862
Vaissière, Revd. Jean Baptiste Camille de la ...	6th. September 1881
Vandamme, Gustave Eugène Stanislas	20th. October 1870
Vang-Tee-San	15th. March 1881
Vass, Francis	9th. June 1891
Vaurigaud, Elie Lucien	12th. March 1875
Véga, Jean Baptiste de la	29th. October 1875
Vergoz, Dauphin Charles Ernest	19th. August 1870
Vidal, Eugène	1st. February 1878
Vien, Jean Baptiste	8th. September 1886
Vien, Louis	1st. April 1887
Villecourt, Joseph Denis Toussaint Corvillon de ...	18th. June 1878
Vuillemin, Mrs. E. née Alice Pignolet de Fresne ...	25th. September 1890
Vinson, Lucien Philippe Eugène...	6th. June 1873
Wallis, John Roland Curtius	9th. June 1891
Weckel, Revd. Nicolas	13th. December 1890
Weisshardt, Gottlieb	9th. June 1891
Wenzel, John Edouard	9th. June 1891
Williams, John	9th. June 1891
Wilson, Francis	9th. June 1891
Wong-Yan	20th. September 1895
Won-Tath-You-Antaye	22nd. November 1894
Wung, Jung	8th. October 1889
Yin-Hong...	26th. June 1895

List of Letters-Patent issued under Ordinance No. 16 of 1875.

No.	Date of Patent.	Patentee's Name.	Subject.	Duration Years.	Expiry.
	1882				
28	May 10	Killieux, Norbert ...	Improvements in evaporating and boiling apparatus employed in the manufacture of sugar and in the application of megasse as fuel, part of which apparatus is also applicable for evaporating and boiling other substances.	14 Years ...	28th. Mch. 1896
29	,, 26	Serrulas, Eugène ...	Treatment of saccharine juice by a new method of concentration by means of congelation and the use of special machinery.	Ditto ...	5th. Mch. 1896
30	July 4	Duval, J. Edmond ...	Improvements in liquoring or cleansing sugar and similar substances in centrifugal machines.	Ditto ...	11th. April 1896
31	Sept. 2	Maurel, Louis Antoine	Disinfection of Petroleum Oil or other mineral Oil and production therefrom of the Oil know as "l'huile cristale."	Ditto ...	31st. July 1896
32	,, 12	Tardieu, Paul ...	The drying of green cane trash, as it comes from the mill to allow of its being at once used as fuel.	Ditto ...	26th. June 1896
33	,, 21	Faure, Pierre ...	Improvements in treating sugar cane to obtain juice therefrom and apparatus therefor.	Ditto ...	21st, Aug. 1896
	1883				
34	Jan. 12	Godillot, Alexis ...	Improvements in Fire Grates for burning dence and filamentous or fibrous fuel.	Ditto ...	3rd. Dec. 1896
35	May 17	P.E. de Chazal, agent and attorney in Mauritius for Allen, Westley Rose.	Improvement in Telephones.	Ditto ...	16th. April 1897
36	July 4	Loumeau, Jules ...	Machine for preparing and cleaning the Aloe Fibre after its extraction from the plants.	Ditto ...	18th. June 1897
37	,, 10	P.E. de Chazal, agent of Achille Gilani.	Improvements in or appertaining to processes for evaporation or concentrating saccharine, saline or other solutions.	Ditto ...	27th. May 1897

No.	Date of Patent.		Patentee's Name.	Subject.	Duration Years.	Expiry.
	1883					
38	May	19	de Barrau, Charles D'Abbadie.	Manufacture of Sulphurous Acid by a new apparatus.	14 Years ...	18th. April 1897
39	August	29	Sicard, Frédéric Isembert, F.C.S.	Improvements in the process of fermenting liquids.	Ditto ...	29th. Aug. 1897
40	Nov.	12	Maclaran, J. F. ...	Improvements in the construction of vacuum pans.	Ditto ...	13th. Nov. 1897
41	August	14	Maurel, L. J. M. D. ...	Process for disinfecting Rum and obtaining therefrom alcohol, brandy and liquors.	Ditto ...	15th. Aug. 1897
42	Dec.	25	Société des Anciens Etablissements Cail.	Frame-work in sheet iron for supporting cane-crushing cylinders, &c.	Ditto ...	25th. Dec. 1897
	1884					
43	July	27	Alex. Smith & Alex. Smith.	Improvements in multitubular steam-boilers.	Ditto ...	27th. July 1898
	1885					
44	March	19	Lesport, Appolydore..	Improving the manufacture of Sugar Cane.	Ditto ...	19th. Mch. 1899
45	,,	20	Dathis fils, Léon ...	Improvements in the manufacture of bread and the apparatus therefor.	Ditto ...	20th. Mch. 1899
46	April	14	Cuisinier, Léon ...	Process for extracting and saccharifying ingredious of amylaceous subtances by treatment with malt.	Ditto ...	14th. April 1899
47	,,	22	Chatel, Rémy ...	Disinfecting rum and alcohols.	Ditto ...	22nd. April 1899
48	March	9	de Barrau, Charles D'Abbadie.	Certain improvements in the manufacture of Sugar as dealing with cane juice.	Ditto ...	9th. March 1899
49	June	17	Kœnig, Henry ...	Making Sugar in using liquid sulphurous acid in cane juices and neutralising it subsequently and using liquid sulphurous acid a second time after the sugar is cooked in the vacuum pan.	Ditto ...	17th. June 1899
50	June	22	Boyer de la Giroday, Charles.	The invention of an Aratory instrument styled 'GratteuseMechanique.'	Ditto ...	22nd. June 1899
51	October	7	Kottman, Gustave ...	Machine called a Sugar Cane diffusion apparatus.	Ditto ...	7th. Oct. 1899
52	October	22	Mc May, David ...	Improving Machines for extracting Aloe fibres and other textile plants.	Ditto ...	22nd. Oct. 1899
	1886					
53	Feb.	16	Stevens, John George	For an improved method of an apparatus or machinery for cleaning & separating the pulpy matters from the fibres of leaves and plants.	Ditto ...	16th. Feb. 1900

No.	Date of Patent.		Patentee's Name.	Subject.	Duration Years.	Expiry.
	1886					
54	March	13	Eynaud, Paul ...	For improving the machinery called centrifugals or turbines and has invented a system of breaks by means of levers beneath the basket.	14 Years ...	13th. Mch. 1900
55	March	13	Eynaud, Paul ...	For improving the machine called centrifugals or turbines and has invented a means of applying steam separated from condensed water into sugar or other substance in the basket.	Ditto ...	13th. Mch. 1900
56	May	4	Fin, Jean Baptiste ...	" Extraction complète de tout le jus contenu dans la canne à sucre."	Ditto ...	4th. May 1900
57	May	17	Bour, François Joseph and Bour, François Numa Alfred.	Improving the manufacture of syrup sugar.	Ditto ...	17th. May 1900
58	July	3	Bour, François Joseph	Injecting steam into the bagasse as well as the water from the condensed steam in the steam pipes from the boilers to the mill.	Ditto ...	3rd. July 1900
59	"	23	Aubin, J. P. Georges.	Diffusion of cane trash or bagasse.	Ditto ...	23rd. July 1900
60	Sept.	22	Hope, Mirza ...	Improved apparatus for the reception of night-soil.	Ditto ...	22nd. Sept. 1900
61	Oct.	1	Castelin, Louis Marie.	Invention of three different kinds of apparatus for converting the cane trash or bagasse from one mill to another in making it pass in a bath imbibition (diffusion) before arriving at a second mill.	Ditto ...	1st. Oct. 1900
62	"	19	Duval, Martin Léonard Edmond.	Improved arrangement of diffusion apparatus applicable to the treatment of sugar cane and bagasse.	Ditto ...	19th. Oct. 1900
63	"	27	Stromberg, Adolphus	Machine for slicing or cutting sugar canes provided with horizontal rotating knives carried by a disc and one or more hoppers by means of which the canes are presented to disc at an acute angle and by the influence of their own right.	Ditto ...	27th. Oct. 1900

No.	Date of Patent.	Patentee's Name.	Subject.	Duration Years.	Expiry.
	1886				
64	Sept. 7	Pochard, Marie Ernest	New process for manufacturing beer and porter.	14 Years ...	7th. Sept. 1900
	1887				
65	January 13	Brin, Louis Quentin and Brin, Arthur,	Improvement in the separation and obtainment of Oxygen and Nitrogen from Atmospheric air.	Ditto ...	13th. Jan. 1901
66	,, 17	Everitt, Percival ...	Improvement in weighing machines.	Ditto ...	17th. Jan. 1901
67	February 21	Eynaud, Paul ...	Extraction of the juice contained in the cane trash or in the rinds (Cossettes) of the sugar canes.	Ditto ...	21st. Feb. 1901
68	February 21	Ehrmann, Léon ...	More complete extraction of sugar from cane trash.	Ditto ...	21st. Feb. 1901
69	......	....	....	......	*Cancelled*
70	March 5	Page, Robert William	Improvements in muscular power or strength testing machines.	Ditto ...	5th. Mch. 1901
71	April 7	de Chazal, P.E., Agent and Attorney in Mauritius for Arthur and Léon Quentin Brin.	Improvements in the manufacture of sugar.	Ditto ...	7th. April 1901
72	May 9	Mc Kay, David ...	For the defiltration of the sugar cane.	Ditto ...	9th. May 1901
73	August 17	Vigier, Louis Auguste	The extraction of the fibres of every kind of textile shrubs or plants aloe or other by means of a new and improved machine.	Ditto ...	17th. Aug. 1901
74	Nov. 22	Vidal fils, Albert Eugène.	A new and improved machine for the washing beating and drying of the aloe and other fibres.	Ditto ...	22nd. Nov. 1901
75	Dec. 15	Messrs. Pipon, Adam & Co., as Agents in Mauritius for "La Compagnie de Fives Lilles" of Paris.	Improvements relating to diffusing apparatus for use in the treatment of beetroot, sugar cane and other substances.	Ditto ...	15th. Dec. 1901
	1888				
76	May 3	Longmore, James & Watson, William Livingstone.	Improvements in the treatment of exogenous fibrous plants, flax, jute rhea and the like.	Ditto ...	3rd. May 1902

No.	Date of Patent.		Patentee's Name.	Subject.	Duration Years.	Expiry.
	1888					
77	May	5	Duchenne, Jean and Mongey, Honoré.	Machine for the extraction of the fibre from the plant known under the name of aloes.	14 Years ..	5th. May 1902.
78	,,	14	Stéphanon, Louis Théodore.	Double acting machine or apparatus for filtering and pressing juice and scums (called filtre-presse à double effet et à lavage mécanique.)	Ditto ...	14th. May 1902.
79	July	24	Bouyer, Frederic ...	Machine for the extraction of fibre from textile plants in general and from the green aloe (Fourcroya Gigantea.)	Ditto ...	24th. July 1902.
80	July	20	Barlow, Frederick William Henry.	Setting up multitubular boilers or other boilers used in Sugar Mills.	Ditto ...	20th. July 1902.
81	August	8	Eynaud, Paul ...	Augmenter considérablement la puissance des appareils évaporatoires connus sous le nom de "Double effet de Triple effet" et annuler la contrepression sur les pistons de machines dont les vapeurs d'échappements sont employées au chauffages des dits appareils.	Ditto ...	8th. Aug. 1902.
82	,,	23	Ruffin, Marie Charles Alfred.	A Process and apparatus for purifying crude spirit and regenerating the purifying agent.	Ditto ...	23rd. Aug. 1902.
83	Sept.	3	Tuyau, Camille and Dauguet, Charles.	New and useful improvements in machinery for extraction fibre from the Agave or Aloes and other textile plants.	Ditto ...	3rd. Sept. 1902.
84	,,	14	Don, Alfred ...	Improved apparatus for the prevention and consumption of smoke and more complete combustion of the fuel in steam boiler and other furnaces.	Ditto ...	14th. Sept. 1902.
85	Nov.	22	Young, Alexander ...	Improved means of generating and superheating steam.	Ditto ...	22nd. Nov. 1902.
86	,,	3	Yaryan, Homer, Taylor.	Vacuum evaporating and distilling apparatus.	Ditto ...	23rd. Nov. 1902

No.	Date of Patent.		Patentee's Name.	Subject.	Duration Years.	Expiry.
	1888					
87	Nov.	23	de Barrau, François Charles d'Abbadie.	An apparatus for drying cane trash (bagasse).	14 Years ...	23rd. Nov. 1902.
88	Sept.	28	Castelin, Louis Marie	A modification and improvement to apparatus No. 2 of his previous invention of three different kinds of apparatus for conveying the cane trash or bagasse from one mill to another in making it pass through a bath of imbibition (diffusion) before arriving at the 2nd. mill.	Ditto ...	28th. Sept. 1902.
	1889					
89	Feb.	20	Stephanon, Louis Théodore, and Chazal Regis de.	A mechanical Filter for Juices and Syrups.	Ditto ...	20th. Feb. 1903.
90	,,	25	de Barrau, François Charles d'Abbadie.	An apparatus for drying cane trash (bagasse).	Ditto ...	25th. Feb. 1903.
91	March	7	Kôhler, Frantz Serapins and Keyling, Ludovig.	Improvements in the manufacture of shot or spheres or globules of iron, steel, metal and in apparatus therefor.	Ditto ...	7th. March 1903.
92	,,	19	de Barrau, François Charles d'Abbadie.	A new apparatus for drying cane trash (bagasse) and straw.	Ditto ...	19th. Mch. 1903.
93	May	8	Raymond, George & Raymond, Albert.	Improvements relating to the pulverization or reduction of mineral or other substances and to apparatus therefor.	Ditto ...	8th. May 1903.
94	,,	9	Godillot, Alexis ...	The disposition of a mode of feeding furnaces with grainy, pulverulent and filamentous fuel.	Ditto ...	9th. May 1903.
95	,,	9	Proks, Charles ...	A filter for the mechanical filtration of syrup and other turbid liquids	Ditto ...	9th. May 1903.
96	July	12	de Barrau, François Charles d'Abbadie.	New apparatus for drying cane trash, (bagasse) Plan I.	Ditto ...	12th. July 1903.
97	,,	12	de Barrau, François Charles d'Abbadie.	New apparatus for drying cane trash, (bagasse) Plan II.	Ditto ...	12th. July 1903.

No.	Date of Patent.		Patentee's Name.	Subject.	Duration Years.	Expiry.
	1889					
98	July	12	de Barrau, François Charles d'Abaddie.	New apparatus for drying cane trash, (bagasse) Part III.	14 Years ...	12th. July 1903
99	,,	12	de Barrau, François Charles d'Abaddie.	New apparatus for drying cane trash, (bagasse) Plan IV.	Ditto ...	12th. July 1903
100	,,	12	de Barrau, François Charles d'Abaddie.	New apparatus for drying cane trash, (bagasse) Plan V.	Ditto ...	12th. July 1903
101	August	5	Daniels, Williams Hoskins.	An improved antiseptic compound for preserving perishable articles.	Ditto ...	5th. Aug. 1903
102	,,	24	Senneville, Edouard de, and Castelin Louis Marie.	Setting up of multitubular cylindrical Boilers with two exterior furnaces.	Ditto ...	24th. Aug. 1903
	1890					
103	January	8	Doty, Henry Harrison	Improvements in the treatment of Rhea or Ramie and other fibrous plants and in an apparatus therefor.	Ditto ...	8th. Jan. 1904
104	Feb.	20	Bouyer, Frederick ...	Extraction of fibres from aloe leaves and other textile plants.	Ditto ...	20th. Feb. 1904
105	March	21	Hyatt, John Wesley.	A method for extracting Liquid or soluble Constituents from Disintegrated vegetable materials.	Ditto ..	21st. Mch. 1904
106	,,	19	Puvrez, Marie and Mathilde.	An improved Mechanical Filter.	Ditto ...	19th. Mch. 1904
107	May	7	Daniel, Achille ...	A combined ploughing Machine (charrue multiple).	Ditto ...	7th. May 1904
108	,,	29	Godillot, Alexis ...	Three inventions for the improvements of the "Four Godillot."	Ditto ...	29th. May 1904
109	June	30	Trébuchet, Louis Gustave Amédée.	A new system of night-soil tubs which he calls "Tinette mystérieuse" for separating Liquids from the solid portions of human dejections.	Ditto ...	30th. June 1904

No.	Date of Patent.		Patentee's Name.	Subject.	Duration Years.	Expiry.
	1890					
110	August	20	Hyatt, John Wesley.	New and useful improvements in machines for disintegrating fibrous substances.	14 Years ...	20th. Aug. 1904
111	,,	20	Potier, J. Chatel and Daudé U.	A new process to prepare vanilla.	Ditto ...	20th. Aug. 1904
112	October	13	Ehrmann, Léon and de Coulhac Mazérieux Prosper.	Filtration of Liquids ...	Ditto ...	13th. Oct. 1904
113	Nov.	21	De la Giroday, Charles Boyer.	A new process for injecting steam in turbines in sugar manufacturing.	Ditto ...	21st. Nov. 1904
114	,,	21	Ehrmann, Léon ...	A new process for the purification of saccharine matters.	Ditto ...	21st. Nov. 1904
	1891					
115	March	3	Léon Pierre Adam ...	A new instrument styled 'Controleur de Charge.'	Ditto ...	3rd. March 1905
116	,,	13	Edouard Carosin ...	A new system of steam injection in Turbines.	Ditto ...	13th. Mch. 1905
117	April	2	L. de Lesconble ...	A new process of preparation and preservation of Vanilla pods by means of sugar.	Ditto ...	2nd. April 1905
118	May	7	Moritz Weinrich ...	An invention for the filtering and purification of saccharine solutions or other solutions or liquids.	Ditto ...	7th. May 1905
119	,,	29	Paul Tardieu ...	An improvement made to the apparatus known under the name of "Four Godillot."	Ditto ...	29th. May 1905
120	June	3	Donald Mc Gregor ...	An invention for cleaning leaves for the manufacture of fibre in general.	Ditto ...	3rd. June 1905
121	August	27	Emile Labat ...	Improvements in the manufacture of sugar.	Ditto ...	27th. Aug. 1905
122	Sept.	22	Ernst Schulze ...	Improvements in slicing Machines for sugar cane and the like.	Ditto ...	22nd. Sept. 1905
123	,,	29	John Norman Spencer Williams ...	Improvements in apparatus for manufacturing sugar.	Ditto ...	29th. Sept. 1905

No.	Date of Patent.	Patentee's Name	Subject.	Duration Years.	Expiry.
	1891				
124	October 22	A. E. Vidal ...	A new and improved machine for the extraction of aloe and other fibres.	14 Years ...	22nd Oct. 1905.
125	December 9	François Charles d'Abadie de Barrau.	An apparatus for digging raw sugar and Turbine supplier " Fouilleuse pour le sucre en tables."	Ditto ...	9th Dec. 1905.
126	" 9	Gaston Rampal ...	A machine styled "Frein instantané pour Turbine."	Ditto ...	9th Dec. 1905.
	1892				
127	Jan. 28	Alfred Chapman ...	"Improvements in apparatus for evaporating saccharine or other solutions or liquids."	Ditto ...	28th Jan. 1906.
128	Jan. 28	Do. ...	Do. do. ...	Ditto ...	Do.
129	Feb. 10	Pierre Faure : commonly known as Pierre Paulin Faure.	"An improved machine for decorticating Ramie and other textile plants.	Ditto ...	10th Feb. 1906.
130	Oct. 11	The Electrolibration Company represented by John Norwood Webb, President.	"Methods of and apparatus for the treatment of Disorders of Human Beings and other living objects."	Ditto ...	11th Oct. 1906.
131	Nov. 17	John Armstrong Chanler.	"Improvement in pavements."	Ditto ...	17th Nov. 1906.
132	Dec. 16	Ernest Hermann and Louis Philippe Cohen.	" Improvements in bagasse Furnaces."	Ditto ...	16th Dec. 1906.
	1893				
133	Jan. 10	P. Tardieu & Co. ...	A "Filtre Presse à toile métallique et à plateaux alternatifs."	Ditto ...	10th Jan. 1907.
134	" 23	Joseph Bour ...	"An apparatus for improvement of sugar cooked in the vacuum pan."	Ditto ...	23rd Jan. 1907.
135	March 27	William and Thomas Hawkins.	"Improvements in and relating to generating fluid pressure for motive power and other purposes."	Ditto ...	27th Mch. 1907.
136	July 20	Mrs Widow Jean Baptiste Fin & Mr. Laurent Christ.	"A new machine for the complete extraction of the juice contained in the sugar cane or in cane trash."	Ditto ...	20th July 1907.

No.	Date of Patent.		Patentee's Name.	Subject.	Duration Years.	Expiry.
	1894					
137	Jan.	5	Oscar Maingard ...	Invention of a new process for reducing to a minimum the loss sustained in the manipulation of sugar on Estates.	14 years ...	5th Jan. 1908.
138	„	17	Léon de Lescouble ...	Invention of a steam apparatus for the preparation and desiccation of vanilla pods.	Ditto ...	17th Jan. 1908.
139	Feb.	14	Messrs Verhaeren and de Jager.	Invention of a " Filtre Décanteur à plateaux horizontaux."	Ditto ...	14th Feb. 1908.
140	May	12	W. Jean Ercole Pellegrin.	" Improvements in the manufacture of sugar and in the apparatus employed therein."	Ditto ...	12th May 1908.
141	„	14	The Miriless Watson and Yaryan company Limited.	" Improvements in the construction of apparatus for the purification of sugar cane juice."	Ditto ...	14th May 1908.
142	June	18	Paul L'Hoste ...	" Invention for making and preparing by the ordinary process of pharmacopiea, a pharmaceutical produce extracted from turtle oil and cocoa and known as " Elixir reconstituant."	Ditto ...	18th June 1908.
143	Nov.	8	Mark Knight Wescott	" An improved process for compressing fodder into blocks."	Ditto ...	8th Nov. 1908.
	1895					
144	June	19	Constant Vankeirsbilck.	Invention of " Glaneuse" to cut sugar cane.	Ditto ...	19th June 1909.
145	„	25	Louis Lachaux ...	Improved means for increasing the evaporating power of certain apparatus " Moyens perfectionnés permettant " d'augmenter la puissance d'évaporation " des appareils dits à " simple, double ou multiple effet ou de tout " autre appareils réchauffeur employé " dans les appareils à " évaporer (à cuire) à " distiller où à rectifier."	Ditto ...	25th June 1909.

No.	Date of Patent.		Patentee's Name.	Subject.	Duration Years.	Expiry.
	1895					
146	Sept.	6	Gérard Cambray ...	A new process for the manufacture of sugar cane juice " l'épuration complète du vesou de la canne à sucre par la double sulfitation. "	14 Years ...	6th Sept. 1909.
147	,,	25	Emanuel Hübner ...	Improvements in the manufacture of white sugar and the like from molasses and in centrifugal apparatus for use therein.	Ditto ...	25th Sept. 1909.
148	Oct.	15	Louis Théodore Stéphanon.	Invention of an apparatus called " Appareil Auto-Compteur-Mesureur " for measuring the volume of juice, syrups and other liquids.	Ditto ...	15th Oct. 1909
149	Nov.	15	Capt. Léon Pierre Adam.	Invention of an " Anémomètre d'Alarme à Signaux Automatiques".	Ditto ...	15th Nov. 1909.

Comparative Statement of the Resident Population of Mauritius according to the Census 1881 and 1891.

Districts.	Census of 1881.	Census of 1891.	Increase of 1891 over 1881.	Decrease of 1891 over 1881.
Port Louis	66,466	62,046	......	4,420
Pamplemousses	37,670	39,147	1,477	......
Rivière du Rempart	20,726	24,151	3,425	......
Flacq	56,022	56,734	712	......
Grand Port	52,982	48,169	.. ...	4,813
Savanne	34,447	34,977	530	......
Plaines Wilhems	46,315	57,591	11,276	......
Moka	29,768	32,552	2,784	......
Black River	15,292	15,698	406	......
Shipping Mauritius	159	123	......	36
Flat, Gabriel and Fouquets Islands ...	27	36	9	......
	359,874	371,224	20,619	9,269

Total increase ... ... 11,350.

A brief description of the Mare-aux-Vacoas Waterworks.

Many changes have been taking place at the Mare-aux-Vacoas during the past four years. The reservoir, which forms a magnificent lake of some 400 acres in extent, was previous to 1891 little better than a swamp, in which many acres of forest had been submerged, has now been entirely cleared of the dead and dying trees, which rotted in the water. The banks of the Mare too, formerly covered with thick bush, scrub and ravenals, which grew down to the water's edge, have likewise been cleared for some distance back, so that it is possible to take a pleasant and agreeable walk of about 5 miles round the margin of the lake, which formerly was impracticable owing to the thickness of the growth and the undrained marshes.

The many works of art designed by Mr. Osbert Chadwick, C.E., for effecting an improvement in the quality of the water, as well as increasing the storage capacity of the lake, are far advanced, indeed fast nearing completion. Among the more important of these works should be mentioned the Great Sluice, and Dam at the head of the Tamarind River, and the new high level and low level outlet chambers. These have all been most substantially constructed in masonry, from stones obtained on the spot, and the workmanship reflects great credit on the creole masons employed on them, under the foremanship of Passooramen the guardian of the Mare, himself an expert Indian mason.

Special notice should be made of the "Great Sluice." This has been imported from England and is known as "Stoney's patent." It was manufactured by Ransomes and Rapier, of Norwich, and is similar to those used on the Manchester ship canal. Briefly, it consists of four flanged steel plates bolted together, and working on roller guides, and is rendered water tight by means of two "staunching rods" of steel which loosely fit into a recess provided for them between the door and the guide plates on either side. The weight of water pressing these rods into place renders the door perfectly watertight. The sluice which is 15' 6" high by 10' wide and weighs 7 tons in all can be readily raised and lowered by one man. It being provided with a counterbalance box, which is slung by stout steel wire ropes passing over pulleys supported on substantial masonry colums 38' above the cill, and a system of geared-motion which is actuated by a light chain passing over a driving pulley. This new sluice replaces one of 2' square which has since been done away with. The object of having this big sluice is to prevent, as far as possible an overflow on the Tamarind Dam by which in heavy rains the good water escapes and is lost. In future the contaminated water will be drawn off from the bottom and when the rains cease good fresh water will be stored.

The Tamarind Dam is being raised 3' 2" above its former level, and is formed of masonry on a solid bed of cement concrete. The raising of this Dam will have the effect of increasing the storage capacity of the Mare to something like 431 millions of gallons, when it will be sufficient to supply a population of 138,500 at the rate of 30 gallons per head per day for 70 days, after allowing for compensation water to the riverains on Tamarind River, and assuming that a drought lasted that time, and that all the streams supplying the Mare had become exhausted, which judging from past record is not a very like occurrence.

The water for drinking purposes is now delivered through a sluice chamber placed in the water directly opposite to the principal streams which feed the Mare. The masonry chamber is provided with six sluices at different levels, so arranged that the water can be drawn off from the surface, instead of from the bottom as formerly, and then flows through an open canal into the Cogliano Stream. The work of excavating this canal was very heavy, and took over 12 months to perform, the greater part of it being thro' solid rock, in places 13 feet deep, but the cost of providing this new outlet has been amply compensated by the improvement in the quality and general clearness of the water delivered thro' it.

The chief works remaining to be done at the Mare itself are the raising of earth embankments for banking off the flatter portions of the fore-shore by means of dykes and directing the tributary streams to the central parts of the Mare and towards the new outlet. These works will yet take some time to complete, but are progressing steadily. The total length of the banks amounts to something like 4000 lineal yards, varying in height from 2 feet to 16 feet but the average embankment is about 5' 6". Most of the banks are formed with slopes of 2 to 1 or 3 to 1 depending on the nature of the soil, and faced on the water side with rough stone pitching. The work is chiefly carried on with the aid of a portable railway, and twelve small tip wagons, which have been imported from England. Without such means the work would become very costly, indeed would hardly be practicable.

The thorough eradication of the "Vonnes" has proved a task of great difficulty, as their growth is most rapid. Recourse has now been had to a Priestman's small stream grab dredger. This has only recently been got into working order, and has not yet had a fair trial, but is likely to be of great service in getting rid of this obnoxious water weed. The plan is to dredge the 'Vonnes" up by the roots, load on to barges, transport them to the shore, and deposit it in suitable places where they will decay without pollution to the water. When the necessary barges are completed it is expected that 400 superficial yards per day will be cleared, or say one acre in 12 working days.

After leaving the Mare the water flows thro' the new cut to the old channel for a distance of about half a mile, when it is intercepted by a masonry dam and then taken by a masonry conduit till it meets the public road leading to Vacoa, &c. From this point the water is conveyed by a 16" cast iron pipe to the filter beds situated at "La Marie."

The works at "La Marie" have been of an extensive character, and are now completed. They consist of a Depositing Reservoir, four Filter Beds, an Engine House, and Superintendent's Quarters, but this latter is only just being started. The works are all substantially built in masonry, much of the stone being brought from a distance, as only a small quantity of that quarried on the spot was found fit for use.

The crude water brought from the Mare by the 16" pipe above mentioned, first passes through the motive cylinders of the Pumping Machinery, and then goes into the Depositing Reservoir, which is 134 feet square by 12 feet deep, and contains about 1,340,000 gallons, entering it at the bottom. It is then drawn from the top by means of a floating pipe, and flows to the filter beds, where it is filtered and then passes into the mains to be distribued to the public. The districts supplied by gravitation are Vacoa, including Highlands Estate, the greater part of Phœnix, also Quatre Bornes, Rose Hill, Beau Bassin, and Petite Rivière as far as the R. C. Church in one direction, and a short distance above Coromandel Police Station in the other. The total length of distributary mains which range from 14" diam. down to 2½ diam. is approximately 44 miles.

The water is pumped to Curepipe by means of 3 hydraulic motors each working a double acting pump, and capable of working either together or separately.

The total height that the water has to be pumped is about 360 feet.

The motors and pumps have been manufactured by Glenfield & Co., of Kilmarnock and exhibit first class workmanship.

For the Curepipe waterworks 3 services reservoirs, each to contoin 150,000 gallons have been arranged for, but up to the present only one, namely that on La Brasserie Hill at an elevation of 2,012 feet has been completed.

The total length of distributary mains amounts to between 17 and 18 miles of cast iron pipes varying in size from 7" down to 2½" diam.

ANALYSIS MADE IN ENGLAND OF THE WATER OF MARE-AUX-VACOAS.

Chemical Laboratory and Testing Works

Broadway,
Westminster, S. W.

London, 9th. February, 1894.

Mauritius Mare-aux-Vacoas Water Works.--Analysis and Investigation.— re Water Purification.

Sir,

Herewith we send you extracts from our report dated May 20th. 1892, re the above matter.

The method of determining "Oxygen absorbed" that was used in this investigation is described in the appendix of the report and is that officially adopted by the Society of Public Analysts. The results obtained by the Flügge method—the necessary reagents for which have been sent to the Colony at your request—are not necessarily identical with those of the process above mentioned. With the particular water now under consideration, experiment shows that the values obtained by the Flügge method are about double those given by the method used throughout the report.

Your obedient servants,

(Sd.) STANGER and BLOUNT.

OSBERT CHADWICK Esq., C.M.G.
7, Carteret Street,
Westminster.

EXTRACTS FROM REPORT DATED 20TH. MAY 1892, UPON INVESTIGATION OF WATER.

Mauritius.—Mare-aux-Vacoas Water Works.

Samples were drawn from each of the four carboys and well mixed care being taken to obtain a proper proportion of suspended matter with each, and the mixed sample used throughout the subsequent investigation.

Analysis of original Sample.

			Grains per gallon.
Total Solids	...	...	... 6.94
Chlorine	...	...	... 0.98

			Parts per 100,000.
Free Ammonia ...	...	...	... .029
Albumenoid Ammonia	...	...	... .031
Oxygen absorbed (after 4 hours)			... 0.43
Nitrogen as Nitrates	...	...	... trace
Nitrogen as Nitrites	...	...	... nil

Hardness... ... $1^{\circ}5$.

Analysis of filtred water. In order to ascertain what improvement had been effected by simple filtration the following determinations were made:

			Parts per 100,000.
Free Ammonia ...	...	...	... .017
Albumenoid Ammonia	...	...	... .013
Oxygen absorbed (4 hours) ...			... 0.22

A reduction in the total amount of solid matter also took place.

			Grains per gallon.
Total Solids	...	...	... 4.93

Treatment with metallic iron. It being apparent that some method whereby the water was rendered capable of more rapid filtration was necessary the action of metallic iron which has been found effective in recent important cases of water purification, was tried.

100 Grams of clean iron turnings were therefore agitated for five minutes with ¼ gallon of water, and the water thus treated filtered. The rate of filtration was much greater than in the case of the untreated water, the time necessary for the passage of the above named quantity being four hours. During the time that filtration was proceeding the water was allowed to stand in contact with the iron turnings but without further agitation.

The filtrate when examined in the 2 ft. tube was light blue in colour and in fact compared favourably with the London supply of Thames water. The degree of improvement in respect of organic purety may be gathered from the following figures.

Analysis of water after treatment.

			Parts per 100,000.
Free Ammonia ...	...	...	... .029
Albumenoid Ammonia	...	...	... .006
Oxygen absorbed...	...	...	... 0.10

The increase in "free Ammonia" as compared with the water merely filtered is the result of the oxidation of a portion of the Albumenoid substances present, the removal of which by this means and by filtration is the cause of the marked decrease in "Albumenoid Ammonia". The total oxidisable organic matter has also undergone a considerable diminution.

Treatment with Clay alone.

The effect of Clay alone was tried on a fresh portion of the water. The quantity taken was epuivalent to :

	Grains per gallon.
Clay	20.

¼ Gall of the water took 5¾ hours to filter.

Analysis of water after Clay treatment.

The filtrate from the treatment described above was a light greenish yellow, but quite bright, it gave the following analytical figures :

	Parts per 100,000.
Free Ammonia	.022
Albumenoid Ammonia	.013
Oxygen absorbed (after 4 hours) ...	0.22
Oxygen absorbed (Flügge method) ...	0.43

It will be seen from these figures that by this very simple process a satisfactory improvement can be obtained.

The method of purification finally chosen must be largely determined by local conditions.

Our belief however founded on such acquaintance with these conditions as we have, is that the best method would consist in agitating, and preferably aerating the water in contact with finely powered burnt Clay—a rich tenacious clay being used—and decanting or filtering according to the reservoir capacity available; passing the effiuent through a revolving barrel containing iron scraps and filtering the water thus treated through an ordinary filter-bed. In the event of the quality of the supply improving, the treatment with iron might be dispensed with as the Clay alone effects a considerable amount of purification.

Mauritius Spa.

It is not generally known by the rising generation that there exists in Mauritius valuable springs of mineral waters which, if we are to believe the analyses made by Dr. J. W. Watson and Mr. Guthrie, formerly Professor of Chemistry at the Royal College, are superior to those of Epsom, Spa and Seidlitz.

The first is that known as Tielmanns a spring of chalybeate water which was discovered on the heights of Champ de Lort in 1818 by Mr. Tielmann.

This water comes from a well 98 feet deep on the property of Mr. Mayer. It was at the time, when servants of the East India Company came to Mauritius to recruit their health, much sought after by persons suffering from enlargement of the Liver and Spleen and Paludien Cachexia. Its fame spread to India, to the Cape and even to Europe and one of the first things asked for by strangers in former days was the waters from this well.

In his work on Mauritius (1862) the Reverend Fleming gives the following analysis of Tielmann's water made by Dr. J. W. Watson from one quart :

Carbonate of Magnesia and Cabonate of Lime	5.50
Muriate of Soda	40.00
Do. of Magnesia	6.00
Do. of Lime	7.75
Sulphate of Magnesia	32.00
Do. of Lime	6.25
Oxide of Iron...	0.75
Silica	1.75
	100.000

Ruisseau Rose.

The water in this locality is highly impregnated with Iron.

Little or no use has hitherto been made of this water probably because it is obtained from sources in the Colony; had it been in the neighbouring Island of Réunion doubtless many Mauritius would have gone there to partake of its health giving qualities.

The first analysis of the Ruisseau Rose water was made by a medical Commission as far back as 1853 which showed that the springs were very rich in Iron. Since then Mr. J. Rouhier, of Comedy Street, Port Louis, who rents the property and who sells the waters of the 3 Springs, has caused these waters to be analysed by Mr. A. H. Boname, the Director of the "Station Agronomique". The following is the result for "Valentine" Spring;

	Gram
Matière minérale par litre	0.118
„ Volatile au rouge	30
Résidu total par litre ...	0.148
Gaz dissons par litre :	Cent. cubes
Acide Carbonique	6.7
Oxygène	1.0
Azote	10.5
	Par litres grammes
Silice	0.015
Chlore	0.036
Acide Sulfurique	0.006
Chaux	0.012
Magnésie	0.009
Soude	0.007
Protoxyde de Fer	00.064

"Mélanie" Spring:

	Grammes.
Fer par litre	0.025
Correspondant à Protoxyde de fer	0.031
Composition :	Grammes.
Fer métallique par litre	0.025
Correspondant a Protoxyde de fer par litre	0.032

Mauritius Tea Experimental Plantation.

Owing to proper cultivation and a good system of pruning and plucking, the old tea fields (5 acres) planted in 1886 and containing mixed shrubs of good and inferior *jât* (quality) have much improved. Their average yield per acre has been 572 lbs. and it is expected to rise to 625 lbs.

The 15 acres planted in 1893 are also steadily improving and with careful treatment will be by far superior in every respect to the old tea fields. The young bushes are just coming into partial bearing with an average of 50 lbs. per acre which will rise to 100 lbs. in 1895.

The plant previously put into the factory, such as the "Sirocco" firing machine and the rolling machine are doing very good work. The quality of the made tea has been raised to a higher standard owing to the uniformity and regularity of the process.

The next desideratum of speedy and cheaper work has been considered and can be arrived at by the addition to the plant of a moter, substituting steam to hand power in working the machines.

The principal plantions are at Chamarel, La Nouvelle France and Curepipe.

The Coloured Earths of Chamarel.

Few strangers coming to Mauritius with time on hand for sight seeing leave without having visited Chamarel Estate in the District of Black River. This Estate is situated on a plateau the height of which is 850 feet above the level of the sea, and the lovely sights from the road winding up from the Black River side once seen are not soon effaced from memory. Here you have a beautiful Cascade with a fall of 300 feet,—a little further on towards the Savanne side is the Tea plantation of which there are 100 acres. Tea from the Estate has already been cured and sent home to England where it is pronounced by experts to be excellent in quality.

On the Black River side, going down towards the Baie du Cap is the spot where there are different coloured Earths arranged in ridges and known as " les côtes de melon ". In the following letter which has been kindly communicated to the Compiler of this Almanac by Mr. W. W. Hay, the late Manager of the Mauritius Estates & Assets Company Limited will be found the Chemical Analyses made by Messrs. Augustus Voelcher & Sons of London of twenty different samples of these earths.

— —

Analytical Laboratory.
22, Tudor Street, New Bridge Street,
London E. C., September 20th. 1894.

W. Riddel, Esq.
Secretary.
Mauritius Estates & Assets Cy. Ld.

Dear Sir,

We beg now to report to you upon the samples of coloured earth sent by you from one of your Estates in Mauritius.

In all, twenty different samples were forwarded to us, with instructions to analyse *two* of these.

The samples varied in colour from yellow and yellowish brown to bright red, purple and corn black. After inspection of them we selected 5 which were distinctly purple in colour, making one average sample of these, and also 3 which were bright red in colour, and we made another average sample of these. These average samples we submitted to analysis and obtained the following results :

(Soils dried at 212° F.)

	Average of 5 purple soils.	Average of 3 bright red soils.
Water of combination, will mere traces of Organic matter...	10.08	10.74
Ferrous Oxide	.29	.25
Ferric Oxide	20.05	22.54
Alumina	28.02	27.47
Lime	.15	.15
Magnesia	.30	.55
Potash	.08	.08
Soda	.09	.04
Phosphoric Acid	.10	.11
Sulphuric Acid	.18	.27
Insoluble silicates & Sand	40.60	37.80
	100.00	100.00
Nitrogen	.03	.03

These results show the soils to be very ferruginous clays of heavy nature, almost devoid of Organic (vegetable) matter, and very deficient in most of the principal elements of soil fertility. Thus, they contain almost no nitrogen, but very little lime, decided deficiencies of Potash, while No. 1 has only a moderate amount of Phosphoric Acid, and No. 2 still less. The absence of Organic matter has been already noted, while in the other hand, the large quantities of Iron and Alumina are unfavourable to the chemical and the physical natures of the soils. It is this deficiency in the main elements of plant food which is, in our opinion, the cause of the soils being so unproductive, coupled with the bad mechanical condition which is characteristic of heavy ferruginous clay like these. The soils are extremely tenacious clays, and we would go so far as to say that, even were they to be well supplied with necessary elements of plant food, their bad mechanical condition and sticky nature would militate greatly against these elements being brought into active availability.

We have examined the soils for the possible presence of ingredients which might directly prove harmful to vegetation, but the result of this is to lead us to conclude that it is not the presence of any harmful ingredient in particular, but the general absence of fertily combined with bad physical condition of the soils that has occasioned the sterility of which you complain.

If the soils are to be cultivated you will have to turn your attention in the first place to the improvement of the mechanical state of these clays and to try and alter their impermeability. Until you have done this it will not be worth while to expend any considerable amount in the endeavour to enrich soils so generally deficient in elements of fertility.

We are, yours faithfully,

(Signed) Augustus VOELCHER & Sons.

The Port Office.

The Port Office is situated on the upper part of the harbour and forms part of the Customs House. It is a two storied building and is easily distinguished by a flagstaff eighty feet above the sea level from which all signals are made in and off the Port. The whole establishment is under the direct control of the Harbour Master. Storehouses are attached for the working plant of the port which consists of warps, lines, blocks, oars, machinery &c. Attached to the Department are two powerful steam tugs, capable of towing the largest men of war. There are also steam launches and mooring launches fitted with winches and appliances for lifting wrecks, anchors or other heavy weights.

This Department is also provided with a life boat and a rocket apparatus for saving life, there are sailing and rowing boats for harbour and sea service.

All hurricane signals are made from the Port Office which is in telegraphic communication with the Observatory at Pamplemousses and are repeated from Fort George. The pilots, who are all master mariners, are under the orders of the Harbour Master. Ships of war are piloted by the Assistant Harbour Master.

No signals are attended to in this Colony but those of the " Commercial Code."

The Light Houses of Mauritius.

In addition to the Light Ship moored at the anchorage of Port Louis, there are three other lights on the coast of Mauritius. The first in starting from Port Louis is that erected on Canoniers' Point at right angles to the existing reef. It has a fixed catoptric light of the first order, and is situated in latitude 20 ° 0' 35" South and longitude 57 ° 35' 24" East, its elevation above the mean level of the sea is eighty nine feet six inches, and it can be seen from the deck of a vessel fourteen feet above the water at a distance of ten nautical miles. This light is a perfectly safe guide in working a vessel up or down the coast between Canonier and Grenadier Points and gives admirable warning by turning red when the vessel is standing into danger.

Flat Island Light House.

The Light house placed on this Island is situated at the South west or highest part of the island in latitude 19 ° 54' 26" South and longitude 57 ° 41' 12" East, its elevation above the mean sea level is 366 feet. The island is about six miles distant from the northern extremity of Mauritius and is used as a Quarantine Station.

The light is a revolving catoptric of the first order and is visible from the deck of a vessel thirteen feet above the sea at a distance of twenty five nautical miles ; the rise and fall of the tide at this place is the same as at Ile aux Fouquets, three feet at full and change. There are two landing places at Flat Island ; one is called the Pass the other the Palisades, both are difficult and sometimes dangerous. The anchorage is not very secure and on signs of a heavy sea, or rollers setting in, ships must immediately get under weigh.

Grand Port Light House.

This is built upon a small island called Ile aux Fouquets, in latitude 20 ° 24' 20" South and longitude 57 ° 45' 9" East ; it marks the Southern entrance to Grand Port Bay and is 800 yards to the East-North-East of Ile de la Passe, there is a small islet between them. The light apparatus is dioptric of the first order, showing a fixed white light from sunset to sunrise visible on every direction from seaward, but dark on the land side ; this light is 108½ feet above mean sea level and in clear weather can be seen at a distance of sixteen nautical miles from the deck of a vessel twelve feet above water.

The Harbour of Port Louis and the Port Department.

The harbour of Port Louis, situated on the west coast of the Island, is about a mile in length, from the Custom House Wharf to a line drawn between the two forts at its entrance, it is almost as broad. It is of irregular form and is bounded on the North by a stone causeway known as "Chaussée Tromlin" which separates the harbour from a large lagoon known by the name of "Mer Rouge." The depth of water in this part of the Harbour is not more than four feet at its deepest parts. The South side of the Harbour is bounded by a shelf of rocks which extend from the shore for about a quarter of a mile. The bottom of this side is of coral with not more than three or four feet of water over it; it suddenly deepens to fourteen feet. The harbour itself varies in depth, but it has accommodation for 150 vessels drawing from 12 to 25 feet, not including coasters, or vessels under 100 tons register, for which accommodation for about 60 more can be found.

There are two dredges constantly at work, the small one is employed to dredge the mouths of the streams that run into the harbour, and the large one is for the heavier and deeper work.

There are moorings laid down for ships of war drawing respectively from 21 to 28 feet. There are also two sets of moorings for large merchant steamers with a span of 400 feet each. Mushroom moorings have been laid down on the South-west side of the harbour for forty vessels. Cargoes are loaded and unloaded by means of lighters varying in size from 25 to 75 tons. The anchorage in the roadstead ranges in depth from 8 to 30 fathoms. It is at this latter depth that vessels are allowed to heave ballast over board. The holding ground is excellent. The best anchorage is about a quarter of a mile to the northward of the light-ship in from 12 to 14 fathoms.

The quarantine anchorage is about a mile southward of the light-ship the depth of water being from 10 to 18 fathoms with fairly good holding grounds: the rise and fall of tide is two feet nine inches full and change.

The latest survey was made in 1877 by Lieutenant J. E. Coglan, R.N., when in addition to careful soundings which were taken all round the Island the "One hundred fathom line" was laid down.

There is a light-ship at the mouth of the Harbour of Port Louis, it is painted white and she can thus be distinctly seen against the dark line during the day. From sunrise to sunset she shows a flashing white light, visible nine miles in every direction from seaward.

Dock Yards.

The Dock Yards which belong to private Companies are built on land belonging to th Colonial Government. They consist of 3 dry docks of the following dimensions:—

	Extreme length.	Extreme breadth.	Depth of Water.
Albion Dock	318	60	20
Hay ,, ...	318½	46½	15½
Stevenson ,, ...	386	60	20

These docks which are excavated in solid basalt with sides nearly perpendicular, are situated in a large basin known as Trou Fanfaron, the entrance to which is protected by a long breakwater, at the extremity of this breakwater is erected the Mariner's Church. The passage leading to the Trou Fanfaron carries as much water as there is on the sill of the largest dock.

By reducing the height of the keel blocks to the level of the inverted arch or sill at the entrance, a vessel of 52 feet broad, drawing 22 feet aft. and 17 feet 4 inches forward with a 260 feet keel can be taken into the Stevenson dock. This dock could easily be lenghtened to 510 feet when 2 vessels could be taken in at the same time. On the 30th. March 1892 this dock was lenghtened by eight feet to enable the French Mail *S. S. Peï-Ho*, 3325 tons to be repaired.

Indeed there is a scheme now under consideration of enlarging and lengthening the Stevenson Dock so as to accommodate the largest seagoing vessel or iron clad afloat. As this scheme cannot at present be carried out by the Colony the Imperial Government has been asked to contribute towards so important a work, and there is now every reason to believe that before long something in that direction will be undertaken. The only difficulty is one of dredging and deepening the Trou Fanfaron.

There are also two Patent Slips in this Basin: one is capable of hauling up a vessel of 450 tons with 9 feet of water forward, the other can only haul up coasters or small vessels of from 100 to 120 tons. There are also moorings for 7 vessels at the head of this basin. The average depth of water in this basin is from 19 to 24 feet english measurement and it is sufficiently large to allow of a vessel of 350 feet in length being turned.

There are also two careening Hulks in the harbour owned by Messrs. Black and Smith capable of heaving down ships of 500 tons.

Harbour Department Storm Signals.

Notice is hereby given that the following Signals will in future be made from the Flag Staff of the Port Office, and repeated by the Flag Staff of Fort George, on the approach of bad weather.

DAY SIGNALS.

First Signal :

A white flag with horizontal blue stripes and ball above at the Port Office, repeated at Fort George and confirmed by a Gun. Send down Top gallant yards and Masts and prepare for bad weather. Ships at the Bell Buoy to go to sea.	*The Masters of all Ships and Vessels in this Port, are required immediately to repair on board their respective Vessels ; and Vessels at the Bell Buoy, ought to proceed to Sea.*

Second Signal :

A red Flag at the Port Office, with Ball above, repeated at Fort George, and confirmed by a Gun.	Vessels in the Port to strike Lower Yards and Topmasts.

NIGHT SIGNALS.

One blue light at the Port Office, repeated at Fort George and accompanied by a Gun.	Vessels at the Bell Buoy, to proceed to Sea, and Vessels in the Port, to make every preparation for bad weather.

Harbour Police.

When the assistance of the Police is required on board any ship, flag H, Commercial Code, should be hoisted at the main. The Police Boat is immediately to repair to any ship making this signal. When this signal is made from land, the boat will proceed immediately to the spot where the signal is made and the non-Commissioned Officer or Constable in charge will ascertain what s wanted.

Storm Signals Railway Department.

The following are the instructions issued by the Railway Department respecting the conduct of the Traffic during Hurricane weather.

On receipt of a telegram from the Director of the Observatory stating that the wind had attained a velocity of 40 miles per hour, the **First Storm signal** warning must be at once given to all stations, this signal, the *Green and White Flag*, is to be exhibited at the Central Station and on the Signal Mountain Port Louis.

On receipt of a Telegram from the Director of the Observatory stating that the wind had attained a velocity of 50 miles per hour, **Second Storm signal** must be sent to all Stations, and the Storm signal, which is a *Red Flag*, will also be exhibited at the Central Railway Station and on the Signal Mountain.

On receipt of the First Storm Signal, the Traffic Superintendent will immediately send a " Bell man " round that portion of the town most frequented by business men who will announce the hoisting of the same. This will also be done on the receipt of the Second Storm Signal Printed notices of both signals should also be affixed in the public places of the town.

Amended Rules and Regulations to be observed in future during the Cyclone or Hurricane Weather.

I. Whenever disturbed, squally, and threatening weather has declared itself in the Cyclone Season, * and there are indications of the approach of a revolving gale, storm, or hurricane, the Director of the Observatory will telegraph the fact to the General Manager of Railways.

II. So long as the weather remains disturbed and threatening, and the barometer is below 29.80 inches at sea-level, the Observatory is to be kept open day and night, and the General Manager shall be on duty the whole time, unless incapacitated by illness, in which case he shall

* The Cyclone or Hurricane Season in Mauritius may be said to extend from the 1st. of December to the 30th. of April and to be at its height in the latter half of February and the first half of March.

be replaced by the Loco : or Traffic Superintendent unless the Director of the Observatory telegraphs that there is no danger.

III. During Cyclone weather, the Observatory will, from time to time, inform, as far as possible, the General Manager of all changes of increase or decrease deemed likely to occur in the velocity of the wind.

IV. If at the Observatory, the wind attain a velocity of 40 miles an hour, the fact is to be immediately made known to the General Manager who thereupon shall, with the least possible delay, stop all trains composed, wholly or in part, of double-story carriages.

V. If the wind, as aforesaid, attain a velocity of 45 miles an hour, the fact is to be immediately made known to the General Manager, who shall, with the least possible delay, stop traffic of every kind, passenger as well as goods.

But no trains are to be run on Grand River Bridge, if the velocity of the wind exceed 40 miles an hour, until it is strengthened in the manner proposed by the Consulting Engineers.

VI. Nothing in these Regulations shall prevent the General Manager from running detached Engines during Hurricane weather, though the velocity of the wind should exceed 45 miles an hour.

VII. The conditions and restrictions laid down in Rules IV, V and VI are to remain in force until the Director of the Observatory announces, by telegram or otherwise, that in his opinion traffic may be resumed.

VIII. When, in Hurricane weather, Passenger traffic has been suspended, no trains composed of empty carriages are to be run later on, even if the velocity of the wind should for a time be below 20 miles an hour, unless the Observatory telegraphs that, with regard to weather, there would be no danger in running such trains.

IX. The relations between the Harbour Master and the Director of the Observatory, during Cyclone weather, shall continue to be those laid down in Government Notice No. 22 of 1876.

X. The Colonial Postmaster is to keep the Port Department, the Railway Department, and the Observatory, in constant direct telegraphic communication day and night during Cyclone weather, unless he be expressly informed by the Director of the Observatory, that there is no necessity for doing so. He is also, during Cyclone weather, to keep the Telegraph Operators at all the Railway Stations on duty from 5 a.m. to 5 p.m., and longer, if the Director of the Observatory requests him to do so.

XI. The Colonial Postmaster, when requested by the Director of the Observatory, will also, as hitherto, forward direct to the Governor, the Officer Commanding the Troops, and the Colonial Secretary, copies of the Weather Telegrams (or Storm Warnings), including probabilities or forecasts despatched by the Observatory to the Harbour Master, and also, if requested, cause copies of these telegrams to be promptly posted up at all Railway Stations, especially the Central Station in Port-Louis. *

XII. The General Manager of Railways, like the Harbour Master (Government Notice No. 22 of 1876,) is to act on his own responsibility in Cyclone or Hurricane weather, subject to the above Rules and Regulations.

All previous Rules and Regulations respecting the joint action of the Director of the Observatory and the General Manager of Railways in Hurricane weather, including those dated the 4th. of March 1884 (M.P. 8987/83), are hereby cancelled.

M. CONNAL,
Engineer and General Manager of Railways.
J. WILSON,
Harbour Master.
C. MELDRUM,
Director of the Observatory,—Chairman

Time-Ball.

The Time Ball on the Signal Mountain (for Chronometer observation) is dropped every Monday, Wednesday and Friday (holidays excepted), at 1 P.M. Observatory mean time.

At 5 minutes before 1 P.M. the Ball is hoisted half mast, and at 2 minutes before 1 P.M. full mast.

The instant of disconnection of the Ball from the cross-head is the time to be observed.

In the event of accident or error, the ball will be rehoisted half-mast, and, if practicable dropped again at 2 P.M. mean time.

According to the latest dermination, the new Observatory, from which the Ball is dropped by electricity, is in Latitude 20° 5' 39" S.' Longitude 57° 33' 9" E., and Longitude in time 3h. 50m. 12s. 6 E.

When the Ball drops at 1 p.m. local mean time, the corresponding Greenwich mean time is 9h. 9m. 47s. 4 A.M.

* Copies of these Storm Warnings have hitherto been sent to the General Manager since 1884.

Table for calculating the maximum pressure of wind during a Storm in pounds on the square foot.

Method of deducing the maximum Pressure of the Wind during a storm from the maximum run of Wind in any one hour during the same storm, together with a Table for converting maximum hourly runs of the wind into maximum pressure calculated from the Formula $\frac{V2}{100}$=P., where V=the maximum run in miles of the wind in any one hour, and P=the maximum Pressure in lbs on the square foot at any time during the storm to which V refers.

Maximum hourly run of the wind in miles.	Maximum pressure in lbs. on the square foot.	Maximum hourly run of the wind in miles.	Maximum pressure in lbs. on the square foot.
40	16.0	71	50.4
41	16.8	72	51.8
42	17.6	73	53.3
43	18.5	74	54.8
44	19.4	75	56.2
45	20.2	76	57.8
46	21.2	77	59.3
47	22.1	78	60.8
48	23.0	79	62.4
49	24.0	80	64.0
50	25.0	81	65.6
51	26.0	82	67.2
52	27.0	83	68.9
53	28.1	84	70.6
54	29.2	85	72.2
55	30.2	86	74.0
56	31.4	87	75.7
57	32.5	88	77.4
58	33.6	89	79.2
59	34.8	90	81.0
60	36.0	91	82.8
61	37.2	92	84.6
62	38.4	93	86.5
63	39.7	94	88.4
64	41.0	95	90.3
65	42.2	96	92.2
66	43.6	97	94.1
67	44.9	98	96.0
68	46.2	99	98.0
69	47.6	100	100.0
70	49.0		

Scale of Velocities of Wind.

Strong Breeze	34 miles per hour.
Moderate Gale	40 ,,
Fresh Gale	48 ,,
Strong Gale	56 ,,
Storm	75 ,,
Hurricane	90 and upwards.

Mauritius Hurricanes and Gales from 1880 to 1895.

KINDLY FURNISHED BY THE HONORABLE C. MELDRUM, C.M.G., L.L.D., F.R.S., DIRECTOR OF THE ROYAL ALFRED OBSERVATORY.
(For previous years, *vide* the Mauritius Almanac for 1878.)

Years.	Months.	Days of Month.	Lowest barometer at sea-level.	Wind.		Rainfall.		Remarks.
				Direction.	Maximum Velocity for one hour.	Inches.	No. of Days.	
					Miles.			
1880	February. .	5	29.700	E. to N.N.E.	30.6	1.56	1	Strong breeze to moderate gale during twelve hours.
,,	December..	17—19	29.919	E.S.E. to N.E.	38.6	3.68	3	Fresh gale during twelve hours.
1881	January ...	19—21	29.669	E. b. S. to N. b. E. ...	50.0	1.88	3	Strong gale during twenty eight hours.
,,	June	30	30.308	E. to E. S. E.	41.5	0.01	1	Fresh gale during six hours.
1882	February. .	8	29.627	E.S.E to S. & S.W. ...	26.4	2.49	1	Strong breeze during thirteen hours.
,,	March ...	10—14	29.744	E.S.E. to S. & W.S.W. ...	32 5	1.58	5	Moderate gale during four hours.
,,	June	14—15	30.155	S.E. to S.S.E.	37.0	0.02	1	Moderate to fresh gale during eight hours.
1883	January ...	20—22	29.581	E. b. S. to S. & S.W. ...	29.2	0.59	2	Strong breezes during three days.
,,	December .	6— 7	27.705	S E. to E , N.E. & N.W....	44.9	2.53	1	Fresh to strong gale during twenty four hours.
1884	January ...	21—23	29.646	S.E. to S. & S.W. b. W. ...	31.2	2.17	3	Strong breezes to moderate gale for twenty hours.
1885	September.	2	30.251	E.S.E. to E. b. N.	29.0	0.29	1	Strong breezes during ten hours.
,,	December..	10—12	29.663	S.E. b. E. to S. & S.W. ...	25.2	1.52	3	Fresh to strong breezes during nine hours.
,,	,,	19—23	29.820	S.E. b. E. to N.E. ...	28.1	0.41	4	Fresh to strong breezes during twenty eight hours;
1886	April ...	5	29.882	E. b. S.	28.5	0.04	1	Strong breeze during eight hours.
	,,	16—17	29.715	S.E. to S. & S.W.... ...	30.1	0.26	4	Strong breezes to moderate gale during eight hours.
1887	June	12	30.072	E.S.E. b. S.	30.3	...	0	Strong breezes to moderate gale during eight hours.
1888	January ...	5	29.664	S.E. to E. b. N.	41.1	4.30	1	Fresh to strong gale for ten hours.
1889	March ...	11—12	29.797	E.S.E. to E. b. N. ...	31.1	4.15	2	Strong breezes to moderate gale for twenty one hours.
1890	August ...	12	30.054	S.E. to E.S.E.	30.1	0.03	1	Strong trade-wind for eight hours.
1891	February. .	5— 6	29.408	S.E. to N.E. & N. ...	37.3	1.37	2	Fresh gale for some hours.
1892	,,	12—13	29.325	E. to N.N.E.	47.5	8.87	2	Fresh to strong gale for five hours.
,,	April ...	29	27.956	N.E. to N. & S.W. ...	103.3	2.44	1	Destructive Hurricane for three hours.
1893	January ...	26—27	29.650	E.S.E. to E. b. N. ...	37.3	0.21	2	Strong breeze to moderate gale for twenty hours.
1894	,, ...	8—14	29.412	S.E.to E.N.E.,S.E.,S.& S.W	41.0	12.84	7	Strong breeze to moderate gale for five days.
,,	February. .	21—22	29.276	E.S.E., S., S.W.	62.2	2.12	2	Strong breeze to strong gale for twenty eight hours.
1895	January ...	13—16	29.514	E.S.E., S.E., S.S.W. & W.	38 8	0.43	4	Strong breeze to moderate gale during twenty two hours.
,,	August ...	24	30.164	S.S.E. to S.E. b. E. ...	35.5	...	0	Strong trade-wind for eight hours.

REMARKS.—From March 22, 1879, to April 29, 1892, the Island was not visited by a hurricane, and only on four occasions by a fresh strong gale. The hurricane of April 29, 1892, has been unprecedented in Mauritius with respect to season, rapidity and amount of atmospheric depression, direction and force of the wind, and loss of life and property. From 3.46 to 3.51 p.m. the velocity of the wind was at the rate of 121.2 miles an hour.

Districts.	1886	1887	1888	1889	1890	1891	1892	1893	1894	1895	Approximate altitudes of stations above Sea-level.
Riv. du Rempart.	inches	inches.	inches	inches	inches	inches	inches	inches	inches	inches	feet.
St. Antoine	23.53	43.18	63.02	61.61	42.75	45.00	47.43	41.35	55.36	......	90
Schœnfeld	29.26	52.52	73.19	74.66	56.64	49.92	61.10	48.06	51.70	57.34	?
Labourdonnais	33.18	59.03	75.53	75.08	64.79	67.01	77.18	......	55.37	67.36	290
Mon Songe	40.63	74,14	94.10	92.60	81.31	74.06	80.30	67.65	69.22	89.67	620
Pamplemousses.											
Observatory	29.74	46.64	52.81	56.19	53.17	44.63	59.12	48.33	48.91	54.16	179
Botanical Gardens ...	46.26	85.12	66.23	58.46	60.55	58.08	69.99	......	53.70	62.29	225
La Grande Rosalie ...	34.66	73.42	89.65	91.76	80.57	77.52	80.46	70 03	68.75	90.31	643.
Flacq.											
Constance (d'Arifat) ...	35.91	60.15	84.17	90.77	65.61	51.66	68.99	59.15	56.96	62.72	?
Union	40.87	66.73	87.34	93.25	72.74	63.38	70.68	63.79	60.51	76.19	500
Sans Souci	81.97	129.19	......	167.24	126.51	128.97	...*	105.16	129.74	157.61	860
Moka.											
Gentilly	......	......	89.70	89.96	88.36	81.00	*...	77.81	74.62	82.75	1150
Lynwood	......	67.04	80.61	91.68	81.31	77.33	*...	75.60	73.83	80.46	1000
Bon Air	35.59	56.76	74.42	79.57	71.43	70.51	82.01	69.96	72.43	77.32	1050
Le Réduit	......	50.98	63.66	64.06	59.43	58.28	56.73	54.49	53.54	60.03	1000
Alma	90.99	134.05	162.05	155.21	137.54	136.99	129.09	114.93	144.50	144.77	1500
Minissy	42.82	63.92	76.88	86.14	78.02	69.69	*...	71.72	69.80	81.77	1150
Plaines Wilhems.											
Trianon	30.68	52.92	71.69	67.73	64.05	59.59	72.04	65.72	69.17	76.42	950
Highlands	35.36	65.18	66.16	78.84	76.42	72.29	*...	66.29	79.95	89.94	1400
Réunion, Vacoas ...	54.15	70.68	98.72	93.41	89.77	96.52	107.57	86.55	101.41	106.10	1420
Henrietta ,, ...	63.07	72.95	94.31	......	85.80	......	99.75	76.37	97.73	103.83	1549
Curepipe Gardens ...	98.29	......	159.41	132.90	127.56	139.32	154.78	119.30	132.93	146.92	1840
Mare-aux-Vacoas ...	......	......	......	139.12	122.16	138.24	163.82	128.16	159.81	173.02	1850
Black River.											
Wolmar	13.84	25.80	50.98	35.22	36.99	29.17	47.31	33.45	36.80	37.88	200
Tamarin	15.71	29.02	50.10	35.99	44.67	36.55	56.89	39.27	39.83	31.87	150
Caselà	.....	......	77.30	49.67	45.36	40.48	59.74	44.75	42.60	37.65	250
Chamarel	58,48	58.65	88.57	77.74	......	......	*...	75.24	......	77.90	850
Grand Port.											
Ferney	47.32	100.51	142.21	125.13	89.57	92.22	85.57	70.49	81.99	......	20
Cluny	95.16	139.64	194.36	173.96	135.84	152.25	165.93	131.24	147.59	167.29	1000
Riche-en-Eau	58.65	102.73	134.89	120.33	93.76	91.62	82.86	73.97	87.65	......	800
Beau-Vallon (Rocheconste) ...	31.49	63.62	93.24	92.82	57.78	71.65	70.55	55.49	67.65	71.24	60
Gros Bois	54.40	94.56	128.97	112.19	90.77	108.60	84.44	76.18	88.25	91.74	500
Savanne.											
Bénarès	33.40	61.84	......	......	......	90.99	79.67	64.37	78.05	74.25	300
Beau Champ	36.94	47.52	89.27	68.65	54.67	61.40	65.26	57.76	53.00	62.59	60
Bel Ombre	47.70	56.97	96.48	70.00	57.10	62.59	73.41	59.70	60.31	65.27	50
Union-Bel-Air	49.68	63.87	125.48	92.50	76.26	80.96	85.65	65.79	67.70	71.27	90

* At most of those stations the Raingauges were damaged or blown away in the hurricane of 29th. April 1892,and no correct record could therefore be obtained.

Rainfall and Temperature from the year 1886 to 1895 at the Royal Alfred Observatory—Height above sea-level 179 feet.

Rainfall.

Years.	1886	1887	1888	1889	1890	1891	1892	1893	1894	1895
Months.	Inches.	Inches.	Inches.	Inches.	Inches.	Inches.	Inches.	Inches.	Inches.	Inches.
January ...	2.13	9.84	8.86	12.74	5.01	4.13	6.96	12.55	14.58	2.14
February ...	4.26	3.37	8.76	5.51	11.02	4.32	13.86	2.42	4.48	2.97
March ...	3.81	12.76	9.83	17.09	11.36	11.74	9.57	6.08	3.99	24.11
April ...	3.12	2.91	1.84	4.65	10.24	7.23	5.68	10.06	6.11	2.62
May ...	1.88	4.68	0.99	1.51	0.82	1.76	1.25	4.13	4.41	3.09
June ...	0.65	1.68	1.64	1.53	1.52	2.55	4.02	2.53	0.76	2.85
July ...	2.22	1.96	1.50	2.21	4.30	2.06	3.10	3.35	2.29	1.12
August ...	0.74	2.11	2.87	3.68	2.22	1.85	3.80	2.06	2.09	4.66
September ...	0.85	0.86	1.03	1.53	0.45	2.50	1.41	0.91	1.88	0.83
October ...	2.58	3.46	1.60	1.20	1.25	1.34	1.39	1.06	1.11	0.64
November ...	1.19	0.60	1.25	1.78	2.80	1.47	1.84	1.78	1.31	2.58
December ...	6.31	2.41	12.64	2.76	2.18	3.68	6.24	1.40	5.90	6.55
Total Rainfall and Mean Temperature	29.74	46.64	52.81	56.19	53.17	44.63	59.12	48.33	48.91	54.16

Temperature of the Air.

*From Max: and Min: Thermometers.

Years.	1886	1887	1888	1889	1890	1891	1892	1893	1894	1895
Months.	°	°	°	°	°	°	°	°	°	°
January ...	79.2	78.5	78.1	77.9	77.5	77.2	79.1	78.0	78.4	80.0
February ...	79.9	76.8	78.1	77.8	77.4	78.6	79.2	78.1	78.5	78.9
March ...	79.3	77.3	76.3	78.1	77.2	76.6	78.1	77.6	77.4	78.0
April ...	77.6	74.4	74.6	76.2	75.0	75.6	77.5	75.2	75.6	76.2
May ...	72.3	71.9	73.3	72.2	70.8	72.1	74.7	72.6	71.8	74.3
June ...	70.6	69.0	70.5	70.2	68.8	69.9	72.2	68.9	68.1	70.2
July ...	68.4	67.9	69.1	69.5	67.2	67.9	69.6	68.0	69.8	69.6
August ...	68.6	66.3	69.6	68.9	67.7	67.7	70.2	68.0	69.8	69.6
September ...	70.2	69.0	69.9	69.6	69.3	70.7	69.9	69.3	70.6	70.5
October ...	72.1	71.4	72.0	72.4	71.2	72.7	72.1	71.7	72.5	73.7
November ...	73.6	74.2	76.1	73.6	74.0	75.2	75.2	72.8	75.3	75.5
December ...	77.0	76.6	77.3	75.9	76.4	77.3	77.1	77.3	78.4	76.9
Total Rainfall and Mean Temperature	74.1	72.8	73.7	73.5	72.7	73.5	74.6	73.1	73.8	74.4

*From observations at 6 a.m. and 3 p.m.

Years.	1886	1887	1888	1889	1890	1891	1892	1893	1894	1895
Months.	°	°	°	°	°	°	°	°	°	°
January ...	78.6	78.0	77.8	77.2	76.8	76.7	78.6	77.4	77.7	79.4
February ...	79.2	76.3	77.6	77.1	76.8	78.1	78.8	77.4	77.8	78.2
March ...	78.7	76.6	75.6	77.6	76.4	76.1	77.7	76.8	77.0	77.7
April ...	77.0	74.2	73.9	75.6	74.4	75.1	76.9	74.4	75.1	75.4
May ...	71.9	71.5	72.7	71.8	70.6	71.8	74.3	72.1	71.3	73.6
June ...	70.2	69.0	70.0	69.7	68.2	69.8	71.8	68.4	67.7	69.8
July ...	67.9	67.6	68.6	69.2	66.9	67.5	69.3	67.4	69.3	69.2
August ...	68.1	66.3	69.0	68.4	67.0	67.4	69.7	67.4	69.0	68.8
September ...	69.3	68.6	69.2	68.9	68.8	70.0	69.1	68.3	69.6	69.7
October ...	71.2	70.7	71.3	71.6	70.5	72.1	71.3	70.9	71.4	72.8
November ...	73.0	73.6	75.8	73.1	73.4	74.9	74.6	72.2	74.4	74.9
December ...	76.2	76.0	76.5	75.5	76.1	76.8	76.7	76.5	77.7	76.3
Total Rainfall and Mean Temperature	73.4	72.4	73.2	73.0	72.2	73.0	74.1	72.4	73.2	73.8

* In a current of air between two open windows in a lofty room.

Royal Alfred Observatory,
15th. February 1896.

Temperature of Air inthe Shade in a Screen on the Lawn, at the Royal Alfred Observatory.—Height above sea-level 179 feet.

YEARS.	1886	1887	1888	1889	1890	1891	1892	1893	1894	1895	1888	1889	1890	1891	1892	1893	1894	1895
MONTHS.	From maximum and minimum Thermometers.										From observations at 6 A.M. and 3 P.M.							
	°	°	°	°	°	°	°	°	°	°	°	°	°	°	°	°	°	°
January	80.8	79.1	79.2	78.9	79.1	79.1	80.7	78.7	79.2	80.5	78.5	78.4	78.5	77.8	80.5	78.0	78.3	80.3
February ...	81.4	77.5	78.4	78.8	78.4	79.8	80.4	79.0	79.1	79.8	77.9	78.0	77.9	79.0	80.1	78.1	78.4	78.4
March	80.4	77.9	77.1	79.3	78.4	77.6	79.4	78.3	77.6	78.1	75.9	78.9	77.4	76.8	78.8	77.4	77.3	78.3
April	78.4	75.0	75.4	77.3	75.9	76.5	78.9	76.2	75.9	76.4	74.2	76.8	75.3	75.8	78.0	75.2	75.6	75.8
May	72.9	72.4	73.9	73.0	71.4	72.9	74.9	73.5	72.0	74.4	73.1	72.4	70.9	72.2	73.6	72.4	70.9	73.9
June	71.7	68.9	71.0	70.8	69.3	71.2	71.9	68.7	67.6	70.1	70.1	69.9	68.3	70.4	71.1	68.1	67.0	70.0
July	68.9	68.4	69.6	70.3	68.0	68.5	69.2	68.1	69.9	69.6	68.7	70.0	67.3	67.8	68.7	67.4	69.2	68.9
August	69.7	66.9	70.7	69.7	68.5	68.9	70.4	68.2	70.3	70.0	69.8	69.2	67.8	68.0	69.6	67.4	69.4	68.8
September ...	72.1	70.1	71.3	70.7	70.6	72.1	70.1	69.6	71.4	71.1	70.0	69.7	69.8	71.2	69.2	68.8	70.2	70.4
October	74.1	72.2	73.5	74.3	72.8	74.1	72.8	72.4	73.4	74.7	72.2	73.2	71.8	73.3	72.3	71.7	71.9	73.6
November ...	75.7	75.1	78.1	75.1	75.8	77.4	76.5	73.6	76.5	76.6	77.8	74.3	74.8	76.8	76.3	72.7	75.9	76.2
December ...	77.8	78.1	78.8	77.4	77.8	79.4	78.2	78.7	79.2	77.6	77.5	77.4	77.4	78.1	78.1	78.1	78.7	77.5
Means... ...	75.3	73.5	74.7	74.6	73.8	74.8	75.3	73.7	74.3	74.9	73.8	74.0	73.1	73.9	74.7	73.0	73.6	74.3

Royal Alfred Observatory,

17th. February, 1896.

Table of Corrections for the 3 principal hurricane months to be applied to a *barometer reading* in Mauritius, for the *diurnal variation*, to reduce it to the 9 A.M. height.

From 8 to 10 A.M. the variation is practically *nil* so that if the *pointer* of the barometer be set in that period and the tabular correction applied (+is add−subtract) it can be ascertained at any hour of the day whether the barometer is really rising or falling, with its rate.

The corrections are according to the observations made at the Observatory during the 18 years ending with 1892 see the Publication entitled. "Meteorological Observations taken during "the year 1892 at the Royal Alfred Observatory."—Page 5.

28th, December 1893. M. CONNAL.

Hour.	A. M.			P. M.		
	January.	February.	March.	January.	February.	March.
	mm.	mm.	mm.	mm.	mm.	mm.
0	+0.18	+0.13	+0.28	+0.56	+0.53	+0.67
1	+0.48	+0.48	+0.58	+0.81	+0.91	+1.12
2	+0.84	+0.86	+0.99	+1.17	+1.27	+1.47
3	+1.02	+1.07	+1.19	+1.42	+1.47	+1.65
4	+1.04	+1.12	+1.32	+1.55	+1.55	+1.65
5	+0.81	+0.99	+1.19	+1.40	+1.41	+1.42
6	+0.66	+0.74	+0.91	+0.99	+1.04	+1.12
7	+0.43	+0.41	+0.61	+0.53	+0.61	+0.71
8	+0.03	+0.13	+0.20	+0.18	+0.20	+0.30
9	Zero	Zero	Zero	−0.10	−0.10	−0.03
10	+0.10	+0.05	+0.05	−0.28	−0.25	−0.10
11	+0.28	+0.18	+0.23	−0.20	−0.18	+0.03
12	+0.56	+0.53	+0.69	+0.18	+0.13	+0.28

The Metric System.

In 1790, Prince de Talleyrand laid a proposal before the Constituent Assembly for a new system of weights and measures which it was hoped would ultimately be a universal one. The British Parliament were communicated with in expectation that this country would join in this much wanted reform, that for this purpose a joint committee should be formed of equal numbers of members of the French Academy of Sciences, and the British Royal Society, but the British Government at that time were not inclined to join France in any joint mesure however beneficial it might be to this country. The French Academy, however, proceeded with the work alone, the first step was to select a fundamental linear measure as a basis; the choice lay between the pendulum vibrating seconds at a certain latitude, a quarter of the equator, and a quarter of the meridian.

The pendulum was laid aside because it could not form a universal standard, and also because it was liable to be affected by vibrations of the earth; a quarter of the equator was also laid aside.

The quarter of the meridian was at last selected. A Commission was appointed to undertake the necessary calculations, which, after great labour, were completed on the 9th. December 1799, and on the 1st. January 1840 the Decimal System was enforced by law. They resolved upon taking the ten-millionth part of a quadrant of a meridian measured by calculation from the north pole to the equator, the entire length being one thousand myriametres.

The computation has since been found not to be quite correct, but this is of little importance as now a standard measure for all countries has been selected and approved of.

A bar of platinum was deposited by the authority of the Government in the French archives on the 22nd. June 1799, where it is still preserved.

An accurate copy of this original standard, also of platinum, belongs to the Royal Society, and was used by the Royal Commissioners for the purpose of obtaing an accurate computation of the length of the metre in English inches. In July 1820 these Commissioners gave in their report to the House of Commons. They stated the metre to be 39·37079 inches, and this is adopted as equivalent to the Frence metre.

In 1855, a society was formed in England under the name of "The International Association for the Promotion of a Uniform Decimal System of Weights, Measures, and Coins on the Basis of the Metric System", and in 1863 the British Association for the advancement of science appointed a Committee for the same purpose. In 1862 a Committee of the House of Commons also recommended the introduction of the Metric System. In 1863 a Bill was introduced to carry out this measure, and was passed by a large majority, but it proceeded no further; in 1864 the same Bill was again passed by a large majority. The Government consented to the passing of this Bill, on condition of its being permissive only, which left the whole matter optional. In this position it now stands, the result being that the Metric System is only used for scientific purposes, and will never come into general use till it is made compulsory by Act of Parliament; but the universal use of the Metric System would be such an immense advantage of the general public that it cannot now be long delayed, a step in the right direction has been taken in the Education Code for 1891, in which are the following instructions;—

"The scholars in Standards V., VI., and VII., should know the principles of the Metric System, and be able to to explain the advantages to be gained from uniformity in the method of forming multiples and sub-multiples of the unit."

To show how widely this system is now in use over the world, the following countries have adopted it:—

France, Netherlands, Spain, Greece, Austria, Germany, Switzerland, Norway and Sweeden, Portugal, United States, Mexico, Venezuela, Argentine Republic, Hayti, New Grenada, Mauritius, and the Congo Free State.

It is permissive in Great Britain, Canada, Chili, and India.

The Weights and Measures in use in Mauritius are the kilogram and its subdivisions and Litre. By Proclamation No. 27 of 10th. September 1894, the weights of 125 and 250 grams although not submultiples of the kilogram were declared to be legal weights.

PROPOSED DECIMAL COINAGE FOR BRITAIN.

10 Mils = 1 cent (marked c.)
10 Cents = 1 florin (marked fl.)
10 Florins = 1 pound (marked £.)

NOTE.—The Pound and the Florin would have the same value as at present. The cent would be worth $2\frac{2}{5}$, and the mil $\frac{2}{2}\frac{1}{5}$ of a farthing. Under this system reduction of money would be very easy. Thus, £17, 9 fl., 6c., 8 mils would equal £17·968, or 179·68 florins, or 1796·8 cents, or 17,968 mils.

Rules for converting Metric to English Measures and Weights.

REDUCTION.

LINEAL MEASURE.

Millimètres to inches :—Annex a cipher and divide by 254.

Inches to millimètres :—Annex two ciphers and divide by 4, the result, increased by $\frac{4}{10}$ of the given number of inches, is millimètres.

Mètres to yards :—Multiply by 70 and divide by 64.

Yards to mètres :—Multiply by 64 and divide by 70.

Kilomètres to miles :—Multiply by 64 and divide by 103.

Miles to kilomètres :—Multiply by 103 and divide by 64.

SUPERFICIAL MEASURE.

Square centimètres to square inches :—Multiply by 31 and divide by 200.

Square inches to square centimètres :—Multiply by 200 and divide by 31.

Square décimètres to square feet :—Annex two ciphers and divide by 929.

Square feet to square décimètres :—Multiply by 929 and cut off two fingers.

Square mètres to square yards :—Multiply by 61 and divide by 51.

Square yards to square metres :—Multiply by 51 and divide by 61.

Hectares to acres :—Multiply by 257 and divide by 104.

Acres to hectares :—Multiply by 104 and divide by 257.

SOLID MEASURE.

Cubic centimètres to cubic inches :—Multiply by 44 and divide by 721.

Cubic inches to cubic centimètres :—Multiply by 721 and divide by 44.

Cubic décimètres to cubic inches :—Multiply by 61.

Cubic inches to cubic décimètres :—Divide by 61.

Cubic décimètres to cubic feet :—Multiply 111 and divide 3143.

Cubic feet to cubic décimètres :—Multiply by 3143 and divide by 111.

Cubic mètres to cubic yards :—Multiply by 310 and divide by 237.

Cubic yards to cubic metres :—Multiply by 237 and divide by 310.

CAPACITY.

Gallons to litres :—Annex two ciphers and divide by 22.

Litres to gallons :—Multiply by 22 and divide by 100.

Litres to pints :—Multiply by 88 and divide by 50.

Hectolitres to pecks :—Multiply by 11.

Pecks to hectolitres :—Divide by 11.

Hectolitres to quarters :—Multiply by 11 and divide by 32; or take the sum of $\frac{1}{3}$ and $\frac{1}{100}$ of the given number of hectolitres.

Quarters to hectolitres :—Multiply by 32 and divide by 11; or multiply by 3 and subtract $\frac{1}{11}$ of the given number of quarters.

AVOIRDUPOIS WEIGHT.

Grams to ounces :—Multiply by 20 and divide by 567.

Ounces to grams :—Multiply by 567 and divide by 20.

Grams to lbs. :—Divide by 454.

Kilograms to lbs. :—Multiply by 1000 and divide by 454.

Pounds to grams :—Multiply by 504 and subtract one-tenth of the product.

Kilograms to cwts. :—Annex a cipher and divide by 508.

Hundredweights to kilograms :—Multiply by 508, and $\frac{1}{40}$ of the given number of cwts. to the product, and cut off the last figure.

Troy Weight.

Grams to grains :—Mulitply by 10,000 and divide by 648.
Grains to grams ;—Multiply by 648 and divide by 10,000.
Grams to dwts. :—Multiply by nine and divide by 14.
Dwts. to grams :—Multiply by 14 and divide by 9.
Grams to ounces ;—Multiply by 29 and divide by 902.
Ounces to grams :—Multiply by 902 and divide by 29.
Kilograms to pounds :—Multiply by 300 and divide by 112.
Pounds to kilograms ;—Multiply by 112 and divide by 300.

BAROMETER SCALES.

Inches.	Millimetres.	Inches.	Millimetres.	Inches.	Millimetres.
31·0	787	29·6	751	28·2	716
30·9	784	29·5	749	28·1	713
30·8	782	29·4	746	28·0	711
30·7	779	29·4	744	27·9	708
30·6	777	29·2	741	27·8	706
30·5	774	29·1	739	27·7	703
30·4	772	29·0	736	27·6	701
30·3	769	28·9	734	27·5	698
30·2	767	28·8	731	27·4	695
30·1	764	28·7	728	27·3	693
30·0	761	28·6	726	27·2	690
29·9	759	28·5	723	27·1	688
29·8	756	28·4	721	27·0	685
29·7	754	28·3	718	26·9	683

(Extract from W. & A. K. Johnson's handbook of the Metric System.)

Absentees.

Persons quitting the Colony of Mauritius without leaving a duly appointed Attorney or Agent, whose appointment must be recorded in the Registration and Mortgage Office, are liable to have their Property taken possession of and administered by the Curator of Vacant Estates. All estates so administered pay a Commission to Government of 5 o/o.

The Mauritius—Zanzibar Cable.

The following information respecting the Eastern Telegraph Company which now has a station at Mauritius may prove of interest to many readers of this work.

The Company started operations as far back as 1870 with only a few stations and an insignificant mileage. At the end of 1894, the total length of Cables of the Eastern Telegraph Company associated with the Eastern Extension and Eastern and S. A. Telegraph Co., exceeded 53,285 miles, exclusive of 1,457 miles of Land Lines and 2,300 miles leased to the Company.

The number of stations is at present 92 and no fewer than 10 steam ships composed of 8 for laying and repairing Cables and 2 store ships are constantly on the move to keep in working order the different lines of communication. These vessels, in addition to their ordinary crews have a doctor and a staff of Engineers and Electricians.

The length of the line from Zanzibar to Seychelles is 1,017 knots or 1,173 English miles and from Seychelles to Mauritius 1,066 knots or 1,229 miles.

The deepest repairs that have yet been made were in 1874 when the Madeira Cable was raised from a depth of 2,900 fathoms or 17,400 feet and repaired.

The annual subvention at present paid for the Mauritius — Seychelles — Zanzibar Line is £ 28,000 divided as follows :—

English Government	£ 10,000
Indian Government	£ 10,000
Seychelles Government	£ 1,000
Mauritius	£ 7,000

The greatest depth in which the Cable from Zanzibar to Mauritius lies is Zanzibar to Seychelles 2,650 fathoms or 15,900 English feet. Seychelles to Mauritius 2,300 fathoms or 13.880 feet.

The following are the Names of the ships belonging to the Company :

Ship	Capitain	Chief Elec.
Amber	R. Grecy	W. Murphy
Electra	H. Scott Smith	H. W. Ansell
John Pender	W. Perkins	F. Ryan
Mirror	G. Pattison	J. Boyes
Chiltern	J. W. Starkey	F. Lilley
Great Northern	V. Fox	C. Shaw
Recorder	R. A. E. Brereton	A. C. M. Weaver
Sherard Osborn	C. O. Madge	J. H. D. Jones

The Zanzibar — Seychelles cable was completed on 11th. November 1893, and the Seychelles—Mauritius Cable was completed on 22nd. November 1893.

A Prise or share of the Mare-aux-Vacoas Water.

A " Prise " or share of water from the Mare-aux-Vacoas is now regulated by Ordinance No. 20 of 1894.

Correspondance with the Government of this Colony.

The following are the rules to be observed in conducting correspondence with the Government :—

1. Two or more distinct subjects must not be included in one letter. Each letter must be confined to one subject.
2. The paragraphs are to be numbered consecutively.
3. If the letter be in reply to any communication marked with a distinctive number, the number of such communication as well as the date thereto is to be quoted in the reply.
4. The paper to be used is to be of Foolscap size ; an inner margin of at least one fourth of the width of the paper to be left blank, and if the communication extends to two or more sheets each page is to be numbered. The ink used should be black and the writing should be large and distinctly legible.
5. The marks of persons unable to write their own names must be properly attested.
6. All communications to the Colonial Secretary's Office should be addressed to the Colonial Secretary whether the letters from the Secretariat are signed by the Colonial Secretary or by the Assistant Colonial Secretary.

Interest on Curatelle Deposits.

Interest on Curatelle Deposits at the rate of 2 o/o per annum is allowed on all sums above Rs. 5 which have been more than six months in hand. (Article 54 of Ord. No. 9 of 1890.)

The Civil Service Widows and Orphans' Pension Fund.

On the 1st. April 1882, an Association was established for providing pensions for the Widows and Orphans of deceased public officers of this Colony. It was conducted on the lines of the Jamaica Fund, pending the preparation by the Imperial Government of a scheme suitable for Ceylon, Mauritius, and other Colonies ; and after working satisfactorily for four and a half years it was absorbed into *The Mauritius Civil Service Widows and Orphans' Pension Fund*, under Ordinance No. 2 of 1886.

According to Ord. 8 of 1893, every public servant on being first appointed to any permanent office under Government, with a salary of Rs. 240 and upwards, has to be registered as an Associate of the Fund.

The pensions are calculated, not according to the discretion of the Directors, but strictly according to the Ordinance, and the tables annexed thereto. There is one pension, payable to the widow only during her widowhood ; after which the widow's pension is divided, share and share alike, among such of the orphan children as are of pensionable age at the death or marriage of the widow, if they are more than three in number ; but if they are three or less in number, each child receives one-fourth of the whole.

The pensions of boys cease at the age of 18 : of girls, at 21 or marriage.

Every Associate is required to contribute, from the date of his registration, a sum equal to four per centum on the amount of his salary ; and the contributions are deducted by the Receiver General. The contributions are payable for thirty five years, or until the officer attains the age of 65 years, after which all abatements cease. When an officer retires from the Service on pension, it is optional for him to pay from that date, abatements either on his pension or on the full salary he was drawing before retiring. The contributions are retained by the Government, and interest at the rate of four per centum is allowed on the mean monthly balances.

The Association is under the direction and superintendence of a Board of 5 Directors who are named by the Governor each year.

The Directors' Report for the year ended 31st. December 1894, shows that on that date there were 986 registered Associates ; and the income for the year was Rs 53,185.57 ; and that the disbursements were Rs. 22,356.70. At that date there were 56 widows and 23 orphans on the pension list.

The cash balance in the hands of the Treasurer, at the close of each financial year since the formation of the Fund, was as follows :

On 1st. January 1883 ...	Rs.	13,607.95		On 31st. December 1889 ...	Rs.	146,617.59
,, 1st. January 1884 ...		31,066.26		,, 31st. December 1890 ...		171,049.31
,, 1st. January 1885 ...		45,850.04		,, 31st. December 1891 ...		195,575.72
,, 31st. December 1886 ...		77,448.75		,, 31st. December 1892 ...		221,877.11
,, 31st. December 1887 ...		97,501.78		,, 31st. December 1893 ...		254,490.34
,, 31st. December 1888 ...		120,806.79		,, 31st. December 1894 ...		285,319.21

Forty five Associates died during the ten past years, the yearly record being :—

In 1882	None.	In 1889...	Six.
In 1883	Four.	In 1890...	Ten.
In 1884	Five.	In 1891...	Nine.
In 1885	None.	In 1892...	Fifteen.
In 1886	Two.	In 1893...	Twenty one.
In 1887	Four.	In 1894...	Seventeen.
In 1888	Five.		

Of the 17 deaths in 1894, ten only gave rise to claims on the Fund.

List of Sworn Weighers.

Sworn Weighers ore appointed under and subject to the provisions on Proclamations dated 29th. April 1816.

E. Banche
J. Curé
D. Masson
L. A. Masson
J. Ithier
J. W. Maya
W. Telère
J. C. Florens
F. W. Calasse
X. Labutte
E. Tonnet
A. C. D. Frédéric
P. Bechet
P. Lavictoire
A. Cupidon
M. J. François
J. E. Brasse
A. Glond
H. Rosse
A. Langlois
A. Cochemée
E. Hubert.

Summary showing the number of Pupils attending Government Schools throughout the Colony, during 1894, andcost of the same.

Schools	No. of Teachers on 31.12.94				No. of Servants.	Average No. of Pupils on Roll during the year.			Average Attendance during the year			Fixed Salaries		Result Grants		Servant's wages		Rent of School buildings and lodging allowances to Teachers		Total Expenditure		Cost of each Scholar per annum calculated on the No. on Roll	
	Masters.	Mistresses.	Assistants.	Monitors.		B.	G.	Total.	B.	G.	Total.	Rs.	c.	Rs.	c.	Rs.	c.	Rs.	c.	Rs.	c.	Rs.	c.
First Grade, 1st division...	10	8	24	43	...	1922	1012	2934	1175	629	1804	42539	07	...	..	2161	50	11088	39	55788	96	19	01
First Grade, 2nd division...	24	8	15	61	...	2792	1311	4103	1812	824	2636	37924	15	5509	05	3329	50	11821	26	58583	90	14	27
Second Grade	22	2	19	3	...	1213	486	1699	750	272	1022	10955	35	1975	...	...	...	6620	...	19550	35	11	50
Second Grade—½ time system	8	...	7	...	...	350	105	455	215	57	272	3244	75	406	93	...	...	2298	...	5919	68	13	07
Training of Teachers for 2nd grade schools ½ time system	...	...	...	...	...	...	...	...	...	...	...	1666	98	...	...	...	...	...	...	1666	98	...	...
Relieving Teacher	...	...	...	...	...	...	...	...	...	...	...	600	...	...	...	...	...	...	...	600	...	...	...
Relieving Monitors	...	...	...	...	...	...	...	...	...	...	...	384	...	...	...	...	...	...	...	384	...	...	...
Drawing Master	...	...	...	...	...	...	...	...	...	...	...	300	...	...	...	...	...	...	...	300	...	...	...
Teacher of Singing	...	...	...	...	...	...	...	...	...	...	...	480	...	...	...	...	...	...	...	480	...	...	...
Personal allowance to Mrs. M. Dromart for training female teachers ...	...	...	...	...	...	...	...	...	...	...	...	240	...	...	...	...	...	...	...	240	...	...	...
Government Schoolmaster assisting the Inspector of Schools	...	...	...	...	...	...	...	...	...	...	...	1946	15	...	...	...	...	240	...	486	15	...	...
Salary of Mr. Ternel for 1 month (special).........	...	...	...	...	...	...	...	...	...	...	...	30	...	...	...	...	...	...	...	30	...	...	...
Totals...........	64	18	65	*107	...	6277	2914	9191	3952	1782	5734	100310 ‡	45	7890	98	5491	...	32067	65	145760	08	...	...

D. J. ANDERSON,
Superintendent of Schools.

* 26 of those are female attendants in 2nd Grade Schools.

‡ Rs. 48 out of this sum were paid as allowance to 2 Head Teachers for supplying water to the pupils.

Summary shewing the number of Pupils attending State-Aided Schools throughout the Colony during 1894, and the amount of Government Contributions.

School.	No. of Teachers on 31.12.94.		No. of Scholars on Roll and in average attendance.						Government Contributions.								Cost of each Scholar per annum calculated on the No. on Roll.		Remarks.
			Average number of Pupils on Roll during the year			Average attendance of Pupils during the year.			Sums paid as										
									Fixed Salaries.		Maintenance Grants.		Result Grants.		Total.				
	Head	Assist.	B.	G.	Total.	B.	G.	Total.	Rs.	c.	Rs.	c.	Rs.	c.	Rs.	c.	Rs.	c.	
Roman Cotholic Schools... ...	58	71	3134	3206	6340	2040	2147	4187	47048	76	10863	50	9492	13	67404	39	10	63	
Church of England Schools ...	27	9	1538	357	1895	984	222	1206	14491	02	2482	58	2357	23	19330	83	10	20	
Presbyterian Mission Schools ...	2	3	96	73	169	73	58	131	1699	92	180	...	191	83	2071	75	12	25	
Mahomedan School	1	1	106	...	106	78	...	78	690	41	154	28	...	...	844	69	7	96	
Drawing Master	...	...	...	...	...	...	...	...	...	...	...	...	...	...	300	...	...	...	
Training of Teachers for Aided Schools	...	...	...	...	...	...	...	...	...	...	...	...	...	...	3031	06	...	...	
Fees to two Examiners in Hindi ...	...	...	...	...	...	...	...	...	...	...	...	...	...	...	10	...	...	...	
Total... ...	88	84	4874	3636	8510	3175	2427	5602	63930	11	13680	36	12041	19	92992	72	...	...	

D. J. ANDERSON,
Superintendent of Schools.

Expenditure on the Government and Aided Schools of the Colony and also on Industrial Education for the year 1894.

Administration	Rs. 23,300.97
Expenditure on Government Schools exclusively	157,225.12
Expenditure on Aided Schools exclusively	92 992.72
Expenditure common to Government and Aided Schools	21,397.33
Industrial Education *	3,446.16
	Rs. 298,362.30

REVENUE.

Government and Aided Schools—Sale of Books... ... ... Rs. 6,703.91

* Five youths for apprenticeships for 5 years in the Railway Workshops and two at the Botanical Gardens for four years are selected annually by the Schools's Committee among the boys of the entire Colony. They receive daily wages from Government increasing in amount each year of apprenticeship.

The amount spent under this heading in 1894 was Rs. 3,446.16.

Oriental Telephone and Electric Company Limited.

OFFICE AND EXCHANGE, 7 PRINCE REGENT STREET, PORT LOUIS.

Mauritius Branch.

Electrician and Manager: E. L. Lalonde, A.I.E.E.

List of Subscribers.

No.	Numerical List.	Address.
1	Baylis & Co.	Church Street
2	Robinson, George	Queen Street
3	Hardware Company	Church Street
4	Commercial Bank of Mauritius	Church Street
5	Oriental Estates Company	Queen Street
6	Collector of Customs	Custom House
7	Rogers, L.	Church Street
8	Merchants' Clerks	Custom House
9	Librairies Coloniales (L. Roussel)...	Church Street
10	Pipon, Adam & Co.	Queen Street
11	Mauritius Engrais Chimiques Company	Church Street
12	Daily Publisher (E. Pezzani)	Comedy Street
13	Blyth Brothers & Co.	Wharf
14	New Mauritius Dock Company	Wharf
15	Civil Service Stores	Desforges Street
16	de Barrau, C.	Church Street
17	Ireland, Fraser & Co.	Pavillon Street
18	Vitry, H. & Co.	Prince Regent Street
19	Colonial Fire Insurance Company...	Comedy Street
20	Goudin, Coutanceau & Co.	Barracks Street
21	Scott & Co.	Corderie Street
22		
23	Elias, Mallac & Co.	Comedy Street
24	Smith, Freeland & Co....	Company's Garden

No.	Numerical List.	Address.
25	Taylor, A.	Wharf
26		
27	Currie, Fraser & Co.	Corderie Street
28	Sulliman, Issop Mamode	Corderie Street
29	Commercial Gazette	Old Council Street
30	Central Dock Company	Pavillon Street
31	Forges et Fonderies de Maurice	Nicolay Road
32	Black, Smith & Co.	Fort George
33	Albion Dock Company...	Trou Fanfaron
34	Compagnie Générale de Quincaillerie	Royal Street
35		
36	Kœnig, R. Notary	Bourbon Street
37	Dry Docks and Slips Company	Trou Fanfaron
38	Goilot, L. & Co.	Royal Street
39		
40	Bank of Mauritius Limited	Place d'Armes
41	Railway Goods Shed	Central Station
42	Minet, A. & Co.	Church Street
43	Minet, A. & Co.	Dumas Street
44		
45	Saboo Sidick & Co.	Hospital Street
46	Harbour Master	Wharf
47	Colonial Engrais Chimiques	Place d'Armes
48	Mauritius Fire Insurance Company	Church Street
49		
50	Manager Telephone and Electric Company	Prince Regent Street
51	Telephone and Electric Cy., Instrument Dept. ...	Prince Regent Street
52	Laurent, V. & Co.	Church Street
53		
54		
55	Antelme, Léopold	Church Street
56		
57		
58		
59		
60	Agricultural Company...	Rempart Street
61		
62	Merchants and Planters Gazette	Pope Hennessy Street
62	Vrai Mauricien	Pope Hennessy Street
63		
64		
65		
66		
67		
68		
69		
70		
71		
72		
73		
74	Municipality of Port Louis	Pope Hennessy Street
75	Mauritius Estates and Assets Company	Comedy Street
76		
77		
78		
79		
80		
99	Officer Commanding Troops	Fort George
100	Commanding Royal Engineer	Line Barracks
101	Central Police Station	Pope Hennessy Street

No.	Numerical List.	Address.
102	Paul & Virginie Police Station	Paul & Virginie Street
103	East End Police Station	Pamplemousses Road
104	Souillac Street Police Station	Souillac Street
105	West End Police Station	Brabant Street
106	Treasury do.	Intendance Street
107	Harbour Police Station	Wharf Square
108	Fanfaron Police Station	Farquhar Street
109	Abercrombie Police Station	Pamplemousses Road
110	Roche Bois Police Station	Abattoir Road
111	Milk Street Police Station	Milk Street
112	Railway Police Station	Railway Station

	Alphabetical List.	No.
A	Agricultural Company	60
	Albion Dock Company	33
	Antelme, Léopold	55
B	Blyth Brothers & Co.	13
	Baylis & Co.	1
	Black Smith & Co.	32
	Bank of Mauritius Limited ...	40
C	Central Dock Company	30
	Collector of Customs	6
	Colonial Engrais Chimiques Company	47
	Colonial Fire Insurance Company ...	19
	Commercial Bank of Mauritius ...	4
	Commercial Gazette	29
	Currie, Fraser & Co.	27
	Co-operative Engrais Chimiques ...	16
	Compagnie Générale de Quincaillerie	34
	Civil Service Stores	15
D	De Barrau, C.	16
	Daily Publisher (E. Pezzani) ...	12
	Dry Docks and Slips Company ...	37
E	Elias, Mallac & Co.	23
F	Forges et Fonderies de Maurice ...	31
G	Goilot, L. & Co.	38
	Goudin, Coutanceau & Co. ...	20
H	Harbour Master	46
	Hardware Company	3
I	Ireland Fraser & Co.	17
K	Kœnig, R.	36
L	Laurent, V. & Co.	52
M	Mauritius Fire Insurance Company...	48
	Mauritius Dock Company New ...	14
	Mauritius Engrais Chimiques Cy. ...	11
	Mauritius Estates and Assets Cy. ...	75
	Merchants' Clerk	8
	Merchants and Planters Gazette ...	62
	Minet, A. & Co., Church Street ...	42
	Minet, A. & Co., Dumas Street ...	43
	Municipality of Port Louis ...	74
O	Officer Commanding Troops ...	99
	Oriental Estates Company ...	5
P	Pezzani, E.	12
	Pipon, Adam & Co.	10
	Police Station, Central	101
	do. Section G., Paul et Virginie..	102
	do. do. H., East End	103
	do. do. D., Souillac St.	104
	do. do. E., West End	105
	do. do. Treasury ...	106
	do. do. Harbour ...	107
	do. do. F., T. Fanfaron	108
	do. do. I., Abercrombie	109
	do. do. K., Roche Bois	110
	do. do. A., Milk Street	111
	do. do. Railway Police Station.	112
R	Railway Goods Shed	41
	Robinson, George	2
	Royal Engineer (Commanding) ...	100
	Rogers, L.	7
	Roussel, L.	9
S	Smith, Freeland & Co.	24
	Sulliman, Issop Mamode ...	28
	Sanitary Improvement	16
	Scott & Co.	21
	Saboo Sidick & Co.	45
V to Z	Taylor, A.	25
	Telephone and Electric Company, Manager	50
	Telephone and Electric Company Instrument Department ...	51
	Vitry, H. & Co.	18
	Vrai Mauricien	62

IN CASE OF FIRE: RING UP Nos. 74 AND 101.

The following are also subscribers to the "Merchants Clerk's Telephone":

	Call No.		Call No.
Albion Dock Company	33	Ireland, Fraser and Co.	17
Blyth Brothers and Co.	13	Merchants and Planters Gazette ...	62
Commercial Gazette	29	New Mauritius Dock Company ...	14
Daily Publisher	12	Pipon, Adam and Co....	10
Forges et Fonderies de Maurice ...	31	Scott and Co.	21
Goudin, Coutanceau and Co. ...	20		

The following are also subscribers to the "Harbour Master's Telephone":

	Call No.		Call No.
Albion Dock Company	33	Ireland, Fraser & Co.	17
Blyth Brothers and Co.	13	Merchants & Planters Gazette ...	62
Commercial Gazette	29	New Mauritius Dock Company ...	14
Daily Publisher	12	Pipon Adam & Co.	10
Elias, Mallac and Co...	23	Scott & Co.	21
Goudin, Coutanceau and Co... ...	20		

There are also 20 Private Lines in Town and Country.

The Central Fire Station in Port Louis is connected on a separate Telephonic system with Fort Adelaide.

The Beau Bassin Central Prisons are also connected on a separate Telephonic system with the Police Station of Beau Bassin.

NOTE.—The Oriental Telephone and Electric Company Ld. in addition to its Telephonic business, now undertakes every kind of work connected with Electricity.

Rules for using the Magneto Bell and Telephone.

1. When you desire to speak with a Subscriber, turn the Bell handle sharply several times.

2. Your call will be immediately answered from the Exchange.

3. Then, and not before, take up the tubes, place them to your ears and call out the number (*never the name*) of the subscriber you wish to be connected with.

4. Wait until you hear the number you have asked for repeated and the words "*ring your bell.*" Then, put your tubes on the hooks, and ring up. When you get the reply take off the tubes and speak through *at once, letting your correspondent know who calls him.*

5. When you have finished speaking, replace the tubes, and give two distinct rings, to notify that you have finished. This should be done *at both ends.* A neglect of this rule may cause great inconvenience to subscribers :—as, for instance, A has been speaking to B. Immediately afterwards he wants to speak to C. If he has not rung off from B he will be still in connection ; and instead of ringing up the Exchange, he will again ring up B. (This has happened frequently). NEVER LEAVE THE TUBES OFF THE HOOKS : BY SO DOING YOU WILL RUIN THE BATTERY, AND RENDER YOUR INSTRUMENT USELESS.

6. The slighest inattention, or incivility, from the Central Office, or any defect in the working of the instruments, should be reported at once to the Manager, who will consider such information in the light of a personal favour.

N. B.—*Always answer a call by ringing your own bell. This will save time. And please keep the telephone covered at night. Dust hinders it from working satisfactorily.*

Death-rates of Mauritius from 1831 to 1895, showing the mortality of the Colony before and after the outbreak of fever in 1867.

Years.	Death-rates.	Years.	Death-rates.	Years.	Death-rates.
1831... ...	26.84	1853... ...	29.66	1875... ...	24.90
1832... ...	31.35	1854... ...	84.61	1876... ...	27.03
1833... ...	27.35	1855... ...	33.01	1877... ...	29.64
1834... ...	39.85	1856... ...	50.56	1878... ...	27.20
1835... ...	35.96	1857... ...	26.08	1879... ...	32.11
1836... ...	30.96	1858... ...	28.09	1880... ...	28.11
1837... ...	37.16	1859... ...	30.88	1881... ...	29.90
1838... ...	30.70	1860... ...	31.64	1882... ...	34.96
1839... ...	38.99	1861... ...	31.34	1883... ...	35.53
1840... ...	30.00	1862... ...	42.05	1884... ...	31.22
1841... ...	41.53	1863... ...	35.56	1885... ...	33.49
1842... ...	42.41	1864... ...	35.06	1886... ...	28.92
1843... ...	34.64	1865... ...	34.55	1887... ...	34.04
1844... ...	58.41	1866... ...	33.38	1888... ...	30.04
1845... ...	39.48	1867... ...	125.11	1889... ...	33.07
1846... ...	32.71	1868... ...	58.95	1890... ...	34.03
1847... ...	29.31	1869... ...	36.89	1891... ...	27.02
1848... ...	26.44	1870... ...	23.70	1892... ...	38.04
1849... ...	30.84	1871... ...	25.41	1893... ...	40.09
1850... ...	31.46	1872... ...	26.78	1894... ...	29.00
1851... ...	26.50	1873... ...	33.78	1895... ...	37.12
1852... ...	28.07	1874... ...	29.52		

Decennial and Quinquennial Periods.

Years.	Death-rates.	Years.	Death-rates.	Years.	Death-rates.
1831—40 ...	32.91	1866—70 ...	52.04	1886—90 ...	32.02
1841—50 ...	36.72	1871—75 ...	26.47	1891—95 ...	34.25
1851—60 ...	36.91	1876—80 ...	28.78		
1861—65 ...	36.77	1881—85 ...	32.17		

Average prices of various articles of Use or Consumption in Mauritius during 1894.

Articles.	Price in January.	April.	July.	October.
Wheaten Flour per 50 kilos	Rs. 7.50	Rs. 7.45	Rs. 7.80	Rs. 7.61
Wheaten Bread per half kilo	0.10	0.10	0.10	0.10
Butter Salt ,, ,, ...	1.13	1.14	1.05	1.05
Cheese ,, ,, ...	1.13	1.14	1.05	1.05
Beef ,, 150 kilos	82.03	81.11	94.55	86.38
Pork ,, 50 kilos	80.83	85.33	90.00	81.83
Rice ,, bag of 75 kilos ...	10.25	10.37	10.05	10.22
Coffee ,, 50 kilos	53.41	62.67	65.00	65.33
Tea ,, pound	0.95	0.95	0.95	0.95
Sugar ,, 50 kilos	Average of last season Rs. 10.00 to Rs. 12.00.			
Salt	Rs. 1.55	Rs. 1.34	Rs. 1.73	Rs. 1.82
Wine per cask	101.66	104.49	103.75	103.75
Brandy ,, case of 12 bottles	23.83	28.00	27.33	27.83
Beer ,, ,, ...	6.78	5.75	6.50	6.00
Tobacco per 50 kilos	160.99	168.50	173.10	192.22

Statement showing the Machinery in the Colony of Mauritius during 1894.

Districts.	Fibre extracting Machines.	Steam Engines.	Cane Mills.	Vacuum Pans.	Triple Effets.	Wetzels.	Centrifugal machines or turbines for drying sugar.	Manure making or Engrais Establishments.	Distilleries.	Remarks.
Port Louis	...	...	...	...	...	...	...	...	1	
Pamplemousses ...	...	27	14	12	4	10	72	8	...	1 diffusion plant.
Riv. du Rempart ...	19	42	17	17	6	16	99	1	...	
Flacq	...	71	28	32	14	45	171	3	1	
Grand Port... ...	...	52	34	34	12	24	173	2	1	
Savanne	2	49	21	25	9	6	125	8	1	1 diffusion plant.
Black River ...	10	7	5	5	1	12	22	2	1	
Plaines Wilhems ...	...	14	15	14	5	3	61	7	...	
Moka	...	20	12	16	3	14	63	2	...	
Total... ...	31	282	146	155	54	130	780	33	5	

Average rates of wages for Labour.

Class of Labour.	Per annum.	Per day.	Per task or Job.
Prœdial	Rs. 66 to 84 with rations, lodging and medical care.	Rs. 0.50 to 0.75.	Varies according to the task given.
Domestic ...	Rs. 120 to 192 with lodgings and medical care.	Rs. 0.75	Not employed by the Job.
Trades	Rs. 240 with lodgings, rations and medical care when on Estates.	Rs. 1 to Rs. 2.50.	Varies according to the task given.

List of Government Contractors for 1895-96.

Fresh Fish, 1895-97	Issop Mamode Olla.
White and Brown Bread, flour, &c., 1896-98	Goolam Hassan Issop.
Fowls and Eggs, 1896-97	Govinden.
Milk (except Plaines Wilhems), 1895-97	Ramjeewon Bussawon.
Milk (Plaines Wilhems), 1895-97	Mrs. A. Ducray.
Vegetables, 1896-97	S. Singaravalloo.
Groceries and General Stores, 1896-98	P. Candasamy.
Cocoanut oil, 1896-98	Mr. Nairac.
Firewood, 1896 97	Kodoruth.
Clothing, 1896-98	Mr. A. Maulgné.
Ironmongery, Tools, Implements, &c., 1895-97	V. Laurent, Mercier & Co.
Transport of Stores, &c, to and from Ile aux Fouquets, 1895-97	Widow Cowie.
Government Gazette, 1896-98	P. Robert.
Job-Printing, 1896-98	E. Pezzani.
Lighterage, 1896-97	Messrs J. Cowin & Co.
Lime, Sand, Coral and Red Earth, 1896-97	Mr. Modally.
Cartage, 1895-97	Widow Cunnoo.
Repairing and Winding up Clocks and Watches, 1896-97	J. Loiseau.
Washing, 1896-97	Salim Hossein.
Charcoal, 1896-97	Dawoodchun Moothy.
Conveyance of Sick Paupers to Pamplemousses and Beau Bassin, 1896-7	Mungroo Lalloo.
Coffins and Hearses, 1896-97	Mr. F. Laurent.
Conveyance of mails and packages weighing not more than 50 kilos, between Petite Rivière and Chamarel, 1895-97	Wid. Roopoo Fakeerah.
Fresh Beef, Tripe, &c., 1896	E. Docinthe.
Wines, Spirits, &c., 1896	Mr. Capeyron.
Cartage for Moka Hospital and for the conveyance of dead bodies to Pailles Cemetery 1896-97	K. Varatharajaloo.
Conveyance of dead bodies at Flacq, 1896-97	Mrs. A. Hector.
Gunny and Flour bags, 1896-97	Amurthalingum.
Book Binding, 1896-98	F. Atisse.
Australian Coals	Blyth Brothers & Co.
English Coals	Ireland Fraser & Co.
Colonial made boats, 1896	A. Sibaly.
Teak in balk, Teak Scantlings, Teak Madriers & Planks and Kawrie timber	Dauban, Desvaux & Co.
Teak shingles, Singapore boards, Swan River Mahogany	Pastourel, Duponsel & Co.
Madagascar and Colonial Timber	Messrs Singery & Co.
Deal madriers & Boards and Singapore planks	Messrs. A. & H. Rousset.

Time at which Money Doubles at Interest.

Rate per cent.	Simple Interest.	Compound Interest.
10	10 years	7 years 100 days.
9	11 years 40 days	8 years 16 days.
8	12½ years	9 years 2 days.
7	14 years 104 days	10 years 89 days.
6	16 years 8 months	11 years 327 days.
5	20 years	15 years 75 days.
4½	22 years 81 days	15 years 273 days.
4	25 years	17 years 246 days.
3½	28 years 208 days	20 years 53 days.
3	33 years 4 months	23 years 164 days.
2½	40 years	28 years 26 days.
2	50 years	35 years 1 day.

Close Season for Game, Wild Birds and Fish.

The following Table gives the "close" time for the different kinds of Game in Mauritius during which it is illegal to kill, destroy or pursue, the game mentioned, all dates inclusive—*Ord. No.* 8 *of* 1869.

The penalty for contravening the provision of the above cited Ordinance is for the first offence a fine not less than Rs. 50 and not more than Rs. 100, but in case an offender shall have been convicted for a second offence within twelve months, the punishment shall be imprisonment for a period not less than 5 days and not more than one month or to a fine not less than Rs. 150 and not more than Rs. 300.

Game.	Periods.
Deer	From 1st. September to 15th. May following.
Partridges	From 15th. September in every year until the 15th. April following.
Wild Guinea Fowls	
Quails	
Wild Ducks	
Sarcelles	

Close Seasons for Oysters, Crabs, Camarons, Rougets, Sardines & Sprats,

all dates inclusive :—

Fish.	Periods.
Oysters	16th. September to 14th. April next following.
Mussels	do.
Crabs—Female	do.
Homards—Female	do.
Camarons—Female	1st. October lo 1st. March following.
Rougets	10th. November to 10th. December.
Sardines & Sprats	1st. August to 31st. January following.

Size of Fish that may be caught.—*Ordinance No.* 42 *of* 1881.

SCHEDULE D. ARTS. 18 & 19.

	Centimeters.		Centimeters.
Anguille, eel...	any size	Perroquet ...	21
Balao ...	27	Poule d'Eau	24
Banane	21	Prêtre	8
Barbet	21	Piment	10
Barrois	27	Rougets	21
Basse Carrangue	any size	Sap-Sap	13
Breton	18	Sardine grosse	any size
Capitaine	27	Do. batarde	any size
Carrangue	any size	Sardes or Brodemare	16
Carandine	13	Sole	18
Cateau	21	Tazar	any size
Champêtre	any size	Trompette...	any size
Chirurgien	24	Vieille de Boue	21
Cordonnier	18	Do. Faraud	21
Dame Berry ...	26	Do. Grise	13
Gueule-Pavée	27	Do. Plate	18
Herring	16	Do. Rouge	16
Licorne	29	Chevrette de mer	8
Lubine	21	Oyster	5
Lune ...	13	Mussel	5
Machoaran	any size	Homard	23
Madras	13	Camaron	10
Mullet...	27	Crabe dit de Carlet *	12
Maquereau or Sizare	16	Crabe de petite espèce	5

* The shell being measured over its greatest length.

Governors of Mauritius.

For the Dutch Republic (1638 to 1710.)

Pieter de Goyer, Commander	1638
Adrain Van der Stel, Commander (Frederick Van der Marrzen, 2nd. in command	1639
First abandonment of the Island by the Dutch	1644
Maximilien de Jong, Opperhoofd, (Governor)	1650
Second abandonment of the Island	1654
Adrin Nieuland Opperhoofd, (Governor)	1659
Dirk, Jonzoon Smient Ditto	1664
George Frederick Wreede Ditto	1668
Hubert Hugo Ditto	1671
Isaac Johannes Lamotius Ditto	1677
Rœlof Diodati Ditto	1692
Abrahim Mommer Van de Velde Ditto	1705
Final abandonment of the Island by the Dutch	1710

For the French East India Company (1721 to 1767

M. Duronguet, Le Toullec, Governor	1st December	1721
Le Chevalier de Nyon, Colonel, Governor and Engineer in Chief	January	1722
M. de Brousse, *Lieutenant du Roi*	December	1725
M. Benoit Dumas, Director General of Commerce for the two Islands (residing at Bourbon)	16th. August	1727
M. de Maupin, Commandant	31st. August	1729
M. Mahé de Labourdonnais, Governor General of the Isles of France and Bourbon)	8th. June	1735
M. Didier de Saint Martin, *pro tem*	February	1740
M. Mahé de Labourdonnais	December	1742
M. Didier de Saint Martin, *pro tem*	March	1746
M. Barthelemy David, Governor General of the Isles of France and Bourbon	8th. October	1746
M. de Lozier Boutet, Do. do. do.	February	1753
M. Magon, Commandant General of the Isles of France, Sainte Marie, Rodrigues, &c.	8th. November	1759
M. Desforges Boucher, General for the King	27th. June	1761

For the French Government (1767 to 1810.)

M. Dumas, Colonel Governor General of the Isles of France and Bourbon	17th. July	1767
M. Steinaur, Brigadier General, Commandant General of the two Islands	20th. November	1767
Le Chevalier des Roches, *Chef d'Escadre*, Governor General of the two Islands	7th. June	1769
M. Steinauer *pro tem*	July to Novemb.	1770
Le Chevalier d'Arzac de Ternay, *Chef d'Escadre*, Commandant General of the two Islands	24th. August	1772
Le Chevalier de Guiran de la Brillane, *Chef d'Escadre*, Commandant General of the two Islands	2nd. December	1776
Le Vicomte de Souillac, Commandant General *pro tem* of the Isle of France.	3rd. May	1779
Le Vicomte de Souillac, Governor General of the two Islands	4th. July	1781
Le Vicomte de Souillac, Governor General of the French Establishments, East of the Cape of Good Hope	15th. February	1785
Le Chevalier de Fresne, Colonel, Commandant *pro tem* of the Isles of France and Bourbon	5th. April	1785
Le Chevalier de Fleury do. do.	28th. June	1785
Le Vicomte de Souillac	November	1785
Le Chevalier Bruni d'Entrecasteaux, *Capitaine de Vaisseau* Governor of the Isles of France and Bourbon	5th. November	1787
Le Vicomte de Conway, *Maréchal-de-Camp*, Governor of the French Establishments East of the Cape of Good Hope	14th. November	1789
M. Davit Charpentier de Cossigny, Maréchal-de-Camp, Governor General of French Establishments East of the Cape of Good Hope	26th. August	1790
Le Comte de Malartic, Lieutenant-General, Governor General of the French Establishments, East of the Cape of Good Hope	21st. June	1792

Le Comte Magallon de Lamorlière, *Général de Division*, Governor General *pro tem* of the two Islands ... ... 29th. July ...1800
M. Charles Decaen, *Général de Division*, Captain-General of the French Establishments, East of the Cape of Good Hope ... ... 26th. September, 1803

"INTENDENTS."

M. Poivre ... ... 17th. July ...1767
M. Maillard du Mesle ... ... 22nd. August ...1772
M. de Foucault ... ... 17th. November. 1777
M. Chevreau ... ... 4th. July ...1781
M. Motais de Narbonne ... ... 12th. October ...1785
M. Dupuy ... ... 17th. August ...1785
M. Thibault de Chanvallon ... ... 6th. November. 1798
M. Léger, *Préfet Colonial* ... ... 26th. September 1803

GOVERNORS FOR GREAT BRITAIN.

R. T. Farquhar, Esquire ... ... 3rd. December. 1810
Major-General H. Warde (*acting*) ... ... 9th. April ...1811
R. T. Farquhar, Esquire ... ... 12th. July ...1811
Major-General J. Gage Hall ... ... 10th. November. 1817
Colonel Dalrymple ... ... 10th. December. 1817
Major-General R. Darling (*acting*) ... ... 6th. February...1818
Sir R. T. Farquhar, Bart. ... ... 6th. July ...1820
Major-General R. Darling (*acting*) ... ... 20th. May ...1823
Hon. Sir G. Lowry Cole ... ... 12th June ...1823
Hon. Sir Charles Colville, K.G.H. ... ... 17th. June ...1828
Major-General Sir W. Nicolay, C.B., K.G.K ... ... 30th. January ...1833
Colonel J. Power, R.A. (*acting*) ... ... 20th. February.. 1840
Sir Lionel Smith, Bart., K.C.B. ... ... 16th. July ...1840
Colonel W. Staveley (*acting*) ... ... 3rd. January ...1842
Lieut.-Colonel Sir W. Maynard Gomm, K.C.B. ... ... 21st. November. 1842
Lieut.-Colonel T. Blancard (*acting*)... ... ... 5th. May ...1849
Lieut.-Colonel H. L. Sweeting (*acting*) ... ... 21st. May ...1849
Sir George William Anderson, K.C.B. ... ... 8th. June ...1850
Major-General W. Sutherland (*acting*) ... ... 19th. October ...1850
James Macauley Higginson, Esquire, C.B. ... ... 8th. January ...1851
Major-General W. Sutherland (*acting*) ... ... 14th. April ...1854
Major-General C. M. Hay (*acting*) ... ... 18th. January ...1855
Sir J. M. Higginson, K.C.B. ... ... 17th. June ...1857
Major-General C. M. Hay (*acting*) ... ... 11th. September. 1857
Sir William Stevenson, K.C.B. ... ... 21st. September. 1857
Major-General M. C. Johnson (*acting*) ... ... 10th. January ...1863
Sir Henry Barkly, K.C.K. ... ... 22nd. August ...1863
Major-General E. S. Smyth (*acting*) ... ... 4th. June ...1870
Honorable Sir Arthur Hamilton Gordon, K.C.M.G. ... ... 31st. January ...1871
Major-General E. S. Smyth (*acting*) ... ... 19th. August ...1871
Hon. Sir Arthur Hamilton Gordon, K.C.M.G. ... ... 29th. September. 1871
Edward Newton, Esquire, C.M.G. (*acting*) ... ... 21st. October ...1872
Hon. Sir Arthur Hamilton Gordon, K.C.M.G. ... ... 28th. October ...1872
Edward Newton, Esquire, C.M.G. (*acting*) ... ... 20th. January ...1873
Hon. Sir Arthur Hamilton Gordon, K.C.M.G. ... ... 20th. October ...1873
Edward Newton, Esquire, C.M.G. (*acting*) ... ... 30th. September. 1874
Lieut.-General Sir Arthur Purves Phayre, G.C.M.G., K.C.S.I., C.B. ... 21st. November.. 1874
F. Napier Broome, Esquire, C.M.G. (*acting*) ... ... 31st. December... 1878
Sir George Ferguson Bowen, G.C.M.G. ... ... 4th. April ...1879
F. Napier Broome, Esquire, C.M.G., *Lieutenant-Governor* ... ... 9th. December. 1883
C. Bruce, Esquire, C.M.G. (*acting*) ... ... 5th. May ...1883
Sir John Pope Hennessy, K.C.M.G. ... ... 1st. June ...1883
H. N. D. Beyts, C.M.G. (*acting*) ... ... 25th. September. 1884
* Sir John Pope Hennessy, K.C.M.G. ... ... 15th. October ...1884
H. N. D. Beyts, C.M.G. (*acting*) ... ... 30th. September. 1886

* Commission suspended by Sir Hercules H. R. Robinson on 14th. December 1886. Reinstated by Sir T. H. Holland, Secretary of State, on 12th. July 1887, and arrived in Mauritius on the 22nd. December 1888.

Sir Hercules H. R. Robinson, P.C., K.C.M.G., Governor ... ... 15th. December. 1886
Major-General W. H. Hawley (*acting*) ... ... 18th. December. 1886
Francis Fleming, Esquire, C.M.G. (*acting*) ... ... 2nd. July ...1887
Sir John Pope Hennessy, K.C.M.G., Governor ... ... 22nd. December. 1888
Colonel Thomas Erskine Arthur Hall (*acting*) ... ... 17th. December. 1889
Sir Charles Cameron Lees, K.C.M.G. ... ... 21st. December.. 1889
Hubert E. H. Jerningham, Esquire, C.M.G. (*acting*) ... ... 12th. March ...1892
Sir Hubert E. H. Jerningham, K.C.M.G., Governor... ... ... 24th. April ...1893
Arthur Anthony King-Harman, Esquire, C.M.G. (*acting*) ... ... 17th. January ...1894
Sir Hubert E. H. Jerningham, K.C.M.G., Governor... ... ... 24th. July ...1894

Chief Judges and Commissaries of Justice.

George Smith ... ... 30th. October ...1814
Edward Berens Blackburn ... ... 10th. January ...1824
James Wilson ... ... 1st. October ...1835
Sir J. Edward Remono, Knt. (*acting*) 6th. March to 20th. June and 1st. Nov. 1858 to 29th. Aug. 1860
Sir Stevenson Villiers Surtees, Knt. (*acting*) ... ... 31st. January ...1857
Sir Charles Farquhar Shand, Knt. ... ... 30th. May ...1860
Sir Nicolas Gustave Bestel, Knt. (*acting*) 19th. January 1868 to 4th. June 1868 and April ...1875
to 6th. June 1876 and 11th. September 1878 to 31st. August...1879
Sir Adam Gib Ellis, Knt. ... ... 1st. September...1879
Sir E. P. J. Leclézio, Knt. ... ... 22nd. November. 1883

Colonial Secretaries.

Colonel Barry ... ... 3rd. December...1814
A. W. Blane (*acting*) ... ... Feb. to Dec. ...1831
G. F. Dick ... ... 27th. December..1831
C. J. Bayley ... ... 26th. December..1849
W. W. R. Kerr (*acting*) ... ... April to June ...1855
J. Dowland (*acting*) ... ... June 1855 to June 1857
H. Sandwith, C.B. ... ... 20th. June ...1857
Stair Douglas (*acting*) ... ... Sept. 1858 to June 1860
Felix Bedingfield, C.M.G. ... ... 1st. September...1860
Edward Newton, C.M.G. ... ... 1st. December ...1868
W.H.Marsh (*acting*) 20th. Jan. to 20th. Oct. 1872, 1st. Oct. to 21st. Nov. 1874, 22 July to 6 May. 1877
F. Napier Broome, C.M.G. ... November 1877, 9th. December 1880 to 4th. January...1883
H. N. D. Beyts, C.M.G. (*acting*) ... ... 31st. December 1878 to 4th April. 1879
to 1st. July 1879 to 24th. May 1880, 9th. December 1880 to 4th. January. 1883
Charles Bruce, C.M.G. ... ... 5th. January ...1883
H. N. D. Beyts, C.M.G. (*acting*) ... ... 3rd. Dec. 1883 to 24th Sept. 1884
16th. Oct. to 2nd. Dec. 1884, 23rd. Aug. 1885 to 5th. February. 1886
Clifford LLoyd Lieutenant-Governor and Colonial Secretary... ... 6th. February ...1886
H. N. D. Beyts, C.M.G. (*acting*) 1st. to 29th. Sept. 1886, 30th. October to 17th. December...1886
F. R. Round (*acting*) ... ...17th. December 1886 to 23rd. February. 1887
Francis Fleming, C.M.G. ... ... 24th. February...1887
H. N. D. Beyts, C.M.G. (*acting*) 2nd. July 1887 to 31st. May, 27th. August to 21st. December..1888
H. Cockburn Stewart (*acting*) ... ... 1st. June to 26th. August ...1888
Francis Fleming, C.M.G. ... ... 22nd. December..1889
E. B. Sweet Escott (*acting*) ... ... 17th. April ...1889
Thos. Elliott (*acting*) ... ... 24th. July ...1889
Hubert E. H. Jerningham, C.M.G. ... ... 21st. December.. 1889
Thos. Elliott, C.M.G. (*acting*) ... ... 13th. May ...1891
Hubert E. H. Jerningham, C.M.G. ... ... 11th. November. 1891
Thos. Elliott, C.M.G. (*acting*) ... ... 12th. March ...1892
C. A. King-Harman, C.M.G. ... ... 2nd. September..1893
Thos. Elliott, C.M.G. (*acting*) ... ... 17th. January ...1894
C. A. King-Harman, C.M.G. ... ... 24th. July ...1894

List of Laureates of the Royal College from 1840 to 1895.

Names.	Years.	Names.	Years.
Kœnig, A.	1840	Dick, Frédérick, C.	1871
Garreau, V.	1841	Bouchet, Louis V. G...	—
Fressanges, H. F.	1842	Paddle, James Isaac	1873
Meistre, A.	1843	Anderson, Daniel Elie	—
Longueville, A.	—	Jean Louis, Nemours	—
D'Emmerez de Charmoy, P. F. Oscar..	1844	Cantin, Louis Alfred	—
Colin, Jules	—	Bell, Herbert John	1875
Barbeau, A.	1845	Wohrnitz, Ferdinand B.	—
Tourrette, C.	1847	Laurent, Eugène	1876
Dick, Charles, M.	—	Hullard, George	—
Dupuy, A.	1848	K/Vern, Victor F. G.	1877
Bardet, T...	1849	Rohan, Virgile	—
Leclézio, E. J.	1850	Newton, Ch. Christian	—
Beaugeard, O.	—	Boucherat, Julien	1878
Allas, Léonce	1851	Suzor, Jean Renaud...	—
Brunet, Fulcher...	1852	Dumat, Fra. Campbell	—
Rouillard, John	1853	Bell, John Ackroyd	1879
Barraut, A. Rodrigues	1854	Despeissis, Louis Henri	—
Rogers, Henry P.	—	Bonnefin, Henri	1880
Beaugeard, Horace	1855	Laurent, Octave	—
Mayer, George C.	—	Despeissis, Antony	1881
Pellereau, Etienne	1856	Kœnig, Etienne	—
Laconfourque, N.	—	Bonnin, Louis	1882
Cox, George	1857	Croft James	—
Coignet, Charles	—	Rouillard, John	1883
Leclézio, Henri	1858	Rouget, Auguste	—
Rogers, William...	—	Serret, Eugène	1884
Guibert, Georges	1859	Pitot, Emile	—
Didier, St Amand, E.	1860	Herchenroder, Alfred F.	1885
Chastellier, Evenor	—	Cochemée, Alfred	—
Newton, William	—	Standley, Alfred	1886
Trouche, William	1861	Rouillard, Louis	—
Dick, George Royer	—	Barbeau, Gabriel	1887
Jenkins, Thomas Lionel	—	Le Juge de Segrais, Paul	—
Cox, Lionel	1862	Martin, Charles	1888
Legrand, Louis	—	Jacques, Volcy	—
Galéa, Henry	1863	Chazal, R. de...	1889
Forder, Joshua	—	Chastellier, G	—
Hermans, Jean	1864	Pitot, Charles Alphonse Robert ...	1890
Lemière Hypolite	—	Kœnig, Paul	—
Dubois, Victor	—	Perdreau, Joseph Arthur	1891
Hobbs, William	1865	Momplé, Robert	—
Lebobinec, Ferdinand	—	Giraud, Pierre Léopold	1892
Pellereau, Elie	1866	Duclos, Joseph Adolphe	—
Brown, Richard Miles	—	Melotte, J. Baptiste Darcet... ...	1893
Forget, Arthur Louis	1867	Rowell, Percy Fitz Patrick ...	—
Thibaud, Arthur Louis	—	Louis, Léon	1894
Mc Donald, Peter	1869	D'Avray, Edward Alfred	—
Hullard, Jean Arthur	—	Desenne, Henri *	1895
Crétin, Eugène	—	Nairac, Edouard ‡	—

* Modern side | ‡ Classical side

Supreme Court.

His Honor Sir E. P. J. Léclézio, Kt. *Chief Judge.*
His Honor J. Rouillard, *First Puisne Judge.*
His Honor L. V. Delafaye, *Second Puisne Judge.*
His Honor F. C. Moncrieff, *Third Puisne Judge.*
The Honorable F. T. Piggott, *Procureur & Advocate General.*
The Honorable L. Rouillard, *Substitute Procureur & Advocate General.*
E. Didier St. Amand, *Master.*
L. G. de Comarmond, *Chief Clerk Master's Court.*
Léonce Isnard, *Registrar.*
W. Bathfield, *Chief Clerk Registry.*

Court of Bankruptcy.

The Master of the Supreme Court, *Judge.*
L. G. de Comarmond, *Registrar.*
G. Newton, *Accountant.*

Supreme Court.

CIVIL SESSIONS.

1st. From 1st. February till 31st. March
2nd. From 16th. April till 14th. June
3rd. From 1st. July till 14th. September
4th. From 16th. October till 14th. December

Assize Court.

CRIMINAL SESSIONS.

1st. ....Tuesday 25th. February.
2nd.........Tuesday 19th. May
3rd.........Tuesday 18th. August
4th.........Tuesday 17th. November

Counsel (*Actually practising*)

	Called to the Bar.		Called to the Bar.		Called to the Bar.
Bax, L.A.R. ...	... 6. 6—94	Jenkins, D....	... 6. 6—83	Newton, Hon. W., Q.C.	6.6—64
Beaugeard, P.	... 6.11—68	Jollivet, Y.P.A.	... 13.11—75	Newton, C. ...	... —80
Chastellier, P.L.,Q.C.	17.11—68	Kœnig, E. ...	... 25. 6—84	Pilot, C. L. H...	... 6.6—94
Chastellier, G.C.	... 26. 1—94	K/Vern, G ...	... 9. 6—88	Pitot, Robt ...	... 25.6—95
Esnouf, A. ...	... 26. 1—94	Laurent, O...	... 6. 6—82	Renaud, E. ...	... 6.6—94
Galéa, H., Q.C.	... 11. 6—67	Leclézio, L. ‡	... 17.11—86	Rouillard, Louis	... 3.7—89
Guibert, Hon. G.,Q.C.	30. 4—64	Leclézio, E...	... 13. 6—89	Rouillard, Edmond	... —89
Herchenroder, Alfred	13. 6—88	Mathews, F.	... 6. 6—72	Sauzier, E. ...	... 28.1—89
* Hugues, L.A.	... 16. 1—78	Martin Moncamp,P.G.	30.4—61	Rochery, Gustave †	... 26.1—90

Attorneys (*Actually practising.*)

Bernard, E. ...	...1889	Ganachaud, E. ...	...—71	Pitot, A. ...	...—63
Bertin, H.	...—64	Goumany, A. H....	...—88	Ritter, G. A. Hon.	...—64
Bétuel, A.	...—63	Halais, J. ...	...—65	Robert, F.	...—57
Bouloux, G. ...	...—76	Hewetson, W. ...	.. —95	Robert, F. junior ...	...—85
Chaillet, E. ...	...—78	Huteau, E. ...	...—82	Rochery, G... ...	...—86
Chaperon, P. O. ...	...—85	Jonas, L. ...	...—94	Rohan, A.	...—64
Chazal, P. E. de ...	...—60	Kœnig G.... ...	...—74	Rousset, C.... ...	...—70
Colin, A. junior ...	...—89	Lafitte, L.... ...	...—79	Sauzier, E.... ...	...—66
Comarmond, A. de	...—67	Lastelle, P. F. ...	...—72	Sicard, N.	...—62
Comarmond, H. de	...—95	Laurent, E. ...	...—49	Simonet, F... ...	...—63
Desjardins, N. ...	...—88	Leblanc, W. G. ...	...—72	St. Pern, L. de ...	...—70
Ducasse, V. ...	...—79	Leblanc, M. ...	...—84	Thatcher, H. ...	...—76
Ducray, V. G. ...	...—64	Leclézio, Hon. H...	...—80	Victor, F.	...—60
Edwards, W. H. ...	...—81	Marjolin, V. ...	...—84	Wohrnitz, L. ...	...—69
Finniss, W. ...	...—53	Pitchen, C. ...	...—85		

List of Ushers.

SUPREME COURT.

Clair, Julius
Camoin, Pierre
Dupont, A.
Lecudenec, Léon
Lamusse, Alfred
Pommerol, Edgar
Remy, Louis
Serret, Victor
Tobin, William

DISTRICT COURT, PORT LOUIS.

Dina, Abou Faride
Dusaulchoy, Henry C.
Moukime, Sakir
Piarroux, E.
Sampson, D. P.
Russie, Joseph

RURAL DISTRICTS.

Pamplemousses ...	E. Don Bastien and H. Dubor
Riv. du Rempart...	M. Marie
Flacq ...	... E. Ferrière and E. Hugon
Grand Port	... E. Upton and L. Poisson
Savanne ...	... M. Hein
Black River...	... E. Mouton
Plaines Wilhems	... D. Mai and A. Góbert
Moka... ...	... V. Dupont
Curepipe ...	... P. F. Mouton

* Is Acg. District Magistrate, Grand Port. ‡ Is Acting District Magistrate, Flacq.
† Is Acting Visiting Magistrate, Oil Islands.

Notaries.

(With a list of the " Minutes " in their possession.)

PORT LOUIS.

Hart, Walter Edward...... 30th. September 1892.

Possesses the Minutes of

Barry ... ... 1863 to 1884	Meistre ... ... 1852 to 1863
Lamusse ... ... 1845 to 1852	Boulanger, A. ... ... 1884 to 1892

Durand Deslongrais, Charles A....... 28th. January 1867.

Possesses the Minutes of

Bussié ... ... 1823 to 1832	Erny [*Port Louis*] ... ... 1832 to 1837
Caiez ... ...1801 [An X] to 1823	Grevint ... ...1781 to 1801 [An X]
Delisle Beauregard [*Pl. Wilhems & Moka*] ... ... 1789 to 1771	Liénard ... ... 1837 to 1855
Delisle Beauregard [*Port Louis*]... 1781 to 1807	Raffray, J. J. ... ... 1862 to 1867
Erny [*Pamplemousses*] ... ... 1831 to 1832	Vigoureux de K/Morvan ... ... 1855 to 1862
	Yardin ... ...1797 [An X] to 1816

Kœnig Robert (*Government Notary*)...... 8th. June 1888.

Possesses the Minutes of

Auffray ... ...1773 to 1802 [An X]	Geffroy, V. ... ... 1864 to 1874
Bombard ... ... 1763 to 1823	Geffroy, L. A. ... ... 1874 to 1884
Bonsergent ... ... 1825 to 1828	Guimbeau, J. B. ... ... 1848 to 1863
Déroullède ... ... 1816 to 1837	Guimbeau, G. ... ... 1884 to 1888
Douand ... ... 1771 to 1793	Kérivel ... ...1785 to 1797 [An X]
Eon ... ... 1802 to 1831	Ledo [*Plaines Wilhems and Black River*] ... ... 1821 to 1825
Geffroy, N. [*Plaines Wilhems and Black River*] ... ... 1821 to 1832	Petit... ... ... 1792 to 1825
Geffroy, N. [*Port Louis*] ... ... 1837 to 1848	

Gimel, Alfred..................20th. November 1874.

Possesses the Minutes of

De Marcy, L. ... ... 1836 to 1839	Herchenroder, L. ... ... 1842 to 1860
Gimel, E. ... . 1860 to 1874	Icery, Charles ... ... 1839 to 1842

Poupinel de Valencé, Albert.........17th. May 1869.

Possesses the Minutes of

Maingard, C. A. Josselin ... ... 1852 to 1867	Ducray, A. ... ... 1857 to 1869
Baro Rivière ... ... 1793 to 1832	Jollivet, Yves ... ... 1822 to 1856
Esnouf ... ... 1857 to 1865	Leforestier ... ... 1781 to 1787
Jollivet, Arthur ... ... 1865 to 1885	Jollivet Adolphe ... ... 1885 to 1889
Poupinel de Valencé, A. [*Plaines Wilhems and Black River*] ... 1869 to 1892	

de Robillard, Edgar............ 26th. April 1895.

Possesses the Minutes of

Audibert ... ... 1789 to 1792	Ducray, M. F. G. ... ... 1874 to 1878
Barry ... ... 1830 to 1842	Durand père ... ...1791 to 1796 [An V]
Bonnefin ... ... 1825 to 1833	Durand fils ... ...1705 [An IV] to 1819
Bouic ... ... 1833 to 1839	Leroy ... ... 1819 to 1825
Chateau de Balyon père 1772	Maingard, C. A. J.... ... ... 1857 to 1872
Chateau de Balyon fils 1791 to 1803 [An XII]	Pepin ... 1799 [An VIII] to 1808 [An IX]
Ducray [*Pamplemousses*] ... ... 1829 to 1834	Pitot, C. J. C. ... ... 1878 to 1884
Ducray [*Grand Port*] ... ... 1831 to 1842	Toussaint [*Grand Port*] ... ... 1791 to 1820
Ducray, J. M. R. G. ... ... 1833 to 1857	Vigoureux de K/Morvan ... ... 1885 to 1888
Ducray, J. M. R. G. ... ... 1872 to 1874	Maingard, J. M. ... ... 1888 to 1895

Piat, Ariste..................... 23rd. May 1893.

Possesss the Minutes of

Bélin père	1785 to 1823	Kœnig	1834 to 1851
Bélin fils	1824 to 1837	Pelte, A. L. S.	1852 to 1880
Duran	1789 to 1798	Montocchio, P. A.	1880 to 1893
Faivre de Bouvot	1817 to 1819		

Levieux, Félix Xavier Schmaltz.........7th. August 1885.

Possesses the Minutes of

Baltan	1793 to 1817	Levieux P. J.	1839 to 1856
Callot [*Pamplemousses*]	1814 to 1816	Maingard	1830 to 1839
Dubor [*R. du Remp. & Pt. Louis*]	1819 to 1830	Pelte	1778 to 1791
Dumat, C.	1856 to 1860	Raoul, L.	1860 to 1885
Guérin père	1791 to 1817	Sylvain Roux.. 1796 [An V] to 1803 [An XII]	
Guérin fils	1817 to 1823	Touraille	1779 to 1791

Baissac, Gustave ....8th. January 1886.

Possesses the Minutes of

Baissac, L. E.	1873 to 1885	Sauzier, Théodore	1868 to 1873
Sevène, G. M. F.	1836 to 1868		

Notaries Public appointed on the 15th. January 1889 for the District of Port Louis under the provisions of Art. 6 of Ordinance No. 25 of 1888.

Ange Edouard Thibaud & François Angelbert Méyépa, junior.

PAMPLEMOUSSES AND RIVIÈRE DU REMPART.

D. L. V. Vèle................................ 1894.

Possesses the Minutes of

Macquet	1836 to 1841	Maingard, J. M.	1866 to 1874
Langlois	1842 to 1863	Planel, J. C.	1874 to 1894
Charmoy, E. D. de	1863 to 1866		

FLACQ.

Gersigny, J. B. A. Brousse de.........11th. March 1875.

Possesses the Minutes of

Arnaud père [*Flacq*].	1791 to 1797 [An VI]	Montocchio, C. J.	1822 to 1857 & 1868 to 1875
Harscher	1797 [An VI] to 1822	Lenior, J. C. Gustave	1857 to 1868

GRAND PORT AND SAVANNE.

Blancard, William Stenio......... 8th. July 1889.

Possesses the Minutes of

Macquet, A. Noël	1842 to 1872	Halais, F.	1872 to 1889

BLACK RIVER, PLAINES WILHEMS AND MOKA.

L. A. Geffroy........... ....15th. July 1892.

English Notaries in Port Louis.

Comarmond, A. D. | François, F.

Minutes formerly deposited in the Registry of Court of Appeal now in the Archives Office.

Allain	1781 to 1784	Fouquereaux	1791 to 1797
Arnaud père	—97 to 1822	Géraud	—63 to —67
Arnaud fils	1823 to —33	Gombaud	—73 to —82
Ballu	1782 to 1797	Jacob	—64 to —70
Bertin	—47 to —49	Kergalet	—30 to —33
Bonnescuille de la Roche Durand	—60 to —62	Lablache, M.	1842 to 1845
Boudeville	—95 to 1811	Lefèvre	—02 to —03
Bourlier	—51 to 1757	Leroux	1728 to 1730
Boussard	—61 to —67	Leroux de Cinq Noyers	—74 to —84
Brun	—91 to —97	Lousteau	—67 to —91
Colas	—57 to —60	Melville de St. Remy	—36 to —44
Colbert	—33 to —43	Mollière	—37 to —51
Delaguette	—76 to —79	Motet	—30 to —33
Describes	—56 to —63	Penchin	—49 to —55
Dusart de la Salze	—30	Rose	—97 to 1811
Dustillet	—67 to —70	St. Martin	—26 to 1730
Fouilleuse	—29 to —30	Trébuchet	1832 to 1842

Sworn Land Surveyors.

Barrant, E.	24th April—95	Laurent, E.	22nd June—86
Bety, Sébert (Seychelles)	1889	Lepervanche, P.	29th Jan.—84
Cauvin, J.	1884	Maillard, Auguste	8th Sept.—70
Coriolis, G. de	17th June—79	Masson, Léon	2nd June—92
Duff, James	3rd Dec.—92	Marion, Paul	11th Augt.—92
Elie, R.	1st Dec.—82	Mathews, V.	6th May—95
Florent, François Eloi	29th June—88	Parsons, F. R.	24th June—90
Forgerays, Antony	2nd Oct.—48	Pougnet, E. D.	24th June—90
Gébert, Gaston	1st May—85	Reid, George Garbert	23rd Feb.—67
Hobbs, S. Barton	10th Sept.—72	Vaudin, W. M.	19th May—90
Langlois, Arthur	10th Dec.—80	Raffray, R.	2nd Dec.—95
Sapet A.	19th July—94	Vincent, C.	25th Oct.—94

Minutes of Land Surveyors in the Archives Office

Balisson	An V to 1837	Lartigue	1769 to 1788
Bataille	1771 to An VI	Lebrun	1793 to An XI
Boudard	1752 to 1756	Lislet	1793
Brisset	1809 to 1829	Magnin	1791 to An VIII
Butler	1851 to 1869	Malliet	1816 to 1829
Chevalier	1783 to 1821	Malavois	1791
Corby	1840 to 1857	Marçon	1809 to 1812
Courbeaux	1836 to 1842	Merle	1758 to 1780
De la Férrier	1774	Mondon	1794 to 1816
Duncan	1857 to 1876	Pastourel	1838 to 1874
Duplesis Lomet	An IV to An XII	Pugin	1794 to 1832
Edwards	1866 to 1867	Sauchet	1773 to 1807
Garnier	An IX to An XII	Schmaltz	An III to An VI
Gourlier	1756 to 1777	Target	1853 to 1871
Guyomar	1741	Tram	1787 to An XI
Hallot, M.	1823 to 1842	Ulliac père, F.	An V to 1840
Hallot, E.	1838 to 1840	Ulliac fils, F.	1827 to 1838
Hoart	1819 to 1834	Vuillemain	1794 to 1827
Imbault	1794 to 1808	William	1843 to 1853
Lacombe Grandon	1817 to 1818	Young	1845 to 1848

Commissioners in Lunacy.

Port Louis	Drs. Rouget and F. Larcher, acting.
Pamplemousses	Drs. Le Jeunne and V. Dubois.
Rivière du Rempart	Drs. A. Menagé and Lejeunne.
Flacq	Drs. Monty and E. de La Roche.
Grand Port	Drs. Portal and Guérin.
Savanne	Drs. Lemerle and E. Desenne.
Black River	Drs. A. Chasteauneuf.
Plaines Wilhems	Drs. Paddle and Laval.
Moka	Drs. E. Vinson and H. Clarenc.

List of Physicians and Surgeons duly authorized to practise Medicine and Surgery in the Island of Mauritius.

Names.	Residence	Qualifications.
Antelme, F.	Civil Hospital	M. D. Faculty of Paris.
Arékion, A.	Rose Hill	Do.
* Barbeau, L. G.	St. George street	M. B. C. M. Edin., D. P. H. London.
Beaugeard, O. Hon.	Lunatic Asylum	M. D. U. Univ. Edin.
Blackburn, C. W. A.	Plaines Wilhems	M. R. Coll. Surg. Eng.
† Bolton, J. G. E.	Curepipe	Do.
Bonnefin, A. E.	Do.	M. D. Faculty of Paris.
Bonchet, G. V. L.	Flacq	Bachelor in Med., Edin., Master in Surgery. Edin.
Bour, E. F.	Savanne	L.R.C. of P. Lond. M.R.C. of S. Eng. L. of the S. of A. London.

* Is Acting Sanitary Warden. | † Is Medical Inspector Immigration Dept.

Names.	Residence.	Qualifications.
Brouard, L. F. H. G. ...	Flacq	M. D. Faculty of Paris.
Castel, A. L.	Plaines Wilhems ...	M. R. C. S. Eng., L. R. C. P. London.
Chasteauneuf, A. ...	Black River ...	M. R. & C. M. Edin.
Chastellier, E. (*a*) ...	Plaines Wilhems ...	M. D. Edinburgh.
Chauvin, P. S.	Grand Port ...	M. D. Edinburgh.
Clarenc, H.	Moka	M. D. Strasbourgh.
De Boucherville, L. E....	Port Louis... ...	Dip. R.C. Phys. & Surg. Edin., Fac. of Phys. & Surg. [Glasgow.
De Chazal, Ed. L. [A.E.	Vacoas	M. D. London.
De Laroche Souvestre, L.	Flacq	Dip. R.C. Ph. & Sur. Edin., Fac. of Ph. & Sur. Glasgow
De Rosnay, A. F. ...	Pamplemousses ...	M. D. Faculty of Paris.
De Senneville, L. E. ...	Mahebourg ...	Do.
Desenne, A. E.	Savanne	Do.
Drouin, L.	Port Louis ...	Do.
Dubois, L. V.	Pamplemousses ...	Lic. R. Coll. Phys. Edin., Lic. R.C., Surg. Edin.
Edwards, W.T.A. Hon...	Plaines Wilhems...	M. D. Faculty of Paris.
Esnouf, C. A. E. (*b*) ...	Port Louis... ...	Mem. R. C. Surg. Eng., Lic. R.C. Surg. Eding.
Fibich, V. E.	Port Louis... ...	M. D. Faculty of Paris.
Guérin, F. O.	Mahebourg ...	Bachelor in Med., Master in Surg. Edin.
Harel, C. P. E.	Plaines Wilhems ...	M. D. Faculty of Paris.
Jacques, Louis V. ...	Port Louis ...	R.C.P.L. R.C.P. Edin. L.R.C.S. do. L.F.P.S. Glasg.
Jauffret, G. H. L. ...	Mapou	Lic. R.C. of Ph. Lond., Mem. R.C. Surg. Eng.
Jollivet, A. B. Y. (*c*) ...	Beau Bassin ...	Lic. Ph. & Surg. Glasgow, Lic. R. Coll. Ph. Edin.
Joly, Joseph A. M. ...	Ditto	Mem. Royal S. Eng., Lic. R. C. Ph. London
Keisler, F. L. (*d*) ...	Port Louis ...	Dip. R.C.Ph. & Sur. Edin., Fac. of Ph. & Sur. Glasgow
Larcher, E. V.	Ditto	Lic. R. Coll. Phys. Edin. Lic. R. C. Surg. Edin.
Laurent, E. A. O. ...	Ditto	B. S. & B.M. London, M.R.C.S. Eng.
Laval, P. C. E. (*e*) ...	Ditto	Lic. R. Coll. of Phys., Lic. R. Coll. of Surg. Edin.
Lejeunne, H.	Pamplemousses ...	M. D. Faculty of Paris.
Le Gall, E. H.	Rose Hill	Do.
Le Merle, J. H. (*f*) ...	Savanne	Bachelor in Med. & Master in Surg. Edin.
Lincoln, J. M.	Curepipe	Do.
Lorans, H. (*g*)	Port Louis... ...	Do.
Lesur, M. M. A... ...	Moka	M. D. Faculty of Paris.
Lesur, P. M. A... ...	Flacq	Lic. R. Coll. Phys. London.
Ménagé. A. (*h*)	Riv. du Rempart...	M. D. Faculty of Paris.
Monty, S. A. R... ...	Flacq	Lic. R. Coll. Surg. Edin., Lic. R. Coll. Phys. Edin.
Monty, J. V.	Seychelles ...	Do. do.
Nalletamby, M. E. X. ...	Port Louis ...	Dip. R. C. Ph. & Surg. Edin., Fac. of Phys. Glasgow.
Paddle, I. J. (*i*)... ...	Rose Hill	F. R. C. S. England, M. D. London.
Penaud, J. C. M. ...	Curepipe	M. D. Faculty of Montpellier.
Pepin, E. A.	Plaines Wilhems...	M. D. Faculty of Paris.
Pepin, C. J.	Ditto	Do.
Pétricher, L. J.... ...	Port Louis ...	Lic. R. Coll. Phys. Edin., Lic. R. Coll. Surg. Edin.
Portal, E.	Ditto	Do. do.
Portal, L. E. (*j*) [C.	Flacq	Mem. R. Coll. Phys. and Surg. Edin.
Poupinel de Valencé, E.	Plaines Wilhems ...	M. D. Faculty of Paris.
Raffray, J. A.	Curepipe	Do.
Rohan, G. V. Hon. ...	Port Louis... ...	Bachelor in Med. and Master in Surg. Edin.
Rohan, M. J.	Ditto	Dip. R. C. of Phys. & Surg. Edin., and Faculty of Phys. & Surg. Glasgow.
Rouget, F. A. (*k*) ...	Ditto	Bachelor in Med. and Master in Surg. Edin.
Roussel, E.	Rodrigues	Do. do.
Sakir, Hassam	Port Louis ...	Do. do.
Sinatambou, B. A. ...	Ditto	Dip. R.C. Ph. & Surg. Edin., Fac. of Ph. & Sur. Glasg.

(*a*) Director of Medical & Health Depart.
(*b*) Is Health Officer.
(*c*) Surgeon Superintendent, Barkly Asylum.
(*d*) Medical Officer in charge of Immig. ships.
(*e*) Poor Law Medical Officer, Port Louis.
(*f*) Ag. Govt. and P. Law Med. Officer, Savanne
(*g*) Medical Officer, Immigration Department.
(*h*) Govt. & P. Law Med. Officer, Riv. du Remp
(*i*) Govt. Medical Officer, Plaines Wilhems.
(*j*) Ag. Govt. & P. Law Med. Officer, Flacq.
(*k*) Police and Prisons Surgeon.

Names.	Residence.	Qualifications.
Tennant, J. J. F. ...	Curepipe	M. D. Faculty of Paris.
Ulcoq, L. A. W. ...	Savanne	Ditto
Villemont, V. (*n*) ...	Port Louis ...	M. D. Hiedelberg.
Vinson, P. L. E. (*o*) ...	Moka	M. D. Faculty of Paris.
Vinson, M. E.	Moka	Ditto

Veterinary Surgeons.

Blancard, N.	Port Louis ...	Mem. Royal College of V. S. England.
Bradshaw, T. C... ...	Ditto	Mem. Royal College of V. S. Edinburgh.
Florens, A. P.	Moka	Mem. College Veterinary Surgeons, London.
Galdemar, C.	Port Louis ...	Dip. Veterinary Coll. Highland & Agric. So. Edin.
Galloway, J.	Ditto	Mem. Royal College of V. S. Glasgow.
Nadal, F. J.	Grand Port ...	Mem. Royal of V. S. Edinburgh.

Dentists.

Mamet, E. E.	Port Louis ...	Cert. de Reception, Faculty of Paris, Surg. Dent.
Périndorge, G. de ...	Ditto	Cert. Jury Med. Dept., Seine, Paris.
Périndorge, C. de ...	Ditto	Ditto ditto
Rohan, R.	Ditto	Cert. to act as Dentist, Med. Council Office.

List and Addresses of the Pharmacies of the Island of Mauritius.

NAMES.	ADDRESS.	MANAGER.	QUALIFICATIONS.
Astruc, J.	Port Louis ...	Minet, J. ...	Pharm. Mauritius.
Baissac, Delisse & Co.	Ditto ...	Baissac, J. ...	Pharm. Chemist, Great Britain.
Curé, E. & Co. ..	Ditto ...	Rohan, R. A. ...	Ditto ditto
Degaye, A.	Mahebourg ...	Degaye, A. ...	Pharm. Mauritius.
Robillard, J. de ...	Flacq ...	Robillard, J. de...	Ditto ditto
Robillard, L. & Co. de	Souillac ...	Robillard, L. de ..	Ditto ditto
Edwards, E. A. ...	Port Louis ...	Boullé, A. ...	Pharm. Chem. Great Britain.
Edwards & Co. ...	Curepipe ...	Watson, J. ...	Ditto ditto
Mrs. Berichon ...	Quatre Bornes ...	Fleury, A. ...	School of Pharmacy, Paris.
Le Cudennec, L. E. ...	Curepipe ...	LeCudennec, L.E.	Pharm. Chemist, Great Britain.
LHoste & Co. P. ...	Port Louis ...	P. LHoste ...	Pharm. Mauritius.
Guiot, E.	Vacoa ...	E Guiot ...	Pharm. Chemist, Great Britain.
Macquet, E.	Rose Belle ...	Macquet, E. ...	Pharm. Mauritius.
Marie, X. & Co. ...	Port Louis ...	Marie, X. ...	Chemist and Druggist, Great Britain.
Merle, E. N.	Pamplemousses ..	Merle, E. N. ...	Pharm. Chemist, Great Britain.
* Minet, A. & Co. ...	Port Louis ...	N. Couve ...	Chemist and Druggist, Great Britain.
* Minet, A. & Co. ...	Pt. Louis (Branch)	Ch. Curé ...	Pharm. Chemist, Great Britain.
* Minet, A. & Co. ...	Rose Hill do. ...	A. Guerandel ...	Pharm. Mauritius.
Naz & Edwards ...	Port Louis ...	Naz, Virgile ...	Ditto ditto
Paoletti, H.	Ditto ...	Paoletti, A. ...	Ditto ditto
Régnier, H.	Ditto ...	Régnier, H. ...	Ditto ditto
Sakir, C.	Ditto ...	Olivier, L. ...	Pharm. Chem. Great Britain.

Midwives.

Baumgarthen, Mrs. ...	Port Louis ...	Dip. Mid. Univ. Montpelier
Rolland, Mrs.	Ditto	Dip. Mid. Comm. de Santé, St. Denis Reunion.
Smith, Mrs. Mary ...	Ditto	Dip. Mid. of Dublin.

(*n*) Resident Surgeon, Civil Hospital.
(*o*) Government Medical Officer, Moka.
* Vide Page 22 of Advertisements.

Names.	Residence.	Qualifications.
Alexis	Port Louis	Examined by Chief Medical Officer, agreeably to law, and permitted to attend simple cases of natural labour only.
Ally, widow	Do.	
Anastasie, widow ...	Do.	
Anodin, Amanda ...	Do.	
Archange, widow ...	Do.	
Aristide, Mrs	Do.	
Arthur, widow	Do.	
Aza, Marie Catherine ...	Pamplemousses ...	
Barbe, Mrs	Do.	
Bernard, Mrs	Port Louis	
Blakeney, widow ...	Do.	
Brilland, Mrs Paul ...	Do.	
Chéry, widow	Do.	
Clermont, Mrs	Do.	
Crépin, Mrs L. M. ...	Do.	
Dantin, Mrs	Do.	
Désiré, Mrs	Do.	
Désiré, widow	Do.	
Dauphine, Mrs	Flacq	
Diagroo, Mrs	Pamplemousses ...	
Georges, Mrs	Port Louis	
Harel, Mrs	Do.	
Hyacinthe, widow ...	Do.	
Jean, Mrs	Do.	
Jeannette, Mrs	Plaines Wilhems ...	
Jolicœur, widow ...	Rose Belle	
Joly, Mrs	Pamplemousses ...	
Joseph, Mrs	Port Louis	
Jupiter, Mrs	Pamplemousses ...	
Labonté, widow... ...	Port Louis	
Lacresse, widow ...	Do.	
Latulipe, Mrs C. ...	Do.	
Louvet, widow	Plaines Wilhems ...	
Maréna, Mrs D. M. ..	Poudre d'Or	
Marie, Mrs M. E. ...	Port Louis	
Marlow, Mrs	Do.	
Moïse, Mrs P. George ...	Do.	
Monique, Mrs	Plaines Wilhems ...	
Mousset, widow ...	Port Louis	
Nunn, Mrs	Pamplemousses ...	
Parah, Mrs	Port Louis	
Renaud, Mrs	Pamplemousses ...	
Reune, Mrs	Do.	
Rivière, widow E. ...	Do.	
Sansdésirs, Mrs... ...	Port Louis	
Sapiane, Séraphine ...	Do.	
Tarah, Mrs	Do.	
Tessier, Mrs	Do.	
Thomas, widow... ...	Do.	
Vincent, Mrs H... ...	Do.	
Walsh, Mrs	Do.	

Government Medical Officers.

Port Louis	Dr. Rouget, Police and Prison Surgeon.
Pamplemousses	,, Dubois.
Riv. du Rempart	,, Ménagé.
Flacq	,, Monty.
Grand Port	,, Portal, acting.
Savanne	,, Lemerle, acting.
Black River	,, Chasteauneuf.
Plaines Wilhems	,, Laval.
Moka	,, Vinson.

Poor Law Medical Officers.

Port Louis	Dr. Sinnatambou, acting.
Pamplemousses	,, Dubois.
Riv. du Rempart	,, Ménagé.
Flacq	,, Monty.
St. Julien	,, Lesur.
Rivière Sèche	,, de la Roche, acting.
Grand Port	,, Guérin, acting.
Savanne	,, Lemerle acting.
Black River	,, Chasteauneuf.
Plaines Wilhems	,, Paddle, acting.
Moka.	,, Clarenc.

Government Vaccinators.

List showing the names of the Government Vaccinators, the District assigned to each, and the places' days and hours for gratuitous vaccination.

No.	Name of District.	Name of Vaccinator.	Places for Gratuitous Vaccination.	Day.	Hour.
1	Port Louis ...	Dr. de Boucherville ...	Police Station, Abercombie ...	Monday	Noon.
			Public Dispensary, West. Suburb.	Thursday	Noon.
2	Pamplemousses .	Dr. Dubois ...	Terre Rouge Police Station ...	Monday	1.30 P.M.
			Pamplemousses do. ...	Wednesday	Noon.
			Powder Mills Hospitals ...	Thursday	10.00 A.M.
			Ruisseau Rose Police Station ...	Friday	3.00 P.M.
3	Riv. du Rempart	Dr. Menagé ...	Piton Police Station	Monday	2.00 P.M.
			Grand Gaube Police Station ...	1st. Tuesday of each month	3.00 P.M.
			Grand Baie do. ...	1st. Thursday of each month	3.00 P.M.
			R. du Remp. Poor Law Hospital .	Friday	11.00 A.M.
4	Flacq	Dr. Monty ...	Prison Hospital, Centre of Flacq.	Monday	11.00 A.M.
			Haut de Flacq Village	Do.	1.00 P.M.
			La Marre	Do.	3.00 P.M.
			Rivière Sèche	Tuesday	1.00 P.M.
5	Grand Port ...	Dr. Guérin ...	Mahebourg	Monday	11.00 A.M.
			Plaine Magnien	Saturday	8.00 A.M.
			Escalier	Do.	9.00 A.M.
			Rose Belle	Monday	8.00 A.M.
6	Savanne ...	Dr. Desenne ...	Souillac	Thursday	1.00 P.M.
			Britannia	Do.	8.00 A.M.
			Chemin Grenier Police Station...	Do.	1.00 P.M.
7	Black River ...	Dr. Chasteauneuf	Black River Police Station ...	Monday	9.00 A.M.
			Poor Law Dispensary Bambous .	Wednesday	11.00 A.M.
			Petite Rivière Police Station ...	Thursday	8.00 A.M.
			Case Noyale Police Station ...	Monday	9.00 A.M.
8	Plaines Wilhems	Dr. Vinson ...	Rose Hill Convent	Wednesday	Noon
			Vacoa do.	Do.	1.30 P.M.
			Curepipe Police Station... ...	Do.	3.15 P.M.
			Pailles do.	Friday	1.15 P.M.
9	Moka	Dr. Vinson ...	Central Police Station	Thursday	11.30 A.M.
			Quartier Militaire Police Station.	Do.	3.00 P.M.
			Pailles Railway Station... ...	Friday	1.15 P.M.

Banks.

The Bank of Mauritius, A. Wemyss, Manager.
Commercial Bank.—E. Spéville, *Secretary*.
The Mercantile Bank of India Limited.—Blyth Brothers & Co., *Agents*.

Merchants.

Barrau C. de
Blyth Brothers & Co.
Baylis, A. G. & Co.
Chauvin, E.
Cugnet, C.
Currie, Fraser & Co.
D'Emmerez, L. & Co.
Elias, Mallac & Co.
Elie, L. D.
Goudin, Coutanceau & Co.
Hugnin fils, P.
Ireland, Fraser & Co.
Jacobs, C. & Sons
Lagesse fils, A.
Laroque, F.
Limonaire, P. & Papou G.
Loumeau, E.
Minet, A. & Co.
Pipon, Adam & Co.
Richer, F. & Co.
Olivier, C. & Co.
Rivière, M.
Schirmer, C. J.
Scott & Co.
Smith, Freeland & Co.
Souchon, L.
Sylva, Adolphe de
Thierry, Thomy
Ulcoq, A.
Vitry, H. & Co.
Vallet; J.

Indian and Chinese Merchants.

Abba Sakoor & Co.
Abdoola Adam
Achim & Co.
Affijee Cassim
Ajum Goolam Hossen & Co.
Allarakia, Hajee Omar.
Allidina, R. & Co.
Ally Bhay Dawood & Co.
Ally Mahomed Hadjee Salay Mahomed
Anhu Korun & Co.
Anhu Low Yean & Co.
Amode Cassim
Appou, J. B. R.
Aroonassalon, K. & Co.
Aroomoogum, V. & Co.
Athoy Chan Kaw
Attime Tchangpen & Co.
Carrimjee Jeewonjee.
Cassim Amode & Co.
Dowjee Cassim Parack.
Esmael Peermahomed & Co.
Goolam Mahomed Ajam.
Goolam Mahomed Jeewa & Co.
Hajee Aga Abdool Rassool & Co.
Hajee J. H. Ahmed.
Hajee Cassim Mamoojee.
Hajee Ahmed Hajee Assam Abdullah.
Hajee Hamode Aboo & Co.
Habib Omar.
Hallen & Co.
Hossein Cassim.
Ibrahim Affijee Cassim.
Ibrahim Ismael Torawa & Co.
Issop Cassim.
Issop Jeewa Atchia & Co.
Issop Mamode Sulliman.
Irlapoullé Valaydon & Co.
Jackariah Jan Mamode Habib & Co.
Mamode Keekabay.
Mamode Essopjee & Hamoodjee Moosajee
Mamode Mamojee Timol & Co.
Mahomed Hadjee Ebrahim Mall.
Mamoojee Hassam.
Moussajee Cassimjee.
Mouladina Hadjee.
Moussajee Ismaljee Hariff.
Moutiachetty V. & Co.
Noormahomed, J. H. & Co.
Rassoul Khan.
Saboo Sidick, H. & Co.
Samtoy & Co.
Sham Tong.
Sulliman Taleb & Co.
Vayapooree, S. & Co.
Venpen, A. & Co.
Visram Ebrahim & Co.

Brokers and Exchange-Brokers now practising.

FIRST CLASS BROKERS.

Antelme, L. *senior*
Antelme, L. *junior*
Artus, A. (on leave)
Boulé, A.
Bougault, L.
Couve, L.
Dalais, Adrien
Dauban, C.
Desvaux, de Marigny
Ducray, H. G. [E.
Giroday, F. B. de la
Harold, L.
Henry, E.
Hourquebie, E.
Hourquebie, L. G.
Jean Louis, J. B.
Labat, G. (on leave)
Labat, L.
Lacoste, E.
Langlois, Paul.
Le Breton, L. *junior*
Le Juge de Segrais, L.
Lincoln, L.
Montocchio, J. E.
Nalletamby, P. I. A. R.
Nicholson, H. E.
Noël, L.
Pascau, E.
Régnard, A.
Régnard, J.
Ribet, V.
Robinson, G. Hon.
Rogers, L.
Rondeaux, J.
Rondeaux, A.
Rouillard, E.
Rousset, J.
Shand, C. F.
Tennant. F.
Trime, L. A. Belcour
Tyack, C.
Vallet, James
Vigier Latour, L. T.
Vigoureux, H.

Second Class Brokers.

Abdoul Cader Abdoul Raman,	Gaud, E.	Pierre, E.
Baptiste, A.	Lahausse, A.	Rayeroux, P. E.
Bouchet, L.	Loumeau, H.	Sénèque, J. C. E.
Galais, Pierre	Maya, G.	Xavier, G. F.

House, Land and Cattle Agents.

Ackbar, Ally Baccus	Lapierre, E.	Rey, Armand
Mamode, A. S.	Letellier, A.	

Maritime Brokers.

Capiron, L. V.	Hutchinson, C.	Olivier, Ed.
Dalais, C. A.	Laurent, T. P.	Pierry, L.
Fleury, A.	Leguen, F.	Victoire, L.
Hervey, William	Mautalent, C.	

Photographers.

Messrs. Drenning and Rambert, Rempart Street and Curepipe.
A. Loumeau, St. George Street, Port Louis.

Auctioneers.

de Valencé, Poupinel G.	Mayer, Oswald	Hardy, F.
Mayer, Edgar *Govt. V. Master*	Poupard, A. (*Master's Delegate*)	Tourrette, Marius

List of Hotels.

In Port Louis :
New Mauritius Hotel, Pope Hennessy street.
Oriental Hotel, on the Wharf.

In the Country Districts :
The Universal Hotel, Curepipe.
The Victoria, Hotel, Curepipe.

Agents for the sale of Peruvian Guano.

Messrs. Scott & Co.—Corderie Street, Port Louis.
,, Blyth Brothers & Co.—Quay Street, Port Louis.

List of Foreign Consuls.

Mauritius.

France	A. Drouin.
Austro-Hungary	F. C. Estill.
Denmark	Hon. Hamilton Stein.
Sweden and Norway	Hon. Hamilton Stein.
Germany	Hon. Hamilton Stein.
United States	John P. Taylor, *Consul.* Hon. A. P. Ambrose, *Vice-Consul.*
Italy...	Hon. A. P. Ambrose, *Consul.* John W. Hollway, *Vice-Consul*
Spain	Jean Simon Léopold Antelme, *Vice-Consul.*
Portugal	Charles Léopold Antelme, *Consul.*
Netherlands	F. C. Estill, *Consul.*
Belgium	John W. Hollway, *Consul.*
Switzerland	G. A. Bourguignon, *Consul.*
Siam	H. E. Patterson (on leave).
Peru	J. Coutanceau, *Consular Agent.*

Seychelles.

France	F. Cheyron, *Vice-Consul*
Italy	Nicolas O. Bonnetard, *Vice-Consul.*
Portugal	N. Jouanis, *Consul.*

Table of Precedency for Public Servants in Mauritius.

1	The Governor.	
2	General Commanding the Troops. Admiral on Station.	According to dates of Commission.
3	Bishop of Mauritius.	
4	Bishop of Port Louis.	
5	Chief Judge.	
6	Officer Commanding the Troops, if a Colonel.	
7	Puisne Judges of Supreme Court.	Ditto if not at variance with previous special provisions.
8	Colonial Secretary.	Being Members of Executive Council.
9	Procureur General.	

Class I.

10	Colonial Treasurer.	
11	Auditor General.	
12	Collector of Internal Revenues.	
13	Collector of Customs.	
	Inofficial Members of Council.	According to dates of nomination.

Class II.

Colonel in the Army. Post Captain in the Navy above 3 years standing Civil Commissioner of Seychelles. Mayor of Port Louis.	According to dates of Commission.

Class III.

Surveyor General. Inspector General of Police. Master of Supreme Court. Substitute Procureur General. Senior Civil Chaplain. Receiver Registration Dues. Rector of Royal College.	These Civil Officers to rank with Lieuts. Cols. in the Army, and Post Captains in the Navy under 3 years standing, and with each other according to dates of Commission, or of previous nomination to an office of corresponding or superior rank.

Class IV.

Registrar of Supreme Court. Military Chaplain. Protector of Immigrants. Harbour Master. Secretary to Council. Asst. Colonial Secretary, "General Branch." Asst. Colonial Secretary, "Despatch Branch." Senior Magistrate, Port Louis. Junior do. do. District Magistrates. Civil Commissary of Port Louis.	Ditto, with Majors in the Army, and Commanders in the Navy, and with each other as above directed.

CLASS V.

Junior Civil Chaplain. Roman Catholic Clergy. Presbyterian Minister. Colonial Postmaster. Curator of Intestate Estates. Stipendiary Magistrates. Deputy-Mayor of Port Louis. Notables. Superintendent of Government Schools. Secretary to Educational Committee. Surgeon to Civil Hospital. Assistants in Departments. Superintendent of Police. Landing Surveyor of Customs.	These Civil Officers to rank with Captains in the Army and Lieutenants in the Navy, and with each other as above directed.

CLASS VI.

Clerks to Districts Courts. Director of Botanical Gardens. Health Officer. Assistant Surgeon to Civil Hospital. Assistant Harbour Master. Inspectors of Police.	Ditto, with each other as above directed.

The Mauritius Government Savings Bank.

This Bank was established on the 1st. May 1837 under the provisions of Ordinance No. 13 of 1836. The Head Office is in Port Louis but there is a Branch Office in each of the Eight Rural Districts and Curepipe. The depositors during the year 1894 were 22,816, and the sums deposited amounted to Rs. 1,149,876 and the withdrawals to Rs. 1,236,678. The total amount at the credit of Depositors on 31st. December 1894 amounted to Rs. 3,253,538.34.

The rate of Interest allowed on Deposits has since the passing of Ordinance No. 24 of 1891 has been reduced to 3½ o/o.

The Invested Funds amounted to Rs. 4,286,436.25. The Revenue amounted to Rs. 121,920 and the Expenditure including interest to Depositors to Rs. 147,651.55.

The cost of management including interest to Depositors amounted to Rs. 113,306.87.

Population of the World according to Religions. *

Protestants	137,000,000	Buddhists & Brahmins	672,000,000
Roman Catholics	216,000,000	Mohammedans	200,000,000
Greek, Armenian & Abyssinian Church	95,000,000	Jews	7,000,000
		Other Creeds	125,000,000
Total Christians ...	448,000,000	Total non Christians ...	1,004,000,000

* From Meyer's Konversations-Lexikon.

List of the Cabinets of England from 1783.

Date.	Prime Minister.	Duration Yrs.	Duration Dys.	Chancellor.	Secretaries of State for the Colonies.	Foreign Secretary.
Dec. 23, 1783	William Pitt	17	84	Thurlow Longhboro	M. of Caermarthen	Grandville
Mar. 17, 1801	Hy. Addington	3	59	Eldon	Lord Hobart Castlereagh	Hawkesbury
May 15,—04	William Pitt	1	272	Eldon	Candem	Harrowby Mulgrave
Feb. 11,—06	Lord Granville	1	48	Erskine	Windam	Charles J. Fox Visct. Howick
Mar. 31,—07	Duke of Portland	2	246	Eldon	Castlereagh	G. Canning
Dec. 2,—09	Spencer Perceval	2	190	Eldon	Earl of Liverpool	Bathurst Wellesley
June 9,—12	Earl of Liverpool	14	319	Eldon	Earl of Bathurst	Castlereagh G. Canning
Apr. 24,—27	George Canning	0	134	Lyndhurst	Goderich	Dudley
Sept. 5—27	Visct. Goderich	0	142	Lyndhurst	Rt. Hon. W. Huskisson	Dudley
Jan. 25,—28	D. of Wellington	2	301	Lyndhurst	Sir G. Murray	Dudley Aberdeen
Nov. 23,—30	Earl Grey	3	238	Brougham	Goderich Standley	Palmerston
July 18,—34	Visc. Melbourne	9	161	Brougham	T. Spring Rice	Palmerston
Dec. 26,—34	Sir Robert Peel	0	113	Lyndhurst	Aberdeen	Wellington
Apr. 18,—35	Visct. Melbourne	6	141	In Comm. Cottenham	Rt. Hon. C. Grant Normandy Russell	Palmerston
Sept. 6,—41	Sir Robert Peel	4	303	Lyndhurst	Lord Standley Gladstone	Aberdeen
July 6,—47	Ld. John Russell	5	236	Cottenham Truro	Earl Grey	Palmerston Granville
Feb. 27,—52	Earl of Derby	0	305	St. Leonards	Packington	Malmesbury
Dec. 28,—52	Earl of Aberdeen	2	44	Cranworth	Duke of Newcastle	Ld. J. Russell Clarendon
Feb. 10,—55	Lord Palmerston	3	15	Cranworth	Herbert Russel	Clarendon
Feb. 25,—58	Earl of Derby	1	113	Chelmsford	Standley	Malmesbury
June 18,—59	Lord Palmerston	6	141	Campbell Westbury	Duke of Newcastle	Russell
Nov. 6,—65	Earl Russell	0	242	Cranworth	Cardwell	Clarendon
July 6,—66	Earl of Derby	1	236	Chelmsford	Earl of Carnarvon	Stanley
Feb. 27,—68	Benjamin Disraeli	0	286	Cairns	Granville	Stanley
Dec. 9,—68	W. E. Gladstone	5	74	Hatherley Selborne	Buckingham	Clarendon Granville
Feb. 21,—74	Benj. Disraeli Earl Beaconsfield	6	67	Cairns	Earl of Carnavon Sir M. H. Beach	Derby Salisbury
Apr. 28,—80	W. E. Gladstone	5	57	Selborne	Earl of Kimberley	Granville
June 24,—85	Marq. of Salisbury	0	227	Halsbury	Colonel Standley	Salisbury
Feb. 5,—86	W. E. Gladstone	0	178	Herchell	Earl Granville	Roseberry
Aug. 3,—86	Marq. of Salisbury	5	334	Halsbury	Hon. E. Stanhope	Iddesleigh
Aug. 4,—92	W. E. Gladstone	1	193	Herchell	Marquis of Ripon	Roseberry
Mar. 10,—94	Earl of Roseberry	1	121	Herchell	Marquis of Ripon	Kimberley
July 2,—95	Marq. of Salisbury	...	...	Halsbury	Jos. Chamberlain	Salisbury.

THE ROYAL FAMILY

Her Majesty VICTORIA, By the Grace of God, of the United Kingdom of Great Britain and Ireland, Queen Defender of the Faith, Empress of India (in India, Kaisar-i-Hind) *born* 24th. May 1819, *succeeded* to the Throne 20th June 1837, on the death of her uncle, King William IV ; *crowned* 28th. June 1838 ; and *married*, 10th February 1840 to his late Royal Highness Francis ALBERT Augustus Charles Emmanuel, PRINCE CONSORT, Duke of Saxony, Prince of Cobourg and Gotha, was *born* 26th. August 1819 ; *died*, 14th. December 1861. Her Majesty has had issue :

1. Her Imperial Majesty VICTORIA Empress Federick of Germany, Adelaide Mary Louise, PRINCESS ROYAL, *born* 21st. November 1840 ; *married* 25th January 1858, to his late Imperial Highness the Crown Prince of Germany afterwards German Emperor *born* Oct. 18, 1831, *died* June 15, 1888, and has had issue—Frederick William, V. A. reigning German Emperor, *born* 27th. January 1859, *married* 27th. February 1881, to Princess Augusta Victoria of Schleswig-Holstein, and has issue—V. E. A. Charlotte, *born* 24th. July 1860, *married* 18th. February 1878 to Hered, Prince of Sax-Meiningen, and has issue—A. W. Henry, *born* 14th. August 1862, *married* 24th. May 1888 to his cousin Princess Irène of Hesse Sigismond, *born* 15th. September 1864, *died* 18th June 1866 ; Victoria, *born* 12th. April 1866, *married* 19th. November 1890 to H. S. H. Prince Adolphe of Schaumburg-Lippe : Waldemar *born*,10 February 1868, *died* 27th March 1879 ; Sophia Dorothea, *born* 14th. June 1870, *married* 27th. October 1889 to the Duke of Sparta and Margaret Beatrice, *born* 22nd. April 1872, *married* 25th. January 1893 to Prince Fred. of Hesse Cassel.

2. His Royal Highness ALBERT EDWARD, Prince of Wales, Duke of Saxony, Cornwall, and Rothesay, Earl of Dublin, &c., *born* 9th. November 1841 ; *married* 10th. March 1863, to the Princess Alexandra Julia, *born* 1st. December 1844, eldest daughter of the King of Den mark, and has had issue—Albert Victor Christian, Edward Duke of Clarence, Lieut. 10th. Hussars' *born* 8th. January 1865, *died* 14th. January 1892 ; George Frederick, Duke of York, Captain R.N., *born* 3rd. June 1865 *married* 6th. July 1893 to Princess Victoria Mary of Teck, *born* 26th May 1867, has had issue a son Edward Albert, 23rd. June 1894 ; Louise, *born* 28th. February 1867, *married* 27th. July 1889 to the Duke of Fife, issue—Alexandra, born 17th. May 1891 and Maud *born* 3rd. April 1893, Victoria, *born* 6th. July 1868 ; Maud, *born* 26th. November 1869 bethrothed 1895 to Charles second-son of the Crown Prince of Denmark and Alexander, *born* 6th. April, *died* 7th. April 1871.

3. Her Royal Highness ALICE Maud Mary, *born* 25th. April 1843 ; *married* 1st July 1862, to His Royal Highness LOUIS IV, Grand Duke of Hesse-Darmstadt, *born* 12th. September 1837, *died* 14th. December 1878, her issue being—Victoria Alberta, *born* 5th. April 1863, *married* 30th. April 1884 to Prince Louis of Battenburg, R.N. ; Elizabeth A. Louise Alice, *born* 1st. November 1864, *married* 15th. June 1884 to the Grand Duke Serge of Russia ; Irène Marie Louise *born* 11th. July 1866, *married* 24th. May 1888 to her cousin Prince Henry of Prussia, brother of the German Emperor ; Ernest Louis, Grand Duke of Hesse, *born* 25th. November 1868, *married* 19th. April 1894 to Her Royal Highness Princess Victoria Melita of Saxe Cobourg ; Frederick William, *born* 7th. October 1870, *died* 29th. June 1873 ; Alix Victoria, *born* 6th. June 1872, *married* 26th. November 1894 to His Imperial Majesty the Czar of Russia and has isssue :—Olga *born* 15th. November 1878.

4. His Royal Highness ALFRED Ernest Albert, Duke of Edinburgh *born* 6th. August 1844, Admiral of the Fleet, 30th. December 1878, *married* 23rd. January 1874, to the Grand Duchess Marie of Russia, and has issue—Alfred A. W. E. Albert, *born* 15th. October 1874 ; Marie A. V., *born* 29th. October 1875, *married* 10th January 1893 to Ferdinand Crown Prince of Romania and has issue—Carol *born* 15th. October 1893 and a daughter Victoria Melita, *born* 25th. November 1876 *married* 19th April 1894 to Ernest Louis, Grand Duke of Hesse and has issue—and Alexandra A. Olga Victoria, *born* 1st. September 1878 betrothed 1895, and Beatrice, *born* 20th. April 1884.

5. Her Royal Highness HELENA Augusta Victoria, *born* 25th. May 1846, *married* 5th. July 1866, to Prince Frederick Christian C. A. of Schleswig-Holstein, born 22nd. January 1831, and has issue—Christian Victor, *born* 14th. April 1867 ; Albert John, *born* 26th. February 1869 ; Victoria Louise, *born* 3rd. May 1870 , Louise Augusta, *born* 12th. August 1872, *married* 6th. July 1871 to Prince Aribert of Anhalt, and Harold, *born* 12th. May, *died* 20th. May 1876.

6. Her Royal Highness LOUISE Caroline Alberta, *born*18th. March 1848, *married* 21st. March 1871, to John, Marquis of Lorne, late Governor-General of Canada, *born* 6th. August 1845.

7. His Royal Highness ARTHUR William Patrick Albert, Duke of Connaught, *born* 1st May 1850 ; Lieut-General, *married* 13th. March 1879, to Princess Louise Margaret, daughter of the late Prince Frederick Charles of Prussia, *born* 25th. July 1860, and has issue—Margaret Victoria Aug. Charlotte Norah, *born* 15th. January 1882 ; Arthur Frederick Patrick Albert, *born* 13th. January 1883 ; Victoria Patricia Helena Elizabeth, *born* 17th. March 1886,

8. His Royal Highness LEOPOLD George Duncan Albert, Duke of Albany, *born* 7th. April 1853, *marrid* 27th. April 1882, to the Princess Helen. daughter of the Prince of Waldeck, *born* 17th. February 1861, *died* 28th. March 1884, his issue being—Alice Mary, born 25th. February 1883 ; Leopold Charles Edward George, Duke of Albany, *born* 19th. July 1884.

9. Her Royal Highness BEATRICE Mary Victoria Feodora, *born* 14th. April 1857, married 23rd. July 1885, to Prince Henry Maurice of Battenburg, *born* 5th. October 1858, and has issue—Alexander. *born* 23rd. November 1886 ; and Victoria Eugenie Julia Ena, *born* 24th. October 1887 ; and Leopold Arthur Lewis, *born* 21st. May 1889, and Maurice Victor Donald, *born* 3rd. Oct. 1891

Royal Princes and Princesses.

His Royal Highness Ernest Augustus W.A.G.F. Third Duke of Cumberland, son of the late King of Hanover, cousin to Her Majesty, *born* 21st. September, 1845 ; *married* 21st. December, 1878, to the Princess Thyra of Denmark ; and has issue—Marie Louisa, *born* 11th. October, 1879 ; George William Christian, *born* 28th. October, 1880 ; and Alexandra, *born* 29th. September, 1882, Olga, *born* 11th. July, 1884. Christian, *born* 4th. July, 1885, and a son *born* 17th. November, 1887. His sisters,— Frederica, *born* 9th. January, 1848 ; *married* 24th. April, 1880, Baron Von Pawel-Rammingen, had issue— Victoria Georgine, *born* 7th. March, 1881, *died* 27th. March, 1881 ; and Marie Ernestine, *born* 3rd. December 1889.

Her Royal Highness Augusta Wilhelmina Louisa, Duchess of Cambridge, daughter of the Landgrave of Hesse-Cassel, *born* 25th. July, 1797, *married* 7th. May, 1818, the Duke of Cambridge who died 8th. July, 1850, and his issue—

1. George William Frederick Charles, second Duke of Cambridge, Field-Marshal Commanding-in-Chief, cousin to Her Majesty, *born* 28th. March, 1819.

2. Augusta Caroline, cousin to Her Majesty, *born* 19th. July, 1822, *married* 28th. June, 1843, Frederick, Grand Duke of Mecklenberg-Strelitz, and has issue—Adolphus Frederick ; *born* 22nd. July, 1848 ; *married* and has issue.

3. Mary Adelaide, cousin to Her Majesty, *born* 27th. November, 1833 ; *married* 12th. June, 1866 Francis Paul Charles, Duke of Teck, *born* 27th. August, 1837, and has issue—Victory Mary, *born* 26th. May 1867 ; *married* 6th. July, 1893 to H.R.H. The Duke of York. Adolphus, *born* 13th. August, 1868 ; *married* 1894 Lady Margaret Grosvenor, daughter of the Duke of Westminster, and has issue ; Franscis, *born* 9th. January, 1870 ; and Alexander George, *born* 14th. April, 1874.

Her Majesty's near Relatives.

Niece and Nephews, by half-sister, daughter of her mother the Duchess of Kent, by her first-husband, Emich Charles, Prince of Lenningen—

1. Charles Louis, *born* 25th. October, 1829 ; *married* morganatically. In the Wurtenberg Army.

2. Herman Ernest, Prince of Hohenlohe-Legenberg, *born* 31st. August, 1832. Lieut.-General in the Prussian service ; *married*, and has issue.

3. Adelide Victoire, *born* 28th. July, 1835, *married* 11th. September, 1856, Prince Frederick Schleswig-Holstein-Sonderburg-Augustenberg, he *died* 13th. January, 1880 and has issue.

Nephews, by half-brother, son of the late Duchess of Kent.—Ernest Leopold Prince of Leningen Admiral in the Royal Vavy, *born* 9th. November, 1830 ; *married* 11th. September, 1858, Princess Marie Amelia of Baden, and has issue ; and Edward Frederick, *born* 5th. January 1833, Captain Royal Imperial Guard of Austria.

Summary of the two Houses of Parliament.

HOUSE OF LORDS.

	Members.
Peers of the Blood Royal	6
Archbishops	2
Dukes	22
Marquisses	22
Earls	121
Viscounts	29
Bishops]	24
Barons	310
Representative Peers of Scotland ...	16
Elected every New Parliament Representative Peers for Ireland ...	28
Elected for life ...	580

HOUSE OF COMMONS.

	Members.	
England & Wales.		
53 Countries in 253 Divisions ...	253	
143 Cities, Boroughs, &c., in 215 Divisions	237	
3 Universities	5	—495
Scotland.		
34 Counties in 39 Divisions ...	39	
7 Cities and towns	18	
13 Districts of Burghs	13	
4 Universities	2	— 72
Ireland.		
32 Counties	85	
9 Cities and Boroughs... ...	16	
1 University	2	—103
Total		670

Annuities to the Royal Family.

Her Majesty		
Privy Purse ...	£ 60,000	
Salaries of the Household ...	131,260	
Expenses of the Household ...	172,500	
Royal Bounty, &. ...	13,200	
Unappropriated ...	8,040	
Total		£ 385,000
Prince of Wales ...		40,000
For the children of H. R. H. ...		*36,000
Princess of Wales...		10,000
Dowager German Empress ...		8,000
Duke of Edinburgh ...		10,000
Princess Christian of Schleswig-Holstein ...		6,000
Princess Louis (Marchioness of Lorne) ...		6,000
Duke of Connaught ...		25,000
Princess Beatrice (Henry of Battenburg) ...		6,000
Duchess of Mecklenburg-Strelitz ...		3,000
Duke of Cambridge ...		12,000
Duchess of Teck ...		5,000
Duchess of Albany ...		6,000
Royal Pensions limited to £ 1,200 per annum...		24.592

Aides-de-Camp to the Queen.

Field-Marshal H. R. H. the Prince of Wales, K.G. (*personal*).
Lieut.-Colonel H. R. H. the Duke of Connaught, K.G. (*personal*).
Field-Marshal H. R. H. the Duke of Cambridge, K.G. (*personal*).

Col. Belper Rt. Hon. Lord.
Col. Lord Blythswood.
Col. B. G. D. Cooke.
Col. G. L. C. Money, D. S. O.
Col. J. Jopp C. B.
Col. F. Howard.
Col. Rt. Hon. Earl of Derby, G. C. B.
Col. William Bell, Royal Guernsey Militia.
Col. James Godfray, Royal Jersey Militia.
Col. Earl of Wemyss, 7th. Mddx, R.V.C. (*super.*)
Col. Sir James G. Baird, Bt., 1st Midloth.A.V.C.
Col. Duke of Westminster, K.G. Cheshire Yeo, Cav. and 13th. Middx. R.V.C. (*super*).
Col. John Ramsay Slade, C.B.R.A.
Col. Arthur John Hammond, V.C.D.S.O.. Indian Staff Corps.
Col. Viscount Oxenbridge, Lincoln Regiment.
Col. Hon. Hallam Parr, C.M.G. Sommerset Lt. Inf.
Col. Marc Sever Bell, V.C. Royal Engineers.
Col. W. Campbell.
Col. Sir R. H. A. Ogilvry, Bart.
Col. M. Protheroe C.B.
Col. A. B. Crosbie.
Col. J. G. Kelly, C.B.
Col. J. Davis.
Col. Sir C. S. Gzowski K.C.M.G.
Col. Earl of Haddington.
Col. Robert Mc Gregor Stewart, R.A.
Col. Lord Claud Jno.Hamilton, Royal Innis. Fus.
Col. Earl of Limerick, Royal Munster Fus.(*super*)
Col. Earl of Home, Lanar. Yeom. Cav. (*super*)
Col. Earl of Mount-Edgecumbe, 2nd Vol. Bat. Devon Regt. (*super*)
Col. Sir Horatio H. Kitchener, K.C.M.G. Royal Engrs.
Col. William J, Thomas, S. Wales Borderers.
Col. Earl of Cork and Orrery, K.P., N. Somerset Yeomanry Cavalry.
Col. Hon. Reginald A. J. Talbot, C.B.
Col. John Palmer Brabazon, 10th Hussars.
Col. Casimir S. Growski, Canada Engrs. (*hon.*)
Col. Reginald Garnett Seaforth Highlanders.
Col. John Henry Barnard, C.M.G. Royal Muns. Fusilier.
Col. John Henry Rivett-Carnac, C.I.E.N.W.P. of India Volunteers.
Col. James Charles Cavendish, Derbyshire Volrs.
Col. Lord Suffield, C.B.K., Norfolk Art. Militia.
Col. Rt. Hon. Earl Percy.
Col. E. T. H. Hutton, C.B.
Col. A. Gaselee, C.B.

* For the proper disposal of this money which will continue to be paid till 6 months after Her Majesty's decease, certain trustees have been appointed who will hold the sum granted under the Act, and any accumulations in trust for all or any of the children of His Royal Highness in such shares and at such times and in such manner and subject to such conditions and powers of revocation, including a condition against alienation as H.R.H. with the consent of the Queen may by order, countersigned by the first Commissioner of H. M.'s Treasury and the Chancellor of the Exchequer, appoint.

The Judges of the English Bench, their salaries, the ages, and date of elevation to the Bench.

					Salary.
The Lord Chancellor (Halsbury)		August	1892	57	£ 10,000
Master of the Rolls (Lord Esher)		August	1868	76	6,000
Baron Pollock		January	1873	80	5,000
Lord Chief Justice Russell		May	1894	49	8,000
Lord Penzance		...	...	...	5,000
Lord Justice Lindley		May	1865	65	5,000
Mr. Justice Hawkins		November	1876	77	5,000
Mr. Justice Lopes		November	1876	65	5,000
Mr. Justice Matthew		March	1881	63	5,000
Mr. Justice Cave		March	1881	61	5,000
Mr. Justice Kay		March	1881	71	5,000
Mr. Justice Chitty		September	1881	65	5,000
Mr. Justice North		November	1881	61	5,000
Mr. Justice Day		June	1882	67	5,000
Mr. Justice Smith		April	1883	56	5,000
Mr. Justice Wills		July	1884	65	5,000
Mr. Justice Grantham		January	1886	58	5,000
Mr. Justice Stirling		May	1886	57	5,000
Mr. Justice Kekewitch		November	1886	60	5,000
Mr. Justice Charles		September	1887	54	5,000
Lord Watson	Lords of appeal in Ordinary.	March	1880	65	6,000
Lord Macnoughten		January	1887	63	6,000
Lord Morris		November	1889	66	6,000
Sir John Rigby		September	1895	50	5,000
Mr. Justice Williams		February	1890	56	5,000
Mr. Justice Lawrence		February	1890	61	5,000
Mr. Justice Romer		November	1890	53	5,000
Mr. Justice Wright		December	1890	54	5,000
Mr. Justice Collins		April	1891	52	5,000
Sir Francis H. Jeune (President)		January	1891	51	5,000
Mr. Justice Barnes		May	1892	45	5,000
Mr. Justice Bruce		July	1892	60	5,000
Mr. Justice Kennedy		October	1892	48	5,000
Mr. Justice Davey		...	1895	49	6,000

Estimated numbers of Religious Denominations amongst English-speaking Communities throughout the World.

Episcopalians	29,200,000
Methodists of all denominations	18,650,000
Roman Catholics	15,500,000
Presbyterians of all Descriptions	12,250,000
Baptists of all descriptions	9,230,000
Congregationists	6,150,000
Free Thought, various	5,250,000
Uniterians under several names	2,600,000
Minor religious sects	5,500,000
Lutherian, German or Dutch etc.	2,800,000
Of no particular religion	17,000,000
English-speaking population	124,130,000

English bids fair to become the universal language; already it is more widely spread and more freely spoken than any tongue. In Europe it is regarded as the language of polite society. On the vast Australian and North America continents it is one speech; and in the East fully 18,000,000 of Hindus, Mahomedans, Buddists and others read and speak English. In point of numbers at the present time, it is exceeded by the Chinese alone.

Secretaries of State for the Colonial and War Departments from 1795 to 1854.

1795 Right Honorable Henry Dundas, afterwards Viscount Melville.
1801 Lord Hobart, Earl of Buckinghamshire.
1804 Earl, late Marquess of Camden.
1805 Viscount Castlereagh, afterwards Marquess of Londonderry.
1806 Right Honorable W. Windham.
1807 Viscount Castlereagh, afterwards Marquess of Londonderry.
1809 Earl of Liverpool.
1812 Earl Bathurst.
1827 Viscount Goderich, afterwards Earl of Ripon.
Right Honorable W. Huskisson.
1828 Sir George Murray.
1830 Viscount Goderich, afterwards Earl of Ripon.
1833 Right Honorable E. G. Stanley, late Earl of Derby, G.C.M.G.
1834 Right Honorable Thomas Spring Rice, afterwards Lord Monteagle.
Earl of Aberdeen.
1835 Right Honorable Charles Grant, late Lord Glenelg.
1839 Marquess of Normandy.
Lord John Russell, afterwards Earl Russell.
1841 Lord Stanley, late Earl of Derby, G.C.M.G.
1845 Right Honorable William Ewart Gladstone.
1846 Earl Grey, K.G., G.C.M.G.
1852 Right Honorable Sir John S. Pakington, Bart., afterwards Lord Hampton.
1852 Duke of Newcastle.

Secretaries of State for the Colonies, 1854 to 1895.

1854	June	10	Right Honorable Sir G. Grey, Bart.
1855	Feb.		Right Honorable Sidney Herbert, afterwards Lord Herbert of Lea.
1855	May	15	Lord John Russell, late Earl Russell, K.G., G.C.M.G.
1856	July	21	Right Honorable Sir William Molesworth, Bart.
	Nov.	17	Right Honorable Henry Labouchere, afterwards Lord Taunton.
1858	Feb.	26	Lord Stanley, now Earl of Derby.
1858	May	31	Right Honorable Sir Edward Bulwer Lytton, Bart., afterwards Lord Lytton, [G.C.M.G.
1859	June	18	Duke of Newcastle, K.G.
1864	April	4	Right Honorable Edward Cardwell, now Viscount Cardwell.
1866	July	6	Earl of Carnarvon.
1867	March	8	The Duke of Buckingham and Chandos.
1868	Dec.	10	Earl Granville, K.G.
1870	July	6	Earl of Kimberley.
1874	Feb.	21	Earl of Carnarvon.
1874	Feb.	4	Right Honorable Sir Michael H. Beach, Bart.
1880	April	28	Earl of Kimberley.
1882	Dec.	16	Earl of Derby.
1885	June	24	Right Honorable Colonel F. A. Stanley.
1886	Feb.	6	Earl Granville, K.G.
1886	Aug.	3	Right Honorable Edward Stanhope.
1887	Jan.	14	Sir H. T. Holland, Bart., now Lord Knutsford.
1892	Aug.		Marquis of Ripon.
1895	July	2	The Right Honorable Jos. Chamberlain.

Dates of some events in the History of the British Colonial Empire.

Newfoundland discovered	1560
Virginia taken possession of by Releigh	1584
India: first Adventure from England	1591
Incorporation of British East India Company	1600
Barbadoes first settled	1605
Massachussets founded by English Puritans	1620
Nova Scotia settled by the Scotch	1632
Maryland settled by English Roman Catholics	1634
Rhode Island settled by Roger Williams	1636
Madras founded	1640
Jamaica taken from the Spaniards	1655
Bombay ceded to Charles II by Portugal	1662
New York conquered from Dutch and Swedes	1664
Transportation of convicts legalized	1666

Pensylvania settled by the Quakers	1682
William Dampier landed in Australia	1686
Calcutta purchased	1698
Gibraltar taken from the Spaniards	1704
Canada taken from the French	1759
Bengal Behar and Orissa ceded	1765
Captain Cook landed at Botany Bay	1770
United States, first so styled 9th. September	1776
United States, Independence acknowledged	1782
New South Wales settled	1787
First Church erected in Australia	1793
Battle of Seringapatam : Death of Tippoo	1799
Malta acquired by conquest	1800
Tasmania (Dan Dieman's Land) organised	1803
Cape of Good Hope taken from the Dutch	1806
Mauritius taken from the French	1810
See of Calcutta founded	1814
Ceylon acquired	1815
Western Australia formed into a province	1829
South Australia formed into a province	1834
Hong-Kong taken from the Chinese	1841
New Zealand made a separate Colony	1841
The Punjaub formally annexed	1849
Victoria formed into a province	1850
Second Burmese War ; Pegu annexed	1852-3
Oude annexed. Lord Canning, Viceroy	1856
Mutiny commenced at Meerut, 10th. May	1857
India transferred to the Crown, 1st. September	1858
Queensland formed into a province...	1859
Transportation of convicts abolished	1868
Queen publicly proclaimed Empress of India	1877
Cyprus taken possession of	1878
English occupation of Egypt	1882
New Guinea divided with Germany	1885
The Colonial Exhibition opened	1886
Burmese Empire entirely annexed	1886
The Queen's Jubilee	1887
Zululand became a British possession	1887
British South African Company Chartered	1889
Western Australia a self-governing Colony	1890
Matabele War	1894
British Guiana-Venezuela dispute	1895
The Pamir Convention	1895

British Orders of Knighthood.

ORDER.	RIBBON.	MOTTO.
1. The Most Noble Order of the Garter, K.G. (1349)	Garter blue ...	*Honi soit qui mal y pense.*
2. The Most Ancient and Most Noble Order of the Thistle, K.T. (1540)	Green ...	*Nemo me impune lacessit.*
3. The Most Illustrious Order of St. Patrick, K.P. (1783)	Sky blue ...	*Quis superabit ?*
4. The Most Honourable Order of the Bath, K.CB. C.B. (1399, 1725)	Crimson ...	*Tria juncta in uno.*
5. The Most Exalted Order of the Star of India (1861)	Light blue ...	*Heaven's Light our Guide.*
6. The Most Distinguished Order of St. Michel and St. George (1818)	Saxon blue with scarlet stripe.	*Auspicium melioris œvi.*
7. The Order of the Indian Empire (1878 ...		
8. Royal Order of Victoria and Albert (1862) ...		
9. The Imperial Order of the Crown of India (1878)		
10. The Victoria Cross (1856)*		
11. Baronets of England		
12. Knight Bachelors		

* For conspicuous bravery.

A Table of the Kings and Queens of England.

Name.	SAXONS AND DANES.	Access	Died.	Age.	Reign.
Egbert	First King of all England	827	839	—	12
Ethelwulf	Son of Egbert	837	858	—	21
Ethelbald	Son of Ethelwulf	858	860	—	2
Ethelbert	Second son of Ethelwulf	858	866	—	8
Ethelred	Third son of Ethelwulf	866	871	—	5
Alfred	Fourth son of Ethelwulf	871	901	52	30
Edward the Elder ...	Son of Alfred	901	925	46	24
Athelstan	Eldest son of Edward	925	940	—	15
Edmund	Brother of Athelstan	940	946	23	6
Edred	Brother of Edmund	946	955	—	9
Edwy	Son of Edmund	955	958	20	3
Edgar	Second son of Edmund	958	975	31	17
Edward the Martyr ...	Son of Edgar	975	959	17	4
Ethelred II	Half-Brother of Edward	979	1016	—	27
Edmund Ironside ...	Eldest son of Ethelred	1016	1016	28	—
Canute	By conquest and election	1017	1035	40	18
Harold I	Son of Canute	1035	1040	—	5
Hardicanute	Another son of Canute	1040	1042	—	2
Edward the Confessor.	Son of Ethelred II	1042	1066	64	24
Harold II	Brother-in-Law of Edward	1066	1066	—	—
	THE HOUSE OF NORMANDY.				
William I	Obtained the Crown by conquest ...	1066	1087	60	21
William II	Third son of William I	1087	1100	43	13
Henry	Youngest son of William I	1100	1135	67	35
Stephen	Third son of Stephen, Court of Blois by Adela, Fourth daughter of William I ...	1135	1154	49	19
	THE HOUSE OF PLANTAGENET.				
Henry II	Son of Geoffrey Plantagenet, by Mathilda, only daughter of Henry I	1154	1189	56	35
Richard II	Eldest surviving son of Henry II ...	1189	1199	42	10
John	Sixth and youngest son of Henry II ..	1199	1216	51	17
Henry III	Eldest son of John	1216	1272	65	56
Edward I	Eldest son of Henry III	1272	1307	67	35
Edward II	Eldest surviving son of Edward I ...	1307	1327	43	20
Edward III	Eldest son of Edward II	1327	1377	65	50
Richard II	Son of the Black Prince, eldest son of Edward III	1377	Dep.1399	33	22
	THE HOUSE OF LANCASTER.				
Henry IV	Son of John of Gaunt, fourth son of Edward III	1399	1413	46	14
Henry V	Eldest son of Henry IV	1413	1422	34	9
Henry VI	Only son of Henry V, died 1471 ...	1422	Dep.1461	49	39
	THE HOUSE OF YORK.				
Edward IV	His grandfather was Richard, son of Edmund, fifth son of Edward III; and his grandmother, Anne, was greatgrand daughter of Lionel third son of Edward III	1461	1483	41	22
Edward V	Eldest son of Edward IV	1483	1483	12	—
Richard III	Younger brother of Edward IV ...	1483	1485	33	2

Name.	THE HOUSE OF TUDOR.	Access	Died.	Age.	Reign.
Henry VII	Son of Edmund, eldest son of Owen Tudor, by Katherine, widow of Henry V; his mother, Margaret Beaufort was great grand daughter of John of Gaunt... ...	1485	1500	53	24
Henry VIII	Only surviving son of Henry VII	1509	1547	56	38
Edward VI	Son of Henry VIII, by Jane Seymour ...	1547	1553	16	6
Mary I	Daughter of Henry VIII, by Kate of Arragon	1553	1558	43	5
Elizabeth	Daughter of Henry VIII, by Anne Boleyn...	1558	1603	70	44
	THE HOUSE OF STUART				
James I	Son of Mary, Queen of Scots, grand-daughter of James IV and Margaret daughter of Henry VII	1603	1625	59	22
Charles I	Only surviving son of James I	1625	1649	48	24
Commonwealth	Commonwealth declared May 19	1649	—	—	—
	Oliver Cromwell, Lord Protector	1653	1658	59	—
	Richard Cromwell, Lord Protector	1658	Res. 1659	—	—
	THE HOUSE OF STUART.—(Restored)				
Charles II	Eldest son of Charles I	1650	1685	55	25
James II	Second son of Charles, died 16 Sept. 1701...	1685	Dep. 1688	68	3
	[Interregnum, Dec. 11, 1688-Feb. 13, 1659]	—	Dec. 1701		
William III ... ... and	Son of William, Prince of Orange, by Mary daughter of Charles I.	1689	1702	51	13
Mary II	Eldest daughter of James II ...	—	1694	33	6
Anne	Second daughter of James II	1702	1714	49	12
	THE HOUSE OF HANOVER.				
George I	Son of Elector of Hanover, by Sophia, daught. of Elizabeth, daught. of James I...	1714	1727	67	13
George II	Only son of George I...	1727	1760	77	33
George III	Grandson of George II	1760	1820	82	59
George IV	Eldest son of George III	1820	1830	68	10
William IV	Third son of George III	1830	1837	72	7
Victoria	Daugh. of Edward, 4th son of George III ...	1837	WHOM GOD PRESERVE.		

Sovereigns of Scotland from A. D. 1507 to the Union of the Crowns.

Names.	Began to Reign.	Names.	Began to Reign
Malcolm (*Ceanmohr*) ...	1057, April	Robert II (Stewart) ...	1371, Feb. 22
Donald (*Bane*)	1093, Nov.	Robert III	1390, April 12
Duncan	1094, May	James I	1406, April 4
Donald (*Bane*) rest	1095, Nov.	James II	1437, Feb. 20
Edgard	1097, Sept.	James III	1460, Aug. 3
Alexander I	1107, Jan. 8	James IV	1488, June 11
David I	1124, April 27	James V	1513, Sept. 9
Malcolm (*Maiden*)	1153, May 24	Mary	1542, Dec. 16
William (*The Lion*)	1165, Dec. 9	Francis and Mary... ...	1558, April 24
Alexander II...	1214, Dec. 4	Mary	1560, Dec. 5
Alexander III	1249, July 8	Henry and Mary	1565, July 29
Margaret	1286, Mch. 19	Mary	1567, Feb. 10
John (Balliol)	1292, Nov. 17	James VI	1567, July 29
Robert I (Bruce)	1306, March 27	(Ascended the throne of England as James I, 24th, March, 1603.)	
David II	1329, June 7		

The Merovingians

Clovis, " The Hairy, " King of the Salic Franks	428
Childeric III, last of the race	737

The Carlovingians.

Pepin, " The Short, " son of Charles Martel	752
Charlemagne " The Great " Emp. of the West	768
Louis V, " The Indolent, " last of the race	986

The Capets.

Hugh Capet, " The Great "	987
Louis IX, " St. Louis "	1226
Charles IV, " The Handsome "	1322

The House of Valois.

Philip VI, de Valois, " The Fortunate "	1328
Henry III, last of the race	1574

The House of Bourbon.

Henry IV, " The Great " King of Navarre	1589
Louis XIII, " The Just "	1610
Louis XIV, " The Great, " Dieudonné	1643
Louis XV, " The well-beloved "...	1715
Louis XVI, (guillotined 21st January 1793)...	1774
Louis XVII, (never reigned)	1793

The First Republic.

The National Convention first sat	24 Sept.	1792
The Directory nominated	1 Nov.	1795

The Consulate.

Bonaparte, Cambacèrès and Lebrun	24 Dec.	1799
Bonaparte, Consul for 10 years	6 May	1802
Bonaparte, Consul for life	2 Aug.	1802

The Empire.

Napoléon, I, decreed Emperor	18 May	1804
Napoléon, II, (never reigned) died	22 July	1832

The Restoration.

Louis XVIII, re-entered Paris	3 May	1814
Charles X, (dep. 30 July 1830 ; died 6 November 1836)		1824
Heir-expectant ; Hon. Comte de Chambord...	20 Sept.	1820

The House of Orleans

Louis Philippe, King of the French ... ... (abdicated 24 February 1848 ; died 26 August 1850).		1830
Heir-expectant, Comte de Paris, born ... ... also heir to the House of Bourbon).	23 Aug.	1838

The Second Republic.

Provisional Government formed...	22 Feb.	1848
Louis Napoléon elected President	19 Dec.	1848

French Dynasties and Sovereigns.—*Continued*

THE SECOND EMPIRE.

Napoleon III, elected Emperor	22 November ...	1852
(Deposed 4 September, 1870, died 9 January 1873)		

THIRD REPUBLIC.

Committee of Public Defence	4 September ...	1870
L. A. Thiers, elected President	31 August ...	1871
Marshall Mac Mahon, elected President	24 May ...	1873
Jules Grévy, elected President	30 January ...	1879
Marie François Sadi Carnot, elected President	3 December ...	1887
(Assassinated 24th June 1894)		
Casimir Perrier, resigned	January ...	1895
Félix Faure, elected President	7 January ...	1895

Presidents of the United States of America.

Declaration of Independence		4 July	1776
General Washington first President	1789	and	1793
John Adams			1797
Thomas Jefferson	1801	and	1805
James Madisson	1809	and	1813
James Monroe	1817	and	1821
John Quincy Adams			1825
General Andrew Jackson	1829	and	1833
Martin Van Buren			1837
General William Henry Harrison (died 4 April)			1841
John Tyler (elected as Vice-President)			1841
James Knox Polk			1845
General Zachary Taylor (died 9 July 1850)			1849
Millard Fillmore, (elected as Vice-President...			1850
General Franklin Pierce			1853
James Buchanan			1857
Abraham Lincoln (assassinated 14 April 1865)	1861	and	1865
Andrew Johnson			1865
General Ulysse S. Grant	1869	and	1873
Rutherford B. Hayes...			1877
General James Abraham Garfield (died 19 September 1881)			1881
General Chester A. Arthur, (elected as Vice-President)			1881
Grover Cleveland			1885
General Benjamin Harrison			1889
Grover Cleveland	March		1893

Population in 1776, including slaves, 2,614,300.
Population in 1881, all free, 50,152,866.
Population in 1890, 62,622,250.

The Establishment of the Colonial Office.

Secretary of State	The Right Hon. Jos. Chamberlain.
Private Secretary	H. F. Wilson.
Assistant „	W. H. Mercer.

UNDER SECRETARIES.

Parliamentary	The Earl of Selborne.
Private Secretary	C. A. Harris.
„ „	
Permanent	Hon. Robt. Henry Meade, C.B.
Private Secretary	John Anderson.
Asst. Under Scretary	John Bramston, C.B.
Do.	Edward Wingfield, C.B.
Do.	Edward Fairfield, C.B.

Chancelor of the Order of St. Michael and St. George : Sir Robt. George Wyndham Herbert, G.C.B.

The Church of Ireland.

Armagh.—Archbishop, Most Reverend Robert Samuel Gregg, D.D....	1894
Dublin.—Archbishop, Right Honorable and Most Reverend Lord Plunket, D.D. ...	1884
Down.—Bishop, Right Reverend Thomas James Welland, D.D.	1892
Limerick.—Bishop, Right Reverend Charles, Graves D.D.	1886
Tuam.—Bishop, Right Reverend James O'Sullivan, D.D.	1890
Derry.—Bishop, Right Reverend William Alexander, D.D.	1867
Cashel.—Bishop, Right Reverend Maurice Fitz G. Day, D.D.	1872
Cork.—Bishop, Right Reverend William Edward Meade, D.D.	1894
Ossory.—Bishop, Right Reverend William Pakenham Walsh, D.D.	1878
Killaloe.—Bishop, Right Reverend Fredlk. Richards Wynne, D.D.	1893
Kilmore.—Bishop, Right Reverend Samuel Shone, D.D....	1884
Meath.—Bishop, Most Reverend Joseph Ferguson Peacocke	1885
Clogher.—Bishop, Right Reverend Charles Maurice Stack, D.D.	1886

The Episcopal Church in Scotland.

Brechin.—Hugh W. Jermyn, D.D. Primus (1886)	1871
St. Andrews.—The Rt. Revd. G. H. Wilkinson, D.D.	1893
Edinburgh.—The Rt. Revd· John Dowden, D.D.	1886
Glasgow.—The Rt. Revd. William T. Harrison, D.D.	1888
Aberdeen.—The Rt. Revd. Honorable A. G. Douglas, D.D.	1883
Argyll.—The Rt. Revd. J. R. A. Chinnery Haldane, L.L.D.	1883
Moray.—The Rt. Revd. J. B. K. Kelly, D.D.	1867

The Established Church of Scotland·

Lord High Commissioner.—Right Honorable the Marquis of Breadalbane.
Moderator of the General Assembly.—Right Reverend Donald Macleod, D·D.
Dean of the Order of the Thistle and of the Royal Chapel.—Reverend James Cameron Lees, D.D.
Deans of the Chapel Royal.—Reverend William Milligan, D.D., Reverend A. F. Mitchell, D.D., Reverend William Stewart, D.D., Reverend Robert Flint, D.D., L.L.D.
Chaplains to the Queen.—Reverend John Stewart, D.D., Reverend Donald Macleod, D.D., Reverend James Mc Gregor, D.D., Reverend Robert H. Story, D.D.
Domestic Chaplain of the Royal Household.—Reverend Archibald Alexander Campbell·

The Roman Catholic Hierarchy.

Pope Leo XIII is the 258th. Pontiff ; counting from St. Peter, born March 2, 1810. Elected February 20, Crowned, March 3, 1878. The full number of the Sacred College is 70; viz, Cardinal Bishops 6 ; Cardinal Priests 50 ; Cardinal Deacons 14. At present there are 6 Cardinals. First Cardinal Bishop, Raphael Monaco, Dean of the Sacred College ; First Cardinal Priest, Gustavus Adolphus Von Hohenlohe ; First Deacon, Theodolphus Mertel. Secretary of State to His Holiness, Cardinal Rampolla.

—

The Roman Catholic Hierarchy throughout the world according to official returns lately published at Rome consisted of 13 Patriarches ,and 191 Archbishops and Bishops. Including 12 Coadjutor or Auxiliary Bishops ; the number of Roman Catholic Archbishops and Bishops now holding office in the British Empire is 159.

R. C. Archbishops in Great Britain and Ireland.

Westminster.—Most Rev. Herbert Card. Vaughan, consecrated 1872.
Glasgow.—Most Rev. Charles Eyre, cons. 31 January 1869.
St. Andrews & Edinburgh.—Most Rev. Angus Macdonald, cons. 1878.
Armagh.—Most Rev. Michel Logue, Primate of Ireland, cons. March 1879.
Dublin.—Most Rev. William J. Walsh, cons. 2 August 1885.
Cashel.—Most Rev. Thomas W. Croke, cons. 5 July 1870.
Tuam.—Most Rev. John Mc Evilly, cons. 8 November 1857.

Bishop of Port Louis.—(Vacant).
Bishop of Seychelles.—The Right Rev. Dr. Marc Hudrisier, Bishop of Teo, cons. 28 Oct. 1890.

Twelve o'clock noon, at Greenwich mean time as compared with the following places.

	H.	M.		H.	M.
Aden	3	0 a.m.	Cairo	2	05 p.m
Alexandria	1	59 a.m.	Copenhagen	0	50 p.m.
Boston, U.S.	7	18 a.m.	Florence	0	45 p.m.
Durban	2	2 p.m.	Jerusalem	2	21 p.m.
Dublin	11	35 a.m.	Madras	5	21 p.m.
Edinburgh	11	47 a.m.	Malta	0	58 p.m.
Galle	5	20 p.m.	Marseilles	0	21 p.m.
Glasgow	11	43 a.m.	Melbourne, Australia	9	40 p.m.
Hong-Kong	7	36 p.m.	Moscow	2	30 p.m.
Lisbon	11	43 a.m.	Munich	0	46 p.m.
Madrid	11	45 a.m.	Port Louis, Mauritius	3	50 p.m.
New York, City Hall	7	4 a.m.	Paris	0	9 p.m.
Penzance	11	38 a.m.	Pekin	7	46 p.m.
Philadelphia	6	59 a.m.	Prague	0	58 p.m.
Quebec	7	15 a.m.	Rome	0	50 p.m.
Kurrachee	4	27 p.m.	Rangoon	6	20 a.m.
Adelaide	9	14 a.m.	Rotterdam	0	18 a.m.
Amsterdam	0	20 p.m.	Tamatave	3	17 p.m
Athens	1	35 p.m.	St. Petersburg	2	1 p.m.
Berlin	0	54 p.m.	Singapore	6	55 p.m.
Berne	0	30 p.m.	Suez	2	10 p.m.
Bombay	4	51 p.m.	Sydney	10	5 p.m.
Brussels	0	17 p.m.	Stockolm	1	12 p.m.
Calcutta	5	53 p.m.	Stuttgardt	0	37 p.m.
Cape Town	1	13 p.m.	Vienna	1	6 p.m.
Constantinople	1	56 p.m.	Zanzibar	2	37 p.m.

Variation of Time depends upon Longitude; every degree East of Greenwich is 4 minutes earlier, and every degree West four minutes later. Note the variation in the U. S. or in British America.

The French Republican Calendar.

This, although reckoned from the 22nd. September 1792, was not introduced until the 22nd. November 1793. It remained in use only till the 31st. December 1805, when the Gregorian Calendar was restored 1st. January 1806 (Nivôse 10, year 14). The months were:

Vendémaire (Vintage month) 23 Sept. to Oct. 22.	Germinal (Budding month) 22 March to April 21.
Brumaire (Foggy month) 23 Oct. to Nov. 22.	Floréal (Flowery month) 21 April to May 20.
Frimaire (Sleety month) 22 nov. to Dec. 21.	Prairial (Pasture month) 21 May to June 20.
Nivôse (Snowy month) 22 Dec. to Jan. 21.	Messidor (Harvest month) 20 June to July 19.
Pluviôse (Rainy month) 21 Jan. to Feb. 20.	Thermidor (Hot month) 20 July to Aug. 19.
Ventôse (Windy month) 20 Feb. to March 19.	Fructidor (Fruit month) 19 Aug. to Sep. 18.

The twelve months were divided into three decades of ten days each but to make up the 365 five were added to the end of September; the 17th. *Primidi*, dedicated to Virtue; the 18th. *Duodi*, to Genius; the 19th. *Tridi*, to Labour; the 20th. *Quartiti* to Opinion; and the 21st. *Quintidi* to Rewards. The leap year called *Olympic*, a sixth day *Sextidi*. " Jour de la Révolution, " was added

The Established Church of England.

Canterbury.—Archbishop and Primate of all England, Right Honorable and Most Reverend Edward White Benson, D. D. 1883
York.—Archbishop and Primate of England, Right Honorable and Most Reverend Dalrymple Maclagen, D. D. 1891
London.—Bishop, Right Honorable and Right Reverend Frederick Temple, D. D. ... 1885
Durham.—Bishop, Right Reverend Brook Foss Wescott, D. D. 1890
Winchestsr.—Bishop, Right Reverend Randall Ths. Davidson, D. D. 1895
Bangor.—Bishop, Bight Reverend Daniel Lewis Lloyd, D. D. 1890
Baths and Wells.—Bishop, Right Honorable, Geo. Wyndham Kennion D. D. 1894
Carlisle.—Bishop, Right Reverend John W. Bardsley, D. D. 1892
Chester.—Bishop, Right Reverend Francis John Jayne, D.D., L.L.D. 1889
Chichester.—Bishop, Right Reverend Ernest R. Wilberforce, D. D. 1895
Ely.—Bishop, Right Reverend Lord Alwine Compton, D. D. 1886
Exeter.—Bishop, Right Reverend Edw. Hy. Bickersteth, D. D. 1885
Gloucester and Bristol.—Bishop, Right Reverend Charles John Ellicott, D. D. 1863
Hereford.—Bishop, Right Reverend John Percival, D. D. 1895
Lichfield.—Bishop, Right Reverend Augnstus Legge, D. D. 1891
Lincoln.—Bishop, Right Reverend Edward King, D. D. 1865
Liverpool.—Bishop, Right Reverend John Charles Ryle, D. D. 1880
Llandoff.—Bishop, Bight Reverend Richard Lewis, D. D. 1883
Manchester.—Bishop, Right Reverend James Moorhouse, D. D. 1886
Newcastle.—Bishop, Right Reverend Edgar Jacob, D. D. 1895
Norwich.—Bishop, Right Reverend John Sheepshanks, D. D. 1893
Oxford.—Bishop, Right Reverend William Stubbs, D. D. 1889
Peterborough.—Bishop, Right Reverend Mandell Creighton, D. D. 1891
Ripon.—Bishop, Right Reverend W. Boyd Carpenter, D. D. 1884
Rochester.—Bishop, Right Reverend Edward Stnart Talbot, D. D. 1895
St Albans.—Bishop, Right Reverend John Wogan Festing, D. D. 1890
St Asaph.—Bishop, Right Reverend Alfred Geo. Edwards, D.D. 1889
St David's.—Bishop, Right Reverend William Basil Jones, D. D. 1874
Salisbury.—Bishop, Right Reverend John Wordsworth, D. D. 1885
Sodor and Man.—Bishop, Right Reverend Norman J. D. Straton D.D. 1892
Southwell.—Bishop, Right Reverend George Ridding, D. D. 1884
Truro.—Bishop, Right Reverend John Gott, D. D. 1891
Wakefield.—Bishop, Right Reverend Wm. Walsham How, D. D. 1888
Worcester.—Right Reverend John James Stewart Perowne, D. D. 1890

States of Europe and the Sovereigns.

WITH YEAR OF ACCESSION AND OF BIRTH.

Austro-Hungarian Empire.—Francis Joseph, Emp. 1848 ; born 1838.
Belgium.—Léopold II, King of Belgium, 1865 ; born 1835.
Denmark.—Christian IX, King, 1863 ; born 1818.
France.—Monsiour Félix Faure, President of the Republic, 1895 ; born 1841.
German Empire.—(Consisting of 26 States), William II, June 1888, Emperor of Germany ; b. 1859.
Great Britain and Ireland.— Victoria, Queen, succeeded her uncle William IV, June 20, 1837 ; crowned June 28, 1838 ; born May 24, 1819.
Greece.—George I, King of the Greeks, 1863 ; born 1895.
Italy.—Humbert, King, 1878 ; born 1844.
Netherlands.—Wilhelmina (a minor) Queen, : born 31 August 1880.
Portugal.—Don Carlos I, King, 1889 ; born 1863.
Roumania.—Charles I, King, 1881 ; born 1839.
Russia.—Nicolas II, 1894 ; born 1868.
Servia.—Alexander Obrenovitch (a minor) King 1889 ; born 1876.
Spain.—Alphonse XIII (a minor) King ; 17 May 1886.
Sweden and Norway.—Oscar II, King, 1872 ; born 1829.
Switzerland.—Confederation of 22 Cantons, Joseph Zemp, President.
Turkey.—Abdul Hamid II, Sultan, 1876 ; born 1842.

Rulers of the Chief Countries of the World.

Country.	Ruler.	Born.	Acceded.
Abyssinia	Menelek, *Emperor* (or Negus)	...	12 Mch. 1889
Afghanistan	Abdur Ramhman Khan, *Amir*	...	1880
Annam	Bun-Lan, *King*...	1862	1 Aug. 1884
Argentine Republic ...	Sinor Uriburnd, *President*	...	22 Jan. 1895
Austria-Hungary ...	Francis Joseph, *Emperor*	18 Aug. 1803	2 Dec. 1848
Beluchistan	Mir Mahmud, *Khan*	...	1893
Belgium	Leopold II, *King*	9 April 1835	10 Dec. 1865
Bokhara	Seid Abdul Ahad, *Amir*	...	23 Nov. 1891
Bolivia	Don Maraino Baptista, *President*	...	1 Aug. 1892
Borneo	Hassim Jalilal Alam Akamaldin, *Sultan* ...	...	May 1885
Brazil	General Dr. Prudente José de Morœs, *Presidt.*	...	15 Nov. 1894
Bulgaria	Ferdinand of Saxe-Cobourg, *Prince*... ...	26 Feb. 1861	11 Aug. 1887
Chili	Admiral Jorge Moutt, *President*	1847	19 Nov. 1892
China	Kuang-Hsü, *Emperor*	15 Aug. 1871	12 Jan. 1875
Columbia	Miguel A. Caro, *President*	...	7 Aug. 1892
Costa Rica	Rafael Iglesias, *President*	...	8 May 1890
Denmark	Christian IX, *King*	8 April 1818	15 Nov. 1863
Dominican Republic...	General Ulises Heureaux, *President* ...	...	1 Sept. 1886
Ecuador	Don Cordero, *President*	...	30 June 1892
Egypt	Abbas II, *Khedive*	14 July 1874	7 Jan. 1892
France	Félix Faure, *President*	30 Jan. 1843	Dec. 1894
Germany	William II, *Emperor*	27 Jan. 1859	15 June 1888
Prussia	William II, *King*		
Bavaria	Otto, *King*, Prince Luithold, *Regent* ...	27 April 1848	13 June 1886
Saxony	Albert, *King*	23 April 1828	29 Oct. 1873
Wurtemberg ...	William II, *King*	25 Feb. 1848	6 Oct. 1891
Baden	Frederick, *Grand Duke*	9 Sept. 1826	5 Sept. 1856
Hesse	Ernest Louis V, *Grand Duke*	25 Nov. 1868	13 Mch. 1892
Anhalt	Frederick, *Duke*	29 April 1831	22 May 1871
Brunswick	Prince Albrecht, *Regent*	8 May 1837	22 Oct. 1885
Mecklenburg-Schwerin	Frederick Françis III, *Grand Duke*... ...	19 Mar. 1851	15 April 1883
Mecklenburg-Strelitz	Frederick William, *Grand Duke*	17 Oct. 1819	6 Sept. 1860
Oldenburg	Peter, *Grand Duke*	8 July 1827	27 Feb. 1853
Saxe-Cobourg and Gotha	Alfred, *Duke of Edinburgh*	6 Aug. 1844	23 Aug. 1893
Waldeck-Pyrmont. .	Frederick, *Prince*	20 Jan. 1865	12 May 1893
Greece	George I, *King*...	24 Dec. 1845	31 Oct. 1863
Guatemala	General Reina Barinos *President*	...	1894
Hawaii	Sanford B. Dole, *President*	...	4 July 1894
Haytii	General Hypolite, *President*	...	18 Aug. 1888
Honduras	Dr. P. Bonilla, *President*	...	1894
Italy	Humbert, *King*	14 Mch. 1844	9 Jan. 1878
Japan	Mutsu Hito, *Emperor*	3 Nov. 1852	12 Feb. 1867
Liberia	J. J. Cheesman, *President*	...	7 Jan. 1892
Madagascar	Ranavalona III, *Queen*	...	13 July 1883
Mexico	General Profirio Diaz, *Président*	...	1 Dec. 1873
Montenegro	Nicolas, *Prince*...	7 Oct. 1841	14 Aug. 1860
Morocco	Mulai Abdul Aziz, *Sultan*	...	7 June 1894
Nepaul ...	Prithivi Beer Bikram Shum Shere Jun Bahador, *Maharaja.*	1875	Sept. 1884
Netherlands	Wilhelminia, (a minor) *Queen*	31 Aug. 1880	23 Nov. 1890
Nicaragua	José Santos Zelaya *President*	...	June 1893
Oman	Seyyid Fesvalbin Turkee, *Sultan*	...	4 June 1888

Country.	Ruler.	Born.	Acceded.
Orange Free State ...	Nicola Pierola, *President*	...	
Paraguay	Equsguiza, *President*	...	25 Nov. 1894
Persia	Nazir-ed-Din, *Shah*...	24 April 1829	10 Sept. 1848
Peru	*President*...	...	
Portugal	Dom Carlos, *King*	28 Sept. 1863	19 Oct. 1889
Roumania	Charles, *King*	20 April 1839	26 Mch. 1881
Russia	Nicolas II, *Emperor*...	18 May 1868	1 Nov. (N.S.)94
Salvator	Rafael A. Gutierrez, *President*	...	June 1894
Sarawak	Sir Charles Johnson Brooke G.C.M.G. *Raja*	3 June 1829	1868
Servia	Alexander (Obrenovitch), *King*	14 Aug. 1876	6 Mch. 1889
Siam	Khoulalonkorn, *King*	21 Sept. 1853	1 Oct. 1868
Spain	Alphonso XIII (a Minor), *King*	17 May 1886	17 May 1886
Sweeden and Norway.	Oscar II, *King*	21 Jan. 1829	18 Sept. 1872
Switzerland	Joseph Zemp, *President*	1884	1895
Transvaal	S. J. Paul Kruger, *President*	18 Oct. 1825	April 1893
Tripoli...	Ahmed Rassim Pasha, *Governor*	...	Nov. 1881
Tunis	Sidi Ali Pasha, *Bey*	1817	28 Oct. 1882
Turkey	Abdul Hamid II, *Sultan*	22 Sept. 1842	31 Aug. 1876
United States, America	Grover Cleveland, *President*	18 Mch. 1837	4 Mch. 1893
Uruguay	Juan Idiarte Borda, *President*	...	21 Mch. 1894
Venezuela	General Ivanquin Crespo, *President* ...	...	14 Mch. 1894
Zanzibar	Hamid-bin-Thwain, *Sultan*	...	5 Mch. 1893

British Ambassadors.

Name.	Salary.	Residence.
His Excellency Marquess Dufferin and Ava, G.C.B., K.P....	£9,000	Paris.
Right Hon. Sir Edmund J. Monson, G.C.M.G., C.B. ...	8,000	Vienna.
Right Hon. Sir Clare Ford, G.C.B., G.C.M.G.	7,000	Rome.
Right Hon. Sir Philip H. Wodehouse Currie, G. C. B. ...	8,000	Constantinople.
Right Hon. Sir F. C. Lascelles, G.C.M.G.	7,500	Berlin.
Right Hon. Sir N. R. O'Conor, K.C.B.	7,800	St. Petersburg.
Hon. Sir Julian Pauncefoote, G.C.M.G.	6,500	Washington.
Sir Henry Drummond Wolff, G.C.B., G.C.M.G. ...	5,500	Madrid.
Henry Nevil Dering, Esq.	3,750	Mexico.
E. H. Egerton, Esq. C. B.	3,500	Athens.
Captain H. M. Jones, V.C.	2,300	Lima.
F. B. Jenner, Esq.	2,000	Bogota.
James Frederick Roberts, Esq.	500	Guatemala
Alexander Gollan, Esq....	1,800	Havana.
Augustus Cohen, Esq.	1,250	Port-au-Prince.
Claude C. Mallet, Esq.	1,285	Panama.
Hon. Sir F. R. Plunkett, K.C.M.G....	3,230	Brussels.
Fred. R. St. John, Esq....	1,650	Berne.
Sir Horace Rumbold, Bart., G.C.M.G.	4,000	The Hague.
Lord Cromer, G.C.M.G., K.C.B., K.C.S.I., C.I.E. ...	6,000	Alexandria.
Sir Spencer B. St. John, K.C.M.G	3,400	Stockholm.

Heights of the principal Mountains in the Several Continents.

Europe	Mont Blanc..................	Switzerland..................	15,781 feet.	
Asia	Mount Everest	Himalayas	29,002 ,,	
Africa	Kilimanjaro	Equatorial Africa	20,000 ,,	(estimated)
America	Mount St. Elias	Russian America	17,500 ,,	
Do.	Aconcagua	Chili	22,422 ,,	

Qualifications of Electors.

§ 15. Every male person shall be entitled to be registered in any year as a voter for any electoral district, and when registered to vote at the election of a Member of the Council for such district, who is qualified as follows, that is to say :—

1.—Has attained the age of twenty-one years.

2.—Is under no legal incapacity, and is in possession of his civil rights.

3.—Is a British subject by birth or naturalization.

4.—Has resided in the Colony for three years at least previous to the date of registration and possesses some one of the following qualifications :—

(*a*) is on the first 1st. day of January in each year, and has during the preceding six calendar months, been the owner of immoveable property within such district of the annual value of Rs. 300 or the monthly value of Rs. 25 above all charges and encumbrances effecting the same ;

(*b*) is at the date of registration paying, and has for six calendar months previous to the 1st. day of January in such year, paid rent in respect of immoveable property situate within such district, at the rate of at least Rs. 25 per month ;

(*c*) has for three calendar months previous to the 1st. day of January in such year resided, or had his principal place of business or employment with such district, and in the owner of moveable property within the Colony of the value of at least Rs. 3,000 ;

(*d*) is the husband of a wife, or the eldest son of a widow, possessing any one of the above qualifications ;

(*e*) has for three calendar months previous to the 1st. day of January in such year resided, or had his principal place of business or employment within such district, and is in receipt of a yearly salary of at least Rs. 600, or a monthly salary of at least Rs. 50 per month.

(*f*) has for three calendar months previous to the 1st. of January in such year resided or has his principal place of business or employment within such district, and pays license duty to the amount of at least Rs. 50 per annum.

Provided—

1.—That no person shall be registered as a voter or be entitled to vote for the election of a Member of the Council who has been convicted of perjury in any Court in Our Dominions, or who has been sentenced by any such Court to death, or penal servitude, or imprisonment with hard labour, or for a term exceeding twelve months, and has not either suffered the punishment to which he was sentenced or such other punishment as by competent authority may have been substituted for the same or received a free pardon from Us

2.—That no person shall be registered as a voter in any year who has within twelve calendar months immediately preceding the 1st. day of January in that year received any relief from public or parochial funds.

3.—That no person shall be registered as a voter in any year unless he shall in the presence of the registering officer or of a magistrate with his own hand subscribe his name to his claim to be registered, and write thereon the date of such subscription, and the qualification in respect of which he claims to be registered.

4.—That no person claiming to be registered in the district in which he resides, in respect of either of the qualifications (*c*), (*d*), (*e*), (*f*), shall be registered in respect of the same qualification in the district in which he has his principal place of business or employment, or *vice versâ*.

Election of Members* of the Legislative Council.

UNDER HER MAJESTY'S LETTERS-PATENT OF THE 16th. SEPTEMBER 1885.

MEMBER FOR MOKA.	MEMBER FOR RIV. DU REMPART.
† Leclézio, Henri	† Antelme, L. E.

MEMBERS FOR PORT LOUIS.

Election held on the 27th. January 1896.

Newton, W. ... ... 1067 votes.
Rohan, Dr. V. ... ... 878 „

MEMBER FOR PLAINES WILHEMS.

Election held on the 29th. January 1896.

Guibert, Georges ... ... 530 votes.

MEMBER FOR GRAND PORT.

Election held on the 30th. January 1896.

de Rochecouste, Louis ... ... 298 votes.

MEMBER FOR PAMPLEMOUSSES.

Election held on the 31st. January 1896.

Sauzier junior, E. ... ... 268 votes.

MEMBER FOR FLACQ.

Election held on the 3rd. February 1896.

Bouchet, Dr. ... ... 224 votes.

MEMBER FOR SAVANNE.

Election held on the 4th. February 1896.

Edwards, Dr. W. T. A. ... ... 191 votes.

MEMBER FOR BLACK RIVER.

Election held on the 7th. February 1896.

Geffroy, Vincent ... ... 72 votes.

Total number of Voters in each District for 1896.

Moka	‡ ......
Rivière du Rempart	‡ ......
Port Louis	1843
Plaines Wilhems	951
Grand Port	498
Pamplemousses	476
Flacq	346
Savanne	373
Black River	120

List of Roman Pontiffs from 1724 to 1878.

(For a complete list from A.D. 67 to 1721, vide Almanac for 1886 page 233.)

Benedict XIII	1724	Pius VII	1800
Clément XII	1730	Leo XII	1823
Benedict XIV	1740	Pius VIII	1829
Clément XIII	1758	Gregory XVI	1831
Clément XIV	1769	Pius IX	1846
Pius VI	1775	Leo XIII	1878

His Holiness Pope Leo XIII (Vincent Joachim Pecci), the 258th. Roman Pontiff, was born at Carpineto, March 2, 1810; consecrated Archbishop of Damiotta. Feb. 19, 1843; translated to the See of Perugia, Jan. 19, 1846; proclaimed Cardinal, Dec. 19, 1853; elected Pope, Feb. 20, crowned March 3, 1878.

* The title of Honorable is given to the members of the Executive and Legislative Councils in virtue of Government notice dated 19th. August 1826.

† No Poll was taken for the Districts of Moka and Rivière du Rempart as only one Candidate was nominated for each of those Districts.

‡ No election took place in these two Districts.

Names of Estates.	Names of Owners.	Names of Managers.	* Acres in cultivation	No. of Laborers.
Pamplemousses.				
Beau Plan	Beau Plan Sugar Est. Cy. Ld.	J. de St. Romain ...	400	355
Belle Vue	W. F. Pilot	A. Lagesse ...	300	431
Belle Vue & Mauricia ...	J. & N. Harel	A. Harel ...	600	343
Constance	Beau Sejour Sugar Est. Cy. Ld.	L. Lagesse ...	400	215
Espérance	E. Lebreton	E. Lebreton ...	325	180
Mon Piton	Beau Séjour Sugar Est. Cy.Ld.	G. Aubin ...	500	316
Maison Blanche & Mon Rocher	The Mon Rocher & Maison Blanche S. E. Cy. Ld.	E. Maurel ...	780	450
Plessis	E. Martin & Co.	E. Carosin ...	400	249
Petite Rosalie	A. Ulcoq	A. Colin... ...	350	213
St. André (A)	Northern Sugar Est. Cy. Ld...	G. Harel ...	400	305
St. André Solitude (B) ...	Do. Do. ...	G. Harel ...	450	291
The Mount	Léopold Antelme... ...	G. Antelme ...	450	210
Rosalie	Mauritius Sugar Est. Cy. ...	C. Montocchio ...	1200	513
Rivière du Rempart.				
Antoinette	G. Martin & Co.	G. Martin ...	1200	656
Belle Vue	L. Maurel	L. Maurel ...	750	438
Bon Espoir	Heirs Tiroumoudy ...	L. Pelletier ...	500	286
Beau Séjour et Mon Choix...	Beau Séjour Sug. Est. Cy. Ld.	G. Aubin ...	1000	686
Espérance	Trébuchet & Co.	A. Ménagé ...	1000	510
Forbach	Mrs. Wiéhé & Souchon ...	A. Wiéhé ...	300	212
Haute Rive	Ile d'Ambre Sugar Est. Cy. ...	F. Rondeaux ...	400	266
Ile d'Ambre	Do. Do. ...	Do. ...	500	216
Labourdonnais	Mrs. Wiéhé & Souchon ...	A. Wiéhé ...	400	377
L'Amitié	L. Maurel	L. Maurel ...	80	132
Mon Loisir Sugar Estate Cy.	Agricultural Company ...	E. Alizart ...	600	566
Mon Songe	Beau Séjour Sug. Est. Cy. Ld.	L. Lagasse ...	800	548
St. Antoine	Messrs. de Chazal & Co. ...	R. D'Unienville fils...	600	535
Schœnfeld	A. Cayeux & Co.	A. de Rosnay ...	1000	454
Flacq.				
Argy	C. Baschet & Co.	L. Baschet ...	700	349
Beau Bois	V. Dupin	R. Dupin ...	500	281
Beau Champ	Mauritius Est. & Assets Cy. Ld.	C. Barlow ...	1000	779
Beau Vallon	Credit Foncier of Mauritius ...	A. Lemaire ...	500	104‡
Bel Etang	Bel Etang & Sans Souci Sugar Estate Cy. Ld.	J. Mazérieux ...	1200	400
Belle Rive	Mauritius Est. & Assets Cy. Ld.	A. Marquay ...	1200	486‡
Belle Vue (A)	Mrs. Widow P. Allendy ...	E. D'Unienville ...	600	456
Bon Espoir	V. Dupin	R. Dupin ...	480	119
Bonne Mère	Queen Victoria & Bonne Mère Sugar Est. Cy.	A. Desvaux ...	800	335
Clémencia	Mauritius Est. & Assets Cy.Ld.	P. Lemerle ...	850	285
Constance & La Gaieté ...	Constance & La Gaieté Sugar Est. Cy. Ld.	A. Dalais ...	400	651

* Compiled from Returns furnished to the Protector of Immigrants under Ordinance No. 12 of 1878. The number of acres in cultivation is only approximate.

‡ Has no mill.

Names of Estates.	Names of Owners.	Names of Managers.	Acres in cultivation.	No. of Laborers.
Flacq.—Continued.				
Constance (Manès) ...	E. Mérandon, A. Desbleds & Co.	E. Mérandon ...	600	596
Deep River	Mazery & Antelme ...	C. Castel ...	600	498
Etoile	Mauritius Sugar Estates Cy...	E. de la Hogue ...	1000	690
La Gaieté	Constance & La Gaieté Sugar Estate Company Limited.	A. Dalais ...	1500	486
La Grande Retraite ...	A. Bourgault Ducoudray ...	M. Carosin ...	600	254
La Lucie	Widow Hardy & Co. ...	N. Langlois ...	600	219
L'Union	A. Régnard	E. Roussel ...	600	382
L'Unité & Mon Rêve ...	Agr. Company of Mauritius ...	N. Raffray ...	800	488
Olivia	Mauritius Est.& Assets Co.Ld.	C. Barlow ...	500	330
Petite Retraite	Mrs. Allendy	E. D'Unienville ...	700	398
Queen Victoria	Queen Victoria & Bonne Mère Sugar Est. Company Ltd.	A. Desvaux ...	1200	713
Richfund	Mrs. M. A. Arnaud & Co. ...	P. Eynaud ...	800	453
St. Julien	Mauritius Est. & Assets Co. Ld.	Léon Daruty ...	1700	590
Grand Port.				
Anse Jonchée	M. Portal and Sisters ...	M. Portal ...	1000	312
Astrœa	Mauritius Sugar Estate Cy ...	A. Daniel ...	900	386
Beau Vallon	A. de Rochecouste & Co. ...	D. de St. Romain ...	1400	774
Beau Vallon	A. Dauban	J. Chéron ...	1000	442
Cent Gaulettes (E. de R.) ...	E. de Rochecouste ..	L. Lorans ...	150	92‡
Cent Gaulettes (O. E.) ...	Oriental Sugar Est. Co. ...	A. Ducray ...	64	472
Cluny	Issop Mamode Sulliman & Co.	A. Desplaces ...	900	596
Deux Bras	Mrs. Robert & Mrs. Edgar de Rochecouste	Du Peloux de St. Romain	800	375
Eau Bleue	Mauritius Land Credit Cy. ...	E. Labat ...	700	278
Ferney	A. Dumontet & Co. ...	A. Ozoux ...	1000	407
Gros Bois	Thierry and Cloupet ...	E. Labat ...	1600	693
Joli Bois	Brouard & Boullé ...	A. D'Unienville ...	800	322
La Barraque	J. B. Guimbeau & Harel ...	A. Mancini ...	950	435
La Rosa	Mauritius Est.& Assets Cy. Ld.	A. Baissac ...	300	260‡
Mon Désert	T. Thierry	A. Maurice ...	800	508
New Grove	Mauritius Est. & Assets Cy.Ld.	A. Baissac ...	800	267
Plaisance	Agricultural Company Ld. ...	J. Martin ...	1000	516
Riche en Eau	E. de Rochecouste ...	L. Lorans ...	1200	650
Rose Belle	Mauritius Est.& Assets Cy. Ld.	A. Baissac ...	1200	650
Rivière Créole	Mauritius Est.& Assets Cy. Ld.	A. Fayd'herbe ...	400	120‡
Sauve Terre	Widow J. B. Colin ...	E. Mariette ...	100	24‡
Savinia	J. F. de Falbaire	F. de Falbaire ...	...	93‡
St. Hubert	Widow Thomas & Ch. Lachambre	L. Harel ...	1200	597
Union Vale	Samouilhan & Co. ...	V. Descombes ...	900	464
Union Park	Samouilhan & Co. ...	A. F. Rault ...	700	402

‡ Has no mill.

Names of Estates.	Names of Owners.	Names of Managers.	Acres in cultivation.	No. of Laborers.
Plaines Wilhems				
Bagatelle	Renaud Desvaux & Co. ...	Renaud Desvaux ...	500	251
Bananes	Mauritius Est. & Assets Cy. Ld.	J. A. Wiéhé ...	800	413†
Midlands	Do. do.	G. Perromat ...	1500	726
Bassin	Widow L. Arnaud ...	J. L. Colin ...	900	550
Henrietta	J. W. Shand-Harvey ...	V. Dupouy ...	1000	587
Highlands	Highlands Sugar Estates Cy ...	C. Dalais ...	1500	895
Réunion	Hon. Geo. Robinson ...	F. Boulle ...	1000	378
Stanley & Ebène ...	Hon. Sir C. Antelme, K.C.M.G.	C. Antelme fils ...	1000	665
Trianon	Belzim & Harel	E. Lagesse ...	1600	584
Black River.				
Albion & Dependencies ...	Mrs. G. Rougier Laganne ...	G. Rougier Laganne..	700	246
* Chamarel	Mauritius Est. & Assets Cy. Ld.	W. W. West ...	300	120
Wolmar	Do. do.	H. Kœnig ...	600	449
Médine & Dependencies ...	Agricultural Company Limited.	B. Kœnig ...	600	366
Tamarin	Mauritius Est. & Assets Cy. Ld.	H. Kœnig ...	500	297
Moka.				
Agrément (Pieter Both) ...	Agricultural Company ...	G. Mackie ...	500	385
Alma	Hon. H. Leclézio	C. de Gorsigny ...	1000	736
Bon Air	W. S. Telfair	W. Telfair ...	500	173
Bar-le-Duc	Hon. H. Leclézio	C. de Gersigny ...	800	455
Bonne Veine	Mauritius Est. & Assets Cy. Ld.	Léon Daruty ...	900	538
Côte d'Or	Desvaux & Co....	E. Desvaux ...	1000	514
La Laura (Pieter Both) ...	Agricultural Company ...	G. Mackie ...	600	738
Mon Désert	Mon Désert Sugar Estate Company.	E. Manès ...	900	611
Minissy	Widow H. Hardy & Cy. ...	L. Hardy ...	500	302
Valetta	Mrs. Th. & L. D'Arifat ...	J. D'Arifat ...	1000	501
Melrose	Mauritius Est. & Assets Cy. Ld.	L. Dugand ...	1200	512
Sans Souci	Bel Etang & Sans Souci Sugar Estates Company.	A. Dalais ...	1000	639
Savanne.				
Beau Champ	Allam & H. C. Mamoojee ...	E. Lemerle ...	800	163
Beau Bois	Société de St. Aubin	E. Nozaïc ...	300	178
Bel Air	Heirs Hardouin...	C. Parisot (acting) ...	560	273
Bénarès	Sir V. Naz & Co.	A. Constantin ...	800	525
Bel Ombre	Allam & H. C. Mamoojee ...	E. Lemerle ...	600	450
Fontenelle	Vve F. Lecourt de Billot ...	A. Lecourt de Billot...	500	223
La Flora	Maur. Land Credit Cy. Ld. ...	E. Piat	800	406
L'Union	Agr. Comp. of Mauritius ...	A. Lagesse	400	355

* This Estate has, besides sugar and other produce, over 100 acres planted in Tea.

† Has no mill.

Names of Estates.	Names of Owners.	Names of Managers.	Acres in cultivation.	No. of Laborers.
L'Union & Bel Air ...	Mrs. T. Vigier Latour... ...	E. de St. Félix ...	800	590
Riche Bois	Maur. Sugar Estate Cy. Ld. ...	L. Nayl	1200	768
Rivière des Anguilles ...	E. de Senneville & Co. ...	E. de Senneville ...	705	273
Savannah	Savannah Sugar Est. Cy. Ld...	H. D. de Riquebourg.	880	788
St. Avold	F. Bour & Co.	A. Bour	780	592
St. Aubin	Société de St. Aubin	F. Nozaïc	800	948
St. Félix	Mrs. E. P. Dumat	E. Dumat	500	301
Terracine	Terracine S. E. Cy.	O. Pilot	1200	590
Chamouny	L. D'Emmerez & Co.	A. D'Unienville ...	800	210
Combo	Highlands Sugar Est. Cy. Ld ..	J. D. Campenon ...	800	431
Britannia	Oriental Estates Cy. Ld. ...	T. W. Innis	1500	905

DISTILLERIES.

Names of Proprietors.	Names of Distilleries.	Districts.
Mrs. H. Legall	Queen	Port Louis.
Hossen Cassim	Balaclava	Pamplemousses.
Heirs Lecudennec	Léonburg	do.
Mrs. C. Pitot	Avenir No. 1	do.
Widow Rouget	Constance	do.
Ahmun and others	Canton	do.
Mrs. H. Legall	Belle Vue	do.
Mrs. H. Legall	Mauricia	do.
F. Béguinot and J. Achard	Union	do.
Gourrège & Co.	La Paix	do.
A. Leblanc	Zund Nadel Gewlher ...	do.
Ww. Frédéric Fleuriot	Von Moltke	Rivière du Rempart.
Acyokoo & Co.	Pékin...	Flacq.
Heirs H. Tostée	Phœnix	do.
Nicles Bestel	Spa	do.
Mauritius Estates and Assets Cy. Ld. ...	Beau Champ	do.
F. Laroque	Bonne Veine	do.
Heirs A. Jadin	Petite Victoria... ...	do.
Mrs. G. Chauvet & Co.	Chauvet	do.
Jules B. de la Giroday	Bon Accueil	do.
T. Thierry	Les Mares	Grand Port.
A. de Rochecouste	Rivière La Chaux ...	do.
R. A. Morel	La Diète	do.
A. Daruty de Grandpré...	Mon Trésor	do.
J. Mortimer & Co.	Victoria	Savanne
James Bax	Belle Etoile	Plaines Wilhems.
A. Constantin	Galathée	do.
A. Arékion	Bonne Terre	do.
E. Victor	Avenir No. 2	Moka.
Baylis & Co.	Cognac	do.
Taw-Chien	Kah-hin	Black River.

Districts.	Name of Factory.	Owners.
Pamplemousses	Massilia	G. Martin & Co.
	Balaclava	Hossen Cassim.
	Léonbourg	Lecudenec.
	Mont Choisy	J. Constantin.
Rivière du Rempart ...	Mare Sèche...	E. Hourquebie.
	Belle Vue	C. Cugnet.
	L'Union	Mrs. A. D'Hotman.
	St. Antoine	de Chazal.
	Vale	Mrs. Cauvin.
	Melville	J. C. Marie.
	Mon Loisir	E. Rouillard.
Black River	Goblet	A. Kœnig.
	Mon Repos	F. D'Unienville.
	Beau Songe	P. Boissard.
	La Cantine... ...	B. Mellotte & Co.
	Charbonnière ...	B. Mellotte & Co.
	Les Rochers ...	Blyth, Brothers & Co.
	Le Bosquet... ...	Blyth, Brothers & Co.
	Gros Cailloux	G. Lagane.
	Palmyre	Blyth, Brothers & Co.
	Yemen	Pépin.
	Rivière Noire	E. Pierrot.
	Malgré Tout	A. Gérard.
	Les Salines...	A. Latapie.
	La Ferme	L. Vigoureux.
	Walhala	A. de Bragard.
	Tamarin	A. Mc Gregor.
	Kahin	Taw Chien & Co.
Plaines Wilhems	Plaisance	P. D'Unienville junior.
	Chebel	William Leblanc.
Flacq	Providence	E. Tostée.
Moka	Les Pailles	A. Martin.

A useful table for measuring land.

To aid in arriving at accuracy in estimating the amount of land in different fields under cul tivation, the following table may be found useful.

Yards wide.		Yards long.	Contains.	Feet wide.		Feet long.	Contains.
5	by	968	1 acre	60	by	726	1 acre.
10	„	484	do.	110	„	396	do.
20	„	242	do.	120	„	363	do.
40	„	121	do.	220	„	198	do.
70	„	69½	do.	240	„	181½	do.
80	„	60½	do.	440	„	99	do.

THE CASTLE MAIL PACKETS COMPANY LIMITED

ROYAL MAIL SERVICE

CAPE OF GOOD HOPE, NATAL, EAST AFRICA, MADAGASCAR, MAURITIUS.

PRO FORMA TIME TABLE—JANUARY TO JUNE 1896.

OUTWARD VOYAGES

London. Dep.	Southampton. Dep.	Cape Town. Dep.	Port Elizabeth. Arr.	East London Arr.	Natal. Arr.	Delagoa Bay Arr.	Madagascar (Tamatave). Arr.	Mauritius. Arr.
Jan. 3	Jan. 4	Jan. 28	Jan. 30	Feb. 2	Feb. 4	Feb. 9	Feb. 18	Feb. 20
Jan. 10	*Jan. 11*	*Feb. 1*	*Feb. 2*	*Feb. 5*	*Feb. 7*			
Jan. 31	Feb. 1	Feb. 25	Feb. 27	March 1	March 3	March 8	Mch. 17	Mch. 19
Feb. 7	*Feb. 8*	*Feb. 29*	*March 1*	*March 4*	*March 6*			
Feb. 28	Feb. 29	March 24	March 26	March 29	March 31	April 5	April 14	April 16
March 6	*Mch. 7*	*March 28*	*March 29*	*April 1*	*April 3*			
March 27	Mch. 28	April 21	April 23	April 26	April 28	May 3	May 12	May 14
April 3	*April 4*	*April 25*	*April 26*	*April 29*	*May 1*			
April‡ 24	Ap. 25	May 19	May 31	May 24	May 26	May 31	June 9	June 11
May 1	*May 2*	*May 23*	*May 24*	*May 27*	*May 29*			
May‡ 22	May 23	June 16	June 18	June 21	June 23	June 28	July 7	July 9
May 29	*May 30*	*June 20*	*June 21*	*June 24*	*June 26*			
June‡ 19	June 20	July 14	July 16	July 19	July 21	July 26	Aug. 4	Aug. 6
June 26	*June 27*	*July 18*	*July 19*	*July 22*	*July 24*			

HOME VOYAGES

Mauritius. Dep.	Madagascar. (Tamatave) Dep.	Delagoa Bay. Dep.	Natal. Dep.	East London Dep.	Port Elizabeth. Dep.	Cape Town. Dep.	Las Palmas. Call	London Arr.
1895			Dec. 17					
Dec. 7	Dec. 9	Dec. 15		Dec. 19	Dec. 23	Dec. 26	Jan. 11	Jan. 17
1896			Jan. 14					
Jan. 4	Jan. 6	Jan. 12		Jan. 16	Jan. 20	Jan. 23	Feb. 8	Feb. 14
Feb. 1	Feb. 3	Feb. 9	Feb. 11	Feb. 13	Feb. 17	Feb. 20	Mch. 7	March 13
Feb. 29	Mch. 2	March 8	March 10	March 12	March 16	March 19	April 4	April 10
Mch. 28	Mch. 30	April 5	April 7	April 9	April 13	April 16	May 2	May 8
Ap.‡ 25	Ap. 27	May 3	May 5	May 7	May 11	May 14	May 30	June 5
My.‡ 23	May 25	May 31	June 2	June 4	June 8	June 11	June 27	July 3
Jne‡ 20	June 22	June 28	June 30	July 2	July 6	July 9	July 25	July 31

Intermediate Service is shewn in ordinary type, Royal Mail Service in Italics.

‡ Call at St. Helena and Ascension.

Madagascar and Mauritius Service—Calls are made at Fort Dauphin, Manauzary, Vatoumandry, and other ports on the East Coast of Madagascar, when inducement offers.

COMPAGNIE DES MESSAGERIES MARITIMES

LIGNES DE L'OCEAN INDIEN

COTE ORIENTALE D'AFRIQUE—MADAGASCAR—ILES MASCAREIGNES

MARCHE DU SERVICE DU 1er JANVIER AU 31 DÉCEMBRE 1896

VOYAGES D'ALLER

Départ de	ARRIVÉES A											
Marseille	Pt. Saïd	Suez	Djibouti	Zanzibar	Mayotte	Majunga	Nossi-Bé	D.-Suarez	Ste Marie	Tamatave	Réunion	Maurice
10 Janvier	15 Jan.	16 Janvier	21 Janvier	28 Janvier	31 Janv.	1 Février	2 Février	3 Février	4 Fév.	5 Février	7 Février	8 Février
25 Janvier	30 Jan.	31 Janvier	5 Février	......	......	......	......	12 Février	......	14 Février	16 Février	18 Février
10 Février	15 Févr.	16 Février	21 Février	28 Février	2 Mars	3 Mars	4 Mars	5 Mars	6 Mars	7 Mars	9 Mars	10 Mars
25 Février	1 Mars	2 Mars	7 Mars	......	......	......	......	14 Mars	......	16 Mars	18 Mars	20 Mars
10 Mars	15 Mars	16 Mars	21 Mars	28 Mars	31 Mars	1 Avril	2 Avril	3 Avril	4 Avril	5 Avril	7 Avril	8 Avril
25 Mars	30 Mars	31 Mars	5 Avril	......	......	......	......	12 Avril	......	14 Avril	16 Avril	18 Avril
10 Avril	15 Avr.	16 Avril	21 Avril	28 Avril	1 Mai	2 Mai	3 Mai	4 Mai	5 Mai	6 Mai	8 Mai	9 Mai
25 Avril	30 Avr.	1 Mai	6 Mai	......	......	......	......	13 Mai	......	15 Mai	17 Mai	19 Mai
10 Mai	15 Mai	16 Mai	21 Mai	28 Mai	31 Mai	1 Juin	2 Juin	3 Juin	4 Juin	5 Juin	7 Juin	8 Juin
25 Mai	30 Mai	31 Mai	5 Juin	......	......	......	......	12 Juin	......	14 Juin	16 Juin	18 Juin
10 Juin	15 Juin	16 Juin	21 Juin	28 Juin	1 Juil.	2 Juillet	3 Juillet	4 Juillet	5 Juilt.	6 Juillet	8 Juillet	9 Juillet
25 Juin	30 Juin	1 Juillet	6 Juillet	......	......	......	......	13 Juillet	......	15 Juillet	17 Juillet	19 Juillet
10 Juillet	15 Juil.	16 Juillet	21 Juillet	28 Juillet	31 Juil.	1 Août	2 Août	3 Août	4 Août	5 Août	7 Août	8 Août
25 Juillet	30 Juil.	31 Juillet	5 Août	......	......	......	......	12 Août	......	14 Août	16 Aout	18 Août
10 Août	15 Août	16 Août	21 Août	28 Août	31 Août	1 Septem.	2 Septem.	3 Sept.	4 Sept.	5 Sept.	7 Sept.	8 Sept.
25 Août	30 Août	31 Août	5 Septem	......	......	......	......	12 Sept.	......	14 Sept.	16 Sept.	18 Sept.
10 Sept.	15 Sept.	16 Septem	21 Septem	28 Septem	1 Oct.	2 Octobre	3 Octobre	4 Octob.	5 Oct.	6 Octob.	8 Octob.	9 Octob.
25 Sept.	30 Sept.	1 Octobre	6 Octobre	......	......	......	......	13 Octob.	......	15 Octob.	17 Octob.	19 Octob.
10 Octob.	15 Oct.	16 Octobre	21 Octobre	28 Octobre	31 Oct.	1 Novemb.	2 Novem.	3 Novem.	4 Nov.	5 Novem.	7 Novem.	8 Novem.
25 Octob.	30 Oct.	31 Octobre	5 Novem.	......	......	......	......	12 Novem.	......	14 Novem.	16 Novem.	18 Novem.
10 Novem.	15 Nov.	16 Novem.	21 Novem.	28 Novem.	1 Déc.	2 Décem.	3 Décem.	4 Décem.	5 Déc.	6 Décem.	8 Décem.	9 Décem.
25 Novem.	30 Nov.	1 Décem.	6 Décem.	......	......	......	......	13 Décem.	......	15 Décem.	17 Décem.	19 Décem.
10 Décem.	15 Déc.	16 Décem.	21 Décem.	28 Décem.	31 Déc.	1 Jan. /97	2 Jan. /97	3 Jan. /97	4 Jan./97	5 Jan. /97	7 Jan. /97	8 Jan. /97
25 Décem.	30 Déc.	31 Décem.	5 Jan. /97	......	......	......	......	12 Jan. /97	......	14 Jan. /97	16 Jan. /97	18 Jan. /97

VOYAGE DE RETOUR

Départs de Maurice	ARRIVÉES A											
	Réunion	Tamatave	Ste. Marie	Diégo Suarez	Nossi-Bé	Majunga	Mayotte	Zanzibar.	Djibouti	Suez	Port-Saïd	Marseille.
15 Fév.	16 Fév.	18 Fév.	......	20 Fév.	......	......	......	......	28 Fév.	4 Mars	5 Mars	10 Mars
1 Mars	2 Mars	4 Mars	5 Mars	6 Mars	8 Mars	9 Mars	10 Mars	12 Mars	19 Mars	24 Mars	25 Mars	31 Mars
15 Mars	16 Mars	18 Mars	......	20 Mars	......	......	......	......	28 Mars	2 Avril	3 Avril	8 Avril
30 Mars	31 Mars	2 Avril	3 Avril	4 Avril	6 Avril	7 Avril	8 Avril	10 Avril	17 Avril	22 Avril	23 Avril	29 Avril
15 Avril	16 Avril	18 Avril	......	20 Avril	......	......	......	......	28 Avril	3 Mai	4 Mai	9 Mai
30 Avril	1 May	3 Mai	4 Mai	5 Mai	7 Mai	8 Mai	9 Mai	11 Mai	18 Mai	23 Mai	24 Mai	30 Mai
15 Mai	16 Mai	18 Mai	......	20 Mai	......	......	......	......	28 Mai	2 Juin	3 Juin	8 Juin
30 Mai	31 Mai	2 Juin	3 Juin	4 Juin	6 Juin	7 Juin	8 Juin	10 Juin	17 Juin	22 Juin	23 Juin	29 Juin
15 Juin	16 Juin	18 Juin	......	20 Juin	......	......	......	......	28 Juin	3 Juillet	4 Juillet	9 Juillet
30 Juin	1 Juil.	3 Juillet	4 Juil.	5 Juillet	7 Juillet	8 Juillet	9 Juillet	11 Juillet	18 Juil.	23 Juillet	24 Juillet	30 Juillet
15 Juillet	16 Juil.	18 Juillet	......	20 Juillet	......	......	......	......	28 Juil.	2 Août	3 Août	8 Août
30 Juillet	31 Juil.	2 Août	3 Août	4 Août	6 Août	7 Août	8 Août	10 Août	17 Août	22 Août	23 Août	29 Août
15 Août	16 Août	18 Août	......	20 Août	......	......	......	......	28 Août	2 Sept.	3 Sept.	8 Sept.
30 Août	31 Août	2 Sept.	3 Sept.	4 Sept.	6 Sept.	7 Sept.	8 Sept.	10 Sept.	17 Sept.	22 Sept.	23 Sept.	29 Sept.
15 Sept.	16 Sept.	18 Sept.	......	20 Sept.	......	......	......	......	28 Sept	3 Octob.	4 Octob.	9 Oct.
30 Sept.	1 Oct.	3 Oct.	4 Oct.	5 Oct.	7 Octob.	8 Oct.	9 Oct.	11 Octob.	18 Oct.	23 Octob.	24 Octob.	30 Oct.
15 Oct.	16 Oct.	18 Oct.	......	20 Oct.	......	......	......	......	28 Oct.	2 Nov.	3 Nov.	8 Nov.
30 Oct.	31 Oct.	2 Nov.	3 Nov.	4 Nov.	6 Nov.	7 Nov.	8 Nov.	10 Nov.	17 Nov.	22 Nov.	23 Nov.	29 Nov.
15 Nov.	16 Nov.	18 Nov.	......	20 Nov.	......	......	......	......	28 Nov.	3 Dec.	4 Décem.	9 Déc.
30 Nov.	1 Déc.	3 Dec.	4 Déc.	5 Déc.	7 Déc.	8 Déc.	9 Déc.	11 Déc.	18 Déc.	23 Dec.	24 Décem.	30 Dec.
15 Déc.	16 Déc.	18 Dec.	......	20 Déc.	......	......	......	......	28 Déc.	2 Jan./97	3 Jan. /97	8 Jan. 97
30 Déc.	31 Déc.	2 Jan./97	3 Jan./97	4 Jan./97	6 Jan. /97	7 Jan./97	8 Jan./97	10 Jan./97	17 Jan.97	22 Jan./97	22 Jan. /97	29 Jan. 97

1er. Janvier 1896.

BRITISH INDIA STEAM NAVIGATION COMPANY LIMITED

CALCUTTA, COLOMBO AND MAURITIUS, 1896.

OUTWARD				INWARD			
LONDON	CALCUTTA	COLOMBO	MAURITIUS	MAURITIUS	COLOMBO	CALCUTTA	LONDON
Mails Leave *Friday*	Leave *Wednesday*	Leave *Saturday*	Arrive *Wednesday*	Leave *Friday*	Leave *Tuesday*	Arrive *Tuesday*	Mails arrive *Wednesday*
17 January	29 Jan.	8 Feb.	19 Feb.	6 March	17 March	24 March	8 April
14 February	26 Feb.	7 March	18 March	3 April	14 April	21 April	6 May
13 March	25 March	4 April	15 April	1 May	12 May	19 May	3 June
10 April	22 April	2 May	13 May	29 May	9 June	16 June	1 July
8 May	20 May	30 May	10 June	26 June	7 July	14 July	29 July
5 June	17 June	27 June	8 July	24 July	4 Aug.	11 Aug.	26 August
3 July	15 July	25 July	5 Aug.	21 Aug.	1 Sept.	8 Sept.	23 Sept.
31 July	12 Aug.	22 Aug.	2 Sept.	18 Sept.	29 Sept.	6 Oct.	21 October
28 August	9 Sept.	19 Sept.	30 Sept.	16 Oct.	27 Oct.	3 Nov.	18 Novemb.
25 Sept.	7 Oct.	17 Oct.	28 Oct.	13 Nov.	24 Nov.	1 Dec.	16 Decemb.
23 Oct.	4 Nov.	14 Nov.	25 Nov.	11 Dec.	22 Dec.	29 Dec.	13 Janu./97
20 Nov.	2 Dec.	12 Dec.	23 Dec.	8 Jan./97	19 Jan./97	26 Jan./97	10 February
18 Dec.	30 Dec.	9 Jan./97	20 Jan./97	5 Feb.	16 Feb.	23 Feb.	10 March

HOME PASSAGE RATES.

From Mauritius.		Single fare	6 Mos. Return.	12 Mos. Return.
Naples	1st. Class	Rs. 600	Rs. 1,130	Rs. 1,265
	2nd. "	" 400	" 790	" 845
London (viâ Naples including railway fare)	1st. Class	" 775	" 1,455	" 1,600
	2nd. "	" 525	" 1,000	" 1,100
Plymouth or London } by sea	1st. Class	" 650	" 1,220	" 1,340
	2nd. "	" 425	" 800	" 870

The periods quoted above for return tickets are calculated from date of embarkation to the time of return to Mauritius.

European Nurse or Maid occupying first class berth but not messing with Stewardess, two thirds of first class fare.

Children of three and upwards to ten years of age, half fare. One child under three years, if with parent, free;—each additional child under three, at quarter fare.

To bona-fide members of one family a reduction of 10 o/o is allowed on single first class tickets if equivalent of three full fares is paid, and 15 o/o for equivalent of four full fares.

Passengers from England, who return within six months from the date of debarkation, are allowed a reduction of 20 o/o on the above rates, and within twelve months 10 o/o, provided full single fares were paid for the outward voyage. Similarly Passengers returning to Mauritius, are allowed the same reduction on the outward sterling rates.

BAGGAGE ALLOWANCE.

1st-Class, 3 cwt. or 40 c. ft. 2nd-Class, $1\frac{1}{2}$ cwt. or 20 c. ft.

Half allowance for children at half fares. Any baggage in excess will be charged for on board at the rate of ten shillings per cwt., or one shilling per cubic foot.

Passengers' baggage must contain their personal effects only, and it is carried at their own risk and under their sole charge. It is particularly requested that all baggage should be clearly marked, and the Company provide labels specially designed for the purpose.

PASSAGE RATES ON LOCAL SERVICE FROM MAURITIUS.

Colombo	... Single fare 1st Class Rs. 200	2nd. Class Rs. 125	
Madras	... "	220	" 140
Calcutta or Bombay	"	250	" 150

Calcutta or Bombay } Return tickets available for six months are issued to first class passengers only at a reduction of 10 o/o on the double fare.

Passengers for Australia tranship at Colombo into the steamers of the Peninsular and Oriental or the Orient Company which leave that port every alternate Monday or Tuesday. Passages can be booked through:—

To Albany, Adelaide Melbourne or Sydney	First Class... Rs. 600.
	Second Class 400.

Ships building for the Royal Navy.

Names.	No. of guns.	No. of Tons.	Horse Power.	Kind of Vessel.	Where being constructed.
Andromeda ...	...	......	......	First class cruiser	Pembroke
Arrogant ...	10	5750	10000	Screw cruiser	Devenport
Brazen	6	......	......	Torpedo-boat destroyer ...	Glasgow
Cæsar	16	14900	12000	Armoured battle ship... ...	Portsmouth
Desperate ...	6	......	5400	Torpedo-boat destroyer ...	Chiswick
Diana	11	5600	9600	Second class cruiser	Glasgow
Dido	11	5600	9600	Do.	Do.
Doris	11	5600	9600	Do.	Barrow-in-Furness
Electra	6	......	......	Torpedo-boat destroyer ...	Glasgow
Fame	6	......	5400	Do.	Chiswick
Fervent	6	......	3850	Do.	Paisley
Foam	6	......	5400	Do.	Chiswick
Furious	10	5750	10000	Second class cruiser	Devenport
Gladiator ...	10	5750	10000	Do.	Portsmouth
Hannibal ...	16	14900	12000	Armoured first class battle ship	Pembroke Dock
Hardy	6	......	4000	Torpedo-boat destroyer ...	Sunderland
Hart	6	......	4000	Do.	Glasgow
Hasty	6	......	3200	Do.	Poplar
Haughty... ...	6	......	4000	Do.	Sunderland
Hunter	6	......	4000	Do.	Glasgow
Illustrious ...	16	14900	12000	Armoured first class battle ship	Chatham
Isis	11	5600	9600	Second class cruiser	Glasgow
Juno	11	5600	9600	Do.	Barrow-in-Furness
Jupitor	16	14900	12000	Armoured first class battle ship	Glasgow (completing)
Mallard	6	......	5400	Torpedo-boat destroyer ...	Chiswick
Mars	16	14900	12000	Armoured first class battle ship	Birkenhead
Opossum ...	6	......	4000	Torpedo-boat destroyer ...	Newcastle-on-Tyne
•Pelorus	8	2135	7000	Third class cruiser	Sheerness
Porcupine ...	6	......	3900	Torpedo-boat destroyer ...	Jarrow-on-Tyne
Powerful ...	14	14200	25000	First class cruiser	Barrow-in-Furness
Proserpine ...	8	2135	7000	Third class cruiser	Sheerness
Quail	6	......	6000	Torpedo-boat destroyer ...	Birkenhead
Ranger	6	......	4000	Do.	Newcastle-on-Tyne
Recruit	6	......	......	Do.	Glasgow
Skate	6	......	4000	Do.	Barrow-in-Furness
Sparrowhawk ...	6	......	6000	Do.	Birkenhead
Spitfire	6	......	4000	Do.	Newcastle-on-Tyne
Starfish	6	......	4000	Do.	Barrow-in-Furness — (completing.)
Sturgeon ...	6	......	4000	Do.	Do.
Sunfish	6	......	4000	Do.	Newcastle-on-Tyne
Swordfish ...	6	......	4000	Do.	Do.
Teazer	6	......	4500	Do.	Cowes
Thrasher ...	6	......	6000	Do.	Birkenhead
Vindictive ...	10	5750	10000	Second class cruiser	Chatham
Virago	6	......	6000	Torpedo-boat destroyer ...	Birkenhead
Vulture	6	......	......	Do.	Glasgow
Wizard	6	......	4500	Do.	Cowes
Zebra	6	......	4500	Do.	Blackwall
Zephyr	6	......	3850	Do.	Paisley

Bonaventure...	10 guns,	4360 tons,		9000 horse power		(carrying the flag of Rear Admirl Edmond Charles Drummond) Captain Richard Nizel Gresley.
Brisk ...	... 6	,,	1770	,,	3500	,,	Commander Fred. St G. Rich.
Cossack	... 6	,,	1770	,,	3800	,,	Commander William B. Fisher.
Lapwing	... 6	,,	805	,,	1200	,,	Lieut. and Commander Richard H. Story.
Marathon	... 6	,,	2950	,,	9000	,,	Capitain Robert, B. Maconochie.
Pigeon...	... 6	,,	755	,,	1200	,,	Lieut. and Commander Montague G. Cartwright
Sphinx*	... 5	,,	1130	,,	1100	,,	Commander Casper J. Baker.

Time and Watch on Board Ship.

WATCH.—For the purposes of discipline, and to divide the work fairly the crew is mustered in two divisions : the Starboard right side, looking toward the head), and the Port. (left) The day commences at noon, and is thus divided.

Afternoon	*Watch*	... ... noon to 4 p.m.
First Dog	,,	... ... 4 p.m. to 6. p.m.
Second Dog	,,	... ... 6 p·m. to 8. p. m.
First	,,	... ... 8 p.m. to midnight
Middle	,,	... ... 12 a. m. to 4 a. m.
Morning	,,	... ... 4. a. m. to 8. a.m.
Forenoon	,,	... ... 8. a. m. to noon.

This makes seven Watches, which enables the crews to keep them alternately as the *Watch* which comes on duty at noon one day has the afternoon next day, and the men who have only four hours'rest one night have eight hours the next. This is the reason for having *Dog Watches*, which are made by dividing the hours between 4 p. m. and 8 p. m. into two *Watches*

TIME.—Time is kept by means of " Bells, " although there is but one bell on the ship, and to strike the clapper properly against the bell requires some skill. The times are 8 bells at noon, at 4. m., 8 p.m midnight, 4. a m. and 8 a. m.

First two strokes of the clapper at the interval of a second, than an interval of two seconds ; then two more strokes with a second's interval apart, then a rest of two seconds, thus :—

BELL, ONE SECOND B., TWO SECS. ; B. s. B. s. s.; B. B. s. s.; B.

1. Bell is struck at 12.30, and again at 4.30. 6.30, 8.30 p. m. ; 12.30, 4.30 and 8.20 a.m.
2. Bells at 1 (struck with an interval of a second between each B. s. B.), the same again at 5, 7, and 9 p. m. ; 5 an 9 a. m.
3. Bells at 1.30 (B. s., B. s.s., B.), 5.30 7.30 and 9.30 p.m. ; 1.30, 5.30, and 9.30 a.m.
4. Bells at 2 B. s. (B. s.s., B.) 6 and 10 p. m. ; 2, 6 and 10 a.m.
5. Bells at 2.30 (B. s., B. s.s., B. s. B. s.s. B. and 10.30 p. m. ; 2.30 6.30 and 10.30 a. m.)
6. Bells at 3 (B. s., B. s.s., B. s., B. s.s., B. s., B·) and 11 p. m. ; 3, 7 and 11 a. m.
7. Bells at (B. s., B. s.s., B. s., B. s. s., B. s., B. s.s. B) and 11.30 p. m. : 3.30,7.30 and 11.30 a.m.
8. Bells (B. s., B. s.s., B. s, B. s.s., B. s., B. s.s., B. s., B.) every four hours as above.

Colours of Government " Blue Books. "

The English Official colour is ...	*Blue*
The French	*Yellow*
The Germain	*White*
The Austrian... ...	*Red*
The Italian	*Green*

Superficial feet in a board or plank.

Is known by multiplying the length by the breadth. If the board be tapering, add the breadth of the two ends together, and take half their sum for the mean breadth and multiply the length by this mean breadth.

The Institute of France.

The French Academy is composed of 40 members elected for life, and is the highest of the five Academies constituted the *Institute of France.*

The special object of this institution is the composition of the historical Dictionary of the French language. It was founded in 1635 by Cardinal Richelieu, and re-organized in 1816. The other Academies are as follows :—

Académie des Inscriptions et Belles-Lettres, founded in 1663, 40 members.

* Paddle Steamer

Académie des Sciences, founded in 1666, divided into 11 Sections, each of which comprises 6 members.

Académie des Beaux-Arts, 5 sections comprising 40 members as follows :—Painting, 14 members; Sculpture, 8; Architecture, 8; Engraving, 4; Musical composition, 6.

Académie des Sciences Morales et Politiques (for the study of questions of social and political economy), founded 1832, 40 members, 5 sections.

All the Academies, with the exception of the Académie Française, elect a certain number of honorary members and of foreign correspondents.

Members of the Academie Française.

Legouvé, Ernest Wilfrid Gabriel Jean Baptiste, born in Paris, 1807, elected March 1855 predecessor Ancelot.
Broglie, Duc de, Jacques Victor Albert, b. in Paris, 1821 e. 20 Feb, 1862, p. Lacordaire (father).
Ollivier, Ollivier Emile, b. at Marseilles, 1825, e. 7 April 1870, p. de Lamartine.
Aumale, Duc d', Henri Eugène Philippe Louis d'Orléans, b. in Paris 1822, e. 30 December 1871, p. Count de Montalembert.
Mezières, Alfred Jean François, b. in Paris 1826, e. 29 January, p. St. Marc-Girardin.
Dumas, Alexandre, b. in Paris 1824, e. 29 January 1874 p. Lebrun.
Simon, Jules François. b. at Lorient, 1814, e. 16 December 1876, p. De Remusat.
Boissier, Marie Louis Antoine Gaston, b. at Nîmes. 1823, e. 8 June 1876, p. Patin.
Sardou, Victorien, b. in Paris, 1831, e. 7 June 1877, p. Autran.
Audifiret-Pasquier, Duc d', Edmond Armand Gaston, b. in Paris, 1823, e. 24 December 1878, p. Bishop Dupanlou.
Rousse, Aimé Joseph Edmond, b. in Paris, 1817, e. 13 May 1880, p. Jules Favre.
Sully-Prudhomme, René François Armand, b. in Paris, 1839, e. 8 December 1881, p. Duvergier de Hauranne.
Cherbuliez, Charles Victor, b. at Geneva, 1829, e. 8 December 1881, p. Dufaure.
Perraud, Adolphe Louis Albert, Bishop of Autun, b. at Lyons, 1828, e. June 1882, p. Augustin Barbier.
Pailleron, Edouard Jules Henri, b. in Paris, e. 7th. December 1882, p. Charles Blanc.
Coppé, François Edouard Joachim, b. in Paris, 1842, e. 21 Febrnary 1884, p. De Laprade.
Bertrand, Joseph Louis François, b. in Paris, 1822, e. 4 December 1884, p. J. Dumas.
Halévy, Ludovic, b. in Paris, 1834, e. 4 December 1884, p. Count d'Haussonville.
Say, Jean Baptiste Léon, born in Paris, 1816, e. 11 February 1886, p. About.
Hervé, Aimé Marie Edouard, born at St. Denis, Island of Réunion, 1835, e. 11 February 1885, p Duc de Noailles.
Gréard, Vallery Clément Octave, born at Vire, 1828, e. 18 November 1886, p. Count de Faloux.
Houssonville, le Comte Othenin Paul Gabriel de Cléron d', born at Guercy-le-Chatel (Seine and Marne), 21 September 1843, e. January 1888, p. Caro.
Claretie, Jules Arnaud Arsène, b. at Limoges, 3 Dec. 1840, e. 26 January 1888, p. Cuvillier-Fleury.
Meilhac, Henri, b. at Paris, 23 January 1830, e. 26 April 1889, p. Labiche.
Vogué, Viscount Eugène Marie Melchior de, b. at Paris, e. 22 November 1888, p. Désiré Nizard.
Freycinet, Charles Louis de, b. at Foix, 14 Dec. 1828, e. 10 December 1890, p. Emile Augier.
Viaud, Jean (Pierre Loti), b. at Rochefort, July 1850, e. 21 May 1891, p. Octave Feuillet.
Lavisse, Ernest, b. at Nouvien-en-Thierache (Aisne), 17 Dec. 1842, e. 2 June 1892, p. Jurien de la Gravière.
Bornier, le Vicomte Etienne Charles Henri de, b. at Lunel, 25 Dec. 1825, e. 3 Feb. 1893, p. Marmier.
Thureau-Dangin, Paul Marie Pierre, b. in Paris, 12 Dec. 1837, e. 2 February 1893, p. Rousset.
Challemel-Lacour, Paul Armand, b. at Avranches, 19 May 1827, e. 23 March 1893, p. Renan.
Brunetière, Marie Ferdinand, b. at Toulon, 19 July 1849, e. 8 June 1893, p. Lemoinne.
Heredis, José Maria de, b. at Santiago de Cuba, 22 Nov. 1842, e. 22 Feb. 1894, p. de Mazade.
Sorel, Albert, b. at Honfleur, 13 August 1842, e. 31 May 1894, p. Taine.
Bourget, Paul Charles Joseph, b. at Amiens, 21 Nov. 1852, e. 31 May 1894, p. Maxime Du Camp.
Houssaye, Henri, b. 1858, e. 6 December 1894, p. Leconte de Lisle.
Lemaitre, Jules, b. at Vennecy (Loiret), 27 April 1853, e. 20 June 1895, p. Duruy.

3 Vacant Fauteils.

Permanent Secretary and Treasurer, Charles Camille Doucet.
Chef du Secrétariat et Agent Spécial, M. Julia Pingard.

Offices: Palais de l'Institut, 23 Quai Conti, Paris.

The Rule of the Road.

The Rule of the Road is a paradox quite
For in driving your carriage along,
If you turn to the left you are sure to go right
If you turn to the right you go wrong.

But in walking the streets t'is a different case ;
To the right it is proper to steer ;
On the left there should be enough of clear space
For the people who wish to walk there.

Another Reading.

The rule of the *path*
To get well along
Is " keep to the right "
And you cannot go wrong

The rule of the *road*
Is a paradox quite
If you keep to the left
You are sure to be right.

Light and Sound,

Light travels at the rate of 186,660 miles per second, and takes 8 minutes, 18 seconds to travel from the Sun to the Earth. Any phenomenon, therefore, occurring on the surface of the sun is not observed by an inhabitant of the globe till that time afterwards.

Sound travels in still air at the freezing point, at the rate of 1,090 feet per second, and the report of gun one mile distant would not be heard till nearly 5 seconds after the flash was seen.

The moisture of the air and the direction of the wind, as well as the temperature, would, to some extent, modify the time elapsing between the flash and the report.

Magnetic Pulleys.

To increase the tug of pulleys a French engineer has magnetised them, so that they can grip the chain passing over them with greater force. The principle has been applied to a number of tow-barges, and fewer pulleys are required than by the old system. Mr. Edison has adopted the same principle in the case of belting for the transmission of power. The belt is made partially of iron, and is therefore attracted to the magnetic pulley.

Greatest Known Ocean Depths.

The greatest known depth of the Ocean is midway between the islands of Tristan d'Acunha and the month of the Rio de la Plata. The bottom was here reached at a depth of 46,236 feet or 8 ¾ miles exceeding by more than 17,000 feet the height of Mount Evarest, the loftiest mountain in the world.

In the North Atlantic Ocean, south of Newfoundland, soundings have been made to a depth of 4.580 fathoms or 27.480 feet while depths equalling 34,000 feet, or 6 ½ miles are reported South of the Burmuda Islands. The average depth of the Pacific Ocean between Japan and California, is a little over 2000 fathoms ; between Chili and the Sandwich Islands 2,500 fathoms ; and between Chili and New Zealand 4,500 fathoms. The average depth of all the Oceans is from 2,000 to 3,000 fathoms.

Facts Worth Knowing.

There are 2,754 languages.
Envelopes were first used in 1839.
Telescopes were invented in 1590.
The first steel pen was made in 1830.
Watches were first constructed in 1476.
The first iron steam ship was built in 1830.
The first lucifer match was made in 1829.
The average humain life is 31 years
Space has a temperature of 200 degrees below zero.
The Telephone was invented in 1861.
The Chinese invented paper, 170 B. C.
The Pianoforte was invented in 1710.
Printing was known in China in the 6th Century, introduced into England about 1474 America 1536.
Two persons die every second,

The Silk Spider.

The *halaba* a large spider of Madagascar, which produces a thick strong silk of a golden hue is being domesticated by the French savants at Antananarivo, in order to make it serviceable for industrial purposes. Very strong and beautiful fabrics can be made from the fibre.

Business Laws in Brief.

Ignorance of the law excuses no one.
An agreement without consideration is void.
Signatures made with a lead pencil are good in law.
A receipt for money paid is not legally conclusive.
The acts of one partner bind all the others.
Contracts made on Sunday cannot be enforced.
A contract made with a minor or a lunatic is void.
Principals are responsible for the acts of their Agents.
Agents are responsible to their principals for errors.
Each individual in a partnership is responsible for the whole amount of the debt of the firm.
A note given by a minor is void.
Notes bear interest only when so stated.
It is not legally necessary to say on a note " for value received."
A note drawn on Sunday is void.
If a note be lost or stolen, it does not release the maker, he must pay it.
It is a fraud to conceal a fraud.
The law compels no one to do impossibilities.
A personal right of action dies with the person.
An oral agreement must be proved by evidence. A written agreement proves itself. The law prefers written to oral evidence, because of its precision.

Help in Case of Accidents.

Drowning.—1. Loosen clothing, if any. 2. Empty lungs of water by laying body on its stomach, and lifting it up in the middle, so that the head hangs down. Jerk the body a few times. 3. Pull tongue forward, using handkerchief, or pin with string if necessary. 4. Imitate motion of respiration by alternately compressing and expanding the lower ribs, about twenty times a minute. Alternately raising and lowering the arms from the sides, up above the head, will stimulate the action of the lungs. Let it be done gently but persistently. 5. Apply warmth and friction to extremities. 6. By holding tongue forward, closing the nostrils, and pressing the " Adam's apple back " (so as to close entrance to stomach), direct inflation may be tried. Take a deep breath and breathe it forcibly into the mouth of the patient, compress the chest to expel the air, and repeat the operation. 7. DON'T GIVE UP ! People have have been saved after hours of patient, vigorous effort. 8. When breathing begins, get patient into a warm bed, give warm drinks, or spirits in teaspoonfuls, fresh air and quiet.

Burns and Scalds.—Cover with cooking soda and lay wet clothes over it. White of eggs and Olive oil. Olive oil or Linseed oil, plain, or mixed with chalk or whiting. Sweet or Olive oil and lime-water.

Lightning.—Dash cold water over a person struck.

Sunstroke.—Loosen clothing. Get patient into shade, and apply ice-cold water to head. Keep head in elevated position.

Mad Dog or Snake Bite.—Tie cord tight above the wound. Suck the wound and cauterize with caustic or white-hot iron at once, or cut out adjoining parts with a sharp knife. Give stimulants, as whiskey, brandy, etc.

Stings of Venomous Insects, etc.—Apply weak ammonia, oil, salt, water, or iodine.

Fainting.—Place flat on back ; allow fresh air, and sprinkle with water. Place head lower than rest of body.

Tests of death.—Hold mirror to mouth. If living, moisture will gather. Push pin into flesh. If dead the hole will remain, if alive it will close up. Place finger in front of a strong light ; if alive, they will appear red ; if dead, black or dark.

Fire in one's clothing.—Don't run—especially not down stairs or out-of-doors. Roll on carpet, or wrap in woollen rug, wet if possible. Cut holes for the eyes. Don't get excited.

Fire from Kerosene.—Don't use water, it will spread the flames. Dirt, sand, or flour is the best extinguisher, or smother with woollen rug, tablecloth, or carpet.

Digestion of Food.

The following Table shows the time in hours and minutes, required for the digestion of the more common articles of food.

Articles of Diet.	Mode of preparation.	Time required for digestion	Articles of Diet.	Mode of preparation	Time required for digestion
		H. M.			H. M.
Gelatine	Boiled ...	2 30	Green corn	Boiled ...	3 45
Pig's feet, soused ...	,, ...	1 0	Fowls, domestic	,, ...	4 0
Tripe	,, ...	1 0	,, ,, ...	Roasted ...	4 0
Brains	,, ...	1 45	Ducks, ,, ...	,, ...	4 0
Venison steak	Broiled ...	1 35	,, wild	,, ...	4 30
Turkey, domestic ...	Roasted ...	2 30	Suet, beef, fresh	,, ...	5 0
,, ,, ...	Boiled ...	2 25	,, mutton	,, ...	4 30
,, wild	Roasted ...	2 18	Butter	Melted ...	3 30
Goose	,, ...	2 30	Cheese, old, strong ...	Raw ...	3 30
Pig, sucking	,, ...	2 30	Soup, Beef, vegetables, bread	Boiled ...	4 0
Liver, Beef's, fresh ...	Broiled ...	2 0	Soup, marrow-bones ...	,, ...	4 15
Lamb, fresh	,, ...	2 30	,, beans	,, ...	3 0
Chicken, full-grown ...	Fricassee ...	2 45	,, barley	,, ...	1 30
Eggs, Fresh	Hard boiled.	3 30	,, mutton	,, ...	3 30
,, ,, ...	Soft ...	3 0	Chicken soup	,, ...	3 0
,, ,, ...	Fried ...	3 30	Oyster	,, ...	3 30
,, ,, ...	Roasted ...	2 15	Hash, meat & vegetables.	Warmed ...	2 30
,, ,, ...	Raw ...	2 0	Sausage, fresh	Broiled ...	3 20
,, whipped	,, ...	2 0	Heart, animal	Fried ...	4 0
Codfish, cured, dry ...	Boiled ...	2 0	Custard	Baked ...	2 45
Trout, salmon, fresh ...	,, ...	1 30	Beans, pod	Boiled ...	2 30
,, ,, ...	Fried ...	1 30	Bread, wheaten, fresh ...	Baked ...	3 30
Flounder, fresh... ...	,, ...	3 30	,, corn	,, ...	3 15
Salmon, salted	Boiled ...	4 0	Cake	,, ...	3 0
Oysters, fresh	Raw ...	2 55	,, sponge	,, ...	2 30
,, ,, ...	Roasted ...	3 15	Rice	Boiled ...	1 0
,, ,, ...	Stewed ...	3 30	Sago	,, ...	1 45
Beef, fresh lean ...	Roasted ...	3 0	Tapioca	,, ...	2 0
,, dry	,, ...	3 30	Barley	,, ...	2 0
,, steak	Broiled ...	3 0	Milk	,, ...	2 0
,, with salt only ...	Boiled ...	2 45	,, ...	Raw ...	2 15
,, with mustard, &c.	,, ...	3 30	Dumpling, apple	Boiled ...	3 0
,, fresh, lean ...	Fried ...	4 0	Apples, sour and hard ...	Raw ...	2 50
,, old, hard, salted...	Boiled ...	4 15	,, ,, mellow ...	,, ...	2 0
Pork steak	Broiled ...	3 15	,, sweet	,, ...	1 30
,, fat and lean ...	Roasted ...	5 15	Parsnips	Boiled ...	2 30
,, recently salted ...	Boiled ...	4 30	Carrot, orange	,, ...	3 15
,, ...	Fried ...	4 15	Beet	,, ...	3 45
,, ...	Broiled ...	3 15	Turnips, flat	,, ...	3 30
,, ...	Raw ...	3 0	Potatoes	,, ...	3 30
,, ...	Stewed ...	3 0	,, ...	Roasted ...	2 30
Mutton, fresh	Roasted ...	3 15	,, ...	Baked ...	2 30
,, ...	Broiled ...	3 0	Cabbage-head	Raw ...	2 30
,, ...	Boiled ...	3 0	,, with vinegar ...	,, ...	2 0
Veal, fresh	Broiled ...	4 0	,, ,, ,, ...	Boiled ...	4 30
,, ...	Fried ...	4 30			

Contagious and Eruptive Diseases.

It will often relieve a mother's anxiety to know how long after a child has been exposed to a contagious disease there is danger that the disease has been contracted.

The following tables gives the *period of incubation*—or anxious period—and other information concerning the more important diseases.

Disease.	Anxious period ranges from	Symptoms usually appear.	Patient is infectious.
Chicken-pox	within 14 days ...	10—18 days ...	Until all scabs have fallen off.
Diphtheria	„ 2 „ ...	2— 5 „ ...	14 days after disappearance of membrane.
Measles	„ 14 „ ...	10—14 „ ...	* Until scaling and cough have ceased.
Mumps	„ 10-12 „ ...	16—24 „ ...	14 days from commencement.
Scarlet Fever... ...	„ 4 „ ...	1— 7 „ ...	Until all scaling has ceased.
Small-Pox	„ 12-17 „ ...	1—14 „ ...	Until all scabs have fallen off.
Typhoid Fever ...	„ 11 „ ...	1—28 „ ...	Until diarrhœa ceases.
Whooping-cough ...	„ 14 „ ...	7—14 „ ...	† 6 weeks from beginning to whoop.

The following points may help to determine the nature of a suspicious illness :—

Character of Rash or Eruption	Date of appearance.	Disease.	Duration in days.	Remarks.
Small rose-pimples changing to vesicles.	2nd. day of fever or after 24 hours' illness.	Chicken-pox.	6— 7	Scabs from about 4th. day of fever.
Diffuse redness and swelling.	2nd. or 3rd. day of illness.	Erysipelas...	......	High fever and severe pain.
Small red dots like flea-bites.	4th. day of fever, or after 72 hours' illness.	Measles ...	6—10	Rash fades on 7th. day.
Bright scarlet, diffused..	2nd. day of fever, or after 24 hours' illness.	Scarlet fever	8—19	Rash fades on 5th. day.
Small red pimples changing to vesicles then pustules.	3rd. day of fever, or after 48 hours' illness.	Small-pox ...	14—21	Scabs from 9th. or 18th. day, fall off about 14th.
Rose-coloured spots scattered.	7th. to 14th. day ...	Typhoid fever.	22—30	Accompanied by diarrhœa.

* In measles the patient is infectious 3 days before the eruption appears.

† In whooping-cough the patient is infectious during the primary cough, which may be three weeks before the whooping begins.

The Queen.

The Queen reigns in her own right, holding the Crown both by inheritance and election. Her legal title rests on the Statute 12 and 13 Will. III C. 3 by which the succession to the Crown of Great Britain and Ireland was settled on the death of King William and Queen Anne without issue, on the Princess Sophia of Hanover, and the " heirs of her body being Protestants."

The inheritance thus limited descended to George I, son and heir of Princess Sophia, she having died before Queen Anne; and it has ever since continued in a regular course of descent.

Guide to the gestation and incubation of Domestic Animals.

KIND.	Age for reproduction.	Duration of reproduction.	Number of Females for one Male.	Period of Gestation and Incubation.		
				Shortest No. of days.	Mean No. of days.	Longest No. of days.
Bull	3 years	5 years	30 to 40	......	......	......
Boar	1 ,,	6 ,,	6 to 10	......	......	......
Bitch	2 ,,	8 ,,	......	55	60	83
Buck Rabbit	6 months	6 ,,	25 to 30	......	......	......
Cow	3 years	10 ,,	......	240	283	321
Cock	6 months	6 ,,	12 to 15	......	......	......
Dog	2 years	9 ,,	......	......	......	......
Doe Rabbit	6 months	6 ,,	......	20	28	35
Duck	9 ,,	6 ,,	......	28	38	33
Ewe	2 years	6 ,,	......	146	154	161
Goose	9 months	7 ,,	......	27	30	33
Hen	9 ,,	3 to 5	......	......	21	24
Mare	4 years	12 ,,	......	322	347	419
Ostrich	4 ,,	......	1	42	42 to 46	50
Pigeon	9 months	7 ,,	......	16	18	20
Stallion	5 years	14 ,,	20 to 30	......	......	......
Sow	1 year	6 ,,	......	109	115	143
Tup	1 ,,	7 ,,	40 to 50	......	......	......
Turkey	......	8 ,,	......	......	......	......

NOTA.— The most favorable season for breeding must be considered in accordance with locality and other particular circumstances of climate and keep.

Hints for the sick-room.

Woollen hangings are quite out of place in bedrooms. They tend to make a room that is slept in both stuffy and unhealthy, by retaining those particles given off by the skin. The window curtains may be made of lined cretonen, which will be as effective in excluding light as woollen fabrics. In case of infectious illness, the carpets and rugs may with advantage be exchanged for Indian matting. The dress of the nurse should be of cotton, if possible, but not starched to such stiffness as will produce a sound of rusling. Anything of this kind likely to act prejudicially upon the nerves, is most earnestly to be deprecated in a sick-room. The bed should have a spring mattress, this being much more cleanly, healthy, and convenient than feathers. It is extremely difficult to keep a patient quite comfortable on a feather bed during a long illness, if he or she is too weak to get up to admit of the bed being thoroughly shaken. Even then, it cannot, as a rule be properly shaken up ; for nothing but the passage of fresh air among the feathers will produce the softness and freedom from lumps so essential to comfort. Everything likely to irritate the patient must very carefully be avoided. Even when in health, none of us like to be kept waiting for things : but during illness, the delay of a minute seems like that of a quarter of an hour. Punctuality is never so virtuous as when presiding over the arrangements of a sick-room. All the appointments of a sick-room should be as dainty as possible. It is very depressing to look round and see a want of neatness— a towel lying across the back of a chair, the table crooked ; the curtains awry, a dirty saucepan in the fender with a spoon in it. Everything should be kept as neat as though the sick-room were the family drawing-room.

The Telautograph.

The *Telautograph* of Mr. Elisha Gray, of Chicago, a telegraph which writes the message down in the autograph of the sender, that is, makes a faithful copy at the far end of the message as written at the near end, has been tried successfully between London and Dover, on the line of the London to Paris telephone. The apparatus, which is too complicated to describe, performed its duty very well.

Fever Warnings.

Scarlet Fever.—(incubation period, 1 to 5 days.)—*Onset symptoms*: sore throat, shivering, fever, skin-heat, thirst, "strawberry" tongue: pink eruption second day. Infective through contact excretions, skin peeling for three weeks after convalescence. *Results to be feared*: dropsy, kidney, ear, and brain mischief.

Typhoid, or "drain fever" (incub., about 20 days).—*Onset*: fever, offensive diarrhœa, headache; pink spots after seventh day. Stools most dangereous. *Results*: relapses, great prostration, brain mischief.

Typhus, or "jail fever" (incub., 1 to 14 days).—*Onset*: fever, headache, constipation, drowsiness, delirium; dark eruption. Breath, evacuations, and all surroundings infectious. *Results*: bronchitis, joint and kidney disease, paralysis.

Smallpox.—(incub. 10 to 16 days).—*Onset*: fever, languor, shivering, headache, sickness, pain in back and loins; pimply eruption third day. Infective through skin and all excretions and surroundings for three weeks. *Results*: pneumonia, ear suppuration, blindness, disfigurement.

Measles.—(incub., 10 to 14 days).—*Onset*: feverish cold in head, chest oppression, cough, mottled eruption fourth day. Infective convalescence, 14 days. *Results*: chest, eye, ear, or joint disease.

N.B.—As soon as fever declares itself, isolate the patient and adopt measures of disinfection. Proper medical advice and good nursing are required. Mild cases may be followed by bad complications, and infect other persons severely.

The Value of Gold.

Gold is divided in 24 parts, or Carats, to the ounce Troy, and the ounce of pure gold being worth 85s., it follows that gold of :—

9	Carats fine to the ounce Troy is worth	£ 1	11	10½
10	,, ,, ,, ...	1	15	5
12	,, ,, ,, ...	2	2	6
15	,, ,, ,, ...	2	13	1½
16	,, ,, ,, ...	2	16	8
18	,, ,, ,, ...	3	3	9
22	,, (British Standard for Gold Coins)	3	17	11
24	,, (Pure unalloyed Gold)	4	5	0

How to remove Tight Finger Rings.

Pass the end of a piece of fine twine underneath the ring and wind it evenly around the finger upwards as far as the middle joint. Then take hold of the lower end of the string beneath the ring and begin to slowly unwind upward, when the ring will gradually move alone the twine towards the tip of the finger and come off.

To find the tonnage of Ships.

Multiply the length of keel, taken within the vessel, or as much of the ship as treads upon the ground, by the length of the midship beam, taken also within, from plank to plank; and that product by half the breadth, taken as the depth. Then divide the product by 94, and the quotient will give the tonnage.

Anti-Toxic Serum.

Thanks to the experiments of Mr. Roux, a pupil of Pasteur, and Professor Behring of Berlin, a preventative and cure of diphtheria and croup has been successfully used, with the result so far that the mortality from these diseases can be reduced to half its former rate, and their is a prospect of a still further reduction. The method of treatment is by anti-Toxic Serum, that is to say, the serum from the blood of animals, preferably horses, which have been " immunised ", to adopt a needful word, against the bacillus of the desease, or in other words, rendered capable of resisting the disease. A horse, for example, can be made to enjoy an immunity from the attacks of the bacillus of diphtheria by injecting weak cultures of the bacillus, attenuated by heat, or by the addition of a small quantity of trichloride of Iodine to the liquid in which the bacilli are cultivated. After undergoing a course of these injections, for 80 days or so the horse is immunised, and the serum of its blood, drawn from the jugular vein, can be used as lymph to inject into the veins of human beings or other animals to prevent them for catching diphththeria, or to cure them if they have already an otherwise mortal dose. This method of treatment, which is due above all to Professor Behring, is likely to become general, and the British Institute of Preventive Medicine have taken steps to provide the serum for injection at cost price.

Useful Bacteria.

Bacteriologists have discovered the bacterium which is instrumental in making butter and cheese. Moreover a German experimentalist in this line has found a bacterium which has the power of rendering sweet milk transparent and at the same time degestible. These useful bacteria are now cultivated for dairy and medical purposes.

Good rules for health.

Never go to bed with cold or damp feet.

Never lean with your back against anything that is cold.

Never begin a journey until the breakfast has been eaten.

Never take warm drinks, and then immediately go out into the cold.

Keep the back, especially between the shoulder blades, well covered ; also the chest well protected. In sleeping in a cold room, establish the habit of breathing through the nose, and never with the mouth open.

Never omit regular bathing, for unless the skin is in active condition the cold will close the pores and favour congestion and other diseases.

After exercise of any kind never ride in an open carriage or near the window of a car for a moment ; it is dangerous to health, or even life.

When hoarse, speak as little as possible until the hoarseness has disappeared, else the voice may be permanently lost, or difficulties of the throat be produced.

Merely warm the back by the fire, and never continue keeping the back exposed to the heat after it has become comfortably warm. To do otherwise is debilitating.

When going from a warm atmosphere into a cooler one keep the mouth closed, so that the air may be warmed in its passage through the nose ere it reaches the lungs.

An Electric Steering Compass.

Lieutenant Bersier, of the French Navy, has invented a highly ingenious compass which steers the ship itself without the aid of a man at the wheel. The needle of the compass card is connected on the secondary circuit of an induction coil, and throws off a stream of small electric sparks which pass to plates of metal round the bowl of the compass. The position of the needle determines the plate which receives the sparks, and this intermittent or sparking current is caused to work an electric motor by which the rudder is turned. If the needle moves to the right of its true position the motor turns the wheel one away, and if it goes to the other side the wheel is moved the other way, so that the ship is kept on its course as set by the navigating officer. The beauty of the devise is that the sparks do not hamper or disturb the needle in its movements as mechanism would do, and the apparatus is said to work well in practice,

Books.

Without books God is silent, justice dormant, natural science at a stand, philosophy lame letters dumb and all things involved in cimmerian darkness.—*Bartholini.*

Among the varied influences amidst which the human race is developped, a book is incomparably the most important and the only one that is absolutely essential. Upon it the collective education of the race depends. It is the sole instrument of registering, perpetuating and transmitting thought.—*H. Rogers.*

Consider, except a living man there is nothing more wonderful than a book; a message to us from the dead; from human souls whom we never saw, who lived perhaps thousands of miles away and yet there, in those little sheets of paper, speak to us, amuse us, terrify us, teach us, open their hearts to us as brothers.—*C. Kingsley.*

Books are the true Elysian fields where the spirits of the dead converse couched on flowers and to these fields a mortal may venture unappalled.—*A. Eneas Sage.*

Nutrition.

Table showing the average quantity of nutritive matter in 1,000 parts of several varieties of animal and vegetable food :

Wheat ...	... 950	Mutton ...	... 290	Cod ...	... 210	Strawberries	... 100
Barley ...	... 920	Grapes ...	... 270	Sole ...	... 210	Carrots ...	... 98
Rice ...	... 880	Chicken ...	... 270	Brain ...	... 200	Cabbage ...	... 73
Rye ...	... 792	Apricots	... 260	Peeches ...	... 200	Milk ...	... 72
Oats ...	... 742	Beef ...	... 260	Gooseberries	... 190	Turnips ...	... 42
Almonds ...	... 650	Potatoes...	... 260	Haddock	... 180	Melons ...	... 30
Bones ...	... 510	Veal ...	... 250	Apples ...	... 170	Cucumber	... 25
Tamarinds	... 340	Cherries...	... 250	Pears ...	... 160		
Morels ...	... 206	Pork ...	... 240	Beetroot...	... 148		
Plumbs ...	... 290	Blood ...	... 215	White of Eggs ...	140		

Tables for converting Centigrade degrees into Fahrenheit

Cent.	Fah.	Cent.	Fah.	Cent.	Fah.	Cent.	Fah.
1	33.8	14	57.2	27	80.6	40	104.0
2	35.6	15	59.0	28	82.4	41	105.8
3	37.4	16	60.8	29	84.2	42	107.6
4	39.2	17	62.6	30	86.0	43	109.4
5	41.0	18	64.4	31	87.8	44	111.2
6	42.8	19	66.2	32	89.6	45	113.0
7	44.6	20	68.0	33	91.4	50	122.0
8	46.4	21	69.8	34	93.2	60	140.0
9	48.2	22	71.6	35	95.0	70	158.0
10	50.0	23	73.4	36	96.8	75	167.0
11	51.8	24	75.2	37	98.6	80	176.0
12	53.6	25	77.0	38	100.4	90	194.0
13	55.4	26	78.8	39	102.2	100	212.0

Thermometer.

Comparison between the scales of Fahrenheit and the Centigrade.

To reduce : Centigrade to Fahrenheit.

Multiply the given temperature by 9 and divide by 5—this gives the required number of degrees Fahrenheit reckoned from the freezing point; then add 32 and the number on the Fahrenheit scale is obtained.

In the same way to reduce from Fahrenheit to Centigrade; Substract 32; this gives the number of degrees Fahrenheit then multiply by 5 and divide by 9 and the required number on the Centigrade Scale is obtained.

Why is food required ?

The question seems almost absurd, so familiar is the fact; and yet the answer to it involves one of the grandest chapters in the history of science. In its simplest form it may be given in hree words; it is fuel. We require food frequenly, for just the same reason that fire requires coal freqnently, and a lamp oil because we are burning away. The air that we breathe into our lungs contains oxygen, and this oxygen combines with, or burns, the muscles or other organes of our bodies just as it does the coals in a fire. About 30 oz. of oxygen a day are thus consumed, requiring about 12 oz. of carbon to replace the waste, or say 3 lbs of bread. The heat produced in a man's body in the course of a day is considerable in quantity, though not very intense in quality. Taking the average, it is enough to raise five and a half gallons of water from freezing point to boiling point, and this is about the heat that would be given off during the burning of a pound of coal. All this heat comes from slow wasting or burning of the substances of the body, so that it is evident that if we did not make up for this constant loss by eating food our organs would soon be wasted away and consumed.

Important to Bathers.

Avoid bathing within *two* hours after a meal.

Avoid bathing when exhausted by fatigue or from any other cause.

Avoid bathing when the body is cooling after perspiration.

Avoid bathing altogether is the open air if, after having been a short time in the water, there is a sense of chilliness with the numbness of hands and feet; but

Bathe when the body is warm, provided that no time is lost in getting into the water.

Avoid chilling the body by sitting or standing *undressed* on the banks or in the boats after having been in the water.

Avoid remaining two long in the water, leave the water immediately there is the slightest feeling of chilliness.

The vigorous and strong may bathe early in the morning on an empty stomach.

The young and those who are weak, had better bathe two or three hours after a meal—the best time for such is from two or three hours after breakfast.

Those who are subject to attacks or gildiness or faintness, and those who suffer from palpitation and other sense of discomfort of the heart, should not bathe without first consulting their medical advisers.

Peculiar Geography of the North Pole.

At the North Pole, there is neither North nor East nor West, but every possible direction therefrom is only South. The Pole being the meeting place of all the Meridians, it is always there any and every hour of the day and the night you please. Your watch there always keeps perfect time, provided only it never moves and ever points to all times of the day-night.

Percentage of Alcohol in Wines and Spirits.

Beer	4.0	Gooseberry	11.8	Ratafia	21.0
Porter	4.5	Champagne	12.2	Madeira	21.0
Ale	7.4	Claret	13.3	Port	23.2
Cider	8.6	Burgundy	13.6	Curaçao	27.0
Perry	8.8	Malaga	17.3	Aniseed	33.0
Elder	9.3	Lisbon	18.5	Maraschina	34.0
Moselle	9.6	Canary	18.8	Chartreuse	43.0
Tokay	10.2	Sherry	19.0	Gin	51.6
Rhine	11.0	Vermouth	19.0	Brandy	53.4
Orange	11.2	Cape	19.2	Rum	53.7
Bordeaux	11.5	Malmsey	19.7	Irish Whisky	53.9
Hock	11.6	Marsala	20.2	Scotch Whisky	54.3

Spirits are said to be " proof " when they contain 57 per cent. The maximum amount of alcohol, says Parkes, that a man takes daily without injury to his health is that contained in 2 oz. qrandy, ¼ pint of sherry, ½ pint claret, or 1 pint beer.—*Mulhall.*

MUNICIPALITY OF PORT LOUIS.

List of Mayors and Deputy-Mayors from 1850.

	Mayors.	*Deputy-Mayors.*
1850	Hon. L. Léchelle	F. Kœnig
1851	Hon. L. Léchelle	F. Kœnig
1852	Hon. L. Léchelle	F. Kœnig
1853	Hon. L. Léchelle	F. Kœnig
1854	(May) Hon. G. Fropier	A. Besnard
1855	Hon. G. Fropier	E. Pipon
1856	Hon. L. Léchelle	E. Pipon
	E. Pipon	Hon. H. Lemière
1857	Hon. H. Lemière	A. Edwards
1858	A. Edwards	F. N. Jouannis
1859	P. N. Charon	D. Sicard
1860	G. de Courson	A. Edwards
1861	G. de Courson	J. Mallac
1862	G. de Courson	E. Marie
1863	Hon. H. Lemière	C. Pitot
1864	Hon. H. Lemière	C. Pitot
1865	P. N. Charon	J. Brodie
1866	C. Pitot	E. Laurent
1867	Hon. C. Pitot	E. François
1868	E. François	E. Ducray
1869	E. François	L. Letard
1870	E. Ducray	J. Barbeau
1871	Hon. E. Ducray	J. Barbeau
1872	Hon. E. Ducray	Dr. W.A.T. Edwards
1873	E. François	A. C. Macpherson
1874	E. François	W. Hazlitt
1875	Hon. E. François	G. F. Poulin
	G. F. Poulin	A. Rolando
1876	G. F. Poulin	W. Hazlitt
1877	L. Hily	E. Bazire
1878	Emile Bazire	L. Hily
1879	Emile Bazire	Dr. L. Allas
1880	Emile Bazire	C. E. T. Pitot
1881	Emile Bazire	Dr. L. Allas
1882	A. Lavoquer	Dr. L. Allas & W. Stanley
1883	A. Lavoquer	C. E. T. Pitot
	C. E. T. Pitot	G. V. K/Vern
1884	C. E. T. Pitot	Dr. W. A. T. Edwards
1885	A. Lavoquer	G. V. K/Vern
1886	A. Lavoquer	G. V. K/Vern
1887	G. V. K/Vern	E. Aubert
1888	G. V. K/Vern	C. E. T. Pitot *resigned*
		E. Aubert
1889	G. V. K/Vern	E. Aubert
	E. Aubert	E. Duponsel
1890	E. Aubert	E. François
1891	E. Aubert	E. Duponsel
1892	E. Aubert	E. Duponsel
	E. Duponsel	E. François
1893	E. François	E. Ganachaud
1894	E. François	E. Ganachaud
1895	E. François	E. Ganachaud
1896	C. E. T. Pitot	R. A. Rohan

Municipal Councillors 1896.

MM. A. Bonnefin
L. J. Pétricher
F. L. Morel
D. Jenkins
C. Newton
E. François

MM. E. Sauzier
L. Souchon
F. Henri
G. Bonic
J. Turner
L. Boullé

MM. A. Poupard
E. Vaudagne
C. Olivier
M. Leblanc.

NOTE.—The Mayor of Port Louis is granted an allowance of Rs. 5000 per annum.

Statement of the number of Municipal Electors and Voters from 1850 to 1895.

YEARS.	ELECTORS.	VOTERS.
1850	600	437
1851	754	462
1852	768	234
1853	773	398
1854	1023	590
1855	1024	538
1856	1036	493
1857	1239	438
1858	1207	281
1859	1192	394
1860	1135	321
1861	884	215
1862	901	268
1863	891	260
1864	938	248
1865	940	149
1866	960	194
1867	882	232
1868	849	288
1869	922	387
1870	1022	387
1871	1023	415
1872	1072	474
1873	1126	475
1874	1145	410
1875	1238	506
1876	1270	507
1877	1234	409
1878	1228	393
1879	1233	430
1880	1236	523
1881	1214	586
1882	1406	770
1883	1449	643
1884	1422	661
1885	1507	833
1886	1747	995
1887	1744	927
1888	1748	869
1889	2442	1579
1890	2547	1319
1891	2573	1386
1892	2537	1408
1893	2586	1325
1894	3572	2050
1895	3685	2008

ESTABLISHMENTS.

J. Henry, Town Clerk ...	... Rs. 4,500	p. an.
J. E. Assy, Sub „ ...	... 2,160	„
L. Le Goy, 1st clerk ...	... 1,240	„
Ch. Geffroy, 2nd „ ...	... 1,200	„
A. Bouisson, 3rd „ ...	... 960	„
H. Devienne, 4th „ ...	... 720	„
M. Henri ...	... 400	„
Doger Spéville, Town Treasurer	4,500	„
F. Canet, Sub „ ...	2,160	„
E. Janson, 1st Clerk ...	... 1,200	„
M. Rayeroux, 2nd Clerk..	... 960	„
M. Bonnabelle, 3rd Clerk ...	Rs. 840	p. an.
G. Leal 4th „ ...	720	„
E. Pitchen, 5th „ ...	600	„
J. Auffray ...	400	„
J. Frédéric, bearer of warrants and inspector for declarations of vehicles and animals ...	1,680	„
F. Delort, do. ...	1,200	„
V. Boutin, Controller ...	3,000	„
L. Olivier, 1st Clerk ...	600	„
H. Mongey, 2nd „ ...	480	„
A. Maillard, Architect and Superintendent of Canals ...	3,600	„
A. Baillache, Inspector of Canals and Inspector of Works ...	1,500	„
L. G. Seriès, Officer in charge of Cadastre and building Surveyor ...	1,440	„
L. Merle, 1st Clerk, and Sub Inspector of Canals ...	1,320	„
F. Haoust, Inspector of Town Hall, with lodgings and Clerk to Architect ...	720	„
Simon, 2nd Clerk ...	300	„

SERVICES EXCLUSIVE OF ESTABLISHMENT.

Slaughter-House.		
J. B. Décube, Inspector of the Slaughter-House ...	1,440	„
C. Galdemar, Veterinary Surgeon ...	1,800	„
Th. Bradshaw, do. ...	1,800	„
H. Fin, Sub-Inspector ...	600	„
Markets		
F. Sébille, 1st Inspector Central Market...	1,225	„
E. Manuel, 2nd do. do. ...	780	„
(*Vacant*) Inspector of Caudan Market ...	380	„
A special constable at Plaine Verte Market ...	240	„
Cemeteries.		
A. Legoy, Inspector of Western Cemetery ...	1,440	„
J. Melies do. Eastern Cemetery ...	600	„
**Inspectors of Revenue.*		
A. Auffray, Superintendent ...	1,800	„
1ST. CLASS INSPECTORS.		
H. Sneeden ...	1,440	„
E. Arnulphy ...	1,200	„
E. Roussel ...	1,200	„
2ND. CLASS INSPECTORS.		
Ch. Sicard ...	960	„
O. Moutia ...	780	„
J. Pitchen ...	720	„
3RD. CLASS INSPECTORS.		
A. Rodesse ...	600	„
E. Sophie ...	600	„
E. Lagane ...	600	„
Fire Engine Department.		
Th. Gibbs, Chief Officer ...	Rs. 6,000	p. n.
H. Ducasse, 1st. Officer ...	1,500	„
E. Panglose, Sub-Officer ...	550	„
E. Manciet ...	550	„
A. Romagou, Engine man ...	625	„
M. Dinnematin do. ...	625	„
Theatre.		
P. Marion de Procés, Keeper of the Scenery of the Theatre ...	600	„
Mrs. P. Diamentaire, Keeper of the Theatre ...	120	„
Public Library.		
E. Prudhomme, Town Librarian ...	1,080	„
A. Geffroy, Assistant Librarian ...	480	„

* Also receive ⅓ of fines recovered in contraventions taken by them.

Name.	Date of Appointment.	Date of Confirmation.	Whether holding any, and what other Civil or Military Office.
	Executive Council.		
Ex-Officio Members.			
Barnard, Major-General William Osborne,	15th. March 1895...	Official Members do not require to be confirmed.	Officer in Command of the Troops.
King-Harman, Charles Anthony, C.M.G.	4th. Sept. 1893...		Colonial Secretary.
Rouillard, Louis	6th. April 1895...		Acting Procureur and Advocate General.
Schmidt, Louis Edouard ...	4th. July 1887...		Receiver General.
Ashley, Edward Charles ...	3rd. Aug. 1894...		Auditor General.
Elected Members of the Council of Government.			
Leclézio, Henry	21st. April 1891...	Sec. S. Despatch "General" 21.4.91.	
Edwards, Dr. Wilbraham Tollemach Arthur.	13th. March 1896...		
	Council of Government.		
	Ex-Officio Members		
Jerningham, His Excellency Sir Hubert Edward Henry, K.C.M.G.—*President.*	21st. June 1893 ...	......	Governor and Commander-in-Chief.
	Date sworn in.		
Barnard, Major-General William Osborne.	25th. Feb. 1896...	Official Members do not require to be confirmed.	Officer in Command of the Troops.
King-Harman, Charles Anthony K.C.M.G.	,,		Colonial Secretary.
Rouillard, Louis	,,		Acting Procureur and Advocate General.
Schmidt, Louis Edouard ...	,,		Receiver General.
Ashley, Edward Charles ...	,,		Auditor General.
Brown, James John	,,		Collector of Customs.
Trotter, John Francis ...	,,		Protector of Immigrants.
De Coriolis, Gustave	,,		Supt. of Public Works and Surveyor General.
	Elected Members.		
	Elected		
Leclézio, Henry	23rd Jan. 1896...	(Date of Elections.)	Member for Moka.
Antelme, Louis Edgard ...	24th. Jan. 1896...		Member for R. du Rempart.
Newton, William, Q.C ...	28th. Jan. 1896...		Member for Port Louis.
Rohan, Dr. Virgile	Do.		Do.
Guibert, George, Q.C. ...	30th. Jan. 1896...		Member for P. Wilhems.
De Rocheconste, Louis ...	31st. Jan. 1896...		Member for Grand Port.
Sauzier, Emile junior ...	1st. Feb. 1896...		Member for Pamplemousses.
*Bouchet, Dr. George ...	4th. Feb. 1896...		Member for Flacq.
Edwards, Dr. Wilbraham Tollemache Arthur.	5th. Feb. 1896...		Member for Savanne.
Geffroy, Vincent	8th. Feb. 1896...		Member for Black River.

* Not yet sworn in.

Name.	Date of Appointment.	Date of Confirmation.	Whether holding any, and what other Civil or Military Office
NOMINATED MEMBERS.			
Ambrose, Ambrose Povah ...	Sworn in on 25th. February 1896.		
* Antelme, Sir Célicourt Auguste, K.C.M.G.	Sworn in on 25th. February 1896.		
Aubert, Edgar, C.M.G. ...	Sworn in on 25th. February 1896.		Poor Law Commissioner.
* Chastellier, Dr. Evenor ...	Sworn in on 25th. February 1896.		Director of the Medical and Health Department.
Dick, George Royer	Sworn in on 25th. February 1896.		Registrar General.
Ritter, Gustave Albert ...	Sworn in on 25th. February 1896.		
Robinson, George	Sworn in on 25th. February 1896.		
Stein, Hamilton	Sworn in on 25th. February 1896.		
† Holland, Captain C. J. ...	Sworn in on 25th. February 1896.		Inspector General of Police.

* Not yet sworn in.

† Is replacing Mr. L. Rouillard who is acting as Procureur and Advocate General.

MILITARY ESTABLISHMENT.

Appointment	Rank.	Names.	Date of present Commission.	Landed in Mauritius.	Residence.
		Staff.			
Commanding Troops ...	Major Gen.	Barnard W. O.	1.2.95	28.2.95	Beau Séjour.
D. A. A. General ...	Captain ...	Hudson, A. T. P. ...	12.10.87	26.3.95	Vacoas.
		Royal Artillery.			
Commanding R. A. ...	Major ...	Vans Agnew, J. F. ...	26.9.95		Not yet joined.
	Captain ...	Thornton, S. V. ...	29.10.86	27.4.95	Q. Bornes.
	" ...	Anderson, R. D. ...	4.1.90	22.8.94	Fort George.
	Lieut. ...	Fraser, L. D.	23.7.90	28.12.91	On leave till 7th. July 96.
	" ...	Last, A. J.	3.5.93	22.8.94	Curepipe.
	" ...	Osborn, L. L. H. ...	10.5.93	2.11.95	Moka.
	" ...	Hope, W. H. W. ...	25.7.93	22.8.94.	Fort George.
	" ...	Muspratt Williams, R.L.	1.11.93	"	"
	" ...	Riddell, R. B.	28.3.95	"	"
		Royal Engineers.			
Commanding R. E. ...	Lieut. Col...	De Wolski, F. R. ...	26.5.93	6.11.94	Q. Bornes.
	Major ...	Bate, C. Mc. G. ...	12.2.94	26.11.95	Moka.
	Captain ...	Tudor E. T.	7.10.92	12.7.95	B. Bassin.
	Lieut. ...	Caulfield, St. George ...	23.7.90	22.3.93	"
		2nd. Bn. York and Lancaster Regiment.			
Commanding Regiment ...	Lieut. Col ...	Boughey, H.	1.7.95	6.2.96	Camp Curepipe.
	Major ...	Broughton, E. C. ...	27.8.94	"	
	Captain ...	Woodford, E. F. ...	1.8.88	"	"
	" ...	Galindo, R. E.	16.9.91	"	"
	" ...	Daniell, F. F. W. ...	30.9.91	"	"
Adjutant	Lieut. ...	Burt, A. G.	17.12.89	"	"
	" ...	Capron, G.	27.8.94	"	"
	" ...	Ashton, F. E.	27.11.94	"	"
	" ...	Colston, H. K.	25.3.95	"	"
	2nd. Lieut ...	Longden, R. J.... ...	17.12.92	"	"
	" ...	Robertson, E. C. ...	28.9.95	"	"
Quarter Master	Lieut. ...	Fuller, J.	31.12.87	"	"
		Army Service Corps.			
Commanding A. S. Corps.	Lieut. Col...	Challice, G. G.	1.11.91	22.8.94	Moka.
In charge of Transport and Supplies.—Curepipe.	Lieut. ...	Ward, H. S.	25.3.91	26.12.94	Curepipe.

Appointment.	Rank.	Names.	Date of present Commission.	Landed in Mauritius.	Residence.
Medical Staff.					
Senior Medical Officer ...	Bde. Surgt. Lieut. Col.	Fraser, J.	31.3.88	22.8.94	Q. Bornes.
Medical Officer, Curepipe...	Surg. Capt....	Colledge, L. R. ...	2.8.84	,,	Curepipe.
Do. Port Louis...	,, ...	Butterworth, S. ...	2.8.84	,,	,,
Do. Curepipe ...	,, ...	Fallon, J.	28.7.86	,,	,,
Ordnance Store Department.					
S. O. S. O. and D. A. C. G. of Ord.	Captain ...	Tracy, W. M.	12.4.91	17.2.95	Rose Hill.
Inspect. of War' Stores ...	Lieut. ...	Waring, R.	14.2.93	22.8.94	Q. Bornes.
Army Pay Department.					
District Paymaster ...	Captain ...	Lindop, A. H.	1.9.86	19.3.94	B. Bassin.

ALPHABETICAL INDEX

OF

THE MAURITIUS CIVIL LIST

FOR

1896.

ALPHABETICAL INDEX.

THE

MAURITIUS CIVIL LIST

FOR

1896.

Governor and Commander-in-Chief. — His Excellency Sir Hubert Edward Henry Jerningham, K.C.M.G. Salary Rs. 50,000 per annum. (*On leave.*)

Appointed 21st. June 1893.

Officer Administering the Government.—His Honor Charles Anthony King-Harman, C. M. G.

Assumed the Government 2nd. March 1896.

Private Secretary.—The Hon. Reginald Walsh, 3,000 per annum. (On leave).

Appointed 16th. July 1894.

Private Secretary and Aide-de-Camp.—Lieut. R. J. Longden, York and Lancaster Regiment.

Appointed 5th. March 1896.

Assistant Private Secretary.—Raoul Lejeunne.

Appointed 5th. March 1896.

Colonial Secretary's Office.

Colonial Secretary.—Charles Anthony King-Harman, C.M.G. Rs. 13,500 per annum.

Appointed 4th. September 1893.

Assistant Colonial Secretary.—William Douglas Young. Rs. 7,200 per annum. (Is Acting Colonial Secretary).

Assumed duties 27th. December 1895.

Chief Clerk.—Frederick Albin Gibson. Present salary Rs. 4,800 per annum. (Is Acting Assistant Colonial Secretary).

Entered the service 1st. October 1875.
Present appointment 25th. March 1894.

Clerk of the Executive Council and of the Council of Government.—William Charles Rae. Rs. 4,000 per annum.

Entered the service November 1876.
Confirmed 25th. March 1894.

2ND. CLASS CLERKS.

Michel Savrimoutou. Salary Rs. 3,600 per annum, and a personal allowance of Rs. 400 per annum. (Is Acting Chief Clerk).

Entered the service 21st. May 1857.
Present appointment 22nd. June 1882.

Arthur Edmund Johnson. Present salary Rs. 3,600 per annum.

Entered the service 13th. September 1878.
Present appointment 1st. January 1895.

3RD. CLASS CLERKS.

George Crétin. Present salary Rs. 2,500 per annum.

Entered the service November 1868.
Present appointment 6th. March 1890.

François Emile. Present salary Rs. 2,400.

Entered the service 1st. January 1868.
Present appointment 29th. November 1894.

4TH. CLASS CLERKS.

Gabriel Lincoln. Present salary Rs. 1,800 per annum (plus Rs. 750 as Secretary to the Woods and Forest Board and Rs. 500 as Secretary to the Station Agronomique Committee).

Entered the service August 1881.
Present appointment 1st. January 1893.

Auguste Maingard. Present salary Rs. 1,800 per annum.

Entered the service July 1885.
Present appointment 29th. November 1892.

Victor Sherwin. Present salary Rs. 1,800 per annum.

Entered the service 6th. may 1884.
Present appointment 11th. May 1894.

5TH. CLASS CLERKS.

Pierre Arokion. Present salary Rs. 1,200 per annum.

Entered the service 1st. January 1888.
Present appointment 1st. August 1892.

Juste Duthil. Present salary Rs. 1,800 per annum.

Entered the service 13th. July 1885.
Present appointment 1st. January 1893.

Raoul Giquel. Present salary Rs. 1,200 per annum.

Entered the service 8th. October 1890.
Present appointment 29th. November 1894.

6TH. CLASS CLERKS.

Léon Kœnig. Rs. 720 per annum.

Entered the service 5th. November 1891.
Present appointment 29th November 1894.

Léonce Isnard, Rs. 720 per annum.

Entered the service 8th. June 1892.
Present appointment 29th. November 1894.

WRITERS at Rs. 300 per annum.

Maurice Rey.

Entered the service 5th. February 1894.
Appointed 29th. November 1894.

Edouard Bathfield.

Present appointment 6th. April 1894.

COPYISTS at Rs. 300 per annum.

Abel Lonneau.

Present appointment 15th. November 1895.

Louis Arthur Albert.

Present appointment 15th. November 1895.

Loan Office.

Secretary.—Edouard Pelte. Salary Rs. 4,800 per annum.

Appointed 1st. November 1894.

Accountant.—Pierre Louis Eugène Lincoln. Salary Rs. 3,600 per annum.

Entered the service 25th. September 1882.
Present appointment 1st. November 1894.

Expert.—Elysée Marot. Salary Rs. 3,600 per annum.

Appointed 1st. November 1894.

Clerk.—Raoul Lejeune. Rs. 2,400 per annum.

Entered the service 24th. September 1884.
Present appointment 1st. November 1894.

Auditor.—F. V. Descroizilles. Salary Rs. 1,200 per annum. (See also Audit Office).

Appointed 1st. November 1894.

Receiver General's Department.

Receiver General.—The Honorable Louis Edouard Schmidt, Rs. 10,000 per annum.

Entered the service 1st. August 1861.
Present appointment 11th. April 1889.

Assistant Receiver General.—Louis Séïde Rathier Du Vergé.

Entered the service 1st. July 1868.
Present appointment 1st. January 1895.

5TH. CLASS CLERK.

Walter L. Argent. Rs. 1,200 per annum, plus Rs. 1,000 personal allowance.

Entered the service 1st. November 1875.
Present appointment 1st. January 1890.

ACCOUNT BRANCH.

FIRST CLASS CLERK.

Albert Fitz Patrick. Rs. 4,800 per annum. (*On leave*).

Entered the service 25th. May 1868.
Present appointment 21st. June 1893.

3RD. CLASS CLERKS.

Edouard Emilien Toussaint. Rs. 2,400 per annum, plus Rs. 600 personal allowance.

Entered the service 1st. January 1867.
Present appointment 1st. March 1885.

Emile Rosse. Rs. 2,400 per annum. (*On leave*).

Entered the service 1st. November 1876.
Present appointment 1st. January 1890.

4TH. CLASS CLERKS.

Félix de Rosemond. Salary Rs. 1,800 per annum. (Acting 3rd. Class Clerk.)

Entered the service 18th. July 1885.
Present appointment 28th. March 1893.

Fritz Vanmeerbeck. Salary Rs. 1,800 per annum.

Entered the service 1st. September 1882.
Present appointment 1st. January 1893.

6TH. CLASS CLERK.

P. A. Moutou. Salary Rs. 720 per annum.

Entered the service 8th. October 1890.
Present appointment 1st. January 1893.

PAY BRANCH.

2ND. CLASS CLERK.

Evariste Crétin. Rs. 3,600 per annum, plus Rs. 400 personal allowance. Present salary Rs. 4,000.

Entered the service 19th. July 1861.
Present appointment 1st. January 1890.

3RD. CLASS CLERK.

Victor Singery. Rs. 2,400 per annum, and Rs. 360 per annum, as Secretary to the Widows and Orphans' Fund. (Is Acting Head Accountant.)

Entered the service 4th. December 1878.
Present appointment 1st. January 1890.

6TH. CLASS CLERK.

Alphonse Planel. Salary Rs. 720 per annum.

Entered the service 8th October 1890.
Present appointment 23rd. April 1893.

RECEIPT BRANCH.

2ND. CLASS CLERK.

Peter Paul Harrison. Salary Rs. 3,600 per annum.

Entered the service 1st. January 1870.
Present appointment 1st. January 1890.

3RD CLASS CLERK.

Luther Crétin. Present salary Rs 2,400 per annum.

Entered the service 20th. July 1874.
Present appointment 23rd. August 1894.

4TH. CLASS CLERK.

Deyevenayegum Canegarayen Maléappa. Salary Rs. 1,800 plus 200 personal allowance.

Entered the service 1st. February 1870.
Present appointment 1st. January 1890.

5TH. CLASS CLERK.

Albert Pierre Mayépa. Salary Rs. 1,200 per annum.

Entered the service February 1883.
Present appointment 17th. October 1891.

6TH. CLASS CLERKS.

Joseph Albert Sicard. Salary Rs. 720 per annum.

Entered the service 8th October 1870.
Present appointment 1st. April 1893.

Floricourt Fanchette. Salary Rs. 720 per annum.

Entered the service 19th. December 1890.
Present appointment 6th. October 1893.

Arthur Bhujoharry. Salary Rs. 720 per annum.

Entered the service 1st. January 1888.
Present appointment 24th. August 1894.

SAVINGS BANK.

2ND. CLASS CLERK.

Louis Alfred Lahausse de Lalouvière. Salary Rs. 3,600 per annum.

Entered the service 22nd. September 1868.
Present appointment 27th. January 1895.

3RD. CLASS CLERK.

Louis Ange Adirouben. Salary Rs. 2,400 per annum, plus Rs. 600 personal allowance.

Entered the service, 1st. November 1864.
Present appointment 1st. January 1890.

5TH. CLASS CLERKS.

Marius Thomas. Salary Rs. 1,200 per annum.

Entered the service 1st. January 1881.
Present appointment 31st. July 1891.

Alcide Assarapin. Salary Rs. 1,200 per annum.

Entered the service 26th. July 1877.
Present appointment 3rd. July 1894.

6TH. CLASS CLERK

Percy Fitz Patrick. Salary Rs. 720 per annum.

Entered the service 9th. September 1890.
Present appointment 6th. April 1894.

WRITERS, Rs. 300 per annum.

Frank Alfred Yerriah.

Entered the service 15th. May 1893.
Present appointment 4th. May 1894.

Louis Joseph Robert Giraud.

Appointed 5th. May 1895.

COPYISTS, Rs. 300 per annum.

B. Cateaux.

Appointed 14th. May 1894.

Alfred Etienne Bruneau.

Appointed 10th. December 1894.

STAMP BRANCH AND WEIGHTS AND MEASURES.

3RD. CLASS CLERK.

Jean Fernand Duchenne. Salary Rs. 2,400 per annum.

Entered the service 7th. February 1876.
Present appointment 28th. March 1893.

4TH. CLASS CLERK.

Charles Louis Félix Lebreton. Salary Rs. 1,800 per annum, plus Rs. 700 personal allowance.

Entered the service 29th. May 1865.
Present appointment 16th. May 1881.

WORKMAN.

Joseph Edgard. Salary Rs. 600 per annum.

Present appointment 15th. July 1890.

DISTILLERY BRANCH.

Superintendent.—Henry Clancy Rawstorne. Salary Rs. 3,600 per annum.

Entered the service 27th. January 1874.
Present appointment 26th. April 1894.

Chief Inspector.—Louis Albert Célestin. Salary Rs. 2,400 per annum.

Entered the service 1st. October 1875.
Present appointment 8th. November 1893.

Inspectors.

Edouard D'Arvoy. Salary Rs.1,800 per annum, plus Rs.700 personal allowance.

Appointed 8th. November 1864.

Adelson Latapie. Salary Rs. 1,800 per annum, plus Rs. 700 personal allowance.

Appointed 10th. November 1864.

Louis Alfred Pougnet. Salary Rs. 1,800 per annum.

Entered the service 13th. May 1876.
Present appointment 1st. January 1890.

Eudoxe Hitié. Present salary Rs. 1,800 per annum.

Entered the service 11th. February 1880.
Present appointment 1st. April 1891.

Albert Letellier. Present salary Rs. 1,800 per annum.

Entered the service 11th. February 1880.
Present appointment 25th. January 1892.

Gustave Rose. Present salary Rs. 1,800 per annum.

Entered the service 8th. June 1881.
Present appointment 27th. March 1893.

Numa Allan. Rs. 1,800 per annum.

Entered the service 10th. June 1885.
Present appointment 1st. September 1894.

Jules Loumeau.

Appointed 3rd. May 1895.

Elphege, Jean Louis.

Appointed 3rd. May 1895.

Second Class Inspectors.—Salaries Rs. 1,200 per annum.

George Rose.

Appointed 17t. October 1889.

Périclès Némorin. (Is Acting Inspector Iuland Revenue).

Appointed 18th. March 1892.

Arthur Luciany. (Is Acting Inspector Inland Revenue.)

Appointed 18th. March 1892.

L. S. Walter.

Appointed 8th. May 1895.

Henri Bonnin.

Appointed 8th. May 1875.

Alcide Loumeau.

Appointed 1st. January 1892.

Lousteau Serret.

Appointed 3rd. June 1893.

*Provisional Inspectors** at Rs. 100 per mensem.

Bruneau, Léon.

D'Arvoy, Gustave.

Montocchio, James.

Poupinel de Valencé, A.

INLAND REVENUE BRANCH.

Superintendent.—David Petrie Garrioch.† Present salary Rs. 4,000 per annum.

Entered the service 9th. April 1863.
Present appointment 6th. March 1890.

Five Inspectors at Rs. 1,500 per annum.

Louis Nemours Lagesse.†

Entered the service 19th. March 1868.
Present appointment 30th. October 1876.

Gustave Letourneur.† (Is Acting District Cashier, Port Louis.

Entered the service 1st. May 1880.
Present appointment 1st. June 1881.

---

* These Officers are employed temporarily and their services may be dispensed with at one month's notice.

† The Superintendent and Inspectors of Inland Revenue receive as travelling allowance the refund of actual expenses and a Railway pass.

John Peter Freeman.†

Entered the service 28th. July 1880.
Present appointment 14th. May 1887.

Gustave Bérenger.†

Entered the service 1st. April 1887.
Present appointment 18th. March 1893.

L. F. L'Estrange.†

Entered the service 7th. October 1892.
Present appointment 21st. October 1895.

Audit Office.

Auditor General.—The Honorable Edward Charles Ashley. Rs. 10,000 per annum.

Entered the service 26th. March 1863.
Present appointment 17th. January 1894.

Chief Clerk.—F. V. Descroizilles. Rs. 5,000 per annum. (Is also Auditor to the Loan Commission with a salary of Rs. 1,200.)

Entered the service 19th. May 1874.
Present appointment 1st. November 1894.

2ND. CLASS CLERKS.

Jules Rozan. Present salary Rs. 3,600 per annum, plus Rs 300 personal allowance.

Entered the service 1st. January 1870.
Present appointment 1st. January 1887.

Polixène Cartier. Present salary Rs 3,600 per annum.

Entered the service 1st. September 1865.
Present appointment 11th. September 1893.

Thomas Carr. Present salary Rs. 3,600 per annum.

Entered the service 1st. October 1882.
Present appointment 4th. May 1894.

Joachim Hyacinthe Daniel. Present salary Rs 3,600 per annum.

Entered the service 26th. May 1877.
Present appointment 5th. July 1894.

---

† The Superintendent and Inspectors of Inland Revenue receive as travelling allowance the refund of actual expenses and a Railway pass.

James Macpherson. Present salary Rs. 2,400 per annum, plus Rs. 400 personal allowance.

Entered the service 20th. October 1874.
Present appointment 1st. May 1895.

3RD. CLASS CLERKS.

P. Léon Ferré. Present salary Rs. 2,400 per annum.

Entered the service 1st. March 1881.
Present appointment 1st. August 1892.

Joseph H. Pilot. Present salary Rs. 2,400 per annum.

Entered the service 24th. August 1881.
Present appointment 11th. September 1893.

Walter Edgar Acton. Present salary Rs. 2,400 per annum.

Entered the service 1st. August 1894.
Present appointment 4th. May 1894.

James Edward Batty. Present salary Rs. 2,400 per annum.

Entered the service 1st. February 1879.
Present appointment 5th. July 1894.

J. Gregory Standley. Present salary Rs. 2,400 per annum.

Entered the service, 3rd. March 1879.
Present appointment 4th. May 1895.

4TH. CLASS CLERKS.

Frédéric Crétin. Present salary Rs. 1,800 per annum.

Entered the service 3rd. January 1877.
Present appointment 6th. August 1892.

Henri Chrétien. Present salary Rs. 1,800 per annum.

Entered the service 1st. December 1883.
Present appointment 1st. August 1892.

5TH. CLASS CLERKS.

Ernest Narcisse. Present salary Rs. 1,200 per annum.

Entered the service 25th. September 1886.
Present appointment 11th. September 1893.

Emmanuel Bouffé, Rs. 720 per annum, plus Rs. 500 per annum, as Secretary to the Railway Board.

Entered the service 1st. January 1888.
Present appointment 26th. September 1895.

6TH. CLASS CLERKS.

T. Lemerle, Rs. 720 per annum.

Appointed 1st. May 1895.

J. Alexander Bruce, Rs. 720 per annum.

Appointed 20th. September 1895.

WRITERS, Rs. 300 per annum.

Henry Kœnig.

Appointed 15th. November 1894.

Michel Alphonse Bruneau.

Appointed 24th. September 1894.

COPYIST, Rs. 300 per annum.

Gaston Labat.

Appointed 9th April 1895.

Public Works Department.

Superintendent of Public Works & Surveyor General.— The Honorable Gustave de Coriolis. Rs. 8,000 per annum.

Entered the service 1st. August 1889.
Present appointment 21st. March 1892.

CHIEF CLERK.

John Behan Bruce. Rs. 3,000 per annum.

Entered the service 1st. February 1862.
Present appointment 11th. February 1884.

PAY CLERK.

Louis Joseph Mazère. Salary Rs. 2,400 per annum, plus Rs. 600 personal allowance.

Entered the service 11th. August 1874.
Present appointment 26th. March 1884.

4TH. CLASS CLERK.

Jean François Evariste Magnien. Salary Rs. 1,800 per annum, plus Rs. 60 personal allowance. (Receives Rs. 300 as Secretary to Mare-aux-Vacoas Water Supply Commission.)

Entered the service 1st. February 1872.
Present appointment 1st. January 1890.

5TH. CLASS CLERK.

Ange François Arokion. Rs. 1,200 per annum.

Entered the service 1st. January 1888.
Present appointment 24th. August 1894.

6TH. CLASS CLERK.

Henry Nicole. (Is Accountant and Storekeeper Mare-aux-Vacoas Water Supply Department with a salary of Rs. 2,400 per annum.)

Entered the service 9th. July 1875.
Present appointment 18th. November 1887.

Georges Piat, *Acting.*

ENGINEERING AND ARCHITECTURAL BRANCH.

Government Architect & Engineer.— Léon Emile Pitot. Salary Rs. 5,000 per annum

Entered the service 10th. April 1889.
Present appointment 20th. May 1891.

Inspector of Works.—Elysée Mangénie. Present salary Rs. 3,000 per annum.

Entered the service 20th. January 1886.
Present appointment 22nd. September 1886.

5TH. CLASS CLERK.

Timekeeper & Overseer.—Oscar Goder. Salary Rs. 1,200 per annum.

Entered the service 23rd. December 1892.
Present appointment 23rd. December 1892.

ROADS AND BRIDGES BRANCH.

Chief Inspector.—Charles Hall. Salary Rs. 3,600 and Rs. 2,000 travelling allowance, plus Rs. 600 personal allowance.

Entered the service 24th. April 1872.
Present appointment 25th. April 1891.

Inspector of Roads.

John Mc Veay. Salary Rs. 3,000 and Rs. 1,000 as horse allowance.

Entered the service 16th. September 1869.
Present appointment 25th. April 1891.

Charles Mazère.* Salary Rs. 3,000 per annum.

Entered the service 4th. July 1876.
Present appointment 10th. October 1892.

---

* Receives also refund of actual travellling expenses.

SURVEY BRANCH.

Government Surveyor.—Stephen Barton Hobbs. Salary Rs. 5,000 per annum.

Entered the service 28th. December 1865.
Present appointment 25th. April 1891.

Assistant Government Surveyor.—Foster Raglan Parsons. Rs. 4,000 per annum.

Entered the service 18th. August 1873.
Present appointment 10th. June 1892.

5TH. CLASS CLERK.

Louis Saminaden. Salary Rs. 1,200 per annum, plus Rs. 300 personal allowance.

Entered the service 5th. September 1863.
Present appointment 1st. January 1866.

Learners.

James Joseph Brunet Duff. Salary Rs. 840 per annum with a personal allowance of Rs. 660 and Rs. 1,500 per annum as Surveyor in charge of Mountain Reserves Lines.

Entered the service 5th. January 1875.
Present appointment 25th. April 1891.

William Marshall Vaudin. Present salary Rs. 720 per annum. (Is now in receipt of Rs. 1,200 per annum as extra Surveyor.)

Entered the service 1st. January 1888.
Present appointment 1st. June 1893.

Desbarrières E. Pougnet. Present salary Rs. 600. (Is Inspector of the Chaussée Works with a salary of Rs. 2,400 per annum.)

Entered the service 1st. January 1888.
Present appointment 25th. April 1891.

A. M. Sapet. Salary Rs. 480 per annum. (Is in receipt of Rs. 1,200 as Extra Suveyor.)

Entered the service 8th. October 1890.
Present appointment 13th. July 1893.

Louis Edouard. Present salary Rs. 480 per annum. (Is Acting 2nd. Learner.)

Appointed 15th. September 1893.

L. E. Belcourt.

Appointed 1st. September 1894.

P. Poupard.

Appointed 1st. September 1894.

Botanical Gardens.

Director of Woods & Forests & Gardens.—William Scott. Rs. 4,500 with quarters and refund of travelling allowance.

Entered the service 9th. February 1881.
Present appointment 1st. August 1893.

Superintendent of Forest Plantations & Assistant Director of Gardens.—Joseph Vankeirsbilck. Rs. 2,500 per annum and quarters.

Entered the service 15th. May 1879.
Present appointment 1st. August 1893.

Overseer.—J. Powell. Present salary Rs. 720 per annum and quarters.

Entered the service 1st. August 1887.
Present appointment 8th. July 1893.

Clerk.—C. L. Harpe. Rs. 500 per annum with quarters.

Appointed 15th. May 1893.

Guardîan.—Charles Lacaze. Rs. 600 to Rs. 1000 per annum with quarters. Present salary Rs. 840 per annum.

Appointed 3rd. May 1889.

WOODS AND FOREST BRANCH.

Assistant Director of Forests.—Paul Randabel. Rs. 2,500 per annum and quarters.

Entered the service 29th. May 1891.
Present appointment 1st. August 1893.

Officer in charge of Reduit Gardens and Plantations.—W. Kennedy. Rs. 1,500 per annum.

Entered the service 28th. February 1888.
Present appointment 24th. October 1893.

Pay Clerk.—M. Alexandre Pougnet. Rs. 1,200 per annum.

Entered the service 15th. December 1882.
Present appointment 24th. June 1891.

Assistant Clerk.—(Vacant). Rs. 720 per annum.

Copyist.—James Montocchio. Rs. 360 per annum.

Appointed 17th. March 1894.

1st. Class Inspectors.

C. M. de Tarnowsky. Rs. 1,500 plus Rs. 600 horse allowance, with quarters.

Entered the service 3rd. June 1874.
Present appointment 8th. August 1882.

Maurice Keisler. Rs 1,500 plus Rs. 600 horse allowance with quarters.

Entered the service 23rd. August 1880.
Present appointment 23rd. June 1891.

E. Fleury. Rs. 1,500 plus Rs. 600 horse allowance with quarters.

Entered the service 6th. August 1886.
Present appointment 18th. February 1892.

R. Deshayes. Rs. 1,500 plus Rs, 600 horse allowance.

Entered the service 31st. May 1881.
Present appointment 23rd. January 1893.

W. Nicole. Rs. 1,500 per annum and Rs. 600 horse allowance.

Entered the service 16th. April 1890.
Present appointment 12th. October 1894.

2nd. Class Inspectors.

B. Hily. Rs. 1,080 per annum and Rs. 600 horse allowance.

Entered the service 16th. April 1890.
Present appointment 27th. January 1893.

E. Roussart. Rs. 1,080 per annum and Rs. 600 horse allowance.

Entered the service 16th. April 1894.
Present appointment 3rd. November 1893.

David Desfosses. Rs. 1,080 per annum and 600 horse allowance.

Appointed 16th. May 1895.

Royal Alfred Observatory.

Director.—Charles Meldrum, C.M.G., L.L.S., F.R.S., F.R.A.S. Present salary Rs. 6,000 with Rs. 1,000 for quarters and a personal allowance of Rs. 1,000.

Entered the service 16th. June 1848.
Appointed January 1875.

1st. Assistant.—F. F. Claxton, Rs. 4,000 per annum and quarters.

Assumed duties on 13th. February 1896.

2nd. Assistant.—Napoléon Figon, Rs. 800 per annum and a personal allowance of Rs. 200 per annum.

Appointed 15th. October 1873.

Museum.

Superintendent.—Albert Daruty de Grandpré, Rs. 2,500 per annum.

Entered the service 1st. June 1876.
Present appointment 7th. December 1878.

Civil Status Department.

Registrar General.—George Royer Dick, M. A. Cantab., Rs. 7,000 per annum and fees.

Entered the service 4th. December 1879.
Present appointment 1st. May 1886.

3RD. CLASS CLERK.

Joseph Clodomir Maingard. Present salary Rs. 2,400 per annum.

Entered the service 28th. October 1861.
Present appointment 1st. February 1896.

4TH. CLASS CLERK.

Edwin Faoulez. Present salary Rs. 1,800 per annum. (Is acting 3rd. Class Clerk.)

Entered the service 1st. July 1884.
Appointed 4th. May 1895.

5TH. CLASS CLERKS.

Vacant.—Salary Rs. 1,200 per annum.

Léon Forget. Rs. 1,200 per annum. (Is acting 3rd. Class Clerk.)

Entered the service 1st. January 1888.
Present appointment 11th. May 1894.

6TH. CLASS CLERK.

Léon Pilot, salary Rs. 720 per annum. (Is acting 5th. Class Clerk.)

Entered the service 1st, January 1888.
Present appointment 8th. June 1892.

WRITER, Rs. 300 per annum.

A. G. Somnarain.

Appointed 6th. April 1894.

COPYIST, Rs. 300 per annum.

Joseph Bestel.

Appointed 21st. November 1894.

OFFICERS AND ASSISTANT OFFICERS OF THE CIVIL STATUS.

A. Marceau, Louis Alfred Bancilhon & E. Oxenham.—Pamplemousses. (See Dist. Magistracy.)

E. Bernon & Bissessur Halooman.—Rivière du Rempart. (See Dist. Magistracy.)

L. Meyer & Pierre Edgard Agathe.—Flacq. (See District Magistracy.)

A. Antoine, C. J. L'Etang & Jules Plassan.—Grand Port. (See Dist. Magistracy.)

A. Toureau & Louis Conway.—Savanne. (See District Magistracy.)

A. Lachesnaye, A. de Luca & S. Gellé.—Plaines Wilhems, Rose Hill Division; L. J. Madelon, Curepipe Division. (See District Magistracy.)

E. Pauquy & Eugène Bernon.—Moka. (See District Magistracy.)

S. Barfoot & William Simonet.—Black River. (See District Magistracy.)

ADDITIONAL OFFICERS OF THE CIVIL STATUS.

Jean Epidariste Morcy for Flacq at Rivière Sèche, Rs. 720 per annum and fees. Also Dispenser and draws Rs. 360 per annum.

Entered the service 1st. May 1883.
Appointed 8th. May 1895.

J. W. Arthémidor for Black River at Chamarel. Rs. 720 per annum with fees.

Entered the service 17th. July 1877.
Present appointment 1st. February 1892.

Abdool Voissile for Grand Port at Old Grand Port. Rs. 720 per annum & fees.

Entered the service 30th. July 1892.
Present appointment 3rd. July 1894.

Félix Moutia for Grand Port at Rose Belle. Rs. 720 per annum & fees.

Entered the service 5th. November 1891.
Present appointment 17th. September 1895.

A. Rose for Moka at Quartier Militaire. Rs. 720 per annum and fees.

Entered the service 8th. October 1890.
Present appointment 4th. July 1893.

A. T. Ferrière for Petite Savanne at Chemin Grenier. Salary Rs. 720 per annum and fees.

Entered the service 29th. January 1892.
Present appointment 1st. August 1892.

Customs Department.

Collector of Customs and Registrar of Shipping.—The Honorable John James Brown. Rs. 9,000 per annum.

Entered the service 20th. August 1863.
Present appointment 16th. January 1895.

Deputy Collector.—Silas Graves. Rs. 5,000 per annum.

Entered the service 2nd. May 1859.
Present appointment 2nd. March 1896.

2ND. CLASS CLERK.

Louis Michel Cartier. Present salary Rs. 3,600 per annum.

Entered the service 13th. May 1858.
Present appointment July 1894.

3RD. CLASS CLERKS.

Vacant. Present salary Rs. 2,400 per annum.

Entered the service
Present appointment

Albert Stuart Upton. Rs. 2,400 per annum. (Is acting Deputy Supt. Mercantile Marine).

Entered the service 4th. May 1866.
Present appointment 14th. March 1891.

4TH. CLASS CLERKS.

Samuel Henry Thatcher. Present salary Rs. 1,800 per annum.

Entered the service 1st. December 1881.
Present appointment 12th. March 1896.

Richard Edward Lamport. Rs 1,800 per annum a personal allowance of Rs. 800. Present salary Rs. 2,600.

Entered the service 1st. February 1878.
Present salary 9th. December 1892.

M. Auguste Ythier. Present salary R. 1,800 per annum.

Entered the service 22nd. August 1884.
Present appointment August 1894.

5TH. CLASS CLERKS.

Joseph Marius Ythier. Present salary Rs. 1,200 per annum.

Entered the service 1st. January 1881.
Present appointment 17th. October 1889.

Moïse Rayépa. Rs 1,200 per annum.

Entered the service 9th December 1887.
Present Appointed 6th. October 1893.

6TH. CLASS CLERKS.

E. Pitchen. Rs 720 per annum.

Entered the service 5th. June 1887.
Present appointment 6th. October 1893.

Georges Merle. Rs. 720 per annum.

Entered the service 8th. October 1890.
Present appointment 11th. September 1893.

P. E. Appou. Rs. 720 per annum.

Entered the service 21st. July 1892.
Present appointment 29th. November 1894.

WRITER, Rs. 300 per annum.

Daniel Standley.

Appointed 12th. August 1895.

COPYIST, Rs. 300 per annum.

J. W. Casse.

Appointed 15th. October 1895.

OUTDOOR BRANCH.

Landing Surveyor, with rank of 1st. class clerk.—Charles Adolphe d'Avray. Present salary Rs. 4,800 per annum.

Entered the service 1st. July 1868.
Present appointment 2nd. March 1896.

Senior Landing Waiter, with rank of 2nd. class clerk.—Seymour Dinnematin. Salary Rs. 3,600 per annum.

Entered the service 4th. May 1866.
Present appointment 2nd. March 1896.

3RD. CLASS CLERKS.

Landing Waiters.—Arthur Chasteauneuf. Present salary Rs. 2,500 per annum.

Entered the service 29th. November 1875.
Present appointment 3rd. April 1886.

James Chasteauneuf. Present salary Rs. 2,400 per annum, plus Rs. 100 personal allowance.

Entered the service 5th. July 1876.
Present appointment 1st. April 1886.

4TH. CLASS CLERKS.

James Emmanuel Aubert. Present salary Rs. 1,800 per annum, plus Rs 700 personal allowance.

Entered the service 1st. February 1877.
Present appointment 1st. April 1886.

Antony Marot. Present salary Rs 1,800 per annum, plus Rs. 700 personal allowance.

Entered the service 12th. May 1880.
Present appointment 1st. April 1886.

Locker.—James Brodie. Present salary Rs. 1,800 per annum.

Present appointment 6th. January 1893.

Storekeeper.—T. William Avice. Present salary Rs. 1,800 per annum.

Entered the service 21st. January 1880.
Present appointment 15th. October 1895.

5TH. CLASS CLERKS.

Searcher.—Charles A. Alexander Standley. Present Salary Rs. 1,200 per annum.

Entered the service 4th. May 1884.
Present appointment 6th. October 1893.

Assistant-Storekeepers.—Lovinski Colombino. Present salary Rs. 1,200 per annum, plus Rs. 300 personal allowance.

Entered the service 23rd. January 1878.
Present appointment 1st. October 1886.

Henry Sullivan. Present salary Rs. 1,200 per annum, plus Rs. 300 personal allowance.

Entered the service 2nd. December 1884.
Present appointment 15th. October 1895.

Tide Surveyor.

3RD. CLASS CLERK.

Henry Serret. Present salary Rs. 2,400 per annum.

Entered the service 15th. June 1873.
Present appointment 15th. October 1895.

4TH. CLASS CLERK.

Isidore Zamudio. Present salary Rs. 1,800 per annum, with Rs. 480 in lieu of lodgings.

Entered the service 10th. January 1870.
Present appointment 15th. October 1895.

TIDE WAITERS*, Rs. 1,000 to Rs. 1,500 per annum.

Honoré Lecornu. Present salary Rs. 1,500 per annum.

Entered the service 17th. January 1879.
Present appointment 1st. August 1883.

E. Baril. Present salary Rs. 1,500 per annum.

Entered the service 17th November 1882.
Present appointment 1st. January 1887.

TIDE WAITERS, Rs. 500 and an allowance of R. 1.50 a day when employed.

A. Allard.

Appointed 17th. November 1882.

A. Demiannée.

Appointed 2nd. December 1884.

C. Loulié.

Appointed 2nd. December 1884.

R. Argent.

Appointed 2nd. December 1884.

G. H. Barnes.

Appointed 2nd. December 1884.

Henry Sullivan.

Appointed 2nd. December 1884.

H. Haddon.

Appointed 13th. January 1890.

---

* On vacancy the salary will be Rs. 500 with an allowance of R. 1.50 a day when employed.

L. Mars.

Appointed 25th. February 1890.

Thomy Leaure.

Appointed 13th. January 1890.

W. Clinton.

Entered the service 1st. October 1888.
Present appointment 13th. January 1890.

A. Havard.

Appointed 22nd. June 1890.

Pascal Havard.

Appointed 1st. August 1891.

Henri Regnaud.

Appointed 22nd. June 1890.

O. Chavry.

Entered the service 25th. October 1884.
Present appointment 1st. August 1893.

William Rose.

Entered the service 15th. June 1885.
Present appointment 16th. November 1893.

E. César.

Entered the service 9th. June 1884.
Present appointment April 1894.

Richard Shaw.

Entered the service 24th. August 1886.
Present appointment 24th. August 1894.

E. Louis.

Appointed 15th. October 1895.

Léon Jacquin.

Appointed 9th. November 1895.

COAST GUARD INSPECTOR.—Rs. 1,800 per annum.

A. Latapie.

Entered the service 1st. October 1886.
Present appointment 1st. July 1888.

Veterinary Surgeon.—Clément Galdemar. Paid by fees.

Appointed 22nd. May 1888.

Harbour Department.

Harbour Master and Superintendent of Mercantile Marine.—John Wilson. Rs. 6,000 per annum, and a personal allowance of Rs. 2,000.

Entered the service 1st. September 1865.
Present appointment 22nd. May 1888.

Clerk and Boarding Officer.—Samuel Joseph Jenkins. Rs. 1,500 per annum, and a personal allowance of Rs. 1,500.

Entered the service 14th. July 1860.
Present appointment 12th January 1876.

Chief Pilot.—Thomas William Ledson. Rs. 3,000 per annum and quarters.

Entered the service 11th. April 1871.
Present appointment 7th. June 1888.

Chief Engineer.—Auguste Coutet. Rs. 2,800 per annum and Rs. 480 as house allowance.

Entered the service 30th. May 1887.
Present appointment 11th. June 1895.

2nd. Engineer.—John Thompson. Rs. 2,200 per annum, plus Rs. 300 personal allowance and Rs. 480 house allowance.

Entered the service 15th. March 1876.
Present appointment 23rd. January 1879.

DREDGING AND TOWING BRANCHES.

1st. Engineer.—François Dedans. Present salary Rs 2,200 per annum.

Entered the service 15th. June 1881.
Present appointment 1st. August 1895.

2nd. Engineer.—Théodule Lebrasse. Rs. 2,000 per annum.

Entered the service 1st. July 1884.
Present appointment 1st, August 1895.

3rd. Engineer.—Victor Constant. Present salary Rs. 1,500 per annum.

Entered the service 1st. July 1884.
Present appointment 1st. August 1895.

ENGINE ROOM ARTIFICERS.—Rs. 1,000 per annum.

J. Grosset.

Appointed 19th. February 1895.

Albert Gassin.

Appointed 1st. August 1895.

Workman.—Alvard Vanmeerbeck. Salary Rs. 500, plus Rs. 500 personal allowance.

Appointed 5th. September 1894.

Blacksmith.—Arthur Etienne, Rs. 1,000 per annum.

Appointed 15th. July 1879.

Mate of Steamer.—Louis Francis Seymour, Rs. 1,000 per annum.

Appointed 17th. July 1895.

Mate.—Rs. 1,000 per annum. (*Vacant*).

Chief Carpenter.—James Isbester. Salary Rs. 1,000 per annum, plus Rs. 500 personal allowance.

Entered the service 13th. June 1871.
Present appointment 1st. October 1878.

CARPENTER, Rs. 800 per annum.

Pierre Honoré Baya. Personal allowance Rs. 200.

Appointed 21st. October 1878.

2ND. CLASS PILOTS, Rs. 1,800 per annum and fees.

John Bonamy Carrington. (Is 1st. Class Pilot.)

Appointed 1st. January 1882.

Provisional 2nd. Class Pilots.

Evariste Dubois.

Entered the service 24th. December 1883.
Present appointment 24th. December 1889.

Louis Chauvet.

Appointed 4th. December 1889.

Chas. Lewis Harris.

Appointed 1st. October 1890.

Charles D'Hotman.

Entered the service 28th. October 1890.
Present appointment 8th. April 1891.

Robert Johnson,

Entered the service 8th. April 1891.
Present appointment 21st. January 1892.

A. Nairn.

Entered the service 16th. March 1894.
Appointed 12th. November 1894.

Light-House Establishment.

FLAT ISLAND.

Chief Light-House Keeper.—Albert Rose. Rs. 1,200 per annum and rations.

Entered the service 1st. March 1883.
Present appointment 11th. July 1894.

1*st. Assistant.*—(*Vacant.*)

CANNONIERS POINT.

Chief Light-Keeper.—Robert Spencer Lucas. Rs. 900 per annum, plus Rs. 100 personal allowance and rations.

Entered the service 20th. August 1872.
Present appointment 20th. March 1875.

1*st. Assistant.*—Louis Oscar Bisergône. Rs. 700 per annum and rations.

Appointed 16th. November 1893.

ILES AUX FOUQUETS.

Light-House Keeper.—Charles Scheffler. Rs. 900 per annum and rations.

Entered the service 1st. January 1884.
Present appointment July 1894.

1*st. Assistant.*—Charles August Johnson. Rs. 700 per annum and rations.

Appointed July 1894.

QUARANTINE GUARD AND LIGHT VESSEL.

Master.—Charles Green. Rs. 1,920 per annum with Rs. 20 per mensem for rations.

Entered the service 16th. May 1883.
Present appointment 7th. April 1892.

1st. Mate.—Ole Severin Davidsen. Rs. 1,000 per annum and Rs. 20 per mensem in lieu of rations.

Entered the service 13th. January 1883.
Present appointment 7th. April 1892.

2nd. Mate.—John Edward Manning. Rs. 840 per annum and Rs. 20 per mensem in lieu of rations.

Entered the service 5th. August 1887.
Present appointment 7th. April 1892.

Mercantile Marine Office.

Superintendent.—John Wilson. (Is Harbour Master).

Deputy Superintendent.—Nemours Decotter. Rs. 2,500 per annum, and a personal allowance of Rs. 1,000. (*On leave.*)

Appointed 27th. April 1893.

Acting Deputy Superintendent.— A S. Upton.

Registration and Mortgage Department.

Receiver of Registration Dues and Conservator of Mortgages.—Napoléon Lesage. Rs. 9,000 per annum.

Entered the service 1st. December 1844.
Present appointment 15th. November 1884.

1st. CLASS CLERK.

Louis Evenor Dupont. Present salary Rs. 4,800 per annum, plus Rs. 1,200 personal allowance.

Entered the service 1st. September 1864.
Present appointment 18th. June 1884.

2nd. CLASS CLERKS.

Paul Ange Eugène D'Emmerez. Present salary Rs. 3,600 per annum, plus Rs. 400 personal allowance.

Entered the service 20th. November 1866.
Present appointment 18th. January 1870.

Stanislas Pitchen. Present salary Rs. 3,600 per annum, plus Rs. 400 personal allowance.

Entered the service 9th. October 1874.
Present appointment 12th. July 1893.

3RD. CLASS CLERKS.

Evariste Margéot. Present salary Rs. 2,400 per annum, plus Rs. 600 personal allowance.

Entered the service 7th. April 1883.
Present appointment 23rd. August 1887.

Charles Edouard Pitrel. Present salary Rs. 2,400 per annum.

Entered the service 1st. August 1865.
Present appointment 1st. July 1889.

Gulbéas Goy. Present salary Rs. 2,400 per annum.

Entered the service 3rd. May 1881.
Present appointment 1st. August 1895.

4TH. CLASS CLERKS.

Félix Serret. Present salary Rs. 1,800 per annum.

Entered the service 1st. August 1881.
Present appointment 11th. August 1891.

Arthur Grégoire. Present salary Rs. 1,800 per annum.

Entered the service 30th. March 1883.
Present appointment 4th. May 1894.

5TH. CLASS CLERKS.

Paul Charles Quéland. Present salary Rs. 1,200 per annum.

Entered the service 8th. July 1880.
Present appointment 1st. January 1891.

Ivan Rupert Mellish. Present salary Rs. 1,200 per annum.

Entered the service 23rd. August 1882.
Present appointment 25th. August 1891.

William George Smith, Present salary Rs. 1,200 per annum.

Entered the service 12th. February 1885.
Present appointment 5th. June 1894.

Maurice Yardin. Salary Rs. 1,200 per annum.

Entered the service 14th. July 1885.
Present appointment 21st. January 1891.

6TH. CLASS CLERK.

Tristan Avice. Salary Rs. 720 per annum.

Entered the service 20th. Febuary 1892.
Present appointment 4th. May 1894.

Archives Office.

Custodian of Archives.—Aimé Duvivier. Present salary Rs. 3,600 per annum.

Entered the service 1st. November 1879.
Present appointment 1st. January 1891.

5TH. CLASS CLERK.

Isis Boucherat. Present salary Rs. 1,200 per annum.

Entered the service 16th. August 1882.
Present appointment 5th, June 1894.

6TH. CLASS CLERK.

Emmanuel Gérard. Present salary Rs. 720 per annum.

Entered the service 1st. April 1893.
Present appointment 5th. June 1894.

Post Office Department.

Colonial Postmaster & Superintendent of Telegraphs.—Louis Martin, Rs. 6,000 per annum.

Entered the service 1st. January 1860.
Present appointment 20th. September 1892.

2ND. CLASS CLERK.

Samuel Stanley. Present salary Rs. 3,600 per annum.

Entered the service 1st. May 1865.
Present appointment 7th. December 1891.

3RD. CLASS CLERK.

Pierre Edgard Robert. Present salary Rs. 2,400 per annum.

Entered the service 25th. May 1877.
Present appointment 12th. February 1889.

4TH. CLASS CLERK.

Edgard Bourelly. Present salary Rs. 1,800 per annum.

Entered the service 1st. January 1878.
Present appointment 12th. February 1889.

5TH. CLASS CLERKS, Rs. 1,200 per annum.

Auguste Lefébure.

Entered the service 1st. July 1880.
Present appointment 12th. February 1889.

Louis François Rivet.

Entered the service 15th. March 1882.
Present appointment 1st. January 1890.

Charles Albert.

Present appointment 1st. January 1890.

Gabriel Viale.

Entered the service 1st. January 1886.
Present appointment 1st. January 1890.

Léon Clair Robert.

Entered the service 15th. May 1881.
Present appointment 1st. January 1890.

H. L. Philippe.

Entered the service 11th. January 1877.
Present appointment 1st. July 1892.

Eugène Hermelin.

Entered the service March 1868.
Present appointment 15th. July 1892.

Alfred Beaupré.

Entered the service January 1871.
Present appointment 21st. September 1894.

TELEGRAPH BRANCH.

2ND. CLASS CLERK.

Postal and Telegraph Inspector.—Clément Joachim. Present salary Rs. 3,600 per annum, plus Rs. 400 personal allowance.

Entered the service 1st. September 1879.
Present appointment 8th. January 1885.

Select Operator.—A. Geffroy. Rs. 960 per annum.

Entered the service 1st. January 1877.
Present appointment 21st. September 1894.

First Class Operators, Rs. 840 per annum.

Albert Goder.

Appointed 1st. January 1877.

Henri Veckranges.

Appointed 1st. January 1877.

Bélisaire Baya.

Appointde 16th. October 1879.

Jules Tailly.

Appointed 1st. January 1877.

Daniel Sullivan.

Appointed 16th. March 1880.

Aldor Larochette.

Appointed 1st. February 1890.

Némorin.

Appointed 21st. September 1894.

S. Johnson.

Appointed 22nd. March 1895

Supreme Court.

Chief Judge.—His Honor Sir Eugène Pierre Jules Leclézio, Knight. Rs. 17,500 per annum, and a personal allowance of Rs. 154.11 per annum for loss of fees as Vice Admiralty Judge. (*On leave.*)

Entered the service 13th. September 1878.
Present appointment 14th. December 1883.

The Hon. F. T. Piggott, (*Acting.*)

PUISNE JUDGES.

His Honor John Rouillard. Rs. 12,000 per annum.

Entered the service 13th. February 1865.
Present appointment 25th. June 1886.

His Honor Victor Delafaye. Rs. 12,000 per annum.

Appointed 15th. October 1894.

His Honor Frederick Charles Moncrieff. Rs. 12,000 per annum.

Assumed duties on 18th. February 1896.

JUDGES CLERKS.

William Mc Irvine. Present salary Rs. 3,000 plus Rs. 500 as Interpreter.

Entered the service 23rd. September 1878.
Present appointment 17th. September 1883.

Léon Huet de Froberville. Present salary Rs. 3,000 per annum. (Is Acting 2nd. class clerk, Registry, Supreme Court.)

Entered the service 18th. June 1878.
Present appointment 23rd. September 1892.

Thomas W. Hanning. Present salary. Rs. 3,000 per annum.

Entered the service 1st. March 1885.
Present appointment 8th. April 1893.

Henry William James Lavers. Present salary Rs. 3,000 per annum.

Entered the service 30th. January 1892.
Present appointment 14th. January 1895.

Short-Hand Writer.—Vivian Israel Bennett. Rs. 2,500 per annum. (Is also Short-Hand Writer to the Council of Government and draws Rs. 2,500 as such.)

Appointed 21st. September 1882.

Master's Court.

Master.—His Honor Ernest Didier St. Amand. Rs. 10,000 per annum.

Entered the service 3rd. April 1869.
Present appointment 25th. June 1886.

Chief Clerk.—Louis Gustave de Comarmond. Present salary Rs. 4,800 per annum with fees as Interpreter of the Master's and Bankruptcy Courts.

Entered the service 27th. April 1865.
Present appointment 8th. April 1893.

Second Clerk.—Ibrahim Piarroux. Present salary Rs. 3,000 per annum.

Entered the service 1st. November 1865.
Present appointment 16th. April 1869.

Third Clerk.—Julius Richard Coombes. Present salary Rs. 3,000 per annum.

Entered the service 11th. February 1865.
Present appointment 1st. October 1874.

Victor Antoine Emile Duvivier. Present salary Rs. 1,800 per annum, plus Rs. 600 personal allowance.

Entered the service 1st. March 1885.
Present appointment June 1893.

Registrar's Office.

Registrar.—François Léonce Isnard. Rs. 7,000 per annum.

Entered the service 11th. May 1854.
Present appointment 1st. March 1892.

Chief Clerk.—William Bathfield. Present salary Rs. 4,800 per annum.

Entered the service 28th. May 1873.
Present appointment 8th. April 1893.

2ND. CLASS CLERK.

Jocelyn D'Emmerez de Charmoy. Present salary Rs. 3,600 per annum. (Is Acting Accountant in Bankruptcy.)

Entered the service 15th. April 1884.
Present appointment 8th. April 1893.

3RD. CLASS CLERK.

Louis Soligny Collet. Present salary Rs. 2,400 per annum.

Entered the service 13th. September 1880.
Present appointment 26th. August 1889.

4TH. CLASS CLERK.

Maxime Boullé. Rs. 1,800 per annum.

Entered the service October 1890.
Present appointment 8th. April 1893.

5TH. CLASS CLERK.

Louis Halais. Rs. 1,200 per annum.

Entered the service 1st. December 1891.
Present appointment 1st. February 1894.

6TH. CLASS CLERK.

Gaston Kœnig. Rs. 720 per annum.

Entered the service 26th. September 1892.
Present appointment 1st. February 1894.

Bankruptcy Court.

Judge.—His Honor E. Didier St. Amand. (Vide Master's Office).

Registrar.—L. G. de Comarmond (Vide Master's Office).

Accountant.—George Newton. Rs. 6,000 per annum. (*On leave*).

Entered the service 18th. August 1882.
Present appointment 7th. June 1884.

Jocelyn D'Emmerez de Charmoy, *Acting*.

5TH. CLASS CLERK.

Ernest Pougnet. Rs. 1,200 per annum.

Entered the service 20th. July 1885.
Present appointment 1st. October 1890.

Procureur General's Department.

Procureur General.—The Honorable Francis Taylor Piggott. Rs. 13,500 per annum. (Is Acting Chief Judge).

Appointed 22nd. January 1894.
Assumed duties 15th. March 1894.

Substitute Procureur General.—The Honorable Louis Rouillard. Rs. 10,000 per annum. (Is Acting Procureur General).

Appointed 1st. September 1886.

Additional Substitute Procureur General.—Louis Arthur Thibaud. Salary Rs. 6,000 per annum. (Is Acting Substitute Procureur General).

Entered the service 4th. May 1885.
Present appointment January 1890.

2ND. CLASS CLERK.

Albert Rae. Present salary Rs. 3,600 per annum.

Entered the service 9th. September 1875.
Present appointment 11th. May 1894.

3RD. CLASS CLERK.

Edgard John Morgan. Present salary Rs. 2,400 per annum.

Entered the service 9th. September 1878.
Present appointment 11th. May 1894.

4TH. CLASS CLERK.

Jules Lalanne. Present salary Rs. 1,800 per annum. (Is Acting 3rd. Class Clerk).

Entered the service 1st. July 1882.
Present appointment 1st. August 1893.

5TH. CLASS CLERK.

John Lesueur Greene. Present salary Rs. 1,200. Is also Translator of Laws for which he receives Rs. 1,500 per annum. (Is acting 4th. Class Clerk.)

Entered the service 5th. January 1886.
Present appointment 1st. July 1890.

6TH. CLASS CLERKS.

J. E. Steggall Florens. Rs. 720 per annum.

Entered the service 3rd. September 1894.
Appointed 8th. April 1895.

Daniel St. Bertin. Present salary Rs. 720 per annum.

Entered the service 6th. June 1893.
Appointed 12th. August 1895.

WRITER, Rs. 300 per annum.

Louis Wilhems Cateaux.

Entered the service 16th. August 1893.
Present appointment 5th. June 1895.

COPYISTS, Rs. 300 per annum.

E. Bazile.

Appointed 15th. May 1895.

G. Clair.

Appointed 2nd. July 1895.

CROWN PROSECUTORS, Rs. 4,800 per annum.

Martial L. A. Noël. (Is Acting Additional Substitute Procureur General.)

Entered the service 15th. March 1889.
Present appointment 1st. March 1892.

A. Herchenroder, (*Acting*).

Eugène Serret.

Appointed 10th. March 1892.

CROWN ATTORNEY'S BRANCH.

Crown Attorney.—Julius Guibert. Rs. 6,000 per annum, plus Rs. 1,500 per annum personal allowance.

Appointed 1st. July 1883.

5TH. CLASS CLERK.

Maurice Bérenger. Present salary Rs. 1,200 per annum.

Entered the service 18th. April 1891.
Present appointment 12th. August 1895.

6TH. CLASS CLERK.

Fritz Rohan. Present salary Rs. 720 per annum.

Entered the service 12th. February 1894.
Present appointment 8th. October 1895.

Curatelle Office.

Curator of Vacant Estates.—Frédéric Poirier. Rs. 4,000 per annum.

Entered the service 23rd. November 1870.
Present appointment 27th. June 1890.

3RD. CLASS CLERK.

Robert Vilbro. Rs. 2,400 per annum, plus Rs. 100 personal allowance.

Entered the service 28th. May 1860.
Present appointment 19th. March 1885.

Senior District Magistracy.

Senior District Magistrate. — George Clifford Mayer. Rs. 7,000 per annum

Entered the service 13th. January 1865.
Present appointment 10th. January 1887.

District Clerk.—Jean François Evenor Desmarais. Present salary Rs. 3,600 per annum, plus Rs. 400 personal allowance.

Entered the service 1st. September 1866.
Present appointment 13th. May 1875.

Joint District Clerk.—Lucien Bouffé. Present salary Rs. 2,500 per annum. (Receives Rs. 500 per annum as Secretary to Central Prisons Board.)

Entered the service 26th. January 1879.
Present appointment 15th. June 1888.

Assistant District Clerk.— Léon Aminthe. Present salary Rs. 1,200 per annum.

Entered the service January 1882.
Present appointment 15th. November 1895.

Extra Clerk.—George Pougnet. Rs. 1,200 per annum.

Entered the service 1st. February 1885.
Present appointment 20th. February 1892.

Cashier.—Alfred Dupont. Present salary Rs. 2,400 per annum.

Entered the service 1st. September 1871.
Present appointment 21st. July 1894.

Interpreter.—Cancalla Rungasamy. Rs. 1,000 per annum.

Entered the service 5th. May 1882.
Present appointment 1st. November 1882.

Junior District Magistracy.

Junior District Magistrate.—Edouard Amand Esnouf. Rs. 7,000 per annum.

Entered the service 5th. February 1870.
Present appointment 1st. August 1884.

Joint District Clerk.—Louis Nicolas Hardy Sénèque. Present salary Rs. 2,400 per annum, plus Rs. 600 personal allowance.

Entered the service 3rd. March 1864.
Present appointment 29th. January 1879.

Assistant District Clerk.—Allan Barraut. Present salary Rs. 1,200 per annum and a personal allowance of Rs. 300.

Entered the service 23rd. August 1882.
Present appointment 28th. October 1890.

Interpreter.—James Bartholomew Englebright. Present salary Rs. 1,000 per annum, plus Rs. 500 personal allowance.

Entered the service 1st. July 1856.
Present appointment 22nd. July 1891.

Police and Additional Magistracy, Port Louis.

Police Magistrate.—John Henry Ackroyd. Rs. 7,000 per annum.

Entered the service 4th. July 1877.
Present appointment 15th. August 1895.

Joint District Clerk.—Edward Mc Gregor. Present salary Rs. 2,400 per annum. (Is Acting District Clerk, Curepipe).

Entered the service 14th. March 1876.
Present appointment 20th. February 1892.

Louis Conway, *Acting.*

Assistant Clerk.—N. Sicard. Present salary Rs. 1,200 per annum.

Entered the service 1st. January 1888.
Present appointment 20th. February 1892.

Interpreter.—Paul Lazarre. Rs. 1,000 per annum.

Appointed 14th. May 1895.

Stipendiary Magistracy, Port Louis.

Stipendiary Magistrate.—Thomas Erskine Dempster. Rs. 5,000 per annum, with Rs. 1,000 for house allowance and Rs. 750 for travelling allowance. (See Stipendiary Magistracy, Pamplemousses).

Appointed 1st. November 1877.

Clerk.—Volny Villemont. Rs. 1,800 per annum. (*On leave*).

Entered the service 30th. April 1879.
Present appointment 1st. July 1893.

L. A. Bancilhon, *Acting*.

District Magistracy.

PAMPLEMOUSSES.

District Magistrate.—Arthur Boucherat. Rs. 6,000 per annum.

Entered the service 20th. November 1884.
Present appointment 29th. November 1890.

District Clerk.—(*Vacant*). Salary Rs. 3,600 per annum.

Joint District Clerk.—Edgard Oxenham. Present salary Rs. 2,400 per annum.

Entered the service 12th. July 1882.
Present appointment 26th. September 1894.

Assistant District Clerk.—L. A. Bancilhon. Present salary Rs. 1,200 p. a.

Entered the service 13th. July 1885.
Present appointment 8th. April 1895.

District Cashier.—Octave Sandapa. Present salary Rs. 2,800 per annum, 2½ o/o commission on certain stamps and Rs. 150 for collecting Direct Taxes.

Entered the service 3rd. October 1877.
Present appointment 1st. November 1889.

RIVIÈRE DU REMPART.

District and Stipendiary Magistrate.—Gustave Pilot. Rs. 6,000 per annum.

Entered the service May 1879.
Present appointment 7th. March 1896.

District Clerk.—Elysée Bernon. Present salary Rs. 3,850 per annum.

Entered the service 21st. August 1863.
Present appointment 8th. March 1887.

Assistant District Clerk.—Bissessur Haloo man. Present salary Rs. 1,200 per annum.

Entered the service 1st. December 1887.
Present appointment 15th. November 1895.

District Cashier.—Raoul Pinguet. Present salary Rs. 2,400 per annum.

Entered the service 26th. October 1876.
Present appointment 29th. April 1892.

Interpreter.—James Pung. Rs. 1,000 per annum.

Appointed 15th. November 1895.

FLACQ.

District Magistrate.—H. Hewetson. Rs. 6,000 per annum.

Entered the service 1st. May 1888.
Present appointment 7th. March 1896.

District Clerk.—Léopold Meyer. Present salary Rs. 4,000 per annum.

Entered the service 1st. May 1861.
Present appointment 6th. January 1886.

Joint District Clerk.—Julius Aubert Allain. Present salary Rs. 2,400 per annum. (Is Acting Joint District Clerk, Pamplemousses.)

Entered the service 18th. June 1880.
Present appointment 1st. July 1893.

Assistant District Clerk.— Pierre Edgar Agathe. Present salary Rs. 1,200 per annum.

Entered the service 18th. August 1892.
Present appointment 8th. April 1895.

District Cashier.— Vincent Léon Salèce. Present salary Rs. 2,950. (Draws Rs. 240 from General Board of Health Funds ; Rs. 200 for collecting Direct Taxes and 2½ o/o commission on sale of certain Stamps.)

Entered the service 27th. August 1866.
Present appointment 1st. April 1886.

Interpreter.—Edward Mootee. Rs. 1,000 per annum.

Appointed 4th. June 1891.

GRAND PORT.

District Magistrate.—L. A. Hugues. Rs. 6,000 per annum.

Present appointment March 1896.

District Clerk.—Alfred Antoine. Present salary Rs. 3,600 per annum.

Entered the service 17th. January 1860.
Present appointment 1st. August 1891.

Joint District Clerk.—J. Plassan. Present salary Rs. 2,400 per annum.

Entered the service 2nd. February 1872.
Present appointment 20th. February 1892.

Assistant District Clerk.—Charles Jules L'Etang. Present salary Rs. 1,200 per annum.

Entered the service 17th July 1877.
Present appointment 16th. November 1891.

District Cashier.—Oscar Richard Coombes. Present salary Rs. 3,000. (Receives also 2½ o/o commission on sales of certain stamps and Rs. 240 per annum from General Board of Health Funds.)

Entered the service 10th. January 1866.
Present appointment 16th. January 1883.

Interpreter.—Daniel Dawson. Rs. 1,000 per annum.

Entered the service 4th. August 1874.
Present appointment 2nd. November 1882.

SAVANNE.

District Magistrate.— Amable Emile Lanougarède Bazire. Rs. 6,000 per annum.

Entered the service 10th. January 1887.
Present appointment 7th. March 1896.

District Clerk.—Aristhène Toureau. Present salary Rs. 3,400 per annum.

Entered the service 5th. August 1858.
Present appointment 5th. June 1888.

Joint District Clerk.—Louis Conway. Present salary Rs. 2,400 per annum. (Is Acting Joint District Clerk, Port Louis).

Entered the service 1st. March 1874.
Present appointment 26th. September 1894.

District Cashier.—Louis Pilot. Present salary Rs. 2,400 per annum.

Entered the service 1st. March 1882.
Present appointment 1st. March 1894.

Interpreter.—J. Savrimoothoo. Rs. 1,000 per annum.

Entered the service 10th. February 1890.
Present appointment 25th. February 1891.

PLAINES WILHEMS.— ROSE HILL DIVISION.

District Magistrate.—Hippolyte Le Mière. Rs. 6,000 per annum.

Entered the service 30th. November 1882.
Present appointment 30th. April 1895.

District Clerk.—Adrien Le Bas de Lachenaye. Rs. 4,000 per annum.

Entered the service 8th. October 1858.
Present appointment 1st. June 1891.

Joint District Clerk.—Seide Gellé. Present salary Rs. 2,500 per annum.

Entered the service 1st. January 1868.
Present appointment 5th. June 1888.

Assistant District Clerk.—Karl Alfons de Luca. Present salary Rs. 1,200 per annum.

Entered the service 28th. January 1885.
Present appointment 23rd. June 1891.

District Cashier.—Alfred Langlois. Present salary Rs. 3,000. (Receives also Rs. 240 per annum from General Board of Health Funds and 2¼ o[o commission on sale of certain stamps.)

Entered the service 1st. September 1858.
Present appointment 8th. June 1868.

Interpreter.—James Peersahib. Rs. 1,000 per annum with Rs. 500 personal allowance.

Entered the service 1st. February 1859.
Present appointment 13th. April 1876.

Usher.—Désir Mai. Rs. 2,000 per annum and Rs. 750 personal allowance.

Entered the service 6th. February 1878.
Present appointment 11th. October 1886.

CUREPIPE DIVISION.

District and Stipendiary Magistrate.—Henri Avice. Present salary Rs. 6,000 and Rs. 750 travelling allowance. (See District Magistracy, Black River.)

Clerk.—Louis Joseph Madelon. Present salary Rs. 2,400 per annum. (*On leave.*)

Entered the service 22nd. May 1877.
Present appointment 30th. January 1890.

Edward Mc Gregor, *Acting.*

Assistant District and Stipendiary Clerk.—Louis Mylius Aza, Present salary Rs. 1,200 per annum. (Is also Assistant Stipendiary Clerk, Black River.)

Entered the service 1st. January 1888.
Present appointment 1st. August 1893.

District Cashier.—Gustave Victor Pitot. Present salary Rs. 1,800 per annum.

Entered the service 19th. November 1880.
Present appointment 1st. March 1894.

WRITERS, Rs. 300.

K. Seewoodharry Buguth.

Entered the service 4th. July 1893.
Present appointment 15th. November 1893.

Interpreter.— Perumal Rada Ramsawmy (Vide District and Stipendiary Magistrate, Black River).

MOKA.

District and Stipendiary Magistrate.— Henry Eugène Desmarais. Rs. 7,000 per annum.

Entered the service 4th. June 1875.
Present appointment 3rd. July 1889.

District Clerk.—Elysée Pauquy. Present salary Rs. 3,600 per annum.

Entered the service 13th. September 1858.
Present appointment 1st. October 1890.

Joint District Clerk.—Eugène Bernon. Present salary Rs. 2,400 per annum.

Entered the service 15th. September 1873.
Present appointment 20th. October 1890.

District Cashier.—James Fernand Arnot. Present salary Rs. 2,400 per annum.

Entered the service 21st. August 1876.
Present appointment 20th. July 1894.

Interpreter.—S. Amoordassamy. Rs. 1,000 per annum.

Entered the service 15th. September 1880.
Appointed 22nd. July 1891.

BLACK RIVER.

District and Stipendiary Magistrate.— Henri Avice. (Is also District and Stipendiary Magistrate, Curepipe). Present salary Rs. 6,000 per annum. and Rs. 750 travelling allowance.

Entered the service 1st. June 1888.
Present appointment December 1889.

District and Stipendiary Clerk.—Samuel Barfoot. Present salary Rs. 3,600 per annum.

Entered the service 22nd. June 1866.
Present appointment 1st. June 1891.

Assistant Clerk and Interpreter.— M. Aza (Vide District and Stipendiary Magistracies, Plaines Wilhems, Curepipe Division.)

Assistant District and Stipendiary Clerk.—William Simonet. Present salary Rs. 1,200 per annum.

Entered the service 23rd. January 1888.
Present appointment 15th. November 1895.

District Cashier.—Jean Nemours Morin. Present salary Rs. 2,400 per annum.

Entered the service 1st. December 1876.
Present appointment 20th. July 1894.

Interpreter.—Perumal Rada Ramsawmy. Salary Rs. 750 per annum with a free Railway contract ticket between Petite Rivière and Curepipe and Rs. 2 per diem for travelling between Petite Rivière and Bambous.

Appointed 25th. March 1890.

Stipendiary Magistracy.

PAMPLEMOUSSES.

Stipendiary Magistrate.—Thomas Erskine Dempster. (Vide Port Louis).

Chief Stipendiary Clerk.—Ernest E. Rae. Present salary Rs. 1,800 per annum.

Entered the service 11th. May 1881.
Present appointment 1st. July 1893.

Clerk and Interpreter.—J. Bruneau. (Vide Stipendiary Magistracy, Plaines Wilhems.)

RIVIÈRE DU REMPART.

Stipendiary Magistrate.—Gustave Pilot. (Is also District Magistrate.)

Chief Clerk.—James Robert. Present salary Rs. 2,000 annum.

Entered the service July 1872.
Present appointment 8th. September 1890.

FLACQ.

Stipendiary Magistrate.—Andrew John La Nauze. Rs. 5,000 per annum with Rs. 1,750 for house and travelling allowance. (Is also Stipendiary Magistrate, Plaines Wilhems.)

Appointed 7th. September 1877.

Chief Stipendiary Clerk.—François Chéry Jonas. Present salary Rs. 2,000 per annum.

Entered the service 27th. August 1876.
Present appointment 5th. April 1895.

Assistant Clerk and Interpreter.—L. Wilmann. Present salary Rs. 1,500 per annum.

Entered the service 1st. September 1883.
Present appointment 28th. October 1890.

GRAND PORT.

Stipendiary Magistrate.—George Albert Baptiste. Rs. 5,000 per annum with Rs. 1,750 house and horse allowance. (Is also Stipendiary Magistrate, Savanne.)

Appointed 1st. December 1877.

Chief Clerk.—Pierre Evariste Simonet. Present salary Rs. 1,800 per annum.

Entered the service 1st. August 1881.
Present appointment 20th. February 1892.

Assistant Clerk and Interpreter.— Edgar Moutia. Present salary Rs. 1,400 per annum.

Entered the service 15th. June 1885.
Present appointment 15th. April 1894.

SAVANNE.

Stipendiary Magistrate.—George Albert Baptiste. (Vide Stipendiary Magistracy, Grand Port).

Chief Stipendiary Clerk. — Henry Juppin de Fondaumière. Present salary Rs. 1,800 per annum.

Entered the service 18th. October 1876.
Present appointment 16th. November 1891.

Assistant Clerk and Interpreter.—E. Moutia. (Vide Stipendiary Magistracy, Grand Port).

PLAINES WILHEMS.

Stipendiary Magistrate.—Andrew John La Nauze. (Vide Stipendiary Magistracy, Flacq).

Chief Clerk.—(*Vacant*). Salary Rs. 2,000 per annum.

Assistant Clerk and Interpreter.—Joseph Bruneau. Present salary Rs. 1,200 per annum.

Entered the service 1st. January 1888.
Present appointment 1st. July 1893.

MOKA.

Stipendiary Magistrate.—H. Eugène Desmarais. (Is also District Magistrate).

Chief Clerk.—Leu Caltaux. Present salary Rs. 1,800 per annum.

Entered the service 22nd. April 1876.
Present appointment 16th. November 1891.

BLACK RIVER.

Stipendiary Magistrate.—Henri Avice. (Vide District Magistracy, Black River and Curepipe.)

[The Clerical duties of this Court are carried on by the Officers of the District Court.]

Ecclesiastical.

CHURCH OF ENGLAND.

Lord Bishop of Mauritius.—The Right Reverend W. Walsh M. A., D. D. Rs. 7,200 per annum with Rs. 1,000 travelling allowance.

Appointed 26th. December 1890.
Consecrated 2nd. February 1891.

Archdeacon of Mauritius and Bishop's Commissionary.—The Venerable Robert James French. Rs. 4,000 per aunnm. (*On leave*).

Entered the service 20th. March 1871.
Appointed 24th. March 1895.

Second Civil Chaplain in Port Louis.—Reverend Adolphus Vaudin. Rs. 3,000 per annum.

Entered the service 6th. May 1860.
Appointed 24th. April 1895.

Civil Chaplain, Vacoas and Black River.—Reverend Louis Napoléon Seichan, Rs. 3,000 per annum.

Appointed 2nd. October 1890.

Civil Chaplain, Curepipe.—Reverend Charles Sumner Harrington, M. A. Rs. 2,000 per annum.

Entered the service May 1890.
Present appointment 4th. October 1884.

Civil Chaplain of Mahebourg.—Reverend A. Kington Finnimore, B. A. Rs. 3,000 per annum.

Appointed 24th. April 1895.

Incumbent of St. Thomas, Beau Bassin.—Reverend Herbert Adney Woolaston Jones A. K. C. L. Rs. 2,500, per annum.

Appointed 24th. March 1895.

Incumbent of St. John's Moka.—Reverend Whylock Pendavis, M. A. Rs. 2,000 per annum. (Is also Religious Instructor at the Royal College for which he receives Rs. 500 per annum.

Appointed 1st. June 1886.

French Chaplain St. James' Cathedral and *Incumbent of St. Barnabas,* Pamplemousses.—Reverend Adrien Lagier, B. in Th. Rs. 3,000 per annum.

Appointed 4th. July 1878.

Incumbent of St. Nicolas (Mariner's) Church Port Louis.—Reverend H. A. Wollaston Jones, Rs. 2,000 per annum.

Appointed 2nd. February 1895.

NATIONAL CHURCH OF SCOTLAND.

Chaplain St. Andrew's Church Rose Hill and Curepipe.— Reverend George Mc Irvine, M. A., Rs. 4,000 per annum.

Appointed 7th. November 1856.

ROMAN CATHOLIC CHURCH.

Lord Bishop of Port Louis.—Rs. 7,200 per annum with Rs. 1,000 travelling allowance. (*Vacant*).

Vicar General.—Very Reverend Canon Patrick Cooney, Rs. 3,000 per annum with Rs. 500 travelling allowance. (Is administrator of the Diocese).

Entered the service 14th. November 1880.
Present appointment 4th. June 1895.

First Class Priests.

Parish Priest of Montagne Longue. — Reverend A. Cleret de Langavant, Rs. 2,000 per annum.

Appointed 12th. April 1894.

Parish Priest of the Immaculée Conception, Port Louis.— Very Reverend Canon Sébastien Marcelli, Rs. 2,000 per annum.

Appointed 9th. September 1867.

Parish Priest of Beau Bassin.—Reverend Cornelius Hogan, Rs. 2,000 per annum.

Entered the service 1st. April 1873.
Present appointment 17th. March 1894.

Parish Priest of the Cathedral.—Reverend Patrick Sweeney, Rs. 2,000 per annum.

Entered the service 14th. November 1880.
Present appointment 1st. January 1887.

Parish Priest of St. Jean.—Reverend A. Haaby, Rs. 2,000 per annum.

Appointed 1st. June 1895.

Parish Priest of Curepipe.—Very Reverend Canon Cornelius O'Loughlin, Rs. 2,000 per annum.

Entered the service 17th. March 1873.
Present appointment 27th. November 1885.

Parish Priest of Vacoas.—Very Reverend Canon Emile Chalvet, Rs. 2,000 per annum.

Appointed 4th. April 1888.

Parish Priest at Rodrigues.—Reverend Joseph Cotonéa, Rs. 2,000 per annum.

Appointed 6th. February 1891.

Parish Priest of Bambous.—Reverend Charles Léon Piffoux, Rs. 2,000 per annum.

Appointed 27th. April 1888.

Vicar of Notre Dame de Lourdes, Rose Hill (Missionary).—Reverend Daniel Connellan, S.J., Rs. 2,000 per annum.

Appointed 12th. August 1883.

Parish Priest of Flacq.—Reverend Patrick Coghlan, Rs. 2,000 per annum.

Appointed 14th. March 1887.

Parish Priest of Pamplemousses.—Reverend Thomas J. O'Neil, Rs. 2,000 per annum.

Appointed 14th. October 1887.

Parish Priest of Mahebourg.—Reverend Aloysius Ditner, Rs. 2,000 per annum.

Appointed 1st. April 1888.

Parish Priest of Poudre d'Or.—Reverend Pierre Bretesché, Rs. 2,000 per annum.

Appointed 1st. November 1890.

Vicar of Curepipe.—Reverend F. Mac Carthy, Rs. 2,000 per annum.

Entered the service 29th June 1883.
Present appointment 7th. August 1895.

Second Class Priests.

Vicar of Mahebourg.—Reverend Michel Béchet, Rs. 1,500 per annum.

Appointed 9th. June 1881.

Vicar of Souillac.— Reverend Alphonse Clément Perraud, Rs. 1,500 per annum.

Appointed 17th. February 1884.

Parish Priest of Souillac—Reverend Lucien Mengelle, Rs. 1,500. per annum.

Appointed 19th. October 1888.

Vicar of Rose Hill—Reverend (Missionary) Victor Malaval. Rs. 1,500 per annum.

Appointed 1st. November 1894.

Vicar of Rose Hill.—Reverend François Guilhen. Rs. 1,500 per annum.

Appointed 1st. November 1894.

Vicar of the Cathedral.—Reverend Jérome Rochette de Lempdes, Rs. 1,500 per annum.

Appointed 19th. April 1889.

Vicar of the Immaculée Conception.—Reverend Benjamin Grimaud. Rs. 1,500 per annum.

Appointed 12th. June 1893.

Vicar of the Cathedral.—Reverend Pierre Joseph Lainé. Rs. 1,500 per annum.

Appointed 1st. March 1889.

Vicar of the Immaculée Conception.— Reverend Joseph Guyot. Rs. 1,500 per annum.

Appointed 10th. October 1890.

Vicar of the Cathedral.— Reverend Auguste Gausserand. Rs. 1,000 per annnm.

Appointed 10th. January 1893.

Parish Priest of Bocage, Director of the Seminary.—Reverend L. Montferran. Rs. 1,500 per annum.

Appointed March 1895.

Parish Priest of Chamarel.—Reverend J. de Souza. Rs. 1,500 per annum.

Vicar of St. Julian's.—Reverend Alphonse Boujon. Rs. 1,500 per annum.

Appointed 1st. November 1892.

Parish Priest of Rivière Sèche.—Reverend François Rellier. Rs. 1,500 per annum.

Appointed 1st. September 1892.

Parish Priest of Rose Hill.—Reverend C. Bruel. Rs. 1,500 per annum.

Appointed 6th, February 1892.

Royal College.

Rector.—Alfred Messervy, M.A. Oxon. Rs. 10,000 per annum.

Appointed 15th. November 1879.

Senior Professor.—William Wymond Hamley, M.A., Cantab. Rs. 6,000 per annum.

Entered the service 9th. January 1879.
Present appointment 21st. May 1887.

Secretary.—Charles Alfred Britter. Rs. 2,400 per annum.

Entered the service 15th. November 1876.
Appointed 17th. February 1893.

Assistant Secretary.—Egbert G. de St. Pern. Salary Rs. 1,200 per annum.

Entered the service 4th. February 1885.
Present appointment 1st. January 1890.

1st. CLASS PROFESSORS.

Alfred Temple Roberts, M. A., Oxon. Present salary Rs. 5,000 per annum.

Appointed 4th. August 1886.

Western Francis Russell, B.A., Oxon. Present salary Rs. 5,000 per annum.

Appointed 4th. August 1886.

Trevelyan Arnold Pope, B.A., Cantab. Present salary Rs. 5,000 per annum. (*On leave*).

Appointed 16th. August 1887.

Louis Favez, B-ès-Sc., Paris. Present salary Rs. 5,000 per annum.

Entered the service 1st. September 1874.
Present appointment 4th. January 1893.

2ND. CLASS PROFESSORS.

Abel Standley. Present salary Rs. 4,500 per annum.

Entered the service 17th. January 1871.
Present appointment 1st. January 1878.

Thomas Woollen Eyre, B.A., Cantab. Present salary Rs. 4,000 per annum.

Appointed 23rd. October 1889.

Professor of Chemistry.—Julius Félix. Rs. 4,000 per annum.

Entered the service 3rd. May 1876.
Present appointment 24th. May 1889.

3RD. CLASS PROFESSORS.

Francis George Patterson. Present salary Rs. 3,000 per annum.

Present appointment 5th. April 1878.

Louis Dorelly Papillon, B.A., London. Present salary Rs. 3,000 per annum.

Entered the service 1st. September 1873.
Present appointment 12th. October 1878.

Fernand André. Present salary Rs. 3,000 per annum.

Entered the service 1st. January 1872.
Present appointment 1st. May 1882.

Julien Boucherat. Present salary Rs. 2,800 per annum.

Entered the service 1st. April 1883.
Present appointment 4th. January 1893.

PROFESSORS OF RELIGIOUS INSTRUCTION.

Reverend Whylock Pendavis, M.A. Rs. 500 per annum. Attached to Royal College, Port Louis. (See Church of England).

Reverend C. Harrington. Rs. 100 per annum, Curepipe. (See also Church of England).

Appointed March 1892.

Very Reverend Canon E. Chalvet. Rs. 800 per annum. Is attached to Royal College, Port Louis. (See also Church of Rome).

Appointed 17th. November 1891.

Very Reverend Canon C. O'Loughlin. Rs. 400 per annum for Curepipe College School. (See also Church of Rome).

Mistress.—Miss C. de Coriolis. Salary Rs. 1,800 per annum.

Present appointment 18th. November 1890.

Drawing Master (Port Louis and Curepipe). — Alfred Avice du Buisson. Rs. 1,800 per annum.

Appointed 1st. June 1884.

Professor of Hindustani.—Taleb Hossein. Present salary Rs. 1,000 per annum. (*On leave*).

Appointed 6th. Febrnary 1889.

USHERS.

First Usher.—John Smith. Rs. 3,000 per annum and quarters.

Entered the service 21st. March 1881.
Present appointment 12th. August 1893.

Second Usher.—James Furlong. Present salary Rs. 1,800 per annum.

Entered the service 22nd. October 1884.
Present appointment 12th. August 1893.

Third Usher.—George Shipp. Present salary Rs. 1,300 per annum and quarters.

Entered the service 17th. February 1887.
Present appointment 12th. August 1893.

Fourth Usher.—John Hudson. Salary Rs. 1,000 per annum.

1ST. CLASS MASTERS.

Adolphe Bernon. Present salary Rs. 2,500 per annum.

Entered the service August 1869.
Present appointment 1st. January 1878.

Hippolyte Morin. Present salary Rs. 2,500 per annum.

Entered the service 11th. July 1871.
Present appointment 1st. January 1878.

Gustave Chaperon. Present salary Rs. 2,500 per annum.

Entered the service 1st. July 1871.
Present appointment 1st. May 1881.

Arthur Cantin. Present salary Rs. 2,500 per annum.

Entered the service 1st. July 1876.
Present appointment 1st. May 1882.

Louis Jules Bonnin. Present salary Rs. 2,500 per annum.

Entered the service 1st. September 1879.
Present appointment 24th. May 1889.

Aristide Lamalétie. Present salary Rs. 2,500 per annum.

Entered the service 1st. July 1875.
Present appointment 1st. July 1889.

A. Maujean, B.A., London. Present salary 2,400 per annum.

Entered the service 1st. June 1881.
Present appointment 6th. August 1890.

Emile Pierre Laval, B.A., London. Present salary Rs. 2,100 per annum.

Entered the service 13th. January 1882.
Present appointment 4th. January 1893.

Joseph L'Etang. Present salary Rs. 2,000 per annum.

Entered the service 9th. April 1869.
Present appointment 26th. July 1894.

2ND. CLASS MASTERS.

Asthon Maurel. Present salary Rs. 1,500 per annum.

Entered the service 1st. March 1870.
Present appointment 1st. January 1882.

Luther Lafond. Present salary Rs. 1,500 per annum.

Entered the service 17th. January 1881.
Present appointment 1st. May 1882.

Angelo Cantin. Present salary Rs. 1,500 per annum.

Entered the service 1st. May 1881.
Present appointment 1st. October 1887.

John Edward Jones. Present salary Rs. 1,500 per annum.

Entered the service 29th. June 1882.
Present appointment 1st. September 1888.

Gellé Ferré. Present salary Rs. 1,500 per annum.

Entered the service, 1st. September 1882.
Eresent appointment 24th. May 1889.

James Avice. Present salary Rs. 1,500 per annum.

Entered the service 12th. January 1885.
Present appointment 15th. September 1889.

Oscar Brémon. Present salary Rs. 1,500 per annum.

Entered the service 11th. January 1887.
Present appointment 1st. January 1890.

Gabriel Herchenroder. Present salary Rs. 1,500 per annum.

Entered the service 29th. May 1889.
Present appointment 1st. July 1890.

Désiré Picard. Present salary Rs. 1,400 per annum.

Entered the service 1st. September 1885.
Present appointment 9th. September 1891.

Désiré Houbert. Present salary Rs. 1,300 per annum.

Entered the service 1st. September 1885.
Present appointment 4th. January 1893.

Oscar Toureau. Present salary Rs. 1,300 per annum.

Entered the service 1st. August 1890.
Present appointment 17th. February 1893.

Rodolphe L'Aimable. Salary Rs. 1,200 per annum.

Present appointment 9th. September 1891.

Jules Augustin de Gaye. Salary Rs. 1,100 per annum.

Entered the service 1st. September 1891.
Present appointment 20th. July 1894.

ASSISTANT 2ND. CLASS MASTERS.

Darius Motet. Present salary Rs. 720 per annum.

Appointed 17th. February 1893.

Eudoxe L'Etang. Salary Rs. 750 per annum.

Appointed 13th. May 1894.

R. L. Némorin. Salary Rs. 720 per annum.

Entered the service 3rd. May 1893.
Present appointment 26th. July 1894.

Instructor of Gymnastics.—J. Brough. Present salary Rs. 1,000 per annum.

Appointed 22nd. May 1893.

Teacher of Book Keeping.—J. E. H. Touche. Present salary Rs. 600 per annum.

Appointed January 1896.

Porter.—Joseph Pung. Salary Rs. 600 per annum and free quarters.

Appointed 23rd. October 1881.

Government Schools.

Superintendent of Schools.—David Julius Anderson. Salary, Rs. 6,000 per annum, and the refund of actual travelling expenses.

Entered the service 9th. July 1867.
Present appointment 10th. January 1888.

Inspector of Roman Catholic Aided Schools.—Anatole de Boucherville.* Present salary Rs. 4,000 per annum.

Entered the service 10th. December 1868.
Present appointment 2nd. June 1882.

Inspector of Government & Non Roman Catholic Aided Schools.—Edouard Mainty.* Rs. 3,600 per annum.

Entered the service 1st. April 1864.
Present appointment 14th. August 1893.

Additional Sub-Inspector of Schools.—Jules Alphonse Blackburn.* Present salary Rs. 2,400 per annum.

Entered the service 1st. April 1874.
Present appointment 6th. November 1893.

Accountant.—Albert Kalle. Salary Rs. 2,400 per annum.

Entered the service 1st. April 1872.
Present appointment 6th. May 1891.

Clerk.—Louis Joseph Arthur Narcisse. Salary Rs. 1,200 per annum.

Entered the service 1st. June 1879.
Present appointment 6th. May 1891.

COPYST Rs. 300 per annum.

P. Loumeau.

Appointed 16th. August 1895.

MASTERS.

Grégoire Aristhène Avice. Rs. 2,000 and Rs. 360 lodging allowance.

First appointment 1st. December 1857.

François Benjamin Constant Boulineau. Rs. 2,000 and Rs. 360 lodging allowance.

First appointment 1st. February 1861.

* Receives also the Refund of actual travelling expenses.

Prosper Thomas Naréna. Rs. 2,000 with quarters.

First appointment 6th. March 1866.

Evariste Augustin. Rs. 2,000 with quarters.

First appointment 1st. July 1866.

Jean Napoléon Rohan. Rs. 2,000.

First appointment 1st. April 1871.

Pierre Julius Ambroisine. Rs. 2,000 with quarters. (Receives for the training of teachers for the ½ time Schools. Rs. 5 per student under training.)

First appointment 1st. April 1872.

Jean François Désiré Huot. Rs. 2,000 and Rs. 240 lodging allowance.

First appointment 1st. October 1868.

Louis Roumas Aubergé. Rs. 2,000 and Rs. 240 lodging allowance.

First appointment 1st. November 1874.

Rodolphe Ternel. Rs. 2,000 and Rs. 240 lodging allowance.

First appointment 1st. December 1881.

Louis Rodolphe Berton. Rs. 1,900 and Rs. 240 lodging allowance.

First appointment 1st. April 1872.

Charles Muette* Rs. 1,500 with quarters.

First appointment 1st. January 1870.

Joseph William Bell.* Rs. 1,500.

First appoiutment 1st. July 1875.

Thomas William Blackburn.* Rs. 1,500.

First appointment 1st July 1875.

Pierre Sarvaya Gnany. Rs. 1,400 and Rs. 240 lodging allowance.

First appointment 1st. March 1868.

James Henry L'Etang.* Rs. 1,200 and Rs. 240 lodging allowance.

First appointment 1st. June 1874.

---

* Paid in addition for results.

Alexis Sauzier,* Rs. 1,200.

First appointment 1st. October 1874.

Pierre Dorestan Morvan,* Rs. 1,200.

First appointment 1st. January 1882.

Edouard François Moutou,* Rs. 1,200.

First appointment 1st. May 1883.

Némours Lisis. Rs. 720.

First appointment 1st. January 1892.

Charles Lebon. Rs. 720.

First appointment 15th. November 1894.

Grégoire Aristide Avice, Rs. 720 and Rs. 240 lodging allowance.

First appointment 1st. January 1873.

Louis Aristhène Henrison,* Rs. 720.

First appointment 1st. September 1875.

William Hector Lyall Shrubsole,* Rs. 720.

First appointment 1st. January 1882.

Louis Jules Moutou,* Rs. 720.

First appointment 1st. January 1882.

Pierre Frédéric Bigaignon.* Rs. 720 with quarters.

First appointment 1st. May 1883.

Louis Senneville Godon.* Rs. 720.

First appointment 1st. January 1885.

Mardaymootoo Mayaveran. Rs. 720.

First appointment 1st. April 1885.

Jean Félix Lebon. Rs. 720.

First appointment 1st. September 1885.

---

* Paid in addition for results.

Lovard Pascal.* Rs. 720.

First appointment 1st. October 1885.

Baichoo Madhoo * Rs. 720.

First appointment 1st. August 1888.

James Pablot.* Rs. 720.

First appointment 1st. January 1891.

Lucien Moutia.* Rs. 720.

First appointment 1st. February 1893.

A. Khodabuksh.* Rs. 720.

First appointment 1st. January 1895.

Courbanally Nassir. Rs. 600 and Rs. 120 lodging allowance.

First appointment 1st. October 1873.

Samuel Barbé. Rs. 480.

First appointment 1st. January 1891.

Louis Ange Catherine. Rs. 480.

First appointment 1st. July 1893.

Isaac Cuthbert. Rs. 480.

First appointment 1st. January 1892.

RELIEVING TEACHER.

Louis Gaston Geneviève. Rs. 600.

First appointment 1st. January 1891.

ASSISTANT MASTERS.

Charles Townsend Young. Rs. 480. (Is special Tamil Teacher).

First appointment 6th. May 1891.

Louis Xavier Pougnet. Rs. 480.

First appointment 1st. January 1892.

---

* Paid in addition for results.

Léon Rey. Rs. 420.

First appointment 1st. January 1893.

B. A. Gaffour. Rs. 360. (Is Hindi Teacher).

First appointment 1st. March 1892.

Ellis Requin. Rs. 360.

First appointment 1893.

Léon Rosalie. Rs. 360.

First appointment 6th. October 1893.

Louis Moody.* Rs. 300.

First appointment 1st. February 1894.

Daniel Rémy Jenkins. Rs 300.

First appointment 20th. July 1894.

Fernand Fauvette. Rs. 300.

First appointment 12th. March 1894.

Noé Glover.* Rs. 300.

First appointment 1st. January 1894.

Barthélemy Julie. Rs. 300.

First appointment 1st. February 1893.

Louis Nellan.* Rs. 300.

First appointment 1st. July 1894.

Wilfrid Joseph. Rs. 300.

First appointment 1st. December 1894.

L. M. Roussel

First appointment 30th. January 1895.

H. Précieux*

First appointment 31st. January 1895.

A. Jacquin.

First appointment 31st. January 1895.

---

* Paid in addition for results.

S. Allybaccus.*

First appointment 31st. January 1895.

L. Lamarque.*

First appointment 31st. January 1895.

D. Jenkins.

First appointment 20th. July 1894.

V. René.

First appointment 1st. January 1895.

MISTRESSES.

Mary Dromart. Rs. 2,000 with quarters and Rs. 240 for training of Teachers.

First appointment 1st August 1862.

Anne Marie Dorliska Dinnematin. Rs. 1,000 and Rs. 240 lodging allowance.

First appointment 1st. July 1851.

Marie Louise Fenn. Rs. 1,000 and Rs. 240 lodging allowance.

First appointment 15th. October 1861.

Rose Marie Louisa Déclass. Rs. 1,000 and Rs. 240 lodging allowance.

First appointment 15th. September 1868.

Marie Julia Constance. Rs. 1,000 and Rs. 240 lodging allowance.

First appointment 1st. November 1868.

Marie Elodie Gébert. Rs. 1,000.

First appointment 1st. January 1881.

Claudine Marie Eléonore Leal. Rs. 1,000.

First appointment 1st. April 1884.

Marie Jeanne Barbé.* Rs. 720.

First appointment 1st. January 1882.

Cécile Emilie Narcisse.* Rs. 720.

First appointment 1st. January 1882.

---

* Paid in addition for results.

Marie Emma Moutou.* Rs. 720.

First appointment 1st. March 1882.

Marie Thérèse Bonnier. Rs 840 (Infant Mistress)

First appointment 1st. June 1881.

Marie Gèneviève Aubergé. Rs. 480 and Rs. 120 lodging allowance.

First appointment 1st. July 1875.

Marie Cécile Rohan. Rs. 480 and Rs. 240 lodging allowance.

First appointment 1st. April 1875.

Rachel Clémence Galais*. Rs. 480.

First appointment 1st. April 1879.

Alice Courbadon.* Rs. 480.

First appointment 1st. May1883.

Elise Mouton.* Rs. 480.

First appointment 1st. January 1890.

ASSISTANT MISTRESSES.

Marie Albertine Ellis Mullens Rs. 480.

First appointment 1st. January 1885.

Marie Eline Lœtitia Thomas. Rs. 420.

First appointment 1st. August 1883.

Marie Amélie Lebrasse. Rs. 420.

First appointment 1st. August 1883.

Marie Antoinette Leal. Rs. 420.

First appointment 1st. January 1884.

Françoise Noémie Marcel. Rs. 360.

First appointment 1st. January 1871.

Lucie Marie. Rs. 360.

First appointment 1st. November 1886.

---

* Paid in addition for results,

Marie Agaritha Ernest. Rs. 360.

First appointment 1st. April 1888.

Marie Maria Marsh*. Rs. 300.

First appointment 1st. January 1886.

Marie Augusta White*. Rs. 300.

First appointment 1st. May 1886.

Marie Elise Davantin. Rs. 300.

First appointment 1st. February 1884.

Amélia Fortuno. Rs. 300.

First appointment 1st. April 1884.

Ulyssia Marie Tranquille*. Rs. 300.

First appointment 1st. April 1886.

Thais Narcisse*. Rs. 300.

First appointment 1st. August 1888.

Elizabeth Pragassa*. Rs. 300.

First appointment 1st. January 1889.

Philomène Gébert*. Rs. 300.

First appointment 1st. September 1890.

Rachel Rémy*. Rs. 300.

First appointment 1st. January 1891.

Dorcilia Thomas. Rs. 300.

First appointment 1st. January 1891.

Marie Bouquet*. Rs. 300.

First appointment 3rd. March 1892.

Albiona Blais*. Rs. 300.

First appointment 1st. January 1871.

---

* Paid in addition for results.

Mary Ann Farrow*.

First appointment 15th. January 1894.

Angèle Fijac*.

First appointment 14th. May 1894.

E. Dinnematin.

First appointment 31st. January 1895.

L. Ross*.

First appointment 31st. January 1895.

F. O'Canna.

First appointment 1st. March 1895.

Medical and Health Department.

Director Medical and Health Department.— The Honorable Dr. Evenor Chastellier, M. D., Edin. Rs. 9,000 per annum.

Entered the service 1st. May 1866.
Present appointment 15th. November 1895.

Medical Inspector.—Dr. H. Lorans. Rs. 8,000 per annum.

Entered the service 2nd. December 1880.
Present appointment 15th. November 1895.

2ND. CLASS CLERK.

Ariste J. Dupré. Rs. 3,600 per annum.

Entered the service 1st. October 1870.
Present appointment 15th. November 1895.

3RD. CLASS CLERKS.

A. T. Alphonse Gaud. Rs. 2,400 per annum.

Entered the service 1st. May 1884.
Present appointment 15th. November 1895.

Pierre J. Camille Rivière. Rs. 2,400 per annum and a personal allowance of Rs. 100.

Entered the service 1st. January 1878.
Present appointment 15th. November 1895.

---

* Paid in addition for results.

4TH. CLASS CLERKS.

J. Benjamin Pérille. Rs. 1,800 per annum.

Entered the service 11th. October 1880.
Present appointment 15th. November 1895.

L. St. Clair O'Sughrue, Rs. 1,800 per annum.

Entered the service 7th. June 1888.
Present appointment 15th. November 1895.

5TH. CLASS CLERKS.

Arthur Caillaud, Rs. 1,200 per annum.

Entered the service 26th. June 1876.
Present appointment 15th. November 1895.

Abdoul Gaffar Courbanally, Rs. 1,200 per annum.

Entered the service 15th. June 1885.
Present appointment 15th. November 1895.

6TH. CLASS CLERKS.

H. Seewoodharry Buguth, Rs. 720 per annum.

Entered the service 1st. October 1892.
Present appointment 15th. November 1895.

Armand Guiot, Rs. 720 per annum.

Entered the service 3rd. October 1892.
Present appointment 15th. November 1895.

Albert George Rickwood, Rs. 720 per annum.

Entered the service 15th. March 1893.
Present appointment 15th. November 1895.

Copyist.—Fernand Saverimoutou, Rs. 300 per annum.

Appointed 15th. November 1895.

Medical Superintendent Civil Hospital.—Dr. F. Antelme. Rs. 7,000 per annum.

Appointed 15th. November 1895.

Assistant Medical Superintendent Civil Hospital.—Dr. Henri Villemont. Rs. 4,000 per annum with quarters.

Entered the service 13th. March 1888.
Present appointment 15th. November 1895.

Dispenser.—W. Beard. Present salary Rs. 1,500 per annum and Rs. 360 house allowance.

Entered the service 12th. August 1870.
Present appointment 27th. February 1875.

Assistant Dispenser.—E. Monvoisin. Rs. 1,000 per annum.

Entered the service 7th. January 1878.
Present appointment 16th. July 1891.

Head Warder.—J. Durand. Rs. 750 per annum and quarters.

Appointed 22nd. June 1891.

Steward & Accountant.—L. Vulgis Tessier. Rs. 1,800 per annum.

Appointed 13th. June 1894.

Warder Clerk.—Moïse Savriacouty. Rs. 750 per annum.

Appointed 15th. January 1877.

GOVERNMENT LUNATIC ASYLUM.—BEAU BASSIN.

Superintendent.—Dr. O. Beaugeard. Rs. 6,000 per annum with quarters.

Appointed 15th. November 1895.

Medical Assistant.—P. Oscar Leclos. Rs. 1,500 per annum.

Appointed 11th. November 1881.

Steward.—Evariste Casse. Rs. 1,800 per annum with quarters.

Entered the service 1st. May 1876.
Appointed May 1891.

BARKLY ASYLUM, BEAU BASSIN.

Medical Superintendent.—Dr. Arthur B. Yves Jollivet, L. R. C. P. Glasgow, L. R. C. P. Edin.

Entered the service 1st. April 1885.
Present appointment 15th. November 1895.

Assistant Medical Superintendent.—Dr. Maurice Joly. Rs. 3,000 per annum with quarters.

Appointed 15th. November 1895.

Dispenser.—A. Savriacouty. Rs. 1,200 per annum with quarters.

Entered the service 15th. January 1877.
Present appointment 23rd. May 1891.

Dispensary Medical Officer (Port Louis).—Dr. V. Monty. Rs. 5,000 per annum.

Appointed 15th. November 1895.

PRATIQUE AND QUARANTINE.

Health Officer.—Dr. Charles Amand Evariste Esnouf. Rs. 5,000 per annum.

Entered the service 19th. September 1885.
Present appointment 15th. November 1895.

POLICE AND PRISONS.

Police and Prison Surgeon and Vaccinator.—Dr. F. Auguste Rougé. Rs. 6,000 per annum. (Is also Commissioner in Lunacy for Port Louis).

Appointed 15th. November 1895.

Medical Storekeeper.—Auguste Noël. Rs. 1,500 per annum.

Entered the service 1st. January 1880.
Present appointment 1st. June 1892.

5TH. CLASS CLERK.

Anthony Thorel. Rs. 1,200 per annum.

Entered the service 28th. August 1885.
Present appointment 15th. November 1895.

QUARANTINE STATIONS.

Steward and Accountant (Flat Island).—Edwin Collins. Rs. 2,000 per annum with quarters and rations.

Entered the service 30th. January 1873.
Present appointment 30th. May 1894.

Steward and Accountant (Cannonier's Point).—E. Dupont. Rs. 1,000 per annum.

Appointed 9th. March 1894.

Government Medical Officers.

PAMPLEMOUSSES.

Dr. Victor Dubois. Rs. 6,000 per annum. (Acts also as Commissioner in Lunacy.)

Appointed 15th. November 1895.

RIVIÈRE DU REMPART.

Dr. E. Ménagé. Is allowed private practice and receives Rs. 1,500 per annum as Government Medical Officer and Rs. 1.50 for each successful vaccination.

Appointed 15th. November 1895.

FLACQ.

Dr. Samuel A. Monty. Rs. 6,000 per annum.

Appointed 15th. November 1895.

GRAND PORT.

Dr. Louis Portal. Rs. 6,000 per annum.

Appointed 15th. November 1895.

Assistant.—Dr. F. O. Guérin. (Is paid by fees and allowed private practice).

Appointed 15th. November 1895.

SAVANNE.

Dr. Henry Le Merle. Rs. 6,000 per annum.

Appointed 15th. November 1895.

BLACK RIVER.

Dr. Edouard Chasteauneuf. Rs. 1,000 and fees. (Is allowed private practice).

PLAINES WILHEMS.

Dr. Evariste Laval. Rs. 6,000 per annum,

Entered the service 11th. August 1880.
Present appointment 15th. November 1895.

Assistant.—Dr. J. I. Paddle. (Is paid by fees and allowed private practice).

Appointed 15th. November 1895.

MOKA.

Dr. P. L. E. Vinson. Rs. 1,500 and R. 1.50 for each successful vaccination.

Appointed 15th. November 1895.

Sanitary Warden.—Dr. John G. E. Bolton. Rs. 7,000 per annum.

Appointed 15th. November 1895.

Assistant Sanitary Warden.—Dr. G. Barbeau. Rs. 5,000 per annum.

Appointed 15th. November 1895.

Engineer.—Célicourt Carbonel. Rs. 4,000 per annum, with refund of travelling expenses.

Appointed February 1884.

Building Inspector.—Eudoxe P. Lolliot. Rs. 2,000 per annum.

Appointed March 1884.

6TH. CLASS CLERK.

Léopold Courau. Rs. 720 per annum.

Appointed 15th. November 1895.

Customs Sanitary Inspector.—Léon Olivier. Rs. 1,800 per annum.

Present appointment 1st. April 1890.

Veterinary Surgeon.—Clément Galdemar. (Paid by fees).

Appointed December 1883.

First Class Sanitary Inspectors. Rs. 1,500 per annum.

Titus William Ware.

Appointed 1st. March 1881.

J. Edouard Pouguet.

Appointed 1st. March 1873.

Anthony Le Goy.

Appointed January 1890.

Elind Mallet.

Appointed 15th. March 1892.

2nd. Class Sanitary Inspectors. Rs. 1,200 per annum.

G. de Casanove.

Appointed 27th. December 1886.

E. de Boucherville.

Appointed 1st. December 1891.

L. Collard.

Appointed 14th. November 1895.

J. Durand.

Appointed 22nd. June 1891.

O. C. Fontenay.

Appointed 5th. February 1885.

D. Léonce.

Appointed 14th. November 1895.

J. Bird Hulm.

Appointed 22nd. December 1881.

J. Latour.

Appointed May 1886.

R. de Boucherville.

Appointed 3rd. February 1880.

3rd. Class Sanitary Inspectors. Rs. 960 per annum.

S. Caltaux.

Appointed 16th. September 1893.

H. Harter.

Appointed 14th. November 1895.

W. Harvey.

Appointed 8th. November 1888.

Police Department.

Inspector General.—Captain Cecil T. Holland. Rs. 9,000 per annum.

Assumed duties 28th. November 1895.

Chief Town Inspector.—Valentine Trew. Rs. 4,000 per annum, plus Rs. 1,000 allowance.

Entered the service 17th. July 1869.
Present appointment 16th. September 1894.

Inspectors. Rs. 4,000 per annum.

Francis Sheppard. (*On leave*).

Entered the service 4th. December 1863.
Present appointment 16th. December 1894.

Vere Alban Butler.

Entered the service 6th. June 1880.
Present appointment 16th. September 1894.

Albert William Fisher Goold.

Entered the service 14th. December 1881.
Present appointment 16th. September 1894.

Walter Chew.

Entered the service 6th. January 1869.
Present appointment 16th. September 1894.

Henry Marshall.

Entered the service 7th. August 1866.
Present appointment 16th. September 1894.

Léonidas Marie Grégoire.

Appointed 18th. May 1895.

Pay Clerk.—Camille Sergent Pasquet. Present salary Rs. 3,000 per annum.

Entered the service 8th. March 1864.
Present appointment 1st. March 1881.

Assistant Pay Clerk.—Allybux Ameeruddeen. Rs. 1,200 per annum.

Entered the service 22nd. January 1881.
Present appointment 16th. September 1894.

Head Clerk.—Emmanuel Maingo. Rs. 1,800 per annum.

Entered the service 1st. December 1885.
Present appointment 15th. July 1892.

Office Clerk.—Henri de Réland. Rs. 720 per annum.

Entered the service 10th. August 1885.
Present appointment 15th. November 1891.

Prisons.

Superintendent of Prisons and Reformatory.—Arthur H. Wyndham Gordon. Rs. 5,000 per annum and quarters.

Entered the Service 28th. November 1889.
Present appointment 21st. August 1892.

5TH. CLASS CLERKS.

Emmanuel Marc Henri. Present salary Rs. 1,200 per annum.

Entered the service 1st. January 1888.
Present appointment 4th. May 1895.

M· Patron. Present salary Rs. 1,200 per annum.

Entered the service 7th. September 1889.
Present appointment 4th. July 1893.

Matron.—Mrs. Y. J. Jollivet. Present salary Rs. 1,500 per annum and quarters.

Appointed 1st. January 1886.

Assistant Matron.—Mrs. S. Mulvany. Rs. 600 per annum and quarters.

Appointed 1st. January 1895.

Chief Warder.—G. Warwick. Present salary Rs. 2,500 per annum.

Entered the service 17th. March 1883.
Present appointment 24th. August 1895.

FIRST CLASS WARDERS.

John Williams. Present salary Rs. 1,320 per annum plus Rs. 480 personal allowance.

Appointed 17th. March 1883.

New Central Prisons.—Henry Hall, 1,800 per annum and quarters and draws a personal allowance of Rs. 480. (Under interdiction)

Appointed 17th. March 1883.

Auguste Labelle *acting*.

Grand Port.—D. H. Mc Guire, Rs. 1,800 per annum with quarters and draws a personal allowance of Rs. 480.

Entered the service 17th. March 1883.
Present appointment 17th. August 1895.

SECOND CLASS WARDERS.

Manuel Abraham, Rs. 960 per annum. (Officer in charge of the Reformatory).

Appointed 20th. February 1889.

Rémy Berger, Rs. 960 per annum, and a personal allowance of Rs. 60. (Quartered at Savanne).

Entered the service 1st. November 1878.
Present appointment 15th. June 1881.

Arthur Bargain, Rs. 900 per annum.

Entered the service 12th. November 1884.
Present appointment 11th. July 1889.

Jean Charles Coutequel, Rs. 960 per annum, and a personal allowance of Rs. 60. (Quartered at Flacq).

Entered the service 1st. July 1867.
Present appointment 1st. July 1867.

George Mounsmie, Rs. 900 per annum, plus Rs. 100 personal allowance.

Appointed 18th. April 1870.

P. Williamson, Rs. 900 per annum.

Entered the service 7th. November 1873.
Present appointment 6th. April 1892.

Edward Barnes, Rs. 900 per annum.

Entered the service 21st. December 1887.
Present appointment 1st. June 1894.

George Léonard. Rs. 900 per annum.

Entered the service 9th. May 1864.
Present appointment 1st. June 1894.

Dorasamy, Rs. 900 per annum.

Entered the service 20th. October 1883.
Present appointment 1st. November 1894.

Government Reformatory.

Superintendent.—Arthur H. Wyndham Gordon. (Is also Superintendent of Prisons).

FIRST CLASS WARDER. Salary Rs. 1,320.

Auguste Labelle. Personal allowance Rs. 480. Present salary Rs. 1,800 transferred to Beau Bassin Prisons, Manuel Abraham, *acting*.

Dispenser and Accountant—Ivanoff Tranquille, Rs. 420 per annum.

Appointed 12th. September 1893.

Master Carpenter.—Marc Arisse, Rs. 600 per annum.

Appointed 7th. January 1881.

Head Teacher.—Léonce Auguste, Rs. 720 per annum and Rs. 120 lodging allowance.

Appointed 24th. January 1887.

Storekeeper General's Department.

Storekeeper General.—George Lumgair, Rs. 8,000 per annum.

Entered the service 1st. November 1862.
Present appointment 1st. April 1892.

Assistant Storekeeper General.—James Angus. Present Salary Rs. 4000 plus Rs. 500 personal allowance.

Entered the service 16th. February 1868.
Present appointment 5th. May 1888.

3RD. CLASS CLERKS.

Charles Clark. Present salary Rs. 2,400 per annum.

Entered the service 15th. July 1873.
Present appointment 19th. July 1894.

Louis Aristide Edouard Sénèque. Rs. 2,400 per annum.

Entered the service 3rd. February 1876.
Present appointment 1st. June 1892.

4TH. CLASS CLERKS.

Joseph Desèze Melotte. Present salary Rs. 1,800 per annum.

Entered the service 1st. September 1874.
Present appointment 1st. June 1892.

Jean Alcide Dupré. Present salary Rs. 1,800 per annum.

Entered the service 1st. January 1877.
Present appointment 9th. June 1894.

5TH. CLASS CLERKS.

Julien Huron. Present salary Rs. 1,200 per annum.

Entered the service 28th. September 1882.
Present appointment 1st. January 1890.

Léonel Audibert. Present salary Rs. 1,200 per annum.

Entered the service 10th. September 1881.
Present appointment 14th. September 1891.

Louis Léodgard Coureau. Rs. 1,200 per annum.

Entered the service 1st. May 1883.
Present appointment 1st. January 1893.

6TH. CLASS CLERK.

François Saminadeu. Rs. 720 per annum.

Appointed 7th. February 1893.

WRITER, Rs. 300 per annum.

M. Collard.

Entered the service 1st. March 1894.
Present appointment 15th. November 1895.

Immigration Department.

Protector of Immigrants.—The Honorable John Francis Trotter, Rs. 9,000 per annum, plus Rs. 1,000 personal allowance and Rs. 1,000 travelling allowance.

Entered the service 1st. May 1881.
Present appointment 1st. May 1881.

Inspectors of Immigrants.

Owen Livingstone O'Connor. Rs. 5,000 per annum and Rs. 2,000 travelling allowance.

Entered the service 11th. September 1862.
Present appointment 7th. February 1883.

Cecil George Hall. Rs. 5,000 per annum and Rs. 2,000 travelling allowance.

Entered the service 14th. November 1868.
Present appointment 7th. September 1886.

2ND. CLASS CLERK.

Louis Elysée Courtois. Rs. 3,600 per annum.

Entered the service 1st. August 1863.
Present appointment 1st. Febuary 1891.

3RD. CLASS CLERKS.

George Adrien. Rs. 2,400 per annum.

Entered the service 1st. September 1862.
Present appointment 1st. August 1889.

L. E. Barbeau, Rs. 2,400 per annum, plus Rs. 100 personal allowance.

Entered the service 20th. June 1872.
Present appointment 4th. June 1875.

4TH. CLASS CLERKS.

Charles Lionel Lamport. Present salary Rs. 1,800 per annum.

Entered the service 1st. December 1875.
Present appointment 23rd. June 1892.

Louis Edouard Furcy Beyts. Present salary Rs. 1,800 per annum.

Entered the service 22nd. April 1881.
Present appointment 13th. August 1892.

Volcy Magnien. Present salary Rs. 1,800 per annum,

Entered the service 26th. October 1880.
Present appointment 13th. August 1894.

5TH. CLASS CLERKS.

Louis Rayépa. Present salary Rs. 1,200 per annum, plus Rs. 300 personal allowance.

Entered the service 1st. January 1879.
Present appointment 10th. October 1881.

Charles Philogène. Present salary Rs. 1,200 per annum.

Entered the service 17th. April 1879.
Present appointment 27th. March 1884.

Joseph Armand. Present salary Rs. 1,200 per annum.

Entered the service 1st. January 1888.
Present appointment 10th. January 1894.

6TH. CLASS CLERKS.

N. Cheriff. Present salary Rs. 720 per annum.

Entered the service 8th. October 1890.
Present appointment 8th. May 1895.

Louis Ethelbert Séricuse. Rs. 720 per annum.

Entered the service 1st. September 1891.
Entered the service 23rd. May 1893.

E. Fidélia, Rs. 720 per annum.

Entered the service 1st. January 1892.
Present appointment 11th. September 1893.

R. Vanmeerbeck, Rs. 720 per annum.

Entered the service 9th. August 1892.
Present appointment 13th. October 1893.

C. Amboule, Rs. 720 per annum.

Entered the service 11th. February 1892.
Present appointment 1st. August 1894.

COPYIST, Rs. 300 per annum.

Arsène Nayna.

Appointed 1st. October 1895.

Depot Superintendent.—Thomy Louis Jacquin. Salary Rs. 1,500 per annum, plus Rs. 300 personal allowance. (Is under interdiction).

Entered the service 22nd. February 1877.
Present appointment 15th. March 1894.

Depot Photographer.—Daniel Sénèque. Rs. 1,200 per annum.

Entered the service 29th. March 1879.
Present appointment 27th. July 1893.

Chief Assistant.—Pierre Narsoo. Rs. 860 per annum.

Entered the service 5th. April 1873.
Present appointment 27th. July 1893.

Printer.—Guanon Pierre. Rs. 600 per annum.

Entered the service 30th. September 1884.
Present appointment 27th. July 1893.

Assistant.—L. E. Savrimoutou. Rs. 300 per annum.

Appointed 27th. July 1893.

Mauritius Emigration Agents in India.

Emigration Agent. Calcutta.—Allen Campbell Stewart, Rs. 5,000 per annum.

Appointed 23rd. July 1888.

MADRAS.

Emigration Agent.—Joseph George Conran. Rs. 4,000 per annum.

Appointed 13th. May 1889.

Railway Department.

General Manager and Engineer.—M. Connal. Rs. 11,000 per annum.

Entered the service 17th. June 1862.
Present appointment 1st. November 1891.

Statistical Clerk.—Eugène Gassin. Rs. 3,000 per annum.

First appointment 1st. August 1886.

Correspondence Clerk.—Ferran Laventure. Rs. 1,200 per annum.

First appointment 25th. October 1882.

Head Accountant.—Ralph William Dowson. Rs. 4,800 per annum and Rs. 1,200 personal allowance.

Entered the service 18th. September 1862.
Present appointment 1st. September 1891.

TRAFFIC BRANCH.

Traffic Superintendent.—Albert Oudin. Rs. 3,500 per annum.

Entered the service 16th. November 1867.
Present appointment 9th. June 1893.

Chief Platform Inspector.—R. H. Jones. Rs. 2,000 per annum.

Entered the service 4th. January 1867.
Present appointment 9th. June 1893.

Platform Inspector.—E. Farla, Rs. 1,500 per annum.

Appointed 1st. October 1874.

Goods Inspector.—E. Aliphon. Rs. 1,500 per annum.

Entered the service 12th. November 1879.
Present appointment 9th. June 1892.

LOCOMOTIVE DEPARTMENT.

Locomotive Superintendent.—John George Watson, Rs. 4,800 per annum.

Entered the service 24th. July 1878.
Appointed 1st. May 1895.

Poor Law Commission.

Commissioner.—The Hon. E. Aubert, C. M. G., Rs. 5,000 per annum.

Appointed 15th. July 1892.

Head Clerk.—Jules Mafurier. Rs. 1,800 per annum.

Entered the service 1st. February 1869.
Present appointment 20th. March 1891.

Accountant and Financial Clerk.—Edouard Bruneau. Rs. 1,800 per annum.

Entered the service August 1882.
Present appointment 20th. March 1891.

Inspector and Issuer—Lucien Ardé, Rs. 960 per annum.

Entered the service 1st. July 1884.
Present appointment 8th. December 1891.

Additional Clerk.—Emile Luquet, Rs. 960 per annum.

Entered the service April 1888.
Present appointment 20th. March 1891.

Copyist.—G. Olivier, Rs. 300 per annum.

Appointed January 1895.

BARKLY ASYLUM, BEAU BASSIN.

Accountant and Storekeeper.—Rostange Noé. Rs. 1,000 per annum.

Appointed September 1884.

Directress of School and Orphan Branch.— Mrs. Emma Bourbon. Rs. 1,200 per annum and quarters.

Appointed 1st. January 1869.

Overseer.—Auguste Larché, Rs. 960 with lodging allowance of Rs. 15 per mensem.

Appointed 31st. May 1892.

RODRIGUES.

Magistrate.—H. B. Colin. Rs. 5,000 per annum. (Is also Postmaster and draws Rs. 120). (*On leave.*)

Entered the service 1st. January 1892.
Present appointment 6th. April 1894.

F. Robert, Junior, *Acting.*

6TH. CLASS CLERK.

L. Seillier. Rs. 720 per annum.

Entered the service 1st. September 1892.
Present appointment 6th. April 1894.

Roman Catholic Priest.—Reverend J. Cotonéa. Rs. 2,000 per annum.

Appointed 1st. March 1895.

Medical Officer.—L. E. Roussel, M.D., Paris. Rs. 2,000 per annum, with quarters and vaccination fees.

Appointed 4th. June 1887.

Schoolmaster at Gabrielle.—James Dove. Rs. 840 per annum with quarters. (*On leave*).

Present appointed 22nd. March 1893.

A. Armand, *Acting.*

First appointment 1st. July 1870.

Schoolmistress.—Mrs. Armand. Rs. 360 per annum.

First appointment 1st. June 1888.

Schoolmaster, Port Mathurin.—J. Butié Rs. 360 per annum and quarters.

Sewing Mistress.—Mrs. J. Butié Rs. 360 per annum.

MINOR DEPENDENCIES.

Police & Stipendiary Magistrate.—(*Vacant*). Salary Rs. 5,000 per annum.

Acting.—Gustave Rochery.

COMMITTEES &c., FOR 1896.

Woods and Forests Board.

Sir V. Naz, K.C.M.G.,—*Chairman.*
The Hon. the Procureur & Advocate General,
— the Receiver General,
— the Surveyor General,
— H. Leclézio,
The Hon. L. de Rochecouste,
E. de Senneville, Esquire,
G. Aubin, Esquire.
The Director of Forests and Gardens.

Official Visitors to the Government Reformatory.

The Hon. the Procureur General,
— the Protector of Immigrants,
The Director of the Medical & Health Dept.
The Inspector General of Police,
The District Magistrate of Moka.
The District Magistrate of Plaines Wilhems (Rose Hill Division.)
The District Magistrate, Plaines Wilhems (Curepipe Division.)
The Stipendiary Magistrate, Plaines Wilhems

General Board of Health.

The Director of the Medical and Health Department,—*President,*
The Hon. the Surveyor General,
— the Protector of Immigrants,
— Hamilton Stein,
His Worship the Mayor of Port Louis,
The Poor Law Commissioner,
Dr. E. F. Bour,
Dr. E. de Senneville,
Dr. A. B. Y. Jollivet,
A. Bonnefin, Esq., D. M. P.
W. Hart, Esq.

Board of Commissioners for the Town of Curepipe.

(Appd. under Proclamation No. 3 of 9th. January 1896.)

Sir V. Naz, K.C.M.G.—*Chairman.*
The Hon. Dr. W. T. A. Edwards,
— L. de Rochecouste,
The Hon. G. A. Ritter,
Aristide Régnard, Esquire,
V. Lamarque, Esquire.

Central Board of Commissioners in Lunacy.

The Director of the Medical & Health Dept.
The Master of the Supreme Court,
Dr. E. L. de Chazal.

Council of Education.

ORDINARY MEMBERS.

The Hon. G. Guibert, Q.C.—*President.*
George Kœnig, Esquire,—*Vice-President.*
The Hon. J. F. Trotter, Protector of Immigrants,
Evenor Chastellier, Esq., M. D.
The Hon. Gustave A. Ritter,
A. Herchenroder, Esquire.
Eugène Serret, Esquire.
E. Laurent, Esquire, M. D.
The Rector of the Royal College,
The Superintendent of Schools,
The Inspectors of Schools.

EXTRAORDINARY MEMBERS.

Sir V. Naz, K.C.M.G.
The Hon. G. R. Dick,
— E. Aubert, C.M.G.
— V. Geffroy,
Pierre Edmond de Chazal, Esquire,
R. Freeland, Esquire,
E. Pelte, Esquire,
Alfred Rousset, Esquire,
Frederick Nash, Esquire.
A. Huguin, junior, Esquire.

College.

The Hon. George Guibert, Q.C.—*Chairman*,
Evenor Chastellier, Esq., M.D.
Eugène Serret, Esquire.
The Hon. Gustave A. Ritter.
The Rector of the Royal College.

Schools.

George Kœnig, Esquire.—*Chairman*,
The Hon. J. F. Trotter,
A. Herchenroder, Esquire,
E. Laurent, Esquire, M.D.
The Superintendent of Schools,
The Inspectors of Schools.

Prison Committees.

Central Prisons Board.

The Senior District Magistrate, Port Louis—*Chairman*.
The Junior District Magistrate, Port Louis,
The Additional & Police Magistrate, Port Louis,
The District Magistrate, Plaines Wilhems,
The District Magistrate, Moka.
Eliacin François, Esq.
E. H. Le Gall, Esquire, M.D.
L. J. Pétricher, Esquire, M.D.
The Hon. L. E. Antelme,
The Hon. E. Sauzier, Junior.

Flacq.

The District Magistrate,—*Chairman*.
The Stipendiary Magistrate,
The Government Medical Officer,
The Inspector of Police,
A. Brousse de Gersigny, Esquire.

Grand Port.

The District Magistrate,—*Chairman*,
The Stipendiary Magistrate,
The Government Medical Officer,
The Inspector of Police.
The Hon. L. de Rochecouste.

Savanne.

The District Magistrate,—*Chairman*.
The Stipendiary Magistrate,
The Government Medical Officer.
The Officer of Police in charge,
Oscar Pilot, Esquire.

Dead Letter Committee.

(Ordinance No. 20 of 1876)

The Colonial Postmaster,
The Storekeeper General.
The Deputy Collector of Customs.

Licensing Committees.

Port Louis.

The Mayor of Port Louis,
The Chief Officer of Police for Port Louis.
The Superintendent of Inland Revenue.

Pamplemousses.

The District Magistrate,
Edouard Le Breton, Esquire,
Eugène Laborde, Esquire.

Riviere du Rempart.

The District Magistrate,
Arthémidor Ythier, Esquire,
Leon Maurel, Esquire.

Flacq.

The District Magistrate,
A. de Gersigny, Esquire,
J. de Robillard, Esquire.

GRAND PORT.

The District Magistrate.
A. Mollières, Esquire.
The Inspector of Inland Revenue.

SAVANNE.

The District Magistrate.
The Inspector of Police.
A. Constantin, Esquire.

BLACK RIVER.

The District Magistrate.
H. Kœnig, Esquire.
L. Lesage, Esquire.

PLAINES WILHEMS.

The District Magistrate.
V. Lamarque, Esquire.
The Inspector of Police.

MOKA.

The District Magistrate.
C. Hardy, Esquire.
William Finniss, Esquire.

Committee on Tenders.

The Hon. the Receiver General.—*Chairman.*
— the Auditor General.
— L. E. Antelme.
— E. Sauzier, junior.
The Hon. A. P. Ambrose.
The Storekeeper General.
The Poor Law Commissioner.

Board of Appeal under the Building Act Ord. 26 of 1875.

The Hon. the Procureur General.—*Chairman.*
— the Surveyor General.
His Worship the Mayor of Port Louis.
The Hon. G. Robinson.
— V. Geffroy.

Civil Service Commissioners.

Hon. C. A. King-Harman, C.M.G.—*Chairman.*
Sir V. Naz, K.C.M.G.
The Hon. E. C. Ashley.
Dr. C. Meldrum, C.M.G., L.L.D., F.R.S.
The Hon. W. Newton, Q.C.
— L. de Rochecouste.
R. A. Rohan, Esquire.

Commissioners of the Mare-aux-Vacoas Water Supply.

Appointed under Ordinance No. 20 of 1894.

Hon. A. P. Ambrose.—*Chairman.*
— G. A. Ritter.
Hon. Vincent Geffroy.
— the Surveyor General.

Société d'Émulation Intellectuelle.

Sir V. Naz, K.C.M.G.—*President.*
A. de Boucherville, Esq. } *Vice-Presidents*
Eugène Serret, Esq. }
A. Gaud.—*Secretary & Treasurer.*

COMMITTEE.

C. Meldrum, C.M.G., M.A., L.L.D., F.R.S.
Hon. William Newton, Q.C.
— H. Leclézio.
— G. Guibert, Q.C.
Jules Félix, Esquire.
Auguste Maingard, Esquire.
Charles Newton, Esquire.
P. D'Agnel, Esquire.
N. Decotter, Esquire.
Angelo Cantin, Esquire.

Municipality.

COMMITTEES FOR 1896.

Finances.

MM. Bonnefin
Bouio
Boullé
François
Henry
Jenkins

MM. Leblanc
Morel
Newton
Olivier
Pétricher
Poupard

MM. Sauzier
Souchon
Turner
Vaudagne

Travaux Publics.

MM. Bonnefin
Bouic
François
Jenkins
Leblanc

MM. Morel
Newton
Olivier
Pétricher
Poupard

MM. Sauzier
Souchon
Turner
Vaudagne

Cadastre.

MM. Bonnefin
Bouic
Boullé
François
Henry

MM. Leblanc
Morel
Newton
Olivier
Pétricher

MM. Souchon
Turner
Vaudagne

Incendies.

MM. François 1
Pétricher 2
Poupard 3

MM. Morel 4
Henry 5
Newton 6

MM. Turner 7
Leblanc 8

Eclairage et Nettoiememt.

MM. Bonnefin
Bouic
Boullé
Leblanc

MM. Morel
Newton
Olivier
Pétricher

MM. Sauzier
Souchon
Turner
Vaudagne

Canaux

MM. Bonnefin
Bouic
Boullé
François

MM. Leblanc
Morel
Newton
Pétricher

MM. Souchon
Turner
Vaudagne

Reglements.

MM. Bonnefin
Bouic
Boullé
François
Jenkins

MM. Leblanc
Morel
Newton
Olivier
Pétricher

MM. Poupard
Sauzier
Souchon
Turner
Vaudagne

Cimetières

MM. Bonnefin
Bouio
François
Leblanc

MM. Morel
Newton
Olivier
Pétricher

MM. Souchon
Turner
Vaudagne

MARCHÉS ET ABATTOIR.

MM. Bonnefin Bouic Boullé François Jenkins	MM. Leblanc Morel Newton Olivier Pétricher	MM. Poupard Sauzier Souchon Turner Vaudagne

THÉATRE.

MM. Bonnefin Bouic Boullé François Henry Jenkins	MM. Leblanc Morel Newton Olivier Pétricher Poupard	MM. Sauzier Souchon Turner Vaudagne

BIBLIOTHÈQUE.

MM. Bonnefin Bouic Boullé François Henry	MM. Jenkins Leblanc Morel Newton Pétricher	MM. Sauzier Souchon Turner Vaudagne

Station Agronomique.

The Hon. H. Leclézio,—*Chairman.*
— W. Newton, Q.C.
— W. T. A. Edwards, M.D.
— G. Robinson,
George Aubin, Esquire.
Edouard Montocchio, Esquire.
Paul Eynaud, Esquire.
C. Antelme, junior, Esquire.
F. Nash, Esquire.
The President of the Chamber of Agriculture.
The President of the Royal Society of Arts and Sciences.

Imperial Institute Committee.

Dr. Poupinel de Valencé, Esquire, President of the Royal Society of Arts and Sciences. —*Chairman.*
F. Nash, Esquire.
R. Freeland, Esquire.
A. Daruty de Grandpré, Esquire, Superintendent of the Museum.
Corresponding Agent.—A. Daruty de Grandpré, Esquire.

The Hurricane Loan Board of Commissioners.

Ex-Officio Members.

The Hon. the Colonial Secretary.
— the Procureur and Advocate General.
— the Receiver General.
— the Auditor General.

Appointed by the Governor.

The Hon. W. Newton, Q.C.
— E. Sauzier,
— W. T. A. Edwards, M.D.
— A. P. Ambrose,
— V. Geffroy.
— G. Robinson.
— G. A. Ritter.

Health Officers for Sea-Board Districts.

Under Ordinance 6 of 1887.

Dr. L. Portal for Grand Port.
Dr. L. H. Lemerle for Savanne.
Dr. S. A. R. Monty for Flacq.
Dr. L. Dubois for Pamplemousses.
Dr. A. Ménagé for Rivière du Rempart.
Dr. Chasteauneuf for Black River.

Pharmacy Ordinance No. 17 of 1869.

BOARD OF EXAMINERS.

Director of the Medical and Health Department,—*Chairman*.
C. E. Poupinel de Valencé, Esq. M.D.
And two Pharmacists chosen each time a Candidate is examined.

Pilot's Ordinance No. 26 of 1881.

BOARD OF EXAMINERS.

The Harbour Master.—*Chairman*.
2nd. Seat vacant.
3rd. Seat vacant.

The Railway Board.

(Constituted under Proclamation No. 2 of 9th. January 1896.)

The Hon. A. P. Ambrose.—*Chairman*.
— L. de Rochecouste.
The Engineer and Manager of Railways.
Edouard Montocchio, Esq.

Chamber of Commerce.

Hon. H. Stein.—*President*.
C. F. Adam, Esquire.—*Vice-President*.
A. Regnard, Esquire.—*Treasurer*.
C. Domergue, Esquire.—*Secretary*.
R. Freeland, Esquire } *Auditors*.
T. Mallac, Esquire }

Hon. Geo. Robinson
— A. P. Ambrose
MM. A. Boullé
John Fraser, C.M.G.
Ed. Hourquebie
C. Sumeire, C.M.G.
L. Pilot
Joseph Coutanceau
F. Laroque
MM. A. Ulcoq
F. Tennant
F. Nash
Affan Tank Wen
E. Piat
E. C. Fraser
L. Raoul
L. Antelme, junior
Allamkhan Rametkhan
MM. J. Regnard
E. Spéville
G. Labat
A. B. Mamode Taher
Ed. Loumeau
A. Wemyss
F. Richer
L. Rogers

Chamber of Agriculture.

Hon. L. de Rochecouste.—*President*.
F. Nash, Esquire.—*1st. Vice-President*.
Hon. Dr. W.T.A. Edwards.—*2nd. Vice-President*.
Hon. G. Robinson.—*Treasurer*.
G. Bouic, Esquire.—*Secretary*.

MEMBERS OF THE COUNCIL OF THE CHAMBER.

Hon. Ritter, G.A.
— Naz, K.C.M.G., Sir V.
— Leclézio, H.
MM. Aubin, G.
Barlow, C.
Dr. Bour, Alf.
Chastellier, P. L., Q. C.
MM. Chazal, Ate. de
Dumat, C.
Giroday, F. B. de la
Hardy, C.
Harel, N.
Mallac, T.
Montocchio, E.
MM. Nash, F.
Regnard, Ade.
Rondeaux, J.
Rochecouste, E. de
Senneville, E. de
Telfair, W.
Ulcoq, A.

Mauritius Civil Service Cooperative Society.

BOARD OF DIRECTORS.

A. Poupard.—*Chairman*.
E. Serret.—*Vice-Chairman*.
F. Duchenne.—*Secretary*.
L. A. Célestin, Esquire.
E. Mayer, Esquire.
R. Lejeunne, Esquire.
W. C. Rae, Esquire.
A. Pougnet, Esquire.
G. C. Mayer, Esquire.
F. V. Descroizilles, Esquire.
Hon. G. A. Ritter.
V. Singery, Esquire.
Joseph Pilot, Esquire.
O. L. O'Conor, Esquire.
Silas Graves, Esquire.

MANAGING COMMITTEE.

Hon. G. A. Ritter.—*Chairman*.
J. Pilot, Esquire.
E. Mayer, Esquire.
W. C. Rae, Esquire.
F. V. Descroizilles, Esquire.

A. E. Cutler.—*Storekeeper*.

Chamber of Notaries.

G. Baissac, Esquire.—*President.*
W. E. Hart.—*Syndic.*
A. Piat, Esquire.—*Reporter.*
E. de Robillard, Esquire.—*Secretary.*

Chamber of Brokers.

Eugène Hourquebie, Esquire.—*Syndic.*
Alphonse Boullé, Esquire.—*Syndic Adjoint.*

MEMBERS.

J. Charles Dauban.
Edouard Montocchio.
Jules Régnard.
James Vallet.
Hon. George Robinson.
E. Rouillard.—*Secretary.*
H. Giblot Ducray.—*Treasurer.*

Mauritius Civil Service Mutual Aid Association.

BOARD OF DIRECTORS.

Hon. G. de Coriolis.—*Chairman.*
— J. J. Brown.—*1st. Vice Chairman.*
C. G. Hall, Esquire.—*2nd. Vice Chairman.*
A. Boucherat, Esquire.
A. Cantin, Esquire.
A. Celestin, Esquire.
F. V. Descroizilles, Esquire.
W. C. Rae, Esquire.
Léon Salèce, Esquire.

F. Duchenne.—*Secretary.*

Auditors for 1896. { P. Cartier, Esquire. A. Rae, Esquire. }

Meteorological Society.

Established 1st. August 1851.

H. R. H. the Duke of Edinburgh, K.G. &c. *Honorary Patron.*
His Excellency Sir H.E.H.Jerningham, K.C.M.G. *Patron.*
Sir V. Naz, K.C.M.G.,—*President.*
The Rev. G. Mc Irvine, M.A. } *Vice-Presidents*
M. Connal, Esquire. }
Hon. Hamilton Stein,—*Treasurer.*
C. Meldrum, C.M.G., M.A., L.L.D., F.R.S., *Secretary.*

COUNCIL.

C. F. H. Adam, Esquire.
J. Fraser, Esq. C.M.G.
O. L. O'Connor, Esquire, F.R. Met. S.
C. F. Shand, Esquire.

Marine Surveyors.

Murdo Mc Donald, Esq. *Lloyd's Surveyor.*
L. P. Adam, Esq. *Surveyor to French Veritas.*
C. Constant Lemeur, Esq. *Surveyor to American Record.*

Sailors Home Society.

President.—The Right Rev. the Lord Bishop of Mauritius.
Vice-President.—Hon. A. P. Ambrose.
Hon. Treasurer.—Captain M. Mc Donald.
Hon. Secretary.—Revd. G. Mc Irvine, M.A.

COMMITTEE.

J. Wilson, Esquire, Harbour Master.
Hon. Hamilton Stein,
N. Lemême, Esq.
Robert Freeland, Esq.
V. Trew, Esq.
G. H. Ireland, Esq.

Board for Examination of Masters and Mates of British Ships.

(*Under Ordinance No.* 15 *of* 1887.)

The Harbour Master.
The Director of the Royal Observatory.
Captain M. Mc Donald.
— Alex. Ritchie.

Marine Board.

The Senior District Magistrate,—*Chairman,*
The Harbour Master,
The President of the Chamber of Commerce, *ex-officio.*
The Agents for Lloyds.
M. Mc Donald, Esq.
(One vacancy.)

Royal Society of Arts and Sciences.

His Excellency Sir H. E. H. Jerningham, K.C.M.G., *Patron*
Dr. Ch. Poupinel de Valencé,—*President.*
Sir Eugène E. J. Leclézio, } *Vice-Presidents.*
Dr. C. Meldrum, C.M.G., L.L.D., F.R.S. }

A. Daruty de Grandpré, Esq.—*Secretary.*
G. Bonic, Esq. } *Vice-Secretaries.*
T. Henry, }
J. Regnard.—*Treasurer.*

COMMITTEE.

Hon. L. de Rochecouste,
J. Fraser, Esq., C.M.G.,
Dr. P. Chevreau,
Dr. H. Lorans,

Hon. Dr. T. W. A. Edwards.
F. Nash, Esquire.
Léon Leclézio, Esquire.—*Auditor.*

Mauritius Turf Club.

Hon. L. de Rochecouste.—*President.*
C. Antelme, Junior, Esq. } *Stewards.*
E. Sauzier, Senior, Esq. }

L. Souchon, Esq.—*Honorary Secretary.*

Mauritius Cricket Club.

Incorporated by Charter under Ordinance No. 11 *of* 1894 *and Proclamation No.* 30 *of* 9*th. October* 1894.

J. Fraser, Esq. C.M.G.—*President.*
The Hon. A. P. Ambrose,—*Vice-President.*

J. W. Hollway, Esq.—*Hon. Treasurer.*
H. M. Blyth, Esq.—*Hon. Secretary.*

Place of Meeting Rose Hill.

Mauritius Archery Society.

COMMITTEE OF MANAGEMENT.

Major C. M. Bate, R.E.
W. S. Telfair, Esq.
G. Dickson, Esq.

Hon. Hamilton Stein,—*Hon, Treasurer.*
W. F. Russell, Esq.—*Hon. Secretary.*

Mauritius Lawn Tennis Championship Club.

COMMITTEE OF MANAGEMENT.

J. Cowin, Esq.—*Hon. Secretary & Treasurer.*
St. G. Caulfield, Esquire, R.E.

A. de Chazal, Esq.

CHAMPIONS.

April	1891	...	...	...	Captain H. H. Rich, R. A.
December	1891	...	...	...	Lieut. E. F. Harding, 64th. Regt.
April	1892	...	...	...	Lieut. E. F. Harding, ,,
December	1892	...	...	...	J. Stein, Esq.
April	1893	...	...	...	Capt. F. W. Hill.
December	1893	...	...	...	H. H. Sutherland, Esq. " Black Watch ".
April	1894	...	...	...	H. Andrew, Esq. " The Black Watch ".
December	1894	...	...	...	R. L. Muspratt. Williams, R.A.
April	1895	...	...	...	,, ,, ,,
December	1895	...	...	...	St. G. Caulfield, Esq., R.E.

REFEREES.

1, Hon. H. Stein | 2. J. Fraser, Esq., C.M.G. | 3. Vacant.

Board of Examiners.

For issuing Certificates under Ord. 32 *of* 1888 (*Boiler Ordinance*).

M. Connal, Esq.
J. Piddington, Esq.
P. Tardieu, Esq.

The Mauritius Civil Service Widows and Orphans' Pension Fund

Under Ordinance No. 2 *of* 1886.

BOARD OF DIRECTORS.

The Revd. G. Mc Irvine,—*Chairman.*
The Hon. G. R. Dick.
— E. C. Ashley.
O. L. O'Connor, Esquire.
F. V. Descroizilles, Esquire.

Acclimatization Society of Mauritius.

For the year 1896.

A. Daruty de Grandpré, Esq.—*President.*
Hon. L. de Rochecouste, } *Vice-Presidents.*
G. Guimbeau Esquire, }
G. Bouic, Esquire.—*Secretary.*
A. Colin, junior, Esquire.—*Vice-Secretary.*
Jules Regnard, Esquire.—*Treasurer.*
J. F. Anderson, Esquire. } *Auditors.*
L. Antelme, junior, Esquire, }

MEMBERS.

Hon. H. Leclézio.
J. Fraser, Esquire, C.M.G.
G. Regnard, Esquire.
Dr. L. Drouin.
R. Kœnig, Esquire.
J. Vallet, Esquire.

Congrégation de St. Joseph.

FONDÉE EN 1856.

Comité pour 1896.

J. Colony.—*Président.*
R. Romain.—*Vice-Président.*
L. Bontemps.—*Secrétaire.*
H. Legéant.—*Trésorier.*
A. André.—*Vice-Trésorier.*

The Club.

Rose Hill.—(Adjoining the Cricket Club).—Founded 15th. April 1895.
Limited to 40 *Members.*
Entrance Fee Rs. 5. Annual Subscription Rs. 60.—Payable in advance.
His Excellency Sir Hubert E. Henry Jerningham, K.C.M.G.—*Patron.*

COMMITTEE OF MANAGEMENT.

Hon. A. P. Ambrose.—*Chairman.*
R. B. Graham, Esquire.—*Hon. Treasurer.*
M. Y. H. Parks, Esquire.—*Hon. Secretary.*
G. I. H. Davidson, Esquire.
Capt. R. D. Anderson, R.A.

Mauritius St. Andrew's Society.

COMMITTEE.

President.—John Fraser, Esquire, C.M.G.
C. Meldrum, C.M.G., F.R.S., L.L.D.
A. Wemyss, Esquire.
Chaplain.—Revd. G. Mc Irvine.
Secretary.—Hon. Hamilton Stein.
Treasurer.—G. H. Ireland, Esquire.

Mahebourg Yacht Club.

(Established 26th. November 1874.)

President.—Hon. L. de Rochecouste.

Vice-Presidents. { Maurice Portal, Esquire. Jean Coutanceau, Esquire.

Treasurer.—A. Doucet, Esquire.
Secretary.—Jos. Letang, Esquire.

Sailing Committee { D. P. Sampson, E. Autard, J. P. Freeman, F. C. Boullineau. A. de la Rochette.

E. Serret, B. Pérille, } *Auditors.*

Société de St. Vincent de Paul.

CONSEIL PARTICULIER.

MM. C. Béguinot, F. André } *Vice-Presidents.*

MM. H. Maingard.—*Secrétaire.*

LA CONFÉRENCE ST. LOUIS.

MM. C. Béguinot.—*Président.*
N. Frappier, L. Christ. } *Vice-President.*
A. Latapie.—*Secrétairc.*

LA CONFÉRENCE DE L'IMMACULÉE CONCEPTION.

MM. R. Keisler.—*President.*
J. Félix.—*Vice-President.*
F. Leguen.—*Secrétaire.*
Bargeolle fils.—*Tresorier.*

Society of the Propagation of Faith.

Reverend J. Guilhen.—*Procureur.*

The Experimental Plantation Committee.

Hon. L. de Rochecouste.—*Chairman.*
Sir V. Naz, K.C.M.G.
A. Daruty de Grandpré, Esq.
Jules Regnard, Esq.
L. A. Hugues, Esq.
Léon Leclézio, Esq.
J. C. Penaud, Esq. M.D.
Aristide Regnard, Esq.
L. Antelme, junior, Esq.
F. Levieux, Esq.
G. Perromat, Esq.

Historical Records Committee.

A. Daruty de Grandpré, Esq.—*Chairman.*
A. Rae, Esq.—*Secretary.*
The Hon. V. Geffroy.
Aimé Duvivier, Esq.
Léon Leclézio, Esq.
Léon de Froberville, Esq.
E. Dupont, Esq.
Alphonse Gaud, Esq.
G. Lincoln, Esq.
A. D'Epinay, Esq.—*Honorary Member.*

Government Teachers' Benevolent Fund.

The Superintendent of Schools.—*President.*

COMMITTEE OF MANAGEMENT FOR THE YEARS 1895, 1896 and 1897.

Messrs. N. Decotter,—*Chairman.*
P. J. Ambroisine,—*Secretary.*
L. J. Narcisse,—*Treasurer.*
T. W. Blackburn.
J. A. Blackburn.

Messrs. L. R. Aubergé.
E. Mainty.
P. D. Morvan, W. Shrubsole, } *Auditors.*

Société Médicale.

Président—Dr. Lesur.
Vice-Président—Dr. G. Bouchet.
Secrétaire—Dr. F. Antelme.
Trésorier—Dr. E. de Chazal.

MEMBRES DU BUREAU.

Dr. H. Clarenc. | One vacancy. | Dr. H. Lorans.

Société Française d'Assistance.

Président d'Honneur—M. A. Drouin, Consul de France, Chevalier de la Légion d'Honneur.

CONSEIL D'ADMINISTRATION.

Exercice 1895.

Président—J. A. Coutanceau, Chevalier de la Légion d'Honneur et de l'Ordre de St. Sylvestre.
Vice-Présidents—MM. H. Clarenc, M.D., Chevalier de la Légion d'Honneur et du Mérite Agricole et E. Hourquebie, Agent de Change.
Secrétaire—Emile Rivière.
Trésorier—F. Henry, Agent d'Assurance.

MEMBRES DU CONSEIL.

MM. A. F. Richer,
J. Rouhier,
G. Papon,
G. Patureau,
G. Bordas,
M. Rivière,
MM. E. de Rochecouste,
Th. Stéphanon,
Camille Sumeire, C.M.G.,
L. M. Castelin,
L. F. Henry.

Couvent de Notre Dame de Bon Secours.

REMPART STREET.

Révérende Mère Supérieure :—Sœur Pierre.

Couvent des Filles de Marie.

LA PAIX STREET.

Révérende Mère Supérieure :—Marie Mère de la Providence.

Couvent des Réparatrices.

ST. FRANÇOIS.

Révérende Mère Supérieure :—Marie du Prétoire.

Couvent de Notre Dame de Lorette.

CORDERIE STREET.

Révérende Mère Supérieure :—Mrs. Hyacinthe.

Catholic Union of Mauritius.

Place of Meeting, 20 Pope Hennessy Street, Port Louis.

MM. Robert Kœnig,—*President.*
J. C. de Mazérieux,—*1st. Vice-President.*
F. André,—*2nd. Vice-President.*
A. de Boucherville,—*Secretary.*
P. Loustau Lalanne,—*Assistant Secretary.*
Aug. Esnouf,—*Treasurer.*
C. F. H. Adam.
Hon. V. Geffroy.
F. X. S. Levieux.
A. J. Colin, junior.
MM. F. Robert.
E. François.
Alfred Rousset.
Gabriel Herchenroder.
Victor Pitot.
L. Clède.
A. Hugnin, junior.
Dr. X. Nallétamby.
Geo. Pierrot.
A. Poupinel de Valencé.

Société de Secours Mutuels des Ouvriers du Gouvernement.

Fondee à Port Louis le 20 Décembre 1879, et Constituée par Proclamation No. 6 de 1894.

SIÈGE AU PARC-A-BOULETS.

Reçoit du Gouvernement une Subvention annuelle de Rs. 500 approuvé par le Secrétaire d'Etat.

Président,—Charles Mazère.
Vice-Président,—J. Dupin.
Trésorier,—Ls. Charlot.
Secrétaire,—H. Nicole.

Alliance Française.

M. A. Drouin, Consul de France,—*Président Honoraire.*
Dr. H. Clarenc,—*Président.*
M. J. A. Coutanceau, } *Vice-Président.*
Hon. H. Leclézio, }
MM. A. Ollivry,—*Secrétaire.*
E. Rivière,—*Secrétaire Archiviste.*
G. Bouic,—*Trésorier.*
L. de St. Pern.

MEMBRES DU COMITÉ.

MM. V. Boullé.
A. Daruty de Grandpré.
L. Drouin, M.D.
E. Mathé.
C. Sumeire, C.M.G.
J. Rouhier.

The Mauritius Religious Tract Society.

President,—The Lord Bishop of Mauritius.
Secretary,—Revd. Geo. Mc Irvine, M.A.

COMMITTEE OF MANAGEMENT.

The Ven. Archdeacon French.
The Ven. Archdeacon Buswell.
Revd. H. A. Wollaston Jones.
Revd. W. Pendavis.
R. Freeland, Esquire.
Chas. Farquhar Shand, Esquire.

Diocesan Church Society.

President,—The Lord Bishop of Mauritius.

Vice-Presidents.

The Ven. Archdeacon French.
The Ven. Archdeacon Buswell.
J. Fraser, Esq. C.M.G.
Honorable A. Povah Ambrose.
His Hon. C. A. King-Harman, C.M.G.
His Hon. Major General W. Osborne Barnard.

Treasurer,—Hon. H. Stein.

Auditors. { W. S. Telfair, Esq.
J. W. Hollway, Esq.

COMMITTEE.

Revd. A. Vaudin.
Mr. C. Boodhoo.
W. Hamley, Esq.
G. H. Ireland, Esq.
A. Rohan, Esq.
Revd. C. S. Harington.
C. F. Shand, Esq.
A. Wemyss, Esq.
J. Wilson, Esq.
A. Messervy, Esq.
Revd. W. Pendavis.

The *Diocesan Church Council* consists of the foregoing, except the Auditors, together with the rest of the Clergy, the Board of Commissioners, and the Churchwardens of the various congregations. The Hon. Secretary is the Ven. Archdeacon Buswell.

Church Missionary Society.

MISSIONARIES.

Venerable Archdeacon Buswell.
The Revd. V. W. Harcourt.
The Revd. C. A. Blackburn.
The Revd. A. K. Finnimore, B.A.

Assistant Missionary,—The Reverend S. S. Sing.

MAURITIUS NATIVE CHURCH COUNCIL.

Patron.—The Right Reverend the Lord Bishop of Mauritius.
Chairman.—Archdeacon Buswell.
Vice-Chairman.—Mr. Charles Boodhoo.
Hon. Treasurer.—T. E. Dempster, Esq.
Secretary.—Reverend John Ernest.

DELEGATES:

PORT LOUIS PASTORATE.

Cathechist Mirza Hope.
Mr. Biproo.
Mr. Nitanuth.

NORTH CENTRAL PASTORATE.

Reverend J. F. Chorley.
Mr. James Peersahib.
Mr. Vincent Nakadoo.

SOUTH CENTRAL PASTORATE.

Catechist Salomon Toolsy.
Mr. Chas. Nankoo.
Mr. J. Nankoo.

NORTHERN PASTORATE.

Reverend John Ernest.
Mr. W. F. Koylessur.
Mr. F. R. Nursoo.

SOUTHERN PASTORATE.

Revd. S. Susunkur.
Mr. Alex. Simon.
Mr. J. Chinien.

MOKA PASTORATE.

Mr. S. Mooteelal.
Mr. D. Ramchurn.
Mr. Koylass.

Mauritius Auxiliary of the British & Foreign Bible Society.

PATRON:
His Honor Major General W. Osborne Barnard,
HONORARY TREASURER.—Hon. Hamilton Stein
The Lord Bishop of Mauritius.—*President.*
Revd. G. Mc Irvine, M.A.—*Vice-President.*

HONORARY SECRETARIES.—Revd. W. Pendavis, Revd. Chas. Blackburn & Captain Murdo Mc. Donald.

COMMITTEE.

Hon. A. P. Ambrose.
James Forester Anderson, Esq.
C. C. Chéron, Esq.
E. C. Fraser, Esq.
Robert Freeland, Esq.
G. Ireland, Esq.
Capt. A. Ritchie, Esq.
Aldor Rohan, Esq.
C. Farquhar Shand, Esq.
Henry C. Smith, Esq.
V. Trew, Esq.
Capt. J. Wilson.

And all Protestant Ministers aiding this Auxiliary.

Mauritius District Branch of the Society for the promotion of Christian Knowledge.

PRESIDENT.

The Lord Bishop of Mauritius.

Ven. Archdeacon French.
Ven. Archdeacon Buswell.—*Secretary.*
Rev. H. A. Wollaston Jones.
Rev. W. Pendavis.
C. Farquhar Shand, Esq.

Society for the Propagation of the Gospel in Foreign Parts.

President : The Lord Bishop of Mauritius.

MEMBERS OF THE COMMITTEE.

Ven. Archdeacon French.
Hon. P. Ambrose,—*Treasurer.*
— E. C. Ashley.
G. Lumgair, Esq.
A. Messervy, Esq. M.A.
Revd. W. Pendavis, M.A.
C. Nash, Esq.
Geo. H. Ireland, Esq.
A. Temple Roberts, Esq. M.A.
Revd. L. N. Seichan.
Revd. A. Vaudin.
Revd. H. A. Woolaston Jones,—*Secretary.*

Diocesan Committee of the Roman Catholic Church.

(*Constituted under Ordinance No.* 31 *of* 1890.)

C. F. Adam, Esq.,—*President.*
Sir V. Naz, K.C.M.G.
S. Pelte, Esq.
F. Robert, Esq.,—*Treasurer.*
J. Delisse, Esq.
F. André, Esq.
F. Galdemar, Esq.
A. Rousset, Esq.,—*Secretary.*

Presbyterial Committee of the Church of Scotland.

(*Constituted under Ordinance No.* 31 *of* 1890.)

H. C. Smith,—*Chairman.*
Revd. George Mc Irvine, M.A.
„ G. Mc Kelvie, M.A.
„ J. J. Lebrun.
„ D. P. Davoine.
James Bappoo.
E. Dupuy.
A. Ritchie.
T. Le Bon.
J. Forester Anderson.
Murdo Mc Donald,—*Treasurer.*
Joseph Standley.
C. Meldrum, L.L.D., F.R.S., C.M.G.
C. A. Standley.
A. Cangy.
F. David.
A. Baptiste.
T. Ledson.
W. Simonet.
J. Lacloche.
H. David.
A. Antoine.
A. Radal.
W. Mc Irvine,—*Secretary.*
A. Parizot.
F. Simonet.

Kirk-Session (Comité des Anciens) St. John's Church.

Moderator.—
Treasurer.—E. Dupuy.
Secretary.—E. Hubert.

MEMBERS :

A. Standley.
J. Standley.
E. Malliaté.
F. David.
L. Félix.
E. Lebon.
C. Chéron.

Protestant Benevolent Institution.

Patron :
Vice-Patron,—His Honor Major General, W. Osborne Barnard.
President,—The Lord Bishop of Mauritius.
Vice-President,—Hon. A. P. Ambrose.
Hon. Secretary,—Revd. W. Pendavis, M.A.
Hon. Treasurer,—F. Estill, Esquire.

MANAGING COMMITTEE.

J. H. Ackroyd, Esquire
Geo. H. Ireland, Esquire
L. Rogers, Esquire
C. F. Shand, Esquire
H. Smith, Esquire
Hon. C. A. King-Harman, C.M.G.
J. W. Hollway, Esquire
Revd. G. Mc Irvine, M.A.
The Venerable Archdeacon Buswell
The Venerable Archdeaon French
Aldor Rohan, Esquire

LADIES VISITING COMMITTEE.

Mrs. Walsh,—*President.*
Mrs. J. Ambrosé
Mrs. Osborne Barnard
Mrs. Kendall
Mrs. C. A. King-Harman
Mrs. Harper
Mrs. Mc Irvine
Mrs. Vaudin
Mrs. Stein
Mrs. Wemyss
Mrs. P. A. Wiéhé
Mrs. Morgan
Mrs. Estill.—*Hon. Secretary*
Mr. J. Coombes—*Auditor.*

The Mauritius Young Men's Association.

(St. Johns Presbyterian Church).

J. F. Anderson, Esquire,—Hon. Secretary.

Church Wardens, Church of England.

St. James Cathedral	L. Rogers, Esq., and Geo. Garbert, Esq.
St. Mary's Port Louis	Messrs. P. Marday and W. Barnabas.
St. Paul's, Port Louis	Messrs. Somaroo and H. Baichu.
St. Nicholas Mariners' Church	Captain Wilson and S. Graves, Esq.
St. John's, Moka	C. Farquhar Shand, Esq. and W. S. Telfair, Esq.
St. Clement's, Curepipe	A. Lanauze, Esq. and S. Dinnematin, Esq.
St. Luke's, Souillac	H. Rogers, Esq. and Mr. B. Samuel.
St. Peter's, Pailles...	Mr. Catechist Humphery.
St. Thomas, Plaines Wilhems	G. H. Ireland, Esq., and Dr. I. J. Paddle.
Holy Trinity Church, Rose Hill	C. A. D'Avray, Esq., and A. Blackburn, Esq.
St. Paul's, Vacoas	J. Coombes, Esq , and A. Messervy, Esq.
Christ Church, Mahebourg	E. Symms Esq., and O. Coombes, Esq.
St. Barnabas, Pamplemousses	W. Scott, Esq., and Mr. F. Nursoo.
St. Peter's, Bambous	Mr. J. Jean.
St. Andrew's, Quatre Bornes	A. Temple Roberts, Esq., and Hon. J. J. Brown.
St. John Baptist, Brisée Verdière	Messrs. F. Valaydon and G. Donat.
St. Mark, Poudre d'Or	Mr. E. Potié.

SEYCHELLES.

St. Paul's, Port Victoria	E. P. Bonstead, Esq. and M. H. Rhode, Esq.
St. Saviours, South Mahé...	Messrs. L. Derobin and L. Payet
St. Mathews, Praslin	Messrs. F. Morgan and Pierre Barbé.

Church of Scotland.

SAINT-ANDREW'S, PORT LOUIS.

Elders... ... ... Messrs, A. Ritchie and W. Mc Irvine

ST. JOHN'S, PORT LOUIS.

Elder ... ... Mr. E. Hubert.

Moka	Elder	Alf. Radal
Grand River...	Elder	
Flacq ...	Elder	A. Galais
Mapou	Elder	H. David
Pointe aux Piments.	Elder...	J. Lacloche
Savanne	Elder...	A. Parisot
Mahebourg	Elder...	H. Rault
Rose Hill		M.Mc Donald & N.Le Même

New Jerusalem Church Society.

N. Lesage, Esquire,—*President.*
Geo. Mayer, Esquire,—*Vice-President.*
Edgar de Chazal, Esquire,—*Secretary.*
J. H. Ackroyd, Esquire,—*Vice-Secretary.*
A. Chasteauneuf, Esquire,—*Treasurer.*

Chinese Congregations for the year 1896.

1—Num-Shum Congregation.

President ...	... Mr. Ahmon	Treasurer ...	... Mr. Ah-Shun
Vice-President	... „ Atoy Chankow	Secretary ...	... „ Quang-how

2—Chan-Cha Congregation.

President ...	... Mr. Thon Kham	Treasurer ...	... Tee Seng
Vice-President	... „ Chan Tee Lone	Secretary ...	... „ Thu-San

3—Fock-Diack Congregation.

President ...	... Mr. Ah-Aun	Treasurer ...	... Mr. A. Wye-Thim
Vice-President	... „ Fock-Tong	Secretary ...	... „ Fook-Taw

4—Sweet-Hang Congregation.

President ...	... Mr. Tang Tong	Treasurer ...	... Mr. Lock-San-Meng
Vice-President	... „ Ho-Ping-Hin	Secretary ...	... „ Ho-Wing

5—Yin-Foo-Fyquan Congregation.

President ...	... Mr. Chan-Ah-Foo	Treasurer ...	... Mr. Keem Yaung
Vice-President	... „ Sew-Chon	Secretary ...	... „ Lam-Che-Woa

---

THE

MAURITIUS COMMERCIAL BANK

(INCORPORÉE PAR CHARTE ROYALE)

CAPITAL : £ 200,000

Formée de 10,000 Actions de £ 20 chacune entièrement libérée

Cour des Directeurs :

MM. P. L. CHASTELLIER, Q.C.,—*Président.*
F. C. ESTILL,—*Vice-Président.*
Sir VIRGILE NAZ, K.C.M.G.
P. E. DE CHAZAL.
Hon. G. A. RITTER.
Hon. H. LECLÉZIO.
MM. TRISTAN MALLAC.
HENRI GIBLOT DUCRAY.
ARISTE PIAT.

Direction de l'Intérieur :

La Direction de l'Intérieur est confiée à M. ED. SPÉVILLE,—*Secrétaire.*

Caissier... ... ... M. MEE. GOUPILLE | *Comptable*... ... ... P. HUGNIN.

Change :

La Banque fournit des Traites sur ces Agents à Londres, à Paris, etc., à 3, 30, 60 et 90 jours de vue, au change du jour. Elle achète les traites du commerce sur l'Angleterre, la France, l'Australie, Bombay, etc., et délivre des lettres de crédit sur Londres, Paris et Calcutta.

Escomptes et Avances :

La Banque escompte toutes valeurs de place. Ces valeurs doivent être revêtues de deux signatures au moins. Elle fait aussi des avances remboursables dans deux mois sur Dock Warrants de sucre, grains, etc ; déposés dans des magasins dûment patentés moyennant le transfert du reçu du magasinier de la Police d'Assurance.

Les ESCOMPTES ont lieu tous les jours à 2 heures p.m., sauf les SAMEDIS.

Comptes-Courants :

Pour toutes sommes au-dessus de Rs. **1,000** il ne peut être ouvert de compte-courant.

Il n'est pas alloués d'intérêts sur les comptes-courants.

Les formes de mandats et les livrets sont fournis par la Banque aux déposants.

Tout mandats tirés sur la Banque ne peuvent l'être pour une somme au-dessous de **20 Roupies** et doivent être faits sur les **formes fournies.**

La clôture des comptes a lieu le 10 Avril et le 10 Octobre de chaque année, et à ces époques, les livrets doivent être envoyés à la Banque pour être balancés. Il serait à désirer que les carnets fussent présentés à la Banque tous les huit ou quinze jours pour être vérifiés.

Actions :

La transmission des Actions ne peut se faire par la voie d'endossement. Lorsqu'une vente a eu lieu, on en opère le transfert à la Banque sur le Registre tenu à cet effet.

N.B.—Les bureaux de la Banque s'ouvrent tous les jours à 10 heures et se ferment à 3 heures. Les SAMEDIS sont fermés à Midi.

Agents à LONDRES	*Lloyds Bank Limited.*
à PARIS	*Mallet Frères & Cie.*
à BOMBAY, MADRAS, KURRACHEE, ADEN et ZANZIBAR	*National Bank of India Limited.*
en AUSTRALIE et NOUVELLE ZÉLANDE ...	*The Union Bank of Australia Limited.*
dans tous les PORTS DU CAP	*The Standard Bank of South Africa Limited.*

ED. SPÉVILLE,—*Secrétaire.*

BANK OF MAURITIUS LD.

CAPITAL £ 125,550

Directors in London:

THE RIGHT HONORABLE LORD STANMORE G.C.M.G.
GEORGE W. DAVIDSON, Esqre.
W. GRAHAM LOYD, Esqre. | MAURICE ULCOQ, Esqre.

London Office:

10, George Yard, Lombard St.
J. A. FERGUSON, Manager.

Directors in Mauritius:

THE HONORABLE SIR CÉLICOURT ANTELME, K.C.M.G.
THE HONORABLE HAMILTON STEIN
GEORGE H. IRELAND, Esqre.

Bankers in London:

Messrs BARCLAY, BEVAN, TRITTON & Co.
54, Lombard Street, London.

Bankers in Paris:

SEMINARIO Frères & Co.
29, Rue des Pyramides.

Bankers in India and China:

THE CHARTERED BANK OF INDIA, AUSTRALIA & CHINA

Agents in Australia:

English, Scottish and Australian Bank.

Agents in New Zealand:

Bank of New Zealand.

Agents in South Africa:

Standard Bank of South Africa.

Business:

Current deposit accounts opened and cheque books supplied.

Fixed Deposits are received.

Bearing interest at 4½ o/o per annum for one year.
" " at 3 o/o " for six months.

Discounts made and loans granted against securities.
Securities bought, sold and received in custody for the Bank's Constituents.
Interest collected on shares and remittances made for constituents.
Bills collected and every description of Banking business conducted by the Bank.

Drafts are granted and Bills negociated on London, Paris, Bombay, Calcutta, Madras, Colombo, Hong Kong, Singapore, Australia and New Zealand.
Telegraphic remittances made.

Alexander WEMYSS,—*Manager.*

George DICKSON,—*Accountant.*

The Oriental Estates Company
LIMITED

CAPITAL DIVIDED INTO

228,262 Ordinary Shares of £ 1 each...	...	£ 228,262
40,902 Preferred Shares of £ 5 each...	...	204,510
		£ 432,772
6 o/o Mortgage Debentures	...	150,000
		£ 582,772

DIRECTORS :

QUINTIN HOGG, Esq.,—*Chairman.*
ALEX : WILLIAM CRIGHTON, Esq.,
NORMAN WILLIAM GRIEVE, Esq.
HENRY KERR RUTHERFORD, Esq.

LONDON OFFICE—SOUTH SEA CHAMBERS, 97 & 98, BISHOPSGATE STREET WITHIN, E.C.

Estates in Ceylon and Mauritius the Property of the Company.

CEYLON.

Bellwood	Haviland	Mahawatte
Craigie Lea	Haddington	Naranghena
Dangkando	Henegahawelle	Newmarket
Darrawella	Hunugalla	Nilloomally 3/4ths
Delmar	Kondesalle	Sinnapittia
Dene	Kuda Oya	Stellenberg
Dodangalla	Lindupatina	St. Coombs
Donoughmore	Lonmay	Summerhill
Forest Creek	Loolecondura	Waloya
Glen Devon	Mahaberiatenne	Wattewalla

Total acreage 12,953 acres.

Under Tea...	4,129 acres.	
,, Coffee	637 ,,	
,, Cocoa	604 ,,	
Under Cinchona	1,158 acres.	
,, Cardamons	80 ,,	
Grass, Forest, &c	6,345 ,,	

MAURITIUS.

Britannia | Cent Gaulettes.

Acreage 3,547 acres.

The Company are also the Principal Proprietors and Managers of the

Beau Séjour Sugar Estate Company Limited | Highlands Sugar Estate Company Limited

Areage 9,103 acres.

BANKERS :—The Commercial Bank of Mauritius,
and Bank of Mauritius.

Manager in Mauritius : FRED. NASH.

The Mauritius Estates & Assets Company

LIMITED

IN LIQUIDATION

SHARE CAPITAL ... ... £ 350,000 | MORTGAGE DEBENTURE £ 350,000

DIRECTORS IN LONDON :

THOS. A. WELTON, 5, Moorgate Street, Chartered Accountant.
J. LIDDELL, (Messrs. Henderson & Liddell), Eastcheap, E. C.
THOMAS BUXTON MORRISH, Leonard House, Upper Tulse Hill, London.

SECRETARY IN LONDON :

A. RIDDELL, 7 & 8, Walbrook, London E. C.

STAFF IN MAURITIUS :

MALCOLM MONRO, Attorney for the Liquidator.

ARTHUR J. BROAD, Accountant.

Estates of the Company :

Beau Champ, in Flacq	... 2960	acres
Olivia „	... 1320	„
Belle Rive, „	... 1350	„
Clemencia, „	... 1305	„
St. Julien and its annexe Bonne Veine, Moka	... 6520	„
Melrose „	... 1240	„
Midlands, Pl. Wilhems	... 2628	„
Bananes, „	... 1280	„
Rose Belle, & annexes La Rosa, New Grove and Mare d'Albert, G. Port	3078	acres
Rivière Créole „	750	„
Tamarin, Clarens } Black River	3250	„
Chamarel, „	... 3000	„
La Louise, Pl. Wilhems	... 1000	„
Total acreage	...29,681	„

Legal Adviser in Mauritius,— HONORABLE H. LECLÉZIO,

Notary „ GUSTAVE BAISSAC.

THE

Credit Foncier of Mauritius

LIMITED

39, LOMBARD STREET, LONDON E. C.

RAMPART STREET, PORT LOUIS, MAURITIUS

CAPITAL £600,000 IN 12,000 SHARES £ 50 EACH

PAID UP £120,000

London Board of Directors:

J. A. LONGRIDGE, Esq.
W. J. TANNER, Esq.
E. H. LUSHINGTON, Esq.,
C. J. L. NICHOLSON, Esq.

Lt. Col. F. A. V. THURBURN.

Manager & Secretary: ALFRED GRŒME DICK, Esq.

Accountant: DAVID F. PARK, Esq., C. A., Edin.

Auditors:

Messrs. TURQUAND, YOUNGS & Co.

Mauritius Board of Directors:

The Hon. Sir C. ANTELME, K.C.M.G.—President.

C. F. A. ADAM, Esqre.
Sir V. NAZ, K.C.M.G.
Léopold ANTELME, junior, Esq.
P. L. CHASTELLIER, Esq., Q.C.
J. de C. MAZÉRIEUX, Esq.

Manager

AMÉDÉE HUGNIN, Esq.

Accountant

AMÉDÉE HUGNIN, junior, Esq.

Legal Adviser

The Hon. GEORGE GUIBERT, Q. C., Barrister-at-Law.

London Assurance Corporation

INCORPORATED BY ROYAL CHARTER, A.D. 1720

MARINE DEPARTMENT

INSURANCES CAN BE EFFECTED IN

LONDON—At the Head Office, No. 7, Royal Exchange.
MANCHESTER—At the Branch Office, 19, Pall Mall
LIVERPOOL—With Mr. S. S. Bristow, 10, Rumford Place.
GLASGOW—With Messrs. Thompson, Dickie & Co., 17, Royal Exchange Square.
NEW YORK—At the Branch Office, 58 Wall Street.

And also with the following Agents abroad:

Hamburg	Messrs. H. J. Burmester & Co., 14, Neueburg.
Bremen	,, Telge & Hinternhoff.
Amsterdam	Mr. Dirk Tollenaar, Hzn.
Rotterdam	,, W. Ledeboer, Wijnbrugstratt, 7.
Antwerp	,, André de Wael, 17, Rue Hockstetters.
Paris	Messrs. P. & G. Desprez, 6, Place de la Bourse.
Bordeaux	Mons. Albert Lançon, 10, Rue d'Orléans.
Lyon	Messrs. Choulet & Schmoll, 9, Rue de la Republique.
Constantinople	,, Maltass & Co.
,,	The Ottoman Insurance Co.
Smyrna	Mr. J. B. T. Datody.
Alexandria	The Bank of Egypt, Limited.
Port Elizabeth	Messrs. Mackie, Dunn & Co.
East London	,, Dunn & Co,
Durban, Natal	,, Ww. Dunn & Co.
Mombassa	The Imperial British East Africa Co.
Mauritius	Messrs. Blyth Brothers & Co.
Kurrachee	,, Ewart, Ryrie & Co.
Bombay	,, Ewart, Latham & Co.
Calicut	,, Peirce, Leslie & Co.
Colombo	,, Carson & Co., The Fort.
Madras	,, Arbuthnot & Co.
Tuticorin	,, Adamson, Mactaggart & Co.
Calcutta	,, George Henderson & Co.
Rangoon	The Arracan Co., Limited.
Penang	Messrs. Hallifax & Co.
Singapore	,, Guthrie & Co.
Padang	The Padangsche Handei Maatschappy.
Batavia	The Borneo Co., Limited.
Sourabaya	Messrs. Scheltema, Bloemendaal & Co.
Macassar	,, Jenny & Co.
Bangkok	The Arracan & Co., Limited.
Saigon	Messrs. Diethelm & Co.
Hong-Kong	,, Arnhold, Karberg & Co
Shanghai	,, Arnhold, Karberg & Co
Hankow	,, Greaves & Co.
Yokohama	,, H. Ahrens & Co., Nachfolger.
Hiogo	,, H. Ahrens & Co., Nachfolger.
Nagasaki	,, H. Ahrens & Co., Nachfolger.
Sydney	Peele & Co.
Brisbane, Queensland.	The British India & Queensland Agency Co., Limited.
Christchurch, New Zealand.	Messrs. Edwards, Bennett & Co
Victoria, Vancouvers Island.	,, Robert Ward & Co., Limited.
Portland, Oregon.	,, Jas. Laidlaw & Co.
San Francisco	,, H. M. Newhall & Co., 309/11, Sansome Street
Valparaiso	,, Vorwerk & Co.
Chicago	,, C. W. Elphicke & Co., 6 & 8, Sherman Street
Montreal	Mr. Robert Hampson, Corn Exchange Buildings.

Policies can be made payable at any of the above or following places:

Havre	Mr. J. Soulsby Rowell.
Adelaide—South Australia.	Messrs. Elder, Smith & Co., Ld.
Launceston—Tasmania	,, C. H. Smith & Co.
Dunedin—New Zealand	,, Dalgety & Co.

All Policies issued abroad, payable in London, are required to be stamped within TEN DAYS next after the same shall have been received in the United Kingdom.

THE

Mercantile Bank

OF INDIA

(LIMITED)

HEAD OFFICE, N° 40, THREADNEEDLE STREET

LONDON, E. C.

ALL EXCHANGE BUSINESS TRANSACTED

BY

THE MAURITIUS AGENTS

BLYTH BROTHERS & C°

PHŒNIX
Fire Assurance Company
LONDON

For insuring every kind of Property at home and abroad

FROM LOSS OR DAMAGE BY FIRE

ESTABLISHED OVER 100 YEARS

CLAIMS SETTLED WITH PROMPTITUDE AND LIBERALITY

— LOSSES PAID OVER £ 20,000,000 —

CHIEF OFFICES : **Lombard Street and Charing Cross, London.**

TRUSTEES AND DIRECTORS :

Joseph William Baxendale, Esq.
Walter Bird, Esq.
Bristow Bovill, Esq.
The Hon. James Byng.
John Clutton, Esq.
Arthur Clarges Loraine Fuller, Esq.
Charles Emanuel Goodhart, Esq.
William James Thompson, Esq.
R. K. Hodgson, Esq.
The Rt. Hon. Sir John Lubbock, Bt., M.P., F.R.S.
Charles Thomas Lucas, Esq.
The Hon. Edwin Ponsonby.
The Hon. E. B. Portman.
The Rt. Hon. the Earl of Radnor.
Dudley Robert Smith Esq.

AUDITORS :

Joseph Francis Lescher, Esq. | Col. Sir Walter George Stirling, Bart
Thomas Douglas Murray, Esq.

JOINT SECRETARIES :

William C. Macdonald. | Francis B. Macdonald.

The **PHŒNIX FIRE OFFICE** was established by a numerous proprietary in January 1872 upon principles of public utility. The promptitude and cheerfulness with which the most important losses have been made good by the Company are well known ; a large capital in Government Securities is at all times held in readiness for the purpose, besides which the private fortune of every individual shareholder in the Company is responsible for its engagements. No person insured in this office is liable for the losses of others as is the case in Contribution Societies.

First Class risks in this Colony are now taken at the same rates as charged in the Local Companies.

BLYTH BROTHERS & Co.,
Agents.

THE GUARDIAN

Fire & Life Assurance Company

LIMITED

ESTABLISHED 1821

HEAD OFFICE : **6, Princes Street, Bank, London, E.C.**

DIRECTORS :

JOHN BIDDULPH MARTIN, Esq.—*Chairman.*
HENRY JOHN NORMAN, Esq.—*Deputy Chairman.*

Henry Bonham Carter, Esq.
William Hill Dawson, Esq.
Charles F. Devas, Esq.
Allan. G. H. Gibbs, Esq.
James Goodson, Esq.
John J. Hamilton, Esq.
Thompson Hankey, Esq.
Richard M. Harvey, Esq.
Granville F. R. Farquhar, Esq.
John Hunter, Esq.
George Lake, Esq.
Rt. Hon. G. J. Shaw-Lefevre, M.P.
David Powell, Esq.
Augustus Prevost, Esq.
John G. Talbot, Esq., M. P.
Henry Vigne, Esq.
Beaumont, W. Lubbock, Esq.
Roderick Pryor, Esq.

Manager of the Fire Department.—A. J. RELTON.
Actuary and Secretary.—T. G. C. BROWNE.

The Subscribed Capital of the Company is TWO MILLIONS Pounds Sterling, of which ONE MILLION is now paid up and invested in First Class Securities.

The Company has now been in successful operation for SEVENTY YEARS, and during that period the Policies issued for Assurances upon Lives have amounted to over £20,000,000. The Life Claims paid have exceeded £6,000,000 besides Bonuses. Its TOTAL INCOME is over £ 900,000 and its TOTAL ASSETS amount to £4,342,000. Its position is therefore, one of the most assured stability.

Copies of the Annual Accounts, showing all particulars of the investments and income, may be had on application.

BLYTH BROTHERS & Co.,
Agents.

LANCASHIRE

INSURANCE COMPANY FOR LIFE AND FIRE

CAPITAL : £3,000,000

ANNUAL INCOME £825,091

Reserve Fund 31st December 1891 over £1,250,000

LIFE POLICIES granted on very MODERATE TERMS

FIRE POLICIES AT THE USUAL RATES

Blyth Brothers & Co.,
Agents.

BOUIC, HAREL & Co.

IRONMONGERS

10, ROYAL STREET, PORT LOUIS

Large and Small Ironmongery of every Description

AND

SPECIALLY FOR THE USE OF SUGAR ESTATES

A LARGE STOCK OF ALL KINDS OF ARTICLES

FOR COACH-BUILDERS & HARNESS MAKERS

ALWAYS ON HAND

HARNESS, WHIPS, CARRIAGE RUGS

&c., &c., &c.

FRENCH MAIL STEAM SHIPS

COMPAGNIE

DES

MESSAGERIES MARITIMES DE FRANCE

UNDER CONTRACT

WITH THE FRENCH GOVERNMENT

MAIL SERVICE

TO

EUROPE, ASIA, AUSTRALIA, MADAGASCAR, REUNION, &c,

TWO SERVICES MONTHLY

FOR DATES OF ARRIVALS AND DEPARTURES, &c.

APPLY TO

BLYTH BROTHERS & Co., Agents.

COMPANY'S OFFICES:

Paris............ Company's Head Office and Booking Office for Passengers 1, rue Vignon (Boulevard de la Madeleine.) Booking Office for Goods, 10, Place de la République.

Marseilles ... 2, Quai de la Joliette. 10, Rue Cannebière for Passengers, &c.

Bordeaux ... 20, Allées D'Orléans.

LONDON AGENCY, 97, Cannon Street, E.C.

LONDON
GUARANTEE & ACCIDENT
COMPANY LIMITED

INCORPORATED A. D. 1869

Guarantee Branch

THIS COMPANY UNDERTAKES TO GRANT SECURITY FOR

Government Employés

And all other Persons receiving or holding money, or entrusted with Property of any kind.

ALSO FOR

Notaries and Land Surveyors.

The guarantees of Companies are now universally accepted in preference to private security. They have for some years been tested by Her Majesty's Government, the largest Railways and other public bodies and found to be immeasurably superior in every way to those of private sureties. A company's guarantee relieves the employed from the necessity of placing himself under an obligation to his friends, and can be obtained, as a matter of course, by any one having a good character, while it gives to the employer absolute security and the greatest facility for recovering any loss he may incur.

The Bonds of the Company are accepted by—

Her Majesty's Government
The Court of Chancery,
The Local Government Board,
The City of London.

and other Municipal Corporations; and by various Banks and Railways, and other large Companies throughout the United Kingdom, India and Australia.

—RATES OF PREMIUM—

As the rates of premium vary according to the nature of the situation and the duties to be performed, reference to the Agent of the Company is unavoidable to ascertain the premium to be paid in each case.

Forms of proposals and every information may be obtained on application to.

Hamilton STEIN,
Agent.

1, Corderie Street, Port Louis.

MAURITIUS FIRE INSURANCE COMPANY

ESTABLISHED 1855

CAPITAL : ONE MILLION DOLLARS

OR

TWO MILLIONS RUPEES

PAID UP: Rs 500,000

DIRECTORS :

Sir Virgile NAZ, K.C.M.G.—*Président.*

G. T. LIONNET,—*Vice Président*
C. NAIRAC.
Adolphe LARCHER.
Evenor GANACHAUD.

MM. L. D'EMMEREZ.
Lodoïc BOULLÉ
E. LACOSTE.
Dr. M. E. X. NALLETAMBY

AUDITORS :

MM. V. RIBET & Ed. LINCOLN.

The Company issues policies, which include the risks of fire caused by lightning or the explosion of, gas or steam, at premiums varying according to the nature of the risk. The Company also insures against the risk of fire from the neighbour (risque du voisin).

The Company renounces all claims and right of action against the insured when a fire accidentally begun on his premises, and shall have caused, to other premises, damages for which the Company is responsible.

The insurance of the Tenant's risk (risque locatif) is one fourth of the ordinary premium, when the property is not already insured by the Company; and one half when the property is not insured by the Company. The premium for the neighbour's risk (risque du voisin) is fixed by mutual agreement.

POLICIES are delivered for a period of Five Years, on the payment of all premium for Four Years, and corresponding reduction is made on the premium for Insurance effected for Three or Four Years.

By order of the Directors,

Léon PITOT,—*Secretary.*

Office: 15, Church Street, Port Louis.

GOUDIN, COUTANCEAU & CIE

NEGOCIANTS & COMMISSIONNAIRES

REPRÉSENTÉS EN EUROPE PAR

GOUDIN FRERES, (EMILE RIEUNIER, SUCCESSEUR)

5, Rue J. J. BEL., BORDEAUX

AGENTS

POUR LE GUANO DES ILES CHESTERFIELD

(NOUVELLE CALÉDONIE)

Compagnie Havraise Peninsulaire

DE

NAVIGATION A VAPEUR

Ligne régulière de Bateaux à Vapeur entre le Hâvre, St. Nazaire, Bordeaux, Marseille, Port Louis (Maurice) et *vice versa* avec escale à Tamatave

DEPART TOUS LES 45 JOURS

ELIAS, MALLAC & Cie.,
GOUDIN, COUTANCEAU & Cie., } Agents.

N. B.—LA COMPAGNIE ASSURE.

SOCIÉTÉ ANONYME

DES

ANCIENS ETABLISSEMENTS CAIL

CAPITAL SOCIAL : VINGT MILLIONS

Siège Social : 15, Quai de Grenelle, Paris

L'agence de Maurice, représentée par MM. ELIAS, MALLAC & Cie., est prête à recevoir toutes commandes de Machineries.

THE COLONIAL

FIRE INSURANCE COMPANY

CAPITAL SOCIAL : $ 500,000 OU Rs 1,000,000

DONT 250,000 PIASTRES, 500,000 ROUPIES VERSÉES

DIRECTEURS :

MM. P. Edmond de CHAZAL, *Président.*
F. TENNANT, *Vice-Président.*
Honorable H. LECLÉZIO.
G. A. RITTER.

MM. Ant. J. COLIN.
A. BROUARD.
Henri Giblot DUCRAY.

AUDITEURS :

MM. L. LEJUGE de SEGRAIS & N. LARCHER.

La Compagnie assure contre l'incendie et contre les incendies causés par le feu du ciel et l'explosion du gaz et de la vapeur à des primes qui varient suivant la nature du risque.

L'Assurance du risque locatif et du ¼ de la prime lorsque l'Immeuble est assuré par la Compagnie, et du moitié lorsque l'immeuble ne l'est pas par la Société.

La Compagnie garantit aussi le risque du voisin. La prime fixé de gré à gré.

Les polices d'assurances sont délivrées pour deux, trois, quatre et cinq années à la condition que l'assuré paie la prime comptant.

Il sera fait une déduction de 20 o/o sur la prime de cinq années, et une remise proportionnelle sera faite sur la prime des assurances pour trois ou quatre années.

Par ordre des Directeurs :

ELIAS, MALLAC & Cie.

Administrateurs.

Rue de la Comédie, No. 4.

E. CHAUVIN

Négociant-Commissionnaire

Représentant de Messrs. COLLEY & Cie de LONDRES

Agent de Messrs. PHILIPPS & SONS

Fabricants de Lits et Coffre-Forts

SEUL RECEPTIONNAIRE DES

HARNAIS de PALISER et du VIN de **BORDEAUX**

Chateau Lambert

Bureau d'Echantillons—rue de l'Intendance, Port-Louis.

THE CENTRAL

PRINTING ASSOCIATION

9—Poudrière Street, Port-Louis—9

The Central Printing Association which is the largest Printing and Lithographic Establishment of Mauritius, can execute every kind of Printing and Lithographic Work — Cheaper, better and quicker than any where else in the Colony.

THE

MAURITIUS SUGAR ESTATES COMPANY

LIMITED

REMPART STREET, PORT LOUIS.

NOMINAL CAPITAL: Rs. 10,000,000

DIVIDED INTO 100,000 SHARES OF RS. 100 EACH

First Issue 25,000 Shares Paid

DIRECTORS:

Hon. Sir C. Antelme, K.C.M.G., *President.*
C. F. H. Adam, Esq.
Alex. Wemyss, Esq.
A. Hugnin, Esq.
E. Montocchio, Esq.
S. Pelte, Esq.
T. Mallac, Esq.

A. Huguin, Esq.—*Secretary.* C. Antelme junior, Esq.—*Manager.*

Commercial Union

ASSURANCE COMPNY LIMITED

OF LONDON

CAPITAL ... ... £ 2,500,000 | RESERVE FUND £ 500,000

Issue Policies on Goods, Specie &c., to all parts of the World at the current rate.

L. PITOT,—*Agent.*

4 Queen & Church Streets, No. 15.

THE

Agricultural Company of Mauritius

LIMITED

17, CHANGE ALLEY, CORNHILL, LONDON, E. C.

REMPART STREET, PORT-LOUIS

CAPITAL : £ 500,000

Directors :

LONDON BOARD	MAURITIUS BOARD
The Rt. Hon. Lord Stanmore, G.C M G.	Hon. Sir C. Antelme, K.C.M.G *Président*
W. John Tanner, Esq.	C. F. H. Adam, Esq.
C. J. Lindsay Nicholson, Esq.	Sir V. Naz, K.C.M.G , Esq.
J. A. Longridge, Esq.	A. Hugnin, Esq.
Walmsley Stanley, Esq.	P. L. Chastellier, Esq., Q. C.
Lieut. Col. F. A. V. Thurburn.	J. de Mazérieux, Esq., *Manager.*
Alfred G. Dick, Esq., *Manager & Secretary*	

Bankers :—THE MAURITIUS COMMERCIAL BANK & BANK OF MAURITIUS

Solicitors :—Messrs FLUX, SLADE & Co.

Legal Adviser in Mauritius :—P. L. CHASTELLIER, Esq. Q. C.

GARGARISME FLORICOURT

CONTRE LA DIPHTERIE

Ce gargarisme dont l'efficacité incontestable est aujourd'hui reconnue par la plupart de nos meilleurs médecins pour combattre la diphtérie et tous les maux de gorge en général, se vend seulement à la Pharmacie A. Minet & Cie, rue de l'Eglise, Port-Louis.

PRIX DE LA CHOPINE Rs : 10

NORTHERN ASSURANCE COMPANY

ESTABLISHED 1836.

LIFE AND FIRE

ACCUMULATED FUNDS £4,293,000

This Company is prepared to issue policies at current rates.

CURRIE, FRASER & Co.,

Office and Warehouse, 34, Corderie street, Port Louis. Agents.

THE HARDWARE

COMPANY LIMITED

CORNER OF

ROYAL AND CHURCH STREETS, PORT LOUIS

HAS ALWAYS ON HAND A LARGE SUPPLY OF IRONMONGERY

ESPECIALLY ADAPTED FOR SUGAR ESTATES.

SPECIALLY IN PALISER'S HARNESS AND OTHER ARTICLES FOR HORSES.

LARGE AND SMALL IRONMONGERY

A, Minet & Coy.

DISPENSING CHEMISTS & WHOLESALE DRUGGISTS

CHURCH STREET, PORT LOUIS, MAURITIUS

BRANCH HOUSES :

MAURITIUS { **Port Louis : Dumat Street.**
Rose Hill (Plaines Wilhems.)

France (Paris) : 15, Rue Grange Batelière.

PARIS:

A. LAURATET, 15, Rue Grange Batelière *

Manager NOEL COUVE Esqre.

Chemist of Great Britain

Twice Medallist of the Westminster Pharmaceutical College of London

GOLD MEDAL MAURITIUS 1895

AGENTS FOR MOST OF THE EUROPEAN & FOREIGN FIRMS

OF

GREAT BRITAIN, FRANCE & UNITED STATES OF AMERICA

Agents for nearly all Medical and Pharmaceutical Publications in Local Papers.

MODERATE RATES

The extensive European relations which for some time past we have been cultivating, place us in an exceptionally advantageous position in offering both Drugs and Chemicals of every description imported from all Points of the World, and in many articles we have materially reduced our prices so as to give our Customers the fullest advantages in purchasing.

SOLE AGENTS AND IMPORTERS FOR:

NEARLY ALL FRENCH & ENGLISH PATENT MEDECINES

A. MINET & Co

* All our European letters to be addressed A. Lauratet, 15, Rue Grange Batelière,

Messrs IRELAND, FRASER & Co

AGENTS FOR

LLOYD'S

The Castle Mail Packets Company Ld.

THE LIVERPOOL UNDERWRITERS ASSOCIATION

The Underwriting and Agency Association Limited
OF LONDON

NATIONAL BOARD OF MARINE UNDERWRITERS OF NEW YORK

THE LONDON SALVAGE ASSOCIATION

The Liverpool Salvage Association

THE GLASGOW SALVAGE ASSOCIATION

THE GLASGOW SOCIETY OF UNDERWRITERS

BADISCHE SCHIFFHARTS ASSECURANZ GESELLCHAFT MANNHEIM

THE BRITISH & FOREIGN MARINE INSURANCE COMPANY LIMITED

THAMES & MERSEY
MARINE INSURANCE COMPANY LIMITED

The Standard Marine Insurance Company Limited

THE MARITIME INSURANCE COMPANY LD.

THE UNION INSURANCE SOCIETY OF CANTON LIMITED

The Equitable Marine & Fire Insurance Company of Cape Town

THE ROYAL INSURANCE CY LIFE & FIRE

THE COMMERCIAL BANK OF AUSTRALASIA

The Baden Insurance Company Ld.

THE CASTLE MAIL PACKETS
COMPANY LIMITED

FORTNIGHTLY SERVICE

BETWEEN

LONDON, SOUTHAMPTON AND THE CAPE

INTERMEDIATE SERVICE

HAMBURG, FLUSHING AND THE CAPE

MONTHLY SERVICE

LONDON, THE CAPE, MADAGASCAR AND MAURITIUS

LONDON

MESSRS. DONALD CURRIE & Co.

3 & 4, Fenchurch Street.

AGENTS IN MAURITIUS:

IRELAND, FRASER & Co

SCOTT AND COMPANY

MERCHANTS

PORT LOUIS, MAURITIUS

Established 1830

Agents for : UNITED STATES LLOYDS.

GERMANISCHER LLOYD. **REGISTRO ITALIANO**

Verein Hamburger Assecuradeure
Bremen Assuranz Verein
Swergies Angfartygs Assurance Forening, GOTEBORG.
Italia Societa d'Assicurazioni Marittime Fluvialle Terresti, GENOVA.
Newcastle Clubs.
North Shields Insurance Associations.
(Equitable Oriental and Tynemouth)
South Shields Insurance Associations.
Sunderland General A. I. Marine Insurance Association.
Union Association of Underwriters, Dundee.
Dundee Mutual Marine Association.
Arbroath Commercial Association.
Montrose Insurance Association.
Scarborough Insurance Clubs.
Western Clubs, TOPSHAM.
Merchants Marine Insurance Company.
Home and Colonial Marine Insurance Company.
North China Insurance Company.
Netherlands India Sea and Fire Insurance Company.
Samarang Sea and Fire Insurance Company.
Java Sea and Fire Insurance Company.
South British Insurance Company of NEW ZEALAND.
Nord Deutshe Versicherungs Gesiellschaften.
Assicurazioni Generali in Trieste.
Triton Insurance Co. Limited.
Straits Insurance Company Limited.

BRITISH INDIA STEAM NAVIGATION COMPANY LIMITED

Chartered Bank of India, Australia and China.
Hong-Kong and Shanghai Banking Corporation.
Commercial Banking Company of Sydney.
Colonial Bank of Australasia.
National Bank of New Zealand.
African Banking Corporation Limited.

BUREAUX OF THE CONSULS FOR

Germany, Sweden & Norway, and Denmark.

AND OF THE AGENCIES FOR

THE STANDARD LIFE ASSURANCE COMPANY

THE LONDON GUARANTEE AND ACCIDENT COMPANY LIMITED

&c., &c,

British India Steam Navigation

COMPANY LIMITED

UNDER CONTRACT WITH GOVERNMENT.

MAIL SERVICE

To India, Europe and Australia viâ Colombo (Ceylon).

Full powered, commodious and well appointed Steamers, built specially for the Trade, owned by or worked under the auspices of the Company, sail fortnightly between

London, Colombo, Madras and Calcutta.

Passengers to and from Mauritius change at Colombo into the Coy's steamers. The Mauritius steamers also connect at that Port with the steamers of *The Peninsular and Oriental Steam Navigation Cy.* and *Orient Company* to and from Adelaide, Melbourne and Sydney.

Homeward Passage Rates:

	First Class.	Second Class.
To Plymouth or London by sea	Rs. 650	**Rs. 425**
London viâ Naples, (including Railway Fare)	Rs. 775	**Rs. 525**

To bonâ fide members of one family a reduction of 10 o/o is allowed on single first class tickets, if equivalent to three full fares is paid, and 15 o/o for equivalent of four full fares.

The Members of *The Mauritius Civil Service* a reduction of 15 o/o is allowed on single first class tickets between Mauritius and London.

Passages may also be booked to England viâ Calcutta :—

1o. By Straits Settlements, Hongkong and the Canadian Pacific Route ;
2o. By Australia, New Zealand, the Pacific Ocean and the United States of America ;
3o. As well as to all ports in India and Burmah, the Persian Gulf, Aden, Zanzibar and Eastern Africa.

SCOTT & Co.,
Agents in Mauritius.

1, Corderie Street, Port Louis.

Smith, Freeland & Co.

Merchants

Shipping & Commission Agents,

Port Louis—Mauritius.

AGENTS FOR :

YANGTSZE

INSURANCE ASSOCIATION LIMITED

HEAD OFFICE : SHANGHAI

Agencies in all parts of the World.

The Southern Insurance Company

LIMITED

HEAD OFFICE : MELBOURNE

With branch Offices and Boards of Directors in Sydney and London

AGENCIES FOR THE ISSUING OF POLICIES AND ADJUSTMENT OF LOSSES

In India, Ceylon,

Straits Settlements, Australia, New Zealand & Mauritius.

MARINE RISKS OF ALL DESCRIPTION AT CURRENT RATES.

THE ALLIANCE ASSURANCE COMPANY

FOR FIRE RISKS

ESTABLISHED IN 1824.

CAPITAL : FIVE MILLIONS STERLING

Chief Office:— Bartholomew Lane London, E.C.

THE

NOBEL'S EXPLOSIVES COMPANY

LIMITED

Messrs PIPON, ADAM & Co

Agents in Mauritius for the undermentioned Companies

BUREAU VERITAS

COMPAGNIE DE FIVES LILLE

THE CLAN LINE OF STEAMERS

ASSUREURS MARITIMES DE FRANCE

ALLIANCE

LIFE AND FIRE INSURANCE COMPANY

FIRE BRANCH

M^ESSRS. H. VITRY & C^O

Négociants & Commissionnaires
REPRÉSENTÉS EN EUROPE PAR

M^ESSRS. STALEY, RADFORD & C^O

Fenchurch Avenue, Londres

AGENCES
- **EDWARD PACKARD & Co.,**—PRODUITS CHIMIQUES
- **RANSOMES, SIMS, JEFFERIES LD,.**—CHARRUES
- **BOAKE, ROBERTS & Co.,**—SUGAR BLOOMS.

M^ESSRS STALEY RADFORD & C^O.

2—FENCHURCH AVENUE, LONDON, E.C.

Commission Agents, Shipping Agents & Insurance Brokers

MAURITIUS AGENTS : H. VITRY & Co.

E. PACKARD & Co.

Sole Manufacturers of

HUGHES' IMPROVED SUGAR CANE AND OTHER MANURES

Registered Trade Mark "**EHRMANNITE**" for the Patent Sugar Processes.

PATENT SUPERPHOSPHATES & SOLID PHOSPHORIC ACID

H. VITRY & CO.—*AGENTS*

A. BOAKE, ROBERTS & Co.,

Manufacturing, Consulting and Analytical Chemists.
MANUFACTURERS OF
The Golden Bloom and

THE IMPROVED GOLDEN BLOOM

H. VITRY & Co.—AGENTS.

WORKS AT ROCHEBOIS, MAURITIUS.

THE MAURITIUS ENGRAIS CHIMIQUES COMPANY

CAPITAL	... ...	**200,000 RUPEES**
RESERVE FUND	... ...	**250,000 ,,**

Board of Directors :

THE HON. SIR CÉLICOURT ANTELME, K.C.M.G.— *President.*

A. WEMYSS, ESQUIRE. | V. HUTEAU, ESQUIRE.

Auditor :

L. MAINGARD, ESQUIRE.

Manager :

E. GOUPILLE, ESQUIRE.

Analytical Chemist :

J. H. MARICOT, ESQUIRE.

The Mauritius Engrais Chimiques Company supplies all the requisite Substances used in the Manufacture of Sugar-Cane Manures and provides all Chemical Manures required to be mixed with Peruvian Guanos and others.

The Mauritius Engrais Chimiques Company, procuring the requisite Substances at the cheapest sources, is able to deliver its fertilizers at reasonable prices.

OFFICE 23, CHURCH STREET, PORT LOUIS.

C. J. SCHIRMER

Négociant et Commissionnaire

A L'ANGLE DE LA RUE DE LA CORDERIE ET PRINCE REGENT

PORT LOUIS

— REPRÉSENTÉ EN EUROPE —

PAR

Messrs. Aust & Hachmann

HAMBOURG

AGENT A MAURICE DE LA

NORTH GERMAN MARINE INSURANCE CO.

HAMBURG

GERMAN LLOYD MARINE ASSURANCE

COMPANY

BERLIN

ET LE

MAGDEBURG FIRE INSURANCE CY.

Magdeburg

MAURICE ALLAIN

Négociant Commissionnaire

25, BOULEVARD POISSONNIERE

PARIS

Prosper Hugnin fils

Agent pour l'ILE MAURICE

PROSPER HUGNIN FILS

COMMISSION AGENT

PORT LOUIS, MAURITIUS

THE NATIONAL

LIFE INSURANCE SOCIETY

Cette Société fondée en 1830, compte actuellement 66 ans d'existence et est aujourd'hui purement mutuelle. Tous les profits appartiennent à ceux qui en font partie, sans qu'ils encourent aucune responsabilité personnelle.

Le Fonds de garantie s'élève à la somme de £ 1,100,000 provenant de l'accumulation des Primes. Les revenus annuels s'élèvent à la somme de £ 150,000.

La Société fait tous les genres d'Assurances sur la Vie.

Les Primes comme le montant

des Polices sont payables en Livres Sterling ou en Roupies.

Une Commission de 10 o|o *sur le montant du* **Prime** *de la première année est accordée aux personnes qui procurent de nouveaux assurés à la Société.*

Pour tous renseignements, s'adresser à

M. Jules ROUSSET,
Agent.

A son bureau, rue de la Reine, Port Louis, Maurice.

The Standard
LIFE ASSURANCE COMPANY

ESTABLISHED 1825

Governor :

His Grace the Duke of Buccleuch and Queensbury, K. T.

Deputy-Governor :

The Right Honorable The Earl of Stair, K.T.
The Kight Honorable The Earl of Rosslyn, K.T.

Financial Position

Annual Revenue over	£ 1,000,000
Invested Funds	8,000,000
Total Profits distributed to policy holders...	5,500,000

Advantages and conditions of Assurances.

Moderate Premiums for Tropical Climates and immediate reduction to Home rates on return to Europe.

War risks covered for Military men by a small permanent extra.

Liberal Terms of revival for Thirteen months without medical certificate.

Policies unchallengeable after Two years.

Fixed surrended values or paid up Policies in exchange.

Paid up Policies in proportion to Premiums paid in the case of Endowment Assurances and **Policies by a fixed** number of payments.

Policies issued in Rupee Currency, or in Sterling Currency at the option of the assured.

NOTE.—**Forms** of application may be obtained on application, as also the Company's prospectus containing full particulars as to the Rates of premium and explanations of the various forms of provisions granted by the Company.

S. C. THOMPSON, B.A., *Manager and Actuary.*

G. OLIVER, *Colonial and Foreign Secretary.*

Port Louis, Mauritius.

BOARD OF DIRECTORS :

A. L. S. PELTE, Esq.—*Chairman.*

ALEX. WEMYSS, Esq., Manager of the Bank of Mauritius Limited.
P. E. DE CHAZAL, Esq. Attorney-at-Law.
J. COUTANCEAU, Esq., Merchant.

Agent and Secretary to the Board : HAMILTON STEIN.

Medical Officer : Dr. I. J. PADDLE.

1,—Corderie Street, Port Louis.

GENERAL AGENCY

FOR

LIFE & FIRE ASSURANCE

Life Assurances of all kinds are affected with the LONDON AND LANCASHIRE LIFE ASSURANCE Cy., of 66, Cornhill London E. C., established in 1862.

The financial position and progress of that Company are shewn by the following increase in its funds during the last five years.

1890	£ 721,000
1891	781,000
1892	840,000
1893	897,000
1894	975,000

The LONDON AND LANCASHIRE being a *Proprietory* Company instead of a MUTUAL Insurance Office, offers to its insured the additional security of a Capital of **£ 1(0,000** and of a Board of Administration responsible before the Shareholders of the good management of their business.

The Company is represented in Mauritius since 1880 by a **General Agent,** Secretary to a LOCAL BOARD having very extensive powers notably that of accepting *finally* proposals from Mauritius, Réunion, Seychelles and Madagascar without reference to the Central Board of London.

Those Assurances may be effected in RUPEES, in FRANCS, or in POUNDS STERLING at the convenience of the assured and the premiums may be paid yearly, half-yearly, quarterly or monthly.

Fire Insurances of all kinds are effected with the Sun Insurance Office of London established in 1710, the oldest Fire Insurance Office in the world.

The rates and all terms are the same as those of Local Insurance Companies for all kinds of risks both in town and in the country.

The following are the sums insured by the office thoughout the world :

1881	£ 270,000,000
1885	327,000,000
1889	338,000,000
1893	395,000,000

The premium income for 1893 was **£ 975,000** and the total claims paid during that year amounted to **£ 732,000.**

The Agent has full power to settle immediately all claims whatever be their amount.

Local Advisory Committee :

MESSRS. C. DURAND DESLONGRAIS,—*President.*
M. MUNROE,
G. BAISSAC.

L. F. HENRY.

37,—CHURCH STREET.

Oh! my FRIENDS WHISKY is the Curse of Humanity

YOU MUST ALL TRY TO PUT IT DOWN

There must be no half measures; if you don't want WHISKY to get the better of YOU. YOU must get the best of WHISKY.

ASK FOR

DAWSON'S
PERFECTION
OLD SCOTCH WHISKY

GUARANTEED free from anything injurious to health and recommended as the most wholesome beverage in the Market.

May be had at ***E. Mayer's*** Auction Mart, and the Leading Hotels and Wine Merchants.

Address Orders to **E. MAYER'S,**

Intendance Street. **Auction Mart.**

MAISON E. SUSTRAC

FONDÉE EN 1860

J. ROUHIER

SUCCESSEUR

VIN, BIERE, PORTER, SPIRITUEUX, LIMONADES ET BOISSONS GAZEUSES

Le plus grand approvisionnement de :

Vins en barriques et en bouteilles de Bieres et Porters

DE LA COLONIE

Recevant directement des lieux de Productions.

Contracteur des gouvernements civil et militaire.

Seul Propriétaire du RHUM J. ROUHIER

Médaille d'Or Exposition Universelle Paris 1889—*Médaille d'Or Maurice* 1884

Fabrique perfectionnée de BOISSONS GAZEUSES

Médaille d'Argent Paris 1889, *la plus haute récompense.*

COMMISSION—EXPORTATION

SPRINGS OF CHALYBEATE WATERS

"PAUL ET VIRGINIE"

AT

"RUISSEAU ROSE", LONG MOUNTAIN

MAURITIUS

MINERAL WATER FOR THE TABLE

CHALYBEATE WATER

A CERTAIN CURE AGAINST ANŒMIA

SOLE AGENT FOR EXPORTATION

M. J. ROUHIER

PORT LOUIS, MAURITIUS

SPRINGS OF CHALYBEATE WATERS

"PAUL ET VIRGINIE"

AT

"RUISSEAU ROSE", LONG MOUNTAIN

MAUITIUS

MINERAL WATER FOR THE TABLE

Mauritius, 5th. January 1896.

I can most highly recommend the use of the Ruisseau Rose mineral waters to all debilitated constitutions—from whatever cause — requiring some preparation of *Iron* for restoring muscular tone and vital energy in all its particulars.

The proportion of iron in those waters is not considerable, and I consider this and its combination with such a variety of saline constituents, as a great advantage; and, when properly bottled, with a high proportion of oxygen, and a fair one of carbonic acid, render it most acceptable by delicate stomachs whose digestive powers are restored instead of being deeply disturbed as is too frequently the case with most mineral waters containing iron which cannot be easily assimilated.

I have repeatedly prescribed those Ruisseau Rose waters in most of the varieties of anœmia; in nervous depression from any cause; in impaired menstruation and its consequences; in slow and painful digestion, especially when coupled with disordered bowels; etc., etc., etc., and most generally with marked success. Improvement soon shows itself; and then proceeds slowly, but surely and continuously.

One great advantage of those waters is that they are so palatable that they can be taken at meals, without the least repugnance; and can be mixed with any table drink without either spoiling the other.

O. BEAUGEARD, M..D, Edin.
Formerly Surgeon in charge of the Civil Hospital, Port Louis, now Superintendent of the Government Lunatic Asylum, Beau Bassin.

Je soussigné, Docteur en Médecine de la Faculté de Paris, certifie avoir conseillé à plusieurs malades, avec le plus grand succès l'usage des eaux ferrugineuses du Ruisseau Rose.

Entre toutes mes observations, je rapporterai brièvement celle de Monsieur X. Européen, qui après un séjour de plusieurs années dans notre Colonie, était atteint de Cachexie Paludéenne, Le Foie et la Rate hypertrophiés débordaient les fausses côtes, l'appétit était nul, l'amaigrissement rapide. La peau recouverte constamment d'une sueur froide et visqueuse, avait une teinte terreuse.

Devant un état si grave, mon pronostic est sombre, et je conseille à Monsieur X. de partir sans retard pour France. Mon client m'affirme que ses intérêts le retiennent à Maurice, et qu'il lui est absolument impossible de s'absenter.

C'est alors que je lui ordonne un séjour d'un mois à la Montagne Longue, sans oublier le traitement hydrotherapique par les bains, et l'eau ferrugineuse en boisson.

Lorsque je revois mon client, à ma grande joie, je retrouve un autre homme, c'est une véritable resurrection; son teint est frais et coloré, l'appétit excellent, l'embonpoint revenu. Si je ne possédais que ce seul fait, je n'hésiterais pas à conseiller les eaux ferrugineuses du Ruisseau Rose dans les Chloroses, les Cachexies, si fréquentes sous notre climat.

En foi de quoi j'ai délivré le présent rapport.

Dr. FIBICH, D.M.P.

Port Louis, le 20 Novembre 1894.

TABLE MINERAL WATER

Polluted water from rivers is, according to doctor's opinions, the cause of all sorts of diseases. The chalybeate water from the "Paul et Virginie" spring, at Ruisseau Rose, is a pure table water which has been filtered immediately after drawing from the spring, in covered recipients, and then bottled up.

Consumers are therefore certain that they use a perfectly pure water. The iron in dissolution which it contains is easily assimilated by the whole system. It is an hygienic and fortifying drink, the use of which is prescribed by all medical men.

TABLE MINERAL WATER

It sometimes happens that molecules of iron get oxidized in water and form globules of iron in the bottles. Consumers need not be afraid of this. Under the influence of carbonic acid, iron is dissolved, when absorbed.

The sediment of iron should be absorbed together with the water. This water is particularly good for delicate people. It is second to none in the cure of diseases of the stomach and chlorosis.

Young Ladies will soon be restored to health if they use it.

SOLE AGENT FOR EXPORTATION—J. ROUHIER.

8, Comedie Street, Port Louis.

The Daily Publisher

ET

LES PETITES AFFICHES

PORT LOUIS, ILE MAURICE

Cette publication, dont l'origine ne remonte qu'à 8 années, a conquis une des premières places dans la presse mauricienne.

Bien que fondé pour donner la plus grande publicité aux annonces, **The Daily Publisher** et **Les Petites Affiches**, dont le tirage journalier est de 3,000 exemplaires, publie chaque matin, tous les bruits et nouvelles de la veille, le mouvement du port et plusieurs fois par semaine, le cour du marché des effets publics, des sucres, des vanilles, des aloës, les importations et exportations, les taux du change, enfin, tous les renseignements nécessaires concernant le commerce et l'agriculture.

THE DAILY PUBLISHER & LES PETITES AFFICHES

reproduit également à l'arrivée des malles, les plus intéressantes nouvelles télégraphiques et publie tous les jours, soit comme feuilletons ou autrement, les faits les plus saillants de l'extérieur et les plus jolies productions littéraires de Paris.

N.B.—Depuis le 1er Mars 1889, *The Mauritius Advertiser* et le *Journal des Annonces* a fusionné avec *The Daily Publisher* et *Les Petites Affiches*, et ces deux journaux ne font aujourd'hui qu'une seule et même publication.

Cette double combinaison a permis d'en faire la publication la plus utile au commerce, par ses renseignements, en même temps qu'elle est devenue le journal de la famille.

Bureaux et Administration :

9—RUE DE LA POUDRIÈRE—9

CURE FOR ALL

HOLLOWAY'S PILLS

A certain Remedy for all disorders of the Liver, Stomach, Kidneys and Bowels.

These purifying Pills are confidently recommended as the most simple and certain remedy for Indigestion, Flatulency, Acidity, Constipation, and all disorders resulting from disordered Stomach or Bowels They act as purifiers, alteratives, and strengtheners of the stomach. Though powerfully tonic and satisfactorily aperient, they are mild in their operation and beneficial to the whole system.

Weakness and debility—Nervous Irritability.

The wholesome effect exercised by these admirable Pills over the Blood and Fluids generally, is like a charm in dispelling low spirits and restoring cheerfulness. Their general aperient qualities well fit them for a domestic medicine, particularly for females of all ages and periods of life. They quickly eject all impurities f rom the system, and regulate every function of the body giving wonderful tone and energy to weak and debilitated constitutions.

Old Coughs, Colds and Asthmatic Affections.

These Pills, assisted in their action by rubbing Holloway's Ointment very effectually twice a day on the throat and Chest and keeping those parts covered with the preparation, will be found the most effective remedy for Asthma, Coughs, Colds, Bronchitis and Influenza.They tranquilize the hurried breathing, soothe the irritated air-tubes, and assist in dislodging the phlegm which stops up the air passages. This treatment has proved wonderfully efficient in not only curing old settled Coughs and Colds, but even Asthma of many years standing.

Complaints of Women and Children.

Any mother, nurse, or young person guided by the directions which accompany each box of Holloway's Pills has at once available means for checking disease, purifying the blood, and expelling from the system all gross humours.

The Pills and Ointment are sold at Professor HOLLOWAY S Establishment, 533, Oxford Street, London ; also by nearly every respectable Vendor of Medecine throughout the Civilized World, in Boxes and Pots at 1s. 1½., 2s. 9d., 11s. 22s. and 33s. each.

Full printed directions are affixed to each Box and Pot, and can be had in any language.

N.B—Advice can be obtained, free of charge, by applying at the above address daily between the hours of 11 and 4 or by letter.

Agents : A. MINET & Co., Pharmaceutical Chemists,
Church Street, Port Louis.

CURE FOR ALL

HOLLOWAY'S OINTMENT

The Universal Remedy for Bad Legs, Bad Breasts, Old Wounds, and Ulcerations of all kinds.

There is no medical preparation which may be thoroughly relied upon in the treatment of the above aliments as Holloway's Ointment. Rubbed upon the surface of the body, over, or near the affected parts it disappears under the friction of the hand, penetrating at once to the source of the evil, and thus performs its healing errand, rapidly, safely and without pain. In all long standing cases Holloway's Pills should also be taken as they purify the blood and expel all depraved humours from the system.

Coughs, Colds, Sore Throats and Bronchitis.

This Ointment is irresistible in the cure of those throat and pectoral complaints which, when neglected, often end in settled Asthma or Consumption. The Ointment well rubbed upon the Chest and Back, night and morning penetrates the skin, and thus absorbed, is carried directly to the lungs, where, in immediate contact with the whole mass of circulating Blood, it neutralizes or expels all impurities. By these means all pulmonary complaints may be cured with rapidity and ease.

Gout, Rheumatism and Stiff Joints.

This invaluable Ointment exercises a more obvious control over Gout and Rheumatism than any other medecine. No one need remain uncured, who will in good earnest, make a vigourous application of this infaillible remedy, according to the printed Instructions affixed to each Pot. All settled aches and pains will likewise be banished by the same treatment.

Skin Diseases, Scrofula and Scurvy.

The beneficial effects of the peerless Ointment are truly wonderful in case of Ringworm, Scurvy and Scrofula or King's Evil and its powers are adequate to the most inveterate Skin Diseases to which the human frame is subject.

The Ointment and Pills are sold at Professor HOLLOWAY'S Establishment, 533, Oxford Street, London; also by nearly every respectable Vendor of Medicine throughout the civilized World, in Boxes and Pots at 1s. 1½d. 2s. 9d., 11s., 22s., 33s., each.

Full printed directions are affixed to each Box and Pot, and can be had in any language.

N.B.—Advice can be obtained, free of charge, by applying to the above address daily between the hours of 11 and 4, or by letter.

Agents: A. MINET & Co, Pharmaceutical Chemists,
Church Street, Port Louis.

www.ingramcontent.com/pod-product-compliance
Lightning Source LLC
Chambersburg PA
CBHW062123160426
43191CB00013B/2182